Monks and Merchants

Silk Road Treasures
from Northwest China

MONKS AND MERCHANTS

Silk Road Treasures from Northwest China

*Gansu and Ningxia,
4th–7th Century*

ANNETTE L. JULIANO

AND

JUDITH A. LERNER

WITH ESSAYS BY

MICHAEL ALRAM, CHEN BINGYING,
ALBERT E. DIEN, LUO FENG, BORIS I. MARSHAK

HARRY N. ABRAMS, INC., WITH THE ASIA SOCIETY

Published on the occasion of the exhibition "Monks and Merchants: Silk Road Treasures from Northwest China," organized by the Asia Society Museum.

Asia Society Museum, New York, October 13, 2001–January 6, 2002

Norton Museum of Art, Palm Beach, Florida, February 9–April 21, 2002

The Asia Society gratefully acknowledges the donors to "Monks and Merchants: Silk Road Treasures from Northwest China" for making the exhibition and its associated catalogue, performances, and educational and public programs possible.

J.P. Morgan Chase & Company
The W.L.S. Spencer Foundation
The Starr Foundation
National Endowment for the Humanities
The Henry Luce Foundation, Inc.
E. Rhodes and Leona B. Carpenter Foundation
National Endowment for the Arts
Individuals of Gansu Dotcom

EDITOR: Barbara Burn
DESIGNER: Joel Avirom
DESIGN ASSISTANTS: Jason Snyder and Meghan Day Healey

Library of Congress Cataloging-in-Publication Data

Juliano, Annette L.
    Monks and merchants : Silk Road treasures from Northwest China, Gansu and Ningxia
    Provinces, fourth–seventh century / Annette L. Juliano and Judith A. Lerner.
        p. cm.
    Includes bibliographical references and index.
    ISBN 0–8109–3478–7 — ISBN 0–87848–089–7 (pbk.)
    1. China, Northwest—Antiquities. 2. Silk Road—Antiquities. I. Title:
    Silk Road treasures from Northwest China Gansu and Ningxia
    Provinces, fourth–seventh century.
    II. Lerner, Judith A. III. Title.

DS793.N6 J85 2001
951'.4—dc21
                                    2001022132

Copyright © 2001 Asia Society

Published in 2001 by Harry N. Abrams, Incorporated, New York

Printed and bound in Japan
10 9 8 7 6 5 4 3 2 1

  Harry N. Abrams, Inc.
100 Fifth Avenue
New York, N.Y. 10011
www.abramsbooks.com

CATALOGUE ENTRY AUTHORS:

MA	Michael Alram
SB	Susan Beningson
AED	Albert E. Dien
ALJ	Annette L. Juliano
JAL	Judith A. Lerner
BIM	Boris I. Marshak
CM	Colin Mackenzie
JS	Julie Segraves
NS,W	Nicholas Sims-Williams
ZG	Zhang Guangda

PAGE 2: Standing Bodhisattva Avalokitesvara (Guanyin), Sui dynasty, late 6th century. Gansu Provincial Museum, Lanzhou (no. 71)

PRONUNCIATION OF CHINESE

The romanization adopted for Chinese in this book is the widely used *pinyin* system. The pronunciation assigned to most of the letters is close to that used in Western languages, but certain sounds are less intuitively represented. In syllables such as *cai, cao*, and *cen*, the initial *c* is pronounced as *ts*; *q* is pronounced as *ch*; *x* as *sh*; and *zh* as *dj*.

CONTENTS

Foreword

The exhibition and catalogue *Monks and Merchants: Silk Road Treasures from Northwest China, Gansu and Ningxia, 4th–7th Century*, tells, from the perspective of China, the story of far-flung cultural and mercantile communication that saw people, religious faiths, and luxury goods move with unprecedented freedom between the continent's diverse civilizations. Along the network of routes that linked China, Central Asia, India, and Europe, now known popularly known as the "Silk Road," myriad luxury goods were traded, yet this was not merely a network of trade routes; side by side with merchants traveled missionaries and pilgrims, spreading new religious beliefs and ethical codes. Of these, it was Buddhism, introduced around the turn of the first millennium, that was to have the most far-reaching and profound influence.

Unlike previous exhibitions of Silk Road art, *Monks and Merchants* focuses on a particular region, one that played a crucial role in this traffic of ideas and luxuries. This region, comprising the present-day province of Gansu and the Ningxia Hui Autonomous Region, constituted the gateway to China and the only section of the Silk Road within China proper. Gansu and Ningxia were thus a melting pot where exotic and indigenous traditions intermingled and cross-fertilized. The resulting richness and diversity of artifacts and styles are fully represented by the works in this exhibition and catalogue.

More than a century ago, when Western scholars and collectors began to take a serious interest in the arts of Asia, it was the "exotic" appearance of the works, differentiated from Western art, that appealed to them. Now, as we move into the new millennium, neither Asia nor Asian art can be see only in terms of differences. *Monks and Merchants* is intended to remind us that cross-cultural exchanges and connections are an integral part of the world we call "Asia." The choice of *Monks and Merchants: Silk Road Treasures from Northwest China, Gansu and Ningxia, 4th–7th Century* to celebrate the opening of the Asia Society's refurbished headquarters and new exhibition spaces (to be named Asia Society Museum) is thus particularly appropriate.

The story in this exhibition—of relationships among cultures and societies through trade and religion rather than through military conquests—has a powerful message for the new millennium: that we cannot live in isolation and rule by military might. It also suggests new avenues for the exploration of the ever-complex world of Asian arts.

Many people have contributed to the successful realization of this exhibition and catalogue. I would like to express my profound gratitude to the curators and catalogue authors of *Monks and Merchants*, Professor Annette L. Juliano and Dr. Judith A. Lerner, who first recognized the potential of Gansu and Ningxia for an exhibition of Silk Road art. I would also like to thank members of the scholarly advisory committee and catalogue contributors—Michael Alram, Susan Beningson, Chen Bingying, Albert E. Dien, Luo Feng, Colin Mackenzie, Boris I. Marshak, Julie Segraves, Nicholas Sims-Williams, and Zhang Guangda.

The Asia Society is also indebted to the many Chinese officials and scholars who have supported the project: the Honorable Sun Jiazheng, Minister for Culture; Madam Meng Xiaosi, Vice-Minister; Vice-Minister Zhang Wenbin, Director General of the State Administration of Cultural Heritage; Ms. Wang Limei, Director of the Foreign Affairs Office; Vice-Minister Zhao Qizheng of The State Council Information Office; and Ambassador Li Daoyu. The Honorable Joseph W. Prueher, United States Ambassador to China, provided invaluable advice at a critical stage in the negotiations.

In Gansu, Vice-Governor Li Chongan has expressed unwavering support for the exhibition. Mr. Ma Wenzhi, Vice Director of the Cultural Department and Director of the Administration of Cultural Heritage, provided overall direction of the project in Gansu, while day-to-day organization was ably supervised by Mr. He Yangzhou, Vice Director of the Administration of Cultural Heritage, Mr. Tsu Shibin, former Director of the Gansu Provincial Museum, and Mr. Han Bowen, Interim Director.

Additionally, I would like to thank Madam Fan Jinshi, Director of the Dunhuang Research Academy, Mr. Wang Hengtong, Director of the Binglingsi Grottos, and Mr. Hua Pingning of the Maijishan Caves Reseach Institute for agreeing to the very special loans from their respective sites. I would also like to thank Mr. Hua and Mr. Zhang Guangtian of the Gansu Provincial Museum for their photography for the catalogue.

In Ningxia, we are greatly indebted to Mr. Wang Bangxiu, Director of the Cultural Department, Mr. Xue Yaping, Deputy Director of the Cultural Department. Mr. Lei Runze, Vice-Director of the Administration of Cultural Heritage, Mr. Luo Feng, former Director of the Guyuan Museum and now Director of the Ningxia Institute of Archaeology, and Mr. Chen Kun, Director of the Guyuan Museum, have coordinated the project with efficiency and enthusiasm.

Monks and Merchants and its associated programs would not have been possible without the support of a large group of generous donors. I would like to make special mention of our lead corporate sponsor, J. P. Morgan Chase & Company. Crucial additional support came from The W. L. S. Spencer Foundation, The Starr Foundation, the National Endowment for the Humanities, The Henry Luce Foundation Inc., the E. Rhodes and Leona B. Carpenter Foundation, and the National Endowment for the Arts.

Very early on members of the Friends of Asian Arts, a membership group for the Cultural Programs Division of the Asia Society, decided to learn about this exciting region and joined us for a study trip. They formed a group called "Gansu Dotcom" and provided early support for the project.

Many members of the staff of the Asia Society contributed to the success of this exhibition: Colin Mackenzie, Associate Director and Curator; Helen Abbott, Exhibitions and Publications Manager; Amy McEwen, Registrar; Nancy Blume, Education Coordinator; Clare Savard, Exhibitions Coordinator; Josh Harris, Galleries Associate; Chae Ho Lee, Graphics Designer; Mirza Burgos, Melissa Buyum, Sunny Huang, and Kaoru Ishizaki contributed their able administrative support; and Neil Liebman lent his editorial expertise.

Rachel Cooper and Linden Chubin of the Cultural Programs Division have developed an exciting array of performances and lectures that enhance the concept of cross-cultural interchange embodied in the exhibition. I would also like to thank Karen Karp and Heather Steliga, who have presented the multifaceted themes of *Monks and Merchants* in a way that has engaged audiences from the Asian American communities. The Development staff of the Asia Society who worked to secure the financial support for the project include Carol P. Herring, Yun Won Cho, and Atteqa Ali.

In conclusion, I want to express my deep gratitude to Nicholas Platt, President of the Asia Society, for his generous and profoundly important support for this often complex and always compelling project.

VISHAKHA N. DESAI
Senior Vice President
Director of the Galleries and Cultural Programs
Asia Society

Statement

On the behalf of the State Administration of Cultural Heritage of the People's Republic of China, I wish to express my warmest congratulations and heartfelt gratitude to the Gansu and Ningxia Administrations of Cultural Heritage and to the Asia Society for organizing "Monks and Merchants: Silk Road Treasures from Northwest China, Gansu and Ningxia, 4th–7th Century."

By requesting this exhibition, the Asia Society has shown great perspicacity and insight. China is one of the countries with the longest history in the world and possesses a rich and profound culture that has been passed down as an unbroken tradition from ancient times. Gansu province and the Ningxia Hui Autonomous Region are situated in northwest China and are traversed by branches of the ancient Silk Road. As communication between China and the outside world increased, Gansu-Ningxia became one of the most flourishing regions for international commerce, bequeathing to the present a rich legacy of historical sites and cultural relics.

The objects presented here are the finest works of art specially selected from the large quantity of cultural relics unearthed in Gansu and Ningxia. Because of their unique geographical location at the crossroads of the Silk Road, the historical relics and sites in these regions reveal a distinctive flavor, compared with other parts of China, a point that will be immediately apparent to visitors to the exhibition. Indeed, "Monks and Merchants" illuminates an important point in the history and evolution of mankind: that the formation of the distinctive cultures of each people and nation has come about through the exchange, assimilation, and blending of different traditions. This process has occurred in the past, is still occurring in the present, and will undoubtedly continue in the future. Therefore, it is our responsibility and obligation to foster the development and advance of mankind and society by devoting ourselves to cultural exchange and collaboration.

As the Chinese government currently carries out its policy of opening up the west of the country, Gansu and Ningxia are important players in implementing this strategy and are at the same time its beneficiaries. Presenting "Monks and Merchants" in the United States at this time will therefore have an even more positive and profound significance. I believe that this exhibition will deepen the understanding of the American people of the richness of China's northwest culture and of the important role that this region played in Chinese history. It will thus be yet another bridge linking the friendship of the Chinese and American people. This is, I believe, the organizers guiding intention and our common hope.

I wish "Monks and Merchants" every success.

ZHANG WENBIN
Director General, State Administration of Cultural Heritage
The People's Republic of China

Message from the Sponsor

JPMorgan Chase is proud to support the reopening of the Asia Society and Museum as it celebrates its newly renovated quarters. Like the Asia Society, JPMorgan Chase has its headquarters in New York City while maintaining a strong presence internationally. And we share a belief in the Society's mission to help educate the world about the rich heritage of the Asian continent.

We are also proud to sponsor the Society's premiere exhibition, "Monks and Merchants: Silk Road Treasures from Northwest China, Gansu and Ningxia, 4th–7th Century. This outstanding exhibition brings some of the finest works of art from the Silk Road to an American audience, many for the first time.

As this beautiful catalogue documents, this exhibition contains elements that will appeal to both the discriminating art critic and broad public alike. The twin themes of the exhibition—commerce and culture—are as relevant today as they were in ancient China, and we are delighted to help to make such an outstanding presentation possible. In keeping with ourlong-cherished tradition of supporting the arts, JPMorgan Chase is especially pleased to support a project that furthers the mutual understanding of diverse cultures of the world.

DOUGLAS A. WARNER III, JR.
Chairman
J. P. Morgan Chase & Co.

WILLIAM B. HARRISON
President and CEO
J. P. Morgan Chase & Co.

Message from the Asia Society

The Asia Society is proud to present "Monks and Merchants: Silk Road Treasures from Northwest China, Gansu and Ningxia, 4th–7th Century." This exhibition and accompanying catalogue inaugurate the opening of the Asia Society's renovated headquarters at 725 Park Avenue, and the addition of the Museum to the new public face of the Society. We are grateful to the government of the People's Republic of China for agreeing to lend these rare and beautiful works of art, the majority of which have never been seen outside China, for this exhibition.

The theme of this exhibition—thriving cultural and mercantile exchange between China and the West—is especially appropriate to this new century, as China continues to open up to the outside world. It is our hope that this exhibition, by showing that the current trend had remarkable precedents in centuries long past, will contribute to a deeper understanding of China's vital role in world history.

MAURICE R. GREENBERG
Chairman
Asia Society

NICHOLAS PLATT
President
Asia Society

Preface

Since 1993, we have been working to combine our expertise on China and Western and Central Asia to unravel the fascinating iconography and cultural context of the stone mortuary couches from northern China, specifically the Miho couch now in Japan. This research raised interesting issues about the nature of cosmopolitanism and intercultural exchange before the Tang dynasty, generally considered the period of China's greatest receptivity to "foreign" peoples and objects arriving by way of the Silk Road. Our goal has been to explore questions of cross-cultural exchange, assimilation, and adaptation through the archaeological and artistic record in the Period of Disunity between the fall of the Han and the rise of the Tang.

After our trip to northwest China in October of 1997, the concept for this exhibition began to take form. But it could never have been realized without the interest and support of many friends and colleagues in China and in the West. Our initial contact was made at the Gansu Provincial Museum, Lanzhou, with Tsu Shibin, who was director at that time, and with Zhang Pengchuan. Also important in the initial stages of the project was the assistance of Ma Wenzhi, chief of the Gansu Historical Relics Bureau. Others in Gansu who gave us their assistance included Fan Jinshi, at the Dunhuang Institute to us; Wang Hengtong at Binglingsi; Hu Chengzu at Maijishan; and Xiong Guoyao at Tianshui. In Ningxia we were fortunate to have the cooperation and generosity of Lei Runze, director of the Committee for Cultural Relics Management, Ningxia Cultural Relics Bureau, Yinchuan, and in Guyuan we are indebted to Luo Feng, Chen Qun, and Zhang Guangdong of the Municipal Museum. In Beijing An Jiayao was a steadfast friend. Last, but very important, Liu "Andy" Yong in Lanzhou and his associate, Chen "Steed" Tianjia, devoted much time and energy to our project; in fact, without Andy Yong's commitment, perseverance, and ability to make things happen, there would be no exhibition.

In the West, we have benefitted from the knowledge and interest of many colleagues and friends. We express special thanks to Osmund Bopearachchi, Emma C. Bunker, Willow Hai Chang, Derek J. Content, Shoki Goodarzi, Antonio Invernizzi, Laura Kaufman, James J. Lally, Cecilia Levin, Lin Meicun, Joan C. Mertens, Tigran Mkrtychev, Shing Müller, Jack Ogden, Elinor Pearlstein, Ariane Perrin, Qian Zhijian, P. Oktor Skjaervø, Suzanne Valenstein, Elisabetta Valtz, and Wu Xin. We are also fortunate to have had as advisors to the exhibition Albert E. Dien, Boris I. Marshak, Julie Segraves, Nicholas Sims-Williams, and Zhang Guangda. All generously contributed their expertise as well as essays or entries for the catalogue. Other contributors to whom we are indebted are Michael Alram, Susan Beningson, Chen Bingying, Luo Feng, and Colin Mackenzie.

We are grateful for the help and support of Asia Society and its staff. In particular, we thank Vishakha N. Desai, Senior Vice President and Director of the Galleries and Cultural Programs. She immediately recognized the value of an exhibition of this scope and gave us her dynamic leadership. We also wish to thank Colin Mackenzie, Assistant Director and Curator of Galleries, for his travels to China and for his negotiating skills. Also at the Asia Society, Helen Abbott, Exhibitions and Publications Manager, and Amy McEwen, Registrar, provided invaluable assistance. At Harry N. Abrams, we are extraordinarily lucky to have had Barbara Burn as our editor; her professionalism and belief in the project have been critical to the publication of this catalogue.

This entire undertaking would not have been possible without the loving support of Joanna and Joseph Geneve and Alan Kornheiser. Indeed, their patience, encouragement, and good humor helped us immeasurably.

ANNETTE L. JULIANO AND JUDITH A. LERNER

Time Line

WEST		SASANIAN DYNASTY (224–651)		EAST	
(Rome, Byzantium)		(Iran, Mesopotamia)		(Afghanistan, Central Asia, China)	
				220	Fall of Han Dynasty
		224–241	Ardashir I	230–330	Fall of Kushan Empire in Gandhara; Sasanians establish rule in Bactria and India
		241–272	Shapur I		
284–305	Diocletian				
313–337	Constantine I (the Great)			311; 313	Fall of Luoyang; "Sogdian Ancient Letters"
330	Constantinople becomes capital of Roman Empire			375–400	Arrival of Hephthalite Huns in eastern Iran, Bactria and northwest India
379–395	Theodosius I (the Great)			386–535	Northern Wei Dynasty
408–450	Theodosius II Visigothic invasions	459–484	Peroz	455, 461, 466, 468	Sasanian delegations to China
453	Death of Attila, king of the Huns	ca. 470	Chinese delegation to Persian court		
		476	Peroz captured by Hephthalites	476	Sasanian delegation to China
				507	Sasanian delegation to China
				510	Sogdiana conquered by Hephthalites
518–527	Justin I			518–522	Sasanian delegations to China
527–565	Justinian I (the Great)	531–628	Khusro I	535–557	Western Wei Dynasty
540	Antioch destroyed by Sasanians			553, 555	Sasanian delegations to China
				558	Allied with the Turks, Sasanians defeat Hephthalites; Sasanian Empire extends to the Oxus; Sogdiana falls to the Turks
568	Turkic-Sogdian delegation to Constantinople	567	Chinese delegation to Persian court	567	Sasanian delegation to China
610–641	Heraclius I	591–628	Khusro II	589–618	Sui Dynasty
611	Antioch captured by Sasanians				
614	Sasanians take Jerusalem, carry off a piece of the True Cross	615	Chinese delegation to Sasanian Iran before Turco-Persian War		
616	Sasanians invade Egypt, take Alexandria			616–617	Turco-Persian War
629	True Cross returned to Jerusalem	632–651	Yazdgard III	618–906	Tang Dynasty
637	Arabs conquer Jerusalem, Antioch			638	Sasanian delegation to China seeking aid against Arabs
641	Arabs conquer Egypt	642	Arabs defeat Sasanians at Nihavend, in Iran		
		651	Yazdgard murdered	662	Yazdgard's son, Peroz, seeks refuge in Chinese court; until mid-8th century, his descendants recognized by Tang emperor as Iranian sovereigns in exile

Chinese Chronology

NEOLITHIC PERIOD	ca. 8000–ca. 2000 BCE
EARLY DYNASTIC CHINA	
Xia Period (Protohistoric)	ca. 2100–ca. 1600 BCE
Shang Dynasty	ca. 1600–ca. 1100 BCE
Zhou Dynasty	ca. 1100–256 BCE
Western Zhou	1100–771 BCE
Eastern Zhou	771–256 BCE
Spring and Autumn Period	771–476 BCE
Warring States Period	475–221 BCE
DYNASTIC CHINA	
Qin Dynasty	221–207 BCE
Han Dynasty	206 BCE–220 CE
Western Han	206 BCE–24 CE
Eastern Han	25–220
PERIOD OF DISUNITY	220–589
Three Kingdoms	220–265
Wei	220–265
Shu Han	220–265
Wu	222–280
Western Jin	265–317
Northern Dynasties	
Sixteen Kingdoms*	304–438*
Northern Wei	386–535
Eastern Wei	534–550
Western Wei	535–557
Northern Qi	550–577
Northern Zhou	557–581
Sui**	581–589
SUI DYNASTY	589–618
TANG DYNASTY	618–906

Detailed chronology of the Sixteen Kingdoms follows.

**Northern Zhou destroyed Northern Qi in 577 reunifying Northern China. In 581, the throne was usurped by a general Yang Jian, who became the Emperor Wendi, the founder of the Sui dynasty.*

Chronology of the Sixteen Kingdoms*

KINGDOMS	PEOPLES	DATES	PROVINCE
Northwest			
Former Liang	Chinese	314–376	Gansu
Later Liang	Di	386–403	Gansu
Southern Liang	Xianbei	397–414	Gansu
Western Liang	Chinese	400–422	Gansu
Northern Liang	Xiongnu	398–439	Gansu
Central			
Cheng Han	Di	304–347	Hebei
Former Zhao	Xiongnu	304–329	Shanxi
Later Zhao	Jie	319–351	Hebei
Western Qin	Xianbei	365–431	Gansu/Shaanxi
Former Qin	Di	349–394	Shaanxi
Later Qin	Qiang	384–417	Shaanxi
Xia	Xiongnu	407–431	Shaanxi
Northeast			
Former Yan	Xianbei	333–370	Hebei
Later Yan	Xianbei	384–409	Hebei
Southern Yan	Xianbei	398–410	Shandong
Northern Yan	Chinese	409–436	Liaoning
Northern Wei**	Tuoba Xianbei	386–535	

The dates may vary depending on the criteria used to define statehood.

**The Xianbei group known as Tuoba established an independent state in northern Shanxi in 386, under the banner of Northern Wei Dynasty, and gradually defeated all rivals in the north by 439.*

Introduction:
Monks, Merchants, and Nomads
in Northwest China

By Annette L. Juliano
and Judith A. Lerner

Sometime about 313 CE, Nanai-vandak, a Sogdian merchant stationed in what is today the city of Lanzhou in Gansu province, wrote home to Samarkand about the chaos that had befallen China (no. 8): "The last emperor . . . fled from Luoyang because of the famine and fire was set to his palace and to the city. . . . Luoyang is no more, Ye is no more!. . . If I were to write to you everything about how China has fared, it would be beyond grief." This eye-witness account provides a rare view of the disintegration and ruin that had replaced the great Middle Kingdom that was the Han empire, already fallen in 220 CE. The Han was not only one of China's greatest empires but also a period fundamental in the formation of the Chinese identity. This national identity was challenged in the period between the fall of the Han and the rise of the Tang empire in 618 by a succession of short-lived dynasties and recurring invasions of different nomadic tribes from the north.

Until recently these nearly four hundred years of political disunity and social upheaval were perceived as an interregnum between two great dynasties—a period in which the north was controlled by nomadic rulers and the south by remnants of the Han imperial tradition. This period has been characterized as China's "Dark Age," a cultural wasteland of strife, invasion, and civil disorder. The reality, however, is quite different. The fourth to sev-enth century was a time of considerable cultural and artistic achievement. During these cen-turies, China's ancient civilization and art was almost totally transformed by the flourishing of Buddhism and by the increased commercial activity of the Silk Road.

The gateway to China for both Buddhism and trade from the West was through Gansu in northwest China, an area that corresponds to the present-day province of Gansu and a portion of the Ningxia Hui Autonomous Region.[1] Sandwiched between the Qilian Mountains of the Tibetan plateau to the south and the Gobi Desert to the north, Gansu was the only passageway connecting the overland routes, popularly known as the Silk Road, from the desert regions of the West with China's heartland and its imperial cities of Changan (present-day Xi'an) and Luoyang. Across this region traveled Buddhist monks, for-eign merchants, and nomads carrying the ideas and objects that profoundly affected the his-tory and culture of China.

As crucial links of the Silk Road in China, Gansu's cities and towns were, from the early fourth century, bustling centers of religion, commerce, and culture. In their lively mar-kets saffron-robed monks from India and Kashmir, "long-nosed" merchants from the far-

OPPOSITE: Buddhist disciple
Kasyapa (no. 62)

15

away cities of Bukhara, Samarkand, and Turfan, and nomadic tribesmen of Hun, Turkic, or Mongol origin intermingled. The symbiotic relationship that developed among these diverse groups encouraged the spread of Buddhist teaching and image-making as well as mercantile activities. Proselytizing monks bearing sutras and votive images impressed the local populace with their abilities to heal, tell fortunes, and perform magical feats. The nomadic elites sought the monks' advice and became avid patrons of Buddhism throughout Gansu, supporting translation centers for Buddhist texts and establishing some of the earliest cave temples and monasteries in China. Among the converts to Buddhism were merchants, some of whom also became translators of Buddhist texts.[2]

The practice of Buddhism often involved donations of precious objects as well as sumptuous decoration of stupas, temples, and reliquaries, the need for which stimulated the Silk Road trade. Merchant caravans imported the requisite pearls, coral, lapis lazuli, and rock crystal; at the same time, they provided safe passage for Buddhist monks and pilgrims. In addition, Buddhist temples and monasteries served as banks and warehouses for the merchants. The nomads were active also in the Silk Road trade, supplying horses and Bactrian camels to merchant caravans, and trading their leather, fur, and livestock for luxury goods from the West. At times, the nomads may have protected the merchant caravans through the often treacherous terrain of the Silk Road.

Despite the vitality of Buddhism and the Silk Road trade during the fourth and into the seventh century, this period remains one of the least-researched in the history of China's art and culture, of concern mainly to those who study Buddhism and Buddhist art. With the exception of the Buddhist cave paintings and sculptures of Dunhuang at the westernmost border of Gansu, scholarship about China and the Silk Road has concentrated on those regions to the west of China proper—present-day Xinjiang—and on the capital of Changan at the end (or beginning) of the Silk Road.

While the romance of the Silk Road has engendered numerous exhibitions that convey the breadth and scope of this great trans-Asian highway, hardly any have focused on a specific section of the Road or on a specific time in its history. Nor have any attempted to analyze the complexity of the cross-cultural relationships among the diverse groups brought together by the Silk Road within China's borders, nor have any focused on the issues of national identity, cultural exchange, and the ways in which foreign artistic and religious ideas were adapted and assimilated into Chinese civilization in the post-Han period. As the main entry to China from the West, it is ironic that so little attention has been paid to Gansu and Ningxia in any Silk Road exhibition. Other than Dunhuang, few of the many and spectacular Buddhist cave sites in Gansu and Ningxia have received the attention they deserve. Despite the number of significant archaeological finds that have been made in Gansu and Ningxia within the last twenty-five years, only Gansu's bronze "Flying Horse," first exhibited in the West in 1974, and the region's Neolithic painted pottery cultures[3] have figured significantly in major exhibitions; little else is known in the West.

The recent archaeological discoveries in Gansu and Ningxia and the increased accessibility and documentation of the Buddhist caves now make it possible to begin to understand the complex cultural interactions that took place in the region between the Han and Tang periods. Our view of the dynamics of the region has been aided further by the parallel expansion of archaeological investigation to the west, in Central Asia; the results of this activity help to illuminate many of the Chinese finds and to clarify artistic developments.[4]

Most of the objects featured in the current exhibition and in this catalogue can be associated with a specific site or area, having been either scientifically excavated or documented soon after their discovery; all but one are in the public collections of Gansu's and Ningxia's provincial capitals or of their local municipalities. Thus, from Gansu come the brilliantly embroidered banner fragments unearthed at Dunhuang and donated by a fifth-century prince (no. 45), sculptures and painting from the major Buddhist caves of the late fifth to late sixth century at Maijishan (nos. 60–66, 68–70), an elaborately painted and gilded late sixth-century funerary couch (no. 106) and the seventh- or eighth-century bejeweled reliquary boxes from the foundations of a Buddhist stupa (no. 120). From Ningxia are included the remarkably eclectic objects from the tombs of the influential sixth-century generals, Li Xian and Tian Hong (nos. 30–44, 97–100) and those of the Shi family, descendants of Sogdian settlers from Central Asia who rose to official positions in the Chinese court in the early part of the seventh century (nos. 80–92, 95–96, 101–105).

These and the other objects in the exhibition reveal the dynamic social, political, and multicultural links that connected the monks, merchants, and nomads in Gansu and Ningxia between the fourth and seventh century. They also offer a rich opportunity to explore issues of ethnic identity (i.e., what is, what is not Chinese), adaptation, assimilation, and sinicization from an art historical viewpoint. The many ideas, styles, and motifs transmitted during the fourth to the seventh centuries—such as an interest in naturalism, the image of the inhabited vine, and decorative beaded borders—were assimilated and transformed by the Tang to create a new, national style that defined the dynasty for the three centuries of its rule.

NOTES

1. Ningxia was part of Gansu until 1928, when it was defined as a separate administrative region, only to be reabsorbed into Gansu province in 1954. In 1958, it reemerged as the Ningxia Hui Autonomous Region.

2. For example, the second-century merchant An Xuan, most likely a Parthian from Central Asia, joined his compatriot, the monk An Shigao in Luoyang to translate Buddhist texts (Zürcher 1972; Chien 1973).

3. Krahl 1999.

4 Litvinskii 1994, pp. xi–xiv and the entire volume.

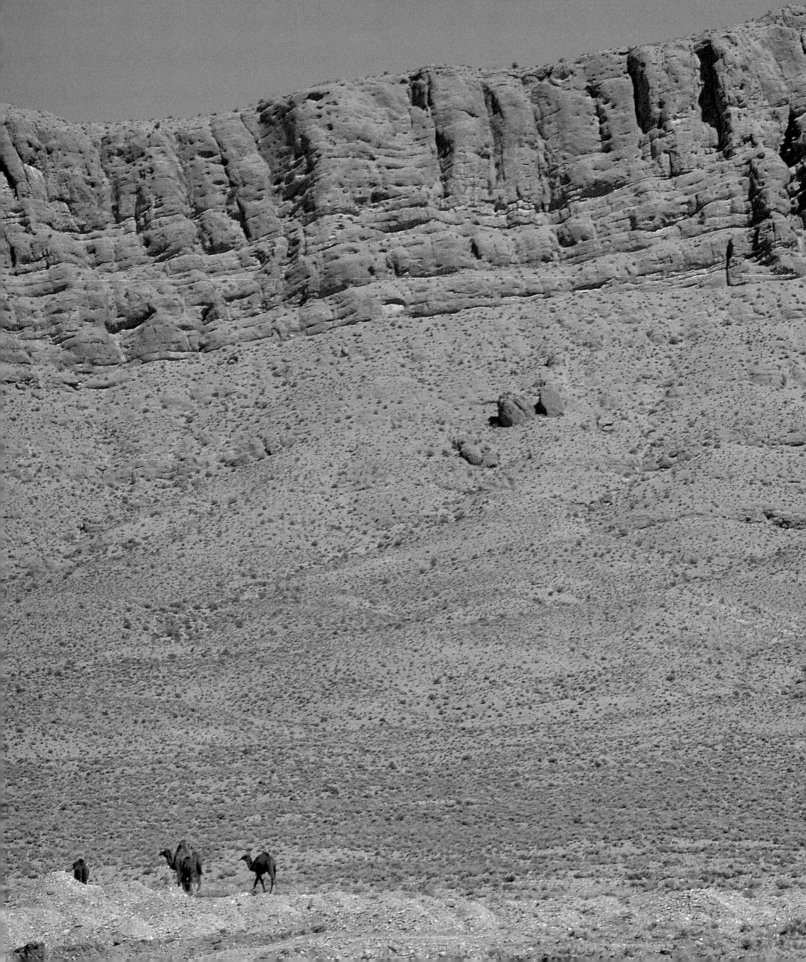

PART I

SETTING THE STAGE

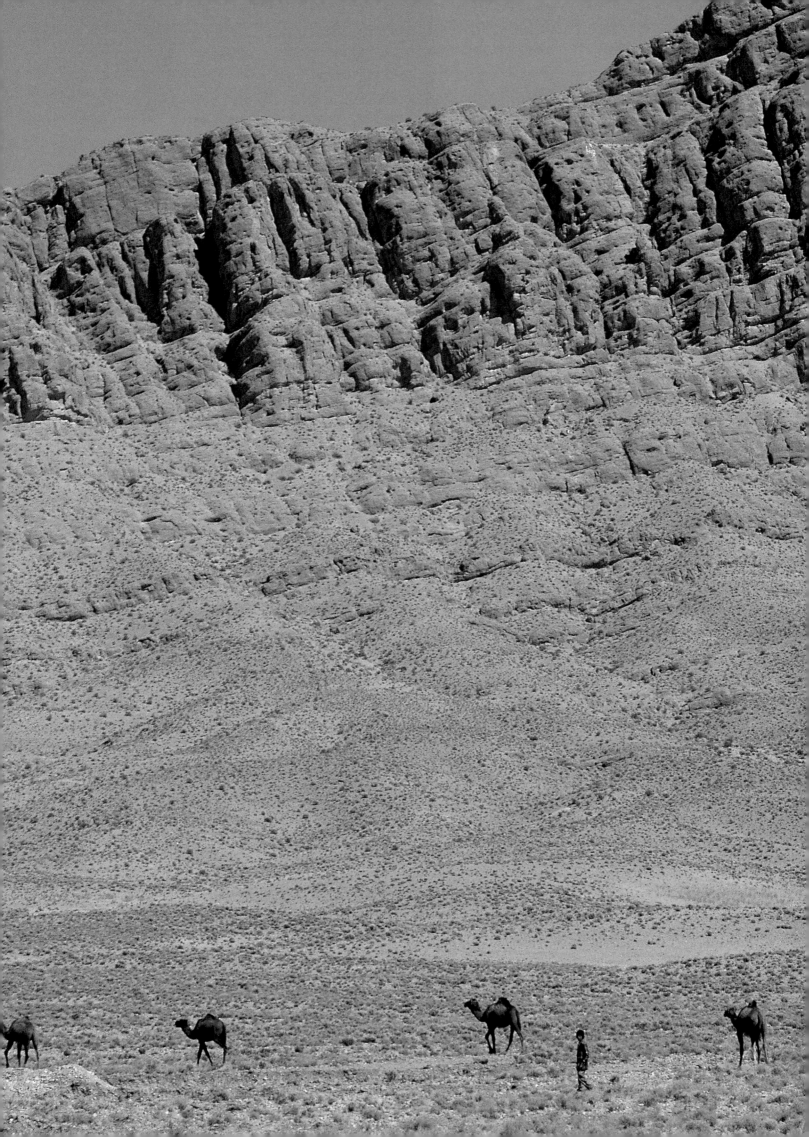

1

The Silk Road in Gansu and Ningxia

ANNETTE L. JULIANO
AND JUDITH A. LERNER

Messengers come and go every season and month,
foreign traders and merchants knock on the gates of the great wall every day.

—*Hou Hanshu*, Official History of the Chinese Han Dynasty[1]

The Trade Routes and Gansu's Role

The term *Silk Road* was coined in the late nineteenth century by the German geographer Ferdinand von Richthofen to describe the system of transcontinental caravan roads that stretched from China to the eastern Mediterranean, a distance of some five thousand miles. This overland trading network linked some of the world's greatest empires—Roman, Persian, and Chinese—but while the Silk Road was the principal means of moving goods, it was by no means the only one. Other "silk roads" went overland, north and south, as well as by sea.[2]

One overland route, similar to the path of the modern Karakorum highway in present-day northern Pakistan, ran north from the upper Indus River Valley in northwestern India to Kashgar in the Tarim Basin of modern Xinjiang (Chinese Turkistan)[3]; from there the route linked up with the east-west transcontinental road to continue east to the ancient Chinese capitals of Changan (present-day Xi'an) and Luoyang or west to Samarkand and beyond. Goods also moved from India through Bactria (present-day Afghanistan), along the Oxus River (the Amu Darya), to and across the Caspian Sea, and along rivers in the Caucasus to the Black Sea.[4] Another overland route, the so-called steppe road, ran from China to Xinjiang through the uplands of Mongolia and southern Siberia, across northern Central Asia (modern Kazakhstan) and along the northern coast of the Caspian and the mouth of the Volga River.[5]

Alternatives to the overland routes were the sea routes from Alexandria in Egypt, by way of the Red Sea, around the Arabian Peninsula, and through the Indian Ocean to India and Ceylon (present-day Sri Lanka); from there ships traveled north across the South China Sea to the ports of Tongking (near present-day Hanoi) and south China. Sea routes combined with land routes so that goods could move by camel caravan from the Mediterranean coast to the Persian Gulf, from whence they could be shipped to India and China; from the south China ports these goods might travel north overland to the Yellow River and its important cities, Luoyang and Changan.[6]

OVERLEAF: Fig. 1. Camel caravan crossing the Iranian plateau on the Silk Road to Central Asia (photo: Judith A. Lerner)

OPPOSITE: View of Cave 169 at Binglingsi (Luminous Spirits Cave Temple), set in the fantastic eroded canyons of the Yellow River in Gansu. This cave, dated to 420 CE, is an extraordinary repository of early fifth-century Buddhist art and contains the earliest known dated cave-temple images. (photo: Annette L. Juliano)

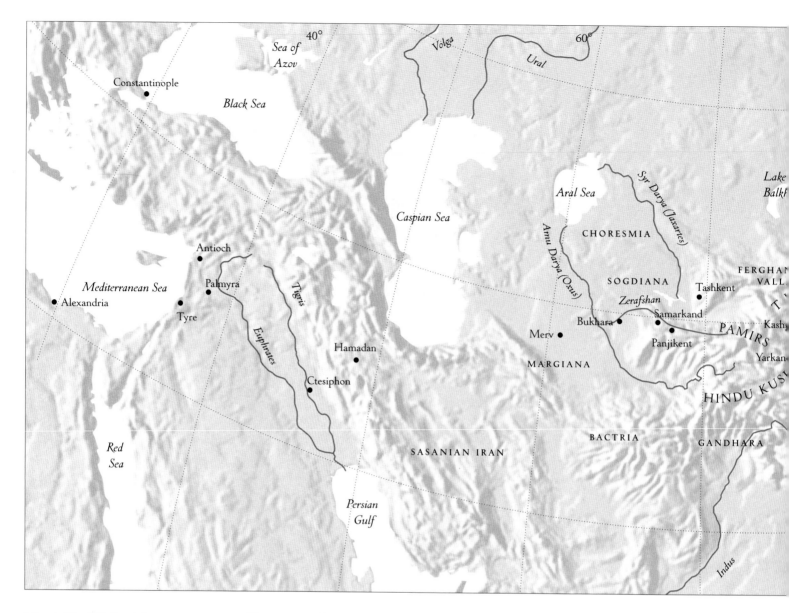

Map 1. The Silk Road from
Constantinople to Xi'an

Fig. 3. Desert landscape in
Xinjiang province (*below*)
(photo: Annette L. Juliano)

To return to the transcontinental overland route, it began (or ended) at the Mediterranean cities of Antioch and Tyre, traversed the many deserts, steppe lands, and mountain
passes of Syria, Mesopotamia, and Iran, to reach the oasis cities of Central Asia (fig. 1).
There, the road passed through Merv (in present-day Turkmenistan), Bukhara, and
Samarkand (in Uzbekistan) and the fertile valleys of Ferghana, home of the swift "blood-
sweating" horses, called *tianma* and prized by the Chinese, to the Tianshan Mountains. To
this point, the route had traversed often difficult and inhospitable terrain, but relatively
benign compared to the next portion, the one that crossed
Xinjiang, the area called by the Chinese the Western
Regions.[7] There, the vast emptiness of the Taklamakan
Desert occupies the center of the arid Tarim Basin. It is an
enormous zone of sand dunes, virtually devoid of vegetation,
ringed by the Tianshan Mountains to the north, the Kunlun
Mountains to the south, and the Pamirs to the west (fig. 3).[8]

It is at the Taklamakan that the Silk Road divides into
a northern and a southern route, both of which pass through
a series of oasis cities strung along the edges of the desert and
bordering on the mountain ranges; in the north, from the
busy market center of Kashgar to Kucha and Kizil with its

MONKS AND MERCHANTS

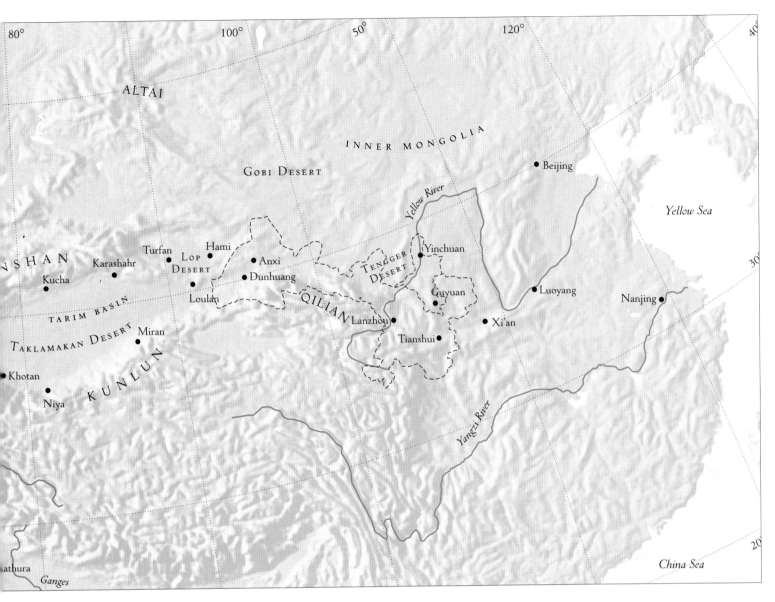

honeycomb of Buddhist caves, then southward through Karashahr (Ming-oi) to Loulan, with a northern fork skirting the forbidding Lop Salt Desert to Turfan and Hami (fig. 4). In the south, the route passed from Kashgar to Yarkand and then through the ancient Buddhist centers of Khotan, Niya, and Miran.

Toward the eastern end of the Taklamakan, the northern route's Karashahr-Loulan road joined with the southern route near Dunhuang. The northern branch of the northern route (the Turfan-Hami road) emerged from the desert somewhat farther east at Anxi.[9] Sit-uated in the midst of a sandy emptiness, the oasis of Dun-huang (called in Tang times Shazhou, "sand district") marks the beginning of modern Gansu province and of westernmost China. Shaped somewhat like a barbell, Gansu is divided into three major zones: desert in the westernmost section corre-sponding to one end of the barbell; a narrow, high-altitude plateau constituting the central bar; and a mountainous region in the east to balance the other end. Much of Gansu is this central portion, a long and narrow panhandle sand-wiched between the Gobi Desert (Map 2, p. 30) on the north and the Qilian Mountains on the south. About a thousand miles long and fifty miles wide, Gansu consists mostly of

Fig. 4. Buddhist cave temples (*below*) at Bezeklik perched precariously on a cliff over-hanging a river valley in the Flame Mountains (Xinjiang), 25 miles southwest of Turfan (photo: Guy A. Weill)

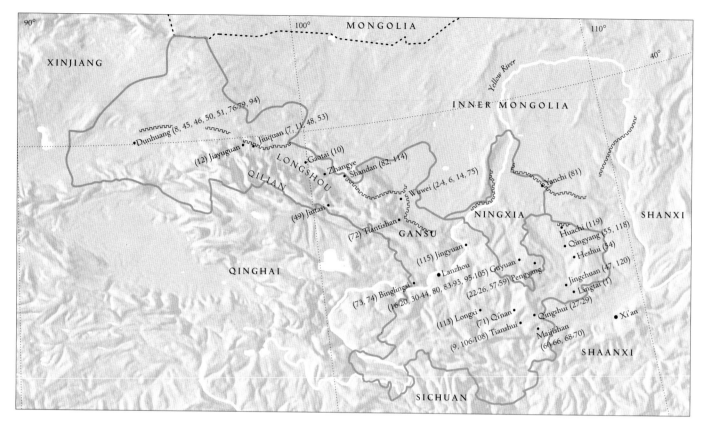

Map 2. Topographical and site map of Gansu and Ningxia, indicating where objects in the exhibition were found

Fig. 5. View of the narrow Gansu corridor (*opposite*) with the Qilian Mountains to the south (photo: Annette L. Juliano)

desert and steppe; its excellent grasslands made it a traditional horse-breeding region, as well as the major corridor for trade and cultural exchange. Also called Hexi ("west of the Yellow River") or Liangzhou ("district of the Liang"), this corridor is actually that part of Gansu that begins at the province's western border and ends at Lanzhou (fig. 5), where the Yellow River first crosses the Silk Road to flow north toward the Mongolian border and then bends to flow south to the area east of Xi'an in Shaanxi province.

With little rainfall, Gansu relies on an extensive irrigation system, developed more than two thousand years ago, that uses the snowmelt from the mountains, which forms streams in the valleys. Along the banks of the resulting rivers, a number of oases developed into towns and cities that served as staging areas and entrepôts for the Silk Road trade. Associated with the development of these inhabited places were numerous Buddhist cave sites, which were established in nearby yet remote areas of the neighboring mountain ranges.

Dunhuang, where a military garrison had been established as early as the first century BCE, was the main center of western Gansu—the last place for caravans to acquire provisions before embarking into the desert and the first stop where they could rest after emerging from it (nos. 10, 13, 45, 46, 50a, 50b, 51, 76–79, 94). It is the site of the wonderful Thousand Buddha Caves (also called Mogao), first established in 366 CE (see p. 127). The next main post of the road is in central Gansu, at Jiuquan (ancient Suzhou and Marco Polo's Sukchur; nos. 7, 11, 14, 48, 53), the oldest of the garrison cities protecting the western entry into China. To its north was the farthest extent of the Great Wall at the site of the modern city of Jiayuguan (no. 12).[9a] To the south of Jiuquan are the network of Buddhist caves of Wenshushan, which were first opened in the fifth century (fig. 6).

From Jiuquan, the caravans passed through lush areas used for breeding Gansu's "heavenly horses" and proceeded to the green oasis of Zhangye (ancient Ganzhou and Marco Polo's Campichu).[10] Associated with this city is the impressive peak of Matishan,

Fig. 6. Wenshushan Mountain (*top*) near the city of Jiuquan, one of the oldest garrison cities in Gansu. These barren red cliffs hide many small Buddhist cave temples. (photo: Annette L. Juliano)

Fig. 7. Xumishan Mountain (*above*) near the city of Guyuan (Ningxia). The view westward through the rock formation known as the Stone Gate reveals a segment of the actual Silk Road traversed for centuries. (photo: Judith A. Lerner)

Fig. 8. Xumishan Mountain (*opposite*) contains cave temples of the same name near the city of Guyuan (Ningxia). This colossal Tang Buddha rises 65 feet from its base. (photo: Annette L. Juliano)

about forty miles to the southeast in the Qilian Mountains, with seven different cave sites in its vicinity. The Jintasi Caves (no. 49) and other sites in the area were founded during the Northern Liang (early fifth century) or Northern Wei (late fifth century) dynasties. Going by way of Shandan on the plain south of the Longshou Mountains (Longshoushan) (nos. 82, 114), the caravans next reached the city of Wuwei (Guzang, also referred to as Liangzhou) (nos. 2–4, 6, 75). Situated in a narrow river valley at the edge of the Tengger Desert (a subdivision of the Gobi), Wuwei was the largest and most prosperous of the central Gansu cities; it was the capital of the Northern Liang dynasty from 412 to 439. Southeast of Wuwei is the Buddhist cave site of Tiantishan (see pp. 296–97) in a valley of the Qilian range (no. 72).

The Gansu corridor ends at Lanzhou (Jincheng, or "Gold City"), where it opens to the mountainous eastern area, called Longxi (no. 113) and Longdong (west and east of the Longshan Mountains, respectively). Here the Silk Road was no longer constricted to the narrow plateau of the Gansu corridor and took several branches. The main route crossed the Wei River and proceeded east to Tianshui (ancient Qinzhou and today Gansu's second-largest city; nos. 9, 106–108), the last major stop in Gansu before crossing over into Shaanxi province and on to the ancient capital of Changan. About thirty miles from Tianshui, amid fertile plains, is the dramatic site of Maijishan (see p. 140), which rises from the plain and is surrounded by richly forested mountains (nos. 61–71).

Southeast of Lanzhou, the spectacular cave site at Binglingsi (nos. 73, 74), founded as early as the late fourth or the early fifth century (see pp. 121–2), was near communication routes that linked southeastern Gansu with the Tibetan highlands of Qinghai, as well as with Sichuan to the south. The route from Sichuan through Gansu was that taken by the early-fifth-century monk Faxian when he set out from Nanjing in southeastern China on his way to India to obtain Buddhist texts.

A more northern route from the Gansu corridor to Xi'an existed from Wuwei or Lanzhou across the Yellow River as it flows south into Shaanxi, into what is today the Ningxia Hui Autonomous Region.[11] The first of the stops was at Jingyuan (no. 115), which led northeast to the important administrative center of Guyuan (ancient Yuanzhou; nos. 16–21, 30–44, 80, 83–93, 95–105), past the colossal Buddha of the Xumishan cave complex to the north of Guyuan (fig. 8). From Guyuan, roads ran north as far as Yanchi (no. 81) right within the Great Wall, and south, passing through Pengyang (nos. 22–26, 57–59) and back into Gansu. There the road continued to Jingchuan (nos. 47, 118, 120) and Lingtai (no. 1) near the border of Shaanxi; it also ran southwest to Tianshui via Qingshui (nos. 27–29) and Qin'an (no. 71).

Although about five thousand miles in length, most of the Silk Road trade came through a chain of short relays, passing from one trader's hands to another's, from one traveling merchant to a local one, so that a particular article might have been bought and sold many times along the way.[12] Some merchants traveled back and forth on only part of the route (see Chapter 6), although others accompanied their caravans for most or all of the entire distance. The exchange of goods basically took three forms: diplomatic gifts or tribute; administered trade organized by government agents at certain agreed places—such as trade fairs or the quarters given over to foreigners in many of the Chinese cities; and market trade carried out by individual merchants.[13] The state's involvement with trade in the Sui period is exemplified by Emperor Yangdi's organizing and attending a twenty-seven-nation trade meeting at Zhangye in 609; delegations not only brought goods for exchange, but performers arrived from Central Asia for a cultural festival that was part of the event.[14]

Gansu in Historical Context

Fig. 9. The aptly named "overhanging" Great Wall, linking Jiayuguan with the Black Mountain, has been recently reconstructed. (photo: Annette L. Juliano)

Before the third century BCE, at the beginning of the Han dynasty, Gansu province was virtually unknown to the Chinese. The area was inhabited by the Xiongnu and other nomadic tribes, who intermittently launched attacks on Chinese agricultural settlements to the east and even threatened the imperial capital of Changan. Chinese recognition of the Gansu corridor's strategic position stemmed from Han military campaigns against the Xiongnu. Related diplomatic ventures into Gansu and beyond into Central Asia were aimed at controlling the approaches to the Han empire and acquiring the much-prized steeds of Ferghana, which the Chinese considered superior to their own steppe ponies. Thus, in 139 and 115 BCE, the Han emperor Wudi (r. 140–87 BCE) sent his emissary Zhang Qian to Central Asia in search of allies to outflank the Xiongnu.[15] Although he returned without an alliance, Zhang Qian brought back word of the many kingdoms and exotic products of the Western Regions, including the Ferghana horses, and paved the way for trade in Chinese silk.

By 100 BCE, the Chinese armies finally succeeded in acquiring a few of these fine animals to present to Emperor Wudi.[16] They immediately became a status symbol and an enduring legend. This western breed of large horse was well known in the later Han empire of the second and third centuries CE and is depicted in the remarkable cast-bronze sculptures of horses in the exhibition (nos. 2–4).[17]

One hundred years later, by the first century CE, the Han army destroyed the Xiongnu threat and gained control of the Tarim Basin and the oasis cities skirting its northern and southern edges. Han military and political dominance of this region led to the opening of the Silk Road, thus beginning the lucrative silk trade with the West. The Great Wall was extended westward into the deserts as far as modern-day Jiayuguan, enclosing what was to become Gansu, including the corridor (figs. 9, 10). To protect access to these Western Regions and defend against nomadic marauders, five Chinese garrisons were established, starting at the far west with Dunhuang near Yumenguan—the "Jade Gate"—and moving eastward to Jiuquan, Zhangye, Wuwei, and Jinching. One million Chinese were forcibly relocated to the Gansu corridor to stabilize this newly acquired territory and to strengthen the Han cultural presence at this end of the Silk Road.[18]

West on the Silk Road, in the second century BCE, the powerful empire of the Kushans emerged in northern India, created by the Yuezhi, a Scythian tribe driven from northwest China by the Xiongnu. The third and most important Kushana king, Kaniskha I (early second century CE), a patron of Buddhism and an energetic builder of religious monuments, facilitated the spread of Buddhism beyond the borders of the Kushan Empire throughout Central Asia to East Asia.[19] In the period from the first century BCE to the first century CE, during the Han dynasty, Buddhism reached China. The domination of Gansu by the Han and of northern India by the Kushans guaranteed relative safety and security to merchant caravans bringing exotic goods from the West to the Han nobility, as well as to proselytizing monks seeking converts.

Despite its achievements, the Han dynasty began to crumble as both internal and external threats challenged Chinese civilization. Weakened by corrupt and inept emperors and by the growing wealth and power of great families, the centralized government failed to quell popular unrest. As the political situation deteriorated, corrosive skepticism turned the educated classes away from their commitment to Confucian ideology, the foundation of the imperial system, and social order. The decline of Confucianism led to the rise of immortality

Fig. 10. Jiayuguan (Gansu). This fort, established in the Han but rebuilt in the Ming (fourteenth century) and refurbished in the modern era, guarded a strategic pass and was considered to be the last major stronghold of the Chinese empire in the west.

cults and alchemy and to the escapism of mystical Daoism; this last provided a window for Buddhism.[20]

The disintigration of Han political and military power opened the door to waves of nomadic invaders in north China and further encouraged the growth of Buddhism, which became an increasingly attractive spiritual refuge. With the final collapse of the Han dynasty in 220, China experienced nearly four hundred years of disunity, disrupted by internal power struggles and nomadic invasions, until stability was restored briefly by the Sui and finally, in 618, by the Tang dynasty. Between the collapse of the Han dynasty and the rise of the Tang empire lies the Period of Disunity (220–589). Often described as an interregnum wedged between two powerful and unified dynasties, the Six Dynasties saw China succumb to political disunity, incessant warfare, internecine strife, and nomadic invasions. These four centuries fall into two significant parts: the first period included the Three Kingdoms (220–265) and the Western Jin dynasties (265–317), and the second encompassed the Nan Bei Zhao, the Period of Northern and Southern Dynasties (304–581), and the Sui dynasty (581–589).

The rulers of the Three Kingdoms warred among themselves and against the growing barbarian menace along the northern and southwestern borders. The contending kingdoms, Wei in the north (220–265), Shu Han (221–265) southwest in Sichuan, and Wu (222–280) in the southeast persisted for some sixty years until that part of China was unified under the banner of the Western Jin (265–317), which tried to rekindle the former glory of the Han empire. The multicultural currents in Gansu during the rule of the Three Kingdoms and Western Jin are evident in the artifacts from the period. These include two seals of a nomadic prince and a king (no. 9); Han-style tomb tiles painted with grazing camels, horses, and donkeys (nos. 10–12); two reclining rams (nos. 14, 15), one made from the coal stone abundant in Gansu and the other from jade probably imported from Khotan; a small bronze nomad lamp with camels (no. 13); and the fantastic unicorns, one of bronze, the other of wood (nos. 6, 7).

The Wei Kingdom that preceded the Western Jin maintained control of the Gansu corridor, and the garrison cities in Gansu had prospered from the lucrative Silk Road trade. The townspeople lived by such trade, and the developing Buddhist communities of Gansu also thrived from the merchants and pilgrims who conducted business and visited the monasteries and cave-temple sites.

During the Western Jin, the reign of the emperor Wudi (r. 265–289) was the most peaceful and prosperous. Around 280, embassies from Shanshan (a desert kingdom that included the important oasis cities of Niya, Miran, and Loulan), Khotan, Kucha, Karashahr, and Ferghana journeyed to Changan, the Western Jin capital, bearing tribute.[21] With the trade and the embassies came more monks ready to propagate the Buddha's teachings by setting up translation centers. In Changan, under the Kushan monk Dharmaraksa (active c. 265–313), the quantity and quality of Buddhist translations reached unprecedented heights; he personally translated into Chinese five of the most important texts of early Buddhism.[22]

After Emperor Wudi died, court intrigues and stabbings exploded in a catastrophic struggle among powerful princes of the Sima clan. Compounded by famine and pestilence, this conflict eventually led to the complete collapse of the north, including Gansu. Sensing weakness in the Western Jin court, a loose confederation of five nomadic tribes—Xiongnu, Jie, Xianbei, Di, and Qiang—sacked Luoyang in 311, an event described with horror by a

Sogdian merchant writing home to his master in Samarkand (no. 8). The nomadic invaders can be glimpsed in the murals and on the painted tiles in Gansu tombs from this period (nos. 10–12). By the final fall of Western Jin, both capitals, Luoyang and Changan, lay in ruins, and the Chinese court fled south, leaving the north to the invaders. Chinese gentry quickly settled in the south and in 317 restored the fallen dynasty under the title of Eastern Jin, with its capital at Nanjing. The Eastern Jin became the standard-bearers of the Han tradition, and the early fourth century marks the beginning of the second half of this period, known as *Nan Bei Chao,* or the Northern and Southern Dynasties.

During the *Nan Bei Chao* (fourth–mid-fifth century), Sixteen Kingdoms period (304–439), sixteen kingdoms, nearly all nomadic, rose and disappeared in the political cauldron of northern China, each lasting an average of twenty-six years. The name "Sixteen Kingdoms" reflects the military and political confusion of this chaotic period, during which, ironically, Buddhism made considerable advances in Gansu. Buddhism and Buddhist art acquired powerful new patrons in the nomadic rulers, particularly under what is called the "Five Liang" Kingdoms: Former Liang (314–376), Later Liang (386–403), Southern Liang (397–414), Western Liang (400–422), and Northern Liang (398–439), all rivals that controlled various parts of Gansu and beyond to Turfan from the late fourth through the early fifth century. During the Western Liang, the Kashmiri monk Dharmamitra journeyed from Kucha to Dunhuang, then the center of the Western Liang, and established a monastery on an unoccupied site.[23] Buddhism also flowered (nos. 19, 20) under Juqu Mengxun (398–433), the ruler of the Northern Liang Kingdom in central Gansu.[24] With his support, the Indian monk Dharmaksema (385–433) opened a translation center with one hundred monks at the capital of Wuwei (Guzang), and important cave-temple building began along the entire Gansu corridor.[25]

In 386, in the northern corner of Shanxi province, the kingdom of Wei was founded by a tribal offshoot of the Xianbei, known as Tuoba. This tribe conquered Gansu by 439 and by the middle of the fifth century had unified the north under the banner of the Northern Wei dynasty. The Tuoba proved adept students of both traditional Chinese culture and of Buddhism (nos. 51–58, 60, 61).[26] Their ruling house, seduced by the Chinese lifestyle, embarked upon a conscious policy of court sinicization, ordering the Tuoba aristocracy to adopt Chinese language, dress, and surnames and encouraging intermarriage with the Chinese gentry. By the early sixth century, this policy of sinicization led to internal struggles between the ruling house and the opposing tribal aristocracy who resented relinquishing their Tuoba heritage. Political disunity and bloodletting returned as the Northern Wei split into rival dynasties in 535, with Gansu coming under the control of the Western Wei (535–553) and then Northern Zhou (557–581); to the northeast, the Eastern Wei (534–550) held sway, followed by the Northern Qi (550–577).

In 581 General Yang Jian, a remarkable figure in Chinese history, reunited northern and southern China for the first time since the Western Jin.[27] With the reunification, Yang Jian, now called Emperor Wendi of the Sui dynasty (r. 589–618), turned his attention to the Tujue Turks, who, through their control of trading routes to the west and north, had emerged as a military and economic force in Mongolia and Central Asia. Wendi sent troops against them to reassert Chinese domination of the Silk Road. Responding to the severe persecution of Buddhism that had occurred at the end of the Northern Zhou, he relaxed the proscriptions against the monks and nuns. Buddhism became the unifying ideology for both north and south China and a vehicle for the breakdown of the strong regionalism and factionalism that the years of disunity had encouraged. Inspired by the model of the early Indian Buddhist ruler Asoka (r. 272–232 BCE), Wendi promoted the construction of stupas across China to enshrine Buddhist relics.

During this short-lived dynasty, Dunhuang's Mogao grottoes experienced a burst of activity with the opening of some seventy or eighty caves embellished by spectacular sculpture and painting, which reflect strong influences from the Indian Gupta Empire (c. 320–650) and Xinjiang. The artistic activity at Gansu Buddhist sites paralleled the growing commercial activity, as exemplified by the organization of the twenty-seven-nations trade fair at Zhangye in 609.[28] Despite these accomplishments, the Sui dynasty did not survive the succession of Wudi's son and fell to the Tang dynasty (618–906), China's second great empire.

The Tang rulers expanded westward into Xinjiang (figs. 11, 12) and beyond to Samarkand; they pushed south into Afghanistan, and to the Indus River Valley of Afghanistan and northern Pakistan. Both land and sea trade grew beyond any level known before, transforming the imperial capital of Changan into a world metropolis that attracted monks (nos. 62, 73), merchants, soldiers, entertainers (nos. 81, 82), and official embassies from all over Asia. Not until the twentieth century was China ever again so tolerant, responsive, and attracted to things "foreign."[29]

With imperial patronage and local support, Buddhism reached its zenith during the Tang. New cave shrines were opened across all of China as Buddhism flourished along with commerce. Gansu benefited from China's military and political control of the Silk Road. This is reflected in the dramatic increase in Buddhist activity at sites such as Dunhuang, which

Fig. 11. Citadel of Jiaohe (Yarkhoto), outside of Turfan (Xinjiang). A garrison town during the Han and the Tang, it is today a ruin with the striking remains of a large Buddhist monastery. (photo: Annette L. Juliano)

added about 210 caves, and Binglingsi, near Lanzhou, which added some 45. Tang sculpture and painting at Dunhuang (nos. 77–79) and at sites such as Tiantishan (no. 72) convey cosmopolitan elegance and subdued sensuality, a blend of India's suave and voluptuous forms contained by the Chinese passion for strong linear rhythms. By the middle of the ninth century (841–845), however, a half-crazed Tang ruler and fanatic Daoist unleashed the most devastating assault ever on the organized Buddhist church and its monuments, not only dealing that faith a crippling blow but also obliterating much evidence of its true impact on China.[30]

What Was Traded?

As the writer Andre Gunder Frank has observed, "The 'silk' road could equally well be called the road of jade. . . . Or the road could be called one of gold, silver; other metals, wood, wool, clay and their manufacturers; spices, grains, and other food stuffs; and especially horses, other livestock, human slaves and a host of other items."[31] It could also be called the "glass" road for the bowls carried from the Roman and Persian Empires (no. 30).[32] Virtually all these products were foreign or exotic, of a special kind or quality; even those that were staples in their homeland became luxury goods in the markets for which they were bound because of their rarity.

The Tang specialist Edward Schafer provides a comprehensive account of the exotic goods brought to the Tang court of China.[33] Not all of these goods figured in the trade of pre-Tang times, nor had some attained the importance or demand they enjoyed under the

Fig. 12. Jiaohe (Yarkhoto), outside of Turfan (Xinjiang). Headless seated Buddhas in the stupa of the destroyed Buddhist monastery. (photo: Annette L. Juliano)

Tang. Among the goods that are most relevant to the current exhibition are glass (no. 30), a variety of precious and semiprecious stones, such as rock crystal, turquoise, agate, lapis lazuli, carnelian, and sapphire (nos. 20, 21, 43, 87, 120); jade (nos. 14, 44, 88); coral (no. 20, 21); jewelry (nos. 32, 85); and metalwork (nos. 31, 115). Pearls from southern India and Ceylon and from Persia came by way of the sea routes from south China or through northwestern India and Central Asia. Pearls were valued in the Roman and Byzantine West and also had great significance for Buddhists, thus figuring prominently in trade and religious donations (no. 120).[34] Among the textiles transported were wool—some of it dyed purple—silk damask, brocades, embroideries, and woolen rugs. The few pieces of silk in the exhibition (nos. 109, 110) present just a fraction of the designs and the quality of the textiles that traveled into and out of China. Unlike its neighbors, Xinjiang to the west and Qinghai to the south, Gansu does not have a climate dry enough to preserve extensive silk remains.

Spices and other edibles also traveled along this historic path. Grapes were first brought to China from Parthia in the second century BCE (nos. 115–117); alfalfa was imported from Central Asia as feed for the Ferghana "heavenly horses." Coins—Sasanian, Byzantine, and their imitations—were used in great numbers as currency, bullion, and even decoration (nos. 93–104). Along with the merchants and monks, others travelers joined the caravans: missionaries, pilgrims, ambassadors, soldiers, scholars, artisans, horse trainers, acrobats, musicians, and dancers. In fact, entertainers from Central Asia were extremely popular in China from at least the sixth century and well into Tang times (nos. 81, 82).

What did China offer and transmit to the West at this time? In addition to silk and other textiles, the most important export was paper technology, carried by merchants as well as by monks. The religious texts and business and other documents discovered at Dunhuang (no. 46) and the Sogdian letter found in the ruined watchtower between Dunhuang and Loulan (no. 8) were written on rag paper. Chinese coins served as the model for the copper coinage used in Sogdiana in Central Asia, possibly as early as the beginning of the seventh century.[35] Perhaps less consequential, but by no means less appreciated, was the rhubarb, used for its medicinal properties, for which Jiuquan was famous.

Fig. 13. The glowing presence of this massive seventy-five foot Tang Buddha (*opposite*) from the early eighth century CE dominates Dunhuang's Cave 130. (photo: Annette L. Juliano)

NOTES

1. Cited by Liu 1988, p. 18.

2. Richthofen actually used the plural, *Seidenstrassen* (silk roads), to refer to this network of "roads," not all of them overland. See Egami, 1988, pp. 12–24.

3. Jettmar 1991, pp. 251–54; see also Chapter 6.

4. Staviskij 1995, pp. 191–92, citing Pliny and Strabo and archaeological excavations on the now-dry Uzboy riverbed.

5. Thierry 1993, p. 121; and Staviskij 1995, p. 192. In contrast to the other routes mentioned, which were well-established in the late first millennium BCE under Roman, Parthian, and Han rule, this route most likely did not become important until the Early Middle Ages, i.e., the seventh century and after (although Staviskij cites second- and third-century evidence for its use).

6. For a summary of the sources, see Pulleyblank 1991, pp. 426–28.

7. Pan 1997, pp. 50–54.

8. Taaffe 1990, pp. 20–22.

9. There is a direct road from Turfan to Dunhuang across the White Dragon Dunes, a particularly inhospitable stretch of total desert.

9a. In February 2001, the official Xinhua News Agency of China reported that the Great Wall is 310 miles longer than previously thought, stretching to the edge of the Lop Desert, and not ending at the Jaiyuguan Pass.

10. It is of interest to note that the first syllables of "Ganzhou" and "Suzhou" combine to make "Gansu."

11. Xu 1995, p. 342.

12. Frank 1992, p. 32.

13. Liu 1988, pp. 76–81. These forms of exchange are not necessarily mutually exclusive. Diplomatic gifts are sometimes called "tribute," as are goods brought by merchants; because of their established trade contacts, merchants were sometimes given ambassadorial responsibilities (see Chapter 6, p. 229 [before n. 11], p. 228, n. 2).

14. Hu 2000, p. 241.

15. A vivid account of Zhang Qian's journey to the west was written by Sima Qian in the *Shiji*. A translation of that section is included in Watson 1962, pp. 264–89.

16. Harrist 1997, pp. 17–18; Morton 1994, pp. 54–56.

17. The Chinese term for these horses, *chibo*, represents the Sogdian word for "quadruped" (Sims-Williams 1996, p. 61 n.

77). The nomadic tribes of north China and Central Asia possessed superior equestrian skills and fine horses. With the pressure of Xiongnu along the northwestern regions, the Chinese were faced with the challenges of learning how to maintain a cavalry and stables of horses (Toronto 1974, p. 119, no. 222).

18. Historians vary on the estimated number of people forced to colonize Gansu, ranging from 700,000 (Reischauer and Fairbank 1960, p. 101) to 2 million (Morton 1994, p. 55).

19. For the most recent dating of the Kushans and of Kanishka, see Cribb 1999, pp. 177–205.

20. For a discussion of the affinities between Daoism and Buddhism, see Ch'en 1973, pp. 48–53; for its absorption into the arts, see Wu 1986, pp. 263–303; Yu 1985, pp. 68–77 (in Chinese), pp. 1375–81 (in English).

21. For a summary of what is known about the Shanshan Kingdom, the important oasis sites, and the surviving Buddhist art, see Rhie 1999, vol. 1, pp. 323–426.

22. Shih 1968, pp. 33–37.

23. Juhl 1995, p. 62.

24. For a discussion of the Juqu Mengxun's biography, see Juhl 1995, pp. 55–82.

25. The major temple sites that were opened along the Gansu corridor are described in Chapter 4.

26. Except for one brief Buddhist persecution in 446, most Northern Wei rulers actively supported Buddhism, opening a number of cave sites across the north: Yungang, near Datong in Shanxi, Longmen, outside of Luoyang in Henan, and Gongxian, east of Luoyang. See Soper 1966b, pp. 241–70.

27. An excellent history is Wright 1978.

28. See note 14 above.

29. The best description of the Tang dynasty's taste for the exotic is Schafer 1951.

30. Reischauer and Fairbank 1960, Vol. 1, p. 175.

31. Frank 1992, p. 30.

32. Egami 1988, p. 19.

33. Schafer 1963. See also Laufer 1914.

34. Liu 1988, pp. 55–58, 100–101. According to Liu, "Buddhist values created and sustained the demand for certain commodities traded between India and China during the first to the fifth century A.D." (p. 175).

35. Yutaka 1996, pp. 70–71: "B. The Date of the Earliest Copper Coins of Chinese Type."

1. *Lead ingots with barbarous Greek inscription*

Chinese Han dynasty, first century BCE–first century CE
Found 1976 in Lingtai county, Gansu
Diameter: 5.52 cm; height: 1.23 cm; thickness (rim): 0. 44 cm; weight: c. 116 g
Obverse: Coiling dragon
Reverse: Circular inscription with barbarous Greek letters and
two small rectangular punches with Chinese characters
Lingtai County Museum, Gansu

1. For a short description of the hoard and further references, see Cribb 1978, pp. 76–78, no. 298; Thierry 1993, p. 96, no. 60; *Put Svile* 1996, p. 105, no. 32..

2. Cribb 1979, pp. 185–209, p. 191, App. II.

3. Cf. Cribb 1978, p. 76.

4. For a discussion of the Changxingzhen hoard and the Chinese references, see Thierry 1995, pp. 304–9.

These two saucer-shaped lead ingots with a concave top and a convex bottom were cast from the same mold. They are part of a hoard that was dug up in 1976 in Lingtai county (Gansu). All together 274 ingots were found with a total weight of 31.80 kilograms, giving an average of about 116 grams per ingot.[1] It has been argued that the shape and size of these ingots are those of one *jin* (16 Chinese ounces, about 250 grams), gold currency ingots known from later Han tombs.[2] Similar lead ingots have been found in Fufeng county (Shaanxi) together with Han *wuzhu* coins and other artifacts giving a first- to second-century CE deposit date (Eastern Han period).[3]

The numismatist Joe Cribb has argued that these ingots, like other imitation ingots made of bronze or clay, are grave goods. He has also convincingly pointed out that the barbarized Greek inscription is copied not from Parthian coins but from Indo-Scythian or early Kushan coins, which circulated in Bactria and northwestern India in the first centuries BCE and CE. In any case, it is taken for sure that these ingots were not imported from Parthia or Bactria but manufactured in China. When the Han emperor Wudi (r. 145–187 BCE) sent Zhang Qian to Bactria in the 130s BCE, the Chinese also came into contact with foreign coins. Contemporary written sources reveal that the Chinese were very impressed with the coins they saw in the Western Regions; thus it is likely that some of these "exotic" coins were brought to China and served as a model for the lead ingots.

In 1990 another hoard was discovered in Changxingzhen (Shaanxi) containing Han *banliang* coins (cast before 118 BCE) and five lead ingots. One of these ingots is round in form with a coiling dragon on the obverse, three are square showing a horse on the obverse, and one is oval with a tortoise on the obverse. Chinese scholars have associated these three ingot types with passages in two of the historical records of the Han dynasty, the *Shiji* (XXX, 1427) and the *Hanshu* (XXIV–2, 1164), which report that, in 119 BCE, Emperor Wudi issued silver coins in three different denominations with the picture of a dragon, a horse, and a tortoise. No examples of such silver coins have survived, but it may be that the images on the ingots refer to these coin types.[4]

MA

2a,b. *Striding cavalry horse with saddlecloth*
3. *Prancing cavalry horse*
4a–c. *Horse-drawn carriage with umbrella and driver*

Eastern Han dynasty, 2nd century CE
Excavated in 1969 from a tomb at Leitai, Wuwei county, Gansu
Bronze
Horses: Height: (2a) 36.5 cm and (3) 38 cm
Horse and chariot (4): Length: 40.7 cm
Gansu Provincial Museum, Lanzhou

The two lively horses and a third horse drawing an umbrella-shaded carriage with driver were excavated from the Han tomb that also contained the "Flying Horse," one of China's most famous archaeological discoveries.[1] Along with the "Flying Horse," these figures form part of a large procession,
some eighty horses, mounted warriors, carts, chariots, chariot drivers, and escorts—all cast from
bronze. During the Han dynasty (206 BCE–220 CE), horses emerge as a significant and favored theme
across northern China preserved in *mingqi* (funerary objects or replicas made specifically for burial),
in other tomb furnishings, and in wall murals. The contents of this Han tomb reflect not only the

no. 2a

Saddlecloth

no. 2b

no. 4a–c

growing passion of the Chinese for fine horses but also the political realities of the period in China's north and northwest, Gansu and Ningxia.

Horses were vital to maintaining Han military strength against the increasing nomadic incursions from the Turkic Xiongnu tribal armies along the northern borders and in the northwest. In the north, China's agrarian-based society shared a poorly defined border with non-Chinese nomads and pastoralists. The Great Wall became not only a defensive physical structure but also a symbolic boundary separating the Chinese from the non-Chinese, the agricultural from the nomadic life, and the civilized from the uncivilized. In 162 BCE, the Han emperor Wen sent an envoy to the Xiongnu with a letter stating that "the land north of the Great Wall, where men wield bow and arrow, is to receive its command from the Shanyu [leader of Xiongnu confederation of tribes], while that within the wall, whose inhabitants dwell in houses and wear hats and girdles, was to be ruled by us."[2]

During the first half of the Han dynasty (from 206 BCE to 23 CE), Han emperors, particularly Han Wudi (r. 141–87 BCE), the "Martial Emperor," pursued an aggressive military policy in the northwest to stop the attacks of the Xiongnu, whose incursions reached withing striking distance of the imperial capital of Changan. Recognizing that the Xiongnu had superior equestrian skills and large numbers of horses, the famous Han dynasty general and horse expert Ma Yuan (14 BCE–49 CE) observed: "Horses are the foundation of military might, the great resource of the state."[3] By the first century BCE, mounted Han armies had ousted the Xiongnu and gained control of the entire Gansu corridor reaching as far as the edge of the Gobi Desert. Han administrative and military garrisons were established along the corridor at Lanzhou, Wuwei, Zhangye, Jiuquan, and Dunhuang to protect against any further Xiongnu threats and to secure passage through the Gansu corridor.

At about the same time, Zhang Qian, an emissary from the Chinese court, returned from his diplomatic missions to Central Asia in 139 and 115 BCE with stories of the amazing "blood sweating" horses called *tianma*, meaning "heavenly horses." These steeds, indefatigable and fleet of foot, were renowned for their stamina and agility, particularly those horses from Ferghana in Central Asia (part

MONKS AND MERCHANTS

of present-day Uzbekistan, Tajikistan, and Kyrgyzstan). The need to acquire this breed of large heavenly horses, considered far superior to China's short, stocky steppe ponies, drove Chinese armies even deeper into Central Asia, beyond the Pamirs to conquer Ferghana in 101 BCE.[4] Acquisition of horses was a priority of early Tang emperors as well.[5] These military campaigns further facilitated China's control of the northwest and the opening of the Silk Road connecting China to Central Asia and countries farther west and extending trade with places as far away as Rome.

These heavenly horses quickly became symbols of prestige and acquired a rich mythology equating their abilities with those of dragons. The concept of this heavenly steed inspired marvelous tomb sculptures and paintings, including the world-famous "Flying Horse," a lively painted version of the horse speeding through the heavens on the ceiling of a Wei-Jin tomb excavated at Jiayuguan in Jiuquan, Gansu, and the popular *sancai* (three-color) Tang stallions.[6] Here, both horses (nos. 2, 3) have been depicted neighing; heads cocked and ears pricked, they paw the ground restlessly as if ready to gallop off. Characteristic of Han sculptural style, the anatomy is captured by tautly rounded but highly stylized forms supported by elegantly slender legs with exaggerated flared hooves.

Over the back of the striding horse is what seems to be an ornamental saddlecloth and a small removable saddle. The saddlecloth is constructed of two very thin square sheets of bronze connected with two strings; one corner of the sheet has been cut off to accommodate the horse's body. Amazingly, there is an image of the flying horse drawn in black on each bronze sheet.[7] In the tomb procession, this horse represented the mount for the deceased and followed the principal chariot in the honor guard; the second horse followed the first.

Alert and poised to respond to the driver's commands, the third horse pulls a two-wheeled carriage known as a *yaoche*, which is shaded by an umbrella. In contrast to the war chariot pulled by four horses, the light carriage has one horse and is used to lead the honor guard. The umbrella was a symbol of authority, and the number of carriages and chariots placed in this and other Han tombs reflects the status of the deceased. By the Han dynasty, the nature of warfare had changed and the chariot had lost its place as the backbone of the war machine, supplanted by cavalry and infantry. Chariots remained important for transport, and the changes in their structure reflect that, with the transition from a single draught to a double draught-pole transport vehicle, like this Wuwei example.[8]

Given the "Flying Horse" and the number of horses, chariots, carriages, and armed horsemen in the procession, the tomb most certainly belongs to a high-ranking official, referred to as a governor in inscriptions engraved on certain horses and referred to also as a general on the seals in the tomb.[9] The tomb itself has three chambers, with vaulted well-type ceilings with a flat square center apex; all three ceiling centers have open lotus flowers with seed pods clearly drawn and painted in the center in red, black, and white. Lotuses, in general, have always been associated with Buddhism in China. Since images of the Buddha begin appearing in the later Han period during the second and third centuries CE in Sichuan and along the eastern coast from Shandong to Jiangsu, often incorporated into a Daoist context, the lotus may be a reference to Buddhism. If so, they are the only Buddhist references from the later Han period in Gansu province known at present. However, a Chinese scholar has suggested that lotuses in square ceiling wells are found in early Chinese palace architecture and were an auspicious symbol to protect buildings from fire.[10]

Internal power struggles and civil disorders severely weakened the power of the Han emperors during the second and third centuries CE, leaving the Chinese empire vulnerable to attack by their northern nomadic neighbors. By the fourth century, nomadic war bands inundated north China. Horsemanship and martial traditions remained important features of life in the north, recorded in the clay infantry and cavalry of fifth- and sixth-century tombs (nos. 22 a–d, 23 a–d, 37a–j).

ALJ

1. Since this horse was discovered in 1969, it has been widely published and exhibited. It was first exhibited in the West at the Royal Ontario Museum in (Toronto 1974, no. 222 and on the cover; see also Sichou 1994, pp. 76–78); the original excavation report was published in *Wenwu* 1972.2, pp. 16–24, pls. 5–8, colorpl. More recently, the two horses and a carriage were exhibited in Lei, Yang, and Zhao 1995, pp. 85, 89, 90. See also *Put Svile* 1996, pp. 110–11, nos. 37, 38 (chariot and horse); p. 118, no. 45 (prancing horse).

2. Emperor Wen in Watson 1962 Vol. II, p. 173.

3. Creel 1965, p. 665.

4. Pirazzoli-t'Serstevens 1982, pp. 88–89.

5. Harrist 1997, p. 18.

6. Wei-Jin tomb, Jiayuguan, near Jiuquan, see *Wenwu* 1979.6, pp. 1–6, pl. I: 2.

7. Goodrich 1984, p. 297.

8. Lu 1993, no. 257, p. 833.

9. Toronto 1974, p. 119, nos. 211–21.

10. Rhie 1999, p. 66.

no. 5a, b

5a–c. *Gold strips and bracteates with turquoise and coral*

Han dynasty (206 BCE–220 CE)
Found in 1983 in a southern suburb of Guyuan, Ningxia
Gold with granulation and inlay of turquoise and coral
a. Gold-foil strip: height: 1.1 cm; length: 9.0 cm
b. Gold-foil strip: height: 2.3 cm; length: 9.4 cm
c. Gold-foil bracteates: each, height: 1.24 cm; length: 0.8 cm
Guyuan Municipal Museum, Ningxia Hui Autonomous Region

These ornaments, made of thin sheets of gold, are embellished with granulation and inlaid stones. Number 5b has a row of granulated diamond shapes that form the outer border of this wider strip and has florets and inlaid turquoise or coral in the center. Each inlay is surrounded by granulation. The narrower strip (no. 5a) has some remaining turquoise stones mounted in granulated circles with a similar diamond granulation border. Number 5c consists of twenty-nine bracteates of a rosette motif similar to that on the wider strip (no. 5b). Bracteates like these are often employed for clothing decoration and have been used in the Near East since about 2000 BCE.

The technique of using gold granulation originated outside China and was introduced into China in two ways. It entered through the Sino-steppe and trans-Asian trade network active at least as early as the fifth century BCE.[1] It also entered via the prosperous sea trade of the Eastern Han.[2] By the end of the Han dynasty, granulation had been mastered as a metalworking technique in China. Turquoise was quite common and had already been extensively used as inlay in belt hooks and bronzes and ritual bronzes going back to much earlier periods. Belt hooks inlaid with turquoise were found in the royal Zhou burials at Jincun in Luoyang, Henan province dating to the third century BC. Turquoise was also found as belt-hook inlays in the second-century BCE tomb of the King of Nanyue in Guangzhou, Guangdong province.[3] Coral, however, was considered a luxury good and was shipped to China through either India or Persia, passing through Central Asia along the Silk Road. Coral was also one of the seven Buddhist treasures identified in the *sapta-ratna*.[4]

SB

1. So and Bunker 1995, pp. 73–74. Also see Chapter 1 in this catalogue.

2. Bunker 1993, p. 33.

3. So and Bunker 1995, p. 153. Also see nos. 20a,b and 21a,b in this catalogue.

4. Liu 1988, pp. 54–57. Also see no. 20a,b and 21a,b in this catalogue.

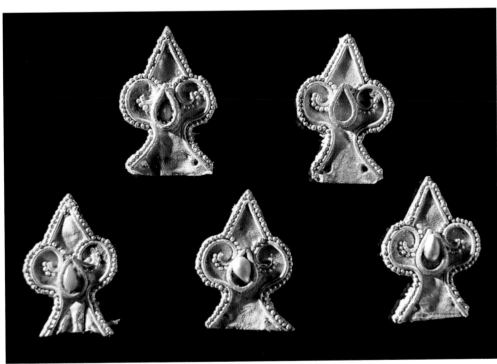

no. 5c

Fig. A. Creature with a spiked horn (*top*), incised in limestone, from the tomb of Yinan in Shandong (after Zeng 1956, pl. 29, no. 8)

Fig. B. Stone tomb doors (*below*), excavated at Guanzhuang, Mizhi county (Shaanxi) in 1971, second half of the Han dynasty (25–220.) (after *Xi'an* 2000, p. 74)

6. *Unicorn*

Han dynasty (206 BCE–220 CE)
Excavated at Mocuizi, Wuwei, Gansu
Wood with black pigment
Height: 39.5 cm; length: 93.7 cm;
length of horn: 22 cm; length of tail: 24 cm
Gansu Provincial Museum, Lanzhou

7. *Unicorn*

Wei-Jin dynasties (220–317 CE)
Excavated at Xiaheqing, Jiuquan, Gansu
Bronze
Height: 24.5 cm; length: 70.2 cm
Gansu Provincial Museum, Lanzhou

Springing from pre-Han and Han cosmology and mythology, fantastic animals ranging from the completely mythical to composite creations constitute a major category in Han art and literature. The *Shan Haijing* (Mountain and Water Classic), an important Han handbook of cosmic geography, is a veritable catalogue of bizarre places and their animal inhabitants.[1] Often deemed both powerful and protective, these imaginary zoömorphs were thought to inhabit the world of the living and the spirit realms of the dead, appearing as auspicious or occasionally inauspicious omens. In particular, the unicorn, known as a *qilin*, became a favorite subject in Chinese art, along with the phoenix, dragon, and turtle, and was a frequent bearer of good tidings.

Traditionally a composite animal, the unicorn has the body of a deer, a bushy ox tail, cloven hooves, scales, and a single horn.[2] *Qilin* became the generic name for both the male *qi* and the female *lin*. Believed to be benevolent, the *qilin*, along with the phoenix, was emblematic of the popular theme of *xiangrui*, or good-omen art, and magical practices pervasive in the latter half of the Han dynasty.[3] The appearance of a unicorn portended the advent of good government or the birth of a

no. 6

MONKS AND MERCHANTS

virtuous ruler. Said to attain an age of a thousand years, the unicorn was perceived as the noblest of creatures and as a symbol of perfect goodness.[4] At the same time, however, the great sage Confucius (sixth century BCE) admitted uneasiness at the sightings or capture of unicorns. He believed that the creatures were harbingers of evil as well.[5]

What is generally believed to be the earliest two-dimensional image of a unicorn is engraved on the wide spout of a bronze *yi*, a low ewer from a Warring States-period (fifth-century to third-century BCE) tomb in Fenshuiling (Changzhi district, Shanxi).[6] This beast has the body of a deer or goat, the tail of an ox, and no scales; with its head and swordlike horn lowered, it appears poised to strike. From the Warring States through the Han dynasty, a variety of single-horned creatures are represented on tomb walls or doors. Several such can be seen cavorting with an extraordinary menagerie of mythical and magical creatures from the spirit realms, all carved on the stone walls of the tomb at Yinan in Shandong dated late Han or possibly post-Han, late third century CE.[7] These single-horned creatures may well be unicorns. One image, in particular, on the north wall of the front chamber, not only has a deerlike body and hooves but also has its head down, leveling a forked horn (fig. A). This form seems to be more closely related to the bronze and wood sculptures in the exhibition than others in the tomb. Carved on the stone tomb doors from Guanzhuang (Mizhi county, Shaanxi) and dating from the second half of the Han dynasty (25–220 CE), two charging unicorns with very bovine bodies have been placed at the bottom of the doors to protect the tomb entrance (fig. B).[8]

no. 7

1. deRosny 1924, pp. 550–86.

2. Mayer 1964, p.127, no. 389.

3. Wu 1986, p. 270.

4. Mayers 1964, p. 127, no. 389.

5. Ibid.; Bulling 1966, pp. 109–10.

6. *Kaogu xuebao*, 1957.1, p. 103 , fig. 2; Bulling 1966, p. 109.

7. Zeng 1956, pl. 29, no. 8, pl.67, no. 55.

8. Stone tomb doors; see *Xi'an* 2000, p. 74.

9. Three wooden unicorns have been published: *Zhongguo* n.d., no. 5, pp. 26–27; Toronto 1974, p. 120, no. 225. Two of the three bronze examples: Sichou 1988, no. 93, *Wenwu* 1958.10, fig 9. and *Kaogu xuebao* 1974.2, p.101, pl. 12:1. For a discussion of wooden sculpture in Gansu including unicorns, see Long n.d., pp. 24–34.

10. *Kaogu xuebao* 1974.2, p. 101, pl. 12:1.

11. Jeannie T. Parker's electronic book *The Mythic Chinese Unicorn Zhi*, available from the Royal Ontario Museum's Web site (www.rom.on.ca), addresses the question of the origin of the Chinese mythic unicorn.

12. Juliano 1980, figs. 24–27; clay representations of unicorns were also placed in tombs undoubtedly as guardians; see Los Angeles 1987, p. 116, no. 37. After the Wei-Jin period, sculptural representations of unicorns are rarely found as *mingqi* in tombs but occur occasionally stamped or painted on tomb tiles.

During the second half of the Han, three-dimensional or sculptural images of unicorns crafted from wood (no. 6), bronze (no. 7), and clay appear for the first time, manifested as tomb guardians. The largest concentration of these unicorn guardians has been found in tombs from the Wuwei and Jiuquan areas in Gansu.[9] These tombs have yielded ten wood and three bronze unicorns. Embellished with black markings, number 6 is one of a pair; the mate is unpainted. Both these wood and bronze beasts display exceptionally coherent and vigorous sculptural forms and share the same aggressive stance, with strongly arched neck and lowered head, their long swordlike horns leveled, ready to charge. Simply modeled, with clear chisel marks, the wood example is constructed in seven pieces, a single trunk and head, with four legs, a tail, and a horn attached with wood dowels. The sculptural form creates a highly charged posture, with the figure balanced on the edges of its hooves, suggesting that it has just leaped into an attack position.

Excavated from Tomb 18 in Xiaheqing near Jiuquan, the bronze *qilin* was not found with the other funerary objects in the rear chamber of the tomb. Instead, the unicorn stood alone in the middle of the front room, its head facing the tomb entrance. With mouth open and tongue out, this animal radiates an extraordinary ferocious energy. The long, spiked horn seems ready to gore unwanted visitors from the world of the living or from the spirit realm. This unicorn is a superb sculpture with a sense of organic integration that effectively conveys its ability to terrorize any threat to the tomb. Another bronze unicorn (fig. C), found at Leitai near Wuwei in a late Han tomb, was similarly positioned just outside the tomb door, also ready to ward off any intruders.[10] Largely constructed like the wood models, the body and head of the bronze unicorn were cast into two halves and joined, the mold seam clearly visible. The legs, the tail, and the horn were made separately and attached. It is clear that both the wood and the bronze forms emerged in the late Han and continued through the Wei-Jin from the third to the fourth century before disappearing. By the sixth century, unicorns became very popular as tomb decor on tiles and epitaph stones but reverted to a more benign concept, galloping rather than threatening, with stubby, less menacing horns.

Many questions about the origins of the *qilin* remain unanswered.[11] How did this form of a single-horned animal emerge? Although such animals appear in mythologies all over the ancient world, there does not seem to be any credible connection between China's unicorn and possible sources in the West.[12] Other intriguing questions remain: Why are all the unicorns depicted in this unique, sculpturally distinctive style found clustered in Gansu province and nowhere else? Finally, why does this particular sculptural concept of the mythic animal simply disappear shortly after the fall of the Han?

ALJ

Fig. C. Bronze unicorn (after *Kaogu xuebao* 1974.2, p. 101, pl. 12:1)

8. *Sogdian Ancient Letter II*

Written by Nanai-vandak in June/July, c. 313 CE

Excavated 1907, at "T.XII.a," a guard post
on the Chinese frontier wall to the west of Dunhuang

Letter: ink on paper; inner wrapper: silk; outer envelope: ink on hemp (?)

Letter: 41.5 x 24 cm; cover: 14 x 9.5 cm

British Library, London, Stein Collection

Find-mark T.XII.a.ii.2; signature Or. 8212/95 (letter); 8212/99.1 (outer envelope),
99.2 (wrapper), 99.3 (paper fragments formerly adhering to the envelope)[1]

This document, never before publicly exhibited, is the most important of a group of letters exca-vated in 1907 by Sir Aurel Stein at the site "T.XII.a" to the west of Dunhuang, a guard post on the wall guarding the western border of China. These documents are known as the Sogdian "Ancient Letters" because they are the earliest surviving texts written in Sogdian, a language of the Iranian family formerly spoken in Sogdiana, present-day Uzbekistan and Tajikistan.

The "Ancient Letters" represent the contents of a mailbag lost in transit (perhaps confiscated by the Chinese authorities) from China to the west. Written by Sogdians in Xinjiang and Gansu and addressed to their compatriots in Sogdiana or Loulan, the letters provide a unique glimpse into the lives and activities of the Sogdian merchants. They refer to Sogdians resident in Luoyang, the Chi-nese capital city, and in some of the major staging posts on the route to China: Dunhuang (where the Sogdians may have had their own Zoroastrian temple), Suzhou (Jiuquan), Guzang (Wuwei), and Jincheng (Lanzhou) (see Map 2, p. 30). Apart from two letters sent by a woman abandoned in Dun-huang by her husband, the letters are chiefly concerned with commerce, naming many commodities including gold, silver, camphor, pepper, musk, wheat, various kinds of cloth (though surprisingly not silk), and perhaps white lead (a costly product, used both as a cosmetic and as a drug).[2]

This particular letter was written by Nanai-vandak, a Sogdian agent stationed in Gansu, perhaps in Jincheng, and addressed to his partners in Samarkand, the capital of Sogdiana, more than two thousand miles to the west. Possibly because of the distance it had to travel, the letter was protected by an inner wrapper of brown silk and an outer envelope of coarse fabric, the latter bearing instruc-tions for the delivery of the letter. After a florid greeting (§1) naming both Varzakk and his father Nanai-dhvar, each of whom is addressed individually in a later paragraph, Nanai-vandak gives news of his associates in various Chinese cities (§2) together with a report on the deteriorating political situation in China. The momentous events described—a severe famine in Luoyang, the flight of the emperor, fighting between the Xiongnu (translated here as Huns) and the Chinese, and the sack of the cities of Ye (307 CE) and Luoyang (311 CE)—are also known from Chinese sources and make it possible to date the Ancient Letters to the years 313–314 CE.[3]

The writer's interest in these events is of course centered on their commercial implications (§3) and their disastrous personal consequences for him and the other Sogdian merchants (§4). Since he considers himself to be "on the point of death," Nanai-vandak asks his correspondents Varzakk (§5) and Nanai-dhvar (§6) to look after a large sum of money that he had left on deposit at home and to invest it on behalf of the "orphan" Takhsich-vandak, presumably his son. He also gives instructions (§7) for dividing the property of Takut, who may be his father. Finally (§8), a note written on the back of the letter gives a date according to the regnal years of an otherwise unknown ruler, perhaps a prince of Samarkand. The date probably corresponds to June or July 313 CE.

Fig. A. The outer envelope bearing written instructions for delivery of the letter to Samarkand. The British Library, London, Or. 8212/99.1 (photo courtesy of the British Library)

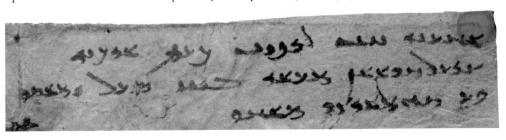

Translation:[4]

(§1) To the noble lord Varzakk son of Nanai-dhvar of the family Kanakk, 1,000 and 10,000 blessings and homage on bended knee, as is offered to the gods, sent by his servant Nanai-vandak. And, sirs, it would be a good day for him who might see you happy and free from illness; and, sirs, when I hear news of your good health, I consider myself immortal!

(§2) And, sirs, Armat-sach in Jiuquan is safe and well and Arsach in Guzang is safe and well. And, sirs, it is three years since a Sogdian came from "inside" [i.e. from China]. I settled Ghotam-sach, and he is safe and well. He has gone to . . . and now no one comes from there so that I might write to you about the Sogdians who went "inside," how they fared and which countries they reached. And, sirs, the last emperor, so they say, fled from Luoyang because of the famine and fire was set to his palace and to the city, and the palace was burnt and the city [destroyed]. Luoyang is no more, Ye is no more! Moreover . . . as far as Ye (these same Huns [who] yesterday were the emperor's subjects! And, sirs, we do not know whether the remaining Chinese were able to expel the Huns [from] Changan, from China, or whether they took the country beyond. And [. . . in . . . there are] a hundred freemen from Samarkand . . . in . . . there are forty men. And, sirs, [. . . it is] three years since [. . . came] from "inside" . . .

(§3) And from Dunhuang up to Jincheng . . . to sell, linen cloth is going [=selling well?], and whoever has unmade cloth or woolen cloth . . .

(§4) And, sirs, as for us, whoever dwells in the region from Ji[ncheng] up to Dunhuang, we only survive so long as the . . . lives, and we are without family, old and on the point of death. If this were not so, [I would] not be ready to write to you about how we are. And, sirs, if I were to write to you everything about how China has fared, it would be beyond grief: there is no profit for you to gain from it. And, sirs, it is eight years since I sent Saghrak and Farn-aghat "inside" and it is three years since I received a reply from there. They were well . . . , but now, since the last evil occurred, I do [not] receive a reply from there about how they have fared. Moreover, four years ago I sent another man named Artikhu-vandak. When the caravan left Guzang, Wakhushakk . . . was there, and when they reached Luoyang . . . the Indians and the Sogdians there had all died of starvation. [And I] sent Nasyan to Dunhuang and he went "outside" (i.e. out of China) and entered Dunhuang, but now he has gone without permission from me, and he received a great retribution and was struck dead in the . . .

(§5) Lord Varzakk, my greatest hope is in your lordship! Pesakk son of Dhruwasp-vandak holds . . . staters of mine and he put it on deposit, not to be transferred, and you should hold it . . . sealed from now on, so that without my permission . . . Dhruwasp-vandak . . .

(§6) [Lord] Nanai-dhvar, you should remind Varzakk that he should withdraw this deposit, and you should both count it, and if the latter is to hold it you should add the interest to the capital and put it in a transfer document, and you should give this too to Varzakk. And if you think it fit that the latter should not hold it, then you should take it and give it to someone else whom you do think fit, so that this money may increase. And, behold, there is a certain orphan . . . and if he should live and reach adulthood, and he has no hope of anything other than this money, then, Nanai-dhvar, when it is heard that Takut has departed to the gods, the gods and my father's soul will be a support to you!, and when Takhsich-vandak is grown-up, give him a wife and do not send him away from you . . . And when you need cash, then you should take 1,000 or 2,000 staters out of the money.

(§7) And Wan-razmak sent to Dunhuang for me 32 vesicles of musk belonging to Takut so that he might deliver them to you. When they are handed over you should make five shares, from which Takhsich-vandak should take three shares, and Pesakk should take one share, and you should take one share.

(§8) This letter was written when it was the year 13 of Lord Chirth-swan in the month Taghmich.

NS-W

1. For the discovery, see Stein 1921, pp. 671–77; IV, pls. CLII–CLIV.

2. For a fuller account of the contents and significance of the "Ancient Letters," see Sims-Williams 1996, pp. 45–67, esp. pp. 46–51.

3. On the dating of the letters, see Grenet and Sims-Williams 1987, pp. 101–22.

4. The only complete translation so far published is that accompanying the first edition (Reichelt 1931, pp. 11–19), now entirely out of date. Even today, in view of the imperfect preservation of the text and the difficulties of its language, many details of the translation are still uncertain.

Fig. B. The letter as it was found (after Stein 1921, pl. CLIII).

2

The Unbroken Thread: Nomads in China

ANNETTE L. JULIANO

Ancient China's amorphous northern border with the nomadic tribes meandered for 1,500 miles, with no clearly defined natural boundary. Instead, China's fertile northern plains gradually metamorphosed into the grasslands and steppes of Mongolia. China's stable agricultural society yielded to the pastoral herds and horse-dominated cultures of the nomads farther north. In the absence of any natural northern barrier, the Great Wall of China provided an artificial border, a line of cleavage, dramatizing the changes in geography, in culture, and in social pattern, dividing what was China from what was not. At the same time, ironically, at and around the Great Wall, the northern tribes and the Chinese created a complex, dynamic, multifaceted relationship that has resonated culturally and historically to the modern day.[1]

China's history can be chronicled not only by the rise and fall of dynasty after dynasty but also by the periodic encounters between the Chinese and their nomadic neighbors.[2] Going back to ancient times, the ambivalent relationship between northern China and the nomads ranged from hostile to hospitable, depending on the circumstances of the moment. Traditionally, the Chinese perceived their country as the center of civilization, beset by barbarian hordes, who were candidates for conquest, assimilation, negotiation, or trade. As Mencius (c. 371–c. 289 BCE), perhaps the most famous disciple of Confucius, pointedly states: "I have heard of men using doctrines of our great land to change barbarians, but I have never heard of any being changed by barbarians."[3] Contemptuous of the northern lifestyle, the Chinese scorned the nomads with their loose-hanging hair not only as wanderers in search of grass and water but also as horse riders who milked mares and ate horsemeat using their hands instead of chopsticks.[4] Traditional Chinese historiographers effectively demonized China's barbarian neighbors. Writings of the Zhou dynasty (c. 1100–256 BCE), particularly the *Zuozhuan*, dating from the third century BCE, often portray the non-Chinese nomads as greedy, aggressive, and cruel, as acquisitive have-nots with a ravenous appetite for Chinese goods.[5] In reality, however, the Chinese and the nomads had a mutually enriching relationship involving military alliances, intermarriages, tribute agreements, and above all trade.

Numerous non-Chinese tribes inhabited a vast arc of marginal land that extended from Gansu province, the Ordos Desert (part of northern Ningxia) through north China and southeastern Inner Mongolia to northeast China, encompassing forests, mountains, deserts, and grasslands.[6] Consequently, the pastoral nomadic economy varied according to local conditions and could involve a mix of herding sheep, goats, horses, cattle, and camels

OPPOSITE: Clay Xianbei hornplayer (c. 420–535) excavated from Pengyang District, Guyuan, Ningxia (no. 26)

along with stock breeding, livestock trading, hunting, fishing, and some subsidiary agriculture. Additional needs, particularly for agricultural products such as grain, were met by
developing strong exchange and commercial ties with their sedentary Chinese neighbors.
Trade became an important facet of this emerging symbiotic relationship.

In northwest China, the foothills of the Nanshan Mountains, which form the southern boundary of the Gansu corridor, and the corridor were highly attractive to pastoral
nomadic peoples. Foothills, valleys, and high plateaus provided excellent grazing for herds
(no. 10). In Chapter 3, Albert E. Dien discusses the favorable conditions of the Gansu corridor itself with its open land, sparse population, and abundant water and grass, which
apparently provided prime conditions to support almost unlimited numbers of horses,
camels, sheep (nos. 14, 15), cattle, and the nomadic peoples who relied on these herds.
Along these northwestern frontiers, the Chinese began trading with the Xiongnu and Qiang
as well as with other nomadic tribes at border markets, known as *guanshi* (barrier market)
or *hushi* (barbarian markets) at a very early date before the Han dynasty.[7] These trading
centers helped diversify the economic basis of the nomadic economy. Although the nomads
sought out Chinese commodities and goods, they also had much to offer in return as this
quotation from a Han imperial official suggests: "Mules, donkeys, and camels enter the frontier in unbroken lines; horses, dapples and bays, and prancing mounts come into our possession. The furs of sables, marmots, foxes, and badgers, colored rugs, and decorated carpets
fill the Imperial treasury."[8]

The accumulating archaeological and literary data provide glimpses of the highly
interdependent nature of these commercial relationships reaching back to at least the late
Zhou or Warring States period (480–222 BCE), and continuing through the Qin dynasty
(221–207 BCE) and the Han dynasty (206 BCE–220 CE). Archaeological finds from the late
Warring States, that is, from the fourth to third century BCE in north and northwest China,
at the Great Wall or beyond, have revealed economic activity from as early as the sixth century BCE with a clear expansion of commercial activities during the late fourth century BCE
and after.[9] These finds point to an extensive sino-steppe trading network, exchange of
coinage, extensive trade in necessities, production of luxury goods for the nomads, and evidence that the nomads supplied China with jade, animal skins, and soldiers. The Chinese
even borrowed nomadic military technology and tactics and for the first time became
mounted warriors accoutered in the nomadic style.

By the fourth century BCE, the state of Qin, the eventual unifier of China, expanded
control over southeastern Gansu (including Lanzhou) and the northeastern part of modern
Ningxia. A late-fourth-century BCE text mentions that several large-scale merchants were
active in this area. One, the merchant Lo, apparently made his fortune by raising cattle and
then exchanging his livestock for silk with minorities in Wushi (Ningxia).[10] Li Si, the famous
legalist who served the Qin in the mid-third century BCE, once noted in a memorial to the
throne that many luxury items, particularly those used by the emperor, were imported from
afar—fast horses from the north, jade from the Kunlun Mountains to the west, and dyes of
cinnabar from western Sichuan.[11] At the same time, Qin supplied the tribes with Chinese
objects and also custom-ordered ornaments, particularly belt plaques.

Manufacturing centers were also established in China to produce objects specifically
designed for the nomadic markets. The site of Yanxiadu (present-day Yixian) in northern
Hebei yielded twenty gold ornaments similar to another lot of gold and silver objects found

at Xigouban in Inner Mongolia.[12] Both groups bear inscriptions in Chinese characters describing the subject matter and the weight of the gold. These inscriptions strongly suggest that the objects were made by northern Chinese specifically for trade with the nomads.

This trading relationship with northern neighbors also gave China economic access to tribes in Inner Asia, a trans-Asian trade that moved both goods and technology before the Silk Road was established during the Han dynasty, second century BCE.[13] When the Silk Road emerged, both the sino-steppe and trans-Asian trade were already active. Objects from the fourth century BCE through the Han reflect intercultural borrowing and adaptation between the Chinese and their nomadic neighbors. Certain of the animal motifs found in the nomadic vocabulary suggest influence from even farther west.

The nomads were a significant factor in the trade dynamic between China and western Asia, periodically controlling critical portions of territory in the northwest regions traversed by monks, merchants, pilgrims, and travelers along the Silk Road. As intermediaries, nomads often played opposing roles, either as traders and even as allies protecting caravans, or as raiders and enemies, seizing trade goods and threatening not only travelers but Chinese settlements and cities. Culturally, they were an important ingredient, introducing horses and related technology and invigorating the arts with new images and new themes.

Notes

1. The Great Wall has a long history beginning with the preexisting defensive walls built by the feudal states of the Eastern Zhou against the periodic incursions of the northern tribes and neighboring feudal states competing for territory. These walls were eventually connected as a single rampart by the Qin emperor Shihuangdi shortly after he unified China. For a full discussion of the Great Wall's complicated history, see Waldron 1990.

2. Barfield 1989.

3. Quoted by So and Bunker 1995, p. 86; Tao 1988, p. 2.

4. Creel 1970, p. 201.

5. Di Cosmo 1994, p. 1092; these unflattering descriptions of the non-Chinese, particularly the Rong and Di, were drawn from two third-century BCE texts, Zuozhuan and Zhanguoce.

6. So and Bunker 1995, p. 20.

7. Yu 1967, p. 95. During the Han, many border markets were run by the army for the convenience of the soldiers stationed at the frontier. Both soldiers and nomads traveled to the common markets in frontier cities such as Zhangye and Jiuquan. Nomadic tribesmen could purchase, most likely through barter, Chinese goods directly from private merchants at these markets.

8. This quote comes from Yantielun (Debates on Salt and Iron) compiled in the first century BCE and translated by Gale 1931, pp. 14–15.

9. Li 1985, p. xx.

10. In the fourth century, the Chinese took to horseback themselves. King Wuling of the feudal kingdom of Zhao is credited with adoption of barbarian or nomadic clothing for riding, that is, trousers, belted jackets, and caps, Creel 1965, p. 655.

11. Hung 1975, p. 10.

12. Hung 1975, p. 10.

13. Wenwu 1980 .7, pp. 1–10; Li 1985, p. 335.

3

Encounters with Nomads

ALBERT E. DIEN

The desert wind moans sadly,
Scudding white clouds.
Poignant the flutes of the nomads
In the bitter, frontier air.

—*Bao Zhao* (412?–466)[1]

The Gansu corridor is largely a land of mountains and deserts that was at first inhabited by nomadic peoples. As Chinese interests expanded into the Western Regions (present-day Xinjiang), traveling merchants, missionaries, and soldiers made their way over the desolate terrain from one oasis to the next. Because of Gansu's location between the Western Regions and the central Chinese heartland, the interaction of the various ethnic groups in the arid wastes of this corridor had a dramatic impact on the political, cultural, and religious history of China.

Geographical Setting

The mountainous complex known as the Nanshan Mountains, which form the southern boundary of the Gansu corridor, comprises a number of ranges, of which the Qilian Mountains are the closest to the corridor (see Map 2, p. 24). A chain of relatively low-lying mountains, the Helishan and Longshoushan, and the Tengger Desert form the northern side of the Gansu corridor across from the Nanshan. The Nanshan are snowcapped mountains, and their melting snows form the source of a number of rivers that run through the valleys between the ranges and empty into the desert to the north. The mountains, which reach a height of more than eighteen thousand feet, block most of the moisture carried by the southern winds, but the foothills, valleys, and high plateaus provide excellent grazing for herds. According to the description in the *Hanshu*, one of the historical records of the Han dynasty, "The land is broad and the people few; water and grass favor animal husbandry, so the cattle of Liangzhou [that is, the Gansu corridor] are the most plentiful in the world."[2] Other sources say the area can support two million head of horses, one million camels, and sheep and cattle without number.[3] It is not surprising that the area was highly attractive to nomadic peoples.

Rainfall in the area is unreliable and sporadic at best, but the rivers provide a reliable source of water with which to irrigate the fertile soil at the foot of the mountains. The

OPPOSITE: The Gansu corridor, with its broad, flat, grassy terrain and supply of water, is still attractive to nomadic peoples for grazing their herds. (photo: Annette L. Juliano)

land is capable of supporting large populations, but extensive labor was required to develop the necessary canals, and great care was needed to maintain them. The series of oases that developed along the corridor formed what the explorer Sir Aurel Stein called a "great natural highway from China towards . . . the Tarim Basin."[4] This is the route that made it possible for Chinese armies to march on the Western Regions and that facilitated the travel of merchants and missionaries.

The area leading into the eastern end of the corridor is the Lanzhou Basin, where trade routes from Tibet to the west, Mongolia to the north, and Gansu and Xinjiang to the northwest converged.[5] Beyond the Liupan Mountains, which run north-south and form the eastern boundary of the basin, is Guanzhong, the North Shaanxi Plateau, and to the south is the Wei River valley, where the major city of Changan (modern Xi'an) was found. Both the basin and the plateau have thick deposits of heavily eroded loess, very little rainfall, and sparse populations. While dryfarming techniques allow for agriculture in the valleys and terraced hillsides, the area in early times also attracted a large number of nomadic groups, making for a heterogeneous array of peoples. This was a frontier area not easily controlled from the capital.

The western end of the Gansu corridor, beyond Dunhuang, opened up to the Taklamakan and the oases that lay at the foot of the mountains north and south of this desert. The area resembled the corridor to some degree, but the oases were more isolated and the mountains provided less forage for animals. North of the Taklamakan the towering Tianshan Mountains are a natural barrier between the oasis farmers and the grassland nomads of the northern steppes, so that there was much less interaction between the two peoples than there was in the corridor.

Yuezhi

Fig. 1 . Armed devotees in Kushan dress, relief panel (939.17.19), grey schist, Pakistan, Gandharan, 2–3rd century CE (photo courtesy of the Royal Ontario Museum ©ROM)

The earliest historical materials concerning Gansu describe the area as dominated by the nomadic Yuezhi, who grazed their herds in the area between the Qilian Mountains and Dunhuang and were said to be able to field more than a hundred thousand warriors (fig. 1).[6] These were a Caucasoid people who most probably spoke an Indo-Iranian dialect. They were displaced sometime before 176 BCE and migrated to the area of modern Uzbekistan. Subsequently, about 130 BCE, they moved across the Oxus River to occupy the northern part of

MONKS AND MERCHANTS

ancient Bactria (present-day Afghanistan), where in time one of their component parts established the Kushan Empire.[7] Those who remained in the Gansu corridor were called by the Chinese the Small Yuezhi. We know much about the Yuezhi culture from the period of their occupation of Bactria and the subsequent Kushan state, but as yet no trace of their stay in the Gansu corridor has been found.[8] We must for the present be satisfied with the statement in the *Hanshu* that their customs were the same as those of the Xiongnu, about whom more is known.[9]

Xiongnu

The emerging steppe power in the early second century BCE was that of the Xiongnu; centuries later they may have been the peoples known in the West as the Huns.[10] The name Xiongnu appears in the Chinese records of the third century BCE, and by the following century the Xiongnu had incorporated most of the other groups into a confederacy that posed a serious threat to the newly established Han dynasty, against whom they conducted border raids and open warfare. Their description in the *Shiji*, the historical record of the Han dynasty, is a typical one in Chinese sources for nomads: they roamed with their herds searching for water and grass; their animals consisted of horses, cattle, and sheep, and to a lesser extent camels, donkeys, and mules. They had no permanent residences and did not farm, although there were defined territories; they had no writing but made oral contracts. The young boys trained by riding sheep and graduated from shooting birds and rodents to rabbits and foxes until they reached manhood, when they all became mounted warriors. Their custom was to herd and hunt but when in straitened circumstances they went to war and conducted raids. Weapons included the bow and arrow, as well as sword and short lance; the Xiongnu saw no shame in retreating when the battle went against them, and according to the *Shiji*, they had no sense of propriety. All levels of their society ate meat, dressed in hides, and covered themselves with felt and fur. The young ate the choicest parts and the old ate the rest, since the Xiongnu honored the strong and looked down on the aged and weak. When a man died, his son would marry his stepmother; widows became the wives of their brothers-in-law.[11] In all these aspects, the customs of the Xiongnu differed from the Chinese, and the *Shiji* description can be seen as an exercise of self-definition by the Chinese historians.

The Xiongnu, who were able to field three hundred thousand warriors, remained a potent force on the northern frontier with some intervening periods of weakness until the second century CE. The Xiongnu Empire consisted of a confederation that brought together many groups of mixed backgrounds. There is evidence that there were some of European background among the Xiongnu, but the core was probably Asian; there is still no certain evidence of the language they spoke.[12]

Fig. 2. Granite horse trampling a barbarian (Hun), from the spirit road approaching the tomb mound of Huo Qubing (d. 117 BCE), Maoling, Shaanxi. He was one of the generals who defeated the Xiongnu in Gansu. (photo: Annette L. Juliano)

Related to the question of European ethnic groups in the north were the Jie, or Lijie, who were listed as a part of the Xiongnu confederation. In 349 CE they were singled out by an enemy group for extermination and were to be identified by their high noses and full beards.[13]

Chinese in the Gansu Corridor

The Chinese under Wudi, the Martial Emperor (140–87 BCE) took to the offensive against the Xiongnu. In an attempt to recruit the Yuezhi to assist in a two-front attack on the Xiongnu, an officer named Zhang Qian was sent to locate them. After much difficulty, Zhang did cross the Taklamakan to reach the Yuezhi just as they were about to move into their newly conquered territory in Bactria, but the Yuezhi had no interest in the Chinese offer. Zhang Qian's report to the throne signals the opening of the Silk Road, and Chinese armies soon marched into the Gansu corridor. The Chinese effort was motivated by two interests: economics, to protect the flow of goods over the Silk Road, and strategic, to counter the pressures from the Xiongnu confederation and to drive a wedge between that enemy and other tribespeople, primarily the Qiang, to prevent a coalition of the two.

The campaigns initiated under Wudi were successful in taking the initiative away from the Xiongnu. The victories of the Han armies under such generals as the young Huo Qubing (d. 117 BCE) succeeded in bringing the Gansu corridor under Chinese control, but it was necessary to establish a Chinese presence if these gains were to be meaningful (fig. 2). For that reason, the Chinese established a chain of settlements beginning in 108 BCE with the establishment of Jiuquan, followed by Zhangye in 102–101 BCE, Dunhuang in 88–87 BCE, Wuwei in 68 BCE, which would become central, and finally, in 81 BCE Jincheng, forming the Five Commanderies.[14] The population within this administrative framework consisted of exiled criminals, the families of those who had been executed, and transported landless peasants, as well as those Qiang tribespeople who came over to the Chinese. Further, to provide logistical support for the armies on campaign, soldiers who farmed when not on call, the so-called military colonists (*tuntian*), put down their roots. The stability of Chinese control depended upon support from the central government, which was not always forthcoming, but during periods of aggressive policy by the Han these settlements thrived.

Qiang and Di

The Qiang were another of the ethnic groups living in the northwest. They have a long history, stretching back at least to the Zhou dynasty (1100–221 BCE) and are found in mountainous areas of western China down to the present. They had close relations with the Chinese, often of a hostile nature, but there is evidence of early intermarriage as well. It has even been suggested that the founders of the Zhou dynasty may have been a branch of these people.[15] Those Yuezhi who remained behind when the Xiongnu forced the Yuezhi to flee were said to have joined with the Qiang who lived in the mountains south of the Gansu corridor.

The Qiang and another closely associated group, the Di, were probably speakers of a Tibeto-Burmese language. They are described as being herders following water and grass, since the areas they inhabited were not suited to agriculture. A Chinese account commented on their ability to withstand cold and suffering, much like that of animals; they were hardy and fearless, having acquired the harsh nature of the place in which they resided.[16] Another early source added that they raised yaks, sheep, and pigs and wove cloth of yak tail and wool for shelter.[17] The term *proto-Tibetan* often applied to the Qiang would seem appropriate.

For centuries during the Han dynasty and after, there were policies in China of allowing non-Chinese peoples from beyond the borders who had capitulated to resettle within China and for forcing border groups who had unsuccessfully rebelled to move closer inland to allow for closer surveillance.[18] There were frequent outbreaks of hostility by the Di and Qiang against the Chinese during the Han period, and numbers of the two peoples were moved closer into the heartland while others on their own volition moved into those areas in search of more favorable land. Warnings were voiced at the court about the dangers these movements foreboded. When the Han dynasty ended in 220 CE, the country fragmented into what is known as the Three Kingdoms period (220–280 CE), but then it was reunited for a time by the Western Jin dynasty (265–317 CE). The stability provided by that dynasty was short-lived as members of the royal family fought among themselves, and the defense of the northern borders weakened, allowing an even larger-scale infiltration of the non-Chinese peoples into north China, joining those already in residence there. In 299 Jiang Tong, in a long and eloquent memorial to the throne, observed that of the more than one million people in the Guanzhong area, half were Di and Qiang. From the memorial, we learn that the Qiang were then living within a 150-mile radius of Xi'an while the Di were even closer, in a 60-mile range. Jiang's suggestion was that the Di and Qiang be moved back to their original homes, but despite the merits of the case that was no longer possible.[19] The Qiang and Di remained a substantial component of the population in the Guanzhong area down through the sixth century, as is demonstrated in the name lists on community-sponsored Buddhist stelae, and they were an important source of recruits to fill the ranks of the armies.[20]

The breakdown of the Jin regime in north China in 317 CE and the emergence of a series of ephemeral regional states established by these non-Chinese peoples, the so-called Sixteen States period, are summed up in Chinese histories by the expression *Wuhu Luanhua* ("The Five Barbarians brought disorder to China"). The "five barbarians" were the Xiongnu, Qiang, Di, Jie, and Xianbei.

Xianbei

The Xianbei were an Asian people speaking an Altaic language; the evidence shows elements of both Turkish and Mongolian perhaps because this was also a confederation of a number of clans and tribes. The Xianbei were basically hunter-gatherers as they began moving south from the far northeast in the opening years of this era, adapting to nomadic herding as they entered suitable terrain. By the middle of the second century CE they had displaced the Xiongnu as the leading force along the northern frontier; many Xiongnu became part of the confederation and adopted the Xianbei designation (fig. 3). A number

Fig. 3. Paintings depicting mounted Xianbei from the west wall in the tomb of Luo Rui, a Xianbei general (d. 557). The riders wear belted tunics over trousers, tall hats, and leather boots (after *Wenwu* 1983.10, colorpl.)

of the ephemeral Sixteen States were founded by the Xianbei; the Tuoba, one of the Xianbei's leading clans, brought that period of fragmentation to an end by uniting northern China in the early fifth century.[21]

History of the Gansu Corridor and History in Retrospect

The Gansu corridor was by no means immune to the disturbances common in the rest of China during the Western Jin dynasty and its aftermath. No fewer than five states were established during the fourth and fifth centuries, each claiming to be the legitimate Liang dynasty:

Name	Founder	Ethnic identity	
Former Liang	Zhang Mao	Chinese	314–376
Later Liang	Lu Guang	Di	386–403
Southern Liang	Tufa Wugu	Xianbei	397–414
Western Liang	Li Hao	Chinese	400–422
Northern Liang	Juqu Mengxun	Xiongnu or Yuezhi	398–439

Eventually the Northern Wei settled the matter by incorporating the territory into its realm in 439. How does one explain this record of continuous warfare and struggle in the Gansu corridor? In any period of loss of central control, whether in the heartland or out on the steppes, there was a struggle by various regional powers to assert their independence and to dominate their neighbors. It may well be that the strongly ingrained martial aspects of the nomadic culture also played a role. Among pastoral peoples, the daily activities of animal husbandry did not require the participation of the males whose role was to guard the herds, to hunt, and to be on call for military adventures. Every adult male normally had the armament, horses, and training to be a warrior, unlike the farmer, and so the military strength of the nomad society in traditional times was out of proportion to its numbers. The agricultural population in the oases also provided the logistical foodstuffs necessary to carry on campaigns. This explains why these oasis inhabitants were considered to be an important body and were moved en masse from one oasis to another as the fortunes of war dictated. The profits to be made from the caravans passing through on the Silk Road were surely another of the factors underlying this constant competition. When the Northern Wei prepared to conquer the area, a list of twelve crimes committed by the Northern Liang was drawn up, and the fourth on the list read, "You know that the will of the [Northern Wei] court is to embrace those far off, and yet you have obstinately opposed [Our] imperial plans; you have severely taxed the merchant Hu [Sogdians] to the extent of cutting off travel." This was listed ahead of the crime of instigating rebellious activity, an indication of its importance at the time.[22]

The eventual effect of all these military and political activities in the Gansu corridor during the fourth and fifth centuries CE is reflected in the course of development of Guzang, the administrative seat of Wuwei Commandery, and of Liangzhou, which served as the capital for several of these states.[23] When the Northern Wei court considered the idea of conquering the Northern Liang with its capital at Guzang, there was a faction at the court that opposed such a plan, saying the region was a wasteland and there was nothing to forage in the surrounding area. Thus, when an army exhausted by its arduous march arrived, it would have difficulty seizing the city. Those advocating the invasion offered as contrary evidence the *Hanshu* description cited earlier. Like the other oases in the Gansu corridor, Guzang was dependent on the flow of water from melting mountain snowcaps, but a number of rivers gave it a more than an adequate and reliable water supply. When the Northern Wei emperor Taiwudi (r. 423–452) decided to go ahead with the campaign in 439 and saw the place for himself, he was impressed with its fertility and abundance.[24] There are no precise numbers, but when the Northern Wei captured the city of Guzang, it is reported to have had a population of 200,000, and, of course, the agricultural resources to support them.[25]

Buddhism and Liangzhou

Liangzhou obviously played an important role in the history of Buddhism in China because the roads between east and west went through it. Many Buddhist monks passed through, as did Chinese pilgrims on their way to sacred India or on their way back, and foreign monks intent on propagating the religion in China. Among the latter were such eminent men as Kumarajiva (350–409 CE),[26] Fotucheng (d. 349),[27] and Dharmamitra (356–442),[28] Liangzhou was also the first area with a largely Chinese population where the new doctrine could be adjusted to the needs of that population before moving on into China proper. Equally as important, the mix of populations and languages there facilitated the necessary translation of the Buddhist sutras, or texts, into Chinese (no. 46).

The translation of Buddhist sutras had already begun during the Former Liang period when 6 chapters of translation are recorded, but this activity expanded greatly during the Northern Liang when 311 chapters were produced. This compares favorably with the 468 chapters credited to the whole of southern China from 317 to 420.[29] One of the greatest translators was Dharmaraksa (Zhu Fahu), born of Yuezhi ancestry at Dunhuang, who spent time in India, and then carried on his activities at Changan and elsewhere, including Jiuquan, from about 265 to 313. As many as ninety-three translations are credited to him in the modern Buddhist canon. Most significant of these is the *Saddharmapundarika Sutra* (*Lotus Sutra*), so important in the Mahayana tradition.

One of the factors favorable to the propagation of Buddhism in the corridor was the encouragement by rulers such as Juqu Mengxun, founder of the Northern Liang. Mengxun was a patron of Tanwuchan (Dharmaksema?), a native either of Kashmir or of central India, who translated eleven works in 140 chapters; one of the works was the *Mahaparinirvana Sutra*, which had an important role in the propagation of Mahayana Buddhism as a "practical, concrete religion with an emphasis on the mystical powers of the Buddhas, the gods, and the mantras." This sutra "preaches not insubstantiality so much as the eternity of the Buddha and the eternal, joyous, personal, and pure nature of nirvana."[30] Unfortunately for the monk, when he was called to the court of the Northern Wei sometime during 428–32, Mengxun did not want that rival state to gain such an important personage and had the monk assassinated on the road.[31] Juqu Jingsheng, either a cousin or a nephew of Mengxun, became a monk and an important translator. The *Chu sanzang jiji* credits him with a number of translations, among which is the *Guan mile pusa shangsheng doushuaitian jing* in one chapter.[32] Dealing with rebirth in Maitreya's Tusita Heaven, it is in a sense a forerunner of the Pure Land school, since it teaches that rebirth, in this case, in the paradise of Maitreya, is brought about by specific meritorious activities.[33]

There was also some Hinayana activity during the Northern Liang. Juqu Mujian, Mengxun's son, set up a team of more than three hundred people, headed by Buddhavarman (Fotuobama), to translate the *Vaibhasa-sastra*, a philosophical treatise (no. 46). But shortly after the translation was completed, the Northern Wei conquered the Northern Liang and close to half of the work was lost. Later, another of Mengxun's sons, Juqu Anzhou, put in order the surviving sixty chapters.[34]

In addition to the activity of making translations, another important contribution of people in the Gansu corridor to the history of Buddhism in China was the emphasis there on meditation leading to visualization as a Buddhist practice. Dharmaraksa, Dharmaksema, and Juqu Jingsheng, all mentioned above, had emphasized *samadhi,* or mental concentration.[35] The list is long of those from this area who brought *samadhi* practices to south China and contributed to its popularity.[36] Meditation required a quiet, peaceful venue, one that may have supplied the initial motivation for constructing the earliest caves such as those at Tiantishan, near Guzang; at Wenshushan, near Jiuquan; and at least two at Dunhuang (Caves 272 and 275) that are credited to the Northern Liang period.[37] The Northern Wei conquest of the Northern Liang in 439 and the subsequent transport of the artisans and craftsmen, among others, from Guzang to the victor's capital at Pingcheng (present-day Datong) are believed to have provided the skills necessary to construct the enormous Buddhas and elaborate decors of the earliest of the Yungang connection at Tanyao Caves. It is also significant in that the head of the Buddhist church, at whose suggestion the caves were constructed, may in the past have been a resident of the Gansu corridor.[38]

Non-Chinese and Chinese

In a basically hybrid society one may ask to what extent there were mutual influences between the ruling non-Chinese elite on the one hand and the general Chinese population on the other. The usual assumption is that the non-Chinese population was assimilated into that of the higher civilization of the Chinese and in time lost its sense of identity. But is that the whole story? There is unfortunately not much information concerning the non-Chinese inhabitants of the Gansu corridor. In terms of material culture, the archaeological reports have by and large been focused on the Chinese population of that period. There was a custom in that area of lining some of the interior walls of tombs with painted bricks depicting scenes of daily life that in some way provided the soul of the dead with necessities. These vignettes provide a vivid picture of many aspects of the life of the time: the deceased with friends at a banquet; kitchen scenes; agricultural activities from plowing and sowing to harvesting; gathering mulberry leaves for the silkworms; tending horses (no. 10), sheep, goats, and camels; hunting with birds of prey or on horseback with spear or bow; and even military units on the march (fig. 4). But there is almost nothing in these scenes to suggest that the non-Chinese inhabitants of the area were involved.[39] The clothing depicted, whether the robes of the elite or those of the ordinary people, seems to be what Chinese were wearing in this period. But when one looks elsewhere in northern China, one sees everywhere evidence of outfits that may be identified as that of the non-Chinese, a style of clothing that seems closely associated with the Xianbei.

The male outfit in the Xianbei style consists of a caftan with tight sleeves, often with wide lapels that can be closed to fit tightly at the neck, and trousers often tucked into boots.

The headgear, a high cap with a neck cloth at the back, is also distinctive. The women wear the same sort of caftan but with a long skirt below and wear their hair in braids or buns.[40] One sees this style of clothing in tomb murals and tomb figurines and in depictions of worshipers in Buddhist settings. The lacquered coffin found at Guyuan (no. 16) is decorated with examples of filial piety drawn from the Chinese tradition, but the figures are depicted in this same Xianbei clothing. A figure representing the deceased is seated holding a goblet in a pose that resembles one found in parts of Western Asia.[41] The combination of Chinese exemplars of filial piety and non-Chinese dress may well represent an accommodation of the two traditions.

Fig. 4. Painted clay tomb tile showing Chinese and nomadic cavalry, from Tomb M5, Jiayuguan, Wei-Jin (220–317 CE) (after Fontein and Wu 1976, p. 72, no. 93)

Li Xian

The tomb of Li Xian (502–569), represented by a number of items in this exhibit, is another example of such an accommodation. Li Xian was from a prominent family of the Guyuan area where the lacquered coffin cited above was found.[42] There is some question as to the ethnic affiliation of the Li family; Turkish, Xiongnu, and Xianbei have all been argued.[43] A tenth-generation ancestor named Yidigui led the way south through the Yin Mountains. Li Xian's family had been in Guyuan for at least three generations and in the Tianshui area before that, so no doubt there had been a long period of adaptation to Chinese culture. The family had an especially close relationship with Yuwen Tai, the de facto ruler of the Western Wei, whose sons, after his death, became emperors of the succeeding Northern Zhou.

Despite some career setbacks due to a nephew's attempt to lead a rebellion, Li Xian held some of the highest military titles in the state and the command of strategic posts on the northwest frontier. His tomb, a joint one with his wife, is typical of northern China, having a long ramp connected to the surface by air shafts, all later backfilled, giving access to a domed tomb chamber (fig. 5). As with many in this area, the entire tomb was carved out of the loess soil and had no brick facing. Despite having been robbed, there were still more than

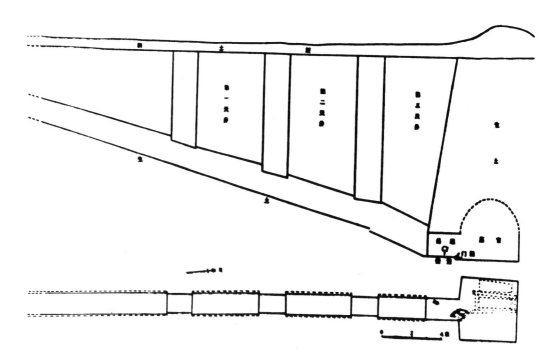

Fig. 5. Cross-section and plan of the Tomb of Li Xian (*above*), showing the position of his and his wife's coffins, Guyuan, Ningxia (after *Yuanzhou* 1999, pl. 40)

Fig. 6. Some of the 255 *mingqi* from Li Xian's tomb (*opposite*), as displayed in the Guyuan Municipal Museum (photo: Michael Alram)

three hundred items included in the grave goods. There are comparatively few pottery vessels, only twenty-one pieces; a few models of buildings and farm implements (including a chicken coop, two stoves, two mills, and two hullers); some pottery animals, including horses, camels, donkeys, a dog, chickens, and an ox (fifteen in all) (no. 40); some metal objects including silver scissors, tweezers, a bowl, and a small pot with handle; and items of bronze and iron that include two gilded buckles, an iron sword (no. 33), and a knife; and a few jade ornaments (no. 34). The most spectacular finds are a gilded silver ewer (no. 31), overlooked by the tomb robbers because the roof had collapsed over it, a Sasanian glass bowl (no. 30), and a ring with a Sasanian seal in intaglio (no. 32), all three of Western origin probably brought over the Silk Road and acquired by Li Xian while serving as governor in the northwest.

By far the most numerous category of the grave goods are 255 figurines, which include male and female attendants, military and civil officials, armored cavalry, and mounted musicians (fig. 6). Thirty-eight of the figurines are described as being Hu attendants, with high brows, deep-set eyes, and prominent noses. Another forty-three wear a hood and cloak worn over the shoulders with sleeves hanging empty, an outfit that is less common than the typical Xianbei attire but it is still distinctively non-Chinese and is found across Asia.[44] One report that describes figurines with this sort of hood and cloak (no. 39 a–d) reads, "The eyes are deep-set, the nose prominent. It is perhaps a Xianbei."[45]

These two categories, the Hu and the hood-and-cloak figurines, may provide a clue as to Li Xian's ethnic identity, but they are common in northern tombs of the period and so cannot bear the weight of an argument one way or another. The same is true of two figures, what are called *zhenmushou*, or animal-like tomb guardians (no. 35), which I have suggested elsewhere were an innovation introduced by the Xianbei but these too were common in the north.[46] To judge by the remaining items among Li's tomb goods, he can be said to have shared in that general hybrid culture of his time, but one cannot be more specific about his ethnic identity.

MONKS AND MERCHANTS

A clearer case can be made for Xianbei influence during the Western Wei and Northern Zhou period on state institutions. One of the most obvious was the practice of awarding Xianbei clan names to men of outstanding merit. There was also an edict to the effect that soldiers were to adopt the name of their commanding officer. On the steppes, the traditional building blocks of the confederacies were the clans in which all members would carry the same clan name and were called into action under the command of the leader of the clan. It is rather clear that the purpose of the Western Wei/Northern Zhou policies was to pattern their military forces on a nomadic clan organization. As the army came increasingly to draw on the non-Xianbei population to fill its ranks, this system had the effect of stretching the traditional Xianbei structure to accommodate them.[47] It has been suggested that this policy went hand in hand with the formation of the *fubing* military organization of the Northern Zhou, a kind of militia, that proved to be very effective and led to the unification of China initially under the Northern Zhou and completed by the Sui in 589 after some three centuries of fragmentation.[48]

Notes

1. Frodsham 1967, p. 151.

2. *Hanshu* 1962, 28B.1645.

3. Zheng 1987, p. 22, citing Gu Zuyu 1956.

4. Stein 1928, p. 508.

5. For more details on the geography of this area, see Dien 1990, pp. 333–35.

6. *Hanshu* 96A.3890,1.

7. There is extensive literature on the Yuezhi. See, for example, Tarn 1951, pp. 270–311; Enoki 1994, pp. 171–89; Narain 1990, pp. 151–73; Chen 1998, pp. 767–84.

8. On the Afghanistan finds, see Sarianidi 1985; Rosenfield 1967. The sculptures depicted in the latter volume give one a clear picture of what must have been the appearance of the Yuezhi.

9. *Hanshu* 96A.3890.

10. The identification of the names seems certain, but whether the peoples known under these names are the same is still debated. See Maenchen-Helfen 1973, pp. 367–69.

11. *Shiji* 1959, 110.2879.

12. Pulleyblank 1983, p. 451. Pulleyblank points to evidence that they spoke a Paleo-Siberian language, of which only Kettish survives today.

13. Maenchen-helfen 1974, citing *Jinshu* 1974, 107.2792.

14. Zhao 1998, pp. 1–5; Cao 1960, pp. 49–57.

15. Pulleyblank 1983, pp. 416–23.

16. *Hou Hanshu* 1965, 87.2869.

17. *Weishu* 1974, 101.22412, 101.2245.

18. Jin 1964, pp. 37–64. Fagen discusses this topic in detail.

19. *Jinshu* 65.1529–34; in particular, p. 1533. His suggestion that the non-Chinese be expelled was not accepted, and as the history concludes, in less than a decade the disaster that he predicted was realized.

20. Ren 1997, no. 2, pp. 20–24.

21. For a discussion of the Xianbei with citations to the relevant literature, see Dien 1991, pp. 40–59.

22. *Weishu* 99.2207. This was cited by Yu 1994, p. 4. For the often deleterious effect of tariffs on caravan trade and the way that such often arbitrary taxes contributed to the non-transparency of the merchant's expenses, thus discouraging mercantile activity, see Steensgaard 1973, pp. 61–67.

23. It served as the capital of the Later Liang from 386 to 401, all during the length of this regime, of the Southern Liang (397–414 CE) from 406 to 410, and of the Northern Liang (398–439) from 412 to 439; see Liang 1987, p. 34.

24. *Weishu* 35.822,23, 4B.108. These and other relevant materials have been brought together in Zheng 1987, pp. 21–29. See also the excellent discussion in Wang and Li 1983, pp. 103–11.

25. *Weishu* 4A.90.

26. Kumarajiva was related to the royal family of Kucha, where he was born, studied in Kashmir, and became famous for his scholarship and magical powers. He was brought to Liangzhou in 384 CE as booty when Kucha was conquered by Lu Guang. After the Later Liang fell, he reached Changan in 402 where he continued to translate texts and purportedly attracted thousands of students; see Zürcher 1972, p. 226.

27. Fotucheng, or Fotudeng, probably a native of northern India, was a wonder worker who became the court-chaplain of the Later Zhao rulers and reached Luoyang in 310; see Zürcher 1972, p. 114; Tsukumoto 1979, 1.254,56; Wright 1948, pp. 321–71.

28. Dharmamitra (Chinese: Tanmomiduo), a native of Kashmir, spent time in Kucha, Dunhuang, and Liangzhou, and finally settled in Nanjing in 424; see *Gaosengzhuan3*, T.50.342c–343a.

29. Wu 1987, p. 81. See also Tang 1963, pp. 389–91.

30. Tsukumoto 1956, 55.2145: 8, p. 60a.

31. Dharmaksema has biographies in the *Chu sanzang jiji*, T. 55,2145: 14, pp. 102c–b, and *Gaosengzhuan* AFMX (Accounts of eminent monks), T. 50.2059, 2, pp. 335c–337b, where alternative transcriptions of his name are given.

32. Senshu 1957, pp. 4–5. This work is in T. 14.452, p. 418 ff.

33. Ibid., p. 5.

34. Buddhavarman, a specialist in this text, was a Westerner who was active in the Gansu corridor area from c. 424–445; see Demieville 1968, p. 248. This work is now T.27.1546.

35. For a discussion of this monastic *dhyana* discipline, see Zürcher 1972, pp. 222–23.

36. Wu 1987, p. 80.

37. Ibid.;

38. The standard biographical sources for the period have no detailed information about the origins of Tanyao but the *Gaosengzhuan* (T.2059: 11, p. 398b). does say he was well known in the Northern Liang period for his acts of meditation. See Tsukumoto 1942, pp. 145–46; also the translation of this section by Tsukumoto 1957, p. 376.

39. It may be that some of the military units depicted are non-Chinese since the soldiers seem to be wearing scale armor, which was not a Chinese type of armor. See Dien 1981–82, pp. 19–20.

40. See Dien 1991, pp. 44–52.

41. *Wenwu* 1984.6, p. 49, fig. 9.

42. Li Xian has biographies in *Zhoushu* 1971, 25.413,8, and *Beishi* 1974, 59.2105,7.

43. See Dien 1990a, p. 362; Dien 1991, p. 50; and the literature cited in those places.

44. See Dien 1997, pp. 968–69.

45. *Wenwu* 1984.4, p. 4.

46. Dien 1991, p. 48.

47. Dien 1977, pp. 137–77.

48. Gu 1962, pp. 34–37.

9a. *Seal with sheep* (Qiang hou)

Western Jin dynasty (265–317)
Found in Xihe county, south of Tianshui, Gansu
Gold
Height: 2.25 cm; width: 2.3 cm; weight: 150 g
Gansu Provincial Museum, Lanzhou

9b. *Seal with camel* (Di wang)

Western Jin dynasty (265–317)
Found at Xihe County, south of Tianshui, Gansu
Gold
Height: 2.25 cm; width: 2.3 cm; weight: 150 g
Gansu Provincial Museum, Lanzhou

A seal with an animal as knob is the typical seal shape of the period. On these examples, the animals appear to be a sheep (no. 9a) and a camel (no. 9b), both kneeling in a conventionalized posture with legs folded and drawn together under the body.[1] This posture, associated with nomadic cultures reaching back at least to the fifth century BCE, is also visible on the jade and coal rams (nos. 14, 15).

On the first seal (no. 9a), a ribbon would have been passed through the hole formed by the body of the sheep. The inscription, in the "Small Seal" style script typically used for this purpose, reads:

1. *Wenwu* 1964.6, pp. 58–59.

2. Seal script refers to a style of early script in general use in the pre-Han period that continues to be used primarily for seals even today.

3. *Hanshu*, 69.2973; and *Hou Han-shu*, 87.2889.

4. See *Wenwu* 1964.6, pp. 58–59. A seal similar to number 9b is in the Shanghai Museum Collection and published in *Zhongguo* 1993, p. 312, no. 117.

5. *Sanguo Zhi*, 33.897.

Jin gui yi Qiang hou, "Marquis of the Loyal Qiang of the Jin [dynasty]."[2] The Qiang are a mountain people who speak a Tibeto-Burmese language and have a long history in China; they are still to be found in Sichuan and Yunnan, in southwest China. They formerly lived farther north, in the mountains of Qinghai and southern Gansu, around Kokonor Lake and in the valley of the Huang River, and there are frequent records of their armed incursions into the surrounding areas. In a number of instances the Chinese historical records trace these uprisings to grievances against the local Chinese officials and magnate families, but perceived weaknesses in the defenses of the Chinese state could also invite such raiding parties. In the first century CE much of the struggle between the Qiang and the Han Empire took place south of modern Lanzhou and into the upper Wei River valley, but, beginning in 36 CE, numbers of the Qiang who had laid down their arms were resettled at Tianshui and even farther east. This led to a gradual infiltration, which by 300 CE resulted in the claim that half the population of the region that approximates modern Shaanxi was made up of Qiang and Di tribespeople, a situation that was to have dire consequences for the ruling dynasty.

The main frontier policy of the Chinese dynasties was to maintain the peace and avoid conflict with the border peoples, sometimes even while pushing into their lands. One of the means to achieve this end was to co-opt the tribal leaders by the presentation of gifts and titles. The history of the Former Han mentions a Qiang leader who in 61 BCE had the title marquis of the Loyal Qiang. *The History of the Han Dynasty* (*Hanshu*) and the *History of the Later Han* (*Hou Hanshu*) record the presentation of a seal and title of marquis to a Qiang chieftain in 115 CE after he led seven thousand of his people to surrender.[3] We have no record of the presentation of the particular seal on display here, but it was undoubtedly a part of this same policy of achieving harmony and mollifying discontent.

The second seal (no. 9b) has a knob in the shape of a camel sitting in a conventionalized posture, with legs folded and drawn together under its body with striations marking the features and the hair, as in the other seal (no. 9a).[4] The inscription in "Small Seal" script reads: *Jin gui yi Di wang,* "King of the Loyal Di of the Jin [dynasty]." The Di, a people living in the mountains of southern Gansu, Qinghai, and Sichuan, were related to the Qiang, mentioned in discussing the first seal (no. 9a), and seem also to have spoken a Tibeto-Burman language. As with the Qiang, the Chinese records list numerous incursions and battles with the Chinese along the frontier and their steady infiltration into Chinese territory in the early centuries of this era. The awarding of such seals and titles by the Chinese was part of a policy called, in Chinese, *jimi huairuo,* "keeping a vassal under control by making a show of conciliation." The Di were divided into many independent groups with no overall organization, and so the title "king" could mean merely the leader of the Di of a particular place. There is an example of one person bearing the title King of the Di of Wudu, west of modern Chengxian, Gansu, who was moved to Guangdu, in Sichuan, near modern Chengdu, bringing more than four hundred families with him.[5]

While one cannot know for certain why these two seals were found near Tianshui, they can serve to symbolize how these two peoples, the Di and the Qiang, had come to settle themselves well within the borders of China while retaining their own identity and organization. The assimilation of the Di and the retreat of the Qiang back to their original location came later when China regained its unity and strength in the late sixth century.

AED

10. *Tomb brick painted with herder and animals*

Wei-Jin period (220–317)
Excavated from tomb at Luotuocheng (Camel City), Gaotai District, Gansu
Clay with pigments
Height: 19.5 cm; length: 39 cm; thickness: 5 cm
Gaotai County Museum, Gansu

Underground tombs built of brick became the characteristic form of burial from the Han dynasty (206 BCE–220 CE) on. These structures ranged from one room to multiple chambers, within which were grave goods, mostly *mingqi,* "spirit objects," replicas usually made of clay (nos. 22–26; 35–40), wood, and sometimes bronze (nos. 2–4) to accompany the deceased. *Mingqi* were deposited together with the coffin or coffins as well as in side storage chambers. The interior walls of these tombs were often decorated, the type of decoration depending on the region. In the north, the murals might be painted on a layer of plaster that covered the brick walls of the larger and more lavish tombs.[1] In the south, where the pervasive dampness would damage such murals, the bricks themselves often had patterns of a wide assortment stamped onto them before being fired. Sometimes, such bricks were assembled like a pieces of a puzzle to create complex panoramas on the tomb walls.[2]

In the northwest, the dryness of the climate permitted painted decoration as in numbers 10–12, but unlike murals, scenes were most often painted on a layer of plaster covering individual bricks. These bricks were set, with the painted side showing, in rows separated by a number of plain bricks or with stamped repetitive patterns set on edge between them. This brick (no. 10) came from a tomb with three chambers; the tomb was about 12 meters long and some three meters high.[3] The tomb contained fifty-eight painted bricks, which depicted life and prevalent beliefs in the area, such as scenes of farming, animal husbandry, feeding pigs, hunting, preparation and serving of food, horse and ox carts, landscape scenes, a portrait of the deceased, and a number of deities, as well as purely decorative designs.

This brick shows a man herding horses with a Bactrian camel and possibly a mule or donkey in the background. Because the man appears to have a mustache, he may represent a non-Chinese person, since Chinese were rarely depicted as hirsute.

AED

1. Wei-Jin tombs at Jiayuguan, Gansu; see Fontein and Wu 1976, pp. 54–78.

2. For stamped clay tiles assembled to create a complex composition of the famous literary theme "Seven Sages of the Bamboo Grove," on two walls of the coffin chamber, see Soper 1961, pp. 79–86.

3. Luotuocheng (Camel City), Gaotai District tomb was published in *Wenwu* 1997.12, pp. 44–51.

1. *Wenwu* 1996.7, pp. 4–38.

2. An observation made by Tsu Shibin, former director of the Gansu Provincial Museum, Lanzhou.

11. *Tomb brick painted with mounted official and woman carrying a basket*

Wei-Jin period (220–317)
Excavated from a tomb at Xigou Village, Jiuquan, Gansu
Clay with pigments
Length: 35.3 cm; width: 17 cm; thickness: 5.5 cm
Jiuquan Municipal Museum

Fig. A. Brick depicting a yurt, Xigou Village, Jiuquan, Gansu (after *Wenwu* 1996.7, p. 32)

This brick came from a large tomb, seven meters long, with an entryway and two chambers connected by a passageway. A ramp was dug six meters deep, and an elaborate brick facade was constructed on the facing vertical wall in which the chambers themselves were dug out.[1] The painted bricks were mounted in five rows on the four walls of the front chamber and in four rows on the back wall of the rear, or coffin, chamber; the remaining walls were undecorated. In all, the tomb contained eighty-seven such painted bricks. These depicted the typical scenes found in most tombs across northern China, such as a banquet presided over by the deceased, complete with musicians, dancers, and singers who provided entertainment; many scenes of food preparation; herding; farming; and harvesting. However, the inclusion of yurts reflects the realities of northwest China with its mixed ethnicities and lifestyles, contrasting the settled farmers and mobile nomads (fig. A).

Representing the entourage of the deceased, mounted figures, often with official titles given as labels, indicate that the deceased must have had high status in his lifetime. This brick (no. 11) shows a mounted rider in the typical style of the time. Since the stirrup had not yet been invented, the saddle has a high pommel and cantle and a heavy saddle blanket to help the rider maintain his seat. The woman, dressed in long robes that must have been a hindrance in performing her duties, may be carrying a water jug on her back, although it may be a basket. Her long black hair divides into two pigtails, thought to be characteristic of non-Chinese, particularly some nomadic tribes.[2]

AED

12. *Tomb brick painted with scene of husbandry*

Wei-Jin period (220–317)

Excavated from Tomb M1, Jiayuguan, Gansu

Clay brick with pigments

Height: 17 cm; length: 34.5 cm; thickness: 4.8 cm

Gansu Provincial Museum, Lanzhou

A number of tombs in an ancient cemetery in the Gobi Desert, east of Jiayuguan, were excavated in 1972–73, and more than six hundred painted bricks were recovered. Tomb M1 was approached by a long slanting ramp 28 meters long, descending some 6.8 meters below the surface. The wall above the tomb's entrance was faced with bricks laid in an intricate pattern simulating a multistory gate tower reaching to the surface level. The ramp was filled in with earth after the burial. The tomb itself con- sisted of a front chamber, 2.8 meters square; two side chambers, each some 1.6 meters square; and a short rear corridor leading to the burial chamber, 2.8 meters by 3.5 meters, where the two coffins of a husband and wife had been laid. This tomb and the others in the cemetery had been robbed long ago but some grave goods remained. The adobe bricks had been laid without mortar in a repeating pattern up to the level at which the domed ceilings begin (fig. A). For three rows the bricks were laid flat in a staggered fashion, in what is called Dutch bond. A fourth row of bricks was then laid on edge, with the large surface showing; these bricks were separated by the short ends of two bricks. Then the pattern was repeated. The painted bricks were those turned on edge with their large surfaces facing in. The images on the bricks in the front chamber include scenes of the deceased hosting a banquet, musicians, servants, hunting, agriculture, and husbandry. The bricks in the rear chamber depict spun silks, clothing racks, silkworm cocoons, and bundles of silk thread, suggesting that this area was in the nature of a storeroom. The inhabitants of the tomb were thus supplied with their daily needs through the grave goods and with scenes of their life on earth painted on the walls around them.

Fig. A. Pattern of bricks (after *Wenwu* 1972.12, p. 27, fig. 5.)

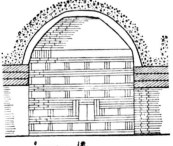

The herder with two oxen and a herd of goats shown on this brick is a typical scene of oasis life. The goats can survive on land too barren for other herbivores and are an excellent source of meat and milk. The oxen would have been used to draw the plows, as shown on other bricks from this tomb.

AED

1. *Kaogu xuebao* 1979.3, pl. 5.5

2. *Zhongguo* 1986, p. 160, pl. 100.5.

3. *Kaogu* 1972.5, p. 33, pl. 8.3

4. *Wenwu* 1987.9, pp. 89, 92, fig. 21

5. *Wenwu* 1984.8, p. 47, figs. 5, 8 (Sichuan); *Kaogu yu wenwu* 1989.1, pp. 42–43 and fig. 8.3.

6. *Kaogu* 1974.3, p. 197, pl. 7.4.

7. Knauer 1998.

13. *Lamp with three camels*

Wei-Jin period (220–317)
Found at Pingliang, Gansu
Bronze
Height: 25 cm.
Pingliang Municipal Museum, Gansu

Interior lighting during this period was either in the form of oil lamps (in which a wick floated in oil) or candles in holders. The largest number of lamps thus far uncovered from south China are of ceramic, usually in the form of candle holders. Bronze lamps, although fewer in number, come in many different forms, ranging from a simple cup with a small handle, probably meant to hold oil and wick, to elaborate candelabra with three lotus flower holders and a lotus-bud base resting on a rectangular table.[1] One may see such candelabra, though of simpler construction, in the lacquer screen from the tomb of Sima Jinlong (d. 484) at Datong.[2] One interesting Northern Wei candle holder has an octagonal stem resting on a plate, with two symmetrically attached small cups fitted into slots in the stem. The candles are placed on the cups and are held upright by two rings at the top; as the candles burn, the cups may be slid up.[3] Another type is a simple cup placed on a stem, resembling a piece of bamboo resting on a larger cup, with or without three short legs, and a curved handle with a dragonhead finial (fig. A). The fragments of a complex structure in the form of a tree, whose branches held lamp pans and peach-shaped leaves, were found in a Wei-Jin tomb in Gansu.[4] Such lamp trees are known from the Han dynasty. Two unusual lamps from Sichuan made in the form of a turtle with a winding snake on its shell represent the symbol of the north. The turtle holds an eared cup in its mouth, and there is a candle socket at the center of the turtle's shell (fig. B).[5] Another interesting lamp takes the form of a small eared-cup shaped vessel with lid, only some seven centimeters long. Half of the cover lifts up and over, thus forming a small cup held in place by a flange. The candle was held by a spindle on the bottom of the movable cup, and a spout allowed melted wax to be poured off into the base. Some holes allowed the object to be suspended by wires or cords.[6]

This lamp (no. 13) is unusual in having three camels on the rim of the bowl and large openings on the base. These two features call to mind the cauldrons of the Central Asian nomads that may have influenced the designer of the lamp. The depiction on the lamp of camels, which rarely appear in the nomadic art, underscores the important role these double-humped Bactrian camels played in the economy of the Silk Road. Their ability to carry heavy loads over the desert wastes that separated the oases from each other was of critical importance in the East-West trade, so it is not surprising that the camel was featured in the art of that part of the world through which the Silk Road passed.[7]

AED

Fig. A. Bronze lamp (*left*), Western Jin (265–317 CE), Shizishan, Wu District, Jiangsu (after *Wenwu ziliao congkan* 1980.3, p. 135, fig. 10.1.)

Fig. B. Bronze lamp (*right*), Three Kingdoms period (third century CE), Honghua Village, Kai District, Sichuan (after *Kaogu yu wenwu* 1989.1, p. 39, fig. 8.30)

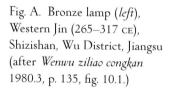

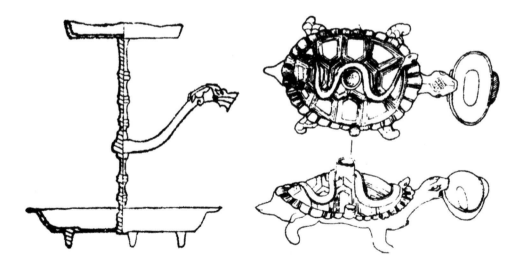

1. Paludan 1992, p. 98.

2. Ibid.

3. Published in *Sichou* 1994, no. 93, and Rawson 1995, p.354, fig. 7. Also published in *Put Svile* 1996, p. 142, no. 65.

4. *Zhongguo*, vol. 4, p. 112, fig. 151, p.111, fig. 150, p. 108, fig. 147, pp. 274–76.

5. So and Bunker 1995, p. 25.

6. Yang 1998, pp. 404–5, no. 135.

7. Paludan 1991, p. 98. Also see *Kaogu yu Wenwu* 2000.3, p. 5, fig. 8, p. 6, fig. 10, for stone rams in the kneeling position, with both legs tucked under them, on the spirit walk at the tomb of Liji (Xu Mao-gong) at the Zhaoling Mausoleum, Shaanxi.

8. Rawson 1995, p. 368.

Fig. A. Stone ram from spirit road of the Tang emperor Taizong (d. 649) at Zhaoling, Shaanxi (after Juliano 1981, p. 15, top)

14. *Reclining ram*

Former Liang dynasty (314–376 CE)
Excavated at Lingjuntai, Wuwei, Gansu
Jade (Nephrite)
Height: 8.5 cm; length: 15.1 cm; depth: 6 cm; weight: 910 g
Gansu Provincial Museum, Lanzhou

Rams have been symbols of auspiciousness throughout Chinese history because the character for "ram," *yang*, is a homophone for *xiang*, the character for "auspicious." Dating back to the Shang dynasty, rams had both sacrificial and ritual associations. Rams or sheep, which are represented by the same character in Chinese, were one of the six sacrificial animals mentioned in both the literary texts *Shiji* (Historical Records of the Grand Historian) and the *Yi Li* (Book of Etiquette and Cere-monial). Rams were sometimes depicted on ritual bronze vessels with the double-ram or four-ram image. Pairs of rams were sometimes lined up along spirit roads approaching imperial, noble, or high-ranking official and military tombs. In the Tang dynasty, military commanders and senior ministers by right were entitled to several pairs of sheep as statuary for their tombs.[1] The sheep or ram was also a symbol of filial piety, kneeling to take its mother's milk, and in the Sui and Tang dynasties this meaning was extrapolated to include virtues of incorruptibility, with stone rams taking the place of stone officials on some spirit roads.[2]

Like the ram in number 15, this jade ram reclines in a conventionalized kneeling posture with legs bent neatly under the haunches. The ram's body reflects a masterful sculptural form conceived in the round and accentuated by the natural coloration of the jade stone and by linear definition. The S-shaped line, created by its raised eyebrows, flows to well-delineated ears, which are emphasized by the looped ram horns, while the bottom line of the horn underscores the powerful line of its jaw. The delicate incised lines, which decorate the ram's pointed chest and the top of its haunches, are typical of Han dynasty jade carvings but are only rarely seen later.[3] The animal-shaped jades from the area of the tomb of Han Emperor Yuandi (r. 48–33 BCE) near Xi'an, Shaanxi province, display this same delicate incising.[4] Nephrite jade of this type was imported into China from Khotan or Lake Baikal across the Silk Road as well from trade with northern nomadic neighbors.[5]

This jade reclining ram combines an inner strength and serenity with the qualities of immor-tality and perfectability that were associated with jade, as a material, from the Han through the Tang period. Hence, according to beliefs, the owner of the ram would be rewarded with good fortune. A bronze ram-shaped lamp, in a similar pose, was found in the Western Han tomb of Prince Liu Sheng.[6] Stone rams graced the paths of spirit roads starting in the Eastern Han and continuing through the Song (fig. A). Statuary on the spirit roads served as guardians and status symbols, as well as providing a link between the physical and spiritual worlds. Rams, in addition, represented incor-ruptibility and often stood in place of stone figures of civil officials on the spirit roads.[7] Ceramic rams were commonly placed in tombs where often a single animal would represent a group of similar ani-mals used in daily life.[6] This ram (no. 14) is more animated and less stiffly postured than its bronze and stone counterparts. It maintains a strong presence surveying the world.

SB

1. *Zhongguo* 1986, p. 118, fig. 26, p. 76.

2. Paludan 1992, p. 43.

3. Rawson 1995, p. 355.

4. *Wenwu* 1988.2, p.41, fig. 36 (bird), fig. 37 (ram).

5. *Wenwu* 1990.1, p. 15, fig. 18.1.

6. Singer 1966–67, pp. 82–83.

7. Weber 1967–68, pp. 73–74.

15. *Ram*

Western Jin dynasty (265–317CE)
Excavated from a Jin tomb, Gansu
Coal stone
Height: 2.15 cm; length: 2.51 cm; width: 1.45 cm
Gansu Provincial Museum, Lanzhou

This coal stone ram strikes a conventionalized kneeling position with forelegs and hind legs folded compactly under its protruding belly. Associated with nomadic cultures along China's northern borders, this distinctive posture dates back to at least the fourth to fifth century BCE and is reminiscent of the hollow-cast bronzes associated with northwestern China, particularly the Ordos region (part of modern Ningxia). Like the jade ram (no. 14), the ram's head and body have been keenly observed and beautifully articulated with delicate incised lines defining the horns. A small hole, drilled through the center of its haunches, enables the ram to be worn close to the body as a talisman to bring good fortune to its owner.

The coal stone ram shown here, kneeling in a nomadic position, is similar in size and pose to a jade ram excavated in 1957 near Xi'an (fig. A).[1] That animal, too, has a similar hole pierced laterally through its body behind its folded forelegs. Such auspicious animals were often worn as talismans.[2] The rise of the widespread use of animal ornaments and toggles from the late Han through the Tang was linked to the intensified search for immortality.[3] Small pendants and toggles in stone or jade were quite common at this time. Small animal-shaped ornaments pierced with small holes were also excavated in a Western Han tomb in Jiangsu province. A small bird ornament, as well as a kneeling ram similar to the one on display here, was found near the neck of the tomb occupant, and had been worn.[4] They are now in the collection of the Yangzhou Museum. Also a small reclining ram of similar shape was excavated from a Han-dynasty tomb in Yangyuan, Hebei province.[5] This ornament was made of dark blue glass and also has a small hole in the same position. There are kneeling rams of similar size, shape, and material in the collections of Dr. Arthur M. Sackler and Dr. Paul Singer.[6] Both are also pierced through their bellies. Other small talismans of this type have been excavated in Lolang, Korea, and near Tangshan, Hebei.[7]

SB

Fig. A. Jade ram, Western Han Dynasty from Jiangsu (after *Wenwu* 1988.2, p. 41, fig. 37)

MONKS AND MERCHANTS

16a–d. *Lacquered coffin*

Northern We dynasty (386–535), c. 470s–480s
Excavated in 1973 at Leizumiao Village, western suburb of Guyuan, Ningxia
Fragments of a lacquered coffin
Length: 180 cm; width: varies from 87 to 105 cm
a. Dongwangfu (King-Father of the East); b. Banquet scene with deceased;
c. Attendants at window; d. Filial piety stories of Emperor Shun
Guyuan Municipal Museum, Ningxia Hui Autonomous Region

no. 16a

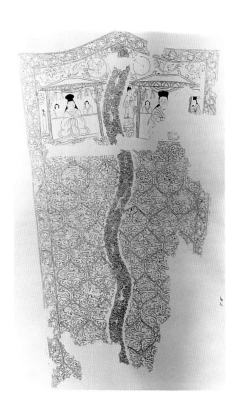

Fig. A. Drawing of the top
of the lacquered coffin (after
Yuanzhou 1999, p. 14, fig. 7)

In 1973, a Northern Wei tomb, probably dated to the third quarter of the fifth century, was discovered near Guyuan, Ningxia, when the water drill of a railway construction team penetrated the roof of the tomb some 5.8 meters below the surface.[1] The construction of the tomb was similar to those at Jiayuguan, consisting of a long ramp leading to a square, domed chamber 3.8 meters to a side and 3.9 meters high. The tomb was lined with plain bricks and was a double burial of a husband and wife (fig. B). Only about sixty burial objects were found in this undisturbed tomb, including an unusually hand-some bronze stove in the form of a tortoise, a bronze wine warmer (*jiaodou*) (no. 19a,b), two oval open-work plaques of curled dragons (no. 18a,b), upper parts of two square animal handles (nos. 17a,b), and a Sasanian silver coin (no. 93).[2] However, the most remarkable aspect of this discovery is that the hus-band's coffin was ornately decorated with lacquer; unfortunately, the water drill caused much damage to what appears to have been a perfectly preserved coffin.

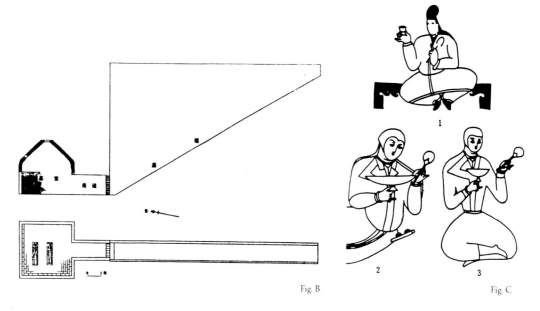

Fig. B

Fig. C

Fig. B. Cross-section and plan of the tomb with the lacquered coffin, Leizumiao Village, western suburb of Guyuan, Ningxia (after *Yuanzhou* 1999, pl. 15)

Fig. C. Line drawings of figures from banquet scenes: *above* (no. 1), lacquered coffin (nos. 2–3); *below*, wall paintings at Balalyk-tepe, southern Uzbekistan (after *Wenwu* 1989.9, p. 41, figs. 1, 3)

The decor of the coffin graphically reflects the multi-ethnic nature of the society of that time. The paintings teem with a lively mixture of traditional Chinese Daoist themes of immortality, Confucian models of filial piety, nomadic clothing, Buddhist elements, an Iranian-style banquet scene, and rich textilelike patterns of Sasanian and Central Asian inspiration. Given the richness of the pictorial and decorative imagery painted on the coffin, only some relevant aspects can be discussed within the context of this catalogue. The top of the coffin represents the Daoist world of the immortals and the vision of the ascent to paradise; the gold-colored River of Heaven (*tianhe*) with swirling waves meanders down the center for the entire length of the top.[3] At the wider head end are two pavilions with hanging curtains and pillars supporting a blue, Chinese-style roof with characteristic owl's tail hooks at each end of the rooftop ridge. Seated in the pavilions are the Daoist deities, Dongwangfu, King-Father of the East, with the sun on his left and his consort, the mythical Xiwangmu, Queen Mother of the West, with the moon on her right. Wearing tall Xianbei hats, Xiwangmu and Dongwangfu preside over the realms of the immortals (fig. A). In this fragment (no. 16a), Dongwangfu is identified by name in the yellow cartouche to the left

no. 16b

Fig. D. Rubbing of the ornament on one of the two small
stone bases found in the tomb
of Sima Jinlong (d. 484),
Datong (Shanxi), Northern
Wei (after *Wenwu* 1972.3, p. 25,
fig. 6)

of the pillar; part of the River of Heaven (the Milky Way) is visible to the right. An overall decorative pattern of repeating, soft-edged, diamond-like lozenges inhabited by fantastic creatures fills the broad open space of the coffin top.[4] Achieving immortality was one of the major themes of the preceding Han dynasty's art[5]; numerous symbols of immortality here include the human-headed birds inside some lozenges, the sun with a three-legged bird, and the scarlet bird with wings outstretched on the roof.[6] All reflect the wishes of the deceased to successfully complete the perilous, after-death journey to the para-dise of the immortals.

On the badly damaged front end of the coffin, a section near the top (no. 16b) depicts another blue-roofed, Chinese-style platform with the deceased, dressed in Xianbei garments with black pointed boots, seated regally on a Chinese-style platform flanked by two female attendants on his right and by two males on his left. In the deceased man's right hand, he holds a wine cup, elegantly clasped in his finger tips with the small finger extended; in his left hand, he has a small circular fan. The female attendant closest to the pavilion also holds a wine cup, using the same delicate gesture.[7] This banquet

1. For the excavation report, see *Wenwu* 1984.6, pp. 46–56, a 1988 monograph, *Guyuan* 1988 and in English (Luo 1990, pp. 18–29); also Karetzky and Soper 1991, pp. 5–18. The coffin has been pub-lished in *Yuanzhou* 1999, pls. 15–18, and *Put Svile* 1996, pp. 197–198 (copy of coffin). See also *Put Svile* 1996, p. 123, nos. 50, 51 (taotie mask); p. 124, no. 52 (dragon plaque).

2. *Wenwu* 1984.6. There were actually three open-work oval plaques with coiled dragons; two are included in the exhibition (no. 18 a,b).

3. The densely packed spirals that define the swirling waters of the heavenly river resemble those used on rugs positioned under the lotus thrones supporting the Buddhas painted on the back section of the north wall of Binglingsi's earliest cave, Cave 169, dated to 420 (See fig. 8, Chapter 4) and *Binglingsi* 1989, pl. 36. Luo Feng in his recent article on the Bactrian silver-gilt ewer in Li Xian's tomb (no. 30) dis-cusses a similar swirling water pat-tern with makara and fish on the bottom of the ewer, as well as other parallels from Dunhuang's Sui Cave 363 (Luo 2000, p. 316, fig. 3). This water pattern also appears in the largest cave temple complex at Kizil. A fragment of a wall painting from the Cave of the Seafarers, c. 500, preserved in the Museum für Indis-che Kunst, Berlin, shows swimmers in water described by similar spiral and swirl patterns, Metropolitan

no. 16c

Museum of Art 1982, p. 75, pl. 15.

4. These fantastic beasts within the lozenges stand above a foliate support formed by a stem that bifurcates into half palmettes. This kind of foliate support appears on Sasanian seals under animal and human heads from the fourth century onward. See Bivar 1969 and Brunner 1978. Such foliate supports also can be found as bases for plump putti-like figures carved in low relief on the small stone bases from the tomb of Sima Jinlong, dated 484, which also included the lacquer screen (*Wenwu* 1972.3, p. 25, fig. 6).

5. See Loewe 1982 and 1979.

6. For discussion of the human-headed bird-bodied creatures, see Juliano 1980, p. 45, n. 208; Luo Feng discusses three-legged and the scarlet birds (Luo 1990, pp. 20–21).

7. Next to the attendant female figure holding the wine cup is what is described as a long-necked wine jar (Luo 1990, p. 21) and "tall caps and . . . a slender-necked flask" (Karetsky and Soper 1991, p. 7). There is no Western long-necked flask next to the attendant. The lacquer fragment has a large crack right near the attendants and the image easily could have been misread. Closer examination reveals the attendant's right arm bent and her right hand holding a wine cup in front of her body. What appears to be the bottom of a wine flask is one of several large lotus buds floating in the air.

8. See Al'baum 1960, banquet scene, figs. 96, 105. It is also interesting to note that stone grave monuments of Turkic warriors found across the steppes of Central Asia, including Xinjiang, virtually all hold some kind of drinking vessel; many grasp small, footed goblets in the same manner as the figure seated on the coffin and at Balayk Tepe. For a compendium of these stone images, see Pletneva 1981, pp. 127–28, and for two examples in Xinjiang, see *Xinjiang* 1975, pp. 91–92, figs. 131–32.

9. The report of the excavation of the Tianshui couch was published in *Kaogu* 1992.1, pp. 46–52. The

no. 16d

scene recalls very similar but more elaborate feasts from surviving fragments of wall paintings in Central Asia, such as those at Balalyk Tepe, a fifth- to sixth-century site in southern Uzbekistan. A number of these scenes show figures sitting cross-legged, holding wine cups in the right hand and small circular fans in the left (fig. C).[8] Feasting and hunting are significant and characteristic themes represented in the ancient Near East and are common in Sasanian and Sogdian art. During the sixth and seventh centuries in China, banquets and hunting scenes inspired by Central Asian sources become part of elaborate pictorial programs, depicting mostly non-Chinese participants, carved onto the back and sides of stone mortuary couches such as the one in Tianshui, Gansu (no. 106k), excavated in 1982, and the sarcophagus from Taiyuan, Shanxi, in 1999.[9]

The side panels of the coffin are divided into three registers: upper, middle, and lower. The upper register has filial piety stories; the middle register, a broad surface some 40 centimeters high, contains three rows of a repetitive textilelike pattern composed of a series of pearled roundels linked by rows of contiguous pearled hexagonals. A somewhat simpler version of this pattern appears as a border on the Dunhuang silk-embroidered banner (no. 45). Pearling can be found throughout Central Asia going back to at least the first century BCE. The technique was adapted into the Chinese decorative vocabulary from the Han through the Tang and is visible on a number of examples in this catalogue (nos. 18a–b, 45, 59, 109, 112, 115). The interstices within the coffin roundels have been filled with pairs of lively putti-like figures with halos, who alternate with ferocious-looking beasts. Parallels to these are plump half-naked figures with halos (some have topknots of hair), who are shown wearing short or long dhotis with looping scarves and who are depicted as flying, hovering, and playing musical instruments; these can be found throughout Caves 6–9 in the Northern Wei Buddhist cave temples of Yungang, Shanxi, dating from the second half of the fifth century (470s and 480s), and on the small stone bases from the tomb of Sima Jinlong, dated 484 (fig. D).[10]

Centered on each of the patterned side panels, a painted window shows two bust-length images peering out from behind a screen or curtain (no. 16c). This window is framed by an intricate pattern of peacock feathers created by soft-edged diamond lozenges filled with graded colors. Chinese scholars identify these figures as servants.

Running horizontally on the side panels of the coffin, familiar Chinese legends of filial piety are depicted and labeled in yellow rectangular cartouches to avoid any ambiguity. Triangles filled with a distinctive flame pattern not only separate each segment of the story but also are integrated into the pictorial composition with figures standing behind as well as between them. While filial piety is a fundamental virtue of a traditional Confucian society, all the figures shown in these stories wear the standard Xianbei clothing as seen on the fragmentary Buddhist silk embroidery found at Dunhuang (no. 45). Even the headgear shows characteristic Xianbei gender differences, the male's hat being taller and leaning slightly backward while the female's has a slight indentation at the top.

The story of the mythological emperor Shun (traditionally 2317–2208 BCE) is told in eight panels; three of which are illustrated here (no. 16d). Shun, the most eminent of all Chinese paragons of filial piety, gained the throne because of his exceptional treatment of his parents. His father had no love for him, and his stepmother favored her own son. To rid themselves of him, they set fire to a granary while he was working in it, but he managed to escape the flames. Next, on a pretext, they sent him down a well and then piled on stones to prevent his escape. He managed to dig his way to an adjoining well and emerged without his parents knowing it. He then fled elsewhere to farm on his own, and he prospered. After the incident at the well, the father went blind. The fragment (no. 16d) picks up the story from here, moving from right to left. In dire poverty, the stepmother is depicted taking a bundle of twigs to the market to sell. She buys rice from Shun, without recognizing her stepson, but he contrives to slip money for her into the rice sack. Later, the father finds the money, surmises that the rice seller is his son, and returns with his wife to the market to seek him out. When confronted, Shun admits his identity, and they embrace. When Shun wipes his father's eyes, the father regains his sight.

According to the myth, Shun's fame spread so far that the emperor Yao, seeking an heir, gave Shun his two daughters in marriage and appointed him the imperial heir. Other panels on the coffin record different classic tales of filial devotion. Models of filial piety were a popular theme during the fifth and sixth centuries and are preserved on major Chinese stone carvings in the west and on a rare lacquer screen dated to 484 from the tomb of Sima Jinlong, in the Tuoba capital of Pingcheng.[11] The use of this theme on the coffin indicates the virtue with which the deceased wished to be associated after his death. Apparently, during the Northern Wei dynasty, the *Book of Filial Piety* (*Xiao Jing*) was translated into Xianbei.[12] However, it is not known whether the occupants of the tomb were originally Xianbei who had been heavily influenced by the Chinese culture or Chinese who were reflecting the hybrid culture of the Xianbei state of that time.[13]

ALJ and AED

discovery of the Taiyuan sarcophagus is discussed in Zhang and Jiang 2000. Another couch is now in the Miho Museum, see Juliano and Lerner 1997b, pp. 247–53. Parts of the stone pictorial panels from another couch said to have come from Zhangdefu, Henan, are now in the Museum of Fine Arts, Boston, with remaining parts at the Musée Guimet in Paris; see Scaglia 1958, pp. 2–28.

10. See *Yungang* 1977, figs. 25 (Cave 6), 37, 38 (Cave 7), 42 (Cave 8), 44 (Cave 9), and *Wenwu* 1972.3, p. 25, fig. 26.

11. Excavated in 1965 in Datong, the lacquer screen preserves, along with the coffin, important information on secular pictorial painting styles during the Period of Disunity. See *Wenwu* 1972.8, pp. 55–60, for the excavation report of the lacquer screen found in the Sima Jinlong tomb dated 484, *Wenwu* 1972.3, pp. 20–29, 64; for a discussion of representations of filial piety scenes in fifth and sixth centuries, see Juliano 1980, pp. 54–58, including the famous Northern Wei stone sarcophagus in the Nelson-Atkins Gallery of Art, Kansas City.

12. Sun 1989, pp. 39–40.

13. On this matter, see Soper 1990, pp. 205–16, in which Soper opts for the latter.

17a,b. *Pair of animal masks* (pushou)

Northern Wei dynasty (386–535), late fifth century
Excavated in 1981 at Leizumiao Village, western suburbs of Guyuan, Ningxia
Bronze, hollow cast
Height: 11.2 cm; width: 10.5 cm
Guyuan Municipal Museum, Ningxia Hui Autonomous Region

18a,b. *Pair of ornamental plaques*

Northern Wei dynasty (386–585), late fifth century
Excavated in 1973 at Leizumiao Village, western suburbs of Guyuan, Ningxia
Bronze, hollow cast
Height: 7.5 cm; width: 11 cm
Guyuan Municipal Museum, Ningxia Hui Autonomous Region

Both the pair of bronze animal masks (*pushou*) and the pair of ornamental plaques (two of the four are illustrated here) were excavated from the tomb containing the marvelous lacquer painted coffin near Guyuan in Ningxia (no. 16). These were probably matched sets, with the plaques hanging from the animal heads. The *pushou* (nos. 17 a,b) and the plaques (nos. 18 a,b) may originally have adorned the coffin that was damaged when the tomb was opened. Alternatively, similar pairs have been found on tomb doors either in cast bronze like this pair or as images carved into stone.[1]

In the center of the plaques and the *pushou* both, stands a small figure, legs planted firmly, almost dwarfed between two confronted dragons. The figure's arms are positioned at its sides with hands down, either touching or grasping the dragons' hind legs or tongue. The rather large head with a high topknot (*ushnisha*), the stance, rounded body, and short dhoti (loincloth) correspond specifically to the iconography of the Infant Buddha and earlier depictions of the Buddha's birth sequence, which first appear in Gandhara narrative panels from the third and fourth centuries CE.[2] The earliest birth sequence identified so far in China occurs on the back of the Xingping stele dated 471 in Shaanxi.[3] Other later birth sequences dated to the late fifth century depict the Infant Buddha with pointed mandorla actually emerging from his mother Maya's side, being examined by a holy man or show him/her standing nearby on the central pillar of Cave 6 at Yungang (Shanxi) (fig. A). An early-sixth-century Northern Wei stele in Cave 133 at Maijishan in Tianshui, Gansu, presents a similarly robust young body wearing a dhoti and enclosed in an aureole.[4]

These Infant Buddhas share strikingly similar stylistic and iconographic features with a small infant Buddha cast from a leaded copper alloy believed to be from Afghanistan and dated to the fifth–sixth century (fig. B).[5] About this time, a nativity cult centered around this blessed event evolved, as suggested by the appearance of independent images of the Infant Buddha, extracted from the Birth Scene, in Central Asia and East Asia.[6] There is now a group of individual Infant Buddha images from the fifth and sixth centuries, including the gilt-bronze Buddha standing on a lotus at the Cleveland Museum of Art, another carved in ivory that was acquired in Khocho and is now at Berlin's Museum für Indische Kunst, and the cast-copper alloy figure attributed to Afghanistan.[7] At this point, it is still difficult to determine with any certainty the origins of this nativity cult in either Central Asia or China.

1. Both *pushou* and plaques have been published in Guyuan 1988, p. XX, col-orpl. 2, top (plaque), bottom, (*pushou*); p. 5, line drawings of plaque (left), *pushou* (right); apparently, three plaques were found in excavation and two *pushou*; Yuanzhou 1999, no. 25 (plaque) and no. 24 (*pushou*). For an extraordinary example of a cast-bronze *pushou* excavated from a Warring States tomb in Hebei see Toronto 1974, p. 87, no. 135. For examples from stone tomb doors, see Xi'an 2000, pp. 74–75.

2. Errington and Cribb 1992, p. 213; Lee 1955, pp. 225–37.

3. Here the Infant Buddha is shown with rounded body, large head, and short dhoti, standing, with a mandorla behind, *nagas* above, and adoring attendants flanking. The *nagas* form a hood of protection and bathe the infant Buddha, see Xi'an 2000, p. 101.

Fig. B. Leaded copper-zinc-tin alloy figurine of the Infant Buddha (*above*) probably from Afghanistan, fifth–sixth century, 10.2 cm high; (after Errington and Cribb 1992, p. 213, no. 208)

Fig. A. Examination of the Infant Buddha by the Rishi (holy man), Asita (*left*), Yungang, Cave 6, from Central Stupa column, north face, lower story (after Mizuno and Nagahiro, vol. 3, pl. 178)

Fig. C. Frontal portrait of a Parthian king, perhaps Mithradates III (r. 57–54 BCE) (after Rosenfield 1967, p. 211, fig. 26: Coin 296)

4. Birth sequences represented at Yungang, Cave 6, located on the corner of the central pillar; Mizuno and Nagahiro 1952–56, vol.3, pls. 178, 200, 201, 204; at Maijishan, stele in Cave 133, proper right of stele, second scene from top, see Sullivan 1969, pl. 59.

5. Errington and Cribb 1992, p. 213, no. 208.

6. The concept of an Infant Buddha or nativity cult has been briefly discussed in Metropolitan Museum of Art 1982, p. 60, no. 3; Errington and Cribb 1992, pp. 213–14; Lee 1955, pp. 225–37.

7. Lee 1955, figs. 1, 2; Metropolitan Museum of Art 1992, p. 60, no. 3; Errington and Cribb 1992, p. 213, no. 208.

8. Wu 1986, p. 270.

9. So and Bunker 1995, p. 71. Bunker makes a connection between *xiangrui*, or good omens, and foreignness when discussing the absorption and sinicization of motifs usually not part of the Chinese repertoire. Because of their foreign origins, motifs from northern tribes in Qin and Western Han became suitable and more powerful *xiangrui*.

10. Rosenfield 1967; see Sahri-Bahlol, Gandhara, nos. 67, 68; a stone sculpture of the God of Wealth, Kubera or Jambhala from Mathura wears the same tunic as this Infant Buddha, no. 48. See p. 211, fig. 26; for a drawing of the Parthian coin with Mithradates, Kushan royal portrait, Mathura, no. 5, and ivory plaque from Begram treasure, no. 97a. The mummy was excavated from Yingpan, Yuli, Xinjiang, *Wenwu* 1991.1, colorpl. inside front cover.

11. *Binglingsi* 1989, pl. 24–25; *Shandong* 1999, pp. 70–71, 132–33.

12. Wu 1986, p. 270 n. 28. Wu Hung cites two examples of *pushou* with Infant Buddha, in the collections of the British Museum and the Asian Art Museum in San Francisco, which have been dated to the fourth century CE.

Here, however, adapted in this Chinese context, the Infant Buddha assumes the auspicious role of "Huan Long Shi, the dragon tamer, a famous character in a traditional Chinese legend."[8] This is related to the traditional Chinese concept of good omens, or *xiangrui*, which suggests that all natural and unnatural phenomena express the will of heaven and that certain strange phenomena, such as the figures depicted in these images, reveal heavenly approval or disapproval. During the late Han dynasty, second and third centuries CE, the Buddha was accepted as a powerful Daoist deity and subsumed into the pantheon of the very popular immortality cults, with their auspicious signs and omens. As the Han dynasty began to crumble, the people became obsessed with the concept of good omens, with any appearance of dragons always considered an extraordinarily positive omen. Since the Buddha and other Buddhist symbols were exotic images, they were readily accepted as *xiangrui*.[9]

On these plaques (nos. 18a,b), the Infant Buddha appears to have wings emerging from his shoulders, a characteristic of the *xian*, Daoist immortals who could fly, change form, and help people attain immortality. The Buddha was also believed to have these abilities. As shown here, the Infant Buddha is an immortal wearing a tight-sleeved tunic, edged with pearling, which also embellishes the dragon's body and the wings and tail of the bird standing on the back of the dragon. Pearl borders can be traced back to Western sources as early as a Parthian coin with the portrait of Mithradates III (r. 57–54 BCE) wearing a pearl-edged, V-necked garment (fig. C). Edging is also found as garment and body embellishment on an ivory plaque with triton and *makara* from the Begram treasure (first–second century CE) and most consistently in depictions of Indo-Scythian clothing on stone relief and sculptural images showing Buddhist devotees from Sahri-Bahlol, Gandhara, and from Mathura, and on the trousers of the Yingpan mummy from Xinjiang (c. second–third century CE).[10] Pearl borders, edging, and pearling seep into Buddhist sculpture in China, adorning mandorlas surrounding the Wu Liang Shou Buddha and flanking Bodhisattvas in the early-fifth-century Cave 169 at Binglingsi in Gansu, on the gray white stone stele from Pengyang, near Guyuan, Ningxia, dated to the early sixth century (no. 59), and on a Northern Qi bejeweled bodhisattva from Qingzhou.[11] By the Sui and Tang dynasties, this decorative motif becomes very popular, occurring also on textiles, ceramics (no. 112), and metalwork.

On the *pushou*, the Infant Buddha stands on an animal mask, the *taotie*, so prominently featured on Shang ritual bronzes from the second and first millennia BCE.[12] In China, the *taotie*, coupled with the images of the dragon and the Infant Buddha immortal, would give this *pushou* extraordinary power to protect the deceased in the tomb on the journey to immortality.

Both the plaques and the *pushou* reflect the adaptation of Buddhist and other foreign elements into a traditional Chinese context.

ALJ

1. *Wenwu* 1984.6, p. 51, figs. 12-13; *Guyuan* 1988 (unnumbered plate); *Yuanzhou* 1999, pl. 21.

2. *Wenwu* 1987.6, pl. 5:2

19a. *Stove (zao) with steamer (zeng)*

Northern Wei dynasty (386–535), fifth–early sixth century
Excavated in 1981 from a tomb at Leizumiao, western suburbs of Guyuan, Ningxia
Bronze
Height: 17.3 cm; length: 20 cm
Guyuan Municipal Museum, Ningxia Hui Autonomous Region

This small stove evokes a quadruped with a long neck that suggested a turtle to the excavators.[1] The "body" of the creature forms the firebox, with an opening at the rear for fuel. Smoke from the fire would have passed up the neck and out of the mouth of the creature. A wide opening on the top of the firebox holds a shallow, narrow-mouthed boiler, with another, of similar shape, resting on its mouth. On top of this sits a deeper basin with a grating to prevent the contents from falling into the boiler. A pair of ogre masks on either side of the basin would each originally have held a handle, enabling the basin to be removed while still hot. The remains of a cake, no doubt prepared for the funerary ceremony, were found in the steamer.

Models of stoves were a popular component of the repertoire of funerary ceramics from Western Han (206 BCE–220CE) onward. Some of these are provided with figures of cooks attending them, which allow the scale of the originals to be roughly gauged. It seems that the originals, no doubt constructed out of brick, rose to almost waist height. The small scale of this bronze stove, however, might have suggested that it too was a model. But traces of soot still visible in the firebox indicate that it had been used. It is possible that the small scale of the piece and its dismantleability reflect its use as a portable stove used on military campaigns or inspection tours. Bronze stoves were not uncommon during the Han period but became rare in graves thereafter. A close parallel to this piece was found in a late Western Han tomb in Shuo County, Shanxi.[2]

CM

1. *Guyuan* 1988, pp. 4, 6.

19b. *Tripod* (jiaodou)

Northern Wei dynasty (386–535), fifth–early sixth century
From the "Lacquered Coffin Tomb" at Leizumiao, Guyuan, Ningxia
Bronze
Height: 10.6 cm; length including handle: 24 cm
Guyuan Municipal Museum, Ningxia Hui Autonomous Region

This vessel possesses the typical features of the *jiaodou* type discussed in greater detail in the entry for number 28. It differs from that piece, mainly in the ornament cast as part of the handle. This consists of a dragon in low relief with its head facing toward the ring and a raised tail, which originally connected with the top of the mouth rim of the vessel. The decoration, like that on the handles of many *jiaodou*, has been gradually blurred by constant use, also attested by traces of soot on its base.

The lacquered coffin tomb at Leizumiao was, by the standards of Northern Wei tombs, relatively rich in bronze vessels. In addition to this piece, the tomb contained a version of the *jiaodou* with an arched dragon handle, the stove (no. 19a), and round and square versions of the *hu*. The tomb also yielded a rare silver version of a traditional lacquer form, the winged cup (*erbei*).[1]

CM

20a,b. *Pair of earrings*

Northern Wei dynasty (386–535), fifth–early sixth century
Excavated in 1991 at Huaping Village, Sanying town, Guyuan, Ningxia
Gold foil with coral and turquoise stones
a. Depth: 3.92 cm; weight: 16.3 g; b. Depth: 3.84 cm; weight: 14.7 g
Guyuan Municipal Museum, Ningxia Hui Autonomous Region

21a,b. *Pair of earrings*

Northern Wei dynasty (386–535), fifth–early sixth century
Excavated in 1987 at Zhaike Village, Ningxia
Gold foil with coral and turquoise stones
a. Depth: 3.25 cm; weight: 8.6 g; b. Depth: 2.58 cm; weight: 6.6 g
Guyuan Municipal Museum, Ningxia Hui Autonomous Region

1. Previously published in *Yuanzhou* 1999, nos. 28, 29; Yang 1998, pp. 104–5, no. 24, Shandong Longshan culture, Neolithic period, 2000 BCE.

2. Liu 1988, p. 54.

3. Ibid, pp. 101, 177.

4. *Sammlung Uldry* 1994, p. 130, fig. 102.

Both pairs of earrings (nos. 20, 21) are hoop shaped and were fashioned from gold foil, which was then pinched at the ends; one pair (no. 21) has small holes still visible at each end. The larger left earring has an ancient repair where twisted gold wire was placed inside the earring in order to reinforce a break.

Alternating coral and turquoise stones, some now missing, were set in teardrop-shaped settings with granulated decoration. The earrings described in entry for number 80b are larger in size and weight and have pinched ends with no holes. They have larger, oval-shaped stones placed in more regular settings, each one framed by a ring of granulation (nos. 5a–c). All the earrings have three concentric rows of turquoise and pearl design.

Turquoise has been used in China for decorative inlay since Neolithic times.[1] Coral was an important luxury good shipped through India to China, along with pearls, glass vessels and beads, perfume, and incense.[2] In addition, coral was one of the seven Buddhist treasures of the *sapta-ratna*. The concept of the seven treasures as symbols of the Buddhist ideal world increased the demand for these luxury goods, and concurrently their trade contributed to the standardization of the *sapta-ratna* concept.[3] A similar pair of earrings was published in a catalogue of the Rietberg Museum, Zurich.[4]

SB

no. 20a, b

no. 21a, b

Detail of earring no. 21a showing ancient repair

1. For the excavation report, see *Wenwu* 1988.9, pp. 26–42; the four warriors, pl. 2, no. 1, and the house, p. 27, fig. 4. A selection of pieces including two of the foot soldiers have been published in *Yuanzhou* 1999, pl. 8.

22a–d. *Four armored foot soldiers*

Northern Wei dynasty (386–535), fifth–early sixth century
Excavated in 1984 at Xinji Village, Pengyang District, Ningxia
Clay with pigment
Height: 37.8 cm
Guyuan Municipal Museum, Ningxia Hui Autonomous Region

This tomb, excavated in 1984, had the usual format of a long, ramped passageway; a couple of shafts to the surface, both of which were filled in after completion; a domed chamber; and a mound mark-ing the site. What was unusual was a model of a house, perhaps half-size in scale, sited precisely over the tomb chamber below and then covered by the tomb's mound.[1] It is made of a dark brown soil, not rammed too solidly, then covered with a layer of rammed yellow loess mixed with plaster, which formed a hard surface. Finally the top and front were covered with a layer of white plaster. It is 4.84 meters long and 2.9 meters wide, the roof at its highest point is 1.88 meters from the surface. The roof is a flush gable one, with layers of simulated tiles and a ridge, slightly sagging in the middle, and ending with rounded projections, somewhat resembling acroteria. There is a double-leaf door at the center and two lattice windows, one on each side. The doors and frames are painted red. There are long, tapered projections emanating from the corners of the windows. The roof has a series of eaves supporting a cushion beam, which holds up the roof.

Among the rich contents of the tomb were more than a hundred pottery figurines, including sixty-five warriors, four of which are displayed here. They are described as having long, thin eye-brows, high nose, deep-set eyes, and facial hair, standard attributes of non-Chinese. They wear a kind of lamellar armor in which the plates overlap upward. The armor covers the upper body and has straps over the shoulders. The figurines seem to wear a heavy garment under the armor that comes up over the throat and is high in back, as well as reaching down to the forearms; such garments were perhaps composed of leather or some other heavy material. The helmet is a type of casque, straight across the brow, covers the ears and back of the head, and has a high protuberance at the top. Very little actual armor of this period has been recovered and one depends on these depictions to trace the development of armor during these years. What little has been found, at the bottom of a moat left over from a battle of 577, matches very well what we see in these figurines. The two arms of each figurine extend from the waist, the hands clenched to form a hole as if to hold a weapon. The head and body were separately molded, and a thin wooden stick was inserted in a round hole at the back of the collar to hold the head firmly in place.

AED

Fig A: *Mingqi* as found in the tomb at Pengyang, Ningxia (after *Yuanzhou* 1999, p. 13, fig. 5)

1. *Wenwu* 1988.9, pp. 26–42; for cavalry, see p. 33, no. 4; pl. 2, no. 2, pl. 3, no. 4. These clay *mingqi* have been published in *Yuanzhou* 1999, pl. 9, *Put Svile* 1996, pp. 128, 129, nos. 56, 57, and see Dien 1981–82, pp. 5–56.

2. Dien 1986, pp. 33–56.

23a–d. *Armored cavalrymen*

Northern Wei dynasty (386–535), fifth–early sixth century
Excavated in 1984 at Xinji Village, Pengyang District, Ningxia
Clay with pigment
Height: 43.5 cm; length: 34.8 cm
Guyuan Municipal Museum, Ningxia Hui Autonomous Region

These figures are more heavily armored than the clay foot soldiers from the same site (nos. 22a–d). The helmet has drawn lines indicating that it is made of metal plates, the collar is higher, and the arms and legs are also covered with iron lamellae.[1] The imbrication, or direction of overlaps is still upward. The horses, too, are covered with armor, the size of the lamellae being larger than those making up the man's armor. This accords well with actual finds of such bard. The red border on the man's suit and that of the horse indicate there was some sort of cloth undercoat to keep the metal armor from chaffing. The head armor of the horse, or chamfron, is the same style down to the same triple-pronged decoration as that found in the broad expanse from Japan and Korea to this outpost in the northwest. Actual examples made of iron enable us to know how it was constructed. What made this sort of heavily armored

cavalry possible was the invention of the stirrup in the fourth century CE during the wars between the Chinese and the steppe peoples.[2] It is not clear to which side credit is to be given: whether the stirrup was the invention of the nomads with their greater experience in horsemanship or of the Chinese in their attempt to match the nomads' riding abilities. This is still a debated question. With the use of the stirrup it was possible for the rider to remain on the horse even when wearing heavy armor, and armor for the horse soon followed. This heavy cavalry, or cataphracti, soon appeared across Asia and initiated a new sort of warfare. As in the case of the infantrymen, the heads and bodies of these figures were made separately. The bodies of the horses are hollow, with the legs and tails added.

AED

24a,b. *Xianbei tribesmen*

Northern Wei dynasty (386–535), fifth–early sixth century
Excavated in 1984 at Xinji Village, Pengyang District, Ningxia
Clay with pigment
Height: 38 cm; width: 39.8 cm
Guyuan Municipal Museum, Ningxia Hui Autonomous Region

1. *Wenwu* 1988.9, pp. 26–42; see also p. 30, fig. 8:2, pl. 3, no. 1; *Yuanzhou* 1999, pl. 13; *Put Svile* 1996, p. 126, no. 53.

2. Dien 1997, pp. 961–81.

There were 26 of this type among the more than 126 figurines in the tomb.[1] Each is described in the tomb report as wearing the hooded headdress of the Xianbei and as having a mustache, sharp nose, and deep-set eyes. Their long, heavy robes, joined at the front, are worn with the lapels turned up. Their left arms are bent forward to hold some long-handled object, no longer present; perhaps it had been an insignia of some sort or a spear. The right arm appears to be kept inside the robe, so that the sleeve hangs empty. The robe may be a form of the Central Asian cape usually worn over the shoulders as a mantle with the sleeves hanging empty. These figures were probably shod in boots.

China at this period was divided between the north, controlled by a variety of non-Chinese peoples who had established a series of states through conquest, and the south, where the Chinese court of the fugitive Western Jin dynasty and its later successors had established their capital at Nanjing in 317. The practice of including a large number of figurines in the tomb was a northern one.[2] Tombs with such figurines ranged as high as 65 percent in Hebei, 40 percent in Shandong, and 35 percent in Henan. Every tomb of this sort had two heavily armored guards at the door; armored cavalry; hooded and caped figures usually identified as Xianbei; foot soldiers with shields; archers; insignia bearers; attendants, both male and female; musicians; and servants. The numbers of such figurines could go as high as 1,064 in a single tomb, with an average of 151. In the north, where the military dominated the society, those buried in these tombs expected in death to be accompanied by the same sort of armed forces to which their offices and status entitled them in life. In the southern dynasty tombs, however, that sort of display would have been out of place, and one finds only a few figurines representing servants or attendants and very few, if any, of the military.

AED

1. *Wenwu* 1988.9, p. 30, fig. 4 (horn player), fig. 5 (drummer); published in *Yuanzhou* 1999, pls. 11 (horn player), 12 (drummer); and *Put Svile* 1996, no. 54 (horn player), no. 55 (drummer).

2. Yi 1981, pp. 85–89.

3. See Akiyama 1968, vol I, p. 181, no. 340.

25. *Xianbei drummer*

Northern Wei dynasty (386–535), fifth–early sixth century
Excavated in 1984 at Xinji Village, Pengyang District, Ningxia
Clay with pigment
Height: 45.3 cm
Guyuan Municipal Museum, Ningxia Hui Autonomous Region

26. *Xianbei horn player*

Northern Wei dynasty (386–535), fifth–early sixth century
Excavated in 1984 at Xinji Village, Pengyang District, Ningxia
Clay with pigment
Height: 39.9 cm
Guyuan Municipal Museum, Ningxia Hui Autonomous Region

Among the 126 complete figurines from this tomb, 10 represent musicians, 8 of whom are horn blowers and 2 are drummers.[1] There were in addition figurines of another drummer, a player of a zither, and another of a player of a mouth organ, which could not be restored, though the pottery models of the instruments were preserved. The present drummer (no. 25) wears a cap that has a projecting crown and folded-up brim. The face is painted white with mustache added in black. He wears a short jacket and trousers. The drum is held at his side and he beats it with one drumstick. Another drummer, not included, had suspended from his neck a drum, which he could hit with a pair of drumsticks. The horn players wear outfits similar to that of the drummer. The horn made of copper or bronze is curved and was based on a steppe nomad instrument not native to China. One source even says that the nomads used such horns to frighten the horses of the Chinese. No surviving instrument of this type has yet surfaced. The horn player (no. 26), with his cheeks puffed out as he blows, was made from three parts: head, body, and lastly both arms and horn as a unit, and then assembled.

The drums and curved horns as well as panpipes and flutes made up the military bands during this period, the number of players and distribution of instruments differing according to period and region.[2] There are depictions of such bands, frequently mounted and accompanying troops on the march. A mounted clay horn player, probably part of a military band, was excavated from a Northern Wei tomb at Caochangbo Village, near Xi'an (fig. A).[3] It is said that they played during battles to bolster the morale of the fighters. These musicians were separate from the units that carried gongs and large drums used to signal the troops to advance or retreat. In real life, strictly enforced sumptuary laws dictated the size of the retinue and type of musical band assigned to those of high rank, and such regulations held for the tomb as well. The figurines of musicians in the tomb together with the large military force not only gave evidence of the status of the deceased but also provided the retinue needed to accompany him for the final procession to the other world.

AED

Fig. A. A mounted clay horn player, probably part of a military band, excavated from a Northern Wei tomb at Caochangbo Village, near Xi'an (after Akiyama 1968, vol. 1, pl. 181, no. 340)

no. 25

no. 26

1. *Wenwu* 1975.6, p. 88, fig. 2:3 (bottle), 6 (cup).

2. Eastern Wei tomb of Li Xizong, Shijiazhuang (Hebei) the set consists of a bronze tray, a gilt bronze *hu* (bottle) with cover, a bronze *jiaodou*, footed silver cup, and five green-glazed stoneware cups that have low ring feet (*Kaogu* 1977.6 , pl. 5:1). Another set was found in the Northern Qi tomb of Kudi Huilu (d. 562), Jiajiazhuang Shanxi (*Kaogu xuebao* 1979.3, pl. 5).

3. See the assemblage of miniature vessels in Juliano 1975, pp. 38–40, nos. 16, 17. A set of four miniature bronze vessels have been found in a Northern Wei tomb, dated 524, in Chuyang (Hebei) (*Kaogu* 1972.5, pl. 8:1–4).

4. Robert J. Herold observed about similar bronze *hu* that "there is clear evidence that the pieces were rotated about their axis and a cutting tool applied to smooth the surface, control the shape, or accentuate a sharp corner .... The incised lines seen on most of the pieces as a decorative device were cut at the same time as the body with a pointed tool" (Herold 19975, pp. 274–75).

5. See note 2 above.

Fig. A. Female votary with cup and decanter, south wall, stupa V, Miran (after Stein 1921, vol. 1, fig. 140).

27a,b. *Bottle and cup*

Late Northern Wei (386–535), c. 529
Excavated in 1972 from the tomb of Wang Zhenbao, Qingshui, Zhangjiachuan Hui Autonomous County, Gansu
a. Bottle: Bronze (hu); height: 16.7 cm; diameter: 12 cm at shoulder
b. Cup: Silver; height: 4.34 cm; diameter: 10.1 cm
Gansu Provincial Museum, Lanzhou

These two utensils, along with the bronze *jiaodou* (footed ladle; no. 28) were part of a ritual set for preparing and serving wine. Most likely used in life, some of these sets accompanied their owners in their tombs.[1] Miniature sets were also used as grave goods in the fifth and sixth centuries.[3]

This bottle is a classic *hu* shape, its form emphasized by six sets of three incised grooves that

encircle the neck and body at intervals: just inside its mouth, on and at the base of its neck, above its shoulder, just below its shoulder and the middle of its body. It was first cast and the surface was then polished and enriched with the grooves, which were made by some lathelike device.[4] The foot was attached separately.

The silver cup consists of a shallow bowl to which a low foot has been soldered. The combination of a drinking vessel with a bottle and *jiaodou* (no. 28) is in keeping with at least one other excavated wine set, that from the almost-contemporary Eastern Wei (534–550) tomb of Li Xizong.[5] A similar cup is held by a female votary in the wall painting of one of the Buddhist stupas at Miran (eastern Xinjiang). She also holds a glass decanter and looks as if she is about to pour its contents into the cup (fig. A).

Wang Zhenbao belonged to the ethnic group known as the Qiang, which had a long history in northwest China stretching back to the Zhou Dynasty; the group is still found today in mountainous areas of western China. The relationship of the Chinese with the Qiang, as with most of their nomadic neighbors, can be characterized as ambivalent, often hostile but also symbiotic. After the fall in 317 of the Western Jin in northern China, the Qiang were one of the five barbarians groups—along with the Xiongnu, Di, Jie, and Xianbei—that brought disorder to China.

ALJ and JAL

28. *Tripod* (Jiaodou)

Northern Wei dynasty (386–535), c. 529
Excavated in 1972 from the tomb of
Wang Zhenbao from Zhangjiachuan Autonomous County, Gansu
Bronze
Height: 9.9 cm. Length including handle: 30.9 cm.
Gansu Provincial Museum, Lanzhou

1. *Wenwu* 1975.6, p. 88, fig. 2:5.
2. See a Western Han example of this type from Sanjiaowei, in Tianchang county, Anhui province (*Wenwu* 1993.9, p. 7, fig. 16:4).

During the course of the Han period, the range of bronze vessels consigned to tombs gradually contracted. With the collapse of the Han, the focus of attention in tombs of the wealthy shifted to vessels in precious metals. Apart from *hu*, the only bronze vessel type that commanded widespread popularity was a flat-bottomed tripod conventionally termed *jiaodou*. The name *jiaodou* is found in Han and later texts and the commentaries describe it as a cooking vessel with a long handle that was taken on military campaigns. Traces of soot on the base of some of these confirm that they were indeed used for cooking or heating.

Jiaodou occur in two versions, one with an S-shaped dragon-head handle and the other with a long flat handle and spout at right angles, as in the piece shown here. The origin of this type is not clear. On the one hand it may be distantly related to globular lidded tripod with handle and spout at right angles that became common during Eastern Han.[1] However, it differs from these by its lack of lid and angular shape. Its frequent occurrence in northern tombs, where militarism was endemic (although it is by no means confined to the north) suggests that it may indeed have had a military function.[2]

CM

1. Five finials were reported from the tomb (*Wenwu* 1975.6, pp. 85, 88, fig. 2).

2. The earliest example comes from Jin period tomb M1 at Jiayuguan (*Wenwu* 1979.6, p. 14, fig. 21). An iron version was found in an Eastern Jin period tomb in Chaoyang in Liaoning (*Wenwu* 1984.6, p. 35, fig. 30:5), and four bronze finials were found in a tomb in the cemetery of the Gao family in Jing County in Hebei (*Wenwu* 1979.3, p. 24, fig. 6:5). Six gilt bronze versions were found in Tomb 1 at Xiguanxingzi in Beipiao County in Liaoning Province (*Wenwu* 1973.3, p. 4, fig. 3:2) and another four in tomb 2 (*Wenwu* 1973.3, p. 20, fig. 21). Of these four, three were found lying slightly overlapping and facing the same way. The remains of a wooden post 60 centimeters long was found in one of them.

3. See Li 1973. Li suggests (p. 9, p. 16 n. 10) that these finials were funerary chariot fittings from which standards were hung.

29. *Dragon-head finials*

Northern Wei dynasty (386–535), c. 529
Excavated in 1972 from the tomb of Wang Zhenbao,
Zhangjiachuan Autonomous County, Gansu
Bronze
Height: 13 cm
Gansu Provincial Museum, Lanzhou

Each finial takes the form of a bowed tube terminating in a striking dragon head depicted in profile.[1] Above the elongated jaw are an eye, a serrated horn, and an ear. The snout, upper jaw, and fangs form a star shape, from which emerges the tongue, which is perforated to form a small ring, from which an object, probably of perishable material, was originally suspended. Remains of an iron pin slotted through a pair of small holes near the base probably served to attach the finial to a wooden strut. Similar dragon-headed fittings ranging in number from one to six have been found in northern tombs dating between the Western Jin (265–317 CE) and Northern Wei periods.[2] Unfortunately, their disposition in the tombs offers only tenuous evidence as to their function. It is possible that they served for hanging standards or formed part of a screen or tent.[3] Since they have no precedent in Han tombs and since they are confined to the north, it seems likely that their origins lie in the cultures of the nomadic peoples who inhabited the border regions.

CM

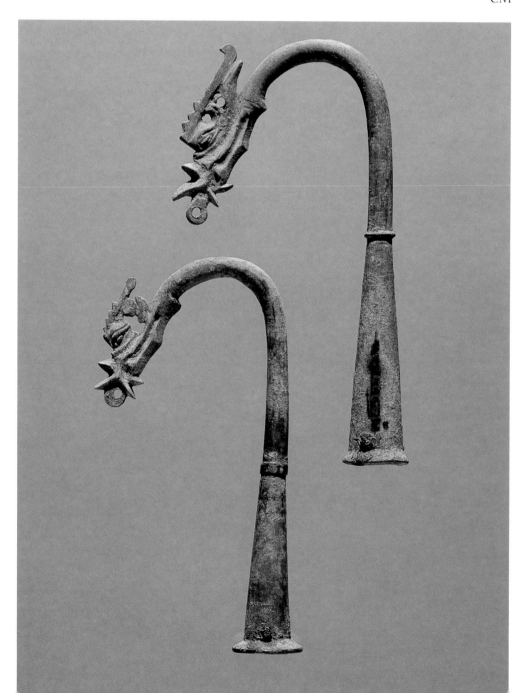

30. *Bowl*

Sasanian Persian, fifth–sixth century
Excavated in 1983 from the tomb of Li Xian (d. 569) and his wife, Wu Hui (d. 547),
western suburbs of Guyuan, Ningxia
Glass
Height: 8 cm; diameter: 9.8 cm; thickness: 6.8 cm
Guyuan Municipal Museum, Ningxia Hui Autonomous Region

This hemispherical clear glass bowl of a greenish tint is decorated with two rows of facets in relief, like protruding roundels; eight are in the top row and six in the bottom. A slightly larger roundel at the base serves as the foot.[1] The blank bowl with its relief pattern was made in a mold, and the surface of each circular facet was then slightly hollowed to a shallow concavity. Similar glass bowls have been found in Gilan province in northwestern Iran and belong to the Sasanian period (224–651 CE).[2]

Circular faceting, in relief or ground into the surface, was a popular way to ornament glass and stone objects in Sasanian Iran, but some scholars have proposed that while glass bowls with this type of decoration were used within Sasanian lands, they were produced in great quantities, mainly for export to the East. Several bowls and fragments with concave circular facets have been found in Chinese tombs other than Li Xian's, but his bowl, with its relief facets, is far less common. Three others are known, one from Xinjiang province, the desert area between China and the West,[3] and the other two from Japan.[4] The distribution of these bowls attests to the reach of the Silk Road as merchants and foreign emissaries traveled eastward with their luxury wares.

The glass bowl was found with the silver ewer (no. 31) between Wu Hui's coffin and the tomb wall. These two objects, along with the intaglio ring (no. 32) and other "exotica" found in the tomb, might have been acquired by Li Xian when he served as governor of Dunhuang, the outpost where the southern and northern branches of the Silk Road join after they emerge from the desert. Valued for its transparency and the way in which its facets catch the light, as well as for its foreign origin, the bowl was probably used for wine. It might well be the kind of wine cup celebrated in the classical Tang verse: "The exquisite grape wine, the night shining cup."

JAL

1. *Wenwu* 1985.11, p. 12, fig. 26, pl. 3:1; An 1986, pp. 173–81; *Yuanzhou* 1999, pl. 78; *Put Svile* 1996, p. 132, no. 59.

2. Fukai 1977, p. 43. One example, the lower half of a similar bowl, was found in southwestern Iran at Qasr-i Abu Nasr; see Whitcomb 1985, p. 157, fig. 58k, p. 205, pl. 43.

3. Laing 1991, p. 111 (at Barchuk, Xinjiang).

4. Complete bowl: *Silk Road* 1998, no. 104; fragments found at the Munakata shrine, on the island of Okinoshima, off the coast of northern Japan: Fukai 1977, pp. 44–45, figs. 40, 41 (dated c. sixth–seventh century).

31. Ewer showing Greek mythological scenes

Tokharistan (ancient Bactria), fifth–sixth century
Excavated in 1983 from the tomb of the Li Xian (d. 569)
and his wife, Wu Hui (d. 547), western suburbs of Guyuan, Ningxia
Silver with gilt decoration on the neck, background of figural frieze, handle, and foot
Height: 37.5 cm; diameter: 12.8 cm
Guyuan Municipal Museum, Ningxia Hui Autonomous Region

The present ewer resembles a typical Sasanian metal shape of the fifth to seventh century (fig. B).[1] It has a pear-shaped body, tall neck, convex molding with pendant leaves demarcating the neck from the body, high pedestal foot, and handle, square in section, decorated with a solid silver ball at its highest point and attached at the top of the vessel to a place immediately below the convex molding on the shoulder and at the bottom of the body at its greatest extension. However, other features of the ewer suggest an origin east of Sasanian Persia, in Central Asia, most likely Tokharistan or ancient Bactria (present-day northern Afghanistan, southern Uzbekistan, and southern Tajikistan): the fluted decoration of the neck and foot; the handle, which is hexagonal in section and has a human head instead of the more typical ball; and the use of beaded decoration—on the convex moldings on the shoulder and on the stem of the foot and around the base of the foot. Such beading is a feature more characteristic of Late Antique ewers of the fourth and fifth centuries than of Sasanian vessels. Also unusual are the terminals of the handle, which are in the form of camels' rather than onagers' heads.

Further distinguishing the ewer from Sasanian models is the division of the body into two registers, the larger one having a frieze of human figures, the smaller register at the base engraved with two mythical figures with the foreparts of tigers and the tails of fish amid a water-and-fish design. This horizontal division of the surface of the body also occurs on Late Antique silver ewers but never on Sasanian vessels. The main register consists of six figures in relief, which represent narrative scenes, with each scene centering on one pair of figures (see line drawing). Although rendered in a classicizing style, the details betray their later date.

Between the fourth and seventh centuries, a group of so-called Bactrian vessels that imitate earlier Greco-Bactrian as well as imported Roman silverware was made in Tokharistan and in the countries to the south of the Hindu Kush. These lands had belonged to the Greco-Bactrian kingdom (mid third century BCE–first century CE). With the rise of the Sasanian dynasty in the third century CE, the art of this region was influenced by that of the Sasanian court. Although the nomadic Hephthalites dominated Tokharistan and adjacent areas in the second half of the fifth and first half of the sixth centuries, Persian artistic influence intensified, owing to the numerous Sasanian silver vessels, along with the great quantity of Sasanian silver coins, that were sent to the Hephthalites, first as ransom for the captured Sasanian king Peroz (r. 457/59–84) and then as tribute paid by subsequent Sasanian kings up to the 560s (see Chapter 9).

Thus, on the ewer there are reminiscences of Sasanian metalwork, but the figural style and imagery derive from the classical world. Episodes from Greek mythology and literature had been a rich source for the decoration of Greco-Bactrian vessels,[2] yet by the fourth or fifth century, though still revered, it was misunderstood. The three pairs of couples represent episodes from the Trojan War. The middle episode refers to the Judgment of Paris, a popular theme in ancient art: Aphrodite, wearing her *stephane* (gold crown) and magic girdle, faces Paris who holds two apples in his hands (31d). The Tokharistan craftsman incorrectly added the second apple and the "scales" on the fruit. The iconography of Paris holding an apple is rare until the Roman period. There are several examples of incomplete depictions of the Judgment of Paris, some of them showing only one goddess instead of three. The standing figure of Paris dressed as a Greek (and not as a Phrygian) is rare but has analogies in classical art.

Fig. A. Development of figural frieze on ewer (*below*) (after *Yuanzhou* 1999, p. 20, fig. 11)

Fig. B. Gilded-silver ewer (*bottom*), Sasanian, sixth–seventh century CE. The Metropolitan Museum of Art, Purchase, Mr. and Mrs. Douglas Dillon Gift and Rogers Fund, 1967, 67.10ab

1. Published in Carpino and James 1989, pp. 71–76; Harper 1991a, pp. 67–84; *Yuanzhou* 1999, pl. 75; Luo 2000c, pp. 311–30 (in Chinese); Luo 1998, pp. 28–33; Marshak and Anazawa 1989, pp. 54–57 (in Japanese; English translation unnumbered); Wu 1989, pp. 61–70; *Put Svile* 1996, p. 131, no. 58.

2. Weitzman 1943, pp. 289–324.

3. This episode was depicted on a Roman sarcophagus in the Palazzo Ducale, Venice. See Gahli-Kahil 1955, cat. no. D 293–294, pl. 6, 4. Some scholars have noted that this second scene resembles the iconography of Hermes (Mercury), perhaps with a soul of a dead woman in front of Charon's bark, but if so, it is difficult to find any logical connection between the episodes.

4. Clairmont 1959, p. 97.

Top row: (left to right):
31a. The human head at the top of the handle; 31b. One of the camel's-head terminals of the handle.

Bottom row: 31c. The embarkation of Helen for Troy; 31d. The Judgment of Paris; 31e. The return of Helen to Menelaus

The episode on the left may represent the Rape of Helen, here shown as Paris and Helen leaving Greece for Troy (31c). She is lifting her leg for the embarkation, but the ship is absent probably because the Central Asian craftsman has omitted this detail, the importance of which he did not understand. The positions of her raised foot, her leg, and her hand may be explained only if she embarks or, in any case, if one of her feet stands much higher than the other.[3] The fingers of Paris touching Helen's chin correspond with the typical Greek love gesture. Both episodes belong to a single story because Helen's love was Aphrodite's payment for the Judgment of Paris.

The third scene may depict the return of Helen to her husband, King Menelaus (31e). Wishing to kill his faithless wife, Menelaus pursued her, but, inspired by Aphrodite, he forgave her when she turned her beautiful face to him. The direction of Helen's feet shows that she is trying to escape; Menelaus is represented as having suddenly stopped with a spear in his hand. The treasures previously stolen by Helen and Paris from her husband's palace are in the box that she holds in her left hand. These three episodes were represented on Greek vases.[4]

Such mistakes as the shield that seems to fall from Menelaus' hand, or Helen's raised foot in the embarkation scene, which seems to hang in the air with no support, show how far removed the craftsman was from the original models when he combined two equally famous exotic styles: foreign Sasanian and ancient Hellenistic.

Like other precious "exotica" in Li Xian's tomb—the Sasanian glass bowl (no. 30) and Sasanian ring (no. 32)—this silver ewer was probably acquired by Li Xian in his capacity as commander of the Dunhuang garrison, from a caravan on its way to the capital at Changan or Luoyang.

BIM

32. *Ring set with a carved stone seal*

Sasanian Persian, fourth–sixth century
Excavated in 1983 from the tomb of Li Xian (d. 569) and his wife, Wu Hui (d. 547),
western suburbs of Guyuan, Ningxia
Gold ring: greatest diameter of hoop: 2.16 cm; nicolo (onyx) seal, diameter: .69 cm
Guyuan Municipal Museum, Ningxia Hui Autonomous Region

The seal stone, which is bezel in form and still in its original setting, is carved in intaglio with a dancing female figure who holds a scarf above her head.[1] A clothed or naked woman, standing or dancing, with a scarf forming an arch over her head and its long ends fluttering to either side, is a frequent image on Sasanian seals.[2] The image is also found on luxury metalwares of the period (fig. A).[3] Unlike the smaller surfaces of the seals, the interior of the silver plate illustrated allows for the inclusion of details that help to identify this figural type. Here the ends of the dancer's scarf turn into luxuriantly curling grapevines that frame her voluptuous naked body. If this figure is not intended to represent the great Sasanian goddess of water and fertility, Anahita, or a priestess of her cult, then it is certainly meant to evoke more generalized ideas of fecundity and abundance.

Finger rings, especially those made of precious metal and set with a seal stone, were not a traditional part of Chinese personal ornamentation. The few rings with stones that have been found in Chinese tombs are all of foreign (and mainly Western) manufacture (see no. 85 in this catalogue).[4]

The ring was found in the coffin of Wu Hui, Li Xian's wife. We may speculate that it was a gift from Li Xian, who most likely acquired it while serving as governor of Dunhuang, possibly from one of the caravans that had to pass through this gateway of the Silk Road as it traveled east into China.

JAL

1. *Wenwu* 1985.11, p. 12, fig. 25, pl. 3:2; *Yuanzhou* 1999, pl. 76.

2. Bivar 1969, CB 3, 4.

3. Similar dancers appear on two pieces of Hephthalite metalwork, dated to the fifth century and found in Sogdian territory, on one a clothed dancer with a scarf above her head is repeated twice as part of a frieze of ladies around the circumference of the bowl; on the other a naked but bejeweled dancer wears a scarf across her shoulders (Marschak 1986, figs. 11–13, 18). Probably of the seventh century and once applied to a nowvanished bowl is a silver appliqué in the form of a nude dancer with a scarf arched over her head (Trever and Lukonin 1987, p. 119, no. 44).

4. In addition to this ring and the intagliocarved stone from the tomb of Shi Hedan (no. 86), at least three other examples of foreign seals, two still set in gold rings, have been found in China. See Xiong and Laing 1991, pp. 165–66, for a discussion of these intaglios; one of them serves as the clasp for Princess Li Jingxun's necklace (see no. 87, fig. A). It is noteworthy that Li Jingxun was Li Xian's greatgranddaughter. The image on the stone from Li Xian's tomb is erroneously identified as "a figure carrying baggage" (p. 165).

Another intagliocarved stone, most likely a seal and heretofore unrecognized as such, was found in the tomb of Kudi Huilou, a military man from a northern tribe (d. 562). Made of agate, it shows a walking lion in a distinctly western style (Wang 1979, p. 393, pl. 11:1 no. 151); it was found at the waist of the deceased's skeleton. For evidence of additional finger rings in China, see the examples cited under number 85.

Fig. A. Silver plate, partially gilded. Sasanian Iran, fifth–seventh century. The Cleveland Museum of Art; purchase from the John L. Severance Fund, 62.295

33. *Sword in its scabbard*

Chinese, sixth century
Excavated in 1983 from the tomb of Li Xian (d. 569)
and his wife, Wu Hui (d. 547), western suburbs of Guyuan, Ningxia
Iron, wood, silver sheets, lacquer
Length: 87 cm
Guyuan Municipal Museum, Ningxia Hui Autonomous Region

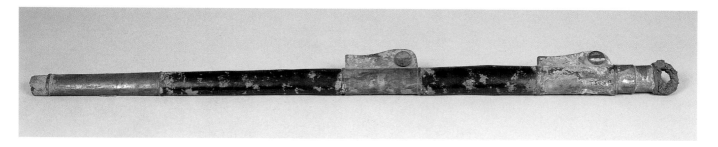

Fig. A. Clay *mingqi* of a warrior leaning on a sword with a P-shaped mount. White-glazed ceramic, Tomb of Zhang Sheng (d. 595), from vicinity of Anyang (Henan), Sui (after Valenstein 1989, p. 60, fig. 53)

This sword is the earliest datable example of a type that is very important in the history of weapons and warfare.[1] The type is characterized by two remarkable features: the ring pommel and two P-shaped mounts on one side of the scabbard. To these mounts were affixed two straps, the one closest to the hilt was short, the other, at the middle of the sword, long. The two straps, in turn, were attached to the swordsman's waist belt. The different lengths of the straps allowed the sword to hang at an oblique angle, which was especially important for warriors on horseback.

The introduction of two P-shaped mounts on the long sword changed the tactics of armies active in the vast territory stretching from Hungary, across Eurasia, through Iran and Siberia, to China and Japan (or wherever the nomadic peoples of the great migration periods roamed). In fact, this type of weapon has been termed the "sword of the Huns." Previously, the long sword had been suspended more or less vertically from the swordsman's belt by means of a slide attached to the center of the scabbard or by straps that passed through loops on both sides of the scabbard. Such vertically suspended swords were the privilege of cavalry, as these swords would drag on to the ground when worn by those who had to fight on foot. Li Xian and other warriors who possessed the swords of the new type could deliberately or under necessity fight as cavalrymen or infantrymen. The loss of their horses in battle did not always mean their final defeat.

In China, in addition to Li Xian's weapon, the sword with P-shaped mounts is attested by a figurine datable to 595 (fig. A), a tomb mural of 577,[2] reliefs depicting Central Asians on a Northern Qi mortuary couch,[3] as well as some actual weapons, dated to about 600 CE.[4]

To the west, at Taq-i Bustan in northwestern Iran, is the only Sasanian depiction of this type of sword. There, on the side of the main rock-cut grotto, is a hunting scene contemporary with Khosro II (r. 590–628).[5] The older, vertical sword is also shown, in the investiture scene of Khosro II on the rear wall of the grotto. He holds this ceremonial sword, standing between the goddess Anahita and the god Ahura Mazda.[6] The sword of new type is much more convenient but probably deemed too barbaric for the highly important religious scene of divine investiture. Below this investiture scene is the statue of an armored horseman, in right profile, so that his sword is almost invisible. However, his quiver and bow case are types that were widespread in the steppes and in the oasis states of Central Asia from at least the fifth century. They were unknown in Iran before a series of wars between the Sasanians and the Turks in the 560s, 580s, and 600s. From about 600, the new type became very popular in Iran; the golden and silver decoration of the hilts and scabbards of these swords show how prestigious they became after a short span of time.[7] In Sogdiana, in the murals of ancient Samarkand (Afrasiab) and datable to the 660s, the oblique swords of warriors and the almost vertical, ceremonial ones, are both represented.[8] In the murals at Panjikent we also see both vertically and obliquely suspended swords. The former are worn by the heroes of the ancient legends,[9] but the very long sword of the epic hero Rustam belongs to the new type.[10]

Oblique-suspension swords are well known also in the nomadic cultures of the steppes, in particular, the Avar culture of Hungary and surrounding areas. The Avars came to Europe from Central Asia in the second half of the sixth century. Beautiful golden and silver P- and M-shaped fittings from swords and daggers are in the Pereshchepina treasure discovered near Poltava in the Ukraine just before World War I.[11] The treasure was hidden sometime after 642, but not later than the 670s. Most archaeologists think that the treasure consists of objects and coins from the tomb of the nomadic chief of the Turkic Bulgars. One of several of the Pereshchepina swords was made by Byzantine court artisans. Each of the separately made golden parts of its hilt and scabbard bears a Greek letter. The alphabetic order of these letters helped the master craftsman assemble the decoration of the sword correctly. Though the two fittings on one side of its sheath are not P-shaped, its pommel formed an oval ring like that of Li Xian's sword. This Pereshchepina sword probably was presented in 630s by the Byzantine emperor Heraclius to his friend Kuvrat, the ruler of the Turkic Bulgars, whose high Byzantine title *Patrikios* has been included into the Greek monogram on his finger rings found in the same "hoard." The other rich swords with ring pommels were Byzantine gifts (in fact, part of the tribute) to the dangerous Avar warlords whose rebellious vassal and, therefore, the ally of the Byzantium was Kuvrat. Later, in the seventh century, the neighboring Khazars forced the most important group of the Bulgars to move into the territory of present-day Bulgaria.

In the Afrasiab mural, oblique swords with the ring pommels and two M-shaped fittings are worn by two North Koreans (from Koguryo Kingdom). In China, the ring pommel was typical in the sixth and seventh centuries, while in Byzantium it came into use only in the first two-thirds of the seventh century, when such swords were executed in the "barbaric" manner for the powerful newcomers from the East. However, the taste of those who received the gifts was taken into account only in general because the decorative details with granulation and glass inlays still remained typically Byzantine.

The plain silver sheets covering the hilt and the scabbard of the sword found in the tomb of Li Xian are very simple because his sword was not a parade weapon. In general, the funerary goods in Li Xian's burial are traditional and even modest except for the Bactrian (Tokharistan) silver ewer (no. 31), the Sasanian Persian glass bowl (no. 30), and the Sasanian finger ring (no. 32). Such modesty, typical for Northern Zhou, contrasts with the important role played by Li Xian in the short history of this dynasty. He was a kind of guardian, almost a stepfather of the future Northern Zhou emperor Wudi, who, according to custom, grew up outside of the palace. Wudi spent six years with the Li Xian family. When Li Xian died, this emperor personally attended his funerary ceremony and mourning. The general was praised as "the pride of the country and the honor of his clan." It seems possible that the simple sword belonged to Li Xian from the earlier stage of his forty-seven-year military career, including twenty-one battles in which he often risked his own life.[12]

One detail of Li Xian's sword seems unusual for its type: only a short upper part of its hilt is free above the scabbard. In this construction the ring pommel could be helpful when the sword was drawn from the scabbard, whereas later such a pommel was merely decorative. Daggers deeply sunk into their sheaths were depicted in Sogdiana, in the Panjikent murals of the late fifth century, but no longer in those of the sixth century.[13]

BIM

1. See Amiet 1967, p. 280; Ghirshman 1963, pp. 293–311; Nickel 1973, pp. 131–42; Trousdale 1975.

2. *Wenwu* 1983.10, pp. 1–23, p. 20, fig. 63 (Tomb of Lou Rui).

3. Scaglia 1958, p. 12, fig. 3.

4. Grancsay 1930–31, pp. 194–96.

5. Ghirshman 1963, p. 197, fig. 237 (royal stag hunt).

6. Ibid., p. 192, fig. 235.

7. Schultze-Dörrlamm and Overlaert in *Splendour des sassanides* 1993, pp. 177–79, nos. 35–41.

8. Marshak 1994, p. 8, fig. 3.

9. Azarpay 1981, pl. 14. The Panjikent scabbards of archaic swords had a hook or a loop on the upper part and two rings symmetrically placed on both sides of it. The "slide scabbard" construction of the early Sasanian swords with only one hook was much simpler. In this case, the scabbard freely moved along one leather sword hanger. Two symmetrical fittings whose function was similar to that of the Panjikent side rings are attested on the Middle and Late Sasanian silver plates with royal portraits.

10. Ibid., pls. 6, 7.

11. Zalesskakaya 1997, pp. 156–57 and 206–8, nos. 40, 82–84. See also pp. 127–137, no. 25 (Byzantine sword).

12. In the tomb of Emperor Wudi (d. 578), whom Li Xian served, has been found a long dagger (length: 32.1 cm) that is very similar to the sword of his general. Its hilt is hidden in the scabbard, which has the two P-shaped fittings (Koch 1999, pp. 575–78, fig. 2, pls. 73, 2).

13. The horizontally attached and slantwise-attached daggers were the predecessors of the oblique swords with two hanger belts of different lengths. Compare Ambroz 1986, pp. 53–73.

1. Jessica Rawson has marshaled impressive literary evidence that jade continued to be highly valued, but was no longer buried in tombs. See Rawson 1995, pp. 75–85, 323–24.

2. *Wenwu* 1985.11, pp. 14–15, figs. 39, 41.

3. See a set of six jade pendants from the tomb of Liu Hong (d. 306) at Anxiang in Hunan (*Wenwu* 1993.11, p. 4, figs. 6–8, pl. 3:1,3) See a set of five graduated arcs from the tomb of Lou Rui (d. 570) near Taiyuan (*Wenwu* 1983.10, p.15, fig. 55) and four similar arcs from a Sui period tomb at Guojiatan in the eastern suburbs of Xi'an (*Wenwu cankao ziliao* 1957.8, p. 66, third illustration from top).

4. See *Tian Hong* 2000, pl. 28.

5. For a discussion of jade pectorals of this period, see Hayashi 1991, pp. 154–56, and Fu 1995, pp. 199–200.

34a–c. *Semiannular and trapezoid pendants*

Northern Zhou dynasty (557–581)
Excavated in 1983 from the tomb of Li Xian (d. 569)
and his wife, Wu Hui (d. 547), western suburbs of Guyuan, Ningxia
Jade (nephrite)
a. Semiannular pendant (*huang*): length: 8.2 cm; b. Larger trapezoidal pendant (*pei*):
length: 12.6–14.2 cm; c. Smaller trapezoidal pendant (*pei*): length: 11.5–12.2 cm
Guyuan Municipal Museum, Ningxia Hui Autonomous Region

The interest of these three objects lies less in their intrinsic appeal than in the questions they raise about the role of jade in this period. From Eastern Han (25–220 CE) until the beginning of the Song period (960–1279), jade is conspicuous by its scarcity. When it does occur, it usually takes the form of small, realistic carvings of animals such as the ram (no. 14), belt plaques, hair pins (nos. 44, 88), and occasionally vessels. Since literary references to jade are still found through this period, it appears that the material continued to be valued and that its scarcity reflects a reluctance to consign it to tombs.[1]

These three pieces evoke forms that had largely disappeared by the end of the Western Han. During the Western Zhou period, semiannular pendants were suspended in tiers with the ends upwards. By the Warring States period (485–221 BCE), they were more often suspended with the ends facing downward. The perforations at the corners of this piece suggest that it would have been suspended in the earlier fashion. The two trapezoid pendants mimic the outline of ritual jade knives common during the Neolithic and Shang periods. However, they lack the sharpened edge of the ear-

lier pieces and seem to have been made in imitation of ancient jades. One of these has been furnished with a bronze hinged loop (now corroded) for suspension.

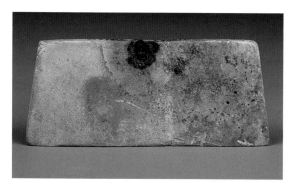

The jades were found placed within the remains of Li Xian's coffin, the semiannular pendant lying on the skeleton's chest and the trapezoid pendants slightly lower down and to the right. On either side of the skeleton were two stone egg-shaped beads, and more than one hundred agate beads were scattered over the upper half of the skeleton. It is possible that these beads were combined with the jades into a single pectoral.[2]

Pectorals of jades are occasionally found in tombs of the Northern and Southern Dynasties.[3] These usually include semiannular pendants together with others of a lobed outline; trapezoid pendants are rarer, but similar examples were found in the tomb of Tian Hong (d. 575).[4] Various reconstructions of the pectorals have been proposed.[5] In some cases, the semiannular pendant may have been hung in a U-shaped arrangement, and in others, they seem to have been aligned vertically in pairs. The trapezoid pendants (some of which have a lobed top edge) may have formed the lower section of the pectoral. Although Sui and Tang dynasty texts refer to the wearing of pectorals, these pieces may have been made purely for burial, since, unlike earlier pendants and, indeed, contemporaneous jade belt ornaments, they are not decorated.

CM

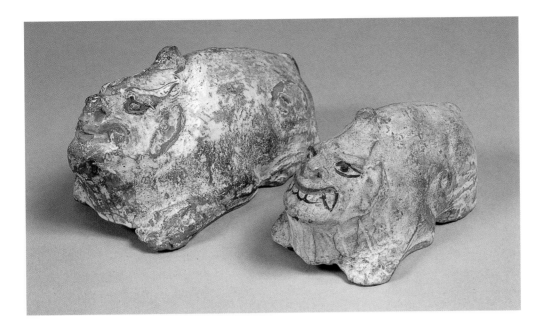

1. *Wenwu* 1985.11, p. 9, fig. 16: 1, 2; *Yuanzhou* 1999, pl. 74.

2. Dien 1987, pp. 1–15.

3. One of the tombs belonged to Chiluo Xie (d. 574), a successful general; Wang Deheng (d. 576) descended from a noble family and held the title of Great General of Yitong of Northern Zhou; Dugu Zang (d. 578), hereditary government official's family and imperial kindsman of the Zhou, Sui, and Tang dynasties; and Wang Shilian (d. 538), held the title of Great General of Northern Zhou. See Yun 1993, pp. 18–19, figs. 22, 23; p. 40, figs. 68, 69; p. 80, figs. 161, 162; p. 114, fig. 211.

35a, b. Pair of tomb guardian beasts

Northern Zhou dynasty (557–581)
Excavated in 1983 from the tomb of Li Xian (d. 569)
and his wife, Wu Hui (d. 547), western suburbs of Guyuan, Ningxia
Clay, white slip, painted details
a. Height: 8.5 cm; length: 18.5 cm; b. Height: 6.9 cm; length: 16 cm
Guyuan Municipal Museum, Ningxia Hui Autonomous Region

Zhenmushou, or tomb guardian beasts of this type, became popular during the Northern Dynasties period and replaced earlier forms such as rhinoceros-like animals popular in the earlier Jin dynasty (265–420 CE), which were armed with two to four horns or spikes along the spine and posed as if ready to charge.[1] Of unknown origins, but perhaps related to Xianbei beliefs, tomb guardian beasts like this pair always had one with an animal head and one with a human head. As time went on, the creatures took on the pose of a seated dog, with a number of spikes along the spine and growing refinement, still in pairs with a human and animal head, until the style reached a kind of baroque magnificence in the Tang period (618–906) during which time its use was abandoned.

Guardians of this sort were necessary because it was believed that the building of a tomb trespassed on the realm of the underworld, which was filled with potentially dangerous beings.[2] All sorts of devices were used to ensure that the sanctity of the tomb would be undisturbed. In many tombs one finds sales contracts, fictitious of course, purchasing the land for all eternity for enormous amounts of money, with the unusual proviso that the spirits of any bodies previously buried in that plot would become the servants of the newcomer. Before the burial, shamans descended into the tomb to exorcise evil demons that might lurk there. In addition, guardians, both in human form and in such grotesque aspects as seen here, were posted at the doorway to keep out unwelcome intrusions. Of course, the real danger was that of grave robbers, and over 90 percent of the tombs, as in this case, had been plundered some time in the past before being archaeologically excavated.

From 1986 to 1990, Shaanxi Provincial Archeological Institute excavated fourteen Northern Zhou graves; eight have epitaphs identifying them as high-ranking generals. Four of the tombs, dating from the 570s and early 580s, contain very similar *zhenmushou* guardian animals.[3]

AED

1. *Wenwu* 1985.11, pl. 14, figs. 14. 15; *Yuanzhou* 1999, pl. 61; *Put Svile* 1996, pp. 134–35, nos. 60–62.

2. Dien 1981–82, pp. 5–56.

3. Yun 1993, figs. 20, 21. In both pairs, one set from Chiluo Xie's tomb and the other from Li Xian's, the individuals within the pair are differentiated in the same way. One wears a helmet topped by a pointed knob; the other has a flat-topped close-fitting helmet.

Fig. A. Line drawing of a pair of clay guardian *mingqi* from the tomb of Chiluo Xie (d. 574), part of the Northern Zhou cemetery found outside Xianyang, Shaanxi (after Yun 1992, p. 18, figs. 20, 21)

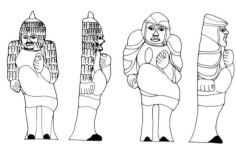

36a, b. *Pair of standing warriors*

Northern Zhou dynasty (557–581)
Excavated from the tomb of General Li Xian (d. 569) and his wife, Wu Hui (d. 547), in the western suburbs of Guyuan, Ningxia
Dark gray pottery, white slip, painted details
Height: a. 18.2 cm; b. 19.2 cm; width: 8.2 cm
Guyuan Municipal Museum, Ningxia Hui Autonomous Region

Some 255 figurines were recovered from this tomb, of which these objects represent the tomb guards who were stationed at the doorway just behind the pair of tomb guardians (nos. 35a,b), hence their fierce appearance.[1] The figurines in this tomb were modeled with flat backs, coated with a white slip, and details added in red, purple, black, and white. The helmets of these two differ slightly, the one on the right having a curved outline at the forehead and a point at the top, perhaps representing a plume. The imbrication of the armor lamellae is upward, as seen in the warriors from Pengyang (nos. 22a–d) but these figures have in addition shoulder guards that extend down to the elbows. They may have held shields in their left hands and some sort of weapon in the right. Made of wood, these items have not survived.

Chinese armor traditionally has been lamellar, that is, made up of small leaves that had holes on all four sides and that were then linked to each other by thongs or strips of leather.[2] Such a method did not require a backing and one would see the connecting links only where they came in and out on the surface, not indicated in these figurines. This sort of armor differs from scale armor which is connected to a backing along the tops of the scales, the linkages covered by the row above. In scale armor the imbrication must be downward. The earliest armor in China was made of leather covered with lacquer, but metal armor began to appear in the Han dynasty (206 BCE–220 CE), perhaps a bit earlier, and by this period metal armor was in general use.

The lack of realism in these figurines is striking, since the artisans of this area were demonstrably able to produce objects that were naturalistic and graceful. It may be that the exaggerated grotesqueness of these figurines was meant to emphasize their martial qualities (fig. A).[3]

AED

37a–j. *Cavalrymen*

Northern Zhou dynasty (557–581)

Excavated in 1983 from the tomb of Li Xian (d. 569) and his wife, Wu Hui (d. 547),
western suburbs of Guyuan, Ningxia

Clay, white slip, painted details

a. Height: 18.0 cm; length: 17.1 cm; b. Height: 18.0 cm; length: 17.6 cm; c. Height: 15.4 cm; length:
14.3 cm; d. Height: 15.0 cm; length: 14.5 cm; e. Height: 15.8 cm; length: 13.9 cm; f. Height: 15.8
cm; length: 14.0 cm; g. Height: 14.4 cm; length: 13.9 cm; h. Height: 14.7 cm; length: 14.3 cm;
i. Height: 14.4 cm; length: 13.5 cm; j. Height: 14.0 cm; length: 13.6 cm

Guyuan Municipal Museum, Ningxia Hui Autonomous Region

1. *Wenwu* 1985.11, p. 5, fig. 7, p. 10, figs. 17, 18.

2. Dien 1986, pp. 33–56; *Yuanzhou* 1999, pls. 63, 64 (no. 37a,b); pls. 72, 73 (no. 37c,d); pl. 71 (no. 37j).

3. Yun 1992, p. 163.

4. Ibid., fig. 28, pp. 19–20.

Among the 255 figurines contained in Li Xian's tomb, 10 were of cavalrymen.[1] Two riders are fully armored with the lamellar armor of the period. They wear full helmets with a double wave outline descending slightly over the bridge of the nose and a hemispherical boss on top, and with full protection of the ears and nape of the neck. Over their suits of armor they wear a sleeved cape, the sleeves hanging empty in the Central Asian mode, called the *szür* in Hungarian. The horses are fully barded. The red lines reveal the parts that made up the horse's armor: the chamfron, or head mask, the neck and chest armor (crinet and peytral) apparently one piece; the side armor, or flanchards; and the crupper, or rump, armor.

With the invention of the stirrup in the fourth century, heavy cavalry with rider and horse encased in armor followed.[2] The numbers of such cavalry increased as time went on, the numbers mentioned going from hundreds to thousands, while at the same time the infantry became increasingly ineffective. It may be that the dominance of the steppe nomads in north China at this time was due to their skill in utilizing this new military technology and their access to large numbers of horses.

At the same time, armor-clad warrior figures on barded horses occur in large numbers, perhaps a reflection of the Northern Zhou emphasis on this mode of warfare.[3] The Northern Zhou destroyed the Northern Qi in 577 and succeeded in reunifying the north. Similar armored cavalry horses and warriors can be found throughout the fourteen Northern Zhou tombs, such as the group from General Chiluo Xie's tomb dated 574, excavated near Xianyang in Shaanxi.[4]

AED

no. 37a

1. For a discussion of clay tomb figurines (*mingqi*) see Juliano 1975 and Dien 1997; for additional examples of specifically Northern Zhou tomb figures, see Yun 1992, which publishes fourteen Northern Zhou graves excavated near Xianyang outside Xi'an dated to the late 570s and early 580s.

2. *Wenwu* 1985.11, p. 8, fig. 11; *Yuanzhou* 1999, pl. 65.

3. *Wenwu* 1985.11, p. 8, fig. 10:1.

4. *Yuanzhou* 1999, pl. 66 (white and caps).

5. *Wenwu* 1985.11, p. 7, fig. 9:3; p. 8, fig. 12; *Yuanzhou* 1999, pl. 70:2 (red jacket).

6. *Wenwu* 1985.11, p. 7, fig. 9:4; p. 8, fig. 12; *Yuanzhou* 1999, pl. 68.

7. *Wenwu* 1985.11, p. 6, fig. 1:2; *Yuanzhou* 1999, pl. 68.

8. *Wenwu* 1985.11, p. 6, fig. 8: 2,4; *Yuanzhou* 1999, pl. 69.

* Two of each are illustrated below, opposite, and p. 110.

38a–f. *Tomb figurines*

Northern Zhou dynasty, 557–581
Excavated in 1983 from the tomb of Li Xian (d. 569)
and his wife, Wu Hui (d. 547), western suburbs of Guyuan, Ningxia
Clay with pigment
a–d. Military officers: height: 12.7 cm; c–d. Civil officials: height: 12.4 cm;
e–f. Non-Chinese: height: 13.4 cm*

39a–j. *Tomb figurines*

a–d. Hooded figures: height: 14 cm; e–h. Figures with tall hats: height: 13.9 cm;
i–j. Female attendants: height: 13.5 cm*
Guyuan Municipal Museum, Ningxia Hui Autonomous Region

The inclusion of figurines of humans in the tomb was long a matter of some debate in ancient China. Confucius is said to have condemned the burial of tomb figurines perhaps because he feared it might lead to the use of human sacrifice or because their resemblance to living humans would make their use abhorrent. Tomb figures as they appeared just after the fall of the Han during the Wei-Jin period (220–317 CE) were simply pale continuations of Han types. But by the end of the fifth century, the quality and variety improved to the point that these grave figurines came to be considered worthy of attention for their artistry. Such figurines provide excellent evidence for the study of many aspects of the material culture, the development of sculpture, and even the social institutions of the Period of Disunity, also frequently referred to as the Six Dynasties period.[1]

The figurines from the northwest, Gansu, and Ningxia, however, lag far behind those from other regions of China in artistic accomplishment and in sophistication. One is tempted to ascribe their crudeness to a lack of skill or simple naïveté in a provincial outpost, but the quality of other products from the northwest demonstrate that the area was not deficient in capable craftsmen or in ability to appreciate a better product. It may simply be that in this area less importance was ascribed to such figurines. At the same time, the numbers remained high and are comparable with the practice across north China.

no. 38a, b

no. 38c, d

MONKS AND MERCHANTS

Aside from the two guardian animals (no. 35a,b), two standing warriors (no. 36a,b), and ten armored cavalrymen (no. 37a–j) from Li Xian's tomb previously discussed, there are nine mounted musicians, a woman rider, eleven mounted riders, twenty-five attendants wearing the "basket" head-dresses, forty-four civil officials, thirty-two military officers, thirty-eight non-Chinese, forty-three members of the entourage wearing hoods, and twenty-eight female attendants. Some examples of these types have been included and discussed below.

The military officers (no. 38a,b) are in court dress rather than in armor prepared for battle.[2] Perched on their head is a small cap with an inserted ribbon called a *pingshance*. They wear a long, wide, sleeved garment; for half of the group, the garment is red, the other half wear a purple one. On the top of this is a jumper-type piece (called a *liangdang*) consisting of a front and back panel connected to shoulders straps and belted. If made of metal, this was a type of armor, but when not at war it was made of cloth. The hands are held together in front of the lower chest, and they held what was possibly some sort of insignia.

The civil officials (no. 38c,d) wear the same sort of perky cap, but their clothing consists of a long inner robe of white, over which is worn a red, wide-sleeved jacket with crossed lapels, belted and reaching almost to the knees.[3] The right hand is held up close to the side of the chest: the left is lowered at the side. The objects that they held, probably made of wood, do not survive. Again, the fig-ures are divided into two equal groups, half with white caps and red lapels, the other with black caps and white lapels.[4]

The facial features set this group of non-Chinese apart (no. 38e–f). They are described as having broad brows, deep-set eyes, and high noses, standard phrases used to describe foreigners. The hair is curled as if braids were piled on top of the head and covered

no. 39i, j

no. 38e, f

no. 39a, b

with a red scarf. Their chests are bare, and they wear a broad-sleeved shirt over which is a red or purple jacket and trousers.[5] Their hands are clasped together in front of them, but what they held has not survived. Given the multiethnic population of the northwest, it is not surprising that Li Xian's entourage would include some who resembled Europeans.

The hooded figures (no. 39a–d) wear standard Xianbei headgear, which consisted of a hood. Beside the hood, these figures are dressed in a round collar shirt, open jacket, trousers, and boots.[6] The hands are clasped together at the front but what they held has not survived. These figures are much more plump and round-faced than the others, which accords with representations of the Xianbei elsewhere.

Figurines with tall hats (no. 39e–h) have a type of headgear that developed in the Six Dynasties period. Called a *longguan,* or "basket hat," it could be worn by men or women.[7] The *longguan* was semi-transparent and probably made of lacquered horsehair like that of the traditional Korean hat. This group of figurines is divided into two types. Members of the first group have a black ribbon, which apparently held the white-colored hat in place, and each wears a shirt with a round collar and wide sleeves. A long red skirt with a multicolored belt is depicted swirling to the right, a rare indication of movement in the figurines and may indicate that they represent women. The other group is similarly clothed, only with no ribbon, the shirt has crossed lapels, and the long skirt is a purple color. Both types hold their hands in front of their chests and once held some object, no longer extant.

Female attendants were divided into two groups (no. 39i–j). The first wears a crossed lapel shirt and a long skirt with a multicolored belt.[8] The hands are held together before the chest, a sign of respect and attention. Except for the hair which is worn piled atop the head, and the indications of facial features, the whole body is painted white. The second group is largely the same as the first, but the hands once held an object that has not survived.

AED

no. 39e, h

MONKS AND MERCHANTS

40a–q. *Models of agricultural paraphernalia and stove, and figurines of farmyard animals*

Northern Zhou dynasty (557–581)
Excavated in 1983 from the tomb of Li Xian (d. 569) and his wife, Wu Hui
(d. 547), western suburbs of Guyuan, Ningxia
Clay with pigments
Guyuan Municipal Museum, Ningxia Hui Autonomous Region

1. *Wenwu* 1985.11, p. 13, fig. 28–34, 36.
Yuanzhou 1999, pls. 56, 58.

2. See the ceramic model of a stove complete with firewood from tomb 168 at Fenghuangshan, Jiangling, Hubei (*Wenwu* 1975.9, p. 6, fig. 7)

In contrast with the 255 military and civilian figures that were arrayed in formation in the antechamber outside the stone doors of Li Xian's tomb, these figurines and models were placed in the southeastern part of the tomb chamber itself. This division clearly reflects the differing roles that these objects were expected to play. While the military figures, like their life-size ancestors, the Terracotta Army located to the east of the tomb of the First Emperor of Qin, clearly fulfilled a symbolic protective role, these figurines and models embodied hopes for the occupants' continuing economic sustenance in the afterlife.

The range encountered here had already become established during the second century BCE. Wells, particularly common in northern tombs, reflected the need for a reliable water supply, while the grain huller and millstone emphasize the central role of agriculture, even in border regions such as Guyuan.[1] From the more detailed models found in other tombs, it is possible to deduce clearly the structure and method of usage of these implements. For instance, some models of hullers show a person stepping on one end of the hinged beam, while models of millstones sometimes show a pole attached to the top by which it was rotated. On some Han-period models of stoves, the food to be cooked is depicted on the top and real straw or twigs representing fuel are placed in the opening of the firebox.[2] On the stoves in this exhibition, the area surrounding the opening was painted gray to represent the soot from the fire. The models of huts take two forms: one with the opening halfway up the front and the other with the opening at ground level. On excavation, the figures of the roosters were found perched on the former, suggesting that these huts represent chicken coops. The other two huts have been identified by the excavators as dwellings for humans.

CM

Top row (from left):
House (h. 6.9 cm), stove
(10.5 cm), well (6.3 cm),
millstone (8.5 cm), chicken
coop (6.9 cm) with hen
(4.5 cm), dog (8.5cm),
Front row: rice husker
(9.7 cm), hens 94–5 cm)

1. *Wenwu* 1985.11, p. 15, fig. 45.

2. So and Bunker 1995, pp. 81–84.

3. White and Bunker 1994, p. 21.

4. Rawson 1995, p. 323. The actual place and time of origin for the buckle with movable tongue are difficult to pinpoint. Roman Ghirshman cites a gilded iron buckle from the first half of the fourth century at Sasanian Susa, in southwestern Iran, but it could have been imported from somewhere else (Ghirshman 1979, pp. 183, 184, fig. 2).

5. For a non-Chinese example of small buckles serving to attach pendant elements to a belt, see the gold pieces of a harness in *Splendeur des Sassanides* 1993, p. 183, no. 44. For a discussion of belts with pendant ornaments, see entry no. 91.

41a,b. *Belt buckles*

Northern Wei to Northern Zhou, first half of the sixth century
Excavated in 1983 from the tomb of Li Xian (d. 569) and his wife, Wu Hui (d. 547),
western suburbs of Guyuan, Ningxia
Bronze
a. Length: 1.7 cm; width: 1 cm; b. Length: 3.21 cm; width: 1.9 cm
Guyuan Municipal Museum, Ningxia Hui Autonomous Region

These bronze buckles reflect the influence of nomadic dress and horse attachments on Chinese costume.[1] The traditional Chinese means of fastening a belt over a robe was by means of a belt hook, typically club-shaped with a button on the underside of one end and a small upturned hook at the other.[2] Beginning at least as early as the sixth century BCE, the earliest examples were small and plain but soon evolved into large and elaborately decorated luxury items; by the middle of the first century CE, however, belt hooks had begun to decline in popularity and were not even listed in the Eastern Han (25–220 CE) official edict of appropriate dress.[3]

Already in the sixth and fifth centuries BCE in north China (present-day inner Mongolia), belt buckles with fixed tongues functioned as belt and harness fastenings and are of northern tribal origin. Round buckles with movable tongues, such as those from Li Xian's tomb, are a development of the third and fourth centuries CE.[4] Both buckles may have belonged to a belt set, which consisted of a buckle and metal plaques affixed to a leather backing (see no. 91). The larger buckle could have secured the belt around Li Xian's waist, with the buckle end of the leather inserted between the two metal tabs that extend from the buckle opposite the tongue. The smaller buckle may have been attached to a short leather strap from which hung decorative plaques, the end of the strap secured by the metal loop at the edge of the buckle, or, the buckle may have been attached to the strap from one of the P-shaped devices of Li Xian's sword (no. 33). The possibility also exists that one or both of the buckles belonged to a part of the harness of Li Xian's horse.[5]

JAL

42. *Miniature mirror*

Northern Zhou dynasty (557–581)
Excavated in 1983 from the tomb of Li Xian (d. 569)
and his wife, Wu Hui (d. 547), western suburbs of Guyuan, Ningxia
Bronze
Diameter: 4.34 cm
Guyuan Municipal Museum, Ningxia Hui Autonomous Region

1. Two iron mirrors were found in the "Lacquered Coffin tomb" at Leizumiao, Western Suburb of Guyuan, *Guyuan* 1988, p. 6 and unnumbered pl. 3.

2. See, for example, a finely cast square mirror dating to the Sui dynasty (581–618) from the Carter Collection in the Cleveland Museum of Art (Chou 2000, no. 48).

3. See *Guyuan* 1996, p. 15, fig. 10:11 (tomb of Shi Shewu); p. 36, fig. 24:8–9 (tomb of Shi Suoyan) p. 81, fig. 59:10–11.

From the Warring States period (475–221 BCE) until the end of the Western Jin period (265–317), bronze mirrors were frequently consigned to tombs. It seems from the themes of their decoration and the auspicious phrases in many of the inscriptions that they were not simply toilet accessories, but also embodied the wishes of their owners for prosperity and good fortune. During the fifth and sixth centuries, however, mirrors were rarely placed in tombs, possibly a consequence of the appropriation of all available bronze for Buddhist images.[1]

Although a small number of finely cast miniature mirrors that may have been intended as portable items have survived,[2] the rather rough casting of this mirror indicates that it is a *mingqi*, or "bright object"—a burial substitute. A number of similar miniature mirrors have been found in Sui and Tang tombs of the Shi family at Guyuan.[3]

CM

1. *Tian Hong* 2000, pl. 35: 7, p. 283, fig. 37 (drawing in situ) and p. 306, fig. 60:81–88.

2. Ibid., pls. 28:1–3, 9, 10, and in-situ drawing. Another *huang*, one disc (*bi*), and two trapezoidal *peis* were found in the passageway to the tomb (pl. 28:4,5, 7,8), p. 285, fig. 39: drawing in situ), probably left by tomb robbers.

3. *Wenwu* 1989.9, p. 76, pl. 8:2.

4. See the rock crystal carving of a mon-keylike man of the Late Shang period (ca. 1200 BCE), excavated at Xiaotun, near Anyang (Henan), which had been pierced to be worn (Rawson 1996, pp. 109–10, no. 49f).

5. In the coffin of the Sui princess Li Jingxun were fourteen rock crystal beads strung on wire and three rock crystal hairpins *Tang Changan* 1980, pls. IX:1 (hairpins) and X:1 (beads). See no. 88, fig. A.

6. Also for fashioning reliquary caskets (Michaelson 1999, ill. on p. 160, p. 161, no. 119).

7. Schafer 1963, p. 227.

43. *Eight beads*

Northern Zhou dynasty (557–581)
Excavated from the tomb of Tian Hong (d. 575) and his wife, western suburbs of Guyuan, Ningxia
Rock crystal
Length: 1.17–1.49 cm; width: .91–1.11 cm
Guyuan District Museum, Ningxia Hui Autonomous Region

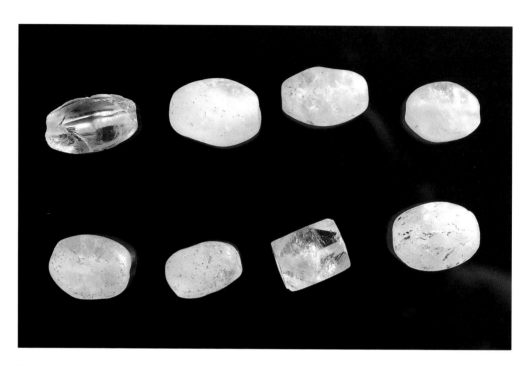

Found scattered in Tian Hong's coffin on and around the chest area of the skeleton, these beads were associated with three semiannular *huang* and two semicircular *pei*, ceremonial jades that were part of Tian Hong's funerary jewelry (see Li Xian's jades, no. 34).[2]

Rock crystal had been used for beads of similar form in China since at least the sixth or fifth century BCE[3] and for small sculptures considerably earlier.[4] The stone continued to be used for beads, as well as for other articles of adornment, such as hairpins,[5] and for decorating Buddhist reli-quaries (no. 120).[6] The pure, transparent properties of rock crystal appealed to the Chinese, who called it "water germ" (or sperm or essence) and likened it to "petrified ice."[7]

ALJ and JAL

44. *Hairpin*

Northern Zhou dynasty (557–581)
Excavated from the tomb of Tian Hong (d. 575) and his wife, western suburbs of Guyuan, Ningxia
Jade (nephrite)
Length: 8.4 cm; width: 2.0 cm; thickness: 1.5 cm
Guyuan Municipal Museum, Ningxia Hui Autonomous Region

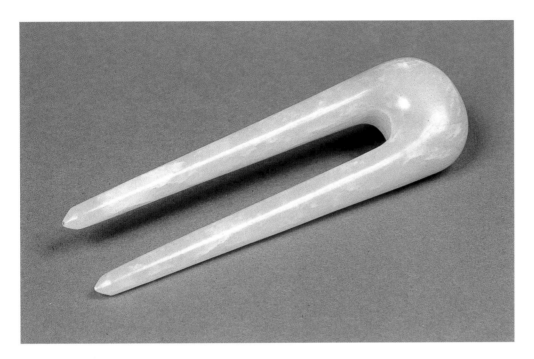

1. *Tian Hong* 2000, colorpls. 19, upper right (in situ) and 28:6; p. 279, fig. 33 (drawing in situ); p. 304, fig. 58:6.

2. Rawson 1996, pp. 110–11, no. 50.

3. Zhou and Gao 1991, p. 71.

4. Yun 1993, p. 101, fig. 201, pl. 231. All four were found in the tomb of Wang Shiliang (d. 583), his wife, Dong Runhui (d. 565), and two nameless concubines. They vary in length from 8.6 to 7.1 cm.

5. Rawson 1995, p. 318, no. 24:6. The jade is 4.6 cm long and 3 cm wide. An even shorter-pronged jade with a flat top (3.2 cm) of perhaps the Han period seems to be a "true" nose plug (Hartman 1975, p. 75, no. 110).

6. Michaelson 1999, p. 64, no. 30 (four jade hairpins).

7. A greenish-white jade hairpin of identical form in the Grenville L. Winthrop collection must also date to this period (Loehr 1975, no. 620).

Hairpins were used by women, and possibly by men, in China from the late Neolithic period (middle of the third to the early second millennium BCE), and those of jade, ivory, and bone are found in profusion in the Shang dynasty (sixteenth–eleventh century BCE).[1,2] They are single-pronged with their upper ends often carved in animal or geometric shapes. Double-pronged hairpins, exemplified by this one, which was found in the coffin of Tian Hong's wife, apparently were not made until the Han period.[3] They were then used through the Wei and Northern Zhou, and were popular in the succeeding Sui and Tang periods. They are typically made of gold, although silver, bronze, and bone are also used.

However, until the recent excavation of Tian Hong's tomb and the discovery of four similar jade hairpins in another Northern Zhou–period burial,[4] double-pronged hairpins were virtually unknown in jade. A jade piece with two short prongs joining it at the wide curved end that dates to the Eastern Zhou or Han period (fourth–second century BCE) may have served as a nose plug rather than a hairpin.[5]

Although double-pronged jade hairpins continue into the Sui and Tang periods, they are more attenuated in shape (see no. 88).[6] This Northern Zhou example and the others have a larger, rounded head, which contrasts with the sharply pointed prongs of the base.[7] The almost bulbous shape enhances the well-polished, milky translucency of the pale green stone and gives this functional yet ornamental object an appealing tactile quality.

JAL

PART II
BUDDHIST MONKS: TRANSMISSION AND TRANSLATION

4

Buddhist Art in Northwest China

ANNETTE L. JULIANO

Go, monks, preach, the Noble Doctrine . . . let not two of you go in the same direction.

—Buddha, Vinaya-pitaka, II, 20–21[1]

Obeying the Buddha's exhortation, his later disciples, Indian and Central Asian monks, carried his teachings out of India through Central Asia to China, arriving during the Han dynasty, at the turn of the first century CE. Often traveling with merchants and diplomatic envoys along various branches of the Silk Road, monks came initially to northwest China, entering the Gansu region and traversing its narrow, thousand-mile long Gansu corridor, the "gateway" to China proper. Gansu's strategic location made it the natural highway for early Buddhist teachers to enter China; later, by the fifth century, Gansu itself had become a major treasure house of Buddhist art. Scattered along the entire length of the province from the far west through the Gansu corridor to the southeast, cave temple sites carved into escarpments and mountains still preserve much of the earliest and the most important Buddhist sculpture and painting in China.

The carved grottoes that transformed mountainsides into cave sanctuaries were an established feature of Indian Buddhism in a tradition most scholars now believe spread to China via Central Asia along with the religion.[2] A long chain of these sites stretches from India eastward through the desert oases of Bamiyan, Kucha, and Turfan to Gansu, where Buddhist cave temple builders began work in the late fourth and early fifth centuries. Today, ten or more major temples survive in Gansu, the largest concentration in any province. The important sites include the world-famous Thousand Buddha Caves at Dunhuang (see Map 3, page 120), the most extraordinary repository of Buddhist art in China, situated at the very edge of the Gobi Desert. At Binglingsi (Luminous Spirits Temple), rows of caves are set deep in the eroded canyons of the Huang He (Yellow River). Lashaosi, with relief carvings more than one hundred feet high, lies almost totally hidden in Wushan. Maijishan (Cornrick Mountain), a haystack-shaped mountain honeycombed with cave temples, is located near the city of Tianshui at the southeastern end of Gansu. The smaller and lesser-known sites of Jintasi (Golden Pagoda Temple) and Matisi (Horse Hoof Mountain), Wenshushan (Manjusri Mountain), Tiantishan (Heavenly Ladder Mountain), and Changmagong are tucked into the foothills of the Qilian Mountains along the southern border of the Gansu corridor.[3] At the eastern end of Gansu near the Shaanxi border are the Longdongsi temples, carved into stone cliffs that gently wind along river valleys southwest

OVERLEAF: Fig. 1. The cave grottoes known today as Binglingsi, called until the Tang Lingansi or Luminous Cliff Monastery, are south of Lanzhou at Yongling, set in spectacular cliffs and steep ravines. (photo: Judith A. Lerner)

OPPOSITE: View of Maijishan Mountain, Tianshui, Gansu (photo: Annette L. Juliano)

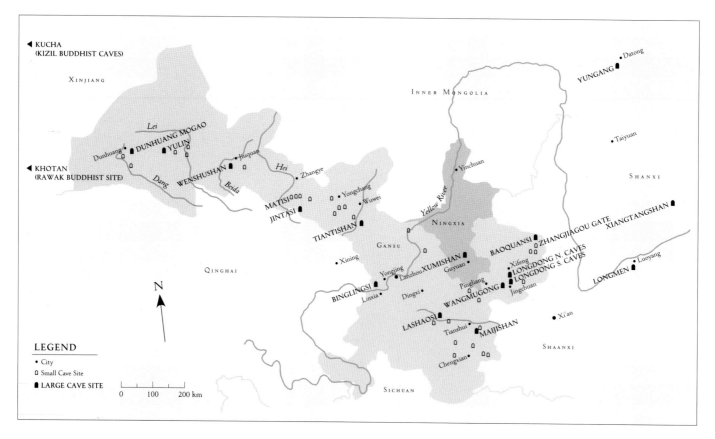

KUCHA
(KIZIL BUDDHIST CAVES)

XINJIANG

KHOTAN
(RAWAK BUDDHIST SITE)

Lei
DUNHUANG MOGAO
YULIN
Dunhuang
Dang
WENSHUSHAN
Jiuquan
Hei
Zhangye
Beida

MATISI
Yongchang
Wuwei
JINTASI
TIANTISHAN

Xining

QINGHAI

N

LEGEND
• City
▢ Small Cave Site
▮ LARGE CAVE SITE
0   100   200 km

INNER MONGOLIA

YUNGANG
Datong

Taiyuan

SHANXI

XIANGTANGSHAN

Yinchuan

NINGXIA

GANSU

BAOQUANSI
ZHANGJIAGOU GATE
LONGDONG N. CAVES
Xifeng
LONGDONG S. CAVES
XUMISHAN
Guyuan
Lanzhou
Pingliang
Jingchuan
LONGMEN
Luoyang

Yongjing
BINGLINGSI
Linxia
Dingxi
WANGMUGONG
Xi'an

LASHAOSI
Tianshui
MAIJISHAN
SHAANXI
Chengxian

SICHUAN

Map 3. Buddhist sites in China (Gansu and Ningxia) and Xinjiang

Fig. 2. The world-famous Buddhist site of Dunhuang (*opposite*), also known as the Thousand Buddha Caves and the Mogao Caves. Located in a river valley at the extreme western end of Gansu, the cliff houses 492 magnificently carved and painted caves, largely concentrated at the southern end. (photo: Annette L. Juliano)

of the town of Xifeng.[4] Located at a cultural crossroads near major trading centers and trade routes, these sites reflect the currents of artistic influence arriving from the west, from Buddhist India and Central Asia, as well as the reverse flow from central China back to Gansu.

The single most famous site in Gansu lies in the extreme western prefecture, bordering Xinjiang and Qinghai provinces. The Thousand Buddha Caves at Dunhuang (fig. 2) also known as the Mogao Caves, have been wrapped in an aura of romance and drama since 1900, when a sealed library of paintings, sutras, and documents was discovered in Cave 17 (no. 46). Beginning in 1907, the expeditions of Sir Aurel Stein and other Western explorers who crossed the Central Asian deserts to Dunhuang acquired scrolls and sutras, which were then taken to the West.[5] Since then, Dunhuang's rich and complex iconography, architecture, sculpture, and wall paintings, located in 492 caves stretching the length of a 1,700-meter cliff, have been the focus of worldwide scholarly attention (fig. 3). Although Dunhuang came under state protection in 1942, the serious conservation efforts of the Dunhuang Research Academy began only after the founding of the People's Republic of China in 1949, with later assistance from international agencies and foundations all working to halt the encroachment of the desert and stabilize this fragile cliff of conglomerate rock. The very process of conservation, which included reinforcing cave entrances and removing accretions of clay and paint applied by later dynasties, often uncovered previously unsuspected nuggets of art and history. In 1965, for example, fragments of a brilliantly colored, embroidered Buddhist banner were found in a crack filled with sand and dry soil extending across the fronts of Caves 125 and 126. This extremely rare find, dated to 487, can be attributed to the donor identified as Yuan Jia, grandson of the Northern Wei emperor (nos. 45a–e).[6]

Nearly all of Dunhuang's celebrated caves are concentrated along the 1,000-meter length at the south end of the cliff; only five cave temples occupy the 700-meter north end,

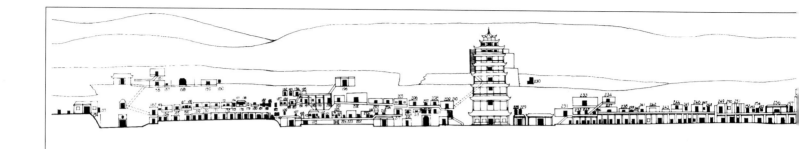

along with many small grottoes long thought to be empty or of little scholarly interest (fig. 4).[7] In recent years, however, excavations and surveys conducted in more than two hundred of these northern caves have opened a new window on the life of the monks and the scope of their activities at Dunhuang. These discoveries have identified cells, each heated by a stove and chimney, for monks and possibly for pilgrims; larger caves with meditation platforms; and public areas, burial caves, and storage caves. Hundreds of relics were found, including many Chinese coins and one silver Sasanian coin of Peroz (no. 94), a stamped clay image on a small Tang votive plaque (no. 76), Buddhist scriptures in many languages, pottery shards, lacquer, silk, cotton, leather, and even clay sculptures, associated with the burial caves. The remains provide a glimpse of the mundane daily activities that surrounded the artistic and spiritual lives of monks, nuns, patrons, pilgrims, and artisans at Dunhuang. The work still under way is part of the continuing effort to explore and systematically document all aspects of this and other lesser-known Gansu cave-temple sites.

During the past twenty years, the early and quite remote Gansu sites of Binglingsi, Matisi, Jintasi (fig. 5), and Wenshushan have been photographed and made more accessible to scholars for study. Recent discoveries and publications by both Western and Chinese scholars have stimulated a re-evaluation of accepted datings and assumptions and generated new avenues of research. For example, the 1963 discovery in Binglingsi's Cave 169 (figs.1, 8–10, pp. 128–30) of the earliest known dated cave temple images, with an inscription dated to 420, supports the thesis that cave temple building began in Gansu in the late fourth or early fifth century.[8] Also, the earliest surviving caves at Dunhuang (Caves 268, 272, and 275) had traditionally been dated to the Northern Wei dynasty, mid- to late fifth century.[9] Since 1980, however, Chinese scholars have begun attributing to these caves an even earlier date in the Northern Liang (398–439), a nomadic kingdom ruled by Juqu Mengxun, an ardent supporter of Buddhism, who controlled central Gansu from the late fourth to early fifth century. Scholars have also broadly defined architectural, figural, and iconographic components that may characterize a distinctive Liangzhou style visible in cave temples opened under the Northern Liang. The term "Liangzhou" also broadly refers to the geographic area of central Gansu occupied by the Liang kingdoms.[10] Still more recent assessments propose assigning Dunhuang Caves 268 and 272 to other nomadic kingdoms in Gansu, contemporary rivals to the Northern Liang.[11]

To the west of Gansu, scientific archaeology and scholarly reassessment have made it possible to revise the dating of some major Buddhist cave sites in Xinjiang. These sites, including the large and important caves at Kizil near Kucha along the northern branch of the Silk Road, (see Map 1, pp. 22–23) contributed significantly to the development of Buddhist

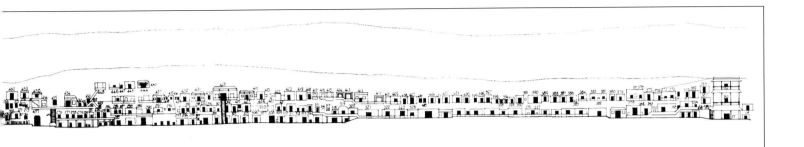

cave-temple art in Gansu. The newly suggested datings as early as the fourth century for some Kizil Caves could help to convincingly place the beginnings of cave-temple art in Gansu back to the mid- to late fourth century, and more clearly identify stylistic, iconographic, and architectural sources.[12] The proposed earlier dating reinforces the importance of the King-dom of Kucha as a thriving Buddhist center and underlines the role of the nearby Kizil Grot-toes as a creative center and formative force in Buddhist art in northwest China.

In many of the Buddhist sites such as Kizil in Xinjiang and the sites in Gansu, the cave sanctuaries have been carved into the stone cliffs. However, because the stone in these regions is often friable and unsuitable for carving sculpture, posing challenges for sculptors and painters alike, the images inside the caves were fashioned from clay and stucco. Most sculp-tures at Gansu cave sites, such as Dunhuang (nos. 50a,b, 51a–c, 76–79), Maijishan (nos. 60–66, 69, 70), and Tiantishan (no. 72), were constructed with an armature of wood or metal, covered with clay mixed with straw, mud, and stucco, sometimes finished with a layer of fine clay, and then painted or gilded and placed in the caves. Walls and ceilings inside the caves were pre-pared with a foundation layer of mud mixed with animal hairs or straw as binders. Several lay-ers of plaster were placed on top to create a smooth surface for painting. Some of these carved

Fig. 3. Site plan of the Dunhuang caves (*above*) (after *Dunhuang* 1981, vol. 1)

Fig. 4. Recently excavated at the north end of the Dunhuang cliff are more than two hundred small caves (*below*), which served as living quarters and spaces for medi-tation, storage, and burials, mainly for the monks, but probably also for pilgrims to the site. (photo: Guy A. Weill)

and painted fragments (no. 68a,b) have fallen off or away from the cave walls or ceilings where they were originally attached, victims of centuries of exposure to the elements, of neglect, of anti-Buddhist vandals and squatters, or of outright theft. The surviving material has been removed from the caves for preservation in research institutes at the sites or moved to local museums.

This exhibition contains nineteen small and large clay sculptures, either constructed with armatures or molded, from Dunhuang, Maijishan, and Tiantishan, and only three carved directly from stone, two from Binglingsi (nos. 73, 74) and one from Maijishan (no. 66). Most had already been removed from the caves, whereas a few others (nos. 77, 78) were found inside large clay stupas under repair around the Dunhuang oasis. These twenty-two pieces as well as others in the exhibition reflect a range of sources, functions, and materials related to Buddhist ritual and practice. The other objects include a reliquary for holding *sarira* or sacred relics (no. 120), fragments of an embroidered Buddhist banner from Dunhuang (no. 45a–e), stone pagodas (stupas) (nos. 48, 52, 53), a clay jar for a monk's ashes (no. 75), a sutra or Buddhist text (no. 46), and stelae dedicated to accrue merit for the donor and his family (nos. 57, 67).

The exhibition extends an opportunity to experience not only the extraordinary Buddhist cave sculpture rarely seen outside of China but

Fig. 5. Western and Eastern Caves of Jintasi, part of the Matishan area in the Qilian Mountains near the border of Gansu and Qinghai (photo: Annette L. Juliano)

also distinctive votive objects such as the Northern Liang sutra pillar and the fragments of a Northern Wei embroidered banner, material largely unfamiliar and unavailable in Western collections. Given Gansu's strategic location, this range of material assembled for the first time makes it possible to explore the complex of sources from the West and from within China that contributed to development of Buddhist art in the northwest and to assess the broader impact of Gansu on north China. The following discussion highlights some of the major themes and artistic developments within the context of the dynamic cultural exchanges from the fourth through seventh century as Buddhist monks and merchants traversed the Silk Road.

Buddhist Monks in Gansu: Transmission and Translation

In many ways, the development of early Buddhist doctrine (dharma) parallels the introduction of Buddhist art—both the art and the religion reached China in fragments.[13] Itinerant monks traveling along the continental highways of the Silk Road, often in company with caravans, carried the Buddhist teachings to China. This Indian religion arrived as "a bewildering array of Mahayana and Hinayana sutras with monastic rules, spells and charms, legends, and scholastic treatises" delivered piecemeal by monks and merchants from different cultures and origins.[14]

Buddhist monks found new opportunities to spread their religion after the fall of the Han Empire in 220 CE. Northern China experienced constant political instability and fragmentation as a succession of nomadic regimes fought for control and as the hatreds among different nomadic tribes and between the Chinese and the so-called barbarian intruders exploded into violence. Amid the tumult, Buddhist monks sought patronage from nomadic rulers who perceived the monks as a new type of shaman with superior magical powers. In exchange for the monks' services as magicians and as political, military, and diplomatic advisors, Buddhism gained powerful new nomadic patrons willing to support image making and translation centers.

Buddhism found eager converts and powerful patrons not only among the northern nomadic conquerors but also in the subjugated Chinese population, and it spread vigorously in the northwest and throughout north China. Northern nomads found this foreign religion attractive on many levels. For rulers, Buddhism offered a common cultural bond that could unite two distinct populations living in the north, bridging the sedentary lifestyle of family-oriented Chinese peasants rooted to the land and the nomadic lifestyle based on horse and herd. For peasant farmers and tribes both, Buddhist monks brought to China potent new magic and herbal medicines. Given the often chaotic conditions in the north, fortune-telling or magical feats were useful tools in winning converts.[15] For the educated classes, Buddhist teachings conveyed challenging new ideas and the fruits of other cultures from the Mediterranean to Iran. Certainly all classes were attracted to the Mahayana promise of personal salvation, which in China increasingly meant salvation not in the elusive state of nirvana but in a very explicit Buddhist paradise defined in newly translated sutras.

The many foreign scriptures, or sutras, in languages such as Pali, Prakrit, and Sanskrit required translation for the expanding body of Chinese converts and clergy (no. 46). Translation centers organized by foreign monks with patronage from nomadic rulers were critical to the continued growth of Buddhism. These translation centers were established as early as the second century CE and became magnets for Parthian monks, Parthian merchants who became monks, Sogdian monks descended from merchant families in China, and Yuezhi monks.[16] At first, spiritual teachers often of Parthian origin, called *acaryas*, translated by reading aloud to Chinese monks who served as scribes. The early translations presented linguistic and philosophical challenges, but by the fourth century, translators developed the concept of *geyi*, a method of matching meanings by searching through Chinese literature, mainly Daoist, for terminology that would better explain Buddhist teachings, a process that gave this foreign religion greater legitimacy.[17] Filtered through Chinese language and philosophy, Buddhism eventually became thoroughly sinicized.

One of the earliest and most influential Buddhist translators and teachers to emerge was the Dharmaraksa (230–304 CE), born at Dunhuang of naturalized Yuezhi, probably to a wealthy merchant family that could afford a literary education in both Buddhist works and the Confucian canon. Known as the Bodhisattva of Dunhuang, Dharmaraksa traveled extensively in the Western Regions, acquiring an extraordinary facility with language. He regularly journeyed to the Buddhist centers of Dunhuang, Jiuquan, Luoyang, and Changan, which became his usual place of residence. Among his collaborators were both Chinese and non-Chinese from India, Kucha, Yuezhi, Khotan, and perhaps Sogdiana.[18] During the second half of the third century CE, his tireless efforts produced translations of the major early Buddhist texts particularly the *Lotus Sutra* in 286 CE, the most influential scripture of Mahayana Buddhism. Mahayana teachings and the popularity of the *Lotus Sutra*, which taught that the act of making images was a work of the highest merit, were a boon to Buddhist art.[19] As a result, lay followers, monks, and nuns often became patrons of art.

The connection between the Gansu corridor and India and Xinjiang was particularly intense during the fourth and fifth centuries, bringing to China such venerated teachers and translators as Kumarajiva, who was born of an Indian father and a Kuchan mother and educated in Kashmir. A renowned scholar and the greatest missionary translator of all time, Kumarajiva was held captive in Guzang (modern Wuwei) in Gansu because of his charismatic powers, and he learned Chinese before reaching Changan in 402.[20] Shortly thereafter, with royal patronage, he established perhaps the largest and most sophisticated translation center; his work included another version of the Lotus Sutra, which made the Mahayana teachings even more accessible to the Chinese.[21] Mahayana Buddhism—the dominant doctrine in China—promises the faithful rebirth in nirvana in the company of celestial beings.[22] Mahayana Buddhism also stresses the concept of the bodhisattvas; enlightened embodiments of compassion who became worthy models for separate worship and devotion. In art, by the mid-sixth century, bejeweled bodhisattvas emerged as popular cult images, particularly Avalokitesvara (Guanyin), "Rescuer from Perils." The Sui dynasty stone Avalokitesvara from the Gansu Provincial Museum (no. 71) offers a rescuer of exceptional beauty, restrained elegance, and repose.

Another central Indian monk, Dharmaksema (385–433 CE), a leader in propagating Buddhist teachings in the northwest, arrived in Juqu Mengxun's Northern Liang capital of Guzang after travels through Kashmir and Kucha. Apparently, he began translating key Mahayana texts at the Xianyu Gong (The Palace for Pleasurable Ease), which was established by Mengxun and supported more than one hundred monks including Mengxun's cousin Juqu Jingshen.[23] His zeal and effectiveness created an unparalleled Mahayana library, which won recognition among the Chinese Buddhists of southern China.[24] Between Dunhuang and Guzang, the Northern Liang had five active sutra translation centers, with the capital housing the largest and attracting an influx of both foreign and Chinese monks. Dharmaksema's talents at fortune-telling were exceptional, as was his ability to use *dharani*, incantations or spells. His accurate predictions about the fortunes of other kingdoms won Juqu Mengxun's confidence, and he was often consulted on affairs of state.[25]

At about the same time, the famous Chinese monk Faxian, motivated by the desire to retrieve sacred books not known in China, began a reverse pilgrimage through the Gansu corridor to India.[26] In 399 CE, according to tradition, he set out from Changan (present-day Xi'an), crossed the mountain passes to eastern Gansu and Binglingsi (fig.1, pp. 116–17; fig.7. p. 128), where his painted image and name appear on the wall of Binglingsi Cave 169, and went on to Dunhuang, Khotan, and Gandhara. Faxian returned to China by sea in a harrowing two-hundred-day voyage and left a fascinating travelogue in his *Record of the Buddhistic Kingdoms*.[27] He was the first to succeed in reaching India and his success encouraged many other Chinese monks to attempt the arduous journey to the holy sites of Buddhism.

In the third and fourth centuries, trade and Buddhism combined to bring relative prosperity and wealth to the frontier garrisons along the Gansu corridor. The major towns of Dunhuang, Jiuquan, Zhangye, Guzang, and Jincheng (modern Lanzhou) flourished as magnets for monks and merchants. By the Sixteen Kingdoms, during the late fourth and fifth centuries, small states in western and central Gansu—the Later, Western, Northern, and Southern Liang—survived on the earnings of trade from Central Asia. The very practice of Buddhism proved a powerful stimulant to trade. Fotudeng, a Kashmiri or Kuchan monk who reached Luoyang by 310 CE, frequently sent his disciples to Xinjiang to purchase incense.[28] After retiring to his homeland from China, the Kashmiri monk Buddhayasas (Fotuoyeshe) sent important sutras to Gansu via merchants.[29] Worship of the Buddha and demonstrations of faith often required donations of precious objects. Reliquaries to hold the sacred *sarira* were crafted from gold, silver, and bronze, often embellished with jewels, and buried deep within the foundations of stupas or pagodas to consecrate the site and structure. A Tang reliquary (nos. 120a–e) consists of three nested coffin-shaped boxes in bronze, silver, and gold with the smallest jewel- and pearl-encrusted box hiding a miniature glass bottle for the *sarira*. Chinese silks for bands, scarves, canopies, banners, or flags were needed along with precious pearls, coral, lapis lazuli, and crystal to decorate stupas, temples, and reliquaries and to make religious offerings.[30] Among other imports, India sought Chinese silk, and China obtained precious stones, glass objects, pearls, and coral. In the Maijishan Grottoes outside of the city of Tianshui in southeastern Gansu, at least three bodhisattvas wear bead ropes that include distinctive copies of branch coral (fig. 6).[31]

Fig. 6. Bead ropes worn by the Western Wei seated bodhisattva from Cave 142 at Maijishan include an example of the distinctive form of branch coral imported from India. (after *Maijishan* 1998, pl. 110)

Early Buddhist Art in the Northwest: Gansu and the Western Connection

Inspiration from Western models was the essential component in shaping early Buddhist art in the northwest. The chapter on religions in the contemporaneous Northern Wei history notes that Northern Liang was deeply permeated by Buddhist teachings and models, particularly in Dunhuang, which "from its contacts with the clerics and laity of the West, obtained therefrom ancient models to follow. Its villages were alike in possessing many pagoda-temples."[32] The precedents help to create an enormously complex range of sculptural and painterly styles during this formative period from late fourth through late fifth century, including the five Liang kingdoms and the onset of Northern Wei. Western models were "transmitted in fragments so to speak by means of small portable images and painting, and iconographic pattern-copy books," which probably arrived in the hands of merchants, monks, pilgrims, or other travelers.[33] These fragments carried some artistic traditions directly from India, the birthplace of Buddhism itself; other traditions arrived filtered and reshaped in the artistic cauldrons of the newer Buddhist hubs in Central Asia.

Early Buddhist sculpture and painting in the oasis kingdoms of Xinjiang and in Gansu were strongly influenced by the art of the Kushan Empire. Located at the western end of the Silk Road, the Kushan Empire began to emerge in the first century BCE, created by the Yuezhi tribes (see Chapter 3) who dominated the western end of Gansu. Driven out of Gansu and pushed even farther westward by the Xiongnu, the Yuezhi took control of Bactria, eventually settled a region known as Gandhara, also at a commercial and cultural crossroads encompassing parts of modern Pakistan and Afghanistan, and moved into north-

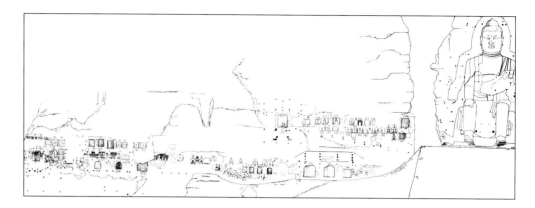

Fig. 7. Site plan of the
Binglingsi caves at Yongjing,
Gansu (after *Binglingsi* 1989)

ern India. The third and most important Kushan king, Kanishka I, became an ardent prop-
agator of Buddhism and builder of Buddhist monuments. By the first century CE, Gandhara's
position on the trade routes facilitated the rapid spread of Buddhism to the oasis kingdoms
of Xinjiang and to China. The peak of the Kushan Empire in the second century CE parallels the Han dynasty's control of the Tarim Basin in Xinjiang. The presence of these two
great empires guaranteed active commercial and cultural exchange across a relatively secure
Silk Road extending back to Rome.

The first iconic images of the Buddha and his life were produced in the two artistic
centers of the Kushan Empire, the Gandharan region, whose stylistic amalgam came mainly
from Rome with Parthian and Iranian elements, and the northern Indian city of Mathura,
with its traditional Indian aesthetic (see Map 1, pp. 22–23). In the art of both centers, the
Buddha first emerges with distinctive iconographic features. Of the thirty-two marks of buddhahood (*lakshanas*), several are adapted to sculpture and painting: a halo behind the head
and body; a cranial protuberance (*ushnisha*) representing transcendent spiritual knowledge,
shown as a large bump on top of the head; elongated earlobes stretched by the weight of
earrings worn during his former life as a prince; a small tuft of hair between the eyes (*urna*),
a sign of spiritual wisdom; a monastic robe; and hands poised in symbolic gestures or
mudras. The Roman elements of Gandharan art are manifested in the realism of the toga-
like monastic robe, which completely envelops the body; this is in sharp contrast to the
Indian style at Mathura where clinging transparent robes reveal rounded, vigorous, and
powerful bodies. Artistic influences from the Kushan Empire, Gandhara, and Mathura
migrated throughout Central Asia to China. Even after the Gupta Empire (320–600) had
encompassed all of north India including Mathura, Gandhara in the northwest continued
producing many more works in stucco in a style reflecting its Roman heritage mixed with
Mathuran, Guptan, and other sources; these later works influenced the Tang.

In Chapter 5, Chen Bingying provides a more extensive discussion of the Gandharan
elements found throughout Gansu, at the earliest caves at Dunhuang (Caves 268, 272, and
275), at Jintasi's Eastern Cave southeast of Zhangye (fig. 5, p. 124), and at Binglingsi Cave
169 near Lanzhou, as well as at Maijishan, southeast of Tianshui (Caves 74 and 78), both in
eastern Gansu. A number of other devotional images and objects such as the stone sutra pillar (no. 48) and the bronze Buddha images (nos. 47, 55) also reveal Gandharan features.

During the third through fifth century, the small oasis kingdoms of Xinjiang, such
as Kucha and Khotan, flourished as commercial and cultural centers and contributed significantly to shaping the style and iconography of early Chinese Buddhist art and architecture in Gansu.[34] Buddhists often fostered commercial interests as monks established temple

complexes within oasis cities and along the trade routes, attracting lay travelers, traders, and pilgrims in a vibrant mix of religion and commerce. Buddhism permeated the cultural life of the Kingdom of Kucha, located along the northern edge of the Tarim Basin. Kucha developed into a creative center for Buddhist thought and for art with the magnificent cave complex at Kizil about forty-four miles west of Kucha.[35] The multicultural character of the Kizil painting style was an inspired blend of Gandharan, Gupta Indian, and Sasanian Persian elements. Although now badly defaced, the sophisticated images remain powerful, painted with a brilliant palette of green and lapis blue or somber cinnabar red, dark brown, and black, their dramatic faces highlighted with white. Painting techniques and styles, architectural elements, imagery, and iconography from Kizil Caves were transmitted to Gansu by the many monks either native to Kucha or from India or Kashmir.[36]

Kizil's artistic presence is most strongly reflected in the fifth-century caves at Dunhuang (figs. 2, 3) and Binglingsi (figs. 1, 7) and in other Gansu cave sites along the Gansu corridor.[37] The connection is apparent when comparing one painted Buddha image on the north wall in Binglingsi's Cave 169, dated to 420 (fig. 8), with the Buddha images enclosed in scalloped diaper patterns on the ceiling of Kizil's Caves 38 and 80, which, according to a suggested new chronology, may date from the fourth century CE (fig. 9a,b). At Binglingsi, the Buddha is seated cross-legged on a lotus, soles of his feet turned upward; his body is surrounded by an aureole; a halo frames his head. Along the top edge of the aureole, a scalloped border is filled with a single row of seven large, open-petaled flowers, with slender, pointed green leaves. Both of the Kizil ceilings show similarities, and Cave 38 depicts the Buddha in the identical posture, with a scalloped border and seven flowers, but the Cave 38 wall paintings also make it clear that this scalloped border, abbreviated at Binglingsi, is actually the top of a tree, undoubtedly the *bo* or *bodhi* (wisdom) tree of enlightenment, rising behind the Buddha's aureole and halo. The flowers at Binglingsi are articulated much like their possible predecessors at Kizil. Finally, the Buddha and flanking bodhisattvas at Binglingsi show dramatic white highlights on the nose, above the eyes, and on the eyelids, in a manner closely resembling the Kizil figures.[38]

Fig. 8. Painting on the north wall of Cave 169, Binglingsi (*left*), rediscovered in 1963 and dated to the Western Qin, 420 CE. Depicted are a seated Buddha with bodhisattvas and kneeling Brahmin. The vegetation, originally the top of a tree visible at the top of the Buddha's mandorla, reflects the strong connection to the major Buddhist cave complex at Kizil, outside of Kucha, on the northern silk route in Xinjiang. (after *Binglingsi* 1989, pl. 36)

Fig. 9a,b. Details of paintings from ceilings of Kizil's Caves 38 (a) and 80 (b) (*center and right*), dated to the fourth century CE, showing a scalloped diaper pattern. Each is filled with a Buddha and has the stylized top of a tree visible just above the mandorla—a configuration that inspired the Binglingsi paintings in fig. 8 (after *Kecier* 1989, vol. 1, pl. 134, Cave 38; vol. 2, pl. 61, Cave 80).

Fig. 10. Paintings from
the north wall of Cave 169,
Binglingsi, dated 420, showing
a seated Buddha, bodhisattvas,
and, to the left, pilgrims
from Korea (after *Binglingsi*
1989, pl. 36)

At the same time, the paintings on the north wall of Binglingsi reflect the multi-
plicity of other styles available to cave temple painters in the fifth century. To the left of
this configuration just discussed, the smaller Buddhas, bodhisattvas, and celestial flying
deities have different Western parentage, while the presence of a Korean donor figure
reveals connections with China's eastern neighbors (fig. 10).[39]

Northern Liang (398–439)

As monks and merchants settled in an increasingly Buddhist Gansu, cave temple building
began in earnest. Many of the earliest sites were initiated in the late fourth and early fifth
centuries under the aegis of the five competing Liang kingdoms. Over the past several
decades, scholars have established the importance of these transient kingdoms, one of
which, the Northern Liang (398–439), founded in central Gansu by the nomadic Xiongnu
or Yuezhi, was pivotal to the spread of Buddhism and Buddhist art within the northwest and
beyond to north China. Northern Liang enjoyed some thirty years of prosperity under the
rule of Juqu Mengxun (398–433), an ardent Buddhist and advocate of Chinese traditional
learning. By 420, Mengxun had stormed Dunhuang, subdued most of his rivals, and unified
the entire Gansu corridor area. Although Mengxun was considered a barbarian, his kingdom was not a provincial cultural backwater. Guzang, the Northern Liang capital, attracted
a diverse population of teaching monks and translators including Dharmaksema. Merchants
from the west joined Chinese scholars and refugees escaping the chaos in central China to
mingle with the local Xiongnu, other nomadic tribes, and the Han Chinese. This rich cultural context compelled sixth-century Chinese historians to concede that the region,
although under barbarian rule since the fourth century CE, was "celebrated for its flourishing Chinese civilization," and that "its refined culture remained unabated."[40]

Juqu Mengxun's enthusiastic patronage of Buddhism was equaled by his lifelong passion
for traditional Chinese histories and classics. In 417 Mengxun built the *Yin Ling Tang* in
Guzang, courted eminent scholars, and hung portraits of the ancient sages around the hall as a
setting for discussions of Confucian texts and biographies with his officials.[41] These dual interests are skillfully integrated on the stone votive stupa sometimes called *jingta*, or sutra pillar,
carved during the Northern Liang (no. 48). Fourteen such pillars, most of which have a form

derived from miniature Gandharan reliquary stupas, have been discovered in the Gansu corridor and the Turfan District of Xinjiang. This fine example belonged to Gao Shanmu and is dated 428, making it one of the five earliest created during the reign of Mengxun.[42] The incised imagery includes eight trigrams from the *Yi Jing*, the ancient Chinese classic of divination and cosmology, a sutra passage inscribed in Chinese script, and the seven Buddhas of the Past, along with Maitreya, the Bodhisattva—or Buddha-to-be. This important correlation of imagery, ancient Chinese trigrams with the eight Buddhas, synthesizes two differing cosmological models, Chinese and Buddhist, both addressing the cyclical nature of life and human existence.[43] This sutra pillar is the earliest representation known in China of the Eight Buddhas (no. 48), a grouping that appears to have originated in Gandhara and remained popular long after the Northern Liang, through the Northern Dynasties.[44] The grouping appears on small stone and bronze stelae such as the two examples (nos. 54, 55) from the Northern Wei dynasty included in the exhibition. Dated to the late fifth century, the earlier bronze (no. 55) places seven smaller figures around the seated Buddha's halo. Another example, an early-sixth-century carving from reddish-brown sandstone (no. 54), shows the Maitreya as a crowned prince, flanked by two bodhisattvas, with seven small seated Buddhas edging the top of the pointed niche. Comparably dated, one of the panels carved in low relief on the five-tiered pagoda from Gansu (no. 52) contains seven Buddhas incorporated into a mandorla, surrounding the crowned Maitreya bodhisattva, seated with crossed ankles, and echoing the bronze votive image (no. 55).

Although still much debated among Buddhist scholars, several cave temple sites along the Gansu corridor have been attributed to the Northern Liang. These include Tiantishan, situated southeast of Guzang, including the Western and Eastern Caves of Jintasi, southeast of Zhangye; and Wenshushan, southwest of Jiuquan (see Map 3, p. 120).[45] This attribution to the Northern Liang is based on a preliminary typological study that observed several common architectural and iconographic features.[46] The first is the plan of the caves, which are usually rectangular, with large-scale images and central-stupa columns that are broader at the top. The second is the iconographic program, which focuses on the seated Sakyamuni and Maitreya images and a standing Sakyamuni and may also include repetitive patterns of the "Thousand Buddhas" covering cave walls.[47]

Stylistically, the Northern Liang images display sculpturally robust torsos; Buddhas and bodhisattvas have round faces and narrow eyes and are attended by large-scale, vivid, and energetic flying *apsaras* (*feitian* or *tianjen*). The most salient feature of the Northern Liang figural style is the long narrow scarves that arch behind heads and haloes, swing forward to pass around arms at the elbow, and then flare out into two-pronged ends, as seen on the bottom row of figures on the sutra pillar (no. 48). These energetic scarves embellish all the figures on the central pillar except the Buddhas. The style is employed with some variations throughout the above-mentioned temple sites in the Gansu corridor and at Tiantishan, as suggested by the painting fragment discussed below (fig. 11).[48] Caves 268, 272, and 275 at Dunhuang, now also attributed to the Northern Liang, have similar billowing scarves adorning most of the bodhisattvas and flying *apsaras*.[49] The scarves persist into the early Northern Wei caves here and in central China at the Yungang Grottoes, particularly Caves 6, 7, 9, and 10, outside of Datong, Shanxi (fig. 12).[50] According to the late art historian Alexander Soper, these buoyant scarves first appeared on Hellenistic sky deities, such as the wind gods, entered the Indian Buddhist vocabulary at Mathura on *apsaras*, donor figures, and then bodhisattvas, and were used in the early caves at the Kizil Grottoes.[51]

Fig. 12. Kneeling *tianjen*, (*apsara*, or heavenly figure) with billowing scarf from the west wall of Cave 17, (*above*), Yungang stone grottoes outside Datong, Shanxi. These billowing scarves reflect influences emerging after the Northern Wei conquest of the Northern Liang in Gansu in 439; large numbers of the Northern Liang population were forced to resettle in Datong (after *Yungang* 1977, pl. 80)

Fig. 11. Northern Liang or early-fifth-century fragment of the wall painting of Maitreya from the central pillar of Cave 4 (*right*), Tiantishan Cave Temples outside of Wuwei (Courtesy of the Gansu Provincial Museum, Lanzhou)

Situated outside the Northern Liang capital of Guzang, the Tiantishan Grottoes have the strongest historical link to Northern Liang and its dynamic founder, Juqu Mengxun, and were believed to have been opened by him shortly after the capital was moved from Zhangye in 412. Here, Mengxun was reputed to have had a colossal Buddha constructed to honor his deceased mother.[52] When the site was restored, the lower legs and feet of a colossus were found in what remained of Cave 16. Believed to be the ruins of the image Mengxun had dedicated, this is one of the earliest colossal images partially surviving in China. In 1927, the cliff sustained severe damage from a major earthquake, and the salvageable sculptures and painting were later hastily removed when the river valley was dammed to create a reservoir.

The Tiantishan Grottoes once held very early Buddhist wall paintings probably similar in date to those of Binglingsi, late fourth to early fifth century. A few remaining fragments now survive at the Gansu Provincial Museum in Lanzhou.[53] Certainly, the most beautiful, fragile, and striking of these is from the central pillar of Cave 4, which depicts Maitreya Bodhisattva holding a vase with the waters of life. He stands with feet apart, left hip thrust outward in an S–curved *tribhanga* posture (see fig. 11). Strongly rooted in the Indian stylistic idiom, the facial features, firm rounded forms, energetic scarf, and dhoti recall early representations of Maitreya in Kushan and early Gupta sculpture from Mathura.[54] However, the vigorously painted line on this fragment speaks of Chinese brush skills, not a foreign hand. Simple bold lines describe and abstract the form and rhythm of the cloth.

Northern Liang (398–439) and Northern Wei (386–535)

In 439 the Tuoba, a tribal branch of the Xianbei, swept into Gansu and drove the Northern Liang ruling house westward to the Turfan Depression. This completed the Tuoba unification of northern China, and the leaders of these nomads ruled as the Northern Wei dynasty. Control of Gansu and the Gansu corridor gave the new Northern Wei rulers access to the Western Regions. A forced migration evacuated the old Liang capital, bringing artistic talents and Buddhist religious zeal to the new Northern Wei capital at Pingcheng (present-day Datong) just inside the Great Wall in northern Shanxi, closer to the Tuoba homeland. Wei history recounts that "when the Liang population was transferred to the capital, the monks came eastward with their Buddhist paraphernalia, and 'teaching by images' spread far and wide."[55] Contemporary accounts suggest the magnitude of this migration, which may have involved tens or even hundreds of thousands of households and three thousand monks.[56] However, within a few years of this massive relocation, the aging emperor Tai Wudi (r. 424–452), spurred on by Daoists, unleashed a fierce Buddhist persecution in 446: "From this day onward, whoever presumes to worship foreign gods and make images either of clay or bronze will be put to death with his whole household. . . . Let those in charge issue a proclamation to the generals, the armies, and the governors, that all stupas, paintings, and foreign sutras are to be beaten down and burned utterly; the *sramanas* [holy men or monk ascetics] without distinction of age, are to be destroyed."[57]

After Tai Wudi's death in 452, the new emperor, in a pentitent reversal, restored state approval to Buddhism, placing it under direct control of the court and appointing a Buddhist superintendent from Liangzhou, the Gansu corridor area.[58] The second superintendent, Tanyao, also from Liangzhou, petitioned the emperor "to chisel a stone wall in the

Fig. 13. The late-fifth-century cross-ankled bodhisattva with a high crown from the rear chamber, south wall of Cave 7 at the Yungang stone grottoes, outside Datong, Shanxi, was probably inspired by Northern Liang prototypes such as one of the earliest known images of cross-ankled Maitreya on the sutra pillar of Gao Shanmu (no. 48) (after *Yungang* 1991, pl. 77)

mountain to Wuchou Pass, west of the capital, open five caves in each of which is to be carved a Buddha statue. The highest statue is to be 70 feet, the next 60 feet, sculpturing and ornamentation to be the most extraordinary, a crowning achievement to the whole world."[59] Such literary evidence underlines the seminal role that monks from Liangzhou played in the revival of Buddhism. With imperial patronage, the first Buddhist cave temples opened at Yungang just outside Pingcheng in the 460s and 470s, largely as a result of influ-ence exerted by Liangzhou monks.[60]

The presence of Liangzhou Buddhists is also suggested by the many individual icono-graphic and stylistic parallels between this first phase of cave temple construction at Yungang, including five colossal images (Caves 16–20) and two sets of paired caves (Caves 7–8, 9–10), and the earlier cave temples along the Gansu corridor including Dunhuang's Northern Liang and Northern Wei caves. These colossal Northern Wei Buddhas at Yungang in the second half of the fifth century may have had their inspiration in the earlier Northern Liang colossal image dedicated to Juqu Mengxun's mother at Tiantishan.[61] The representation of the seated, crossed-ankled Maitreya with tall crown as carved on the Northern Liang sutra pillar (no. 48), became popular at Yungang, Cave 7 west wall (fig. 13), and later at Longmen, the second Northern Wei cave temple opened after the capital was moved to Luoyang in the late fifth century.[62] Visible on carved figures at the base of the votive stupa is the narrow billowing scarf that may mark Northern Liang figural style; such scarves are pervasive on bodhisattvas in early Yungang caves (fig. 12). Soper observes that "the sculpture from these caves are over-whelmingly western in their iconography and style."[63] For the most part, the sculptural ele-ments reflect Gandharan and Mathuran inspiration transmitted through Xinjiang oasis cities.

Northern Wei (386–535)

The admixture of Western elements in iconography and style that characterized the North-ern Liang continued to mature during the Northern Wei in the fifth century. The Northern Wei artistic presence is visible throughout the major cave sites of Gansu. During the last two decades of the fifth century and in the early sixth century, Northern Wei Buddhist sculpture and painting developed an innovative stylistic idiom, with elongated forms articulated in an intensely mannered linear style often identified as distinctively Chinese. This changed style has traditionally been associated with the transformation of the Tuoba nomadic regime as the

Fig. 14. Maijishan is a stun-ning haystack-shaped moun-tain (*opposite*) that rises 142 meters and is honey-combed with caves filled with sculp-ture, stelae, and paintings, of which 194 survive. (photo: Annette L. Juliano)

Fig. 15. Site plan of the Maijishan stone grottoes (*below*) (after *Maijishan* 1998)

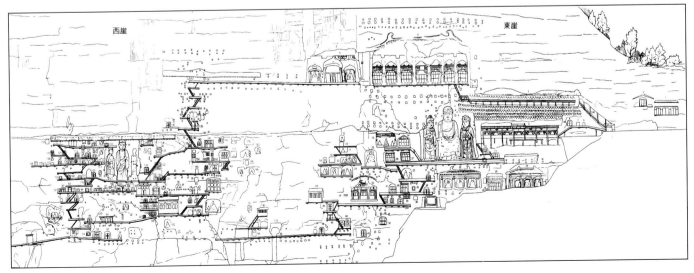

西崖　　　　　　　　　　　　　　　　東崖

ruling house of Wei, seduced by Chinese cultural heritage and lifestyle, embarked upon a conscious policy of sinicization. Under the reign of Xiao Wendi, the capital was moved in 493–94 from Pingcheng near the Great Wall to Luoyang, the ancient capital near the Yellow River in the heart of north China (Map 3, p. 120), which had been devastated by the sack of 311 (no. 8).[64] In this rebuilt metropolis, Chinese became the only court language; Tuoba aristocrats were also ordered to adopt Chinese dress, customs, and surnames and were encouraged to intermarry with the Chinese gentry. Soper proposes that this stylistic shift, which is visible in the later caves at Yungang, resulted from the influence of Buddhist art at the Chinese court in the south.[65] Certainly, throughout the fifth century, embassies presenting "regional objects" or "tribute" were regularly exchanged between the Northern Wei and the Southern dynasties of Liu Song and Southern Qi, which had remained under Chinese rule.[66]

This early-sixth-century change in style is expressed not only through the attenuation of the body but also through the treatment of the Buddha's garments. Northern Wei sculptors clothed Buddhas and bodhisattvas in a tailored Chinese gown with wide sleeves, open at the front, a style also adopted at the Northern Wei court and perhaps borrowed from the elite of the Southern dynasties' Chinese court at Nanjing.[67] Superficially, the costume consists of a loose outer robe over a sashed undergarment and resembles the requisite attire for the *sangha*, or community of Buddhist monks.[68] But this dress was actually a Chinese reinterpretation of the Buddhist robe, mixing Chinese and Indian elements. The new focus was on aesthetic elaboration with fishtail splaying, and rhythmic pleating and patterning of the skirt, robes, and shawl. The complex cascades of drapery folds abandon the thin, revealing robes of Kushan Mathura and early Gupta, which enemies of Buddhism in their polemics against this foreign faith had targeted as barbaric or immodest.[69] The abstract drapery patterns can be seen on the small stele from Pengyang in Ningxia, on which the body virtually disappears beneath cascades of pleated cloth (nos. 58, 59).

Maijishan Cave Temples: Northern Wei (386–535) and Western Wei (535–557)

Although battered over the centuries by tremors and earthquakes, 194 caves have survived at Maijishan, the remarkable haystack-shaped mountain rising 142 meters from terraced farmlands near the city of Tianshui in southeastern Gansu (figs. 14, 15). The site preserves an extraordinary range of sculpture, largely but not exclusively in clay, stone stelae, and painting fragments, offering superb examples of the exquisite early-sixth-century Northern Wei style, not limited to large grotto sculpture (fig. 15).[70] This strongly sinicized Northern Wei style focused on attenuation of sculptural forms and on drapery patterning. The pair of small attendant bodhisattvas (no. 60a,b) and the flying *apsara* (*feitian*) (no. 61) exhibit the hallmarks of the Northern Wei style at its best. The attenuated and swayed bodies of the bodhisattvas recede beneath the layers of drapery that form thin and elegant, low-relief, patterned folds, falling to a gentle flare at the base. Rather large heads are slightly bowed; the figures appear reverent with enigmatic smiles and typically blissful expressions captured in the high, arched eyebrows over half-closed eyes.

Maijishan bodhisattvas and *apsaras* were relief sculptures with completely flat backs that were attached to the cave walls or ceilings. Although others remain in place, the *apsara* (no. 61) in this exhibition fell from the ceiling of the large and important Cave 133. The drap-

ery animates the entire arched body, flowing over and sweeping behind, creating a powerful sense of energy and movement. These early-sixth-century caves are filled with inventive drapery on sitting and standing images; sculpted fabrics fall over the dais in looping zigzag patterns, swaying or splaying outward. Many of these same stylistic elements have been translated from sculpture into painting by the brush and vivid color, as seen in one of the somewhat later painting fragments (nos. 68a, b) from the walls of Maijishan Cave 78. The *apsara* in this fragment plays a musical instrument, and the figure's elongated body floats effortlessly among trailing ribbons and narrow shawls. This distinctive new drapery style became synonymous with Northern Wei sculpture and painting throughout the Wei Empire, creating almost a national style that continued to shape sculpture through the mid-sixth century in north China.

Fig. 16. Kasyapa, detail of no. 62. Distinctive portrait of the Buddha's oldest disciple, marked here as a foreigner by the beaklike nose. Front part of the right wall, Cave 87, Maijishan stone grottoes (photo courtesy of Maijishan Art Research Institute)

On the sculpted *apsara* (no. 61) from Cave 133, the trailing scarves are decorated with a small, floating, five- or six-petaled open flower. A nearly identical painted flower is positioned at regular intervals around the *apsaras* playing music on the Buddha's halo in Western Wei Cave 127 and can be found utilized in very much the same fashion along the garland in a third-century CE painting from Miran, eastern Central Asia (Xinjiang).[71] A similar flower also appears in a more repetitive form as a decorative border on Gandharan reliefs.[72] Also in Cave 127, two attendant bodhisattvas display elegant palmettes hanging from their torque necklaces. Many imported motifs such as these floral images, both sculpted and painted, continued their assimilation into the Chinese decorative vocabulary.[73]

With the collapse of the Wei, China divided into west and east. Western Wei (535–557) was followed by Northern Zhou (557–581) in the same region; both had their capitals at Changan (present-day Xi'an), due east of Maijishan and Tianshui. Maijishan benefited enormously from proximity to the imperial capital, developing a special connection with the Western Wei rulers that led to their rapid opening of twenty new caves. In another example of this close relationship, when the Western Wei empress died, a special cave, called the *chiling*, or silent cave, was carved at Maijishan to temporarily house her body before it was transferred to her husband's tomb in Changan.

Like other grotto sculpture in the northwest, Maijishan's sculpture was often fashioned with armatures and mixtures of clay and straw and conveys an extraordinary sense of freshness and inventiveness, successfully balancing the immediacy of direct hand modeling of clay with the timelessness of the artistic form. These qualities are exemplified in the images of the two famous monks: Ananda (no. 63) from Cave 102 and Kasyapa (no. 62) from Cave 87 (fig. 16). Ananda and Kasyapa represent the Buddha's original monastic community and usually form the basic iconographic unit, the triad, the Buddha flanked by his bodhisattvas. Although additional monks and bodhisattvas may appear, the triad remains most popular across north China from Dunhuang to Longmen in Henan.

Kasyapa was the eldest of the Buddha's disciples (no. 62, fig. 16). A simple monk's robe drapes over the figure's slender, almost emaciated body. Kasyapa's shaved head, bent humbly over hands clasped in prayer, clearly conveys his advanced age and intense spirituality. The large beaked nose, framed by a bridge of drooping eyebrows, emphatically states his foreign origins. In contrast to Kasyapa's lined visage, the smooth full face of Ananda (fig. 16), the youngest of the Buddha's disciples, conveys an air of serenity, which emanates from the enigmatic smiling mouth and eyes. At the same time, Ananda's robe (no. 63), captured by the sculptor as it slips off his right shoulder, suggests a sense of immediacy and a powerful physical presence.

These figures of Ananda and Kasyapa from the first half of the sixth century reflect the best of late Northern Wei sculpture at Maijishan and its close stylistic continuity of the transition into Western Wei and are exceptional achievements in clay sculpture. They typify the complexity and refinement of the Buddhist sculptural tradition at Maijishan, which clearly retains elements of Western influence but by this date is being reshaped largely by indigenous Chinese elements along with a newly emergent naturalism. The sophisticated elegance of Maijishan sculpture from the Northern Wei and Western Wei surpasses most work produced in Gansu and in north China and may have its origins in Buddhist sculpture of the Southern dynasties.[74] This possible connection between Maijishan and Southern dynasties sculpture may have been facilitated by Maijishan's location in southeastern Gansu and further by its proximity to the trade routes that connected to south China.

Late Buddhist Art in Gansu

The dissolution of the Wei Empire divided north China into rival eastern and western factions; this internecine rivalry was particularly ferocious between the Northern Zhou (557–581) in the west and Northern Qi (550–577) in the east, successor dynasties to the Western Wei (535–557) and Eastern Wei (534–550), respectively. Savage battles for succession left the north reeling as hundreds of thousands of real and imagined traitors and enemies were slaughtered. At the same time, the Turkic peoples were gaining power in Central Asia. As Turkic sovereignty spread, making travel and trade safer, Sogdian traders began reaching the Northern Zhou capital of Changan in 564 and 576 and Turkic embassies began arriving in 557.

Complex political and religious struggles continued during the fifty years between the achievements of the Northern Wei and the Tang Empire. Under the first two Northern Zhou rulers, devout followers of Buddhism, temple economies in Gansu and Ningxia flourished. However, the third emperor of this non-Chinese ruling house decided to demonstrate how fully Chinese he was in his thinking. Uncomfortable with the widespread popularity of this foreign religion, he acted to suppress Buddhism and, surprisingly, Daoism as well in 574. More than forty thousand temples were destroyed, and two million monks were returned to secular life.[75] Maijishan, although located near the capital, remained unaffected, as did most of the cave sites in Gansu, perhaps because many local officials were devout Buddhists who continued to protect the cave temples.

Both stylistically and iconographically, the mid-sixth century through the early seventh century represents an important transitional period for Chinese Buddhism and Buddhist sculpture in north China. Sculpture and painting at Maijishan reflect a growing interest in naturalism, with softer, columnar, and more forcefully modeled bodies, sometimes covered with clinging drapery. At Maijishan, this trend is illustrated by a group of images dating from the Northern Zhou through Sui Dynasty, mid-sixth through early seventh century (nos. 65, 66, 69, 70a,b). Found in Cave 135, the seated clay Buddha's rounded body demonstrates this new interest. His robe falls in simple, natural, clothlike folds, which enhance the sculptural harmony and air of gentle dignity expressed by the entire image (no. 65). The hands resting on his chest seem to touch the robe in an unusual gesture, a fleeting but humanizing moment of immediacy, so characteristic of the best of Maijishan clay sculpture. The aesthetic of Northern Zhou moves away from the Northern Wei's attenuated elegance and cascades of abstracted drapery to a mixed vocabulary that retains elements of this earlier Wei style but shifts decidedly back toward the West and India.[76]

Typically, during the second half of the sixth century, Northern Zhou images of the Bodhisattva Avalokitesvara gain volume and an almost columnar solidity and replace the complex patterns of heavy pleated and splayed drapery with thinner, clinging cloth, decorated with beaded medallions, pendants, cabochons, plaques, pearl-like clusters, and linked, thick strands of beads. The jewelry often becomes massive and even ponderous. Bodhisattvas from the northwest, however, tend to simplify the complexity created by the elaborate jewelry of other Northern Zhou images.[77] The tall stone bodhisattva from Cave 47 captures the unique quality of the Maijishan and northwest cave temple sculptural style, exquisitely balancing the strong and solidly columnar body against the cloth ribbons, pleated and layered from the shoulder to the feet and crisscrossing below the knees (no. 67).[78] Jewelry here is often lighter, as in this restrained combination of torque necklace and long multistrand rope of beads punctuated with larger beads or plaques (no. 66). These beads suggest Indian origins and resemble a more abstract version of the bead ropes painted around the neck of Avalokitesvara on the wall of Ajanta Cave I in central India dating to the fifth or sixth century.[79]

By the late sixth century, the Sui dynasty (589–618) succeeded in unifying China for a brief time. The growing interest in naturalism typical of Sui is beautifully expressed in two examples of bodhisattvas at Maijishan. The elegantly slender body of the bodhisattva from Cave 161 (no. 69) assumes a relaxed asymmetrical position, hip thrust back and knee flexed, the curves of the body echoed by the movement and loop of her shawl. The subtle naturalism typical of the last decade of the sixth century is also evident in the superb stone Avalokitesvara (no. 71), found not far from Maijishan. Avalokitesvara holds a bottle in the left hand and the fragment of a lotus flower in the right; the strong columnar body is soft-ened at the waist by a few folds of cloth around the hip. A thin shawl loops over the arms, falling in overlapping layers to zigzag folds near the feet. The repetitive pattern of the long loops of beads and rosette medallions counterpoints the smoothness of the forms.

The Sui laid the foundations for the political and cultural unification of the Tang Empire by beginning to repair the deep fissures of regionalism. Buddhism, with its follow-ing in the north and south among both peasants and privileged classes, helped to close the cultural gap between the Chinese-controlled south and the nomad-ruled north. This once-foreign religion became the vehicle for reuniting the two cultures, and Buddhism flourished for the first two centuries of the Tang. Together the Sui and the Tang dynasties are often cited as the Golden Age of Buddhism and Buddhist art in China. During these years, the subtle signs of naturalism blossomed, transforming Buddhist deities into images more sculp-turally intimate and human. This new spirit is eloquently captured in the quietly sensual forms and softly draped garments of the life-size Tang bodhisattva salvaged from Tiantis-han grottoes (no. 72; see fig. 16) and in the stone Tang monk from Binglingsi Cave 10 who wears an enigmatic smile worthy of a teacher of the dharma (no. 73). With figures like these, the Tang produced a national style of painting and sculpture that is immediately identifi-able as belonging to the period.

Conclusion

By virtue of its unique geographic position on China's western borders and its unusual phys-ical configuration as a natural corridor, Gansu secured a major role in the development of Buddhist art in the northwest and throughout north China. From the fourth through the sixth century, against a landscape of war and politics, monks and merchants were drawn to this gateway and moved through or later settled this cultural crossroads, already home to nomadic herders and Han Chinese farmers. Monks from India, Parthia, Kashmir, Kucha, and Khotan, carrying their Buddhist sutras, votive images, and copy books, found a receptive audience among the nomadic kingdoms and others battling for control of the Gansu corri-dor. With the support of the nomadic rulers, the builders of temples, pagodas, and cave sanc-tuaries began the transformation of Gansu into an extraordinary repository of Buddhist art.

Gansu's geographic configuration naturally created three zones of cave-building activity. The first zone, at the westernmost end, is dominated by a desert landscape and Dunhuang; the second, the narrow corridor with its mixed terrains of deserts, mountains, and grazing and farmland, contained a string of distinctive and isolated smaller cave sites, including Jintasi, Tiantishan, and Wenshushan, ending at the deep ravines of Binglingsi. The eastern end of the corridor widens to join the fertile plains of central China with Maijishan rising to the southeast and Longdongsi farther east, a region shaped not only by influences from the west and central China but also from south China through Sichuan. All three areas were formed by the centuries-long ebb and flow of peoples and historical forces emanating from the West and from central China as well.

Through ten major cave sites and dozens of smaller sites, and in countless individual images and objects, Gansu preserves diverse sculptural forms and styles ranging from the more robust western forms shaped by Gandhara and Mathura, to the sinicized, elegantly attenuated forms of Northern Wei and the exquisitely restrained naturalism and sensuality of Tang. This wealth of artistic treasures makes Gansu province a veritable museum of early Buddhist sculpture and painting. As new sites are discovered in the remote foothills of the Qilian Mountains, and as known sites are more fully documented and better understood, the perception of Gansu's role in the development of early Buddhist art in China will continue to evolve. Finally, however, Buddhism did leave a lasting legacy in Gansu and an indelible imprint on China's non-Buddhist artistic traditions, introducing a new vocabulary of ideas, deities, and motifs, many of which retained their vitality for centuries.

NOTES

1. Zürcher 1962, p. 221; for an alternate translation, see Conze 1954, p. 33.

2. Michael Sullivan mentions the long tradition of loess cave dwellings in north China (Sullivan, 1969, p. 1); Eberhard 1969, p. 136, notes that the Tuoba nomads also cut caves into cliffs to bury their leaders.

3. For a comprehensive list of the cave temples in Gansu province, see Zhang 1994 and Nagel 1978, pp.20–76 (Gansu and Ningxia).

4. Longdongsi consists of two groups of caves in eastern Gansu. The northern caves of Qingyang County are located at the confluence of the Pu and Ru Rivers. Cave 165 was opened in 509; the southern caves, opened in 510, are located north of city of Jingchuan; see Longdong 1987.

5. A catalogue of selected material acquired by Stein was published by Whitfield and Farrer 1990. Stein published accounts of his three expeditions of 1900–1, 1906–9 and 1913–16 in several works, Stein 1904, 1912, and 1921.

6. The original excavation report was published in *Wenwu* 1972.2, pp. 54–60.

7. From 1988 to 1995, the survey and excavation of the north end caves was undertaken by the Dunhuang Research Academy under the direction of Peng Jinzhang, Research Fellow, and Sha Wutian, Assistant Research Fellow. The complete report was published in *Wenwu* 1998.10, pp. 4–27.

8. *Binglingsi* 1989; Dong 1994.

9. Akiyama and Matsubara 1968, Vol. II, pp. 20–21, nos. 1, 2, 6, p. 205, no. 5, p. 206.

10. Soper 1958, pp. 131–64; Abe 1990, pp. 1–20; Su 1986, pp. 435–46.

11. Rhie, 1998, p. 114.

12. Howard 1996, pp. 68–83. The new chronology is based on Su Bai's thirty years of studying the Kizil Grottoes, considering architectural features as well as decorative motifs and iconographic programs. His study and carbon-14 tests of wood and straw fragments on the plastered walls confirm an earlier date of 300 to 600. However, not all scholars agree with this redating. *Kecier* 1989, pp. 10–23.

13. Zürcher 1972, p. 1.

14. Ibid. p. 2.

15. Zürcher 1991, p. 12; Zürcher summarizes areas of innovation in the development of Buddhism that took place in the Chinese cultural environment, particularly the role of famous images as concrete links between China and India, the special importance of miraculous powers of these images as sacred objects, and the political use of iconography.

16. An Shigao, a Parthian monk believed to be of royal lineage, arrived in Luoyang c. 148 CE and founded a translation center which attracted foreign and Chinese monks including a compatriot, An Xuan, who converted to Buddhism. Ch'en 1964, p. 43–44, and Zürcher 1972, p. 23.

17. Ch'en 1964, p. 68.

18. An important source of information about early Buddhism in China is provided by the monks' biographies, *Gaosengzhuan*, (*Biographies of Eminent Monks*) compiled by the monk Hui Qiao about 530 CE. The first installment of the early translators has been translated into French and published by Robert Shih (Dharmaraksa's biography, no. 8 in Shih 1968, pp. 33–37).

19. Two recent articles discuss secular and religious patronage at Dunhuang's three earliest caves (Ning 2000, pp. 489–529) and women as patrons including empresses, aristocrats, gentry, and others during the Northern and Southern dynasties (Wong 2000, pp. 535–564); see also Zürcher 1991, p. 9; Liu 1988, p. 165.

20. Shih, 1968, Kumarajiva's Biography, pp. 60–81.

21. For an excellent translation of the *Lotus Sutra* from Kumarajiva's version, which apparently has more clarity than the earlier one by Dharmaraksa, see Hurvitz 1976.

22. Mahayana, also known as the "Greater vehicle" is one of

the three bodies of Buddhist doctrine; the others are Hinayana, the "Small vehicle," and Vajrayana, the "Indestructible vehicle." The ideal figure of Mahayana is the bodhisattva, a being that embodies compassion and renounces complete entry into nirvana until all beings are saved.(Bercholz and Bertolucci 1993, pp. 315 and 319).

23. Juhl 1995, p. 75.

24. In 426, Mengxun's envoy to the southern court at Nanjing requested copies of the *Yi Jing* (Book of Changes) and works of the early Chinese philosophers. He was given 475 *juan* (chapters or scrolls) to take back to Gansu. In 436, the second and last Northern Liang king sent to the southern court a library of valuable manuscripts as a return offering (Soper 1958, p. 134).

25. Mengxun was said to have had Dharmaksema killed, fearing that Dharmaksema, who had decided to leave court, would use his magic against him if he let him go. Juhl 1995, p. 67; Abe 1990, pp. 2–3; Zhang and He 1994, p. 102. In the north, Buddhism became a state religion and monks such as Dharmaksema served as advisors to the king. Another monk, Xuangao, advised the ruler of Western Qin and then served Juqu Mengxun, who paid him great honors. Juhl 1995, p. 73. In contrast, southern Buddhism remained independent of the state and monks solicited support from the educated elite and landed gentry competing with Confucianism and Daoism (Ch'en 1964, p. 78).

26. The journey to India was so arduous and dangerous that it is estimated that only 2 percent of the Chinese pilgrims to India ever returned. A more inviting alternative was to worship before sculpted scenes on pagodas or wall paintings in Buddhist caves. These sites could serve as a surrogate for the whole trip. Huntington 1987, p. 55, discusses the concept of the pilgrimage.

27. See Giles 1956.

28. Liu 1988, p. 143.

29. Ibid.

30. Ibid., pp. 92–96.

31. *Maijishan* 1954, Cave 127, Western Wei, pl. 106; Cave 87, Northern Wei, pls. 73, 74.

32. Soper 1958, p. 141; Soper 1960, p. 55.

33. Soper 1960, p. 56. Tang copybooks, called *baimiao gao* or (*bihua*) *fenben,* and used by artists to paint the murals at Dunhuang, were found in the Sutra Cave. Although these are the earliest found at Dunhuang, there must have been examples from pre-Tang periods as well, see *Dunhuang yanjiu* 1998.4, pp. 19–28. These artist's sketches point to a "high level of organized professionalism in the artist's practice within the medieval atelier" (Fraser 1996, pp. 60–69).

34. Giles 1956, p. 4. Faxian visited Khotan and described this kingdom as "prosperous and happy; its people are well-to-do; they have all received the Faith, and find their amusement in the religious music. The priests number several tens of thousands, most belonging to the Greater Vehicle (Mahayana)."

35. Howard 1991, pp. 68–83; *Kecier* 1989; *Wenwu* 12 (1984), pp. 4–22.

36. Howard 1991, pp. 80–81.

37. Abe 1990, pp. 1–20. Abe discusses the iconography of Dunhuang Cave 254 and Kizil Cave 80, Cave 254's relationship to Gansu Buddhist art, the popularity of Maitreya in Northern Liang, and the characteristics of what he refers to as "Liangzhou Buddhism."

38. The stone at Binglingsi is suitable for carving; nearly all the caves have carved stone images, with one exception: the earliest cave, Cave 169, has stucco images inspired by Gand-

haran prototypes. Other stylistic and iconographic parallels between Binglingsi and Kizil Cave 38 and Cave 80 are too numerous to detail here.

39. *Binglingsi,* pl. 36; Zhang 1997, p. 27, fig. 28.

40. Wang 1999, p. 74.

41. Zhang 1994, p. 107

42. The literature on the votive stupas has dramatically increased in the last several years. A very comprehensive article discussing twelve of the known fourteen was done by Durt, Riboud, and Lai 1985, pp. 92–106. Most articles in Chinese have been writtten by Yin Guangming and have been included in the bibliography. When Northern Wei conquered the capital at Guzang (Wuwei) in 439, the Northern Liang King Juqu Mujian surrendered but his younger brothers continued resisting and moved to the western end of the Gansu corridor. The middle brother occupied Dunhuang and dispatched the younger brother, Anzhou, to the west to conquer the Kingdom of Shanshan. The Northern Liang Kings reestablished an independent Kingdom, the Daliang, in the eastern part of the Turfan depression, and held sway over the entire Hexi region. A Buddhist shrine to Maitreya was built by Anzhou between 445 and 449 in the Turfan region (Rong 2000a, pp. 318–21).

43. Yin 1998, pp. 87–107. For a full discussion of the merging of the two cosmological systems, see Wang 1999, pp. 70–91.

44. Small clay Buddhas and bodhisattvas, cross-ankled and cross-legged, were originally attached to the aureole surrounding standing Buddhas from Khotan and from Rawak, a Buddhist site northeast of Khotan. The elongated ears on the seven seated Buddhas from Gao Shanmu's stupa are also found on the clay Buddhas from Khotan, see Rhie 1999, figs. 4.68d,e (Khotan) and fig. 4.78a,b (Rawak); Stein 1907, pl. LXXXVII. The robes of the seated Buddhas on the Gao Shanmu stupa drape over both shoulders in Gandharan fashion, although the crossed ankles, jewelry, and hat of his Maitreya resemble the Rawak bodhisattvas (no. 48, fig. D).

45. The Gansu Cultural Relics and Archeological Institute dates most of this material to Northern Liang and discusses smaller sites such as Changmagong near Yumen City and Xiaguanyin and Tongziba in Minle county, also in the Zhangye area (*Hexi* 1987). Other articles discuss the Northern Liang dating of these caves in *Dunhuang yanjiu* 1997.1, pp. 42-56; 1997.4, pp.92–109; 1996.1, pp.22–36; and *Wenwu* 1956.4, pp. 37–44.

46. Su 1986, pp. 435–46. The complex iconography and stylistic features of Wenshushan and Jintasi have presented scholars with an interesting challenge in dating works to Northern Liang or Northern Wei. See Angela Howard's article based on Su Bai's initial seminal observations about the "Liangzhou style," Howard 2000, pp. 235-278.

47. The iconographic configuration of Sakyamuni and Maitreya seems to originate in Kushan, as seen on a large relief from Shotorak, near the ancient city of Kapisa (modern Begram) in Afghanistan. This relief combines Sakyamuni in the bottom register with Maitreya in the top register represented in Tushita heaven and flanked by *devas.* Maitreya is shown seated in a monastic robe but with princely necklaces and earrings. (Rosenfield 1967, pp. 233–34).

48. Soper 1958, p. 144; see *Hexi* 1987examples from Jintasi, pls. 85–87 and from Wenshushan, pls. 115–17.

49. Although Dunhuang's earliest Caves 268, 272, and 275 have been redated from Northern Wei to Northern Liang and depict Sakyamuni and/or Maitreya, they lack central columns. These begin to appear in Northern Wei and persist through the Northern Dynasties caves as late as the Sui dynasty (589-618). Abe, discussing Dunhuang Cave 254 (Abe

1990, p. 5), suggests that early square central columns which can be circumambulated replicate the original central shaft inside the stupa.

50. *Yungang* 1988, Cave 6, pls, 71, 73, 74; Cave 7, pls. 81–84; Cave 9, pls. 98, 100; Cave 10, pls. 105, 108, 109.

51. Soper 1958, pp. 144–45. Examples of the billowing scarf can be seen on a crossbar from a stupa gate from Kushan Mathura, dating to the first century CE (Rhi 1994, fig. 14) and on a clay tile with a figure from the Three Kingdoms period from Pingan, Qinghai (Rhie 1999, fig. 2.24).

52. The remains of a large colossus believed to be the image dedicated to Juqu Mengxun's mother have been published in Zhang 1994, p. 106, figs. 2, 3.

53. Most of the clay sculpture salvaged from the Tiantishan Caves dates from the Tang and is in the Gansu Provincial Museum awaiting repair and conservation.

54. For development of the iconography of the Bodhisattva see Rhi 1994, pp. 202–6.

55. Soper 1958, p. 141.

56. Juhl 1995, p. 63. Marilyn M. Rhie comments that the movement of families and monks from the Liangzhou area to the Northern Wei capital of Pingcheng (modern Datong) after the conquest of Northern Liang by Northern Wei was "one of the most significant events of the time and had a major impact on the Buddhism and Buddhist art of the northern Wei for generations after 439." Rhie 1995, p. 98.

57. Mizuno and Nagahiro, *Yungang*, supplementary vol. 16, pp. 65–69.

58. Tsukamoto 1957, pp. 363–97.

59. Ibid., p. 374.

60. Ibid., pp. 380–82.

61. Zhang 1994, figs. 2, 3, p. 106.

62. *Longmen* 1991, Vol. I, Guyang Cave, p. 176, figs. 10, 15, p. 178, figs., 27, 25, p. 179, fig. 29.

63. Soper, 1960, p. 56. Abe (1990, pp. 2–3), points out that the Tanyao and Liangzhou migrations may have created a complex and intimate relationship between Liangzhou Buddhism as practiced in Gansu (particularly evident in Dunhuang Cave 254) and Yungang Caves 7–8, 9–10. Soper believes that the central stupa pillar configuration at Yungang could only have been borrowed from Gansu. However, the actual pillar form is based more on constructed pagoda forms, imitation of wood and tile forms as seen in Caves 1, 2, and 39, and more fantastic variations in Caves 6 and 11. The Gongxian sixth-century caves opened by the Northern Wei after they transferred the capital to Luoyang retain more features from the Gansu practice (Soper 1958, p. 158).

64. In a paper presented at a recent conference in Beijing, Shing Müller discussed the emerging Tuoba culture in Northern Wei's first capital at Pingcheng. She proposes that Xiao Wendi's decision to move the capital just after the dowager empress Wenming's death was driven not just by a desire to support sinicization but by a need to escape the dowager's power base of Buddhism and the growing strength of the Tuoba culture. When Xiao Wendi reached Luoyang, he permitted the construction of one pagoda, Yongming, in the royal city and prohibited Xianbei dress; see Müller 2000, p. 37.

65. Soper 1960, pp. 47–112. Few examples of Buddhist sculpture from southern China survive, since more perishable materials such as lacquer and wood were commonly used.

66. Bielenstein 1997, pp. 108–10.

67. Yang 1978, pp. 331–37; Soper 1960, pp. 47–50.

68. Griswold 1958, p. 121.

69. Soper 1960, pp. 57–58; Griswold 1958, pp. 121–27.

70. A classification and dating of the Maijishan caves has been done by Dong 1983, pp. 18–33; for a discussion of the early caves see *Maijishan* 1998, pp. 219–29.

71. *Maijishan* 1998, pls. 152, 153; Rowland 1960, p. 38, fig. 12 (Miran, Eastern Central Asia).

72. Rowland 1960, Host of Mara, no. 14, p. 55 (dated second century CE, Lahore, Central Museum).

73. *Maijishan* 1998, pls. 155, 156, 158.

74. In 1996, a remarkable cache of 400 Buddhist statues dating from the Northern Wei through Northern Qi was unearthed at the site of the Longxing temple at Qingzhou, Shandong province. Some Buddhist scholars in China believe that the Qingzhou sculptures reflect stylistic influence from Southern dynasties Buddhist sculpture. These superb works share with Maijishan a fluid elegance of style and a relationship not yet fully understood, despite known iconographic and stylistic links between Qingzhou and Maijishan. For example, to date, Maijishan and Qingzhou are the only two Buddhist sites from this period that show coral represented in bodhisattvas' looping necklaces. *Shandong*, 1999, p. 52 (coral), p. 55 (hair style), and Zhao 1999, p. 11 fig. 11, p. 39 fig. 32.

75. *Dunhuangxue jikan* 1998.2, pp. 103–8; *China Archeology and Art Digest*, vol. III, no. 4 (June 2000), pp. 251–52.

76. Cave 141 has two seated Buddhas; both have robes reminiscent of the Gandharan mode, covering both shoulders. However, the one on the left has a string fold which is derived from Guptan Mathura and Gandharan sculpture from the Swat Valley in Afghanistan (see *Maijishan* 1998, pl. 208). The other employs an incised line fold that commonly appears in stucco sculpture of north India and Central Asia (see *Maijishan* 1998, p. 207). The string fold also occurs in Dunhuang Cave 275's seated Buddha, and the incised line fold occurs in several Gansu sites, Binglingsi and Dunhuang, as well as in Yungang, Caves 6 and 7 (Rhie 1976, pp. 450, 454, 457–58).

77. Leidy 1998, pp. 88–103; Rhie 1982, pp. 27–54 (in particular see p. 35 for discussion of Shaanxi's more independent beaded style).

78. Rhie 1982, p. 37. Rhie writes: "Generally speaking, the images from Maijishan show less interest in complexity than the Shaanxi images and less geometric subtlety of form than Hebei images in lieu of emphasis on rather bold, sometimes repetitive drapery configurations, and simply molded and rebounded form that is heavy and slender. The result is a fresh and vigorous style showing a mixture of warmth and naturalism with abstract purity while eschewing the extremes of either."

79. Singh 1965, p. 26.

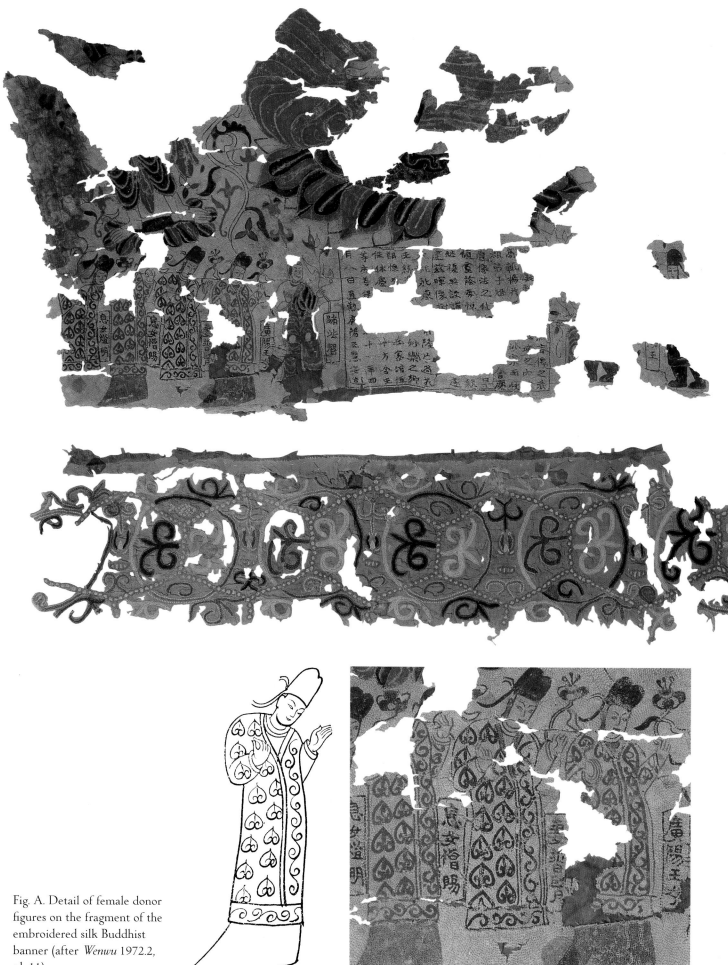

Fig. A. Detail of female donor figures on the fragment of the embroidered silk Buddhist banner (after *Wenwu* 1972.2, pl. 11)

45. Fragments of Buddhist banner with Xianbei donors

Northern Wei dynasty (386–535 ce), dated to 487

Dunhuang Mogao Caves, outside Caves 125 and 126, Gansu

Silk embroidery

Height: 75 cm; width: 51 cm

Dunhuang Research Institute, Gansu

This extraordinary embroidery was found at the Mogao Caves at Dunhuang in the far northwest of Gansu. In 1965, while excavations were under way to clear away debris accumulated over the centuries, several fragments of embroidery were discovered in a sand- and dry-soil-filled crack in the cliff-side in front of Caves 125 and 126.[1] Only a small part of this large temple banner, originally meant to hang inside a cave temple, survives; however, enough remains to determine the contents. The main fragments include a floral border, a scene of a sermon by the Buddha with two accompanying bodhisattvas, the text of a prayer, and several worshipers.

Under the Buddha's multi-petaled lotus pedestal embroidered with alternating red and green colors, two lines of worshipers are ranked on either side of the large rectangular cartouche containing the prayer. The first figure to the right appears to be a monk; of the second figure, only a head and leg are visible and only the word "prince" remains of his title. The right side most probably consists of the males of the party, whereas the women of the entourage are at the left. The first female is a nun named Fazhi (Wisdom of the Law); the second carries the label "Mother of the Prince of Guangyang"; the third is identified as the donor's wife, Puxian; while the last two are daughters named Sengci and Dengming. On the basis of a partial date and the name "Prince of Guangyang," the donor can be identified as the Prince Yuan Jia, the grandson of an emperor of the Northern Wei dynasty; the date the banner was donated was 487.

After the Jin dynasty lost control of the north in 317 ce, there followed a time of fragmentation and warfare as many of the non-Han peoples who had moved into China established a series of ephemeral kingdoms known as the Sixteen Kingdoms. The Tuoba (Turco-Mongolian Tabgach), a group of the Xianbei people, were able to defeat all their rivals and united northern China, establishing the Northern Wei dynasty in 386 ce. Their first capital was far to the north, at Shenglo (in present-day Inner Mongolia); in 398 ce, they moved it to Pingcheng (present-day Datong, Shaanxi) and finally in 494 to Luoyang, where it remained until the end of the dynasty in 535.

Yuan Jia, prince of Guangyang, the donor of the embroidery, has a biography in the *Wei Shu*, the standard history of the period. He had a distinguished career, at one point serving as co-regent for a young emperor. His biography mentions that he and other princes would accompany the emperor, eating and drinking the whole night, thoroughly enjoying themselves. Yuan Jia liked to drink wine and became drunk and boisterous in the presence of the emperor but was forgiven because he was an elder of the royal family. The emperor even condescended to visit him at his home, a great honor. Yuan Jia loved pomp, and his carriage and clothing were unusually splendid. It was said that in processions he carried himself so well that he elicited admiration from the onlookers. He was also praised for promoting the careers of those whose talents were still unrecognized.

Other than empresses, women are only very rarely mentioned in these official histories, but Yuan Jia's wife, who may be the Puxian included in the embroidery fragment, came from a high family and is said to have been extremely intelligent, supportive, and successful in advancing the fortunes of the family. They had a son, Yuan Shen, who may be the person whose boots can be seen standing behind the prince. Shen became an important general and governor but lost his life in the disturbances and rebellions that marked the end of the Northern Wei dynasty.

The clothing that we see depicted on this banner is that of the Xianbei elite. The women behind the nun wear tall purplish-brown caps with ribbons and long narrow-sleeved robes fastened down the center and ornamented with peach and honeysuckle patterns, with a long skirt below the coat, all of this in a range of colors (fig. A). The first woman is labeled as the mother of the prince, the second

Fig. B. Female Xianbei donor figures in Cave 11 of Yungang (*top*), on the east and west sides of the light window (after *Yungang* 1977, no. 63)

Fig. C. Male Xianbei worshiper holding a lotus flower (*above left*) in Cave 78 of Maijishan (after *Maijishan* 1998, pls. 12, 13)

Fig. D. Female banqueters wearing robes with a pattern of inverted hearts or leaf shapes (*above right*), on wall painting, Balalyk Tepe, southern Uzbekistan, fifth–sixth century (after Al'baum 1960, fig. 109)

is his wife, and the third and fourth are daughters. The men, whose figures are not as well preserved, also wear tall headdresses, coming down in the back to cover the neck, and like the women, a long narrow-sleeved robe, fastened in front, but with trousers and boots below. The men's hats have smooth rounded tops; in contrast the women's have an indentation in the center creating two bumps, a distinction also observed on the lacquered coffin (no.16d).

Both the men and women are wearing clothing characteristic of the Xianbei before the emperor Xiaowen decreed a change to Chinese-style apparel, particularly at court and among the elite, after the capital was moved to Luoyang in 494. This style of dress can be found in north China at the Buddhist cave temples of Yungang near Pingcheng and at Maijishan near Tianshui as well as painted on the lacquered coffin fragments excavated from a tomb near Guyuan, Ningxia. Yungang's Cave 11 has two rows of female Xianbei donor figures on the east and west sides of the light window (fig. B) others appear on Cave 18's east wall.[2] In Maijishan's earliest known cave, Cave 78, two rows of worshipers holding lotus flowers decorate the painted base of the Buddha's dais (fig. C).[3] Several scenes from the lacquered coffin (nos.16a–d) depict Xianbei clothing, including the scene showing the deceased drinking while seated on a Chinese-style platform, in a pavilion flanked by male and female attendants (no. 16b) and scenes depicting the filial piety stories of Shun (no. 16d).

The long robes worn by the women donors show a distinctive peach-shaped honeysuckle textile pattern described in the excavation report. Examples of this pattern can apparently be found among the early Northern Wei caves in Dunhuang but also appear in a slightly simplified version as a Sogdian textile motif in a wall painting of the fifth to sixth century from Balalyk Tepe (in present-day southern Uzbekistan) (fig. D).[4] As discussed in the lacquered coffin entry (no. 16a–d), textiles from Central Asia and farther west, easily portable luxury items, may well have been one of the main sources that enriched the decorative vocabulary of the Buddhist and traditional non-Buddhist arts of China.

The surviving section of the banner fragment's border is composed of a series of roundels linked by rows of contiguous beaded hexagons, with floral stems and vines filling the interstices. Similar decorative borders, in varying degrees of complexity, embellish other cave temples of this period as well as other Dunhuang caves and also appear on the lacquered coffin, in the closest parallel (no. 16c). In a more complex version, the circles become roundels with beaded borders connected by beaded hexagons. More densely packed floral motifs as well as plump, putti-like figures, dragons, and human-headed birds fill the spaces between roundels. The colors of the embroidery, applied to a light yellow silk, are green, purple, and blue. Other than at the border, the stitches are so closely made that they completely cover the cloth.

The official histories rarely mention Buddhism, and Yuan Jia's biography is no exception. It is doubtful that Yuan Jia himself visited Dunhuang to present this piece. More likely, this was made as an offering and carried to Dunhuang by an emissary. Chinese scholars propose that this banner was brought from the Northern Wei capital of Pingcheng, possibly by a monk, to hang inside one of the Dunhuang cave temples.[5] At the time, banners were hung in temples as offerings to be used by monks in their teaching.[6] Yuan Jia's religious dedication is mentioned in a Buddhist source that tells of his having read all the sutras three times, of his having dedicated a temple, and of his having had fifteen chapters of sutras copied out, all activities by which one accrues religious merit. This banner is further evidence of his Buddhist faith.

ALJ and AED

1. *Wenwu* 1972.2, pp. 54–60, pl. 11, 12; a copy of the coffin and the paintings were exhibited in Zagreb, see *Put Svile* 1999, pp. 197–98.

2. *Yungang* 1977, no. 63 (Cave 11); and Mizuno and Nagahiro 1952–56, vol.10, pl. 31.

3. *Maijishan* 1998, pls. 11–13. p. 230, no. 11. When the layers of accretions from later dynasties were removed in 1965, these very important early donor paintings were uncovered.

4. *Wenwu* 1972.2, p. 56, figs. 2:2, 3 (Dunhuang Caves 251, 260); Frumkin 1970, p. 118, fig. 28; p. 120, fig. 29.

5. According to Luo Feng in his article on the Guyuan lacquered coffin, there is general agreement that the embroidery was brought from Pingcheng in Shanxi. This idea is further supported by the fact that this style of dress is not found on figures in wall paintings at Dunhuang. See Luo 1990, p. 26.

6. *Wenwu* 1972.2, p. 58.

46. *Section of* Faju Jing *(Dhammapada Sutra)*

Before 368 CE

Discovered in 1900 at Dunhuang, Cave 17, Gansu

Height: 24.9 cm; length: 135 cm

Handscroll, ink on paper

Gansu Provincial Museum, Lanzhou

This scroll is one of the earliest dated manuscripts among the hoard of paintings, banners, and sutras found in Cave 17 at Dunhuang and is thus of great significance for the study of the early history of Buddhist texts in China. It is also one of the earliest handscrolls in existence and provides important evidence for the style of calligraphy current during the fourth century.

The text of the scroll comprises two chapters of the *Faju Jing* (Expressions of the Law). The first column entitles the first of these chapters "Daoxing (Way of Virtue), chapter 38 in 28 sections." The second, entitled "Nihuan (Nirvana), chapter 39 in 25 sections, " begins at the thirtieth column (identifiable by the smaller-scale calligraphy and the blank space in the lower half). These chapters correspond closely to chapters 28 and 36 of the *Faju Jing* as it has survived in the Buddhist Tripitaka.[1]

At the end of a scroll, a faintly visible colophon (two columns after the end of the sutra) inscribed by the Buddhist novice (*sramanera*) Jingming, states that the text was recited intensively by him during the twelfth year of the *shengping* reign period, a date equivalent to 368. Another, more visible colophon (see detail), also inscribed by Jingming, refers to a subsequent recitation on the twentieth day of the tenth month of the third year of the *xian'an* reign period, a year equivalent to 373. It is unlikely that Jingming himself transcribed the sutra, since the calligraphy of the colophons is noticeably different from that of the sutra itself. The scroll itself could therefore be a few decades earlier than 368.

The existence of this scroll and the two colophons supports the belief of scholars that the *Faju Jing* in its various revisions enjoyed wide popularity in China at this time.[2] The *Faju Jing* is a composite work derived mainly from the *Dhammapada* (Way of Righteousness), a collection of ethical verses that form part of the canon of Hinayana Buddhism and which exists in Pali (*Dhammapada*), Sanskrit (*Dharmapada*), and other versions. The central portions of the *Faju Jing* (chapters 9–32 and 34–35) correspond in their titles, sequence, and content to the twenty-six chapters of the Pali *Dhammapada*. The other thirteen chapters (including the two in this scroll) and additional stanzas added at the end of each chapter derive mainly from the Sanskrit *Dharmapada* known as the *Udānavarga*.

The transmission of the *Dhammapada* into Central Asia seems to have begun early. A manuscript of the *Dhammapada* in the Ganhara Prakrit language dating to the first or second century was found at Khotan in Xinjiang.[3] According to the preface of the *Faju Jing*, a version of the *Dhamma-*

pada comprising five hundred verses was brought from India to Wuchang, China, in 224 by a monk of Indian origin, Weqinan, who translated it with another Indian monk, Zhu Jiangyan. Mention is also made of a third monk, Qian, as redactor. Qian should probably be identified with the famous Indo-Scythian *upasaka* Zhi Qian who was probably the anonymous author of the preface, revised the text, and built up the new framework by adding the thirteen chapters. The preface mentions three other *Dhammapada* recensions familiar to the redactor containing nine hundred, seven hundred, and five hundred verses respectively. The preface also indicates that another Chinese version transmitted by a certain Ge, probably the well-known monk Tanguo, was in existence, but this earlier version has not survived.[4]

Paper had been invented by the early Han dynasty, but it was not until the third century that it replaced bamboo or wooden strips as the primary vehicle for texts. This shift was coincident with the gradual replacement of *lishu* (clerk script) by *kaishu* (regular script). The calligraphy of this manuscript is transitional between the two. The square proportions are typical of *kaishu*, but the emphasis on horizontal axes and on broad flourishes is characteristic of *lishu*. It is particularly noticeable that there is no attempt to hide the point of the brush, as was to become the norm in *kaishu*. It is not certain where this transcription of the *Faju Jing* was executed. It is possible that it was done at the capital of the Liang dynasty at Guzang (present-day Wuwei) and only later brought to Dunhuang. At any rate, the scroll was already more than six hundred years old when it was consigned to Cave 17 at Dunhuang.[5]

ZG

1. *Faju Jing* Compare with the revision of the *Faju Jing* in the Taisho edition, vol. 4, p. 201.

2. Levi 1912, pp. 203–94.

3. For a study of this manuscript, see Brough 1962.

4. A number of recensions of the *Dhammapada* and the *Udanavara* have survived in the Chinese Buddhist canon (the *Faju Piyu Jing, Chuyao Jing,* and *Faji Yaosong Jing*), but these are all later than the *Faju Jing*.

5. Cave 17 is believed to have been sealed off about 1035.

47. Seated Buddha with parasol

Sixteen Kingdoms, Western Qin dynasty (365–431), dated to 430–431
Found at Yudou, Jingchuan County, eastern Gansu
Gilt bronze
Total height: 19 cm
Jingchuan County Museum, Gansu

Fig. A. Seated gilt-bronze Buddha with parasol (*top*), latter half of fourth–early fifth century, excavated from a cemetery at Beisongcun village, eastern outskirts of Shijiazhuang (Hebei) (after Akiyama 1969, p. 185, no. 187)

Fig. B. Seated gilt-bronze Buddha (*above*), latter half of the fourth–beginning of the fifth century; found in Baoding area (Hebei) (after *Wenwu* 1998.7, colorpl. I, no. 1)

Without question, the vast majority of Buddhist bronzes cast from about the fourth to the seventh century have been lost. What has survived in China are groups of smaller images, most likely from home altars and private shrines, which could easily be hidden or carried. The dominant type depicts a single figure of a Buddha or bodhisattva, often identified by inscription. Most of the sculptures were gilded to suggest the radiance of the Buddha's visible body.

This elegant gilt image belongs to a well-known type among the surviving early bronzes dating from the fourth and fifth centuries. All share the same basic stylistic and iconographic configuration: a Buddha seated in a cross-legged meditation posture on a high, square lion throne with hands held in an unorthodox version of the meditation (*dhyana*) mudra. Covering both shoulders in typical Gandharan fashion, the robe falls across the body in symmetrical and rhythmic folds much like the pleated robe ends that fan out over the forearms. A round lappet covers the feet. Although the robe and disproportionately large head, bent slightly forward, along with the high *ushnisha*, display Gandharan origins, the strong overall pattern of the abstract drapery folds, coupled with the insistent symmetry of the entire image, reflects Chinese adaptation.

A large, separate parasol protects the seated Buddha. In many cultures, parasols, umbrellas, or canopies have traditionally been emblems of status, elevated rank, or authority. Certainly in China, processions of high officials were often accompanied by servants holding parasols. In Buddhism, however, the precious parasol is one of the eight sacred symbols associated with the Buddha and offers protection from evil.

Many of these images have holes or lugs attached to the back, indicating that other parts such as the aureole were cast separately and attached, although few have survived. Happily, in addition to the Buddha itself and the separately cast lion throne, three other attachments remain: a four-legged dais, an aureole, and the parasol, all of which neatly assemble. A lug on the back of the image fits into the socket in the aureole and is secured in place by the handle of the parasol. On each side of the Buddha is a small hole that pierces the dais, suggesting that a pair of small bodhisattvas or monks could have been inserted. The tiny holes around the edge of the parasol probably held hanging beads or teardrop-shaped bits of bronze, like those preserved on the example from Shijiazhuang cited below.[1]

Similar but somewhat more elaborate images were excavated from a tomb at Beisongcun village, on the eastern outskirts of Shijiazhuang, Hebei (fig. A). In one of these examples, the parts became detached; another intact figure came from the Baoding area of Hebei (fig. B).[2] Both the Shijiazhuang and Baoding Buddhas are apparently so close in detail that Chinese scholars from the Hebei Province Research Institute believe that both images were cast in the same place or possibly even from the same mold.[3] The Shijiazhuang Buddha not only has a parasol with hanging petals or possibly beads still attached but also is flanked by two monks or two *apsaras* on the aureole. The examples excavated from Hebei share two distinctive features with this bronze Buddha unearthed in the Jingchuan District of Gansu. First, all the eyes have been depicted with a "double lid," which is not commonly seen but also appears on the 338 CE Buddha in the Asian Art Museum of San Francisco.[4] Second, the pleated folds of the robe fall down the shoulder and upper arms in wedge-shaped jagged silhouette. This distinctive fold can be found on images from the Butkara I in the Swat Valley, Afghanistan, and seems to have been widely adopted for small Chinese bronze sculpture of the late fourth and early fifth centuries.[5] This second feature is definitely found on images from the Hebei

1. Published in Li Jingjie, *Kaogu* 1995.5, pl. 7, no. 2; *Sichou* 1994, Gansu Provincial Museum, no. 97; *Wenwu ziliao congcan* 1983.3, pp. 74–76. This image and the Shijiazhuang images as well as others indicate that many of these small gilt-bronze figures were quite elaborate with parasols and beaded tassels.

2. See Akiyama and Matsubara 1969, vol. II, pp. 185–86, figs. 187, 188. A third image (fig. 189) considered slightly later in date, early to mid-fifth century, was also unearthed in Hebei, a region in which the manufacture of gilt bronzes flourished from the fourth century CE into the Tang.

3. *Wenwu* 1998.7, pp. 67–68.

4. d'Argence 1974, no. 19, pp. 64–65. Marylin Rhie has suggested that "it may be a local version and/or of limited duration" (Rhie 1995, p. 92).

5. Rhie 1995, pp. 442–43.

6. Akiyama and Matsubara 1969, vol. II, p. 239, no. 189.

7. See *Wenwu ziliao congcan* 1983.3, p. 76.

area; according to Akiyama, Hebei was a region in which the manufacture of gilt-bronze Buddhas flourished from the fourth century to the Tang.[6] This image was found in a cache burial with some bronze vessels, bronze bells, and a gilt-bronze seal. On the basis of the seal, the burial has been dated to 430 to 431, just before the destruction of the Western Qin, one of the Sixteen Kingdoms. It is very possible that this image was cast in Hebei and perhaps carried to eastern Gansu by a monk, merchant, or pilgrim.[7]

ALJ

48. *Miniature stupa or scripture stupa* (jingta)

Northern Liang dynasty (398–439), dated by inscription to 428

Found Jiuquan District, Gansu

Dark gray limestone with incised line drawing, Chinese text, and low-relief sculpture

Height: 44.6 cm

Gansu Provincial Museum, Lanzhou

Fourteen scripture stupas, also called sutra pillars (*jingta*), have been discovered so far in the Gansu corridor and in the Turfan District of Xinjiang; most are housed in the collections of the Gansu Provincial Museum and of the Dunhuang, the Jiuquan, and the Wuwei Municipal Museums. Two from the Turfan District remain in Berlin's Museum für Indische Kunst.[1] Of the fourteen, seven have dates ranging from 426 to 436, and nine bear names of the lay Buddhist donors who commissioned them. All but two were made under the Northern Liang dynasty (398–439) during the thirty-year rule of Juqu Mengxun, an ardent Buddhist who also admired traditional Chinese culture. Probably votive in function, most scripture stupas have been found at sites of former temples; this kind of scripture stupa is found only in Gansu and Turfan and is not known in north-central China.[2] The type disappears from Gansu after the Northern Liang but survives briefly in Turfan with the remnant of that dynasty.

Commissioned by Gao Shanmu and dated to 428, this votive stupa, originally found in Jiuquan, is one of the best preserved, with both the architectural form and the clarity of the carved imagery

1. Of the fourteen scripture stupas, five were from the Dunhuang District, including the earliest one from 426; and six are from Jiuquan District. Two from the Turfan district were originally found in the ancient city of Qoco (Khocho) by the German expeditions of Grunwedel and Von Le Coq (1902–5) and are now in Berlin's Museum für Indische Kunst. Turfan was the last refuge of the remnants of the Northern Liang regime that managed to escape westward after the dynasty fell in 439 and retained control of this eastern Turfan Depression until 460. The last one of unknown provenance remains in the Wuwei Municipal Museum. See Yin 1997a, pp. 84–94; *Sichou* 1994, p. 94; Soper 1958, pp. 131–64. This sutra pillar or votive stupa has been widely researched, interpreted, and published by both Western and Chinese scholars. Many of the publications are included in the notes, but additional sources appear in the bibliography.

2. *Wenwu* 1977.1, p. 185.

3. *Sichou* 1994, p. 94. Below the sutra passage on the base, an inscription reads: "This pagoda of the enlightened Sakyamuni was erected by Gao Shanmu in honour of his parents on the first year of the Chen Xuan (428 CE).

4. Wang 1999, p. 85.

5. Although there are only six Buddhas and the capitals on the colonnets differ, Gao Shanmu's seven seated Buddhas are reminiscent of the wooden lintel with four complete and two partial Buddha niches from Loulan about the third century CE. See Rhie 1999, fig. 5.55.

6. Abe 1990, pp. 1–31. Abe does a thorough analysis of Dunhuang, Cave 254, the most completely preserved fifth-century cave, and the Sakyamuni Buddha/Maitreya bodhisattva theme and its parallels to the Central Asia site of Kizil, Cave 80. Other early caves at Dunhuang also reflect this theme; Caves 251, 253, 257, 259, as well as Yungang, at Datong, Shanxi.

7. The cosmology on this sutra pillar closely resembles the traditional Chinese cosmological model of the universe, often depicted in other media on the *shi*, or cosmic board, incorporating a larger square (symbol of earth) with a smaller circle in the center (symbol of heaven), four heavenly gates, twelve months, Heavenly stems, and Earthly branches, Twenty-eight Lunar Mansions, and the central Big Dipper. One such cosmic board, made of lacquered wood, was excavated from a later Han (25–220 CE) tomb in Wuwei (ancient Guzang), Gansu; *Wenwu* 1972.12, p. 15, fig. 8; Wang 1999, pp. 82–87.

8. *Dunhuang* 1981, pls. 6–17.

9. *Yungang* 1977, figs. 33–35.

10. Rowland 1960, p. 40, fig. 14.

11. Zwalf 1985, no. 273.

12. Giles 1956, p. 4.

13. Soper 1958, pp. 147–48. Apparently King Mengxun sent an envoy to the capital of the Chinese Song dynasty in Nanjing in 426 to ask for a copy of the divination classic.

14. *Sichou* 1994, p. 94, and Yin 1997b, pp. 81–89.

15. Wang 1999, pp. 70–91. Wang discusses this combination of Chinese and Buddhist cosmological systems as expressed on the Northern Liang miniature stupas. This combination may be connected to the development of the Sino-Japanese mandala of the Two Worlds. In *Japanese Mandalas, Representations of Sacred Geography,* Elizabeth ten Grotenhuis points to the possible link between Chinese pre-Buddhist concepts of sacred geography and the cosmological system of the five elements (diagrammatic form) as possible sources for the concept and iconography of the Two-World mandala, ten Grotenhuis, pp. 53–57.

and calligraphy essentially intact.[3] Composed of four discrete tiers, the stupa sits on an octagonal faceted base bearing a frieze of adoring deities described by fine incised lines (fig. A). These haloed deities display two distinct styles of dress: one group of four, with feet apart in a lunging stance, have bare torsos with short dhoti-style skirts reaching mid-thigh; the other four have floor-length skirts and tight, long-sleeved, hip-length jackets. All eight are further embellished with long, narrow scarves that arch behind their haloed heads, then swing forward to pass around their arms at the elbows before flaring out into two-pronged ends. Each deity also presents an offering; these include the flaming jewel or lotus pearl raised in both hands above the right shoulder. Just above the left shoulder of each deity is incised a trigram from the ancient Chinese classic, *Yi Jing* (Book of Changes).

The octagonal base supports the second tier, a circular column engraved with vertical lines of carefully written Chinese characters, which quote a sutra passage from the Buddhist *Ekottaragama Sutra* (Book of Gradual Sayings). The same passage is carved onto all fourteen Northern Liang stupas; the complete sutra was translated into Chinese by Sanghadeva during the Eastern Jin (317–420) and preaches the endless chain of causality in life with only transcendence of the cycle ending all the care and anxiety.[4] In a third tier, above the carved sutra passage, sit seven meditating Buddhas and one cross-ankled Maitreya, or future Buddha (see detail), in eight arched niches, separated by colonnets.[5] This iconographic configuration, the seven Buddhas of the past including the Historic Buddha, Sakyamuni, juxtaposed with the Buddha of the Future, Maitreya, is popular on small stone stelae and bronze images (nos. 54, 55) in early Buddhist art of the northwest and north China. On a larger scale, the themes of Sakyamuni Buddha, including depictions of events in his life and *jataka* tales of his previous lives, join with celestial imagery of Tusita Heaven and Maitreya Bodhisattva to influence the iconographic program of painting and decoration in fifth-century caves in Gansu.[6]

This third tier is clearly the focal point of the sutra pillar, separated from the script below by a curved ledge and from the top by a collar of eight large lotus petals. The conical top, composed of seven horizontal raised bands and divided by undercut recesses, is capped with a rounded disc incised with the Big Dipper constellation filled in with gold leaf.[7] This conical top reflects a simplified translation of an Indian *chattravali*, a pinnacle formed by a mast supporting multiple tapering umbrellas, an important iconographic feature that rises from the tops of Indian stupas.

no. 48 (detail)

Stylistically, the worshipful deities on the lowest tier, with their looping, pronged scarves and lung-ing stance, point to the development of the Northern Liang figural style, which is also visible in the early caves at Dunhuang, in particular Caves 268, 272, and 275.[8] Echoes of this style are also visible in the early Northern Wei sculptures in Cave 7 at Yungang, undoubtedly reflecting the transfer of the Liang population, including Buddhist monks, from Gansu to the Northern Wei capital near Yungang.[9]

These sutra pillars exemplify the strategic geographic position of the Northern Liang dynasty, controlling the Gansu corridor and access to the West. The figural style of the adoring deities and the Buddhas reflects crosscurrents of influence that ultimately derived from several sources, Gandhara, Mathura, and Central Asia before reaching Gansu. The multitiered form and decorative details of the sutra pillar reveal strong connections to miniature stone stupas from Gandhara, such as the slate stupa from Loriyan Tangai, second to third century (fig. D).[10] Judging from these miniature versions, Gand-haran stupas typically emphasized the *chattravali*, the slender pinnacle formed by a stack of evenly spaced flat rings tapering to a point. These Gansu and Turfan sutra pillars may resemble stupas or stu-palike wooden posts that have been found in Loulan, Central Asia (fig. B).[11] In the account of his pil-grimage to India, Faxian, the famous Chinese monk, mentions a cult of stupas in Central Asia.[12]

In addition to Western influences, there are unquestionable Chinese elements visible on this pil-lar as well as on the others, notably the eight trigrams incised above the left shoulder of the deities in the bottom frieze. Their presence can at least partially be explained by the Northern Liang ruler Mengxun's passion for traditional Chinese scholarship, particularly the *Book of Changes,* which is repeatedly mentioned in the literary evidence about Northern Liang.[13] Some Chinese scholars asso-ciate the second distinctly Chinese feature, the Big Dipper constellation incised on the very top of the pillar, with the Daoist teaching of *fengshui,* or geomancy. Others propose that the alignment of the trigrams reflects creation, spring, and dawn, passing through to winter and the final days, and beyond to the new world, rebirth, and the future Buddha, Maitreya.[14] The incorporation of this ancient Chinese cosmological system into the Buddhist system reflects the complex process of adap-tation, a way for early-fifth-century China to gain deeper understanding of Buddhist teachings and perhaps the reverse.[15]

ALJ

Fig. A. Ink rubbing from this stupa (*opposite left*), showing the four discrete tiers of the carving (courtesy of the Gansu Provincial Museum, Lanzhou)

Fig. B. Miniature wooden stupa from Loulan (Xinjiang) (*oppo-site right*) (after Stein 1921, vol. 3, pl. 32)

Fig. C. Small clay cross-legged bodhisattva (*above center*) from a nimbus from Rawak, north-east of Khotan (Xinjiang), dated c. third century CE (after Stein 1907, pl. LXXXVII, R.Ixxiv.) a possible source for the cross-ankled maitreya carved on this sutra pillow—compare with detail of no. 48 (*top left*).

Fig. D. Miniature stupa from Loriyan Tangai, Gandhara (*above right*), second–third century CE, in the Indian Museum, Calcutta (after Rowland 1960, p. 40, fig. 14)

49. *Head of Buddha*

Northern Liang (401–439) or possibly early Northern Wei dynasty (386–535),
mid- to late fifth century
From Jintasi Cave temple, in Matishan area, Zhangye;
probably from Eastern Cave, central pillar
Painted red clay with white, red, and black pigments
Height:16.5 cm; width: 11.5 cm
Gansu Provincial Museum, Lanzhou

Lacking the identifying iconographic attributes, the rounded bump on the head (*ushnisha*), and elongated ear lobes, this head of Buddha originally belonged to a small image on the central pillar in the
Eastern Cave at Jintasi Temple site (fig. A). Jintasi (Golden Stupa Temple), in the Matisishan area,
is located about sixty miles southeast of the city of Zhangye, one of the original Han garrisons in
Gansu and later an important trading center.[1]

Carved into coarse red sandstone cliffs, this site sits in splendid isolation at three-thousand
meters tucked into the Qilian Mountain range. Two hundred steps hewn from the face of the cliff
rise to a ledge that offers an unparalleled view of the snow-capped mountains and the Eastern and
Western Caves. Both caves have a central pillar-style configuration: a large, square column of rock,
rising from floor to ceiling, has been left in the center of the cave and decorated with relief carving

Fig. A. A small Buddha (*below*)
on the central pillar of the
Eastern Cave at Jintasi Temple
(after *Hexi* 1987, pl. 57)

and painting. This formation can be found in the fifth- and sixth-century caves at sites across north China, such as Yungang and Tianlongshan in Shanxi, Gongxian in Henan, and Wenshushan, Matisi, Tiantishan, and Dunhuang in Gansu, as well as in Central Asia, at Kizil in Xinjiang.[2]

Central pillars are equated with the Indian stupa, a funerary monument that marked the burial of the relics of the historic Buddha and also became an iconographic symbol of Buddhism and its universe. Stupas can be either free standing or carved inside a worship cave, known in India as a *chaitya* hall. The ritual of circumambulation is usually performed around a stupa or central pillar with the devotee circling on foot in a clockwise direction, keeping the right side toward the sacred shrine, an act that bestows merit. Although there are few references to circumambulation in Chinese sutras or in Chinese biographies of monks, this ritual was probably one of several associated with the central pillar.[3]

In Jintasi's Eastern and Western Caves, the central pillars literally teem with large and small sculptures rising up the column in three tiers on all four sides. In the Eastern Cave, a large Buddha image fills the main niche on each side of the central pillar on the bottom tier; one bodhisattva stands on the ledge at the base of the pillar on either side of the main niche. Two unusual small Buddhas with heads like the one shown here perch between the Buddha's mandorla and the bodhisattvas' halos. Since the small Buddhas on the western face of the pillar remain intact, this head would have come from one of the small Buddhas on the other three faces.[4] The exaggeration of the iconographic attributes; the high, rounded *ushnisha;* and the large, very elongated, wide ears make these heads distinctive, as does the atypical treatment of the robes. To the right of the main image, the small Buddha seems to be leaning forward, feet together and arms outstretched beseechingly, while the robe, which covers both shoulders, billows out behind and against the body as if a stiff breeze is blowing.[5] The small Buddha to the left sits on a high rounded seat in the *siwei* posture with the left leg pendant and the right foot resting on the left knee. This would be the earliest representation known to date of this *siwei* posture, which became very popular in sixth-century China and eventually in Japan.[6]

A hint of a smile lies on the slightly pursed red lips, and the half-closed eyes are painted as black half moons below the high, arched brows on this round face. The Buddha's expression conveys a self-absorbed and blissfully rapturous state, an expression shared by most of the sculpture in this cave.[7] Similar styles of faces can be found on the remains of Buddhist sculpture from the third- to-fourth-century Buddhist monastery at Miran, with some resonance from Karadong images as well.[8]

In the broadest context, the general style at Jintasi is consistent with other early fifth-century sites, such as Tiantishan and Wenshushan.[9] This early site, like others in Gansu, manifests complex iconographic configurations and rich styles that reflect the mingling of Indian and Central Asian sources flowing into the Gansu corridor at this time, posing a challenge for Buddhist scholars to unravel.

ALJ

1. Photographs of this site are available in *Hexi* 1987, figs. 4–100, and Zhang 1994, pp. 28–41.

2. The eminent Chinese Buddhist scholar Su Bai has identified the central pillar-style cave as a principal feature of a Liangzhou-type cave under the Northern Liang dynasty; see *Kaogu xuebao* 1986.4, pp. 435–45. The initial ideas presented in this article have never been fully developed (*Kecier* 1989, vol. 1, pp. 10–23).

3. Abe 1990, p. 5.

4. *Hexi* 1987, p. 5, fig. 4.

5. Ibid., fig. 5. The description of these small Buddhas on the right side notes the highly unusual treatment of the robes, in which the cloth moves freely, like silk. The way this image has been made is rarely seen in stone cave temples.

6. This posture had come to be associated with the Maitreya but actually can refer to all bodhisattvas who are Buddhas-to-be waiting to come down to earth. Leidy 1989.

7. Some of the characteristics, large ears, and finely shaped nose, and lips, evident in Jintasi's eastern cave are echoed by the colossus in Yungang's Cave 20, see *Yungang* 1977, figs. 92, 93.

8. Stein 1921, MII, fig. 121; Rhie 1999, fig. 5.44; Debaine-Francfort, Idriss, and Wang 1994, pp. 34–52 ; Idries and Zhang 1997, pp. 39–42.

9. Rhie 1999, p. 108.

50a. *Small Buddha*

Northern Wei dynasty (386–535), late fifth–sixth century
Dunhuang, Mogao Caves, from a central pillar
Unbaked clay mixed with organic matter (straw) and painted pink, black, and blue
Total height: 23.8 cm; width: 15.5 cm
Gansu Provincial Museum, Lanzhou

The following entry (no. 51a) includes additional discussion of these molded bodhisattvas and Buddha images affixed to the central stupa pillars at the Dunhuang Caves. The walls of the earliest caves at Dunhuang, Caves 268 and 275, as well as later caves from the Northern Wei through to the Tang (fifth–eighth century), are often painted with a grid filled with repeated images of small seated Buddhas, referred to as the "Thousand Buddhas."[1] This Buddha is unusual, in that far fewer caves place small Buddhas in relief on the central pillar; most central pillars are decorated with kneeling bodhisattvas.

All these Buddhas recall the small early Buddha images (no. 47) that were cast in bronze. Whether painted or made of molded clay, these "Thousand Buddha" images are shown wearing a typical Gandharan-style robe covering both shoulders and looping down the front with drapery ends falling over the forearms and covering the legs. The hands are invariably overlapped in a somewhat unorthodox version of the *dhyana* mudra symbolic hand gesture for meditation. This object has a light red mandorla encircling the entire image, with a halo just behind the Buddha's head. Summary blue brushstrokes emphasize the drapery folds of the white robe. The eyes seem to be painted white, a feature seen on painted "Thousand Buddhas" from Northern Wei through Northern Zhou.[2]

Where this pattern is painted, the wall is often divided into a grid of horizontal and vertical lines with one Buddha filling each square of the grid. To maintain the repetitive and uniform nature of the pattern, a stencil or similar device must have been used.

The "Thousand Buddhas" decorative motif also appears at Yungang Caves 16 to 20 in northern Shanxi. The pattern's appearance at Yungang may show influence from Liangzhou Buddhists who were forced to move to Datong after the Northern Wei conquest of Gansu in 439. Whether painted on the wall, applied in relief, or carved all over the interior and exterior wall, the images concretely symbolize the Buddha's omnipresence through time and space. Scholars have suggested that an important feature of the Buddhist practices in fifth-century Gansu was visualization. Appearing inside caves at Dunhuang, the "Thousand Buddhas" were settings or classrooms for or related to the advanced practice of visualization techniques, involving mental construction of an eidetic image, with the eventual goal of the practitioner learning to visualize a chamber full of Buddhas.[3]

ALJ

1. Cave 259 may have had small "Thousand Buddha" or kneeling bodhisattva relief sculptures originally attached to the central pillar, but this is difficult to determine from the marks remaining on the cave wall; see *Dunhuang* 1981, vol. 1, pl. 20.

2. It is possible this figure came from the Northern Zhou Cave 428, an unusual cave with relief Buddhas forming the "Thousand Buddha" grid on the north and south walls. See *Dunhuang* 1981, vol. 1, pls. 160, 161 (Cave 428). Among the repetitive small Buddhas visible on a fragment of a wall painting from Dunhuang's Cave 263, dating from the Northern Wei, one image shows similarly painted robes, dark blue folds broadly defined on a light blue robe. Ibid., pls. 51, 57 (Cave 263). This fragment is now in the State Hermitage Museum, St. Petersburg; see *Silk Road* 1988, p. 75, no. 68.

3. Abe 1990, p.8; Abe's article discusses visualization as a special characteristic of Buddhism that evolved in the earlier fifth-century practice during the reign of the Liang Kingdoms, particularly Northern Liang, pp. 5–9.

50b. *Small Buddha*

Northern Wei (386–535) to Western Wei dynasty (535–557),
first half of the sixth century
Dunhuang, Mogao Caves, from a central pillar
Unbaked clay mixed with organic matter (straw) and painted pink, black, and blue
Total height: 23.5 cm; width: 15 cm
Dunhuang Research Institute, Gansu

The entries for numbers 50a and 51a include discussions of these molded bodhisattvas and Buddha figures attached to the central stupa pillars in the Dunhuang Caves. In addition to the colors, this example differs from number 50a in two ways: the white face shows the eyebrows, mouth, nose, and eyes, which have pupils painted in black. There are three dark blue dots evenly spaced along the edge of the Buddha's robe. To date, these details are visible elsewhere only on the small Buddhas on the central stupa of the Western Wei Cave 288.[1]

ALJ

1. *Dunhuang* 1981, vol. 1, pl. 108.

1. For examples of central pillars with attached bodhisattvas still remaining, as well as the spots where the images fell off or were removed, see *Dunhuang* 1981, vol. 1, pl. 26, Cave 254; pl. 38, Cave 257; pl. 46, Cave 251; pl. 58, Cave 260; pl. 66, Cave 435; pl. 83, Cave 248.

2. There are several interpretations of the actual hand position and meaning of the *anjali* mudra. See Bunce 1997, p. 12.

3. Soper 1958, p. 145.

4. Rhie 1999, figs. 4.66, 4.68 a–d, 4.77, 4.78a, b.

5. Rhie 1999, p. 313. Rhie dates this part of the Rawak site to late fourth–early fifth century (p. 313).

Fig. A. View of northeast corner of the central pillar (*below*), Dunhuang Cave 251, Northern Wei dynasty (386–535) (after *Dunhuang* 1981, vol. 1, pl. 47)

Fig. B. Fragment of a bodhisattva (*bottom*) from nimbus of standing Buddha from Rawak (after Gropp 1974, fig. 116: B)

51a. *Kneeling bodhisattva holding lotus buds*

Northern Wei dynasty (386–535), late fifth–early sixth century
Dunhuang, Mogao Caves, from a central pillar
Unbaked clay mixed with organic matter (straw) and painted dark green, light green, dark gray
Total height: 33 cm; width: 17.5 cm
Gansu Provincial Museum, Lanzhou

As discussed in the entry for number 49, caves with central stupa pillars, large square columns of stone rising from floor to ceiling, are a distinctive architectural formation that dominates early temple sites along the Gansu corridor during the Northern Liang or early Northern Wei dynasty. At Dunhuang this formation appears in the early Northern Wei caves such as Caves 251, 254, 257, 260, 435, and 248 and persists into the late sixth century. Central stupa pillars, the visual and ritual center of the cave, were covered with stucco as a ground surface, and then richly decorated with paintings and large and small sculptures. Along with two other bodhisattva forms (nos. 51b, 51c), this type of kneeling bodhisattva, lined up in tightly packed rows on all four faces of the central pillar, originally filled the spaces above and around the main images in these caves (fig. A).[1]

In a typical pose, the figure kneels with the right leg up and left bent backward partially tucked under the robe. The arms assume one of the three positions that can be found on the same column. Here, the right arm bends in front of the body holding a lotus bud at the center of the chest, while the other arm raises the lotus bud up alongside the halo near the top of the head. Although only part of number 51c survives, and one arm has been broken off, the remaining left arm similarly holds a lotus bud at the chest. The other figure, number 51b, has both hands pressed together in the center of the chest in the *anjali* mudra, a symbolic hand gesture of prayer or devotion.[2] The third and last

figure raises the lotus bud to the right shoulder using both hands. The garment scarf drapes over the softly rounded body in one of two standard forms of Gandharan-style dress, crossing the body from the right thigh and over the left shoulder, while exposing the right shoulder.[3]

There is little doubt that these figures, produced by the hundreds, were made from molds. They are reminiscent of the small molded bodhisattvas and Buddhas, mostly surviving as fragments, affixed to the nimbus of standing Buddha images from Rawak, a site northeast of Khotan.[4] Enclosed by a simple halo, the head of number 51a recalls a fragment of molded bodhisattva head from Rawak (fig. B).[5]

ALJ

51b. *Kneeling bodhisattva*

1. Rowland 1934, p. 23, fig. 1.

Northern Wei dynasty (386–535),
late fifth–early sixth century
Dunhuang, Mogao Caves, from a central pillar
Unbaked clay mixed with organic matter (straw)
and painted dark green, light green, and pink
Total height: 24.5 cm; width: 12.5 cm
Dunhuang Research Institute, Gansu

Please see the discussion in the entry for number 51a of these molded bodhisattva figures attached to the central stupa pillars in the Dunhuang Caves. In Gandharan fashion, the bodhisattva's garment scarf covers both shoulders and the hands are held in the *anjali* mudra. An almost identical figure from the central pillar in Dunhuang Cave 257 is at Harvard University.[1]

ALJ

51c. *Fragment of kneeling bodhisattva*

Northern Wei dynasty (386–535), late fifth–early sixth century
Dunhuang, Mogao Caves, from a central pillar
Unbaked clay mixed with organic matter (straw) and painted pink, black, and blue
Total height: 22 cm; width: 10 cm
Dunhuang Research Institute, Gansu

Please see the discussion in the entry for number 51a of these molded bodhisattva figures attached to the central stupa pillars in the Dunhuang Caves. In contrast to numbers 51a and 51b, the face of this bodhisattva has painted features, half-lidded eyes in black, tiny red lips, and bright blue hair. A wooden stick was added to the back to stabilize the sculpture.

ALJ

52. *Five-stone pagoda* (ta)

Northern Wei dynasty (386–535), late fifth–early sixth century
Zhuanglang county, Eastern Gansu
Beige sandstone with relief carving
Total height: 217 cm; height of each stone ranges from: 32.6–52 cm; width: 31–43 cm
Gansu Provincial Museum, Lanzhou

(below, left to right)

Fig. A. Three-tier Western Wei Stone pagoda dated 536 found in Qinan county, Eastern Gansu (after *Sichou* 1994, no. 103)

Fig. B. Stone pagodas carved on face of cliff, late Northern Wei Xiwo stone caves, in Xinan district, western area, Henan (after *Wenwu* 1997.10, p. 66, fig. 3)

Fig. C. Drawing of hipped roof pagoda painted on wall in Dunhuang Mogao, Cave 254 (after *Kaogu* 1976.2, p. 114, fig. 7.4)

In Chinese, the character *ta*, translated as "pagoda," refers to a tall square multistoried tower with Chinese-style tiled roofs, which inherited most of the functions of the Indian stupa, so central to early Buddhist practice. Buddhist texts refer to the stupa as a burial monument, usually an egg-shaped mound, designed to contain relics, either human remains or objects once connected to the deceased.[1] Over time, this distinctive architectural and iconographic symbol of the Buddhist faith has acquired multiple layers of meaning. Beginning as a burial mound containing relics of the historical Buddha Sakyamuni, the stupa subsequently became a structure used to commemorate sacred places, to house objects for worship, and to embody cosmological reflections of the Buddhist universe. The simple mound evolved into more elaborate structures with hemispherical domes, described in modern Chinese as "overturned rice bowls," which contained *sarira*. The Great Stupa at Sanchi from the first century CE in central India is one of the earliest and most famous of this type. The stupa spread through Central Asia modifying its shape in response to local practices and traditions.

This pagoda consists of a stack of five trapezoid-shaped stones that narrows from the base as it rises to its peak. Chinese-style tiled roofs, with either a straight roof line (fig. B) or hipped roof ends (fig. C), give the pagoda its unmistakable profile. Originally, this five-tiered stupa probably had Chinese-style straight roofs and had been constructed like another stone pagoda discovered in Gansu at Qin'an and dated by inscription to 536, the beginning of Western Wei (fig. A).[2] This three-tiered pagoda from Qin'an has been assembled from separately carved stones, including a base, three blocks, three roofs, and a top stone. According to Tsu Shibin, the director of the Gansu Provincial Museum, similar roof pieces once existed for the five-tiered pagoda but were too damaged to salvage.

Each face of the five stones portrays stories or legends related to the Buddha or his life, which have been carved into shallow niches. Along with the typical triads depicting a seated or standing Buddha flanked by two bodhisattvas, several faces represent the great events that epitomize the life of the historic Sakaymuni Buddha, his birth and ritual cleansing with water by a hood of *nagas*, serpent kings, his departure from his father's palace, and his

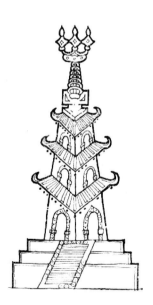

RIGHT: Conversation between the bodhisattva Manjusri and the learned Vimalakirti, on the fourth tier

FAR RIGHT: Resplendent bodhisattva flanked by two monks with *apsaras* flying above, on third tier

OPPOSITE TOP LEFT: Death, or *parinirvana*, of the Buddha with grief-stricken monks in attendance, on fourth tier

OPPOSITE BOTTOM RIGHT: Drawing of the scenes depicted on the four sides of no. 52 (after Dong n.d., p. 36)

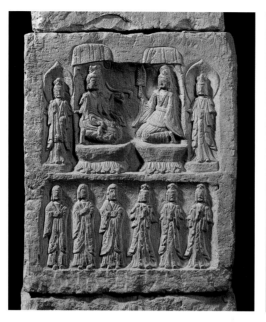

1. De Marco 1957, p. 229. This five-tiered stupa has been published in Dong n.d., pp. 35–39; *Sichou* 1994, no. 102; *Maijishan* 1992, no. 72.

2. The Western Wei stone stupa dated inscription to 563 CE and found in Qin'an County, Eastern Gansu, see *Sichou* 1994, no. 103. At the Yungang Temple site, the interiors of Caves 51 and 52 have central pillars carved in the form of a pagoda, with Chinese-style tiled roofs, columns, and bracketing. In Cave 51, the central pagoda pillar narrows as it rises. Each corner of the central pillar in Cave 6 becomes a tapered pagoda as well; for Caves 2 and 51, see *Yungang* 1977, pls. 5, 106, respectively; for Cave 6, see *Yungang* 1988, p. 12, fig. 47.

3. The Vimalakirti sutra is a philosophic discourse written about the first century CE in which basic Mahayana principles are presented in the form of a conversation between two famous Buddhist figures, Vimalakirti, the humble householder, and Manjusri. This text was translated into Chinese by Kumarajiva in 401 and became immensely popular in China. As Arthur F. Wright observed, this wealthy and powerful aristocrat and respected householder could possess such a pure and disciplined personality that he affected all whom he met for the better, becoming a new model for aristocratic lay Buddhists. Vimalakirti attracted aristocrats who found Buddhist ideals desirable but did not want to renounce their worldly pleasures (Wright 1971, p. 52). The earliest representation of this famous conversation has been found on the walls of Cave 169 at the cave temple of Binglingsi, dated to 420 CE (Dong 1994, pl. 31, p. 8, fig. 12).

death, or *parinirvana*. An iconogaphic configuration, Maitreya plus the seven Buddhas of the Past, which frequently recurs in Gansu and across north China in the fifth and sixth centuries, appears here on one face of the bottom stone. Wearing the characteristic high crown of the Buddha of the Future, Maitreya, flanked by bodhisattvas and monks, is shown seated cross-ankled with the seven Buddhas arranged above and around his head in the mandorla. This configuration is also found on a votive stupa (no. 48), dated to 428, a reddish-brown sandstone stele (no. 54), and a bronze image (no. 55). The scene on the fourth stone depicts the famous conversation between the Bodhisattva of Wisdom, Manjusri (Wenshu), and the wealthy aristocrat and ideal lay buddhist, Vimalakirti, central figures in the influential sutra of the fifth and sixth centuries, the *Vimalakirti-nirdesa*.³ Bodhisattvas with halos flank the conversants, while three monks and three more bodhisattvas line up below to listen.

Other faces of the five stones display a range of interesting stylistic or iconographic features and anomalies. A figure supporting a plate of fire on its head squats between two bodhisattvas. The representation of the infant Buddha in his role as the dragon tamer, *huanlongsi*, visible on the bronze coffin or door ornaments from Guyuan and discussed in the entries for numbers 17a,b and 18a,b is shown here, although with lionlike creatures rather than dragons. One of the most dramatic and effective compositions is the *parinirvana* of the Buddha. Ananda, Sakyamuni's youngest and favorite disciple, sits tenderly holding the Buddha's head while his oldest disciple, Kasyapa, kneels by his feet. The Buddha's horizontal body cuts the composition into two parts. Above are six wailing mourners all with arms raised, wearing garments reflecting Gandharan style. Below, three figures seem to be making noise or playing music. The center figure appears to be shaking and moving as if clanging the bells he holds, while the two kneeling figures wearing dhoti blow rhyton-shaped horns. Finally, a resplendent bodhisattva stands in full glory on the third stone with streaming ribbons, flowing flowers, and flapping *apsaras*. The two monks standing to the right and left are probably Ananda and Kasyapa.

Overall, the pagoda reflects a stylistic eclecticism, with the most dominant aspect being a rather naive and provincial version of the innovative early-sixth-century style of the Northern Wei, discussed in Chapter 4, mixed with Gandharan and Gupta elements. Characteristic of this Northern Wei style are elegantly elongated figures receding behind layers of complex drapery patterns. Here, complex drapery covers figures with less elongation and elegance; they seem almost squat with large, square, somewhat blocky heads sitting on short necks. This early-sixth-century style is often combined with the mid- to late-fifth-century stylistic features particularly visible in the rendering of the *apsaras*, who fly through the heavenly realms above the heads of Buddhas or bodhisattvas. In several scenes, they are shown wearing long dhotis; they have naked chests, squat bodies, and narrow shawls arching over their

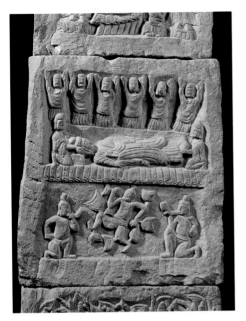

heads and backs recalling the *apsaras* from the early fifth-century Northern Liang cave temples at Jintasi, Gansu, and from the Northern Wei mid- to late-fifth-century Cave 6 at the Yungang Cave temple site near Pingcheng (present-day Datong).[4] Both the mourners and the seated Manjusri and Vimalakirti wear drapery articulated with folds that are a possible variation of the embedded string fold, which can also be found in ivories from Begram, in Gupta Mathura sculpture, in some Gandharan images, and in Swat pieces from Afghanistan.[5]

In China, the earliest representation of this type of multi-storied pagoda occurs on a fragment of clay tile from Baiguo Village just north of Chengdu. The fragment is believed to date from the Han dynasty, late second to third century CE.[6] It shows a three-story tower positioned on a high, square platform; the tower has Chinese-style roofs and a mast rising from the top decorated with three umbrellas and a ball-shaped finial. The tall towerlike pagoda differs markedly from the round domed form of the Indian stupa. The assumption has been that the pagoda evolved from the Indian hemispherical form and that the transformation occurred in Gandhara or Central Asia before the stupa reached China. However, the evolution of the pagoda has yet to be satisfactorily resolved.[7]

According to Buddhist teachings, a pilgrimage to the sacred sites in India associated with the Buddha's life produces merit that will benefit the pilgrim and all of the faithful. However, making this journey was time-consuming, expensive, and very dangerous, as Chinese pilgrims from China often learned. Many never came back; of those who braved the challenge, only 2 percent returned.[8] A more inviting alternative to making the actual journey was to perform devotions in front of images depicting these great events in the Buddha's life. Stupas became ideal monuments to serve as surrogate pilgrimage sites.

Pagodas or stupas were typically incorporated into temples or monastery complexes. Today in China, however, many pagodas of this scale and much larger, often too tall and heavy to even consider moving, now remain isolated monuments in museums or in newly incongruous contexts, dwarfed by tall modern buildings or factory chimneys, forlorn reminders of the grand temples or monasteries that dominated ancient cities and hillsides.[9]

ALJ

4. *Hexi* 1987, colorpls. 13–16; *Yungang* 1977, figs. 32–36 (Cave 6)

5. Rhie 1976, p. 458; Czuma 1985, no. 47, pp. 118–20.

6. This tile fragment with a rubbing of the image has been published by Rhie 1999, vol. 1, fig. 1.34a,b, and discussed on pp. 61–62. For the original Chinese report of the discovery written by Xie 1967, p. 62, as well as subsequent discussions in the same journal, see *Sichuan wenwu* 1992.11, p. 40, and 1993.3, p. 16.

7. According to Nancy Shatzman Steinhardt, when the stupa reached China, the form had already changed, becoming much taller and thinner, still capped with a domed top and finial (see Steinhardt 1998, pp. 41–44). This later more towerlike stupa was adapted into the traditional Chinese architectural system and modeled after the Chinese watchtower. However, Marylin Martin Rhie suggests that there were two architectural traditions originating in India, the hemispherical stupa and another kind of shrine. The pagoda may relate more directly to this tall square or round multi-storied shrine with a square base, railings, and balconies, and a rounded top depicted in second-century Kushan reliefs from Mathura (Rhie 1999, vol. 1, pp. 62–64, figs. 1.35a, b, c, d, e, Kushan Mathura) and 1.36 (Gandhara).

8. Huntington 1987, pt. 1, p. 55.

9. Whitfield 1989, p. 131.

53. *Three-tiered votive pagoda* (ta)

Northern Wei dynasty (386–535), late fifth century, possibly 496

Found in Jiuquan in 1964

Dark gray limestone with relief carving

Carved by Cao Tianhu, attributed to the twentieth year of Taihe, or 496

Height: 38 cm; width: 16 cm

Jiuquan City Museum, Gansu

In contrast to the dark gray miniature limestone votive stupa of Gao Shanmu, dated to 428 or Northern Liang (no. 48), which clearly derives from Gandharan or Central Asian protoypes, this example reflects the Chinese version of a stupa, a multi-storied tower called a pagoda (see no. 52). Carved from one piece of limestone, this miniature square pagoda has three stories divided by Chinese-style tile roofs. Considerable damage was sustained along one edge and at the four corners of each roof, strongly suggesting that these corners were hipped or curved upward (see no. 52, fig. B). The present object stands on a square platform with an inscription by the sculptor Cao Tianhu, repeated on four sides. Reflecting his piety, the inscription describes how the Buddhist believer Cao Tianhu spent all of his savings and carved this stupa.[1]

Characteristic of Buddhist cave-temple architecture of the fifth and sixth centuries, there is a visible blending of Indian and Chinese architectural motifs and details.[2] Each face is divided into three parts, the central or middle section reserved for predominantly single Buddha images sitting crossed-legged in shallow niches with a horseshoe-shaped frame and an imported Indian *chaitya* arch. Some niches have pillars running alongside the arch with U-shaped Chinese brackets at the top to hold up the roof. Flanking the central images are either one bodhisattva or two small meditating Buddhas. The single images are depicted with both hands placed in the lap in a *dhyana* mudra, a sign of meditation, or the right raised in the *abhaya* mudra, "do not fear," and the left hand in the *vara* mudra, "bestowing or charity," open with the palm up resting on the knee with fingers extended and pointing downward. All the Buddha's robes either cover both shoulders with a roll of cloth framing the neck or leave the right shoulder bare in typical Gandharan fashion. Although asymmetrically pulled across the chest and legs, the robe is defined by evenly spaced pattern of lines forming its folds. The drapery reflects styles common during the fifth century and visible in Binglingsi Cave 169.[3]

On the bottom tier, the central section depicts scenes from the Sakyamuni's life, including his birth and the ritual cleansing of the infant Buddha by the nine *nagas* or serpent kings. The scenes are similar to those represented on the five-tiered sandstone stupa discussed in the previous entry (no. 52). The top tier contains the very popular seated Maitreya with crossed ankles and tall crown and a far less common, seated image of the skeletal, fasting Buddha.

There is no record of the sculptor Cao Tianhu, and the year designated in the inscription as *yimao* occurs twice during the Northern Wei in 436 and 496. Chen Bingying of the Gansu Provincial Museum dates this miniature stupa to 496 based on the stylistic characteristics that the sculpture and iconographic configuration share with Dunhuang Mogao Caves and Yungang Caves of the mid- to late fifth century.[4] A fragment of a very similar pagoda with a meditating Buddha, fasting Buddha, and the pair of Buddhas, Sakyamuni and Prabhutaratna, is in the collection of the Palace museum in Beijing (fig. A).[5]

It is possible that Cao Tianhu may be related to another known stupa carver, Cao Tiandu, from Shuoxian county in Shanxi.[6] The works of both are similar. Chen speculates that they both may have come from the same family or were even brothers.[7] When Northern Wei defeated Northern Liang in 439 and forcibly resettled thousands from Gansu to the Northern Wei capital at Pingcheng (modern Datong), Cao's family members were probably moved to Shanxi. Eventually, Cao Tianhu returned to his hometown, Jiuquan, in Gansu bringing back the Buddhist styles from Yungang cave temples in Shanxi. This may provide rare evidence of exchange and transmission of styles between the northwest and central China.

ALJ

1. Chen 1988, p. 83.

2. Steinhardt 1998, p. 46.

3. Dong 1994, pl. 45, niche 21, pl. 47, niche 20, east side.

4. Chen 1988, pp. 84–85, 93.

5. *Gugong Bowuguan yuankan* 1986.4, pp.30–31.

6. Shi 1980, pp. 68–71.

7. Chen 1988, p. 93.

Fig. A. One view of a fragment of a pagoda, in dark limestone in the Palace Museum, Beijing (after *Gugong Bowuguan yuankan* 1986.4, pp. 30–31)

1. *Maijishan* 1992, p. 91, no. 70, p. 121.

2. The early-sixth-century Guyang Cave at Longmen, outside of Luoyang, contains a number of Maitreya figures and provides the closest parallels with very similar stylistic elements along with figures from the Northern Wei caves at Binglingsi Grottoes in Gansu (*Longmen* 1991, vol. 1, pp. 146, 162; *Binglingsi* 1989, pls. 126, 132). A very large number of bodhisattvas in the Yungang Grottoes in Shanxi have the crossed scarves with flared points at the shoulders but are missing the circular ornament at the waist, except for one example in Cave 11 (*Yungang* 1977, pls. 54, 55, 65). At Yungang, the crossed scarves without the center circular ornament are dominant as well as in Dunhuang's Western Wei Cave 285; see *Dunhuang* 1981, vol. 1, pls. 123–26. A very elegant example of scarves crossing through a circular ornament can be found on seated Manjusri from Western Wei Cave 102 at Maijishan in the exhibition, no. 64.

3. This region may also be broken down further into smaller stylistic subsets such as the "Yellow earth plateau sculptural style" described in *Xumishan* 1997, pp. 23–24, and discussed in reference to nos. 58, 59. A close analysis still needs to be done to understand the dynamic of these regional stylistic variants and the formative and continuing sources of influences. Certainly, given the proximity of northern Sichuan to southeast Gansu and Shaanxi, the interaction with sculptural styles in northern Sichuan will also be a factor.

4. See *Longdong* 1987, Bifosi, figs. 118–130.

5. *Longmen* 1991, vol. 1, pp. 143, 153.

54. Seated Maitreya

Northern Wei dynasty (386–535), fifth–sixth century
Heshui county, Chengguan, Eastern Gansu
Reddish-brown sandstone
Height: 36.5 cm; width: 23 cm
Heshui County Museum, Gansu

This seated, cross-ankled Maitreya with the right hand raised in the *abhaya mudra* ("do not fear") and left hand done in the *vara* mudra ("charity" or "giving") sits in the center of a shallow pointed niche attended by two bodhisattvas and two small lions in atypical postures.[1] As Buddha-to-be, Maitreya and attendant bodhisattvas wear a style of garment, with a scarf crossing at the waist and forming an X, popular from the mid-fifth through early sixth century and visible in cave temples across north China.[2] On the Maitreya, the dhoti tied at the waist forms a long skirt with symmetrical pleats that bend with the knees. A long scarf covers both shoulders and crosses through a circular ornament (probably from a jade original) at the waist, leaving just a small segment of the bare chest visible. The thin ribbonlike ends of the scarf loop around the knees and flow up over the Maitreya's forearm. In a characteristic feature of this style of garment, the figure's shoulder is emphasized by a stylized, pointed flare of the scarf. Overall, the style is a simplified, abstract, and rigidly symmetrical variant of the dominant Northern Wei style of the early sixth century. This variant seems to be part of a regional style of sculpture that occurs where eastern Gansu, southern Ningxia, and Shaanxi provinces share both geographic proximity and the more traditional farming cultures of the fertile yellow earth plateau of the Central Plains.[3] A number of stylistic parallels and connections are visible in the remains of a stone pagoda and stelae from the destroyed temple site at Bifo near Pingliang in eastern Gansu.[4]

Above the niche, a row of seven small seated Buddhas, each also enclosed in a pointed niche, forms a prominent border. As discussed in Chapter 4, this iconographic configuration of the seven Buddhas of the Past including Sakyamuni, the historic Buddha, plus the Maitreya appears for the first time on the Northern Liang votive stupas (no. 48). Maitreya, as the future Buddha, is waiting in Tusita Heaven until the historic Buddha Sakyamuni passes into nirvana and will take his place as the next Buddha. In the fifth and sixth centuries, this configuration was popular throughout northwest China and appears not only in the Gansu Cave Temples but also in Longmen in central China and in Yungang on the extreme northern borders of Shanxi.[5]

ALJ

55. *Seated Buddha*

Northern Wei dynasty (386–535), 470s–490s
Qingyang, eastern Gansu
Bronze
Height: 21.8 cm; width: 10.9 cm
Qingyang Regional Museum Storage, Gansu

With a high *ushnisha* and pronounced long ears at the side of his head, this Buddha sits cross-legged in a meditation posture and mudra, reposing on a simple molded "Sumeru throne" supported by a dais with four squat legs.[1] On the front of the dais, a floral vine, possibly honeysuckle with a saw-toothed edge, fills the horizontal space; each leg has a standing figure holding a long-stemmed lotus. The figure on the right side wears clothing associated with the nomadic Xianbei female elite: a tall hat with ribbons, a long narrow-sleeved robe fastened down the center, and a long pleated skirt under the robe. On the left, the male figure, somewhat less clear, seems to have a tall headdress, a long robe fastened in front with trousers below, and boots. A more elaborate version of this Xianbei noble can be seen in the donor figures depicted on the embroidered Buddhist banner, dated to 487, found at Dunhuang (no. 45). The back and sides of the dais seem to be undecorated, but serious corrosion may have obliterated any images on the back legs of the dais.

Edged with a tiny pearl border, the pointed mandorla has an outer area filled with U-shaped flames; the inner area has a smaller mandorla also edged with a pearl border and seven small seated Buddhas arranged around the large Buddha's halo and shoulders. On the back of the mandorla are

back view

1. Published in *Maijishan* 1992, p. 120, fig. 68.

2. Soper 1958. These two bodhisattvas on the back of the mandorla in their proportions and in their relaxed postures are reminiscent of the two ascetics depicted on a relief from Butkara I, Swat; see Rhie 1976, fig. 26; Rhie also draws parallels between this Butkara I relief and a standing Buddha from Binglingsi, Gansu, Cave 169, dated 420; see p. 451, fig. 24.

3. Rhie 1999, p. 312.

4. Matsubara 1966, pls. 331, b, and fig. 14; Rhie 1976, in which Rhie discusses the group of images with this abstract schema of drapery using the terminology "Serried Incised Fold," pp. 458–60. She also suggests that this style of drapery ends in a major, though provincial, school of sculpture in Shaanxi and Shanxi during the early sixth century (Rhie 1999, p. 312).

5. See *Longdong*, 1987, figs. 164, 165, p. 21. The Buddha appears to be sitting in *bhadrasam* position with both legs pendant or down, which is also referred to as "European style." The robe covers both shoulder, and the folds are articulated in close parallel line; here, the drapery is asymmetrical pulling diagonally across the chest toward the left shoulder; .Zhang 1999, pl. 150.

6. *Longdong* 1987, surviving pagoda fragments and stelae from Bifo temple in Pingliang County, figs. 118-130, pp. 16–17.

Fig. A. Fragment of a stone pagoda, dated 503, depicting a seated Buddha, two bodhisattvas, and seven female donors, from the temple of Bifo in Pingliang county, eastern Gansu (after *Longdong* 1987, fig. 124)

two standing bodhisattvas with three small seated Buddhas above their heads, all enclosed in an arch ending in dragon or serpent heads. This iconographic configuration, the seven Buddhas of the Past, including Sakyamuni, plus Maitreya, was popular during the fifth and sixth centuries in Gansu and north China and can be seen on several examples in the exhibition. While the Maitreya is usually differentiated from the seven Buddhas of the past and shown as a bodhisattva with a high crown and cross-ankled as in number 54, they are all shown here as Buddhas. The earliest representation occurs on the votive stupas from the Northern Liang dynasty (no. 48). The two barefooted bodhisattvas with disproportionately large, square, haloed heads wear long dhotis and scarves that loop around the back of the heads, over their arms and down, in the "Liangzhou figural style" found on the base of the votive stupa (no. 48) and discussed in Chapter 4.[2] Corrosion on the back of the mandorla has completely obscured some details and made it very difficult to read others.

In typical Gandharan fashion, the Buddha's robe covers both shoulders with the folds descending in V-shaped, closely set parallel lines on the axis of the body. The sleeves form lappets that virtually cover the knees and legs, which have almost completely disappeared beneath the garment. This distinctive, abstract schema using "combed" lines to articulate drapery can be found in Palmyrenean, Gandharan, Swat, Rawak, and Chinese sculpture.[3] This style apparently first appears on Chinese bronze Buddhas from about the mid-fifth century onward. A number of small bronzes, dating from the 470s–480s, not only continue this combed-line definition of their drapery but also have similar donor or devotee figures on the legs of the dais and a single deity, paired deities, or an elaborate scene including more deities on the back of the mandorla as well. Two very similar bronze Buddhas, their drapery articulated with "serried" parallel lines, have been identified by Matsubara as characteristic of a style group from the Gansu and Shaanxi areas.[4] Near the Gansu-Shaanxi border, the rock-cut cave temple site of Baoquan, opened in 491 and the earliest in eastern Gansu, preserves some images with serried-style drapery. A seated Northern Wei Buddha in Niche 5 (Chapter 5, fig. 8) shares very similar facial features, tall *ushnisha*, and long ears, as well as this serried drapery.[5] On a fragment of a stone pagoda from the destroyed temple of Bifo in Pingliang County, eastern Gansu (fig. A), a seated Buddha and bodhisattvas appear very similar with large ears, broad shoulders, narrowed and tapered waists, and the serried drapery style.[6]

Undoubtedly, only a very small number of bronze sculptures cast during the fourth through seventh century have survived; even works of considerable size in bronze are few. Most small Buddhist bronzes, with an occasional exception such as number 47, are very vulnerable unless preserved in the relative security and protection of tomb burial; the bronzes fall victim to a range of catastrophes, including political unrest, Buddhist persecutions, and melting down. In the evolution of Buddhist art in China, the stylistic and chronological interrelationship between bronze and stone sculpture, whether part of a cave temple or not, and paintings has yet to be fully understood.

ALJ

56. *Buddhist stele with bodhisattva*

Northern Wei dynasty (386–535), sixth century
Found Xingji Township, Pengyang, Ningxia
Sandstone
Height: 49.6 cm; width: 14 cm at base
Guyuan Municipal Museum, Ningxia Hui Autonomous Region

This striking and atypical bodhisattva stands on a high plinth and is tightly framed by a narrow, pointed mandorla.[1] There are no attendant figures. A long pronounced nose dominates the face, with its small compressed lips, reminiscent of the possibly non-Chinese Northern Zhou faces at Xumishan.[2] The head and shoulders, modeled in higher relief, appear almost massive in comparison to the flat, lower portion of the slender body with its tiny feet visible below the robe. The head is further emphasized by an unusually elaborate headdress, with what appear to be braids, or perhaps enormous earrings, and a large thick necklace, torque, or cowl. Slender hands and forearms hold an offering, as is customary for bodhisattvas from this time period in both paintings and sculpture (for example, in other figures at Dunhuang and Maijishan).[3]

This figure wears a long dhoti, tied at the waist, which fishtails at the base. Also, a narrow scarf wraps around the shoulders, descends in a symmetrical X shape across the front of the figure, and wraps back up over the forearm to trail down the sides of the figure. Additional forms of curled ribbon below and outside the elbows lend an almost flamelike edging where the robes blend into the mandorla. The robes themselves, along with the sash and the scarf, are elegantly

articulated by incised, parallel lines both horizontal and vertical. Similar lines mark the sharp V of the scarf as it reverses at the level of the knee. Aside from these markings, the lower part of the body is barely defined beneath the drapery. Although the combed lines used to articulate the bodhisattva's robes seem less abstract, this technique may relate to number 55 and reflect the same local style that developed and peaked in the Gansu and Shaanxi areas in the early sixth century.[4]

Both this standing sandstone bodhisattva and the sandstone stele discussed in the entry for number 57 were found in a storage pit near the city of Pengyang, southern Ningxia, very close to both the Gansu border and the Shaanxi border.[5] The handling of the drapery and body on this figure suggests a Northern Wei date.

ALJ

1. With the exception of one small bronze votive image, believed to date from the mid- to late fifth century, the storage pit contained stone images including one piece similar to this bodhisattva but less elaborate. Of the images published, two were definitely Daoist; *Kaogu yu wenwu* 1984.6, pp. 34–35, 55, pl. 5:4; also published in *Xumishan* 1999, pp. 23–24, figs. 24, 25.

2. See monograph *Xumishan* 1988, Northern Zhou Cave 51, pls.10–12.

3. Rhie 1976, pp. 458–60; Rhie 1999, p. 312. She believes this provincial style developed in the Shaanxi-Shanxi region, while Matsubara called it a Gansu-Shaanxi regional style.

4. A monk and a nun carry offerings for the Buddha in Western Wei Cave 92, *Maijishan* 1998, pp. 193–94; an animated bodhisattva gestures toward the Buddha with an offering in hand, Western Wei Cave 127, pl. 158. In Dunhuang wall paintings, the bodhisattvas nearest the Buddha carry an offering, as in Northern Wei Cave 248, front chamber, north wall, pl. 84; west wall, north end, of Western Wei Cave 285 (*Dunhuang* 1981. vol. I)

5. *Kaogu yu wenwu* 1984.6, pp. 34–35, 55, pl. 5:4.

57. *Buddhist stele*

Northern Wei dynasty (386–535), dated by inscription

Jianming, second year, or 531

Found Xinji Township, Pengyang, Ningxia

Sandstone

Height: 48 cm; width: 20.8 cm

Guyuan Municipal Museum, Ningxia Hui Autonomous Region

1. *Kaogu yu wenwu* 1984.6, pp. 34–35, pl. 5:1.

2. Ibid., p. 34.

3. Hurvitz 1976, pp. 185–89.

4. *Longdong* 1987, p. 20, fig. 160.

Both this sandstone stele and the standing sandstone bodhisattva discussed in the entry for number 56 were found in a storage pit near the city of Pengyang, southern Ningxia, close to both the Gansu border and the Shaanxi border.[1] The flat back of this small votive stele bears an inscription and date, Jianming second year, 531, near the end of the Northern Wei dynasty, which relates that the General of the Western Regions commissioned two stelae.[2] Only this one has survived.

The shallow carved niche is filled by two tiers of figures clearly divided by a horizontal bar or floor. The bottom tier is dominated by a large bodhisattva figure framed by a narrow mandorla, flaring slightly at the peak, the very tip of which extends into the upper tier. Six smaller figures flank the bodhisattva in identical groups of three. On each side at the bottom is an attendant whose youthfulness is indicated by the two topknots of hair. These attendants are fully visible and they face inward. The two lowest attendant figures have robes that curve back over the edge of the niche at the base. Above on either side are two partially hidden figures, overlapped by the young attendants; only their heads and upper chests are visible. These figures face outward, rather than inward.

The upper tier itself depicts the famous scene from the Lotus Sutra of the historic Buddha, Sakyamuni, in conversation with the Buddha of the Past, Prabhutaratna. Their presence together on the same platform symbolizes their mystical identity and the concept of Sakyamuni as eternal, and their presence together manifests in Buddhist art in many different forms.[3] These two major figures face inward and are seated on a platform, which resembles the stone mortuary couch (no. 106). Four smaller figures are aligned between the two Buddhas; they appear to be monks, faces turned inward, perhaps listening intently to the conversation. The two Buddha figures and the six attendants below wear the traditional Chinese robes discussed in greater detail in chapter 4. The robes of the two Buddhas splay out over the base of their couch, overlap the edge of the carved niche, and disappear behind the peak of the bodhisattva's mandorla, lending the stele a three-dimensional quality.

Stylistically, these figures represent the end of Northern Wei at the moment of transition to the later Western Wei style. As discussed earlier in number 54, Buddhist sculpture from southern Ningxia has many stylistic ties to Shaanxi and eastern Gansu as visible on the stele from Shaanxi (fig. A) dated Western Wei (535–557) in the squareness of the heads and faces, heavy-lidded eyes with incised lines, and the concept of the composition. Very similar facial features can be found on three surviving Buddhas carved in the Chenjia stone caves now partially collapsed in a gorge just below Longyan Mountain in Zhuanglang county, Gansu.[4]

ALJ

no. 57. backview

Fig. A. Sandstone stele with Sakyamuni and attendants (obverse) (*below*), Western Wei (535–557) (after Institute for the Protection of Cultural Relics, Xi'an)

1. Published in *Xumishan* 1997, pp. 23–24, fig. 24.

2. See *Binglingsi* 1989, pls. 81 (Cave 124, 125), 94 (Cave 132), 99 (Cave 132).

3. *Xumishan* 1997, pp. 24–25.

4. A large number of white marble images, some 2,200, many with inscriptions, were found in the base of a ruined Song dynasty (960–1126) pagoda at Xiudesi in Chuyang; see Akiyama and Matsubara 1969, vol. II, pp. 239–40, nos. 190–96.

58. *Seated Buddha*

Northern Wei dynasty (386–535), late fifth–early sixth century
Found in Pengyang county in 1985, Ningxia
White smooth soft stone (gypsum?)
Height: 18.9 cm; width: 9.0 cm; thickness: 4.5 cm
Pengyang County Museum, on loan to Guyuan Municipal Museum,
Ningxia Hui Autonomous Region

A shallow, pointed niche cradles this striking, white, starkly simple Buddha image, seated cross-legged on a high dais.[1] A single incised line emphasizes the curves of the drapery, and cross-hatching on the covered hands relieves the smooth creamy-white surface of the stone. Tilting forward, the fully modeled head contrasts with the almost flat low-relief definition of the elongated body, which recedes behind the rhythmic pattern of scalloped angular folds of the robe. The intensely linear and abstracted pattern formed by the drapery, which spreads symmetrically over the dais, characterizes the Northern Wei style that emerges in north China during the late fifth century and early sixth centuries. Across north China, these complex drapery patterns retain the identifiable hallmarks of this Northern Wei style but do develop distinctive variations from Buddhist site to Buddhist site, reflecting regional variants. Here, the rigid symmetry and simplification of the drapery suggest a regional variant of this style.

As noted in the entry for number 54, this new style is associated with the Northern Wei emperor Xiao Wendi's attempts to sinicize his court and force Tuoba aristocrats to adopt Chinese dress and cus-

toms. This modified version of the traditional monk's robe was believed to have been adapted from the garments of the Southern dynasties elite, which are long Chinese-style robes with full sleeves and a vertical opening at the chest, worn over an undergarment tied at the front. This Northern Wei style, which remained popular during the first half of the sixth century, moved decidedly away from the earlier Northern Liang (nos. 48, 49) and earlier Northern Wei (no. 51), styles inspired almost exclusively from Western sources. The engaging simplicity of this Buddha finds its closest parallel in the sixth-century images at Binglingsi near Lanzhou, with their sharply pointed and scalloped patterned drapery.[2] Belying its small scale, this Buddha has a compelling presence.

This is one of eight stone images found in an underground storage pit at Pengyang in 1985 along with number 59. Pengyang is south of Guyuan, just at the Ningxia-Gansu border. These three contiguous geographical areas, Pengyang in Ningxia, Longdong in Gansu, and northern Shaanxi are part of the "Yellow Earth Plateau" style of carving in which smooth forms are embellished with folds defined by single or closely raised parallel lines.[3] Both small white Buddhas (nos. 58, 59) have been carved from this unusually soft white stone, which may have been chosen because of its similarity to white marble, a popular material for carving Buddhist sculpture, particularly in Hebei province.[4]

ALJ

59. *Seated Buddha*

Northern Wei dynasty (386–535)–Western Wei (535–557),
early to mid-sixth century
Found in Pengyang county in 1985
White smooth soft stone (gypsum?)
Height: 18.0 cm; width: 11.4 cm; thickness: 6.5 cm
Pengyang County Museum, on loan to Guyuan Municipal Museum,
Ningxia Hui Autonomous Region

A shallow and rounded but damaged niche encloses this handsome white Buddha image, seated cross-legged on a high dais flanked by bodhisattvas. The right hand, also damaged, is partly raised and open in the *abhaya* mudra ("do not fear"), while the left is open, palm up, pointing down in the *vara* mudra ("charity" or "giving"). A single beaded border embellishes the larger mandorla, while the smaller halo has a double one. Beading is also used in what remains of the flame pattern along the right edge of the mandorla. Pearl borders can be traced back to Central Asian clothing worn by earlier Parthians and Kushans (see nos. 17, 18, figs. C, D) and becomes incorporated into Buddhist art of Central Asia and then Gansu and north China. Pearls were highly valued as one of the *sapta-ratna*, or seven Buddhist treasures, along with lapis lazuli and coral.[1]

Worship of the Buddha and patronage of Buddhism involved offerings of tangible gifts. Pearls were not only an important form of wealth for monasteries but were used to encrust reliquaries holding Buddhist treasures (no. 120). During the fourth through seventh century, pearl borders and pearling become pervasive parts of the Buddhist decorative vocabulary in China,[2] visible on other examples in the exhibition such as number 18, the ornamental coffin plaques or door handles, and number 112, a Tang clay *hu* vessel.

Although the drapery falls over the dais of this figure in a Northern Wei-styled, abstract drapery pattern, the actual modeling of the Buddha reflects new elements that begin to emerge in the mid-sixth century. The robe appears to combine the traditional Indian-styled monk's robe (*kasaya*), which wraps across the chest and around the shoulder, with the complex drapery patterns favored by Northern Wei. However, even the patterned folds at the base of number 59, although abstract, still hint at a style less rigid than that of number 58.

Despite being quite worn and difficult to read, the fully modeled rectangular head and the distinctive facial features, including pronounced nose and lips, echo the features of the Northern Zhou Buddhas in Cave 51 at Xumishan. There is also a suggestion of foreign ethnicity about these features.[3]

This figure along with number 58 is one of eight stone images found in an underground storage pit at Pengyang in 1985. Pengyang is south of Guyuan, located just at the Ningxia-Gansu border. These three contiguous geographical areas, Pengyang in Ningxia, Longdong in Gansu, and northern Shaanxi, are part of the "Yellow Earth Plateau" style of carving in which smooth forms are embellished.

ALJ

1. The *sapta-ratna* originally only referred to the seven marks of the *chakravartin*, or universal ruler, in India; Bunce 1997, pp. 260–61. It is not clear when they became associated with the seven treasures, pearl, gold, silver, lapis lazuli, crystal or quartz, a red precious stone or red coral, and agate or coral; Liu 1988a, pp. 92–94.

2. A comparable but painted pearl border adorns the mandorlas surrounding the Wu Liang Shou Buddha and flanking bodhisattvas in Cave 169 dated 420 at Binglingsi in Gansu (*Binglingsi* 1989, pl. 24–25). Another example occurs on the Yungang Colossus in Cave 20, dated late fifth century (*Yungang* 1988, pp. 178–79, pl. 171). Pearl borders and pearling are extensively used in both painting and sculpture in the Sui Caves at Dunhuang (*Dunhuang* 1981, vol. 2, pls. 139, 140, 143 [Cave 140]; pls. 147, 148, 150, 153 [Cave 396]).

3. *Xumishan* 1988, pls. 10, 11, 12.

1. Published in *Sichou* 1994, no. 101. Because of the topknot of hair and flowing robes with the crossed X-shaped scarves, they have been identified in this Chinese publication as bodhisattvas. During the reign of Xiao Wendi, the Northern Wei capital was moved in 493–494 from Pingcheng (modern Datong) to Luoyang, ancient Chinese capital in the heart of north China. At the new capital, the Tuoba aristocrats were ordered to adopt Chinese style dress. This change in dress style is also reflected in the robes worn by both Buddhas and bodhisattvas during the late fifth century to the mid-sixth century. Bodhisattvas and female donors share similar clothing styles and sculptural styles except for the crossed scarves. There was considerable stylistic and iconographic cross-fertilization between Buddhist art and traditional Chinese non-Buddhist arts. Buddhist elements in clothing and style entered *mingqi* at this time. See Juliano 1975, pp. 13–17, 48, no. 23.

2. *Gongxian* 1989, Cave 1, pl. 4.

3. Juliano 1980. See pottery in figs. 130, 131 and bricks in figs. 19, 49. Also see *Kaogu* 1973.4, p. 219, figs. 4.1,2, 5.1,2 for figures with similarly oval shaped heads and long cylindrically shaped necks from the Northern Wei tomb of Yuan Shao, now in the collection of the Loyang Museum.

4. Zhou and Gao 1991, p. 208, fig. 272.

5. *Maijishan* 1998, pls. 77, 80.

60a,b. *Two bodhisattvas*

Northern Wei dynasty (386–535), late fifth–early sixth century
From Maijishan Caves, Tianshui, Gansu
Unfired clay with traces of pigment
a. Height: 35.2 cm; b. Height: 36.1 cm
Gansu Provincial Museum, Lanzhou

These two bodhisattvas are made of unfired clay that still retains traces of pigment, especially on the hair. One gracefully leans right, and the other left (probably flanking a Buddha image). They could easily be mistaken as donor or secular figures, e.g., procession of attendants on walls of Longmen and Gongxian, but the distinguishing feature is scarves that cross forming an X particularly in Northern and Western Wei sculpture (nos. 52, 54, 56, 57, 65).[1] Their forms are elongated, and each is made from molds in two parts, with the head separate and inserted into a long cylindrical neck. Their hair is in small chignons on the top of their heads (Buddha-like qualities). Their faces are long and oval, enhanced with delicate lips and eyes in low relief, which brings descriptive clarity to the figures. The figures are conceived two-dimensionally, with a flat back with little indication of a bodily form beneath their clothes with each figure only showing one hand. The drapes of their clothing move toward left or right with the posture of each figure. Although there is some damage and discoloration on the figures, it does not mar the refined execution of the figures or their ethereal presence.

Donor figures in the processions of the emperor and empress in Cave 1 at the Gongxian Caves in Henan province (fig. A) maintain a similar tilted posture and flowing robes as do these figures from Maijishan.[2] Flowing robes with ribbonlike elements are also evident in the tiles excavated in the tomb at Dengxian, also in Henan province. Both the figures in the carved tiles on the walls of the tomb and the ceramic figures placed in this Six Dynasties tomb reveal the same style of elongated heads with narrow necks as the Maijishan donors and similarly fluid, draping robes with a round neck.[3] Such costumes are evident in the painted-lacquer screen from the tomb of Sima Jinlong in Datong, Shanxi, which also dates from the Northern Wei period.[4] These donor figures, like many sculptures still situated in the Maijishan Caves, are typical in the way their slender, elongated forms reveal both delicacy and spirituality with their sensitively modeled faces and graceful postures.[5] They are also reminiscent of the same style as portrayed in the Six Dynasties painting of Gu Kaizhi.

SB

Fig. A. Courtiers and attendants in the procession of the Empress, Gongxian, Cave 1, upper tier, west side of the south wall, Northern Wei, early sixth century (after *Gongxian* 1989, pl. 4, Cave 1)

1. This *apsara* has been published in *Maijishan* 1992, p. 39, no. 15. *Maijishan* 1987, pls. 152–53. Cave 127 Buddha slightly later, dating from the Western Wei (535–557), which follows the Northern Wei split dividing the north into Western and Eastern Wei.

2. Reischauer and Fairbank 1960, vol. 1, pp. 152–53.

3. Before the Northern Wei style shifted at the end of the sixth century, the typical painted or sculpted *apsara* at Gansu Buddhist sites—including Binglingsi, Dunhuang, Jintasi, and Wenshushan and also visible at Yungang in Shanxi and at Kizil outside of Kucha in Central Asia—reflects strong influence from Western prototypes. Figures have naked chests, long dhotis, plump rounded body forms in a V-shaped posture with arms fully extended to each side and wrapped in a thin scarf. See *Hexi* 1987, p. 19, which provides a comparison of apsaras from these different Gansu sites.

4. *Longmen* 1991, figs. 4–34 (Binyang Cave), figs. 46–66 (Lianhua Cave).

5. *Maijishan* 1998, pl. 85 (Cave 248), pls. 62, 64 (Cave 437).

6. Juliano 1980, pp. 55–56, figs. 57–59; for Danyang, see *Wenwu* 1977.1, p. 66, fig. 4:4, *Wenwu* 1974.2, pp. 44–56, and Bush 1976, pp. 49–83. The strong similarity between the Maijishan *apsara* and the example from Danyang supports Dr. Alexander Soper's theory, proposing that this new Northern Wei style was actually reflecting influence from Southern dynasties buddhist art. In addition, Emperor Xiao Wendi's edict moving the court to Luoyang contributed to the Xianbei becoming "more Chinese." Since Maijishan is situated near Shaanxi and Sichuan, influence could have come along the Yangtze River from the southern capital of Nanjing or up through Sichuan directly. See Soper 1960, pp. 47–112, and plates.

61. Apsara (tianjen or feitian)

Northern Wei dynasty 386–535, early sixth century
Cave 133, Maijishan Caves, Tianshui, Gansu
Clay with traces of black, red, and white pigment
Height: 20.7 cm; length: 24.3 cm
Maijishan Art Research Institute, Tianshui, Gansu

Swooping effortlessly through the air trailing thin ribbons of drapery, this *apsara* from Cave 133 is a superb example of the distinctive style that emerges in the north during the Northern Wei from the late fifth to the early sixth century. A group of these flying celestial beings, inhabitants of the Buddha's heavenly realm, was originally attached to the bottom edge of the ceiling where it meets the wall in Cave 133. These elegant *apsaras* often play music, present offerings, or just hover near the Buddha. Cave 127 also at Maijishan has a seated Buddha wearing a large halo filled with these music-making celestial beings.[1]

Stylistically, this piece is characteristic of the Northern Wei, following the move of the capital to Luoyang and Emperor Xiao Wendi's policy of sinicization.[2] The new style, which appears in the late-fifth-century caves at Yungang, near the original capital of Pingcheng (modern Datong) in northern Shanxi, moves decidedly away from rounded, rather plump body proportions and clothing influenced by Western prototypes to elongation with emphasis on highly mannered, elegantly conceived abstract patterns.[3] This style is fully exploited at the new cave temples at Longmen, opened just outside of Luoyang in Henan.[4]

As discussed in Chapter 4, this Northern Wei style spreads across the north and is quite visible in Gansu Buddhist sites, particularly at Maijishan. Among the sites, the exquisite execution at Maijishan cannot be matched by any other examples known in Gansu at this time, although Dunhuang has a few vibrantly energetic examples of this style painted on the ceiling of Northern Wei Cave 248 and some sculpture on the central pillar just above the Buddha's niche in Northern Wei Cave 437.[5] At Dunhuang, aspects of the clothing and style retain a connection with Western sources. Interestingly, the most telling comparisons are found in the early-sixth-century Guyang cave at Longmen, Henan, on stamped clay tiles from the northern Chinese tomb at Dengxian in Henan, and from a late-fifth-century Southern Dynasties tomb at Danyang in Jiangsu province.[6]

All three examples from Maijishan, number 61, Dengxian (fig. B), and Danyang (fig. A) share basic characteristics: a C-shaped vertical position with legs scissored and drapery flying freely behind. The Maijishan *apsara* has a slender neck and small head with a tied loop of hair. This small and quite fragile *apsara* sustained damage in several places, probably when it fell from the cave ceiling. The head is broken at the neck, and a crack crosses the trailing drapery.

ALJ

Fig. A. Drawing of an *apsara* from a tile (*above*) from the tomb at Huqiao, Danyang (Jiangsu) (after *Wenwu* 1977.1, p. 66, fig. 4:1)

Fig. B. *Apsaras* on a clay tomb tile from Dengxian tomb (*right*) in Henan (after *Dengxian* 1959, p. 27, fig. 33)

62. *Buddhist disciple Kasyapa*

Northern Wei Dynasty (386–535)
Cave 87, right wall of Maijishan Caves at Tianshui, Gansu
Clay
Height: 107 cm
Maijishan Art Research Institute, Tianshui, Gansu

1. *Maijishan* 1992, pp. 48–49, no. 27; p. 117; *Maijishan* 1954, pl. 75.

2. For a discussion of representation of Kasyapa at Dunhuang, see Baker 1999, pp. 77–81.

3. Sekel 1964, p. 250.

4. *Maijishan* 1998, pls. 135, 136 (Cave 123, Western Wei, both monks); pl. 112 (Northern Wei, Cave 142, just Ananda); pl. 92 (Northern Wei Cave 133, possibly Ananda).

This compelling figure of the Indian monk Kasyapa, eldest of the Buddha's disciples, usually stands in Cave 87 at Maijishan.[1] Sharply defined sculptural forms create an extraordinarily accomplished portrait of the aged monk.[2] A simple monk's robe covers his slender almost emaciated body with repetitive loops of folded cloth. The shaved head, bent humbly over the hands clasped in prayer, clearly conveys his advanced age, non-Chinese ethnicity, and intense spirituality. The large beaked nose, framed by a bridge of shaggy, drooping eyebrows, emphatically states his foreign origins. During this period, exaggerated noses, long or beaked, became the single stereotyped facial feature used by Chinese artists to identify the "foreignness" of Westerners. Other examples of these distinctively non-Chinese noses can be seen throughout the exhibition and include the nomadic herder painted on a third-to-fourth-century clay tile (nos. 10, 12) from Jiayuguan in Gansu, the sixth-century clay figure of a Central Asian or Indian (no. 114), the seventh-century small bronze figure (no. 82), from Shandan in Gansu, and two eighth-century dancing Sogdians carved on stone tomb doors (nos. 81a,b).

Already in his eighties prior to meeting the Buddha, Kasyapa was a renowned Indian ascetic with a large following of his own. The Buddha, traveling around India and attracting growing numbers of believers, met and converted the stubborn Kasyapa and his five hundred disciples in an historic encounter. Kasyapa became one of the Buddha's ten leading disciples along with Ananda, the Buddha's cousin and youngest disciple. The two are frequently paired in Buddhist sculpture and painting, symbolically representing all the Buddha's disciples.[3] The exhibition also includes a superb sculpture of young Ananda from Cave 102 at Maijishan (see no. 63).

Although images of both monks exist from this period at Maijishan, fewer of Kasyapa have survived. Together, the elder Kasyapa and the younger Ananda become part of a standard iconographic arrangement commonly found in caves dating from the Northern Wei (386–535) and Western Wei (535–557) dynasties. In a typical triad, the main Buddha image, flanked on either side by bodhisattvas, forms the fundamental iconographic unit and is always expanded by adding the two monks, Kasyapa and Ananda, and sometimes two lay worshipers, one on either side. This configuration is very popular at Dunhuang as well.[4]

The clay figure of Kasyapa has sustained severe damage and is broken at the neck and chest; a large piece of his chest is missing, undoubtedly detailing his protruding collar bone and rib cage; the lower part of the robe and feet are missing as well. The head remains in remarkable condition, with exceptionally sharp modeling, while the robe evidences general surface wear and damage with pitting, pocking, and chewed drapery edges. None of the damage can diminish the focused power and energy of the monk's portrait.

ALJ

1. There are many books and articles that recount the story of the Buddha's life and his encounters with Ananda, including Coomaraswamy 1964, pp. 66–67; Basham 1959, pp. 256–58, discusses the story of the Buddha's life and its influence; Snelling 1998.

2. Published in *Maijishan* 1998, pl. 132, and *Maijishan* 1992, pl. 29.

3. Getty 1962, p. xxiii.

4. A *parinirvana* carved on the east wall of the Northern Wei Cave 132 at Binglingsi, Gansu, shows Ananda kneeling near the head of the reclining Buddha (*Binglingsi* 1989, pl. 101).

5. Sculptural representation of Ananda and Kasyapa can be found at Yungang, Cave 18 (Northern Wei, late fifth century), see *Yungang* 1977, pls. 85, 86; at Longmen Grottoes, Binyang Cave (Northern Wei, early 6th century), see *Longmen* 1991, vol. 1, pls. 7, 12, 13; and Dunhuang, Cave 439 (Northern Zhou), *Dunhuang* 1981, vol. 1, pls. 158, 159.

63. *Buddhist disciple Ananda*

Western Wei dynasty (535–557)
Cave 102, Maijishan Caves, Tianshui
Clay with traces of pigment
Height: 120 cm
Maijishan Art Research Institute, Tianshui, Gansu

Renowned for his encyclopedic knowledge of the teachings, Ananda was chosen by the Buddha to be his personal servant and also became his favorite.[1] Described as the "Beloved Disciple" of the Buddha, the radiant young Ananda stands to the right, between the main image and a seated Manjusri, or Wenshu (no. 64), the Bodhisattva of Wisdom, in Maijishan Cave 102.[2] His fully modeled head and columnar body reflect the growing interest in naturalism of Western Wei sculpture. Ananda's youthfulness is captured in the smooth rounded forms of his shaved head, and his spirituality is evident in his intently focused gaze. The crisply articulated features coupled with an enigmatic smile suffuse his face with a calm, knowing intelligence. The figure's strong sense of presence is further enhanced by a feeling of immediacy, evoked by his robe, which appears to have just slid off one shoulder.

As described in the entry for number 62, Ananda is frequently paired with Kasyapa, the eldest of the Buddha's disciples; both were incorporated into the standard iconographic unit of the Buddha with two bodhisattvas, usually as individual sculptural images, with the youngest monk always on the right and the oldest on the left. At times, both monks are also incorporated in the death scene of the Buddha, the *parinirvana*. Knowing he was about to die, the Buddha lay down on his right side, with his head turned toward the north, and gave his faithful disciple Ananda his last instructions for the organization of the Buddhist community.[3] Ananda is often depicted in sculptural reliefs and in wall paintings of the death scene, sitting next to or tenderly touching the Buddha's head while Kasyapa, collapsed with grief or reverently bowing, kneels near his feet (see *parinirvana* scene on large stupa, no. 52).[4] This basic triad, often with two other monks, became quite popular in northern China and is found in Northern Wei cave temples dated from the late fifth through early sixth century, and stretching from Longmen near the ancient capital of Luoyang in Henan through the Gansu corridor to Dunhuang.[5]

Although described as belonging to the Sakya, a tribal people from the border of modern Nepal to whom the Buddha himself belonged, Ananda, the Buddha Sakyamuni's cousin, has been represented by the sculptor as definitively Chinese, while Kasyapa (no. 62), an Indian Brahman holy man, has a distinctively Western profile. The exceptional characterizations of Ananda and Kasyapa exemplify the mastery of the Maijishan sculptors.

Like the figure of Kasyapa, the clay figure of Ananda has been damaged, with part of the bottom of the robe and the feet missing. Although the neck was broken, the head remains in excellent condition, retaining sharpness and clarity of modeling, whereas the robe evidences general surface wear with pitting, pocking, and chewed drapery edges.

ALJ

1. *Maijishan* 1992, pl. 28, p. 117, no. 28; *Maijishan* 1998, pl. 102.

2. Getty 1962, p. 110. When the bodhisattva image emerged in India, it was definitely male. By the time the image reached China, it had become more androgynous and feminine. However, during the fourth to seventh century, bodhisattvas are still male, which is often indicated with a painted mustache. Consequently, gender references are sometimes confusing.

3. Davidson 1954, p. 33.

64. *Seated Bodhisattva Wenshu* (Manjusri)

Western Wei dynasty (535–557)
Cave 102, right side, Maijishan Caves, Tianshui, Gansu
Clay
Height: 130 cm; width: 59 cm; thickness: 44 cm
Maijishan Art Research Institute, Tianshui, Gansu

Maijishan's Cave 102 contains an exceptional group of Western Wei sculpture, two of which (nos. 63, 64) have been included in this exhibition. As described in the previous entry, Ananda, the youngest disciple, stands to the right of and in between the main Buddha and the majestic seated figure of the Manjusri (Wenshu), the Bodhisattva of Wisdom.[1] Manjusri, who represents the Buddha's transcendent wisdom, was the first bodhisattva mentioned in the Buddhist scriptures and often appears in the *Lotus Sutra* in connection with the historic Buddha, Sakyamuni. According to Chinese Buddhism, Manjusri was told by the historic Buddha that it was his duty to turn the Wheel of the Law for the salvation of the Chinese from the mountain of the five peaks, Wutaishan, in Shanxi.[2]

Sculpture at Maijishan during the first half of the sixth century evolves from Northern Wei to Western Wei without any sharp stylistic or iconographic breaks. Certainly, as mentioned in Chapter 4, Maijishan enjoyed the patronage of the aristocracy and a close relationship with the Western Wei court and its capital at nearby Changan (present-day Xi'an). The thin, flatter, and more linear forms with the abstracted drapery patterns and cascades so characteristic of Northern Wei assume somewhat rounder and less rigid forms in Western Wei. In particular, the heads with smooth helmetlike hair supporting a three-petaled crown become almost square; soft, fleshy cheeks are set off by the crisply defined features. Still complex, the configuration of the robe involves a dhoti tied at the waist, an undergarment covering one shoulder, and a series of shawls that covers the shoulders and crisscross in front of the body through the central ornamental ring. The left side, now broken off, originally draped up over the forearm. Two additional disks at either side of the torque necklace seem to secure additional ribbons of drapery. The drapery patterning is still complex but falls and twists with more naturalism, enlivening the rather flat and somewhat stiff body.

There are fifth- and sixth-century representations of Manjusri and Vimalakirti engaged in their historic debate, an event described at length in the *Vimalakirti-nirdesa Sutra*. Across from the Manjusri in Cave 102 sits an image of Vimalakirti, whom the text describes as a pious layman who had acquired divine powers but was ill. Only Manjusri had the courage to converse with him and, in the course of the discussion, ask: "What is the essence of Buddhism?" Vimalakirti answered, "A silence like a clap of thunder," a famous response reflecting the profundity of his knowledge.[3]

Although the neck was broken and repaired, Manjusri's relatively undamaged face retains a focused glance and a gentle smile of benign tolerance. As with the other clay sculptures from Maijishan (nos. 60–65, 69, 70), parts of this sculpture show not only wear, including scraping and chipping, but also breakage and loss, with missing feet and drapery ribbons.

ALJ

1. *Maijishan* 1992, pp. 60–61, pl. 34; *Maijishan* 1998, pl. 174; *Maijishan* 1954, pl. 141.

2. A small leaded-copper alloy image of the Infant Buddha believed to be from Afghanistan and dated to the fifth century holds its right arm bent at the elbow, with the right hand placed on the chest, palm facing inward. This same hand position is sometimes assumed by Gandharan figures of the Buddha and monks and occasionally by Buddha images from China, as in Cave 169, east wall, at Binglingsi near Lanzhou in Gansu and from Central Asia. However, this does not reflect any known Buddhist mudra or gesture (Errington and Cribb 1992, pp. 213–14, pl. 208). The rare Buddhist icon from Panjikent, actually a mold, shows a figure with the left arm bent at the elbow; the hand rests palm down on the chest as well (Marshak and Raspopova 1997–98, pp. 297–305).

65. *Seated Buddha*

Northern Zhou (557–581)
Cave 135, main wall, left niche, Maijishan Caves, Tianshui, Gansu
Clay
Height: 84 cm; width 32 cm; thickness: 26 cm
Maijishan Art Research Institute, Tianshui, Gansu

Modest in scale but monumental in effect, this Buddha dating from the Northern Zhou sits tucked among the sculptures in the left-hand niche, nearly lost among the rather large and magnificent Western Wei Buddhas in Maijishan Cave 135.[1] Clearly, this was not its original location, which unfortunately remains unknown.

Maijishan sculpture during the mid-sixth century continued to evolve toward greater naturalism, with sculptural forms becoming more robust, covered by robes that drape more like actual cloth than like the earlier schematic patterns of the Northern Wei. This Buddha wears the traditional Buddhist garment rather than the adapted early-sixth-century Chinese style robe (no. 58). The figure's hands rest on the chest, in what appears to be an informal gesture, perhaps grasping the robe but not in positions associated with any known Buddhist hand gestures or mudras; the meaning if any remains obscure.[2] Although the lower part of the sculpture has been lost, the Buddha has both legs pendant, *bhadrasana*, in what is usually referred to as a Western or European manner. The simple, smoothly rounded forms and the calm introspective facial expression give the figure a sense of spiritual power. Northern Zhou sculpture is less known and perhaps less appreciated than its Northern Qi counter-

parts. This Buddha presents a strong argument for the power and subtlety of Northern Zhou sculpture at its best.

The piece, highly vulnerable because it is sculpted from clay, has unfortunately been badly damaged. Part of the *ushnisha* may have been broken off the top of the head; the face has been damaged; the neck was broken and repaired; and the left hand has also been gouged and scraped, all suggesting that the figure may have fallen over.

ALJ

66. *Bodhisattva, Avalokitesvara or Padmapani*

Northern Zhou dynasty (557–581)
Cave 47, Maijishan Caves, Tianshui, Gansu
Stone with pigment
Height:145 cm; width: 36 cm; thickness: 24 cm
Maijishan Art Research Institute, Tianshui, Gansu

1. *Maijishan* 1992, no. 37, p. 118.

2. Bodhisattvas from Northern dynasties grottoes at Yuanzishan in Shanxi province definitely have jutting ribbons but the heads have been damaged, making it difficult to determine what the crown was like (*Wenwu* 1997.2, pp. 68-72); a Southern dynasties cross-ankled Maitreya with tripartite crown and ribbons excavated at Xi'an road in Chengdu, Sichuan (*Wenwu* 1998.11, pp. 4–20).

As discussed earlier in Chapter 4, the stone of Maijishan Mountain was not suitable for carving. Thus, the technique of constructing large-scale sculpture with armatures of wood or metal and clay reinforced with organic materials was adopted. Although most of the sculpture at Maijishan is made of clay with armatures, a few images were carved from local stone and placed in the caves. Standing on a lotus base, this carved example, a tall stone bodhisattva now in Cave 47, holds the stem of a rose lotus, one attribute of Padmapani, a manifestation of the bodhisattva Avalokitesvara. (see also no. 71).

Large-scale, bejeweled Avalokitesvara images became enormously popular in north China, reflecting both stylistic and iconographic innovations during the second half of the sixth century. Stylistically, Northern Zhou Avalokitesvara gain volume and exhibit almost columnar solidity, whereas the complex patterns of heavy pleated and splayed drapery of the early Northern and Western Wei periods are replaced with thinner, clinging cloth. The Northern Zhou figures wear heavy harnesses of jewels from the neck to the feet and thick strands of linked beads laden with beaded medallions, pendants, and cabochons. Although jewelry often becomes massive and even ponderous on these Northern Zhou images, bodhisattvas from Gansu, like this example from Maijishan,[1] tend to simplify the complexity.

This Avalokitesvara wears a dhoti, gathered and tied at the waist. Cloth ribbons, layered from the shoulder to the feet, strongly reinforce the columnar body form while multi-strand ropes of beads pinched at intervals with single larger beads or plaques provide a textured counterpoint. The bead configuration suggests Indian origins and resembles a more abstract version of beaded ropes painted around the neck of Avalokitesvara on the wall of Ajanta Cave I, dating from the fifth to the sixth century (fig. A). This Padmapani (no. 66) captures the singular quality of Maijishan and the northwest cave temple sculptural style in the exquisite balance achieved by the columnar form covered in layers of clothing and embellished with strings of textured beads.

A simple round halo with a lotus formed of overlapping petals frames the head, which has delicately painted facial features. Just above the lip is painted a black wispy mustache, a reminder of the masculine gender of bodhisattvas, despite the often elegantly feminine sculptural images typical of China. The tripartite crown and ribbons that jut out at the sides of the head are features found on Southern Dynasties sculpture to the southwest in Sichuan and on Northern Dynasties examples farther east in Shanxi province.[2]

ALJ

Fig. A. Painting of Avalokitesvara (*below*) from Cave I, Ajanta (fifth–sixth century), showing the strings of beads that become more abstracted in Northern Zhou versions such as no. 66 (after Singh 1965, pl. 26)

67. "Wang Lingwei" dragon stele

Northern Zhou dynasty (557–581), dated 573
Zhangjia Hui Autonomous county, Eastern Gansu
Stone
Height: 113 cm; width: 42 cm
Gansu Provincial Museum, Lanzhou

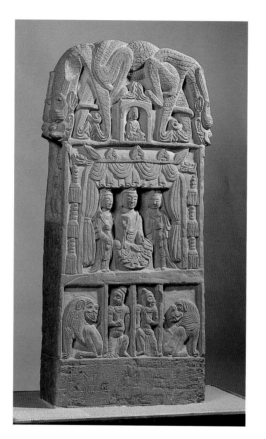

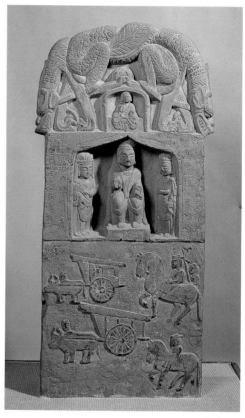

back view

Writing and the art of writing have long occupied an exalted and revered position in Chinese culture. Stelae, stone tablets with inscribed characters and images, provided permanency to written texts such as the Confucian classics, commemorated historical events, and preserved the memory and deeds of noted individuals.[1] Stelae erected above ground, called *bei*, are in the form of an upright stone tablet, often with a base. The tablet itself has two parts, the upper part usually bearing some descriptive title often embellished with designs of tigers, dragons, or birds, and the lower part displaying the inscribed text and possibly other images.[2] Buddhists adapted the stele into their practice and worship, commissioning votive stelae, which became sculptural and increasingly ornate. These Buddhist votive stone stelae are known as *huanyuan fobei* and were usually erected in temples but could also be positioned at roadside sites, in monasteries, in nunneries, in cemeteries, or in private family compounds. Geographically, stelae are found from eastern Gansu across north China to eastern Shandong and south to Chengdu and Jiangsu province.[3]

Donors, including Buddhist monks and nuns, frequently pooled their resources to commission the carving of a stele in honor of the Buddha, or of their families, in the belief that they were thus securing benefit for their families and ancestors, as well as earning merit toward the achievement of enlightenment. Family groups ranging from small to extended clans remained consistent donors of stelae. This stele was commissioned in 573 by Wang Lingwei for the benefit of his family, who is believed to be Xianbei by the dress of the figures depicted on the back of the stele.[4] Apparently, the

MONKS AND MERCHANTS

intent was to seek blessings for the deceased, especially several dead children, in particular, two dead sons who are probably represented on the back as figures riding horses and following ox-drawn carts.[5]

The front of the stele is divided into four parts: an inscribed lower portion; a second tier with two lions[6] and two vigorous, muscular, and topknotted *dvarapala* guardian figures; a third tier that is the main focus, almost stagelike in appearance, with a Buddha figure flanked by bodhisattvas in a deeply cut niche bordered by curtains and large beaded chains issuing from dragons' mouths; the fourth, or top tier has a very small central Buddha in another deep niche, surmounted by a striking pair of intertwined crouching dragons. Both sides of the stele exhibit wonderful dragon heads, on one side hanging over a seated Buddha, probably Sakyamuni, and on the other side, over a cross-ankled bodhisattva, probably Maitreya. Stylistically, the stele begins to reflect the evolution of Northern Zhou sculpture from earlier Northern Wei and Western Wei predecessors. Although the forms on this stele are somewhat softer, rounder, and more solid in the Northern Zhou characteristic style, the vocabulary remains in large part that of Northern and Western Wei. This is especially evident in the linear patterns of falling drapery and scarves, far more typical of the earlier Wei styles than of Northern Zhou. The configuration of the main Buddha's niche framed with its draped curtains and beaded chains recalls the earlier Northern Wei stele in Maijishan's Cave 133 (fig. A) and the entrances to Northern Zhou Cave 4 with their heavy beaded chains and guardians.[7]

On the back of the stele, at the top, a servant leads a closed ox cart carrying two passengers, who are visible through the two windows on the side of the cart. The inscriptions around the back indicate that the figures in this procession were riding to worship the Buddha and demonstrate their sincerity and respect. The larger mounted figure, apparently the older deceased son, rides behind; his status as the older is indicated by his large horse and by the servant protecting his head with a long-handled umbrella or parasol. Below, another ox cart precedes a smaller mounted figure, with no attendant. Both horsemen wear small boat-shaped caps, trousers, boots, and tight-sleeved and belted tunics, typical Xianbei clothing.[8]

Ox carts as an alternative to horse-drawn carriages came into favor during the Han dynasty. Apparently, just after the fall of the Qin dynasty and the establishment of the Han, economic conditions were harsh and neither the emperor nor court officials could observe strict protocols defining the carriage and horses appropriate to each particular rank. In fact, the emperor himself faced difficulty in finding four matching horses to pull his carriage. Han ministers and noblemen were forced to use ox carts, lending the ox cart prestige as an alternate form of transport. However, horse-drawn carriages were still held superior, and wall paintings in Han tombs preserve images of the processions of the literati ruling class in their horse-drawn carriages.

With the collapse of Han and incessant warfare during the Northern and Southern Dynasties (Period of Disunity), ox-drawn carts gained currency through the north and south.[9] It appears that this mode of transportation became popular first in the south and was slower to take hold in the north. The northern Xianbei rulers whose nomadic lifestyle and military prowess were tied to their equestrian skills resisted the ox carts.[10] By the mid-sixth century, however, ox-drawn carts became commonplace in the north, and pottery models were standard burial objects. The ascendancy of full-size ox carts as suitable transport for the upper classes, however, ended with the Tang.

ALJ

1. Tsien 1962, pp. 70–71.

2. *Xi'an* 2000, p. 21.

3. Li 2000, p.398. Stylistically, there appear to be four independent centers of development, in the northwest, the eastern part of the central plains, northeast, southern Jiangsu and Chengdu region (p. 397).

4. *Wenwu* 1988.2, pp. 69–71, esp. pp. 69, fig. 1 (sides of stele), 70, fig. 2, (back), fig. 3 (rubbing of inscription); *Sichou* 1994, no. 104.

5. *Wenwu.* 1988. 2, pp. 70–71.

6. Not indigenous to China, lions were received as tribute to the court from about the first century CE. Symbols of kingship and the Buddha's spiritual power, lions became pervasive from the fourth century through the Tang, as Buddhism flourished. Lions form part of the Buddha's Lion Throne (no. 47) or as guardians flank the Buddha's throne. On this stele, the lions have been placed on the base with the guardian figures. Atypically, they face outward rather than inward, toward the Buddha. The lion on the right is the male, distinguished by his larger size and full curled mane; the female is smaller and the mane is combed back.

7. *Maijishan* 1954, pls. 110 (Cave 133), 224 (Cave 4); this stele also resonates stylistically with the Northern Zhou sculpture from the cave temple site at Xumishan in Ningxia. Although badly eroded and damaged, Cave 46 shares a similar engaging naiveness in form and facial expression as well as a curtained niche with heavy beaded chains (*Xumishan* 1997, no. 85). This stele shares two possible connections with the smaller sandstone stele (no. 54) from Heshui, also from eastern Gansu. The bodhisattvas' three-part scalloped crown is also worn by the three bodhisattvas on the sandstone stele; in addition they share almond-shaped heavy-lidded eyes.

8. *Wenwu* 1998.2, p. 71.

9. Soper 1967b, p. 54. Soper proposes that incessant warfare in the north virtually annihilated well-bred horses and left ox-drawn carts as the only viable alternative.

10. Liu 2000, pp. 274–88. Liu agrees that at times horses were in very short supply but discusses a broader cultural context as well.

Fig. A. Sandstone stele (no. 16) in Cave 133 (*below*), Maijishan, Northern Wei, early sixth century (after *Maijishan* 1998, pl. 101)

68a,b. *Fragments of wall paintings*

Northern Zhou dynasty (557–581) to Sui (589–618)
Cave 78, Maijishan Caves, Tianshui, Gansu
a. fragment with flaming deity: height: 40cm; width: 60 cm
b. fragment with *apsaras*; height: 48 cm; width: 40 cm
Maijishan Art Research Institute, Tianshui, Gansu

In sharp contrast to the dry desert environment of Dunhuang Mogao cliffs, the wetter climate, greater exposure, and frequent earthquakes of Maijishan have inflicted considerable damage on wall paintings there. The materials and techniques used also have contributed to the damage. Initially, a thin layer of mixed organic material—clay, mud, and straw—was applied to the stone walls of the caves, sometimes with a thin finishing layer of plaster to create a more suitable surface for painting. These organic materials never bonded properly to the rock wall, and moisture seeped down between the rock surface and the paintings, causing many sections to fall off the wall. Despite these losses, the original grandeur of the murals is still perceptible, even in the faded and damaged fragments remaining on the walls, particularly Cave 127's Western Wei paintings and Cave 4's Northern Zhou *apsaras*. These two surviving fragments of splendid wall paintings from Cave 78 (no. 68a,b) heighten our awareness of what was lost and further suggest that the combination of Maijishan's superb sculpture (nos. 60–67, 69, 70) and such brilliantly colored paintings must have been dazzling.[1]

In the sixth century, the walls and ceilings of Maijishan were adorned with richly colored and energetically painted panoramic processions of high-ranking donors or with images of gods and god-

no. 68a

MONKS AND MERCHANTS

desses, such as Xiwangmu in her sled pulled by winged dragons and surrounded by immortals and phoenix birds; dragons swept across the ceiling walls and lotus flowers swirled around Buddhas and bodhisattvas.[2] The rich imagery is also reflected in painting techniques. Black modulated brush-strokes deftly defined forms that were then filled with color; or forms were created by washes of color without the enclosing descriptive boundaries of black brushstrokes, a technique know as "boneless" painting. A far less familiar technique incorporates extraordinarily low-relief carving with two dimensional boneless painting to create the exquisitely executed *apsaras* on the walls outside of the Northern Zhou Cave 4.[3]

These two fragments (no. 68a,b) were found in Cave 78 in 1978, when workers from the Mai-jishan Cultural Relics Preservation Institute were cleaning debris from around the Buddha's throne. Fortuitously, the fallen fragments had been covered by earth and debris, which helped preserve the brilliance and intensity of the original colors—blue, green, white, red, orange, and purple—and pro-tect the clarity of the brushwork and images. Of the two fragments, the first (no. 68a) presents the most intriguing imagery.[4] A fantastic figure ablaze with brilliant red-orange flames commands the center of the fragment, while donors hold lotus flowers or buds below to the right and haloed monks stand below to the left. This figure has been identified by the Maijishan Art Research Institute as Ucchusma, the Purifier, or by the alternate Chinese name of *Huotou*, or Fiery Head,[5] one of the Bril-liant Kings of Wisdom, also known in Chinese as Mingwang and in Sanskrit as Vidyarajas.[6] This *Huotou*, Fiery Head, offers a rare pre-Tang representation of one of the Brilliant Kings, a minor eso-teric Buddhist deity. With a mustache and small goatee, Ucchusma has a bare green chest and wears a long red dhoti; deep bluish-purple thin ribbon shawls loop over each arm. His head is aflame, and

1. *Maijishan* 1998, pls.157, 159, 160–71 (Cave 127), pls. 239–244 (Cave 4); *Mai-jishan*1992, pp.11, 12, 114.

2. *Maijishan* 1998, pl. 168 (Cave 127), Xiwangmu; pl. 178 (Cave 110) swirling lotus blossoms.

3. Ibid., pls. 242, 243 (Cave 4); details of the Northern Zhou flying *apsaras* on the wall above the niche, faces, the upper bare body, arms, hands, and feet are defined in the most exquisite and delicate low-relief sculpture, which blends harmoniously with the painted body and flying ribbon scarves. In flight, they play the lute, or other musical instruments or carry footed cups. Exam-ples of this technique occur in Maijis-han's Cave 127 and enrich the Northern Zhou painting in the Shuiliandong Cave of Lashaosi (north of Wushan in south-eastern Gansu); Zhang 1997, p. 186, and the related very low relief mural of the seated Sakyamuni, 36 meters high and dated to 559; Zhang 1994, p.162. Nothing comparable exists at Dun-huang. Michael Sullivan suggests that this kind of low relief sculpture com-bined with painting might offer exam-ples of "relief painting" which is known

no. 68b

only from literary evidence as being practiced by foreign painters in China in the late sixth and early seventh centuries (Sullivan 1969, p. 55 n. 2).

4. Angela F. Howard discussed the images of the canonical set of eight Brilliant Kings that developed in Yunnan and Sichuan during the early Tang and into the Song. In addition to their portrayal as single deities, they are also depicted as sets of five or eight. Although there is no evidence to date of this set of eight deities in northern China, northern clergy generated sets of five or individual images during the Tang. This painted image of *Huotou*, or Fiery Head, may represent one of the earliest images of an individual Brilliant King in northern China (Howard 1999, pp. 93–107).

5. *Maijishan* 1998, p.231, no. 14.

6. Vidyarajas possess the understanding of the sacred formulas or mantras, part of the practice of the esoteric form of Buddhism (ten Grotenhuis 1999, pp. 62–63).

7. *Maijishan* 1987, pls. 14, 15 (Northern Zhou to Sui); *Maijishan* 1992, p. 14, nos. 11, 12 (Northern Wei).

8. *Maijishan* 1998, vol. 2, p. 231, nos. 14, 15 (Northern Zhou to Sui). This volume utilizes the same photographs and articles as the 1992 Japanese edition.

9. *Dunhuang* 1981, pl. 121 (Cave 258).

10. The straight-necked lute was introduced into China during the Northern Wei, the early sixth century, apparently during the reign of Xuan Wudi (r. 499–515) via Gandhara and Kucha. (Wolpert 1981, p. 97). According to the Chinese Musical Research Institute publication (*Zhongguo Yinyue* 1964), the bent-necked lute was also played by celestial musicians by the late fifth century appearing on the walls and ceilings of the cave temples of Dunhuang Caves 288, 290 (p. 14, figs. 5, 7); Yungang Caves 6, 11, 16, and 21 (p. 14, figs. 10–12, 15, 17, 18); Longmen Guyang Cave (p. 15, fig. 20); and Gongxian Caves 1, 21 (pp. 15, 25, 31).

his raised hands literally hold the fire. Confident brushstrokes, modulated in thickness, describe the muscular chest and stomach of this *Huotou*, while more delicate strokes capture the exquisite transparent halos behind the two monks' heads. In spite of damage to the face, the image of the monk to the left conveys a sense of calm and an intensity of focus not unlike that of the Ananda sculpture from another Maijishan cave, Cave 102 (no. 63).

The second fragment (no. 68b) depicts traditional Buddhist imagery of music-making celestials, or *apsaras*, the forms often found painted on the cave ceiling or on walls near the ceiling. This painting preserves the upper half of one *apsara* playing a bent-neck lute and the headless body of another. Here, both painterly approaches to defining forms have been used: black descriptive outlining around the form of the *apsaras*, which also have filled-in color, and the boneless method using white pigment with accents of color to paint the two wisps of cloud. When first included in a Japanese volume on Maijishan in 1987, these painting fragments were dated to a period from Northern Zhou to the Sui dynasty; in 1992, when they were exhibited in Japan, they were redated to Northern Wei.[7] The recent Chinese publication of the site in 1998 attributed a Northern Zhou-to-Sui dynasty date.[8] In Chapter 4, the general discussion of Buddhist art notes that Maijishan shares many features of style and iconography with other cave sites in Gansu such as Dunhuang, as well as showing similarities to sculpture and painting from grottoes in central north China such as Yungang, Longmen, Gongxian, and links to the recent finds in Shandong province. At the same time, Maijishan possesses many other distinctive features suggesting connections with southern dynasties Buddhist art. With these multiple sources of influence and with so many of Maijishan's paintings lost or damaged, a coherent context for these fragments is difficult to reconstruct.

Cave 78, where the fragments were discovered, is one of the earliest surviving caves at Maijishan with late-fifth-century paintings of donors, sculpture, and the deep vermilion red background that characterizes Northern Wei Buddhist paintings. Later additions were apparently made to this cave during

the Northern Zhou and Sui. The style and iconography of painting on the two fragments are more consistent with a somewhat later dating to Northern Zhou to Sui. For example, the *apsaras'* bodies, particularly the gently rounded swelling at the waist, appear more substantial than the ethereal forms of the early-sixth-century *apsara* also from Maijishan (no. 61). The increased softness is also visible in number 68b, in the fluttering, narrow ribbon shawls that languidly loop and turn rather than creating the angular shapes and points so characteristic of *apsaras* from Northern Wei to Western Wei (fig. B). Fragment 68a also exhibits softer, fuller forms, which are quite evident when Maijishan's figures are compared to the haloed monk in Dunhuang Cave 285 dated to Western Wei (fig. A).[9] There is a significant change in garb visible in the fragments as well; they show

not long-sleeved Chinese style robes of the early sixth century but rather a long dhoti and short-sleeved upper garment covering one shoulder. One *apsara* plays a bent-necked lute rather than the straight-necked lute; both kinds of lutes begin to appear sculpted and painted on the walls of caves as early as the Northern Wei.[10]

ALJ

Fig. A. Monk (*above*) painted in the south side of the southern niche on the west wall of cave 285, Western Wei (after *Dunhuang* 1981, vol. 1, pl. 121)

Fig. B. *Apsara* (*right*) painted on ceiling of Dunhuang Cave 285, Western Wei (after *Dunhuang* 1981, vol. 1, pl. 144)

69. *Bodhisattva*

Sui dynasty (589–618), c. 600
Cave 161, Maijishan Caves, Tianshui, Gansu
Clay with traces of white and green pigment
Height: 89.5 cm; width: 24 cm; thickness: 12 cm
Maijishan Art Research Institute, Tianshui, Gansu

This standing bodhisattva came from Cave 161, as did the guardians, or *dvarapalas*, in number 70, and was one of two bodhisattvas flanking the Buddha, probably the figure to the right. The two *dvarapalas* flanked the bodhisattvas, and as guardians stood closest to the entrance of the cave.

As discussed in the entry for number 71, a distinguishing feature of Mahayana Buddhist teachings was the bodhisattva, the embodiment of the ideal of compassion. During the second half of the sixth century, the bodhisattva known as Avalokitesvara became very popular.

Strikingly beautiful in its simplicity, the long-waisted slender body stands in a relaxed stance with the right hip thrust back and the left leg flexed.[1] The figure wears a standard undergarment, which covers the left shoulder and pulls across the midriff, accentuating the soft swell of the stomach and tucking in at the waist. In an atypical fashion, the top of the dhoti rolls over in a thick belt-like effect resembling actual cloth;[2] incised loops define the ripple of the folds down both legs. Thin shawls cover the chest and both shoulders and curve across the legs. The earlier slender Northern Zhou bodhisattva from Cave 10 of the Thousand Buddha Cave in eastern Gansu provides the closest parallel. Except for the more rigid posture, this figure is almost identical in style of garments, tripartite crown, and facial features (fig. A).

Unfortunately, this handsome image has sustained considerable damage, losing the left arm completely as well as the additional shawls or ribbons that would cascade down the side from the round disks at each shoulder. Only the left disk remains. Another Northern Zhou bodhisattva from Maijishan's Cave 141 shares a similar dress configuration and facial features.[3] Although the figure from Cave 141 is also damaged, more details are visible, such as a bracelet with a beaded pattern. The right arm of the figure from Cave 161 bends up to rest on the chest and also has a bracelet at the wrist. The broken fingers with part of a stem visible most likely held a lotus flower, which would identify this bodhisattva as Avalokitesvara in the form of Padmapani, the lotus bearer, typically represented as slight and youthful.

There are some interesting structural details visible from the damaged areas. Iron armature is exposed near the hand used to support the lotus. On the *dvarapala* in the following entry (no. 70a), the armature protrudes from the arm, to support the hand. While not visible as a separate element on this bodhisattva, heads were often crafted separately, inserted in the neck, and secured with additional clay fill.

Although the short-lived Sui dynasty lasted for less than thirty years, Sui sculptural styles evolved rapidly.[4] The strongly columnar and abstract flatness of the earlier Northern Zhou style, reflected in the preceding stone bodhisattva, also from Maijishan (no. 66), gives way to the delicately sweet features and face, graceful ease, and evocative stance of this bodhisattva, with the budding naturalistic shaping of the body. Although Sui succeeded in unifying China politically, it did not last long enough to diminish the impact of the entrenched regional artistic styles. Maijishan's sculpture not only reflects evolution of Sui style from stiff frontal poses to the softer incipient naturalism but also the crosscurrents of regional elements from Gansu and nearby Shaanxi and other parts of eastern and southern China. The survival of such stylistic variations, created in response to multiple sources of influence during the very few years of the Sui, underscores the importance of Maijishan's rich and provocative legacy.

ALJ

1. An even more relaxed version of this stance can be seen on the late Sui bodhisattva from Cave 14 (*Maijishan* 1998, pl. 264); this figure and two *dvarapalas* were published in *Maijishan* 1992, p. 39.

2. Sui bodhisattvas in Dunhuang's Cave 304 also have a thick, rounded roll of cloth at the waist. *Dunhuang* 1981, vol. 2, pl. 20.

3. *Maijishan* 1998, pl. 206, Cave 141.

4. Rhie 1982, pp. 27–54.

Fig. A. Stone bodhisattva with extensive remains of pigment, from Cave 10, Thousand Buddha Cave, eastern Gansu, Northern Zhou (557–581) (after Zhang 1994, p. 168)

70a,b. *Guardian figures (*dvarapalas *or* lishi)

Sui dynasty (589–618)
Cave 161, Maijishan Caves, Tianshui, Gansu
Clay with traces of green, white, and cream pigment
a. Height: 74 cm; width: 23 cm; thickness: 17 cm
b. Height: 78 cm; width: 32 cm; thickness: 21 cm
Maijishan Art Research Institute, Tianshui, Gansu

Throughout the history of ancient world art, guardians are a universal phenomena providing order and protection, symbolically controlling access to sanctified and ceremonial places. The role of guardian can be performed by human, animal, or mythical beings or groupings thereof. In the Buddhist context, guardians perform essential ritual functions, protecting main deities and temples, as well as the *dharma*, or teachings, and themselves manifesting aspects of the Buddhist universe. Two types of guardians developed significant roles in Buddhist art, the *dvarapala* or *dharmapala* (no. 70a,b), guardians of gate or temple, and the *lokapalas* (nos. 74, 78), guardians of the world, the four

194

M O N K S   A N D   M E R C H A N T S

cardinal points of the universe. *Dvarapalas*, known in Chinese as *lishi* or *jingang lishi*,[1] are divine beings who protect the entrances to the temple and shield people from demons; they usually are represented as bald, half-naked, fearsome, muscular athletes with grotesque, almost demonic, faces; they sometimes brandish a thunderbolt (*vajra*). Their ferocity is reserved for external threats, while their benevolence was always available to the Buddha. In contrast, the *lokapalas* (nos. 74, 78), who also display grimacing bulging-eyed facial expressions, wear full-dress armor, boots, and helmets, and brandish weapons.

The triad consisting of the Buddha and two bodhisattvas constitutes the nucleus of every larger configuration in Buddhist art. It may be enlarged to a group of five with the addition of two monks, usually Ananda and Kasyapa, Sakyamuni's two principal disciples and representative of the monastic community. Although groups of five were extremely popular, the number of monks and bodhisattvas could be considerably increased. On the periphery, usually in a group of five or more, a place was often given to the *lokapalas*, two guardian kings and/or two *dvarapalas*, the gate guardians. In Maijishan's Cave 161, these two gate guardians were most likely flanking the bodhisattvas (no. 69) but, in their protective role, were positioned closest to the entrance to the cave.

In Maijishan, *dvarapalas* appear in a number of Northern Wei, Northern Zhou, and Sui caves, with the largest concentration in Northern Wei Caves 83, 85, 112, 139, 142, and 154.[2] With the more slender build characteristic of Northern Wei, the guardian in Cave 112[3] stands with right arm raised and bent across the chest and left arm lowered but perhaps bent up at the elbow. This posture suggests that these were the original positions of the missing parts of the broken arms of guardian number 70a. *Dvarapalas* evolve from this pair of vigorously elegant warriors to the massively powerful guardians of the Tang with their bulging, exaggerated, and sharply defined musculature as seen in the pair guarding the Myriad Buddha Cave, dated to 680, at Longmen and in the surviving figure from Fengxiansi, dated 672–677, also at Longmen, Henan.[4] The ferocious form that these guardians achieved by the end of the Tang is familiar, because of its prevalence in the later gate guardians of Japanese temples.

Although both guardians have sustained severe damage, including loss of the feet and arms, the bodies and heads (no. 70a,b), still convey a forceful posture, a fierce lunge expressed by the thrust forward of the leg and the twisting torso. A dhoti tied at the waist with cloth turned down in the form of a rippled pattern accented by green pigment emphasizes the bulging stomach and bare chest. The sense of movement is further underlined by the diagonal accents of the drapery pulled up over the bent leg and echoed by the incised loops falling down the outstretched leg. The dynamism of the body culminates in the massively square and magnificently articulated head with sharply etched features and remnants of a topknot of hair. Under a furrowed brow, the gaze of the deeply set, wide open, and diamond-shaped eyes is riveting. Echoing the bodhisattva from the same Cave 161 (no. 69), the minimized ornamentation, the smooth roundness of form, and the simple repetitive accents of drapery embody the distinctive elegance of Maijishan sculpture, particularly that from the Sui dynasty.[5]

ALJ

1. The prefix *jingang* means *vajra*, or thunderbolt, which also has metaphysical connotations of what is eternal and incapable of discord or decay.

2. Published in *Maijishan 1992*, pls. 40, 41. In a pair, one guardian has an open mouth while the other's mouth is closed. Apparently, there is no definitive interpretation of this polarity. As with yin and yang, this feature may refer to the inhaling and exhaling of the breath or vital energy.

3. *Maijishan 1998*, pl. 74.

4. Akiyama and Matsubara 1969, vol. II, figs. 144–45; *Longmen 1991*, pl. 8.

5. Rhie 1982, p. 37; *Maijishan 1954*, pl. 110 (Northern Wei Cave 142); p. 176, fig. 31 (Cave 62); pls. 71, 72 (Cave 85); pl. 73 (Cave 83); pl. 274 (Cave 112); pls. 69, 70 (Cave 154); pl. 103 (Cave 139); pl. 251 (North Zhou Cave 48); pl. 264 (Sui Cave 14); pl. 263 (Cave 67)

71. *Standing Bodhisattva Avalokitesvara* (Guanyin)

Sui dynasty (589–618), late sixth century
Found in Qin'an county, Gansu province
Granite
Height: 144 cm
Gansu Provincial Museum, Lanzhou

One of the distinguishing features of the Mahayana Buddhist teachings was the concept of the bodhisattva, which embodies the idea of compassion. A bodhisattva, an enlightened being, makes a
compassionate resolution to aspire to Buddhahood solely to assist others, to free them from the toils
of suffering. Having attained enlightenment, the bodhisattva rejects nirvana and voluntarily chooses
to remain in cycles of rebirth until all sentient beings achieve enlightenment. Iconographically, bodhisattvas had all the spiritual marks of the Buddha, such as the *ushnisha* and *urna* but were distinguished by more elaborate clothing, crowns, and jewelry, reminders of their continuing worldly
connection. Although Bodhisattva Manjusri was mentioned first in the Buddhist scriptures, Avalokitesvara, known in Chinese as Guanyin, was far more popular as a savior in times of trouble.

1. For an excellent English translation of the *Lotus Sutra*, see Hurvitz 1976. This translation is based on Kumarajiva's work.

2. Ibid., 1976, p. xv.

3. Ibid., chap. 25, pp. 316–19. When bodhisattvas originated in India, they were definitely males, but they gradually acquired more feminine characteristics as they cross Central Asia. In China by the tenth to eleventh century, Avalokitesvara, as an elegant goddesslike, white-robed Guanyin, is adopted into the Chan pantheon (Fontein and Hickman 1970, pp. xxvi, 47).

4. Giles 1956, pp. 76–77.

5. *Dunhuang* 1981, vol. 2, pls. 81, 82 (Cave 419); pls. 63, 65 (Cave 420).

6. Rhie 1982, p. 27.

7. *Wenwu* 1998.6, p. 54, fig. 8: left image from the third niche.

8. *Dunhuang* 1981, vol. 2, pls. 81, 82 (Cave 419); pls. 63, 64 (Cave 420); *Maijishan* 1954, pl. 271 (Cave 37); *Maijishan* 1992, p. 67, no. 38.

9. The Maijishan bodhisattva from Cave 37 has similar ropes of jewelry composed of two parallel strings of beads (see note 8).

Fig. A. Head and torso of stone bodhisattva from Maijishan, Sui (589–618) (after *Maijishan* 1992, p. 67, no. 38)

The *Lotus Sutra* (*Saddharmapunarika*), translated in China by Dharmaraksa in 286 and by Kumarajiva in 408, emphasized the importance and power of bodhisattvas.[1] Salvationist cults developed around Maitreya (Milo), Manjusri (Wenshu), and Avalokitesvara (Guanyin). In chapter 25 of the *Lotus Sutra*, the Buddha tells listeners about the efficacy of invoking Avalokitesvara, and about his munificence and compassion for others.[2] Avalokitesvara gained popularity for his virtues, which enabled him through thirty-three different manifestations to solace the faithful, saving travelers and other devout Buddhists from drowning, shipwreck, malicious demons, fire, lust, anger, false beliefs, and delusions.[3] This chapter of the *Lotus Sutra* became an independent text; Avalokitesvara's saving and curing powers became legendary. By chanting this chapter, the Northern Liang ruler Juqu Mengxun supposedly invoked his help to cure an illness, and the famous pilgrim Faxian sought his protection from shipwreck during a harrowing voyage from Ceylon to China.[4]

During the second half of the sixth century, single, large-scale images of the bejeweled Bodhisattva Avalokitesvara become a prominent feature of Buddhist sculpture in China. This Avalokitesvara, identified by the small Buddha Amitabha in the front disk of the crown, was discovered at a site just northeast of the Maijishan Grottoes in Tianshui (fig. A). This Sui dynasty image holds a bottle in the right hand below the hip; the left arm is bent at the elbow, the raised hand holding what was perhaps the stem of a broken-off lotus, perhaps a rose-shaped lotus flower. Comparable sculptures and painted images from Dunhuang, particularly in Caves 419 and 420, and a Northern Zhou stone image from Maijishan, Cave 47 (no. 67), hold a rose lotus in the left hand, a reference to the "lotus holder" or Padmapani, an epithet of Avalokitesvara.[5]

The columnlike form of this bodhisattva is exquisitely articulated by thin layers of clothing, shawls, ribbons, and jewelry, all draped to reveal the gently rounded body. The dhoti is tied around the waist, revealing the soft swell of the midriff, and falls to the feet, defining the shapes of the legs. These early and subtle signs of naturalism seem to be characteristic of Sui sculpture of the late 590s and of the northwest region.[6] The beaded patterns of the looped jewelry chains punctuated by floral disks, and the edges of the shawl animate the smooth surfaces of the body. Rising on a tall slender neck, the large and almost rectangular head is particularly striking, not only for the crown bearing four disks, but for the full rounded face contrasting with the sharply chiseled features.

Interestingly, this figure recalls the earlier examples from Tuoshan Grottoes in Shandong province.[7] Stylistically, and in details of drapery, jewelry, and crowns, the figure relates most strongly to sculpture

and paintings in Dunhuang's Caves 419 and 420 and to sculpture in Maijishan Cave 37. A fragment of a bodhisattva, preserved in the Maijishan Art Research Institute, shares the same serene features, torque necklace and double strand beads (fig. A).[8] All three sites, Dunhuang and Maijishan in Gansu and Tuoshan in Shandong, and this figure from Qin'an, share with stone images from Maijishan's Cave 37 a more restrained style and a columnar body exhibiting varying degrees of naturalism and more organically integrated features.[9] None reflects the interest in heavy harnesses of jewelry often associated with these images of bodhisattvas, especially Avalokitesvara, from the mid-sixth century onward.

Ranking among the very best Buddhist sculptures in this exhibition, this standing Bodhisattva Avalokitesvara combines an elegantly abstract simplicity with a degree of subtle naturalism; together, these characteristics lend the figure its quite monumental and arresting presence.

ALJ

72. *Bodhisattva*

Tang dynasty (618–906), eighth century
Tiantishan Caves, near Wuwei, Gansu
Clay or stucco with pigment
Height: 180 cm; width: 43 cm
Gansu Provincial Museum, Lanzhou

The Tiantishan, or Celestial Ladder Mountain, cave temple site has been carved into a spectacularly situated red sandstone cliff in the Qilian Mountain range, southeast of Wuwei, the most prosperous city of Gansu and the capital of the Northern Liang from 412 to 439. Most scholars agree that this site has the closest historical connections with the ardent Buddhist supporter and ruler of Northern Liang (398–439), Juqu Mengxun.[1]

Overlooking a broad river valley, the site has thirteen numbered caves, numerous small niches, and a colossal seated Buddha niche. In 1927, the cliff sustained severe damage from a major earthquake; in 1958, the broad river valley just below the cliff was dammed to create a reservoir, which flooded some of the caves. At that time, the most salvageable sculpture and wall paintings, including some superb fragments of early-fifth-century wall painting (see Chapter 4, fig. 11), were removed to the Gansu Provincial Museum in Lanzhou.[2]

Most of the Tiantishan sculpture and painting fragments preserved in the Gansu Provincial Museum date from the Tang. The best objects are from the late seventh and eighth centuries, in styles characteristic of the high, or flourishing, Tang to the late Tang. Like the majority of the cave temple sculpture at Dunhuang and in Gansu, most of the Tiantishan images were constructed with armatures overlaid with clay mixed with organic materials. As discussed in Chapter 4 and in the concluding Chapter 10, the development of Tang sculpture reflects intensifying naturalism captured sculpturally in more sensual forms accentuated by layers of draped garments that cling, caress, and define the body.

These qualities embodied in this bodhisattva from Tiantishan become richer, softer, heavier, and more complex. The figure stands on a double lotus base with hands pressed together, palms touching, in the *anjali* mudra of prayer and devotion. The fleshy forms of the broad face are emphasized by the heavy-lidded eyes, while the rounded stomach protrudes between the sash tied at the waist and the dhoti tied below the waist. The hair has been pulled up into a topknot, fanned, scalloped, and ridged like a seashell, and falling in loops on the shoulders. Garments have multiple layers; looping ribbon shawls and ties drape with an exquisite tactile sense of the thickness and texture. Typically, many bodhisattvas display ribbons of cloth. In this instance, three ribbons, perhaps the elongated ties from inside the waist of the dhoti, emerge in front over the waist of the dhoti, falling between the legs and tied at mid-thigh in a series of knotted bows. Eighth-century bodhisattvas at Dunhuang, such as the figure in Cave 194 and another painted on the wall in Cave 199, share a number of these stylistic features with Tiantishan examples.[3]

One of the hallmarks of Tang sculpture is the perfect balance achieved between naturalism and abstraction, between the human and the ideal. In this bodhisattva, the balance begins to shift toward increased naturalism, with the image becoming more intimately human and accessible.

ALJ

1. Zhang and He 1994, pp. 104–8; Howard 2000, pp. 250–51; Rhie 1998, p. 106. The connection between Juqu Mengxun and Tiantishan is first referred to in the monk Dharmaksema's biography (Shih 1968, p. 102).

2. According to the director of the Gansu Provincial Museum, the curatorial staff at the time were given very short notice to remove sculpture and painting from the site before it was flooded. Consequently, the documentation of the original iconographic grouping and configurations of the caves is scant at best. With the exception of a few choice fragments of painting from the early fifth century, the bulk of the salvaged material is Tang sculpture. Some sculpture and painting fragments from the site have been published in *Sichou* 1994, pl. 106 (late polychromed clay seated Buddha); Zhang 1994, pls. 51–54; Zhang 1997, pp. 88–93.

3. *Dunhuang* 1981, vol. 4, pls. 42 (Cave 194), 49 (Cave 199). For a discussion of the characteristics of Tang sculpture from the seventh through mid-eighth century and Indian, Kashmiri, and Central Asian sources, see Rhie 1988.

1. *Binglingsi* 1989, pl. 200 (Cave 10).

2. *Hexi* 1987, Matisi, Qianfotong, Cave 6, pls. 111 (south wall, Ananda) and 112 (west wall, Kasyapa). At first glance, there do not seem to be significant differences between the two monks in Cave 6. However, closer examination reveals that younger Ananda has a smooth, full, rounded head without the furrowed brow, and his neck has horizontal lines suggesting a fleshy neck. The Tang sculpture at Binglingsi, with rounded but somewhat squat figures with proportionately large heads, seems similar to the material found at the Huata temple site, Taiyuan, Shanxi, *China* 2000, no. 174.

3. Sui dynasty (589–618) examples of the definition of the neck on portraits of Kasyapa can be found in Cave 439 and Cave 419 (*Dunhuang* 1981, vol. 1, pl. 159 [Cave 439], vol. 2 [Cave 419].

73. *Buddhist Disciple Kasyapa*

Tang dynasty (618–906)
Cave 10, north wall, Binglingsi Caves, Gansu
Sandstone
Height: 75 cm
Binglingsi Research Institute, Gansu

Often characterized as the golden age of Buddhist art, the Tang dynasty saw the full flowering of Chinese Buddhist art, both in sculpture and in painting. Buddhism enjoyed extensive imperial and popular patronage as cave temple building resurged across China. Under Tang patronage, existing sites in Gansu and Ningxia experienced significant new cave temple-building activity with the most intense at Dunhuang, which added more than two hundred caves to the cliff. Binglingsi, known as Lingyansi (Luminous Cliff Monastery) under the Tang, added more than eighty caves. This sculpture of a monk from the early Tang Cave 10 reflects the increasing naturalism of form and greater emphasis on human and individual qualities that make Tang sculpture eminently appealing.[1]

The figure's informal stance, with both arms folded at the waist, hip thrust outward, and head tilted

Fig. A. Interior of Cave 10 (*above*), Binglingsi, showing the original location of the monk and the guardian (no. 74) (photo: Judith A. Lerner)

in almost quizzical fashion, conveys a sense of immediacy and naturalism. In contrast, the drapery that articulates the monk's body appears far more abstract than the other elements of the sculpture. Except for the uncovered head, bare chest, and exposed sternum, the robe reveals and yet conceals as it falls over the body, the drapery folds defined by abstract patterns of double lines. This often exquisite balance between naturalism and abstraction is quite characteristic of Tang sculpture.

The rather large rounded head rising from a somewhat stylized neck is counterpointed by a comparatively slender body; these characteristics are shared with the early Tang monk figures in Cave 5 at Qianfotong, part of the Matisi complex near Zhangye, also in Gansu.[2] This Tang monk in Cave 5 shares the same physical definition, rounded head and full face with furrowed brow and the vertical line or ridges running down the neck and defining the breastbone and ribs. In spite of the roundness of the head and face, these anatomical details identify this sculpture as Kasyapa, the oldest disciple of the Buddha, rather than the youngest monk, Ananda[3]; this is a portrait strikingly different from the earlier Northern Wei example from Maijishan (no. 62).

ALJ

74. *Guardian or Heavenly King* (tianwang *or* lokapala)

Tang dynasty (618–906)
Cave 10, north wall, Binglingsi Caves, Gansu
Sandstone with remains of pigment
Height: 76 cm
Binglingsi Research Institute, Gansu

Besides the *dvarapala* (no. 70), the second type of Buddhist guardian is known as a *lokapala;* in Sanskrit, *loka* means "world" and *pala* means "guardian." *Lokapala* refers to a distinct set of guardians that protected the four cardinal points of the universe. The Buddhist *lokapala* evolved out of the variety of pre-Buddhist deities in India. According to tradition, these four guardians are believed to dwell on the slopes of the quadrangular mountain, Mount Sumeru, which in ancient Indian cosmology was the vertical axis at the center of the universe. Adapted into Buddhism, guardians not only secured the four entrances to the Buddhist stupas, temples, and altars, but they also were involved in all important events in the Buddha's life, from assisting at his birth to being present at his *parinirvana* (death). They were typically represented in full armor standing on demons.

1. Of the four great celestial kings (*sida-tianwang*), the Vaisravana, protector of the north, was the only one worshiped singly and developed as a separate deity that became very popular in China and Japan (Shi-tenno). This deity is identified by the stupa or pagoda held aloft in his raised hand and often by a bird with outstretched wings on his helmet. Many Chinese legends incorporate interventions of Vaisravana in battles, and in Japan he became one of the seven gods of good fortune (Getty 1928, pp. 166–68; Bunce 1997, p. 165).

2. Fong 1991, p. 99.

3. See *Binglingsi* 1989, pl. 203 (Cave 10), pl. 143 (Cave 38).

4. Ibid. pl. 200 (Caves 10, 38, 64).

5. *Dunhuang* 1981, vol. 3, pl. 17. Cave 322 has a magnificent pair of *lokapalas* with turquoise-color-edged helmets. A marvelous Tang carved wooden *lokapala* still brilliantly painted was excavated from Tomb 206 in Astana burial complex outside modern Turfan, which has been discussed by Baker 1999, pp. 53–57.

6. *Dunhuang* 1989, vol. 1, pl. 165 (Cave 428).

7. Ibid., vol. 2, pl. 46.

8. See Fong 1991, pp. 100–1.

In spite of their Indian roots, the growth and popularity of the four *lokapalas* were largely developed in Central Asia and the Far East, particularly the cult that developed around the guardian of the north, Vaisravana (in Chinese *Bishamen*).[1] In China, the four *lokapalas* were connected to existing cosmological symbols of the four directions, the seasons, specific colors, and animals, as well as other identifying emblems like a sword, and they are also known as the *Sidatianwang* (Four Great Heavenly Kings).[2] Dressed in elaborate armor and helmets, they strike energetic poses with one arm raised and fist clenched, sometimes turning and twisting for dramatic effect, enhancing their martial belligerence; each stands on a dwarfish, demonic creature that squirms under foot.

Although this stone *lokapala* from Cave 10 in Binglingsi does not stand on a demon, his stalwart stance is conveyed by a hip thrust to the right, left arm down with fist clenched and the right hand raised but damaged.[3] One of a pair, his exaggerated mustache and bearded human features, bulging eyes, and furrowed brows further emphasize the menace. The figure is fully outfitted in heavy, molded leather armor. The breastplates, or cuirass, are held in place by ropelike straps descending from a high, stiff curved collar to three straps encircling the midriff; a hip protector and stomach plate are held in place by a girdle tied beneath the bulging stomach. Parts of the tight-sleeved under-tunic flare out at the forearms, and the pleated cloth cascades between the legs. The trousered legs are covered by tight-fitting boots and shin guards. In addition to the sculptural definition of the armor, more detailing was painted on the surface.

Tang sculpture at Binglingsi possesses many of the "classic" stylistic elements associated with Tang; bodhisattvas with voluptuous bodies stand in a sinuous S-curved *tribhanga* posture; faces are full cheeked accentuated by the heavy-lidded eyes, heart-shaped lips, double chin, three-ringed short, fleshy neck, and large topknots of hair.[4] At the same time, since the short necks support proportionally rather large heads, overall sculptural proportions appear somewhat squat and blocky as seen in this *lokapala*. The elegance of the sculpture rests in the languid reverie conveyed by the heavy-lidded eyes and stocky proportions.

A pair of *lokapalas*, not all four, become a standard part of the iconographic configurations in Tang caves, particularly visible in Dunhuang, and the standard group of five—Buddha with pairs of monks and bodhisattvas—becomes seven with *lokapalas* placed at the outside edge of the niche.[5] One of the earliest representations of the four *lokapalas* is preserved on the walls of Dunhuang Cave 428, dated to the latter half of the sixth century, where pairs of guardians flank the Diamond throne pagoda in the middle tier of the west wall.[6] Sculpted images of the heavenly kings are found in the Dunhuang Sui Cave 427 dating from the early seventh century.[7]

By the seventh century, the Four Heavenly Kings gained increasing popularity, and their iconography of the warrior subduing a demonlike creature or large animal such as the bull seems to carry powerful apotropaic connotations. The Buddhist *lokapalas* in full armored regalia replaced the indigenous tomb-warrior tradition and became spectacular *mingqi*, or grave goods, as well.[8] Buddhist guardian figures and tomb guardians became virtually indistinguishable.

ALJ

75. *Funerary vessel*

Tang dynasty (618–907), eighth century
Excavated from a monk's tomb, Wuwei, Gansu
Gray clay with beige slip and paint
Height: 58 cm
Gansu Provincial Museum, Lanzhou

1. *Wenwu* 1997.1, p.13, fig. 31.

2. *Kaogu* 1965.8, p.384, fig. 3.

3. *Huaxia kaogu* 1989.3, p.109, figs.3, 4, details two Tang tombs in Sanmenxia Muncipality; Henan. *Kaogu* 1992.11, p.1010, fig. 2, p.1011, fig. 1, pl. 4, describes a Tang tomb in Yanxi county, Henan. Also see *Wenwu* 1999.2, p. 46, fig. 8, for the roll-out of a floral decoration from a similar vessel of the mid-Tang dynasty.

4. Tokyo 1988, p. 71, fig. 276 (listed from Gansu province) and fig. 277.

5. See *Treasures of Chang'an* 1993, pp. 108–9, fig.29. This *sancai* pagoda-shaped vessel is decorated with stories of filial piety. It is in the collection of the Shaanxi Historical Museum in Xi'an.

6. Vainker 1991, p. 57.

This vessel is made of gray clay with a beige slip and has a lotus decoration painted in dark gray, orange, and red colors. It is made in three pieces. The vessel itself is an ovoid jar with a narrow base that fits in a stand. The stand has cutout patterns and two horizontal lines of fluting that decorate its base. The lid is shaped like a pagoda and has red and black stripes painted vertically down its highly pointed and stepped finial.

Many vessels of similar shape and type have been excavated both singly and in pairs from Tang dynasty tombs.[1] They are often decorated with floral patterns, although the pierced base shown here is quite unusual. A vessel with the same bulbous-shaped body was excavated in the eastern suburbs of Xi'an from the tomb of an imperial granddaughter of the founder of the Tang dynasty. This vessel is also dated to the eighth century. The Gansu Provincial Museum's vessel is in much better condition, and the painting is more intact, but both vessels have almost identically shaped finials. Another Tang tomb also from the eighth century was excavated in Xi'an, and much pottery was found, including two vessels comparable in shape with lotus decorations painted on a white slip ground.[2] Vessels with similar finials have also been excavated from two different tombs in Henan (fig. A).[3] All have flower and lotus decorations, and all are made in three pieces. Two vessels similar in

both shape and finial decoration are in the collection of the Tokyo National Museum. Both of these have painted lotus flowers, and one is said to be from Gansu province.[4] This type of vessel has also been found decorated with a *sancai*, three-color lead glaze.[5] A pottery vessel from the Six Dynasties of similar shape and green glaze, also in three parts, is in the collection of the British Museum.[6]

SB

Fig. A. Clay urn with painted flowers (*above*) from Sanmenxia, Yanxi county (Henan), Tang dynasty (after *Kaogu* 1992.11, pl. 4)

1. *Wenwu* 1998.1, pp. 4–21 and from pp. 22–27, is a discussion about the Sasanian silver coin of Peroz found in one of the caves.

2. Ibid., pp. 13–19.

3. Ibid., colorpl. I:3, p. 14, fig. 19; p. 17.

4. Soper 1950, pp. 75–78.

5. There are two examples of images carved from wood with the Buddha's radiance indicated by raised beveled lines fanning out from the image and filling the mandorla and halo. The first, now in the Musée Guimet (*Sérinde* 1995 p.16, no. 14), is from Kucha, and the other, a standing Buddha from Turfan, is now in the Metropolitan Museum of Art, New York (Ibid., p. 34, no. 35).

6. In Tibetan Buddhist practice of much later date, small clay votive images were placed in relic boxes and worn strapped across the chest if large or at the neck if small. The clay was often mixed with sacred substances such as body relics and could be placed inside large images to consecrate them (Reynolds 1999, pp. 58–59).

7. *Wenwu* 1998.1, p. 17.

76. *Votive plaque with Buddha*

Tang dynasty (618–907)
Cave 142, northern end, Dunhuang Mogao Caves
Unbaked clay with traces of black and red pigment
Total height: 9 cm;.width: 5.4 cm
Dunhuang Research Institute, Gansu

Carved into the eastern side of the Mingsha Mountain, Dunhuang grottoes are divided into a northern and a southern group. Nearly five hundred caves in the southern group have life-size or larger statues of the Buddha, bodhisattvas, monks, and lay devotees and also magnificent paintings of the Buddha's former lives or the promised paradises covering their walls and ceilings. For the most part, the northern group appeared to have only empty and abandoned caves. From 1988 through 1995, systematic surveys and excavations and close study of some 250 caves from the northern group revealed that these were meant for living, storage, meditation, and burial for monks and probably nuns, pilgrims, and artisans[1]; some must have been permanent residents at Dunhuang. The artifacts collected include a Sasanian silver coin of Peroz (no. 94), fifty bronze and iron Chinese coins, and numerous documents and Buddhist scriptures in Chinese, as well as Tibetan, Sanskrit, Mongolian, Uighur, and Tocharian. In addition, the caves yielded leather, textiles including silk and cotton, pottery, and porcelain mostly in the form of pottery jars and lamps, small clay Buddhas, relief sculptures, lacquer, and wooden furniture.[2]

Found in the second room of Cave 142, this small votive plaque depicts Buddha standing on a double lotus base in a rounded, arched niche.[3] Raised parallel lines emanating from the Buddha and filling the mandorla and smaller halo symbolize the mystical or luminous radiance of the Buddha.[4] This technique of fanning parallel lines in relief to articulate the radiance derives from carved wooden images found in Kucha and Turfan dated to the sixth and seventh centuries.[5] The Buddha's robe is draped in traditional Gandharan fashion, covering both shoulders with folds looping down to

the feet and conveying the sense of fullness of the body. In his right hand at his side, the figure holds a tall, narrow-necked vase, a *kalasha*, containing the waters of life, and in his left hand, raised to his chest, he grasps prayer beads, or *malas*, which are used in religious practice by all Buddhists both lay and cleric.

Small votive plaques like this example are made by pressing clay into a mold and are probably air dried. Clearly portable, these small images were most likely used for lay practice and could quite easily be carried by believers on pilgrimages or acquired at the sacred sites visited.[6] Sometimes, the flat back has inscribed mantras, or a mystic syllable, or a date. The details on this plaque, from the drapery folds to the hands holding the prayer beads and vase, are quite sensitive and beautifully articulated.

This votive plaque has been dated to the late Tang, based on the full round form of the Buddha's head and the stocky body and on its similarity to the standing image in Mogao Cave 492.[7]

ALJ

77. *Bodhisattva*

Tang dynasty (618–906), c. 684–755
From Dunhuang Cave site, Gansu
Clay with extensive pigment and painting
Height: 67 cm without wooden base
Dunhuang Research Institute, Gansu

1. No additional information was available from the Dunhuang Research Institute about the context of the discovery of these two clay images. Apparently, the heavenly king and the bodhisattva were found many years ago and no documentation exists.

2. *Dunhuang* 1981, vol. 4, pl. 1 (Cave 320); pl. 21 (Cave 384); pl. 46 (Cave 194).

3. Ibid., pl. 1 (Cave 320).

4. Rhie discusses Tang Buddhist sculpture from the early seventh to mid-eighth centuries, and notes that the process of receptivity to and incorporation of influences from Xinjiang, Afghanistan, India, and Southeast Asia into the framework of Tang style continued (Rhie 1988, pp. 5–41).

Fig. A. Clay bodhisattva (*above*) from Dunhuang Cave 320, early eighth century (after *Dunhuang* 1981, vol. 4, pl. 1)

As discussed in the entry for number 78, this handsome sculpture of a bodhisattva, both of whose arms are missing just below the shoulder, was found with the guardian in the base of one of the many large stupas dotting the Dunhuang cliff site.[1] This bodhisattva reflects the characteristics of the mature, essentially Chinese, Tang style of the eighth century, marked by the curving S-shaped stance with left leg flexed and by sensuously rounded and expansive forms balanced by stylization and abstraction. Here, a long dhoti, rolled and tucked at the waist, clings to the body, with the edge of the fabric falling in a sinuous fold between the legs; raised U-shaped folds loop down on each leg. The fabric of the dhoti is reddish brown with bands of floral patterns painted on a white ground; these patterns also run vertically down the leg and across the bottom edge. A narrow scarf crosses the chest diagonally. One end of the scarf, now broken away and missing, would have fallen grace-fully down the missing left arm. Although Tang bodhisattvas often wear a wide variety of necklaces, composed of disks, beads, and dangles as well as armlets, the examples preserved here are quite dis-tinctive. Each armlet is composed of two separate ridged bracelets, possibly with a beaded pattern, joined together with disks; other disks hang from the lower ring of the bracelet. Flat plaques in a variety of shapes also hang from the double strands of the necklace.

This bodhisattva shares similarities in stance and in drapery detail, as well as a common style of lotus base, with the three bodhisattvas on the west wall of the image niche of Dunhuang Caves 320, 384, and 194.[2] For example, the flat, open-petaled flowers that occur on the white bands of the dhoti can also be found on a number of images in Cave 194; similar large floral blooms occurred in other mediums during the Tang, including the probably eighth-century stupa jar (no. 75).

However, rather than displaying the classic Tang head and face, round with plump cheeks, high arched brows, and puckered, heart-shaped lips, this bodhisattva has a large head with a much squarer shape, a narrow forehead, and full cheeks; the gently arched brows form a continuous line or ridge down the nose. The socket on the top of the head suggests that a looped and tied topknot of hair was made separately and inserted but is now lost. Painted black remnants of a mustache survive above lips less puckered than is usual for the Tang. The head of the bodhisattva in Cave 320 corresponds most closely (fig. A).[3] Both combine a fluid gracefulness and restrained sensuality with a forceful presence, the impact shaped by the subtle undercurrents of continuing interaction with more exotic foreign styles from Central Asia. Tang China maintained its active interest in Central and West Asia until the middle of the eighth century, when the An Lushan rebellion weakened the central government and led to the defeat of a Chinese army by the Arabs at Talas in Central Asia.

This exhibition assembles numerous bodhisattvas from northwest China, with examples ranging from the farthest west in Dunhuang (no. 51) through the Gansu corridor to the southeast in Tianshui (nos. 60, 66, 69, 71, 72, 77), as well as from farther east in the Guyuan area of Ningxia (nos. 56–57), and farthest east almost to the Shaanxi border (no.54). These figures afford the opportunity to see in the broadest terms the evolution and major developments of Buddhist sculpture in the northwest. The sculptural forms clearly reflect the complex stylistic and iconographic elements arriving from Xinjiang and farther west, outside of China, and the internal response of borrowing, rejection, adap-tation, and eventually a synthesis that emerges in the Tang dynasty.[4]

ALJ

78. *Heavenly or Guardian King* (tianwang *or* lokapala)

Tang dynasty (618–906), c. late seventh–mid-eighth century
From Dunhuang Cave site, Gansu
Clay with extensive painting and gilding
Height: 80 cm without wooden base
Dunhuang Research Institute, Gansu

Fig. A. Clay Heavenly King
(*above*) from Dunhuang Cave
194, eighth century (after
Dunhuang 1981, vol. 4, pl. 47)

1. Tang caves at Dunhuang are replete with iconographic groupings of seven typically, including two *tianwang*, see *Dunhuang* 1981, vol. 3, Caves 322, pl. 73, 46, pl. 149; 66, pl. 165.

2. Very little early Buddhist architecture other than cave temples has survived in China. Some of the grandeur of temples in the Chinese capitals was reconstructed from contemporary descriptions and from the early temple structures preserved in Japan, such as Todaiji in Nara, that were based on the Chinese architectural standards. Dating from the late Nara period (710–784) and reflecting Tang style, the four clay guardians in the Kaidanin, Todaiji temple complex in Nara, are positioned on the four corners of the altar. This probably reflects a practice prevalent in the Tang Chinese temples long destroyed by persecution and political upheavals. See Paine and Soper 1975, p. 61, no. 28, pp. 291–323, for a discussion of early Japanese Buddhist architecture.

3. Mary Fong pointed out that the tomb guardians made specifically for burial have identical tunics and trousers hanging down between and over the legs. She suggested that these outfits "impractical for combat, must have been modeled on the costume of Tang palace guards, especially in the tomb of the Tang aristocratic class [which] was designed to resemble the residence of the deceased in real life" (Fong 1991, p. 99).

4. *Dunhuang* 1981, vol. 4, pl. 4, Cave 194, west wall, dated eighth through mid-ninth century.

5. Rhie 1988, pp. 23–25, includes reign of Empress Wu (684–705) and Emperor Xuanzang or Minghuang (713–755).

6. Many, if not all, the stupas dotting the landscape near the Dunhuang Caves are constructed of stucco and could have sustained damage over the centuries, which required rebuilding the entire structure. The history recorded on the stone reliquary container (no. 120) provides some insight into the complex history of pagoda deposits. At the same time, since the iconography and form of the *tianwang* and tomb guardians became virtually indistinguishable, this example could also have been a *mingqi*. This guardian figure is stylistically and iconographically very close to the one in Cave 194.

In their role as guardians of the four directions, *lokapalas*, known as *tianwang* in Chinese, naturally occur in groups of four as discussed in the entry for number 74. However, during the Tang, often only one pair of *tianwang*, not all four guardians, was included in the iconographic configurations particularly visible in Dunhuang caves. Going beyond the standard group of five, which typically comprised the Buddha with a pair of monks and a pair of bodhisattvas, the group became seven in number, with one *lokapala*, or *tianwang*, flanking each of the bodhisattvas at the outside edge of the niche.[1] The two figures may have come to symbolize all four protectors of the Buddhist universe, much as the pair of monks, usually Ananda and Kasyapa, represented the entire monastic community.[2]

Like Binglingsi's guardian (no. 74), the Dunhuang figure has no visible demon to subdue but still assumes the standard aggressive contrapposto stance with legs spread, hips thrust to the right, and right arm raised with one fist clenched. The missing left arm may have been forcefully extended, with the hand open in a gesture perhaps meant to repel or halt any intruder. This figure's menacing and fleshy face, with bulging eyes, furrowed brows, and grimacing mouth, are further emphasized by the frame of his tight-fitting helmet with upturned flaps. A stump of clay on top of the helmet must be the remains of a post that originally had a small plume emerging from the top. Although his armor is very similar to that of number 74, more details of its construction and of embellishments remain visible, the greater definition heightened by color and floral patterning Here, for example, two straps, one on each shoulder, show buckles that secure the stiff, curved collar, which protects the neck, to the breastplate. Both the breastplate and girdle have low-relief plaques elegantly scalloped and scrolled. Fastened under the bulging stomach, a girdle secures the hip-guard, which has a thick, protective underline visible here in an edge of pleats. The shin guards have been covered with floral patterned fabric that has been pulled up in the front and tied just under the knee, an element found on later *tianwang* dating from the eighth century.[3] An almost identical life-size *tianwang* found in Dunhuang Cave 194, dating from the eighth century,[4] displays the same pattern on the leg fabric: single seven-petaled flowers spaced at regular intervals (fig. A). One of the most striking features of this guardian is the vividness of some colors, particularly the turquoise, which strategically accents the armor and fabrics, enhancing its vigor and its visual energy. The *tianwang* and following bodhisattva (no. 77) were produced during the period often referred to as the "Flourishing Tang," when the dynasty reached its apogee of power, prestige, and culture.[5]

In contrast to Binglingsi's stone *tianwang* (no. 74), this clay example has been articulated more fully in the round. This difference is in part due to the materials and the skill of the Dunhuang sculptor. The stone forms at Binglingsi remain more contained; spaces between the legs and the body and arms have not been completely carved out, limiting the sense of movement, while Dunhuang's guardian has a more exaggerated contrapposto, with the legs not only spread farther apart but also completely defined in the round. The layers of cloth hanging down from the undertunic flare out toward the right in response to the figure's movement.

According to the Dunhuang Research Institute, both this *tianwang* and the bodhisattva in number 77, also sculpted from clay and about the same scale and style, were found during the course of repairs to the base of one of the large stucco stupas built near the cliffs during the Song dynasty.

Since the context of these figures is unclear, one key question remains unanswered: Where did these images originally come from? Given their small size, were they originally in a modest niche in Dunhuang that was destroyed, or were they made specifically as an offering for a Tang stupa that was damaged, later rebuilt, and the objects reburied?[6]

ALJ

79. *Head of a bodhisattva (?)*

Tang dynasty (618–906), c. eighth century
Dunhuang Cave site, Gansu
Clay with gilding and traces of pigment
Height: 13 cm
Dunhuang Research Institute, Gansu

Buddhism reached its peak in China during the Tang. Under Chinese military might, this new empire was created, and the Turkic tribes in control of Central Asia were defeated. China reestablished political control over Xinjiang, stimulating a renewed surge of trade, religious, and other contacts with the West. Gansu province, and Dunhuang in particular, flourished with more than two hundred additional cave temples. The Tang dynasty has consistently been characterized by historians as the period in Chinese history that was most receptive to foreign influences.[1] All of this is evident in the sculpture and painting at and around the Dunhuang cave temples.

This head embodies the cosmopolitan elegance, sensuality, and renewed interest in naturalism that characterized the Tang style. Indian influences, from late Gandhara and the Gupta Empire, are evident in the softer, more rounded forms of the head; the half-closed eyes suggest introspection and meditation, retaining a certain aloof quality despite the more naturalistic forms. The gilding gives the head a compelling divine radiance.

It is very difficult to determine whether this head belonged to a Buddha or a bodhisattva. However, the head closely resembles that of the standing bodisattava, also from Dunhuang (no. 77).

ALJ

1. The cosmopolitan atmosphere of the Tang capital at Changan (modern Xi'an) and the interest in exotic goods have been brilliantly documented by Schafer 1963, pp. 7–39.

5

Gandhara in Gansu

CHEN BINGYING

Between the first and fourth century CE, the Buddhist art of Gandhara flourished, developing an eclectic style dominated by classical Western sources mixed with Indian, Iranian, and other elements. This Gandharan style owed much to the region's unique geographic position at a crossroads of commerce and religion. By the first century CE, the powerful Kushan Empire controlled territory from northern and northwestern India into the Central Asian regions. Their territory encompassed Gandhara, the portions of what is now Pakistan and Afghanistan are where the ancient trade routes connecting the Roman Mediterranean world to the Indian subcontinent in the south and to China in the east came together (See Map 1, pp. 22–23).[1] Gandhara, heavily influenced by Rome, became one of two prominent artistic centers of the Kushan Empire; the other center was in and around the northern Indian city of Mathura with its heritage of indigenous Indian traditions. Some of the first images of the Buddha and his life were sculpted in stone or in stucco in the Gandharan cities of Taxila and Peshawar and crafted in stone or clay in Mathura.[2] More traditional Gandhara not only made an important contribution to the development of Buddhist imagery and iconography but also achieved a significant position in the history of world art.

Although separated from Gandhara by several thousand miles, Gansu province was situated on the eastern end of the same major overland mercantile and cultural artery linking China with Central Asia, India, and ultimately the Roman Empire. Moreover, Gansu was particularly receptive to Buddhism, with the religion and its supporters garnering patronage from Buddhist nomadic rulers. More early Buddhist cave sites survive in the Gansu region than in any other part of China. The Buddhist sculpture and painting preserved there, mostly in cave temples (see Map 3, p. 120) were inevitably influenced by the movement of Gandharan art across the trade routes. Since Gansu's earliest known cave temple sculpture and painting date from the fifth century, the work is contemporaneous with the development of the later phases of Gandharan art, when absorption of Indian elements, mainly those derived from Mathura, gradually reflect a more Indianizing style.[3] Add to this strong Indian influence the absorption of new elements during the transmission of Gandharan forms across Central Asia and the modification of style and content within China, and it is not surprising that in the surviving Buddhist art in Gansu, the Chinese and Mathuran traits are more pronounced than early Gandharan ones. However, if one examines the art in detail, it is not difficult to discover within Gansu's more than one-thousand-mile length many examples of early and later Gandharan stylistic features. These are discussed below with examples drawn largely from sculpture and paintings in Gansu cave temples but from other small votive images as well.

OPPOSITE: Standing Buddha, painted clay and stucco, south end of niche 6 of Cave 169, dated 420 CE at Binglingsi Cave Temple, Gansu (photo: Annette L. Juliano)

211

Among the most famous Buddhist caves in Gansu are those at Dunhuang Mogao; these caves at the extreme western border of Gansu on the periphery of the Gobi Desert are also closest to Gandhara via the trade routes. All three of the earliest caves, Caves 268, 272, and 275, date from the Northern Liang (398–439) and display Gandharan features. For instance, the main Buddha images in Caves 268 and 272 both have the countenances characteristically found on Gandharan sculpture: serene faces; long, straight noses that connect directly with the line of the finely arched eyebrows; long, tapered, half-closed, almond-shaped eyes; delicate lips; and tall, elaborately waved *ushnishas*, or cranial protuberances (figs. 1, 2).[4] The modeling of the anatomy is powerful, and proportions are basically naturalistic. On each figure, the robe drapes across the body in the typical Gandharan "open mode," which leaves the right shoulder bare, while the robe crosses the chest and covers the left shoulder.[5] The folds are delineated with curved raised ridges, but the edge of the robe falling over the left shoulder conveys the weight and feeling of pendant cloth. Both images have round haloes.

In Cave 268, the sides of the main Buddha's niche on the west wall are flanked by pillars topped with the Ionian-style capitals of ancient Greece. The posture of the cross-legged Buddha with inward-pointing toes, identified by most scholars as a Maitreya or Buddha-to-be, is very reminiscent of certain third-century CE Gandharan relief carvings.[6] Cave 275 is dominated by several cross-ankled bodhisattvas, including the large main image on the west wall (fig. 2) and two flanking figures, each sitting in a niche, in the north and south walls.[7]

Fig. 1. Seated Maitreya, painted clay and stucco (*left*), main image, west wall, Dunhuang Cave 268, Northern Liang (398–439) (after *Dunhuang* 1981, vol. 1, pl. 6)

Fig. 2. Seated Maitreya, painted clay and stucco (*right*), main image, west wall, Dunhuang Cave 275, Northern Liang (398–439) (after *Dunhuang* 1981, vol.1., pl. 6)

Above these images, in an upper tier on the north and south walls, are two more bodhisattvas tucked into niches, one sitting cross-ankled and the other in a meditating posture with one foot resting on the opposing knee and one hand gently touching the chin. All these bodhisattvas have been identified as images of Maitreya, suggesting that this cave was consecrated to Maitreya. Maitreya images were already relatively common in third- and fourth-century CE Gandhara, and the emphasis on Maitreya in Cave 275 could represent a direct borrowing from the Gandharan artistic repertoire.[8] In this instance, however, it may be that the popularity of sutras featuring Maitreya within the Gansu corridor itself was an even more important factor contributing to the decor of the cave than any direct link back to Gandhara.[9]

The surprisingly strong connections between these early Dunhuang Mogao Caves, particularly the large central cross-ankled image of Cave 275, and the Gandharan sculptural and iconographic vocabulary are visible in comparisons to the Gandharan schist relief dated to the third century CE found in Charsadda (Pakistan) and now in the Museum für Indische Kunst in Berlin (fig. 3).[10] This Berlin relief depicts a bare-chested and cross-legged bodhisattva with a powerfully modeled physique wearing a dhoti with a single loop of beads and a pectoral ornament. While the folds of dhoti on the Dunhuang Maitreya from Cave 275 have been delineated by applying strips of clay, the Gandharan relief displays another variant of this type of fold.[11] Cave 275's definition of the folds with lines of clay in raised relief clearly imitates the relief carving of drapery in Gandharan art. A particularly striking similarity is visible in the nearly identical backs of two thrones, a form best described as an inverted triangular backrest with a halo just above, positioned behind both the Dunhuang Maitreya and a possible Gandharan predecessor, also a Maitreya.[12]

Maitreyas are often identifiable by a small Buddha represented in the crown. To cite one example, in Dunhuang Cave 275 the Maitreya wears a crown composed of three disks; the center disk contains a small seated Buddha in a meditation posture. This type of crown is perhaps a transformation of the stupa-shaped ornament worn by Gandharan images of Maitreya and inspired by the brief mention of a crown adorned with Buddha images in the *Sutra of Maitreya Ascends to the Tushita Heaven*.[13]

In 439 CE, the Tuoba Wei, who had conquered nearly all of north China, succeeded in defeating the Northern Liang and driving the remnants of the Northern Liang ruling family farther west into Central Asia. During the Northern Wei era, which followed the Tuoba victories, cave-building activity continued to thrive. Some of the Northern Wei caves, particularly those dating from 465–495, continue to exhibit Gandharan elements that are especially noticeable in Cave 254.[14] The image of Maitreya on the upper level at the front of the south wall has an imposing bare chest with a torque necklace ending in confronting serpent heads. This image refers to the story of the Buddha subduing the black serpent.[15] In the story and in the Gandharan portrayals, the Buddha subdues the serpent, which crawls into an alms bowl; however, in the hands of the Dunhuang sculptors, the serpent has been transformed into ornament.[16] This transformation symbolizes the equality of all living things, with the taming of the serpent a manifestation of the Buddha's power.

Fig. 3. Maitreya preaching to an audience (*top*), stone relief, Gandhara, c. third century CE, said to have been found at Charsadda (Pakistan), (photo courtesy Museum für Kurst Berlin)

Fig. 4. Seated Buddha with white robe (*above*), painted in middle section of the west wall, Dunhuang Cave 254; Northern Wei, second half of the fifth century CE (after *Dunhuang* 1981, vol. 1, pl. 30)

Painted images, such as the imposing white-robed Buddha image (fig. 4) painted on the center of the west wall of Cave 254, possess many of the same stylistic features that have been discussed above. The folds of the Buddha's robe hang in thick, irregular, densely packed, painted arcs conveying the impression of a heavy fabric and recalling the strong naturalism of Gandharan sculptural drapery style.[17] Although no examples of Gandharan wall paintings have yet been discovered, this image may suggest that Dunhuang mural painters adopted some of the Gandharan sculptural traits into wall painting.

The use of high-relief sculpture in the Dunhuang Mogao Caves of the Northern Liang and Northern Wei dynasties, the use of applied ridges to model drapery folds, and the general appearance of the images of these periods are all evidence of the influence of Gandharan art on Dunhuang.[18]

Sutra Pillars

Carved exclusively during the Northern Liang kingdom (3980–439), the miniature stone votive stupas sometimes known as sutra pillars (421–439) from Dunhuang, Jiuquan, and Wuwei also preserve Gandharan elements. For example, the configuration of the seven Buddhas of the Past and the Maitreya represented on the central register of the sutra pillar dedicated by Gao Shanmu and dated to 428 (no. 48) refers to a theme that had already appeared in Gandharan art in the second and third centuries CE. Despite the small size of the Buddhas, their strongly rounded bodies are clearly articulated by robes covering both shoulders, falling into slightly asymmetrical, densely packed loops across the chest and legs, and conveying an impression of thick cloth. The treatment of these robes and the meditation postures of the seated Buddhas, coupled with the oval faces, tall *ushnishas*, and long ears, reflect a fusion of Gandharan and Mathuran characteristics.

On the octagonal base of the sutra pillar stand the eight "Divine or Spirit Kings," who attended Sakyamuni's passing into Mahaparinirvana.[19] The four male and four female deities function as guardians of the Dharma Law and occur in Gandharan and later Mathuran art. Here, the male figures with their haloes have bare chests and wear short dhotis, while the females wear long narrow-sleeved and narrow-waisted tunics and long skirts and stand with hips thrust to the right; all share similarities with the earlier sword-bearing female figures on the railings of the Gandharan period stupas. The Dragon Kings on the Gao Shanmu stele hold bottles in the pendant left hands, while the raised right hand holds a hill-shaped object of flower petals, features clearly derived from the Dragon King images that appear in late Gandharan art who also hold bottles in the left hand and flowers in the right. The trident held by the Divine Kings originates in Hinduism, where it symbolizes Shiva, but in Gandharan art, the trident had already become a weapon generally associated with warriors.[20]

Other Cave Temples: Matisi, Jintasi, and Binglingsi

East along the Gansu corridor from Dunhuang, the Matisi cave temple complex including Jintasi is near the city of Zhangye, whereas the Binglingsi Caves are even farther to the east. Believed to be Northern Liang (398–439), the early caves at these sites such as Cave 2 of the Thousand Buddha Grottoes at Matisi

Fig. 5. Standing Buddha (*below*), stucco with paint, north wall back section, Binglingsi Cave 169, dated 420 (after *Binglingsi* 1989, pl. 18)

and the two eastern and western caves at Jintasi all reveal elements of Gandharan style in their iconography and in the anatomy and dress of the images. One striking example is the image of the ascetic Buddha from the central pillar of the Eastern Cave at Jintasi. Cave 169 at Binglingsi in Yongjing bears an inscription dated "first year of Jian Hong" (equivalent to 420), which is the earliest known dated cave in China. The images in this cave exhibit a mix-ture of different styles. The face of the standing image on the north wall (fig. 6) is in Chi-nese style with a relatively large *ushnisha*, while the drapery is in Mathuran style, clinging and clearly defining a powerful physique. The image wears a Hellenistic-style outer gar-ment; the edges of the sleeves are rendered as frills, which lend a sense of weight and thick-ness to the garment. The folds of the inner garment are rendered as curves, a few executed in relief. All the above characteristics are closely related to the Gandharan style. The large standing Buddha in Cave I also exhibits the same features, and its almond-shaped eyes are even more characteristic of Hellenistic and Gandharan sculpture.

Maijishan

The grottoes of Maijishan are regarded as one of the four great cave temples of China and have been lauded as a "museum of East Asian sculpture."[21] The sculpture of the early caves again combines many stylistic elements, including Gandharan features. The columnar torsos with upright heads, the large *ushnishas* with wavy hair, the serene and dignified expressions, the oval faces with fine lips, the long noses joining directly with the foreheads in an arc, the almond-shaped eyes with long eyebrows, and the large ears are all Gandharan characteristics. The main image in Cave 78 in the lower middle tier and the bodhisattvas on either side of the main image in Cave 74, which are the earliest images at Maijishan, dating to the period 445–502, possess these same characteristics. Moreover, the modeling of the high-relief images in the early caves also reveals connections with Gandhara.

Baoquansi and Londongsi

Baoquansi and Londongsi cave temples are at the extreme western end of Gansu province. The image of the Buddha in Niche 5 at the Baoquansi caves in Heshui county (fig. 6) also combines Gandharan and Chinese elements.[22] Although the face is predominantly Chinese in style, the tall *ushnisha*, the square proportions of the head, the straight nose, fine lips, and large ears reflect Gandharan models. Most noteworthy, however, is the *kasaya* robe covering the whole body. The drapery folds on this are carved in densely packed grooves, giving the appearance of relief. These folds form curved arcs in an asymmetrical arrangement that is typical of the Gandharan style of drapery. In addition, both the theme of the Seven Bud-dhas and the treatment of drapery on the images in Cave 165 of the Northern Grottoes at Qingyang and Cave I at the Southern Grottoes at Jingchuan, dated 509 and 510, respec-tively, are inspired by Gandharan models.

Bronze Images Showing Gandharan Style

Early bronze devotional images of the Buddha in the exhibition also betray features derived from Gandhara. The zigzag pattern on the parasol of a gilt-bronze image of Buddha from

Yudou in Jingchuan (no. 47) dated to the Later Qin period (384–417) closely resembles the linked sawtooth pattern appearing on Gandharan objects. Other features of this same piece such as the lion throne, the high *ushnisha,* the full face, the prominent nose, the elongated eyes and the treatment of the folds as concentric U-curves spilling over the throne are very close to those found on a comparable Gandharan sculpture from the Loriyan Tangai region.[23] The treatment of the rather square base of the Yudou image is similar to that in third-century CE Gandharan art.[24] The early Northern Wei bronze Buddha (no. 55) from the Qingyang District Museum also has many features that reflect the influence of Gandharan art: the tall *ushnisha* with "snail curls," the long ears, and the protruding eyes are all reminiscent of Gandharan Buddhas. The robe fully covers the body in a series of dense parallel curves, and the scarf is twisted at the neck and falls down behind the shoulders to emerge from between the arms and body, traverses the wrists, and falls across the corners of the throne. The use of incised twin lines produces an impression of drapery folds in relief. Aspects of the decoration on the throne, particularly the flaming halo and the *tribhanga* stance of the Heavenly Kings on the rear of the mandorla, have clear precedents in Gandharan Buddhist art.[25]

In summary, the influence of Gandharan art on Gansu Buddhist art was multifaceted. It included iconography, appearance, posture, drapery, and architecture as well as sculptural technique. The characteristics of Buddhist images of eastern and western Gansu were somewhat different, and this difference very likely reflects the degree to which indigenous traditions were incorporated, the different periods at which other cultural elements were absorbed, the routes by which they arrived, and the strength of the outside influence.

Fig. 6. Seated Buddha, stone, niche 5, Baoquan Caves, Northern Wei, late fifth–sixth century (after *Longdong* 1987, pl. 165)

Notes

1. Errington and Cribb 1992, p. 1.

2. There has been much debate about the cultural compo-nents that shaped Gandharan art, particularly if Greek or Roman influences contributed more; for various perspectives, see Czuma 1985, pp. 20–25; Errington and Cribb 1992, pp. 36–41, 43–48; for a summary of fairly recent research in Gandharan art, see Taddei 1998, pp. 51–56.

3. Czuma 1985, pp. 38–39.

4. Although there may have been some restoration to the head, it has not been completely remodeled and remains a valid research specimen.

5. Griswold 1958, pp. 92–111, fig. 3.

6. See, for example, the two stone reliefs depicting the story of Nanda, the Buddha's half brother, who is shown in the cross-ankled position, and the interpretation of Maya's dream in which King Suddhodana is also depicted in cross-ankled position, both illustrated in Marshall 1960, figs. 116 and 54, respectively. The cross-legged position of the legs resting against the chair with the toes facing inwards is third century BCE Hellenistic, resembling the cross-legged Buddha described above. See Zhu 1960, pl. 361. The coinage of the Saka people (Pre-Kushan) who controlled northwestern India in during the Parthian period also depicts personages seated in the cross-ankled position.

7. The central part shows a *jataka* story, while the lower part shows donors, *Dunhuang* 1981, pl. 12.

8. Marshall 1960, pp. 103 ff. Although many scholars believe that the cross-ankled position of the legs of an image indi-cates a Maitreya, the identification of these cross-legged images as Maitreyas is far from certain. See Abe 1990, p. 1 n. 13, where Abe summarizes the existing points of view.

9. In 303 CE, Zhu Fahu translated the *Mile xia shengjing* (Sutra on Maitreya's Rebirth [Descent]) into Chinese, see Sponberg and Hardacre 1988, pp. 38, 87, 133, 166, 176, 229, 242, 272; in 402 Jiu Moluoshen (Kumarajiva) translated into Chinese the *Mile Dacheng Fojing* (Sutra of [Maitreya] Attain-ing Buddhahood) and *Mile xiasheng chengfojing.*(Sutra on [Maitreya] Achieving Buddhahood Below), see ibid., pp. 97, 100, 176, 225, 229, 272. In 455, Juqu Jingsheng (brother of the Northern Liang ruler Juqu Mengxun) translated the *Guan Mile Pusa shang sheng Doushuaitianjing* (Sutra on Visual-izing Maitreya's Rebirth above in Tusita Heaven) into Chi-nese; see ibid., pp. 45, 97, 99–100, 106, 176, 272. All these sutras were very popular in Gansu.

10. "Maitreya Preaching to an Audience," in Metropolitan Museum of Art 1982, p. 58, no. 1.

11. Rhie 1976, p. 457.

12. See Takashi 1990, appended fig. 16.

13. For stupa-shaped ornaments on Gandharan images of Maitreya, see Takashi 1990, pls. 4, 9, 13, 14.

14. *Dunhuang* 1981, pls. 26–37.

15. See ibid., vol. 1, pl. 209.

16. See Marshall 1960, pl. 113, for a depiction of Buddha taming the Black Serpent at Rajagriha. In the Buddhist alms bowl there is a coiled snake and beneath it two more snakes raising their heads. The serpent is a mysterious and powerful creature that instills fear in people, so in China, Greece, India, and many other countries, there exist myths concern-ing the worship of snakes. For instance, in the Museum of Fine Arts, Boston, there is a mid-second millennium BCE carved ivory figure of a Cretan priestess who holds in her hands two gold-foil plaques in the form of snakes (see Zhu 1960, p. 103, fig. 235).

17. *Dunhuang* 1981, pl. 30.

18. Before the reforms of the Taihe period (477–499), most of the physiques are full-bodied, with little sense of move-ment; the faces are round, or oval, the eyebrows are long, the eyes bulging, the nose is bowed, the shoulders are wide, and the chest is flat.

19. Scholars have divided opinions about the identification of these figures. For a brief summary of some of the interpreta-tions, see Wang 1999, pp. 70–91.

20. See Yin Guangming, *Dunhuang yanjiu* 1996.4, pp. 8–19; 1997.1, pp. 81–89; 1997.3, pp. 84–94.

21. For a compendium of photographs of the sculpture and painting from Maijishan, see *Maijishan* 1998.

22. For some photographs of the Baoquansi site, see *Longdong* 1987, pp. 162–67.

23. See Marshall 1960, pls. 118, 120, 135, 136, 98, 116, 117, 133.

24. Ibid.

25. Ibid.

PART III

FOREIGN MERCHANTS: FROM COLONISTS TO CHINESE OFFICIALS

6

The Merchant Empire
of the Sogdians

Judith A. Lerner

Men of Sogdiana have gone wherever profit is to be found.

Xin Tangshu (New Tang History)

The impetus for the cross-cultural exchange that marks the period between the fourth and seventh century was mainly economic, facilitated by the activities of merchants and their caravans. Although Persians, Syrians, and Indians, among others, engaged in the trans-Asian trade, the main actors were the Sogdians, an Iranian people who inhabited the region of Transoxiana (in present-day Uzbekistan and Tajikistan) in Central Asia. This dry but fertile land incorporated the two great rivers of the Amu Darya (known to the Greeks as the Oxus and to the Arabs as the Jayhun) and the Syr Darya (the Jaxartes, or the Sayhun). While the traditional center of Sughd was the region between these rivers, dominated by the city of Samarkand, Sogdiana was actually larger, defined by those areas where the Sogdian language was spoken. It extended west to the oasis cities of Bukhara and Paikend, not far from the Oxus, east to the Ferghana Valley, and northeast to Shash (present-day Tashkent, Uzbekistan) and beyond, to Semirechye (in present-day Kazakhstan and Kyrgyzstan) in the foothills of the Tianshan Mountains that mark the border with Xinjiang (Chinese East Turkestan).

Unlike the Sasanian Empire in neighboring Iran, with its centralized system of government, Sogdiana was a land composed of small city-states rather than a single polity. It functioned as a feudal society with an active and important mercantile class (see Chapter 7). Although Samarkand was its most important city, and at times dominated the area, the Sogdian city-states developed independently, with local princes sometimes owing allegiance to more powerful rulers. Perhaps as early as the fifth century, and certainly by 510, Sogdiana came under the domination of the Hephthalites, a nomadic people who had moved west from northwest China and, by the mid-fourth century, had penetrated into eastern Iran and northwest India, alternating between being allies and enemies of the Sasanians. In the middle of the sixth century, Sogdiana fell to the Turks, another nomadic group, who joined with the Sasanians to defeat the Hephthalites. Dividing the former Hephthalite lands with the Sasanians, the Turks established their empire (*kaghanate*) in the northern portion of Hephthalite rule, stretching from the Black Sea to the Chinese border and including Sogdiana. Throughout these vicissitudes, the Sogdian city-states, despite the initial ravages of conquest, appear to have thrived.

OVERLEAF: Remains of a Sodgian citadel in the Zerafshan Valley, vicinity of Samarkand, Uzbekistan (photo: Aleksandr Naymark)

OPPOSITE: Some of the life-size statues of foreign dignitaries that flank the entrance of the mausoleum of Emperor Gaozong (d. 683) at Qianling, outside Xi'an. Represented are members of the deposed Sasanian royal family, as well as kings, princes, and emissaries of foreign countries associated with the Tang court. (photo: Judith A. Lerner)

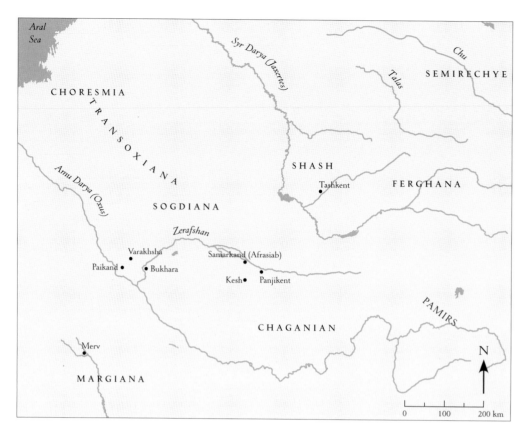

Map 3: Map of Sogdiana and
surrounding regions

The basis of Sogdiana's economy was agriculture, relying on artificial irrigation from its major rivers. However, agriculture alone could not ensure Sogdiana's prosperity, and from at least the early centuries CE it relied on trade. With the Late Roman–Early Byzantine and Sasanian Empires to its west, the Russian steppes and Perm region to its north (the "Fur Road"), Bactria (present-day Afghanistan) and India to its south, and China to its east, Sogdiana was ideally located to establish the vast trade network that allowed its citizens to serve as the prime middlemen in the exchange of goods, as well as ideas, from one civilization to another. Thus, from at least the third century, Sogdian merchants were traveling regularly to and from the upper Indus River region (present-day Northern Pakistan), where they met their Indian counterparts arriving from Kashmir or from the lowlands of Gandhara.[1] They traded textiles and other wares in the north Caucasus and, from the mid-sixth century, had direct trade relations with Constantinople.[2] Sogdian trading activity to the east in Xinjiang and in China proper was well-established by the early fourth century CE, as attested by the so-called Ancient Letters, dating to 311 (no. 8), and by contemporary Chinese chronicles.[3] The Sogdians' overlords, whether Hephthalites or Turks, supported their mercantile activities by making the roads safe, as the successful trade established by the Sogdians also benefited them; even before Turkic rule, nomadic mercenaries protected the Sogdians' caravans.

So dominant were merchants of Sogdian origin that the Sogdian language became the lingua franca of the Silk Road. The Khotanese applied the term *sūlī* (Sogdian) to any merchant, regardless of his ethnic origin.[4] The Chinese viewed the Sogdians as a merchant race and told anecdotes to illustrate their sharpness:

> Mothers give their infants sugar to eat and put paste on the palms of their hands in the hope that when they are grown, they will talk sweetly and that precious

objects will stick [to their hands]. These people are skillful merchants; when a boy reaches the age of five he is put to studying books; when he begins to understand them, he is sent to study commerce.

They excel at commerce and love profits; from the time a man is twenty, he goes to neighboring kingdoms; wherever one can make money, they have gone.[5]

Yet the Sogdians were not the only merchants who plied the Silk Road, despite their apparent control over it. Traders from other nations—Persia, Choresmia (the region north-west of Sogdiana), Syria (mainly from Palmyra), and India attached themselves to the Sog-dian caravans.[6] Of these nationalities, it would seem that the Persians, coming from one of the most powerful countries in the known world, would have been far more dominant.

Established in 224 CE, Sasanian Iran was a centralized state, ruled by a King of Kings, whose supreme authority was based upon his claim to divine descent and whose sovereignty was supported by Zoroastrian clergy (fig. 1). According to the Zoroastrian texts, Sasanian society was divided hierarchically by professions: priests, warriors (the nobility), scribes, peasants, and artisans. Merchants were ranked at the bottom of the "lower" professions, although commercial activity was regarded as a necessary and legitimate pursuit.[7]

Sasanian trade seems to have been in large part state-supported. Like its predeces-sor, the Parthian state, the Sasanian central government established a monopoly on those sections of the trade routes that passed through Iran, thereby preventing direct contacts between the Sogdian caravans and the trading centers of Byzantium in the West.[8] After unsuccessful attempts to gain Sasanian permission to travel through Iran to sell silk directly to the west, the Sogdians appealed to their new overlords, the Turks, to enter into a trade agreement with Constantinople; the Turkic-Sogdian embassy to Constantinople of 568 resulted in the opening of a new trade route across the Caucasus, avoiding Iran.[9]

Fig. 1. Investiture of the founder of the Sasanian dynasty, Ardashir I (r. 224–241 CE) by the god Ahura Mazda, rock relief at Naqsh-i Rustam, Iran. The Sasanian King of Kings right to rule was divinely granted, here symbolized sculpturally by Ahura Mazda, on the right, handing Ardashir a diadem. (photo: Judith A. Lerner)

There is some dispute regarding the degree to which the Sasanians and Sogdians acted in concert or in competition in the Silk Road trade. That they were in competition is attested by the Sasanians' closing their territory to foreign caravans, but it seems that, until the middle of the sixth century, the Sogdians dominated the overland route across Central Asia, while the Sasanians' state-supported trading network developed the maritime route to the East (see Chapter 1).[10] With the ascension of Khosro I (r. 531–579) to the Sasanian throne and his reassertion of a strong centralized rule, the Sasanians began to expand their influence in the overland China trade. The annexation of former Hephthalite territories gave the Persians a firm foothold in Central Asia, while successive diplomatic delegations to the Chinese court helped to establish and strengthen Persian influence, political, and, most likely, economic.[11] While these missions began in the middle of the fifth century, evidence of direct Persian overland trade with China does not appear until late in Sasanian times and after. Not until the Tang period is there evidence of a number of Persians trading with and settling in China. This number increases, so that at the height of the Tang (prior to the rebellion of the general An Lushan in 755),[12] Persian merchants and artisans were as active as Sogdians in China—however, these are no longer "Sasanian" Persians, but Persians now living under Arab rule.[13]

This absence of a direct Persian trade until relatively late in the Sasanian period may explain the paucity of actual Sasanian goods found in tombs in China contemporaneous with the period. With the exception of Sasanian coins (see Chapter 9 and nos. 93–95) and glassware found in pre-Tang Chinese tombs (no. 30),[14] there is little that can be identified as purely "Sasanian" (an example is the ring from Li Xian's tomb, no. 32). Such metalwork as the silver hunting plate from the Northern Wei tomb of Feng Hetu (d. 504) is only Sasanian in appearance and was most likely made east of Iran[15]; the silver wine cup from another Northern Wei tomb, that of Li Xizong (d. 540) and his wife, has Roman rather than Sasanian affiliations.[16] Indeed, as the historian Shih Hsio-yen has observed, "[I]t is striking that none of the well-established indicators of Sasanian silverwork are to be found among the Chinese discoveries."[17] Only with the upswing in diplomacy between the Sasanian and Chinese courts does Sasanian art begin to impact on Chinese art, and then, not until the Tang period.[18] It would seem that the Sasanian influences observed in Tang sumptuary and other arts—textiles (no. 110), ceramics (no. 111), and gilded bronzes (no. 119)—resulted from the gifts or "tribute" brought directly to the Chinese court by the Persian diplomatic mission rather than from the goods brought as items of trade.

The "exotic" objects buried with Chinese officials or found in hoards or temple deposits made their way along the Silk Road, not necessarily moving from their places of origin or manufacture directly to some ultimate destination, but traded from one town or entrepôt along the route to another. Thus, the silver platter, elaborately decorated with intertwined ivy and grape leaves and the image of Dionysus reclining on a feline (no. 115), was made somewhere in East Roman territory, exported to Bactria where it acquired its inscription, and then brought to Gansu; the ewer in Li Xian's tomb (no. 31) was fashioned in Bactria and transported to China, most likely intended for the market in the capital, Changan, but first was acquired by Li Xian as it passed through the border station of Dunhuang. Of course, the possibility should also be considered that the ewer was a royal gift to Li Xian from the founder of the Northern Zhou, Yuwen Tai or his son, the emperor Wudi, who spent part of his boyhood in Li Xian's home.[19]

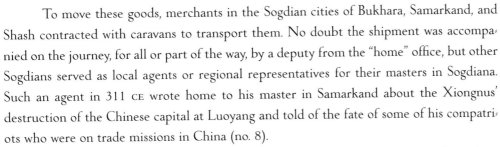

To move these goods, merchants in the Sogdian cities of Bukhara, Samarkand, and Shash contracted with caravans to transport them. No doubt the shipment was accompanied on the journey, for all or part of the way, by a deputy from the "home" office, but other Sogdians served as local agents or regional representatives for their masters in Sogdiana. Such an agent in 311 CE wrote home to his master in Samarkand about the Xiongnus' destruction of the Chinese capital at Luoyang and told of the fate of some of his compatriots who were on trade missions in China (no. 8).

For the purposes of local trade and to ensure the continued movement of merchandise to its destination, Sogdians founded a string of settlements along the Silk Road: from the western part of the trade route in Xinjiang, such as at Gaochang and Toyok (in the Turfan area) and Hami on the northern route and at Khotan on the southern,[20] into China proper and the oasis cities of Gansu (such as Dunhuang and Wuwei), in the capital cities of Changan and Luoyang, as well as in major inland centers such as Yangzhou, the entrepôt at the southern end of the transport canal joining the Yellow River to the Yangtze.[21] At Yuanzhou (present-day Guyuan, Ningxia Hui Autonomous Region), an important administrative center on a branch of the Silk Road leading north to Datong, a Sogdian colony was established in the fifth century (see Chapter 8).

Living in their own communities, these foreigners—some large-scale traders, others local shopkeepers, and even artisans—were controlled by their own headmen and subject to their own laws.[22] A member of each foreign community, known as *sabao*, presided over the

Fig. 2. Interior of a house at Panjikent (*above left*), showing wall-painting of the four-armed goddess, Nana, enthroned on a lion, Sogdian, seventh century. Nana was the most prominent deity in the Sogdian pantheon. Her pose on her lion mount imitates Sasanian royal images, but her four arms draws upon Hindu iconography. (drawing by B. I. Marshak)

Fig. 3. Clay ossuary with molded relief decoration (*above*). Shown on the walls are priests in front of the sacred fire, and on the pyramidal cover two females hold plants in their hands (perhaps the sacred *homa*); above them are a crescent and sun (or the planet Venus). Sodgian, from Mulla-kurgan, Uzbekistan, seventh to eighth century. (after Pugachenkova 1994, p. 236, fig. 7)

Fig. 4. Stone funerary couch from the tomb of An Qie (d. 579), northern suburbs of Xi'an, Northern Zhou. An Qie was of Sogdian origin and came from the Guzang (Wuwei) area, which had a large population from the Western Regions. He held the office of *sabao*, the local official in charge of the affairs of Sogdians and other foreigners in a community, as well as Area Commander-in-Chief. (after Yin, Li, and Xing 2000, p. 15, fig. 1)

community's civic and religious affairs and had Chinese official rank[23]; the forefathers of several of the Shi family buried at Guyuan held this office (no. 83: translation of Shi Shewu's epitaph). Like the Sasanians, the Sogdians were Zoroastrians, but in contrast to their western neighbors, they did not practice Zoroastrianism as an organized state religion. This seems to explain the worship of patron deities by individual families and communities, as well as that of non-Zoroastrian divinities.[24] Several of the gods of the Zoroastrian pantheon, including the highest, Ahura Mazda, were equated with and assimilated into different Hindu deities, while the ancient Mesopotamian deities Inana/Ishtar and Tammuz have their counterparts in Sogdian religious imagery (fig. 2).[25] Sogdian mourning rituals and Hindu-style iconography were departures from the strict Zoroastrianism as defined by Sasanian belief and practice. Yet the Sogdians considered themselves Zoroastrians; as such, Sogdian emigrants living in the colonies along the Silk Road would have adhered to the religious practices of their homeland, although little evidence of such practices in China has survived.

For example, the Zoroastrian proscription against inhumation for fear of polluting the earth (one of the four sacred elements) led to the exposure of the dead body and the subsequent placement of the bones in clay or stone ossuaries (*ostodans*). In Sogdiana (as well as Choresmia) the ossuaries, often elaborately decorated, were placed in mausoleums or kept at home (fig. 3).[26] Some three hundred examples of such ossuaries have been recovered from sites across Sogdiana and Choresmia, and into Xinjiang, their decoration reflecting local artistic and religious traditions; however, none has yet been found in China.[27] Instead, it is possible that the elaborately carved and painted stone funerary couches, which come from tombs of Sogdians or other Central Asians, and of which number 106 is one of four known from northwest and north China (along with a recently discovered stone sarcophagus), may have served to protect the bodies from direct contact with the earth (fig. 4).

Nonetheless, the Sogdians had temples and revered the sacred fire; indeed, accounts from the Tang period tell of Chinese fascination with the Zoroastrian temples and the ritual dancing—associated with the Sogdians—that took place there. Before the Tang, the official recognition of Zoroastrianism in China is linked to the arrival of the Persian embassies; this is not surprising, however, since these were official contacts rather than private trade missions and, as such, are mentioned in the Chinese dynastic histories. Thus, Zoroastrianism was officially recognized early in the sixth century; there may even have been a Zoroastrian priest at the Northern Wei court.[28]

Despite the syncretistic nature of their religion, and the religious tolerance that they practiced, the Sogdians in their homeland were not always well disposed toward Buddhism, and the Buddhist faith never truly flourished there.[29] This is ironic since the Sogdians are credited with being the major translators of the Buddhist sutras into Chinese (as well as being the translators of Manichaean and Christian texts). Apparently, some of the Sogdians who were exposed to Buddhism while passing through Bactria, northwest India, or Xinjiang on their way to China were so attracted to Buddhism that they became converts (no. 67), with some even becoming monks who spread the new faith eastward (see Chapter 2 and note 1 of this chapter).

There may be another reason why Sogdians involved themselves in translating Buddhist texts. As traders, they were conversant in many other languages, and many were literate; they could thus function commercially as translators. It is possible that to please their Chinese hosts and as a source of income Sogdian scribes translated Buddhist texts. Shi Hedan, whose ancestors were Sogdian, worked as a high-ranking translator in the Imperial Secretariat (no. 80c).

Because cultural exchange invariably accompanies the commercial kind, the Sogdians, as the major trading group, were also major transmitters of ideas and traditions. Not only were the luxury products of the West (including those of Sogdiana) that were brought by the Sogdians' caravans of value in their own right, such products were a source of new artistic ideas and religious imagery for the Chinese. Thus, Sogdian metalwork had a strong influence on Chinese metalwork as well as on ceramics (no. 111).[30] Further, the safety provided by the Sogdians' caravans for traveling monks and pilgrims allowed new ideas to spread across the Silk Road and into China. People other than monks and pilgrims also traveled in the caravans, some exporting their services, others exported as actual products, that is, as "gifts" by local rulers or as slaves. Sogdian acrobats, dancers, and musicians were greatly valued by the Chinese, the dancers from Shash being in greatest demand (nos. 81, 82).

1. Jettmar 1991, p. 252. Jettmar proposes that a trade fair had been established at a specific site in the region where merchants of the different countries could meet; Sims-Williams 1996, pp. 52ff. Evidence of trade activity in this region consists of the more than six hundred short rock inscriptions in Sogdian at sites on either bank of the Indus; associated with these inscriptions are those in Indian languages as well as some in Chinese, Tibetan, Bactrian, Parthian, Middle Persian, Syriac, and Hebrew. The monk Kang Senghui, who is credited with introducing Buddhism to southern China, came from a Sogdian family that had settled in India; his father was a merchant in south China, where Senghui was born (Bagchi 1955, p. 39).

2. Hannestad 1955–57, pp. 433, 449; the account of the Turkish-Sogdian embassy to the Byzantine court that opened up direct trade is in Blockley 1985, fragment 10, 1 (pp. 111–15). See Kuznetsov 1996, pp. 202–3, for possible evidence of a Sogdian colony or trading outpost in the north Caucasus, though probably not earlier than the eighth century. The kinds of textiles that moved across this route are shown in Jerusalimskaia and Borkopp 1996.

3. Soper 1958, p. 134.

4. Sims-Williams 1996, p. 46.

5. Chavannes 1903, pp. 133 n. 5, 134. These passages from the Tang histories are often misquoted.

6. Sims-Williams 1996, p. 56. Sims-Williams notes the comparative rarity of inscriptions in languages other than in Sogdian scratched into the rocks in the upper Indus River region.

7. de Menasce 1973, pp. 75–76 (bk. 3, chap. 69). Because the *Dēnkard* is a ninth-century, and therefore post-Sasanian, Zoroastrian text, it may not accurately reflect the social structure that existed in Iran under Sasanian rule. Listed among the dignitaries of the Sasanian court in the third century CE, is a "master of the market" (*wāzārbad* = "bazaar"). I am grateful to P. O. Skjaervø for these references.

8. See Lukonin 1983, p. 740, for the Parthians' control of the trade routes. The Sasanians had maintained an absolute monopoly on silk traveling to Byzantium.

9. See note 2 above, and Chapter 9 n. 32; also Sinor 1990, pp. 302–3.

10. Grenet 1996, p. 75. For a contrasting view, see Frye 1993, pp. 75, 77. For the establishment by the Sasanian state of a network of fortified trading posts to control the maritime trade, see Kervran 1994, pp. 325–51; Pulleyblank 1991, p. 428, for the role of the Persians in pre-Tang maritime trade.

11. The first known mission to the Northern Wei capital took place in 455. Nine successive Sasanian delegations visited the Northern Wei court between 461 and 522, to the contemporary southern dynasty, Liang, in 533 and 535, and to the Western Wei in 555. The object of these missions was to strengthen Persian influence in the east as a counter to the Hephthalite power or to impress the Chinese court with the power of the Sasanian ruler. The Northern Wei sent an envoy to Persia c. 470; one hundred years later, in 567, a Chinese delegation visited the Persian court, and in 615 the Sui emperor sent another, which was then accompanied back to China by a Persian delegation. These diplomatic exchanges ended with the 638 Persian delegation to China seeking aid against the invading Arabs. Aid was refused, but the Tang emperor granted refuge to Peroz, the heir to the deposed and murdered Sasanian king, Yazdgard III (r. 632–651). See Harmatta 1971, pp. 369–76: "The Persians only joined in the caravan trade much later, when after the fall of the Hephthalite Empire it became possible for the Persian merchants themselves to visit China on the 'Silk Route.' The settlement of Persians in higher numbers in China began at that very time, in the course of the sixth century" (p. 370). The 638 delegation is disputed by Antonino Forte, as not attested by the Chinese sources (Forte 1996, p. 190 n. 16). For a summary of the sources, see Pulleyblank 1991, p. 426.

12. By the early part of the eighth century, the Tang government was already experiencing difficulties, and the coup d'état staged by An Lushan, though quickly put down, certainly quickened its demise. Interestingly, An Lushan was the son of a Sogdian father and a Turkish mother (Mair and Skjaervø 1991, pp. 466–67).

13. It is often difficult to determine from the Chinese sources if a Persian from Iran is actually intended or a person who is Iranian. The Chinese used the term *Bo-si* (*Po-ssu*) to designate Persians, but they also used it for any people coming from the Persian Gulf area, Iranians as well as Arabs. Similarly, the Chinese called the Sogdians *Sute*, but they also used the more generalized designation, *hu* ("barbarian"). This term, which, under the Han had been applied to the nomadic horsemen of the north, came to refer to all Iranians: Persians, Sogdians, and natives of Western Turkestan (Xinjiang) (Schafer 1951, p. 409; and Pulleyblank 1952, pp. 318–19).

14. The earliest examples of Sasanian glass come from late-third- to early-fourth-century graves. See Laing 1991, pp. 109–11.

15. Harper 1990, pp. 51–59. Harper believes that the plate was "made east of Iran in a region strongly influenced by Sasanian culture and art"; *Wenwu* 1983.8, figs. 4, 5.

16. Rawson 1986, p. 33; *Kaogu* 1977.6, pl. 5:4.

17. Shih 1983, p. 71.

18. The lack of purely Sasanian objects in Chinese tombs calls for a reassessment of the tendency to attribute any vaguely Western, i.e., Iranian, style or motif to "Sasanian influence." While somewhat over-

stating the case, Souren Melikian-Chirvani remarked perceptively almost twenty-five years ago, "Iranian metalwork itself provides remarkably little evidence to support the contention" that "Sasanian silver actually had an influence over T'ang metalwork" (Melikian-Chirvani 1976, p. 12).

19. Louis 1999, p. 79. Yuwen Tai had given Wu Hui to Li Xian as his bride, accompanied by sumptuous gifts; further, as emperor, Wudi had paid Li Xian the honor of two personal visits to his home: could the ewer have been a gift on one of those occasions? (Anazawa in Marshak and Anazawa 1989, p. 51.)

20. Emmerick 1983, pp. 270–73.

21. Pulleyblank 1991, pp. 426–27.

22. Twitchett 1979, p. 30. A parallel for these local merchant communities, and their relationship to the private firms they represented, based back in Sogdiana, may be drawn with the Old Assyrian colony at Kanesh, which flourished in the nineteenth century BCE in Anatolia as a trading center for the city-state of Ashur, in northern Mesopotamia (present-day Iraq). The traders were "organized in a *karum*, a term that denotes both the physical reality of a special merchant quarter and the community of traders in the town. This was led by a royally appointed man through whom the contacts with the central authorities were regulated" (Larsen 1987, p. 49). Regarding foreign artisans in the colonies, An Jiayao notes evidence of Bactrians making glass in the Datong area in the mid-fifth century, while, in Changan, a Sogdian glassblower earned the admiration of the Sui emperor Wudi (An 1984, pp. 23–24).

23. The *sabao* has traditionally been identified as a Zoroastrian religious official, but this view has recently been questioned; by the Sui and Tang periods, it seems to have been an official title of the administrator of the Central Asian and Persian immigrant communities in the various localities, who was typically of Iranian ancestry. Of non-Chinese origin, the term has been thought to derive from *sāt-pāu* (Khotanese, *spāta* "leader, captain") or from *sārthavāk* (Sogdian "caravan leader"), or Sanskrit, *sārthavāha*. (Luo 2000, pp. 165–91; Dien 1962, pp. 335–43)

24. Marshak and Raspopova 1991, pp. 187–91. Grenet 1994, pp. 47–50.

25. Grenet and Marshak 1998, pp. 5–18. In Mesopotamia, the cult of Nana/Nanaia was linked from the second millennium BCE to that of the goddess Inana/Ishtar (Grenet and Marshak 1998, p. 7; see Black and Green 1992, pp. 108–9 [Inana], p. 134 [Nanaya].

26. For a review of the Sogdian ossuaries, see Pavchinskaia 1994, pp. 209–25, and Pugachenkova 1994, pp. 227–43.

27. Grenet 1986, pp. 236–37, with a map showing the distribution of ossuaries from Margiana and Choresmia in the west along the northern branch of the Silk Road in Xinjiang in the east. I am grateful to Lin Meicun for informing me of three specific sites in the Turfan area of Xinjiang that have yielded ossuaries (Toyok, Jimsar, and Karashahr); he notes that the round wooden box from Kucha, found by the Otani Mission, may be considered a Buddhist reliquary; the color scheme of the painted decoration, according to Boris Marshak, is akin to that of Sogdian painting (although the style and iconography is Kuchan: Kossolapov and Marshak 1999, p. 68). To these containers should also be added the round box in the Musée Guimet, also from *Sérinde* 1995, nos. 99, 100, and that from Kalpin, Xinjiang (Ma, Qi, and Zhang 1994, no. 69: pp. 40, p. 216). On the southern route, a possible ossuary—a tubular clay container with lid, containing the bones of an adult skeleton—is attributed to Shanshan (an ancient oasis kingdom comprising Niya, Miran, and Loulan; ibid., no. 68, pp. 40, 215). Recently, a rectangular house-shaped ceramic container in the Palace Museum in Beijing has been identified by Shi Anchang (Shi 2000, pp. 80–81) as an ossuary "probably excavated from a cemetery of Sogdian immigrants in China"; this attribution needs to be more fully explored.

28. Liu 1976, pp. 12–14; Leslie 1981–83, p. 288. Evidence for some form of Zoroastrian worship in the later sixth century, in the Northern Qi court, is given by Scaglia 1958, pp. 26–27.

29. Grenet 1994, p. 47. Although a Buddhist sutra has been read on a ceramic vessel found at Panjikent, according to Boris Marshak, no true Buddhist cult iconography has been recorded in Sogdiana (Marshak and Raspopova 1990, pp. 151–53). See also Marshak and Raspopova 1997/98, p. 298f. In addition to Zoroastrianism or Mazdaism, religions that were followed in Sogdiana were Hinduism, Manichaeism, Christianity, and Judaism.

30. For Sogdian vessels found in China, see Marshak 1999b, pp. 105–6.

7

The Sogdians in Their Homeland

BORIS I. MARSHAK

Although Samarkand is often considered the traditional capital of Sogdiana, each district or city in Sogdiana developed relatively independently. Power generally was in the hands of local princes, at various times owing allegiance to a more powerful ruler or, as in the fifth and sixth centuries, coming under the domination of nomadic conquerors, the Hephthalites and the Turks. But Sogdian society was not feudal: in contrast to the social order in contemporary Sasanian Iran where the official place of the merchants was the lowest, in Sogdiana merchants were placed socially and politically between the nobility and "the workers," according to their actual significance. Indeed, merchants rivaled land owners in wealth and influence.

This is no better exemplified than by the walled town of Panjikent, about forty miles east of Samarkand, which for the last sixty years has been excavated by Russian and local Tajikistan archaeologists (fig. 7).[1] Panjikent's founding in the fifth century reflects the increasing prosperity of Sogdiana after the Hun or Chionite invasion in the fourth century CE. Panjikent flourished during the sixth, seventh, and first half of the eighth centuries. In the seventh and eighth centuries, the most striking feature of Panjikent was its large and spacious dwellings—not palaces, but houses of the rich townspeople. Built of clay and mud brick, these two- or three-storied residences were decorated on the inside with elaborate wall paintings, along with wooden sculptures and ornamental carvings. At least one house in three was so generously ornate in its architecture and decoration that these sumptous town houses resembled the rulers' palaces discovered at Panjikent itself and at other Sogdian sites. The similarity between the palaces and the houses of the petty landlords and merchants reflected a characteristic aspect of Sogdian social structure, in which a significant role was played by individual urban communities, each with their own officials and revenues.[2]

The mural decoration of the private houses combined religious imagery (ritual scenes and the divine image of a god who was the household's patron deity) with scenes of Sogdian daily life and episodes from epics and fables. This last group of images reveals the far-reaching connections of Sogdian art and culture. The illustrated episodes derived from a number of sources—Greek (Aesop's *Fables*), Indian (stories from the *Panchatantra* and the *Mahabharata*), and Iranian (the exploits of the hero Rustam, which were later incorporated into the Persian national epic, the *Shahnama*)—while the secular painting was, in part, indebted to Chinese painting (figs. 2, 3). The range of Sogdian secular literary works, fragments of which were found in Dunhuang and Turfan, confirms the close ties between the Sogdian colonies established along the Silk Road and the Sogdian metropolis. Fragments of the Hindu *Panchatantra*, Aesop's *Fables*, the Iranian tale of Rustam, and fairy tales show that

OPPOSITE: View of the Zerafshan Valley from the site of Panjikent (photo: Aleksandr Naymark)

Fig. 1. The citadel of Panjikent (*top*) showing the remains of the royal residence, viewed from the east (photo: Boris I. Marshak)

Fig. 2. Chinese couple (*above*), Room VI/42, Panjikent, late seventh century

the literature read by the Sogdians living in Dunhuang and illustrated by the Sogdian artists in Panjikent was almost the same.[3]

Three major factors determined the complexity of Sogdian culture. First, the Sogdians inherited ancient Iranian traditions; Sogdian is an eastern Iranian language, and the teachings of Zoroaster very early penetrated into Sogdiana. Second, ancient Near Eastern cultural tradition influenced Central Asian cultures from prehistoric times, especially during the period from the six to fourth century BCE when Sogdiana and adjacent countries belonged to the Persian Achaemenid Empire. Last but not least was the lack of political centralization in Sogdiana. From the late third century BCE, Sogdiana was neither a powerful state itself nor firmly subjected to any of the adjacent empires; nevertheless, it was closely connected with all these neighboring empires through trade and culture.

In such circumstances, the ideological control could not be as strong as it was in Sasanian Iran with its Zoroastrian hierarchy and beliefs supported by powerful monarchs. Alongside the Zoroastrian gods, the Sogdians worshiped several other deities, among which the most important was the goddess Nana (Nanaia), whose cult was known in Mesopotamia as early as the third millennium BCE (Chapter 6, fig. 2).[4] Christianity and Buddhism had their adepts in Sogdiana.[5] However, in Sogdiana proper there were only small communities of Christians, Buddhists, and perhaps also followers of the prophet Mani, who had lived in Iran during the third century CE. Missionaries of these religions attained much greater success among the Sogdians living in Semirechye and in Xinjiang and Gansu, where the colonists sought some support from coreligionists among the local population and from the international community of caravan merchants.

During the fifth, sixth, and seventh centuries, the Sogdians enriched the iconography of their gods, both Zoroastrian and non-Zoroastrian. Works of art as well as written sources have preserved several layers of the loan elements in the local religion of Sogdiana: ancient Near Eastern, Hellenistic, Kushano-Sasanian, and Hindu. Thus, the ancient Near Eastern goddess Nana (whose main attribute is a lion) in her sixth-century pictorial representations wears semi-Greek attire, while her pose is royal Sasanian and her four arms are borrowed from an Indian model (see Chapter 6, fig. 2).[6]

The paradoxical aspect of the Sogdian religious practices is the contrast between the Zoroastrian funeral ritual on the one hand and the non-Iranian appearance of the Sogdian gods on the other. In Zoroastrian belief, the corpse must be exposed to vultures or dogs in the place where the earth (but not stone), water, fire, or wind cannot be polluted by it. In Sogdiana there were dogs that ate the corpse's flesh. After this, the "clean" bones were collected and put into the special ceramic ossuaries. The sides of many ossuaries were decorated by the stamped reliefs among which there are several depictions of the stationary temple fire-altars of Sasanian type and Zoroastrian priests, along with other religious scenes with clear Zoroastrian meaning (see Chapter 6, fig. 3). However, in the paintings of the houses and the temples of Panjikent we see only portable fire-altars before the images of the deities, and the figures of laymen and laywomen near these small altars. These same people faced death as pious Zoroastrians, yet they worshiped Nana (the goddess's four-armed figure is even placed on an ossuary from southern Sogdiana).[7] Houses frequently contained special rooms where the eternal fire was kept at the fireplace, but in the reception halls of the same houses there were scenes of the worship of the iconic images of the deities. Most probably, the majority of the Sogdians considered themselves Zoroastrians, but in their everyday life they mostly tried to receive protection from the more immediate gods of their family or their community and rarely appealed to Ahura Mazda, the Zoroastrian supreme deity of the whole world.[8]

In the scenes of banquets, processions, and hunts, foreign iconographic influence was minimal, but the complex patterns of rich Iranian or Chinese silks were precisely copied by the Sogdian painters. In several houses of Panjikent the wall paintings demonstrate that much of the known world had been absorbed into the events represented in their reception halls. Thus, in the house of the owner of a large granary there are paintings of the crops distributed after the harvest and the banquets of at least four kings feasting with their subjects (fig. 4).[9] Also in Panjikent, in Temple II, the group of several kings approaching the temple is shown on the side wall of the portico in the main building.[10] These murals help us to understand the Tang Chinese description of a Sogdian building with the murals showing the kings of different countries, including the emperors of China alongside the Sasanian Persian, Byzantine, Indian, and Turkic monarchs.[11]

The autonomy of Sogdiana could only be preserved as a protectorate of one of the powerful empires dominating the Central Asia caravan routes. From 510 to 563, when the

Fig. 3. Chinese orchestra. Room VI/42, Panjikent, first half of eighth century (on a later level of clay plaster)

Hephthalites ruled in Sogdiana, the caravans of the Sogdian merchants arrived in northern China disguised as Hephthalite official envoys. At the end of the fifth and the first third of the sixth centuries, the nomadic Hephthalites, whose native land was probably in present-day northeastern Afghanistan, held possession of Tokharistan (ancient Bactria in the middle Amu Darya Valley), Xinjiang, the lands to the south of the Hindu Kush Mountains, and the northwestern part of India. They even took tribute from such a powerful state as Sasanian Iran. The brief domination of the Hepthalites had an impact on the cultures of those countries that had been conquered by them, as the "Hepthalite Bridge" connected India with Sogdiana and Sasanian Iran. In the sixth century, the influence of post-Gupta Hindu iconography reached Sogdiana while the earliest illustrations of such Indian stories as the *Panchatantra* and the prototype of the *Sindbad-nama* appeared on the walls of the Panjikent houses; at the same time, these secular works were translated into Middle Persian and became well known in Sasanian Iran. In the 560s, the Hephthalites were defeated by the Turks who came from the Altai Mountains and, in one decade, established a vast empire in the steppe zone extending from Mongolia to the Crimea. The king of Samarkand became the vassal of the Turks as well as the petty Hephthalite rulers. Kashmir, transversed via an important route, which is marked by hundreds of Sogdian rock inscriptions, in the late sixth century still belonged to the Hephthalite dynasty.[12]

Throughout the fifth, sixth, and seventh centuries, the Sogdians supported those rulers of different origins who were strong enough to maintain the peace on the caravan routes. In the sixth century, as the councilors to the Turkic Kaghans, the Sogdians pursued above all their own commercial interests and initiated the unsuccessful Turco-Sogdian mission to Iran, followed by the more successful one to Byzantium (see Chapter 6). On the one hand, Sogdian officials played an important role in the administration of the Turk Empire. On the other hand, from the sixth through the eighth century, many Turks penetrated into Sogdian society and became members of the local nobility; in fact, at the end of the seventh century, one of the rulers of Panjikent was a Turk.

When the Tang dynasty consolidated its power over China in 618, the Sogdians immediately recognized its power. In the 620s, when the Turks still held sway over Sogdiana, the king of Samarkand sent a mission to China requesting Chinese protection. The Chinese emperor rejected this request. Yet in the 650s, the Chinese conquered the Turks, and the king of Samarkand, Varkhuman (or Vargoman), was appointed governor of his own kingdom. Thus, he became an official of the Tang Empire. Sogdian merchants, whose status in China had been low because they were mere foreigners, received the desired Chinese citizenship.

The best manifestation of Sogdian political thought are wall paintings discovered at Afrasiab, the archaeological site of ancient Samarkand, and datable to about 660.[13] On the walls of the reception hall of an aristocratic house, probably belonging to a man closely related to King Varkhuman, processional scenes of foreign dignitaries and ambassadors are depicted. On the west wall opposite the entrance, foreign envoys are shown paying homage to the gods of Samarkand.[14] On the white coat of a male figure is a long Sogdian inscription, which, according to Vladimir A. Livshits's reading, contains a fragment of an official account. It states that King Varkhuman had approached the envoy from Chaganiyan (a principality in Tokharistan), and that the latter addressed him with the usual greetings and introduced himself. Then this ambassador persuaded the king not to be afraid of him because he knew the gods and the writing (scripture?) of Samarkand. The end of the text states that after him the ambassador of Shash (Tashkent) also began his speech, which is, however, absent because there was no more space in the white spot chosen for the inscrip, tion. From this text we learn that the envoys from several countries had been represented on the wall. Note that the king approaches the envoy and is not depicted seated on his throne. This confirms that the upper part of the wall (unfortunately completely gone) had been allotted to divine images, but not the enthroned king. Below them, in the center, the most important Chinese delegation is shown presenting silk cloths and threads. The dele, gation is flanked by groups of Turkic warriors from the military escort of the Chinese mis, sion (in the mid,seventh century Turk contingents were included in the Chinese army). Koreans with their headgear adorned by a pair of feathers are also represented in the mural, as are richly clad envoys from several Central Asian oasis states.

The subject matter of the mural on the south wall is the long procession of the king of Samarkand, who is shown visiting a shrine probably dedicated to his ancestors. On the north wall are depicted the royal hunt of the Chinese emperor and Chinese court ladies in a boat, who are providing musical entertainment and feeding fish. Unfortunately, the paintings on the east wall are very poorly preserved. However, the compositions on the west, south, and north walls make the main ideas of the pictorial program quite understandable. The murals show that Varkhuman was worthy of being a king of Samarkand, demonstrating his devotion to the gods of the Samarkand city,state and their international prestige during his reign, then displaying his devotion to his parents (or ancestors), illustrating the might and the splendor of the Chinese Empire, which protected his relatively small kingdom. If we com, pare the programs of the wall paintings in the houses of so modest a town as Panjikent with those in the aforementioned metropolitan residence of the Samarkand magnate, we can see their striking similarity. In Panjikent, without any political motivation (unlike in Samarkand), the owners of the houses commissioned paintings that show kings of distant countries and their subjects.[15] This iconography was also continued by Sogdians who lived and died far from Sogdiana, in colonies situated in northwest and northern China. The sev, eral funerary couches and a sarcophagus that relate to the Tianshui couch in this exhibition (no. 106) depict the deceased accompanied by royal feasts and processions, led by Turkic and Hephthalite rulers.

Among the many motifs of the Panjikent paint, ings, one is particularly connected with the theme of this exhibition. This is a row of horses led by their grooms, a motif found in two houses. Such murals executed about 740 decorated a corridor (Room XXIV/2–3) between the iwan with the front door and the reception hall with the murals showing the kings of the world, each of them feasting with his subjects (fig. 5).[16] The other example, datable to the first quarter of the eighth century, is the mural in the small vaulted vestibule (Room XXIII/28) of a large house.[17] In this vestibule one of the figures is shown

Fig. 4. View of Room XXV/28, Panjikent, early eighth century

Fig. 5. Horse led by groom (*right*). Room XXIV/3, Panjikent, first half of eighth century

Fig. 6. Kneeling man (Chinese?) (*below*). Room XXIII/28, Panjikent, first quarter of eighth century

kneeling before a ruler and holding a narrow tablet. Similar tablets were held by the Chinese officials and the palace servants before or at the audience of the emperor. The face and especially the sparse beard of the man resemble the Sogdian depictions of Chinese (fig. 6). Both murals are the Sogdian counterparts to the well-known and numerous Chinese representations of Westerners as grooms (fig. 5). It is quite possible that the owners of these Panjikent houses had an opportunity to sell or train horses in China, as did many of their countrymen.

On the wall of a room in another Panjikent house (Room VI/42), a Chinese couple is depicted (fig. 2). The seventh-century painter certainly knew Chinese pictures showing palace servants. Even the garments are similar to those in the Tang paintings. However, he did not know the Chinese reality and depicted a bearded man holding a tablet, instead of a eunuch, accompanying a beautiful court lady. Her round breasts correspond to the Sogdian but not Chinese ideal of female beauty. In the first half of the eighth century this painting was covered with an additional layer of clay plaster. Then, in the renewed murals of the same room, in the cornice, a whole orchestra of Chinese women musicians was represented. In Tang China Western musicians, musical instruments, and dancers had become very popular (nos. 81, 82), and the Panjikent artist quite realistically gave to one of his Chinese musicians a Central Asian lute.

The horse harness, the armor, and the weaponry in the sixth, seventh, and eighth centuries were very similar in Sogdiana, the Turkic states, and China.[18] Such details as rectangular and semicircular belt plaques with a rectangular split for the attached pendant belts appeared in Sogdiana and the Turkic steppes in the second half of the seventh century but are attested in China already under the Sui dynasty just after 600 (no. 91) and continued to be used by Tang warriors and officials in the seventh to ninth century. The Turks and the Sogdians began to wear these belts in the seventh century when both were, though not for long, the vassals of the Tang emperors.

Sogdians not only transported the beautiful silks of Iran and China to sell in other countries, they imported them for their own use.[19] During the fifth and sixth centuries, the majority of garments depicted in Sogdian paintings were plain or with simple ornamentation. In the third quarter of the seventh century, the Afrasiab paintings show many richly decorated, multicolored silks with Iranian patterns, alongside plain Chinese fabrics. These Iranian patterns are attested to in Panjikent, too (fig. 7). From the late seventh century

Fig. 7. Lion silk textile pattern (*left*), Sasanian motif. Room X/12, Panjikent, c. 700

Fig. 8. Rosette silk textile pattern (*right*), Tang motif. Room XXV/28, Panjikent, early eighth century

through the first half of the eighth century, in Panjikent and Varakhsha (near Bukhara), Tang rosette silks and damask became very popular (fig. 8; no. 109).

By the mid-eighth century Sogdiana had become the most eastern part of the Arab caliphate, and after the civil war of the 750s within China the isolationistic trend in China became more and more intense. Thus it is the Sogdian archaeological sites of the previous period that reveal the picture of intensive and fruitful contacts between Western and Eastern civilizations.

NOTES

1. Among the numerous publications on Panjikent are the following: Azarpay 1981; Belenitskii 1973; Belenizki 1980 (Belenitskii); Belenitskii 1954; Belenitskii 1959).

2. Raspopova 1990; Livshits 1962, pp. 69–70; Belenitskii, Marshak, and Raspopova 1979, pp. 19–26.

3. Marshak 1999a, pp. 134–35, 146–47, figs. 188, 201–8.

4. Grenet and Marshak 1998, pp. 5–18.

5. Marshak and Raspopova 1997/98, pp. 297–305.

6. Grenet and Marshak 1998, pp. 10–16.

7. Ibid, p. 11, fig. 6.

8. Marshak and Raspopova 1991, pp. 187–95; Grenet 1986, pp. 97–131.

9. Marshak and Raspopova 1990, pp. 157–72, figs. 12, 19, 27–34.

10. Azarpay 1981, p. 42, fig. 12.

11. Barthold 1966, p. 206 (after the *Tangshu*).

12. Sims-Williams 1989–92.

13. Marshak 1994, pp. 1–20.

14. This fragmentary composition is decipherable because at Panjikent there are many similar rooms where the place of honor opposite the door was allotted to the divine patrons of the house surrounded by the worshipers (Marshak and Raspopova 1991, pp. 187–95).

15. Marshak and Raspopova 1990, pp. 171–72.

16. Belenizki 1980 (Belenistskii), pp. 120–21.

17. Belenitskii, Marshak, Raspopova, and Isakov 1977, p. 177.

18. Raspopova 1980, pp. 94, 97, 103–9.

19. However, those silks, which in the archaeological literature are named Sogdian (or Zandaniji), are completely alien to the Sogdian culture. Their date in the late eighth to ninth century corresponds with the period of the radical transformation of the Sogdian culture into the Islamic civilization of Transoxiana with its international, mostly west Asian, roots. Marshak (forthcoming on the silks of Zandaniji) and Raspopova (forthcoming on textiles represented in the Sogdian murals).

8

Sogdians in Northwest China

LUO FENG

Our knowledge of the Sogdians in China during the fourth through seventh century derives from documents written in Sogdian (see no. 8) and later in Arabic, as well as from Chinese historical records. In the past several decades, these sources have been supplemented by the archaeological excavation of tombs belonging to the descendants of Sogdians who had settled in the trading centers and other important cities along the Silk Road.[1] In the Chinese records, these Sogdians are called *zhaowu jiuxing ren* (people of the nine place-names), referring to the Chinese surnames that Sogdians commonly adopted and which reflect the region in Sogdiana from which they came. Thus, the surname An is the Chinese name for Bukhara, Kang the name for Samarkand, Shi(石)is Tashkent, and Shi(史)is Kesh.[2] The Sogdian communities were under the jurisdiction of the Chinese government, each community overseen by an official, called *sabao*, who was in charge of local affairs. By the Tang period, a number of Western, or "barbarian," administrative districts had been established in which Sogdians and probably other foreigners lived. They included the region called Liuhuzhou (Six Foreign States), Changan (Xi'an), Luoyang, Taiyuan, and Yuanzhou. In the fifth century, Sogdians from Kesh (present-day Shahr-i-sabz, south of Samarkand, Uzbekistan) settled in the district of Yuanzhou (present-day Guyuan, Ningxia) and took the sinicized name of Shi.[3] By the Sui and early Tang periods, their descendants had become middle- and high-ranking officials of the Chinese court. Since the 1980s, tombs of Shi family men and their wives have been under excavation; so far seven have been discovered.[4]

The biographies on their epitaphs allow us to reconstruct the family histories of those who bear the Shi name and to trace their rise as military men and court officials. The earliest of the tombs so far discovered belongs to Shi Shewu, who died in 609 (nos. 83–85, 95), followed by one of his sons, Shi Daoluo (d. 658) (nos. 101, 105). They and Shi Shewu's eldest son, Shi Hedan (d. 669; buried with his wife in 671)[5] (nos. 86, 89, 103), and a grandson, Shi Tiebang (d. 666; buried in 668) (no. 96) form one genealogy. Tombs of what may be another branch of the family are those of Shi Suoyan (d. 656) (nos. 87, 88, 102) and Shi Daode (d. 678) (nos. 90–92), who may have been his nephew.

According to Shi Shewu's epitaph (no. 83), his great-grandfather Miaoni had come from the "Western Regions," most probably during the Northern Wei, in the latter half of the fifth century. He had held the administrative office of *sabao*, as did his son and Shi Shewu's grandfather.[6] Shi Shewu himself held several titles; at his death at age sixty-six, he was Cavalry General of the Right Palace Guard. Shi Shewu's eldest son, Shi Hedan, was originally a military officer under the Sui, but in 626 he used his language ability to become a translator in the Imperial Secretariat, rising to Gentleman for Court Discussion and retir-

Fig. 1. View of Shi Shewu's
tumulus. Height: 62 meters;
diameter: 20 meters. Guyuan,
Ningxia. The smaller tumuli
are modern tombs. (photo:
Judith A. Lerner)

ing in 666 to be governor of a prefecture, in charge of military affairs. His son Shi Daoluo
and grandson Shi Tiebang had military careers. The latter had been a low-grade bodyguard
in the imperial court and became an officer in charge of horses; at his death, he was man-
aging a large army horse-breeding farm in Guyuan, which was the largest horse-breeding
base in China. Shi Suoyan first served in the Tang court as an imperial bodyguard and, after
a successful military career, he retired to Guyuan. Shi Daode came from a military family
and according to his epitaph had authority over the Gansu and Qinghai regions; he seems
to have held secretarial posts and became a supervisor of the imperial school.

The adoption of Chinese place names by the Shi and other Sogdian immigrants, as
well as their military and government careers, suggests some degree of sinicization, but the
extent of their assimilation is still an open question. Indeed, there is no broad agreement
among scholars whether the Sogdians completely retained their national customs after they
entered China, kept some of their customs, or were completely assimilated by the local culture. The scientifically excavated tombs of the Shi and of other Sogdian descendants in
northwest and north China have yielded important material that can help us resolve such
issues. In addition to the epitaphs with biographical information, the actual tomb construc-
tions and the tomb contents allow us to conclude that Sogdian immigrants in China had at
least partially accepted the Chinese funerary custom of underground burial, in contrast to
the traditional Zoroastrian practice in Sogdiana of exposing the corpse and storing the dis-
articulated bones in an ossuary, which is then typically placed in a mausoleum.[7]

At Guyuan, the tombs, each marked by a mound of earth like the shape of an inverted
bowl, are arranged in a row with the oldest (Shi Shewu's) on the west and the more recent
(Shi Tiebang's) to the east. A long approach leads to the burial chamber, and multiple shafts
pierce the approach (figs. 1–3). This format begins in the period of the Sixteen Kingdoms
(fourth to early fifth century); none of the Sogdian tombs so far known in China are earlier
than this date. Indeed, the earliest so far known is that of An Qie, which was recently discovered in the northern suburbs of Xi'an, and dates to 579 in the Northern Zhou (see Chap-

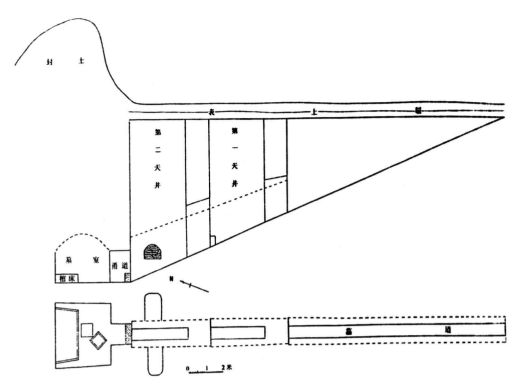

封土

表　上　缺

第二天井　第一天井

墓室　甬道

棺床

N

墓　道

0　1　2米

ter 6, fig. 4).[8] The tomb has five shafts and a single burial chamber. This form continues into the Tang with the tomb of the Sogdian An Pu, at Luoyang (Henan province).[9]

A departure from this form of burial is a cemetery of the High Tang period (first half of the eighth century), excavated at Yanchi in Ningxia, that belonged to members of the He, a family with origins in Kushaniya, west of Samarkand. As excavated, it contains six tombs, arranged chronologically from west to east (nos. 81, 89b).[10] In contrast to the Shi tombs, an earthen tumulus did not seem to cover each grave. Instead, the tombs were carved into a low gypsum outcropping that resembles a mound. The form of the tombs differs from that of traditional tombs of the period. Instead of being entered by a long ramp, with a number of shafts cut into it from the ground surface, each tomb is entered by means of a ramp that begins on the level ground some distance before the outcropping and was then exca-

Fig. 2. Cross-section and plan of Shi Shewu's tumulus and tomb (*above*) (after *Yuanzhou* 1999, pl. 83)

Fig. 3. Cross-section and plan of Tomb M1 (*below*), in the He family cemetery at Yanchi, Ningxia, showing the side burial chambers (after *Wenwu* 1988.9, p. 44, fig. 4)

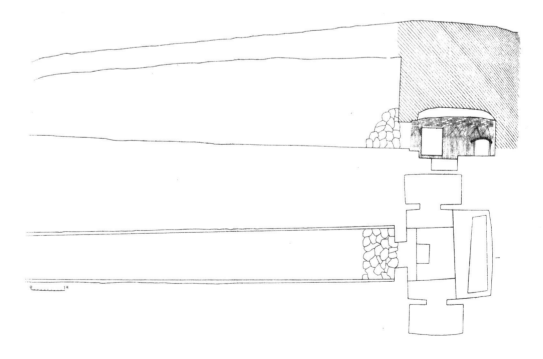

Fig. 4. Entrance to Tomb M2,
Yanchi (*top*), with blocking
stones removed (photo courtesy of Luo Feng)

Fig. 5. Central room and rear
niche of Tomb M3 (*above*),
Yanchi (photo courtesy of
Luo Feng)

vated down at an angle until it reached the outcropping itself. The tomb structure was then dug out from beneath the outcropping (figs. 4, 5). The tomb door was sealed by a stack of stones; the structure within contained a central chamber, square or rectangular, with a ceil-ing height of two meters. Engraved on the walls are simple forms like triangles, squares, trapezoids, and circles. Subsidiary, nichelike rooms, two to five in number, were carved into the walls of the tomb chamber. Typically, for those of Sogdian descent, husband and wife were buried together; this was also true of the Chinese. However, in the He family tombs, there are single burials, couple burials, and group burials. In Tombs M4 and M6 four peo-ple are buried, while in M5, there are more than ten.

It remains to be decided whether the special structure of the He family tombs in Yanchi reflects a local tradition or burial practices from Sogdiana. The use of multi-niches certainly serves some functional need. That each body occupies a niche in the Tang tombs at Yanchi could be a variation of the Sogdian practice of keeping ossuaries with the bones of the deceased in mausoleums.[11] Although identifiable ossuaries have not been found in China proper,[12] the possibility exists that exposure of the dead prior to burial was practiced. In one of the niches of Tomb M4, two upper arm bones were found, each of which was encircled by a thread. The diameter of the loop made by each piece of thread as it was tied to the bone was only two centimeters, which suggests that the bones had been tied in this way after the flesh was removed.

Other funerary practices also differentiate these Sogdian descendants' tombs from traditional Chinese in-ground burials. In Shi Daoluo's tomb at Guyuan, tiles that covered the ceiling led the excavators to postulate a pavilion or some other architectural structure for a stele or epitaph stone, built outside the burial chamber. Three meters below this structure was the skeleton of a dog.[13] The dog was held sacred by the Zoroastrians and figured in the funerary rite (fig. 6),[14] although the significance of this dog burial remains to be analyzed.[15] Evidence of a deliberately set fire was found in the corridor and burial chamber of An Qie's tomb. This was apparently set prior to burial and installation of the funerary couch, which is the main feature of the tomb. These divergences from traditional burial practices in China are extremely varied. They may reflect local customs in Sogdiana or changes and modifications made to those customs by these descendants of the Sogdian settlers.

In further contrast with Chinese burial practice, only one of the tombs at Yanchi, and none of the tombs at Guyuan, contained coffins or wooden remains that could be so identified.[16] Instead, a platform of brick, stone, or earth supported the remains of the deceased. Other tombs that could well be Sogdian contain stone funerary couches, with elaborately carved screens on three sides. Some of these couches seem to have supported a wooden coffin, others most likely not. The couch in the An Qie tomb may be the earliest and is definitely that of a Sogdian (see Chapter 6, fig. 4). That from Tianshui (no. 106) is among the latest, as it seems to belong to the Sui period.[17] While there is no positive evidence that the Tianshui couch, nor two other couches with carved screens, belonged to Sogdians, a comparative study of the carvings leads to the conclusion that all of these types of funerary couches come from Sogdian tombs.

Along with their adoption of in-ground burial, the Chinese Sogdians also followed the Han custom of burying objects, such as *mingqi*, and ceramic vessels that are similar in style to those in "Chinese" tombs.[18] All of the Shi family tombs had been robbed, but enough remained to give an idea of the range of grave goods. In the tomb of Shi Daoluo (the most scientifically excavated of the tombs), as well as that of An Pu, the *mingqi* and ceramics are no different from those in "Chinese" tombs. In fact, the tomb occupants would not be easily identifiable as non-Chinese if their epitaph stones had not been found. In addition to the more traditional objects, the Shi also buried purely foreign ones, perhaps family heirlooms or imports that specifically recalled for them their western heritage (nos. 85–87, 89a). Moreover the Shi tombs as well as that of An Pu included foreign coins, Byzantine and Sasanian, held by the deceased in the hand or mouth (see Chapter 9).[19]

The remembrance of their Sogdian roots may account for the imagery on the stone funerary couches, which shows, among other scenes, feasting and hunting, themes that were popular in Sogdian painting (see Chapter 7). However, we cannot exclude the possibility that such images, while clearly imported from the West, became popular among non-Western people in China. This can be exemplified by the Central Asian dancers on the stone doors from one of the Yanchi tombs (no. 81). Similar "barbarian" dancers are represented on the An Qie and Miho Museum funerary couches[20]; the stone sarcophagus of Yu Hong, discovered in Taiyuan[21]; and in Cave 220 at Dunhuang.[22] Sogdian dance was extremely popular among the Chinese and was for them the most representative feature of Sogdian culture (nos. 81, 82).

The Sogdians introduced a new artistic style and imagery into China. As this "barbarian" style was accepted into mainstream Chinese society, the distinctive cultural characteristics of the Sogdian descendants were reduced. Yet the Shi family retained their physical distinctions, even if culturally they, as did other Sogdian descendants, assimilated with the local populace. The remains of Shi Daoluo's skeleton have been identified as not Chinese, but Western.[23] From their epitaphs, too, we know that they married women who were also of Sogdian lineage. Shi Daoluo; his father, Shi Shewu; and his oldest brother, Shi Hedan, all married women with the family name of Kang (i.e., Samarkand).[24] Shi Suoyan, possibly another branch of the family, married An (i.e., Bukhara) Niang; according to her epitaph, she came from Qizhou in Shaanxi province, and her father and grandfather were, respectively, court officials in the Northern Zhou and Sui courts.

Despite the preservation of their physical distinctiveness, the Shi family and, undoubtedly other Sogdian descendants, were integrated into the Sui and Tang societies. Evidence of the Sogdian burials adds considerably to our attempts to reconstruct the history of Sogdian immigrants in China.

Fig. 6. A rare depiction of the Zoroastrian funerary rite, the *sagdid*, from a marble funerary couch, second half of the sixth–early seventh century, Northern dynasties, Sui dynasty. A priest stands before a fire altar, accompanied by a dog whose glance at the body of the deceased is believed to drive away the spirit of defilement. (photo: Miho Museum, Shigaraki)

MONKS AND MERCHANTS

NOTES

1. A convenient summary in English of Sogdian studies by Chinese scholars, written before 1995, is Cheng 1996. More recent studies, in Chinese, are Yong 1999, pp. 27–86; Luo 2000a, pp. 235–78.

2. See Pulleyblank 1952, pp. 319–323. Reference to the Nine States is in the *New Tang History* (*Xin Tang-shu* bk. 2, "Western Biography," p. 221). The other states mentioned are Mi (Maimargh), Huoxun (Choresmia), Wudi, Cao (Kabudhan), and He (Kushaniyah); the last two have been identified as near Samarkand. However, nine could be an approximate number.

3. For Kesh, see Chavannes 1903, pp. 146–147.

4. Luo 1996; *Tomb of Shi Daoluo* 2000. Three other tombs have been discovered in this cemetery. One belonged to Liang Yuanzhou and dates to the Tang dynasty; the other two were without epitaph stones to identify the owners and had few grave goods, but because of their locations, we can surmise that they were those of Shi family members.

5. The reconstruction of the Tang dynasty pronunciation of the character in his name (x₂) results in the modern pronunciation *he*, but an alternate modern pronunciation of *ke* is also used.

6. Luo 2000, pp. 170–71. Shi Shewu's epitaph suggests that his great-grandfather and a grandfather held the office of *sabao* while still in Central Asia, the first time that a reference to the post of *sabao* in Central Asia has been found.

7. See Grenet 1984, pp. 123–28, 157–86, 235–39.

8. Only preliminary reports are so far available: Yin, Li, and Xing, 2000. The official rank of An Qie was *da dudu* (Great General) and *sabao* of Tongzhou.

9. *Zhongyuan wenwu* 1982.3, pp. 21–26 ("Tomb of Mr. and Mrs. An Pu of the Tang Dynasty in Longmen of Luoyang," Luoyang Municipal Relics Team).

10. The Museum of Ningxia Autonomous Region, "Excavation of the Tang Tombs at Yanchi, Ningxia," *Wenwu* 1988.9, pp. 43–56.

11. See Chapter 6, p. 226–27 for further discussion of Sogdian funerary customs. V. D. Gorjačeva discusses mausoleums with multiple side-chambers for the deposition of the deceased's bones in Semirechye (Kyrgyzstan) (Gorjačeva 1987, pp. 77–79). Apparently, the corpse was not exposed prior to its placement in the tomb; rather, it was allowed to decompose in the corridor and then the bones were moved to an interior chamber.

12. But see the possible ossuary in Beijing (Shi 2000).

13. *Shi Daoluo* 2000, p. 62, fig. 15.

14. Lerner 1995, p. 185.

15. For dog burials in Zoroastrian contexts in Choresmia and Sogdiana, see Grenet 1986, pp. 247–48.

16. Tomb M1 at Yanchi contained a coffin. In the first five excavations of Shi family tombs, it was assumed that the coffins had rotted away, as traces of wood and some nails were found. The remains of a wooden coffin had been postulated for Shi Shewu's burial [Luo 1996, p. 9]. But with the excavation of Shi Daoluo's tomb, it was realized that none of the Shi tombs had burial containers. The discovery of several iron nails in the An Pu tomb at Luoyang also led the excavators to postulate the use of coffins, but the situation might be similar to that of the Shi tombs.

17. References for these couches are in the discussion under number 106.

18. An exception is the Northern Zhou tomb of An Qie, which, according to its excavators, was not robbed but contained few burial objects.

19. The "obol of Charon," a legacy of the Greek period in Bactria and Central Asia, may have been brought by Sogdian immigrants to China (Boyce and Grenet 1991, pp. 66, 191). A gold Byzantine coin, a *solidus* of Justin II (r. 565–78), was found in the Sui-dynasty tomb of Dugu Luo and his wife. The couple was not Sogdian, but had lived for a long period in an area near the Western Regions where they held high positions. It is quite possible that they adopted this foreign custom (see Xia 1961).

20. Yin, Li, and Xing 2000, p. 29, fig. 7; Juliano and Lerner 1997.

21. Xu and Zhang 2000, illus. on p. 8.

22. *Dunhuang* 1981, vol. 3, pl. 27.

23. The Chinese researchers characterize the Daoluo skeleton as "Ural," based mainly on the skull, as the rest of the skeleton, along with that of Shi Daoluo's wife, was in too poor condition to analyze. The Ural categorization was so named by Russian anthropologists and is associated with their "Central Asian of the Two Rivers" category (*Shi Daoluo* 2000, pp. 288–91). In discussing the epitaph of He Wenzhe, Lu Zhaoyin points out that the descendants of the *zhaowu jiuxing* who served as important Tang officials and generals were already sinicized but still married women who also bore one of the "nine place-names" (*Kaogu* 1986.9, pp. 841–48).

24. Shi Hedan's wife, Lady Kang, was his first. He later married a Lady Zhang, which is a Han name.

no. 80a, b

80a,b. Tomb doors and frame

Tang dynasty (618–906), dated 664
From the tomb of Shi Suoyan (d. 656, buried 664), and his wife, Anniang (d. 661),
southern suburbs of Guyuan, Ningxia
Limestone
Total height of both leaves of door: 134 cm; width 55 cm; thickness: 9 cm
Guyuan Municipal Museum, Ningxia Hui Autonomous Region

80c. Rubbing from tomb door

Tang dynasty (618–906), dated 669
From the tomb of Shi Hedan (d. 669) and his wife, Lady Zhang,
southern suburbs of Guyuan, Ningxia
Ink on paper
Rubbing of left tomb door: total height: 122 cm; width: 44.5 cm
Guyuan Municipal Museum, Ningxia Hui Autonomous Region

Chinese burial practices shifted by the end of the Western Han (206 BCE–24 CE) from shaft or pit burials to horizontal plans, with long entrance ramps leading to subterranean burial chambers outfitted with fine stone funerary furniture, coffins, couches, and epitaphs, and packed with *mingqi* made specifically to accompany the deceased. The scale of the tomb and its contents are a direct reflection of the deceased's rank. Marked by mounds above ground, each tomb was conceived as a replica of a house or palace and as a microcosm of the universe. The ceiling was reserved for images of the celestial regions and the walls more for earthly reminders, often a mix of auspicious or cosmological symbols, such as the animals of the four directions with incidents connected to the deceased's life. A cemetery in the southern suburbs of Guyuan contains the six tombs of the Shi family. Descendants

1. Many Tang tombs, including those of Yong Tai and other princes and princesses at Qian Ling in Shaanxi outside Xi'an, have side niches opening off the ramp to store *mingqi* or other grave goods. Both Shi Shewu (no. 88) and Shi Suoyan (nos. 80a,b) have two side niches. (*Yuanzhou* 1999, pl. 83 [Shi Shewu], pl. 102 [Shi Suoyan]).

2. Tomb of Shi Suoyan and his wife, Anniang, excavated in the northern suburbs of Guyuan at Yangfang Village (*Yuanzhou* 1999, pl. 104, p. 193; Luo 1996, pp. 31–55, p. 41, fig. 31).

3. The form of the Red Bird, once established in the late fifth–early sixth century, remains remarkably unchanged throughout Tang. Its early-sixth-century version can be found on clay tiles in the Dengxian tomb in Henan (Juliano 1980, *Dengxian*, fig. 16). Birds of this type are often generically called phoenixes; however, the term phoenix as Jessica Rawson points out covers two bird types, the Red Bird of the South, or *zhuniao*, and the grand mythical bird, the *fenghuang*, usually translated as phoenix. Except when the animals of the four directions are together, it is not always clear whether a given image is a Red Bird of the South or a phoenix (Rawson 1984, p. 99).

4. Chinese artists, unfamiliar with actual lions, have over the centuries created a distinctive Chinese version of the Buddhist lion. This is a hybrid combining the lion and winged *bixie*, stone tomb guardians placed on spirit roads of nobles around the Nanjing area during the late fifth and early sixth centuries (Paludan 1991, pp. 52–76).

5. Rawson 1992, p. 5.

6. Joint burial, Shi Hedan and wife, from southern suburbs of Guyuan at Xiaomazhuang Village (*Yuanzhou* 1999, pl. 117 [right], p. 194; Luo 1996, pp. 55–77, esp. p. 67, fig. 51).

7. Harada 1967, pp. 28, 38.

8. *Wenwu* 1966.1, pp. XX; Zhang 1998, pp. 44–49.

9. Juliano 1980, p. 53.

no. 80c (detail)

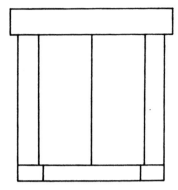

Fig. A. Drawing of stone frame and tomb doors (*above*) from Shi Suoyan's tomb (d. 664), Guyuan (Ningxia) (after Luo 1996, p. 39, fig. 26)

Fig. B. Drawing of the incised decoration on the doors from Shi Suoyan's tomb (*near right*) (d. 664), Guyuan (Ningxia) (after Luo 1996, p. 42, fig. 32)

Fig C. Detail of the head of the helmeted guardian from the stone coffin of Li He (*far right*) (d. 582) (after Zhang 1998, p. 47, no. 6)

of Sogdian immigrants, the Shi had achieved official positions at the Tang court. All their tombs have typical Tang tomb plans. At the bottom of the long ramp, there is a short, level tunnel that leads directly to a single burial chamber.[1] In this short tunnel, the epitaph stone and cover have been placed just in front of the stone doors, the entrance doors to the burial chamber.

Both the actual doors and the frame from Shi Suoyan's tomb have survived.[2] The complete door structure involves two leaves set into a frame composed of six stones: a lintel across the top is supported by vertical side posts with a three-part door jam, one stone under each post and one under the doors (fig. A). Each door has two stone posts that have been cut away at top and bottom with holes inserted at the top and bottom of the door frame, creating pivot posts, which allow the door to open and close. Two holes at about the middle of the door held some type of handle, bronze or perhaps iron rings.

The entire surface of the doors is covered with very low-relief leaf-incised decoration depicting confronted creatures arranged in three registers adorned with floral, cloud, and landscape motifs (fig. B). The top and middle registers contain two of the symbolic animals associated with the four directions; above is the Red Bird of the South[3] and below the Green Dragon of the East, both very auspicious. A grotesquely fanged, horned, and winged felinelike creature with a large, curved tail occupies the third and bottom register and has been identified only as a monster. Given the first two animals, it is surprising that this third one is not the White Tiger of the West or a pair of lions.[4] The dragon and beast stand on a stylized landscape of overlapping triangles fringed with vegetation, while the Red Bird stands on an oval lotus flower resting amid the hills.

The space around the creatures has been completely filled with a mixture of carved, wind-blown, hybrid cloud and floral sprays, as well as a border consisting of a rather distinctive leafy scroll along three edges. With the floral sprays and vigorous beasts, the entire door teems with movement and intense energy, a stylistic continuity from the mid-seventh century that harks back to the sixth century. By the early eighth century, floral elements begin to shift toward peony scrolls and sprays that become elegant and luxuriant. Both the vegetal scrolls and the floral elements along with the concept of confronted pairs of creatures may ultimately have been introduced from the West and Central Asia through Buddhism and commerce.[5] However, this configuration, the execution, and the style reflect a Chinese aesthetic and a synthesis of visual ideas that contributed to the development of the international Tang style.

MONKS AND MERCHANTS

Animal and human guardians are probably the most common decorative theme on tomb doors, reaching back to the Han dynasty. This rubbing has been made from the left-hand door of Shi Hedan's tomb (d. 669), depicting one of a pair of guardians (no. 80c).[6] With hands resting one on top of the other, these tall imposing figures, with non-Chinese beards and mustaches, wear formal court dress. The tunic, here trimmed with a zigzag border, has long, loose sleeves and may be belted over the baggy trousers; traditional cloud-toed shoes curve up at the edge of the trousers. A heart-shaped hat with a horizontal bar across the front is probably a *pingshance*,[7] which was worn at court by military officers or courtiers (see illustration on page 270). A floral border, very similar to the hybrid floral cloud scroll incised on Shi Shewu's epitaph cover (no. 83), runs along the inner edge and single floral sprays fill the background. The face is depicted with a large nose, one characteristic feature that defines the non-Chinese. This same device of a large nose can be seen on the helmeted and also bearded guardians engraved on the front end and on the doors of Li He's stone sarcophagus (fig. C). Li He, who died in 582 just after the founding of the Sui dynasty, was apparently an eminent member of the Northern Zhou and Sui courts with a family lineage of service for generations.[8]

These figures recall the guardians that line the walls of the earlier Dengxian tomb excavated in Henan and dating from the late fifth to early sixth century; the Dengxian faces show small noses, but have wispy beards and mustaches and the same clothing, including the *pingshance* hat, a tunic with long, loose sleeves over loose pants, and cloud-toed shoes.[9]

ALJ

81a,b. *Two tomb doors*

Tang dynasty (618–906), c. 700
From Tomb M6 of the He family cemetery at Yanchi,
Ningxia Hui Autonomous Region
Gray stone
Height: 89 cm; width: 43 cm; thickness: 5 cm
Ningxia Provincial Museum, Yinchuan,
Ningxia Hui Autonomous Region

These outer faces of the doors that guarded the tomb chamber of M6 are unique in their decoration.[1] Tomb doors of this period are typically decorated with scrolls and fantastic animals, in the manner of Shi Suoyan's (no. 80a,b) or with guardian figures, as was Shi Hedan's (no. 80c). In contrast, each of the Yanchi doors is incised with a Central Asian dancer who stands on one leg, the other raised away from his body or crossed behind his supporting leg. The dancer on the left door raises his right arm above his head and extends his left for balance; that on the right clasps both hands above his head and snaps his fingers in time to the music, much the way many Iranians and Central Asians dance today.

In addition to their postures, the physiognomies and clothing of the Yanchi dancers characterize them as Central Asian: mustache, short curly hair bound by a fillet or covered by a cap, leggings, boots, and long, skirted jackets. Dancer A's coat opens at the neck to form two lapels, a common ren-

Fig. A. The doors in situ
(*above*) (after *Wenwu* 1988.9,
p. 50, fig. 13)

Fig. B. Drawing of the dancers
on the doors from Tomb M6
(*right*), He family cemetery
at Yanchi (Ningxia) (photo
courtesy of the Ningxia
Provincial Museum)

dition of Central Asian dress, while dancer B wears a more unusual tight-fitting jacket, closed at the neck, and bound around the hips by a long, fluttering scarf. An even longer scarf weaves around each dancer's arms and frames his figure, reminiscent of earlier dancing female figures from the Iranian world, exemplified here by number 32. Each dancer performs on a small, circular, fringed rug.

The dancers' postures and appearance, along with their use of the rugs, identify their dance as the *huxuan wu*, popularly known as the "Sogdian whirl." While *hu* was broadly used by the Chinese to designate "barbarians" from the north, as well as peoples to the west—Kucheans, Khotanese, Persians, Sogdians, and later Arabs—in this context, it indicates a "dance composed of gyrations, the specialty of Sogdiana."[2] Indeed, contemporary historical and literary accounts of the dance describe whirling, gyrating motions:

> Iranian whirling girl, Iranian whirling girl—
> At the sound of the string and drums, she raises her arms,
> Like swirling snowflakes tossed about, she turns in her twirling dance.
> Whirling to the left, turning to the right, she never feels exhausted,
> A thousand rounds, ten thousand circuits—it never seems to end. . . .
> Compared to her, the wheels of a racing chariot revolve slowly and a whirlwind is sluggish.[3]

The best dancers came from Shash (Tashkent), Kesh, and Samarkand. As chronicled by the official *Tang shu* (Tang history), in the first half of the eighth century, rulers of these and other Sogdian principalities presented these whirling dancers to the Tang emperor Xuanzong (r. 685–762). However, the dance had been known in China even before the Sui dynasty, when an envoy of the emperor

Fig. C. Brown-glazed earthenware *bian hu* decorated in molded relief with Central Asian musicians and a dancer. From the tomb of General Fan Cui (d. 575) at Anyang (Henan), Northern Qi (after *Wenwu* 1972.1, pl. VII)

Yangdi brought back from Sogdiana ten female dancers. These "Western Twirling Girls," so admired by the Chinese court, had their rivals in other Central Asian dancers, both male and female, who entertained with apparently other versions of this vigorous dance. A description of the "Western Prancing Dance," usually performed by boys from Tashkent, has them "girded with long belts whose ends floated high and free, as they crouched, whirled, and leaped to the rapid accompaniment of lutes and transverse flutes,"[4] much in the manner of Yanchi dancer B. Such dancing was popular not only in court circles; according to contemporary accounts, ordinary Chinese were fascinated by it, and flocked to see the ritual dancing that took place in the Zoroastrian temples.[5] The general An Lushan (703–757; also known by the Iranian name of Rokhshan), a favorite of the emperor Xuanzong, was renowned for his ability to dance the Sogdian Whirl, despite weighing four hundred pounds.[6]

The panegyric verses composed about the *huxuan wu* describe both male and female dancers, but most of the visual representations of it depict men and are found in funerary contexts: on the stone funerary furniture belonging to those of Sogdian or other western origins (see Chapter 10, fig. 1),[7] in a wall painting in a Sui tomb,[8] on ceramic pilgrim flasks (*bian hu*) of the mid-sixth to the ninth century (fig. C),[9] and among the *mingqi* of the Tang period.[10] Female *huxuan wu* dancers seem to occur only in the early and middle Tang paintings of Buddhist paradise scenes.[11]

The rug on which the dance was typically performed was probably of Central Asian manufacture and is described in the following Tang verse:

The body leaps gyrating as on an axle, the jeweled belt jangles.
The feet move in rapid motion, the embroidered boots are soft.
. . . Wildly jumping on the new carpet of pure white and crimson wool.
It appears as if some light flowers have spilled over a red candle.[12]

The verse is a good description of the fringed rug with floral decoration on which the Yanchi dancers perform. When depicted on some of the early pilgrim flasks, the rug takes the shape of a lotus flower, the fringes transformed into petals.[13] The motif of dancers performing on a lotus flower continues into the Tang. It is often joined to that of a phoenix, which also stands on a lotus-flowerlike rug, as on the doors to Shi Suoyan's tomb (no. 80a,b).[14]

JAL

1. *Wenwu* 1988.9, p. 50, fig. 13, p. 54, figs. 24, 25; Luo 1994, pp. 50–59.

2. Mahler 1959, p. 147, with sources cited.

3. The first verse of a poem by Po Chu-yi (772–846) translated by Mair 1994, p. 486. Another late Tang poet, Yuan Chen (779–831), also gives a detailed description of the dance: "A wildly dancing whirlwind, sleet in space" (Mair 1994, p. 487).

4. Schafer 1963, p. 55. See also discussion under no. 82.

5. Pulleyblank 1991, p. 429.

6. Mair and Skjaervo 1991, pp. 466–67.

7. Juliano and Lerner 1997a, p. 253: E, and p. 249; Juliano and Lerner 1997b, p. 75, fig. 4; Scaglia 1958, fig. 4 (Zhengdu couch panel); Yin Li and Xing Li 2000, p. 29, fig. 7 (An Qie couch); Yetts III 1929, no. C40, pp. 56, 57, pls. XXVI, XXVII (white marble, possibly the base of a couch). The base of a Buddhist stele of the Northern Zhou period shows a male Central Asian dancer, accompanied by Central Asian musicians, opposite a Chinese girl performing the Chinese "long-sleeved dance" (*changxiu wu*) to the music of a Chinese orchestra (Juliano and Lerner 1997b, p. 76, fig. 6).

8. Shandong Provincial Museum 1991, p. 123, no. 147 (a feasting couple is entertained by a whirling Central Asian dancer).

9. The dancer is accompanied by musicians in the following representations: the golden brown-glazed earthenware flask discovered in the Northern Qi tomb of Fan Cui (d. 575) (Han 1985, pp. 39–41; Watson 1991, p. 49, fig. 24, fig. C in this entry); the green-glazed flask in the Museum of Fine Arts, Boston) Fontein and Wu 1973, p. 148, no. 71); the brown-glazed flask in the British Museum (Watson 1984, p. 144, no. 123); dark green-glazed miniature flask in the Myron S. Falk Collection (Schloss 1969, no. 62); a dark green-glazed flask found in the course of a building excavation in Guyuan, Ningxia (*Yuanzhou* 1999, p. 30, fig. 2)

10. Schloss 1969, no. 33 (identified as a Choresmian dancer).

11. *Dunhuang* 1981, vol. 3, pls. 27 (Cave 220) and 75 (Cave 331).

12. Quoted by Han 1980.

13. On the flasks from Fan Cui's tomb (fig. C) and in Boston, the rug has become a lotus flower, which rests on a volute support; on the British Museum and Falk flasks, the identification of what the dancer is on is ambiguous (see note 7 above). A fringed rug, clearly rendered with a diamond pattern, is the base for male dancers and two musicians on an agate belt plaque of the seventh–eighth century (Rawson 1987, p. 118, fig. 261).

14. Luo 1996, pp. 52–53. The most complete rendition of the phoenix and dancers on rugs, all linked by a vegetal scroll, is on a stone stele from a Xi'an, dated to 721 (ibid. p. 52, fig. 4)

1. *Put Svile* 1996, p. 156, no. 79.

2. Schafer 1963, p. 54.

3. It is interesting to note that in the early eighth century, the local prince of Kesh, the city of the Shi family's ancestors, sent dancing girls to the Chinese court (as well as spotted leopards) (Chavannes 1903, p. 145).

4. Also Azarpay 1981, p. 97. Frantz Grenet has attributed this hat to Sogdians in his identification of a group of donor figures belonging to a Buddhist relief from Ku Bua in Thailand (Grenet 1996, pp. 69–76, pp. 68–69, figs. 1–4. He also cites a similar hat on coinage from Sogdian Shash (Tashkent) (p. 76, fig. 8), and in Cave I at Ajanta (p. 72, fig. 5). Another version of the peaked hat has earflaps and is worn by a dancing male figure repeated in the stucco decoration of the second-century Parthian palace stronghold of Qaleh-i Yazdigird in western Iran; the figure also wears the Iranian tunic and trousers (Keall 1983, pp. 40, 43). His stance, however, with one leg bent over the other, one hand on the hip and the other in the air, bears no resemblance in the *huxuan wu*. Of an earlier period (first millennium CE) is the tall, peaked felt hat worn by one of the Indo-European (Indo-Iranian? Tocharian?) mummies discovered in the Tarim Basin of Xinjian (Mallory and Mair 2000, p. 215, fig. 127).

5. Mahler 1959, pl. XIXa–c (identified as from northeastern Iran); Schloss 1969, no. 58 (identified as a Western Turk); Grenet 1996, p. 74, figs. 6, 7.

6. See note 12 of no. 81. Schafer also cites poetic accounts of dancing boys from Tashkent "wearing tight-sleeved Iranian shirts and high-peaked hats sewn with sparkling beads" (Schafer 1963, p. 55).

7. Rawson 1982, p. 15.

8. Cf. So and Bunker 1995, p. 71; and Wu 1986, p. 270.

Fig. A. The double gourd or calabash in the foreground of this photograph is like the one worn by the figure in number 82 and was a traditional part of the equipment of Iranian and Central Asian dervishes. Often itinerants, dervishes were members of any of the numerous religious orders of Islam. The early twentieth-century dervish dress shown here belongs to the Bukhara State Historic-Architectural Museum (after *Bukhoro* 1991, fig. 102).

82. *Dancing Central Asian*

Tang dynasty (618–906), seventh century
From vicinity of Shandan, Gansu province;
acquired by Rewi Alley in Shendan between 1945 and 1980
Bronze figure, gilded (?) bronze base
Total height: 13.7 cm; greatest width: 8 cm
Shandan Municipal Museum, on loan to the Gansu Provincial Museum, Lanzhou

An expression of the Tang interest in the exotic, this Central Asian is shown in the characteristic posture of the *huxuan wu,* or "Sogdian whirl."[1] The bronze figure balances on one leg, with the hem of his tunic fluttering around him, his raised hands hidden by his long sleeves, which also flap with the movement of his dance. On his back he wears a double gourd or calabash, suggesting that he is an itinerant entertainer (fig. A). Although many of the foreign entertainers in the Sui and Tang periods were sent as gifts to the Chinese court from Central Asian rulers, there were numerous independent musicians and dancers who performed for the people.[2] As noted in the discussion under number 81, the most valued dancers were from Sogdian principalities, especially from Shash (Tashkent), Kesh,[3] and Samarkand.

That this dancer is from the West is attested by his non-Chinese physiognomy, particularly by his large nose. That he is from Sogdiana is indicated by his dress, especially by his peaked hat with turned-up brim. A variant of the so-called Phrygian cap, often seen in classical and Byzantine art to depict an Iranian, similar hats are worn by some of the male figures on the Panjikent paintings (see no. 106, fig. F).[4] Several Tang *mingqi* of Central Asian grooms wear such headgear, which might indicate that they, too, are Sogdian.[5] Indeed, both the cap and the tight sleeves of the dancer's tunic are noted by the Tang poet Liu Yanshi in his description of an Iranian dancing boy:

The Iranian from Tashkent appears young.
He dances to the music before the wine goblet, as rapid as a bird.
He wears a cloth cap of foreign make, empty and pointed at the top,
His Iranian robe of fine felt has tight sleeves.[6]

The dancer perches on a lotus-petal base, which may not be original to the sculpture. It may replace the small carpet upon which the dance was said to have been performed, or it may represent the lotus-shaped support on which similar dancers appear on the *bian hu* flasks of the period (see no. 81, fig. C). The shape of the petals recalls the lotus thrones for bronze Buddhist images of the Tang period, although the lotus was used as a support for other auspicious creatures.[7] Its use for this foreign performer is unusual but may be associated with the concept of *xiangrui* ("good omen"), which imbued foreign, strange, and unusual beings with good fortune.[8]

JAL

1. Tsien 1962, p. 70.

2. Luo 1996, pp. 7–19; *Yuanzhou* 1999, pls. 91 (epitaph cover) and 92 (epitaph stone).

3. Luo 1996, p. 8, fig. 3; p. 14, fig. 9.

83. *Epitaph stone and cover* (muzhi)

Sui Dynasty (589–618), early seventh century
Tomb of Shi Shewu (d. 609), southern suburbs of Guyuan, Ningxia
Limestone
Cover: length: 46.5 cm; width: 47 cm; height: 10 cm
Stone: length: 46.4 cm; width: 45 cm; height: 6 cm
Guyuan Municipal Museum, Ningxia Hui Autonomous Region

By the sixth century, stone memorial tablets and their covers were often placed in the tombs of the Northern nobility, a practice that continued through the Sui and Tang. At first, the form of these commemorative stones, called *muzhi* or *muzhiming* (grave inscriptions) resembled the traditional above-ground vertical stele or *bei* (see no. 68), but this horizontal version became the dominant form and the new standard by the sixth century CE.[1] These stone epitaphs are composed of a base and a cover. The square base or tablet has long texts inscribed on its smooth flat surface (*bottom*), which was then covered by another flat stone with beveled edges. The typical cover has a square central field surrounded by decorative floral and animal images and is usually inscribed with nine Chinese

characters in seal script, a formal ornamental style used to record the honorific titles of the deceased. Sometimes, knobs or large metal rings were inserted in the four corners to facilitate sliding back the cover to reveal the epitaph. These stones are positioned at the base of the tomb's entrance ramp in the short corridor that leads to the burial chambers.

Shi Shewu's tomb, dated to 609, is the earliest of the Shi burials in the cemetery discovered to the south of Guyuan.[2] Rather than residing in the corridor outside the burial chamber, the epitaph stone was placed inside the burial chamber directly in front of the coffin platform.[3] The twenty characters in seal script on the cover are enclosed by an interesting border filled with a hybrid cloud and floral vine. During the fifth through seventh centuries, the long, stylized, scalloped cloud scrolls that filled the celestial realms were mixed with a luxuriant vocabulary of lotus flowers, twists, and vines, the decor that arrived with Buddhism and soon appeared in non-Buddhist settings. Here, at regular intervals along the undulating vines, there are nodes from which grow stylized cloud puffs rather than the expected palmettes or lotus flowers.

The sloping sides of the cover have been filled by animals of the four directions or *siling*, drawn or rather incised in perfunctory fashion. The Green Dragon of the East, White Tiger of the West, Black Tortoise and Snake of the North, and Red Bird of the South cavort through stylized landscape edged at the bottom with stylized cloud scrolls, as floral twists blow through the sky above. Representations of these four animals, regarded as rulers of the seasons and quadrants, first appear during the Western Han and remain popular until the fourth century. After a hiatus, these beasts experience a resurgence in the late fifth and early sixth centuries and were often featured on tomb walls, mirrors, sarcophagi, and epitaph covers.

ALJ

The epitaph cover and stone have been translated by Zhang Guangda:

COVER: "The Inscription of the Epitaph of the Late His Excellency Shi Shewu, Grand Master for Proper Consultation (*zhengyi daifu*), Cavalry General of the Right Palace Guard (*you lingjun piaoji jiangjun*) of the Grand Sui Dynasty"

EPITAPH STONE: "Late His Excellency Shi, respectably named (*hui*, literally the tabooed name) Shewu and with a courtesy name (*zi*) Pantuo, was a native of Pinggao County of the Pingliang Prefecture. His ancestors were originally from the Western Regions. His great grandfather, Miaoni, and his grandfather, Boboni, served this country in the capacity of the *sabao*. His father, Renchou by name, idled away his life, accomplishing nothing in his official career.

"His Excellency was smart and intelligent when he was young. He was of refined feeling with a straightforward demeanor (*fenqing shuanwu*). He excelled in vigorous and valiant spirit and displayed unrivaled bravery.

"In the fourth year of Baoding [564 CE] he waited upon the Jindang Duke (*Yuwen Hu*) in his eastern military expedition. In the first year of Tianhe [566] he followed the Pinggao Duke to Hedong, stationing there in the garrison. In the first month of the second year [of Tianhe, 567] he was awarded the title Commander-in-Chief (*dudu*). In the second month of that year, he was dispatched to be in attendance on the Yanguo Duke in the latter's campaign to take the town of Wangbi. In the fifth year of Jiande [576] he followed the Shenguo Duke and captured the Zhiguan Pass and granted a high reward.

"In the first year of Xuanzheng [578], in the suite of the Prince of Qi, [named] Xian, who held also the military rank of the Supreme Pillar of the State (*shangzhuguo*), he participated in the punitive expedition against the alien Ji people (*jihu*). In the second year of Kaihuang [582], as an attendant of Li Gui, the Qizhang Duke, Supreme Commander (*shang kaifu*), he headed to the city of Liangzhou [present-day Wuwei, Gansu], where he fought the battle against the Turks to the north of the city, and acted in cooperation with Shi Wansui to outflank and check the fleeing troops. In the third year of Kaihuang [583], he volunteered to join the Supreme Commander Yao Bian of Shangkai government on a northern expedition, following him everywhere to stamp out rebellion. Then he followed Gao Yue, the Anfeng Duke to encircle the enemy in the elite forces.

"In the first month of the tenth year [590], as a retainer, he attended upon the Emperor [literally, 'the Imperial Carriage'] at Bingzhou [near present-day Taiyuan, Shanxi]. In the fourteenth year [594], he was transferred to the post of Commander-in-Chief (*dudu*). In the seventeenth year [597], he was promoted to Grand Area Commander-in-Chief (*Da Dudu*). In the nineteenth year [599], he again followed [Yang] Su, the Duke of Yueguo, into the desert, where he routed and vanquished the ferocious faction, without leaving any alive among all living beings. For this reason, he was honored with the award of the honorific post of Commander Unequaled in Honor (*kaifu yitongsansi*) as a reward for his special exploit. In the eleventh month of that year he was appointed Cavalry General by imperial edict. In the twentieth year [600], once more, he penetrated into the desert in attendance on the Prince of Qi.

"In the fourth year of Renshou [604], he was awarded with 1,000 *shi* [1 *shi* = 1 hectoliter] of millet, a living quarter of the first class, and a number of male and female servants and retainers, together with tall piles of silk and gauze. In the first year of Daye [605], he was transferred to Cavalry General of the Right Palace Guard (*you lingjun piaoji jiangjun*) and given a grant of 300 bolts of silk (*wu*) and 200 bushels (*hu*) of rice. In the same year, he waited upon the emperor in Yangzhou and received a grant of 400 bolts of silk and 60,000 copper coins.

"On the twenty-fourth day of the third month of the fifth year [609] he became ill and died in his personal residence at the age of 66. On the day of Jiashen, which fell on the twenty-second day of the first lunar month (whose first day was Guihai) of the sixth year [610], which was the year of Gengwu, he was buried in the [graveyard] of Xianliang Neighborhood of Xianyang Canton (*xianyang xiang*) of Pingliang Prefecture [present-day Guyuan]. Oh, what an acute sorrow!

"His eldest son, Hedan, and the younger ones, in order of age, Changle, Anle with the prestige title of Grand Master for Court Audiences (*chaoqing daifu*), Daxing, Hulang, Daole, and Juda are all worthy progeny with filial piety. All of them are keenly anxious for the long-lasting safety and peace of their father's graveyard. For fear of negligence through changes, we compose an epigraph as follows:

"[Just in the same manner as] a huge river flows out of its sources from the steep mountains, the propitious [genealogical] sequence [of the Shi] traces its origin long back to the blessed past. The family hewed out its good fortune from the stone coffins [of their ancestors]; the clan flourished in the Western Regions. It was only owing to the birth of His Excellency that the family and clan became prosperous. He started his career by joining the cavalry. Brandishing sword, he headed for serving the emperor. Posts were offered for his military merits and rewards were conferred for his loyal sincerity. Having been promoted to the post of Supreme General, he was on the point of being nominated to the Central Censurate. Who would have expected that a sudden gale burst in on him and carried him swiftly away like the last lingering light of the setting sun! But the pines and catalpas on his graveyard would perish only after an infinite duration."

1. Luo 1996, p. 15, fig. 10: 9 (teardrop) and 10 (bar); pl 8; *Yuanzhou* 1999, pls. 94 (teardrop-shaped ornament) and 95 (bar-shaped ornament).

2. Ierusalimskaja 1996, p. 85, fig. 99; Frumkin 1970, p. 120, fig. 29.

3. Zhao 1997; Sheng 1999, p. 51.

4. On a Tang ewer found at Xi'an, an inverted palmette terminates the lower end of the handle (Rawson 1982, fig. 49a).

84a,b. *Inlaid ornaments*

Sui dynasty (581–618), early seventh century
From the tomb of Shi Shewu (d. 609) and his wife, Lady Kang, southern suburbs of Guyuan, Ningxia
a. Teardrop-shaped ornament
Gilt bronze with glass and paste inlays
Height: 5.2 cm; greatest width: 4.12 cm
b. Bar-shaped ornament
Bronze with pearls and glass inlays
Length: 8.77 cm; width: 1.35 cm
Guyuan Municipal Museum, Ningxia Hui Autonomous Region

Both ornaments consist of bronze cells of different shapes that have been filled with stone, glass, and paste; the bronze strip has been embellished further with a row of pearls.[1] The teardrop, also described as "peach-shaped" in Chinese, consists of a beaded border that encloses a rosette and a three-leafed palmette. The bar-shaped ornament has a single beaded border of actual pearls that runs parallel to a line of lozenge-shaped glass inlays. The top (or bottom) of the bar ends in a palmette that is also inlaid with glass.

Rosette and palmette forms are popular motifs found on the textiles that were traded along the Silk Road from the northern Caucasus to China (see no. 109).[2] Beaded or pearled borders, used for medallions and for frameworks to enclose individual motifs, are ubiquitous on textiles produced in Persia, Sogdiana, and Xinjiang.[3] These textiles served as transmitters of motifs and decorative schemes into works in other media, such as metalwork and ceramics (nos. 111, 112).

One cannot surmise the original use of these two ornaments from the excavated remains, nor is their original orientation evident. Indeed, either one or both might have graced the objects to which they were attached, inverted from their positioning as shown here.[4]

ALJ and JAL

85. *Finger ring*

Probably Gandharan, fourth through sixth century BCE
From the tomb of Shi Shewu (d. 609) and his wife, Lady Kang,
southern suburbs of Guyuan, Ningxia
Gold
Overall height: 2.76 cm; diameter of hoop: 2.8 cm;
diameter of bezel: c. 1.84 cm; weight: 30.2 g
Guyuan Municipal Museum, Ningxia Hui Autonomous Region

Finger rings, along with necklaces, were not typical items of Chinese personal adornment.[1] The finger rings so far found in China for this and earlier periods can be identified as imports from the West, either from Sasanian Iran (see no. 32) or Rome (at least some by way of Gandhara)[2]; there are no metal rings at this time that appear to be Chinese made. References to finger rings in Tang literature mainly note them as imports (that is, gifts from Southeast or Central Asia to the emperor) or as "funerary jades."[3]

The ring has a raised circular bezel setting that once held a stone, now missing. Without the stone as a clue for the ring's origin, the ring must be identified by its most salient feature, the way in which the bezel appears to join the hoop. However, the ring was not fabricated from separate pieces but from a single sheet of gold. The back of the bezel was highlighted by two raised circular elements to form a figure eight. In side view, these elements appear as a V in relief, curving from just under the bezel to the center of the hoop. Rings of this type have been reported to come from areas in present-day Afghanistan, Pakistan, and northwest India, the territory that made up ancient Gandhara, and have been dated to the fourth through sixth centuries.[4]

The ring, which was on the floor of the burial chamber and away from the burial platform, apparently had been dropped or overlooked by tomb robbers when they scattered the objects in the tomb. The stone might have fallen out then, although the roughened edge of the empty bezel suggests that the stone had been pried out. Whether robbers would have taken the time to do this when they could have easily pocketed the ring, or the ring had lost its stone before Shi Shewu's burial, is impossible to determine; when the ring was found, earth had already filled the empty bezel. As an exotic object from another place, the ring would have been valued by Shi Shewu or Lady Kang even without its stone.

JAL

1. Luo 1996, pp. 14, 15, fig. 10:3.

2. The other finger rings are:

   1. Gold, with a square bezel set with a small pyramidal stone, from the fifth-century tomb near Nanjing (*Wenwu* 1972.11, pl. 5:2).

   2. Silver, with a raised circular bezel that once contained a stone, found in the Northern Wei stone coffin buried in 481 under the pagoda at Dingxian (Hubei). In *Kaogu* 1966.5, pl. 5:7, a second ring with an engraved stone is reported as "broken."

   3. Gold, with a deer carved in intaglio on the blue stone set into a circular bezel (Tomb of Li Xizong [d. 540] and his wife, Lady Cui, in *Kaogu* 1977.6, p. 388, pl. 6:5).

   4. Gold, with an intaglio stone set flush into the hoop, from a sixth–seventh-century grave in Inner Mongolia (Xiong and Laing 1991, p. 166, fig. 5).

3. Schafer 1963, pp. 221 (a diamond finger ring from the fifth-century ruler of Kelantan, Java), 238 (a jade or chlorophane ring from the Sogdian state of Maimargh), 247 (red coral from the West). A gold ring with elaborate granulated decorations on the hoop and around the bezel and set with an agate intaglio was surely an import into Tang China (*Sammlung Uldry* 1994, p. 209, no. 233).

4. I owe this information to Derek J. Content (personal communication, January 2001).

1. For the publication of the seal, see Luo 1996, pp. 61, 240–47, colorpl. 18; *Yuanzhou* 1999, pl. 122; and Lin 1997, pp. 170–71.

2. The lion's pose is also characterized as "sleeping" or "dead"; in the latter case, it may be likened to some of the lion victims on the Sasanian silver plates depicting royal lion hunts (see Amorai-Stark 2000, pp. 205–6. Although the author brings together much information about the motif, her conclusions about the seal, its significance, and its relation to the Shi family are untenable).

3. Brunner 1978, pp. 94–96.

4. Ibid., pp. 115–17; Marshak 1998, pp. 88–89.

5. The plates have been brought together by Marshak 1998, pls. XIc and XIIIa, c, and by Luo 1996, p. 245; Marshak 1999b, p. 107.

6. The legend appears to begin just above the lion's right eye. I thank P.O. Skjaervø for his help, as well as Philippe Gignoux, who also looked at an impression of the seal and with whom Professor Skjaervø consulted. This reading is markedly different from that proposed by Lin Meicun (Lin 1997, p. 171: "Freedom, Prosperity, Happiness").

86. *Inscribed seal stone*

Sasanian Persian, fourth–sixth century
From the tomb of Shi Hedan (d. 669) and his wife, Lady Zhang, southern suburbs of Guyuan, Ningxia
Nicolo (onyx)
Diameter: 1.56 cm; thickness: 0.46 cm
Guyuan Municipal Museum, Ningxia Hui Autonomous Region

The seal, carved in intaglio and in the form of a circular flat bezel, is made of nicolo, a type of banded agate with a blue top layer and dark brown bottom layer (the same material as no. 32).[1] The image of a reclining lion with frontal head is popular in Sasanian glyptic art, although a lion reclining before vegetation is considerably less so.[2] In the art of the ancient Near East and western Asia, the lion is accorded royal status as well as heroic and solar significance. Zoroastrianism, however, does not give the King of Beasts mythic or astrological meaning, yet its frequent occurrence on Sasanian seals seems to be auspicious.[3] In Sogdiana, the lion was the animal of the goddess Nana, the most important deity of the local pantheon (see Chapter 6, fig. 2, and Chapter 7, p. 233). The upright tripartite tree with tuliplike flowers is also a frequent image on Sasanian seals: the tulip flower, associated with Zoroastrian ideas of prosperity and well-being, and a blooming tree with the Zoroastrian "tree of all fruits."[4] A lion (or other animal) in front of a plant or tree occurs on Sasanian and Sogdian silver plates as a kind of "visual benediction," the animal–plant combination symbolizing the universe in which the owner of the seal or plate should prosper.[5]

The inscription that surrounds the image is written in Pahlavi, the language of Sasanian Iran. However, the script diverges significantly from the fourth- to sixth-century standard and is therefore not easily read. P. Oktor Skjaervø proposes a tentative reading of "generosity, generosity, generosity" for the legend.[6]

The edges of the stone show no signs that it had ever been set in a ring or some other mount; thus, it would have been difficult to impress and use it as an actual seal. Although it was found on the coffin platform, the tomb had been disturbed, making it impossible to know whether the seal belonged to Shi Hedan or Lady Zhang. However, the associations with Zoroastrian and Sogdian imagery may suggest that the seal was of significance to Shi Hedan and Lady Zhang and not merely an exotic item to treasure.

JAL

260

87. *Pendant*

Central Asian, possibly Choresmian or Sogdian (?), sixth–seventh century
From the tomb of Shi Suoyan (d. 656, buried 664) and his wife, Anniang (d. 661), southern sub-
urbs of Guyuan, Ningxia
Sapphire set in gold
Length: 4 cm; width: 2.6 cm; thickness at thickest part: 1.2 cm
Guyuan Municipal Museum, Guyuan, Ningxia Hui Autonomous Region

Set in a roughly oval gold mount, the stone is pebble-shaped, with an irregular surface. The mount bears the remains of a loop from which the stone would have hung.[1] A similar pendant hangs from the necklace of the Sui princess Li Jingxun, who died in 608 and was buried in Xi'an (fig. A).[2] The princess's elaborate piece of jewelry, made of elements of varied foreign manufacture, has a central, jeweled medallion to which is attached a small bead; below this is a large pendant teardrop of polished stone set in a beaded gold mount. Like Shi Suoyan's pendant, this stone is a blue color and has the same irregular surface. The stone has not been identified with certainty, but it could also be a sapphire.[3]

A necklace with a similarly shaped pendent jewel is worn by a goddess on a seventh-century Choresmian silver bowl, dated by its inscription to 658.[4] Further evidence of a necklace with teardrop-shaped pendant in a Central Asian context appears in one of the processional scenes painted on the walls of the seventh-century palace at Old Samarkand (Afrasiab). A bearded emissary from Chaghanian, a principality on the Oxus River in present-day southeastern Uzbekistan and within the Sogdian sphere, and the women who accompany him, wear necklaces with a central jeweled medallion from which hangs a teardrop- or pear-shaped stone (Fig. B).

Although Li Jingxun's pendant is part of a multi-jeweled necklace, we have no way of knowing whether the pendant in Shi Suoyan's tomb originally also hung from a necklace with other decorative elements or was simply worn as a separate piece. We also do not know if the pendant was a family heirloom, harking back to a time more contemporary with Li Jingxun, or even earlier.[5] Before the Sui, necklaces were rarely worn in China; the fashion seems to have been introduced from the West.[6] The pendant may have come from Sogdiana, the country of Shi Suoyan's forefathers, as well as that of his wife, as her name reveals her ancestry in Bukhara. The pendant may have been hers, either brought by her forbearers from Sodgiana or acquired in China.

Whether the sapphire was made into a pendant jewel in Central Asia or in China, the source for such stones is Ceylon, which is further evidence of the extensive trade networks of the period.

JAL

1. The pendant is published in Luo 1996, where it is described as "blue crystal;" p. 36, no. 12, colorpl. 13; *Yuanzhou* 1999, pl. 114.

2. *Wenwu* 1987.10, p. 77; Xiong and Laing 1991, p. 165, fig. 3.

3. Although sapphires are not easily identifiable in Chinese sources of the period, the actual stones exist in at least a Tang context: a hoard of precious stones, excavated at Hejiacun, southern suburbs of Xi'an, contains several sapphires. They "have a high transparency and vary in color from dark to light blue." Their surfaces are polished and irregular, similar to Li Jingxun's pendant and that of Shi Suoyan's (Michaelson, 1999, no. 84, pp. 120–21).

4. St. John Simpson, in *Weihrauch und Seide* 1996; Azarpay 1969, pp. 186–200, pl. 2.

5. Because Li Jingxun was the great-granddaughter of the Northern Zhou general Li Xian, her necklace or some of its foreign elements may also have been family heirlooms.

6. Rawson 1987, p. 115.

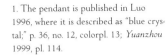

Fig. A. Necklace of Li Jingxun (d. 608), with crystal-like pendant (*above*) (after *Tang Changan* 1980, colorpl. 1)

Fig. B. Chaganyan emissary wearing necklace with pendant (*left*), detail of a Sogdian wall painting from Afrasiab (Old Samarkand), seventh century (after Al'baum 1975, pl. xxiv)

1. Luo 1996, p. 36, no. 14, pl. 28; *Yuanzhou* 1999, pl. 115.

2. Michaelson 1999, p. 64, no. 30.

3. *Tang Changan* 1980, pl. VIII: 1. The shorter rock crystal hairpins range from 2.9 to 3 centimeters in length, and the three longer jade hairpins from 6.8 to 8.1 centimeters.

88. *Hairpin*

Tang dynasty (618–906), seventh century
From the tomb of Shi Suoyan (d. 656, buried 664) and his wife, Anniang (d. 661),
southern suburbs of Guyuan, Ningxia
Jade (nephrite)
Length: 2.82 cm; width: 1.86 cm; thickness at the top: 0.5 cm
Guyuan Municipal Museum, Ningxia Hui Autonomous Region

This double-pronged hairpin, which belonged to Shi Suoyan's wife, Anniang, is a type made of jade that first appears in the Northern Zhou period (see no. 44) and, by the Sui dynasty (589–618), develops into a thin elongated shape with a somewhat flat, curved head.[1,2] Many similar plain jade hairpins have been found dating to the Tang dynasty. It is difficult to tell whether Anniang's hairpin was of this elongated form, its lower half broken off, or was originally of this shorter length. Among the hairpins worn in death by the Sui princess Li Jingxun were three of rock crystal of nearly identical size and shape, along with three jade hairpins with longer prongs (fig. A).[3] Unlike other stone hairpins, Anniang's is notched on each prong. If, in fact, the hairpin was of the longer type, the missing lower portions of the prongs may have had additional notches, perhaps to help secure the hairpin in the piled-up hairstyle that was fashionable among women in the Tang.

As early as the Warring States period (475–221 BCE), girls were given hairpins and other ornaments for dressing their hair as they entered adulthood. It is likely that such gifts marked this rite of passage when Anniang became a young woman.

JAL

Fig. A. The skull of the princess Li Jingxun (*above*) showing her rock crystal and jade hairpins; 608, Sui (after *Tang Changan* 1980, pl. VIII:1)

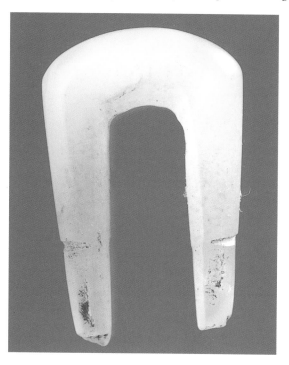

89a. *Cantaloupe-shaped cup*

Chinese, Tang dynasty (618–906), seventh century
From the tomb of Shi Hedan (d. 669)
and his wife, Lady Zhang, southern suburbs of Guyuan, Ningxia
Glass
Diameter: 3.8 cm; height: 2.0 cm
Guyuan Municipal Museum, Ningxia Hui Autonomous Region

89b. *Gourd-shaped* hu

Chinese, Tang dynasty (608–906), seventh–eighth century
From Tomb M6 of the He clan, at Yanchi, Ningxia
Glass
Diameter: 4.0 cm
Ningxia Provincial Museum, Yinchuan, Ningxia Hui Autonomous Region

The two blown-glass vessels are Chinese made. The cup was one of at least ten glass vessels buried with Shi Hedan and Lady Zhang, and is one of two that have survived whole.[1] Originally of a deep green color, the cup is cantaloupe-shaped, its surface divided into six sections, or lobes. Its distinctive form was achieved by blowing the glass into a mold. The thin walls and small size of the cup and the others in the tomb are characteristically Chinese.[2] The Chinese glass specialist An Jiayao notes that most non-Chinese glass vessels were used for serving food and wine and so are relatively large, the majority over 10 centimeters across the mouth.[3]

The *hu*, which retains its deep green tone, seems to have been blown without a mold. Globular, neckless, glass vessels are attributed to the Tang period,[4] but the roughness of the small opening of the vessel suggests that it has lost its neck. If so, its original shape is difficult to determine. It may have had a short conical top similar to the dark green hollow glass object that was found in the Northern Qi tomb of Kudi Huilou (d. 562).[5] Alternatively, it may have resembled the small gourd-shaped bottles with globular bodies, long necks, and mouths modeled into a short hook that were part of the foundation deposit, dated 481, of a Northern Wei pagoda in Hebei province in northeastern China.[6] These vessels can be linked to the slender-necked, globular-bodied blown-glass bottles of Tang date, such as that found in the triple-casket reliquary (no. 120).

Although the Chinese made glass even before Han times, they cast it in molds. Blown glass was not introduced until the mid-fifth century under the Northern Wei dynasty, presumably by foreign craftsmen from the West. An Jiayao cites the *Wei History*'s account of Bactrians manufacturing glass at that time, as well as certain features not found earlier in Chinese glass but known in Roman and Sasanian examples.[7] After the Northern Wei, glass vessels were mainly blown.

JAL

1. *Yuanzhou* 1999, pl. 123; Luo 1996, p. 60, fig. 12, pp. 235–37, pls. 50, 51.

2. As is the small (1.18 cm long) eight-lobed, slightly elliptical, greenish glass cup in the Museum of Fine Arts, Boston (Tseng and Dart 1964, vol. I, no. 144). A nearly complete six-lobed glass cup, 4 centimeters in diameter, was found in the tomb of Shi Daoluo (d. 658) in the Shi family cemetery at Guyuan. The cup sits in a kind of cage made of bronze strips that rest in the vertical depressions formed by the lobes (*Shi Daoluo* 2000, p. 174, fig. 50, p. 29, col-orpl. 28: lower right).

3. An 1984, p. 16. An also cites the small glass cups in two Sui-period tombs, one of them that of the princess Li Jingxun.

4. Thus, the green glass bowl in the British Museum (*Glass* 1968, no. 164).

5. *Kaogu xuebao* 1979.3, p. 393, pl. 11: 3 (27). The glass was described by its excavators as being "in the form of a jewel" and very much resembles a Christmas tree ornament.

6. An 1984, p. 14, fig. 32. The color of all three bottles is a "pale transparent blue." (Also see the published report in *Kaogu* 1966.5 of the foundation deposit of the Northern Wei pagoda at Dingxian [Hebei], pl. 7:3.). The possibility exists, however, that our example belongs to a later period: a green glass gourd-shaped vase consisting of two attached globes of glass, the top smaller than the other, was excavated from the foundations of a Song-period (960–1279) pagoda also at Dingxian (Hebei) (An 1984, p. 20, fig. 44).

7. Ibid., pp. 14, 23.

1. Luo 1996, pp. 89–92, 103–5, colorpl. 20; *Yuanzhou* 1999, no. 133; *Put Svile* 1996, p. 165, no. 88.

2. The earliest of the Western gold masks so far known are those from the shaft graves at Mycenae, dating some-time shortly after 1600 BCE. For a survey of masks found in the ancient western Asia, see Curtis 1995, pp. 226–31.

3. Jade plaques of various shapes found in tombs in China that date to the Neolithic period (c. 3000 BCE) may have been used to cover the body and face of the dead (Rawson 1996, no. 14, pp. 48–49).

4. The practice of assembling jade plaques of different shapes to cover the face is attested in Western Zhou (c. 1027–771 BCE) and Eastern Zhou (770–221 BCE) periods; they may be wired together, as the jades from a Western Zhou tomb in Henan (*Zhong-guo* 1993, pl. 68), or sewn on to cloth, as from one of several Eastern Zhou tombs in Henan (Rawson 1996, no. 72, p. 154; also Rawson 1995, pp. 314–16). However, a single piece of jade occurs as a full-face mask with pierced eyes, nostrils, and mouth and engraved hair, eyebrows, and a possible nose decora-tion in a fifth-century BCE tomb at Qin-jiashan (Hubei) (*Wenwu* 1999.4, p. 24, figs. 13, 14). Jade was also fashioned into plugs for the nine bodily orifices used in the Eastern Zhou and Han (206 BCE–220 CE) periods (see Rawson 1995, p. 318, fig. 24:4–6) and full jade burial suits, made from hundreds of jade wafers, encased the bodies of Western Han nobility of the second century BCE to second century CE (for example, Raw-son 1996, no. 81, pp. 170–71).

5. A flat piece of gold with V-shaped holes for the eyes and mouth was found in the Northern Yan period tomb of Feng Sufu (d. 415) at Xiguanyingzi (Liaoning province) accompanied by several pieces of Roman glass and four seals similar to nos. 6 and 7 in this cata-logue (*Wenwu* 1973.3, p. 22, fig. 35). The bronze masks from the eleventh- to tenth-century BCE tombs in the Yan State cemetery (early Western Zhou period), with their varied and stylized features, most likely had some ritual use rather than protection for the deceased's face (Rawson 1996, no. 52, pp. 114–16).

6. Benkó 1992/93, p. 120. Benkó men-tions a gilded iron mask with several holes in the corners for sewing to a cloth, discovered in the Astana ceme-tery (Turfan oasis, Xinjiang) and now in the State Hermitage Museum, St. Petersburg.

7. Curtis 1995, pp. 226–29.

8. Alekseyeva 1987, p. 171, no. 91, nos. 253–255; these are from male and

90. *Elements of a mask*

Tang dynasty (618–906), seventh century
From the tomb of the Shi Daode (d. 678), southern suburbs of Guyuan, Ningxia
Eleven gold foil pieces that form a face with headdress
Overall height when assembled: 28.4 cm; width: 21.2 cm
Guyuan Municipal Museum, Ningxia Hui Autonomous Region

Originally sewn on to a cloth (most likely silk), these pieces when assembled served as a mask for the face of the deceased Shi Daode.[1] The custom of covering all or a part of a dead person's face has a long history and is widespread in the ancient world, beginning at least as early as the second mil-lennium BCE, with evidence of the practice extending from the Mediterranean[2] to China.[3] The appearance of this mask in Shi Daode's tomb may represent a merging of this custom with other funerary practices and may offer some insight into the nature of the Shi family's adaptation to Chi-nese society.

A number of ways existed for protecting or preserving the features of the deceased's head—ears, nose, and especially eyes and mouth, needed in the afterlife to hear, breathe, see, eat, and speak—ranging from full-face masks to eye covers or "spectacles" (two eye-shapes joined together by a narrow band) and mouth covers. Similarly, a variety of materials were employed at different times and places. From the Mediterranean into Central Asia, gold was used extensively because of its pre-cious and durable nature, while in China, jade was the preferred material because of its similar prop-erties[4]; however, gold masks also occur in China.[5] Silver, ceramic, wood, painted plaster, and cloth

are other materials used for full face masks and eye-covers in areas of Central Asia, southern Siberia, and Xinjiang.[6]

In the West, face masks of gold become widely known in the sixth through the second century BCE in Macedonia, in northern Greece, and on the northern coast of the Black Sea; contemporary with them or somewhat later may be gold masks from the area of Sidon, on the eastern coast of the Mediterranean. Such face masks continue into Roman-Parthian times with the gold funerary masks excavated at Nineveh (northern Iraq) in the second to third century CE.[7] The Nineveh masks were accompanied by gold eye coverings and mouth coverings, the former in the shape of spectacles, which may have been placed directly on the corpse and then covered by the mask. Separate gold "eye plates" and "mouth plates" occur in burials dating to the same centuries, such as those from the classical city of Gorgippia, north of the Black Sea.[8] Nevertheless, the joining of the eye plaques into spectacles seems a more popular form and is found in burials from the Caucasus into Central Asia.[9]

In contrast to the masks and the eye covers of western Asia, which were attached to the corpse by wires tied around the head, the face masks, eye covers, and mouth covers found in Xinjiang and China were sewn on to a silk face cover, which was wrapped around the head of the deceased. According to the *Ili*, or the Book of Ceremonials, which dates from the late Eastern Zhou period (771–256 BCE), part of the funerary ritual involves a square piece of fabric (*mingmu*) to close or cover the eyes of the deceased; the *mingmu* was attached by a ribbon. The commentary on the *Ili*, the *Ili i shu*, adds that the entire head should be enveloped by a veil (*yen*), a piece of plain silk that is tied at the back of the head.[10] An early example of this practice is the late-second-century BCE burial of the Han prince Lui Sheng, in which a pair of jade eye covers has holes for attachment to a now-vanished fabric.[11]

As demonstrated by excavated tombs in Xinjiang and China, various means of covering the entire face or part of it were practiced from at least Han times and well into the Tang: eye covers (*mingmu* or *tzi*), face covers (*fumian*), and masks (perhaps *bujin*); in recent Chinese discussions of these finds, the terms used for the different variants are not very precise. All three types of coverings occur in the sixth- to eighth-century burials at Astana (Turfan oasis, Xinjiang), with the most frequent being silver or bronze "spectacles" (*yanzhao*) sewn on a silk face cover (*fumian*) that was wrapped around the corpse's head.[12]

Associated with the practice of covering the face in this way is the placing of a coin, the so-called Charon's obol, in the deceased's mouth. This Mediterranean custom seems to have fused with the ancient Chinese one of wrapping the head in silk. The coins at Astana are Sasanian silver *drachms* or Byzantine gold *solidi* (real and imitations), as are the coins found in the Shi family tombs (nos. 101–104). The remains of Shi Daode's corpse actually held an imitation *solidus* in its mouth (no. 104).

Shi Daode's mask, with its individual elements meant to be attached to fabric so as to form a realistic, if stylized, face, could fit well within the Chinese tradition of *fumian* and separate plaques for facial features. Yet it is puzzling that Shi Daode, as a descendant of Sogdian emigrants who were most likely Zoroastrians, should follow this burial custom. However, the use of a burial mask consisting of facial elements sewn onto cloth is not alien to some of the cultures of Central Asia.

As early as the Han period, the use of face covers had been adopted in regions to the west of China; for example, in the Minusinsk Basin of southern Siberia, silk was wrapped around the heads and then covered by clay burial masks.[13] Between the first or second and the seventh century CE in cemeteries of the so-called Kenkol culture of the upper Talas River region (present-day Kyrghyzstan), the dead were buried with masks, eye covers, and mouth covers sewn onto silk.[14] The cemeteries may reflect a mix of local and Xiongnu peoples, so it is difficult to know if the masks' eye covers and mouth covers were characteristic of a particular ethnic group or if the practice had been adopted by one from the other and then shared by both. Particular noteworthy are the elements of a face mask from one of these burials: a Y-shape for the eyebrows and nose and a long horizontal strap with a circular piece in the center for supporting the chin.[15] The mask elements from Shi Daode's tomb may stem from this burial custom.

female burials. Pairs of gold-foil breasts were also found in the female burials (cat. no. 256).

9. Benkó 1992/93, p. 116. He attributes the "melting" of the two eye covers together "with a golden ribbon" to the Parthians.

10. Cited by Riboud 1977, pp. 440–41.

11. Rawson 1995, p. 318, fig. 1, and also the pair of eye covers in no. 24:7.

12. Riboud 1977, pp. 441–45. The earliest *fu-mien* at Astana seems to be that from Tomb 303, dated 551 CE, on which was sewn two bone beads for the eyes and an agate bead for the mouth. A flap on the *fu-mien*, typically of a polychrome patterned silk, covers the *yen-chao*; these pieces of cloth have helped textile experts to suggest dates and to attribute other textiles to Sasanian, Central Asian, Byzantine, or Chinese workmanship.

13. Benkó 1992/93, p. 119, n. 23. The masks are of plaster, each fashioned and painted as if to individualize the deceased, and belong to the burial practices of the Tashtyk culture of the Minusinsk area between the first and fourth century CE (see *The Silk Road* 1988, nos. 150, 151).

14. Benkó 1992/93, p. 119. See also Zadneprovskiy 1994, pp. 469–70. Full face masks of gold also exist in Kyrghyzstan burials, as represented by one from Shamshi that is dated to the fourth to fifth century CE. An additional layer of gold leaf forms the long nose, while the eye sockets are filled in with carnelian; white paste emphasizes the "tree of life" motifs on the cheeks and nose, possibly imitating tattoos (*The Silk Road* 1988, no. 158).

15. Benkó 1992/93, p. 122, fig. 5a; Zadneprovskiy 1994, p. 470, fig. 3.

16. Tomb of Shao Zhen (d. 520), near Tianshui in Gansu, Northern Wei dynasty: *Wenwu cankao ziliao* 1955.12, pp. 59–65. I owe this reference and other information on the use (or lack) of chin straps in China to Shing Müller.

17. Michaelson 1999, no. 41, p. 73. Citing the tomb of He Ruo's wife, near Xi'an, in which a gold chin strap was part of an ensemble that included an elaborate headdress, Michaelson notes the possibility that the gold chin strap was "an ornament worn in life and taken to the grave" (p. 74).

18. Mallory and Mair 2000, pp. 191, 193. The two traditions of face mask or face cover on the one hand and of chin strap on the other combine on the mummy excavated from a tomb at Yinpan (near Lopnor, Xinjiang) in which the head of the sumptuously dressed deceased was covered by a hemp mask

on which the eyebrows, eyes, and mustache are painted black and the lips red;
a broad gold foil strip was pasted across
his forehead. The burial may date to the
second to third century CE; based on the
textiles and grave goods, Chinese excavators have speculated that the deceased
was a rich Sogdian merchant, but there
is no evidence of his ethnicity (ibid., pp.
201–3; *Wenwu* 1999.1, p. 13).

19. Sarianidi 1985, pp. 239, 250, 252.

20. Cheng 1996, p. 25 for references;
Luo 1988, pp. 92–94.

21. Grenet 1984, p. 101, fig. 24. The crescent is flanked by wings, which may be
represented, in abbreviated form in, the
side elements of Shi Daode's headdress.
Some of the other astral emblems on the
Tok-kala ossuaries are illustrated on p.
100, fig. 23. The crescent and sun (or
morning star) also crowns the Sogdian
ossuary from Mulla-kurgan (see Chapter
6, fig. 3).

22. Azarpay 1969, p. 200, pl. 7.

23. Filanovič 1991, p. 210. Other examples of Sogdian metalwork have been
found near Bartym, which is not surprising as it was on the northern "Fur Road"
and such silver must have figured into
the commercial exchanges of the route.

Like the mask of the Kenkol culture, that of Shi Daode has a chin strap (a double one made of two gold strips joined together by two quatrefoil bosses on each of the sides). While the use of a metal chin strap to support or bind the jaw of the deceased is found in China, it does not seem to be a Han Chinese tradition. Metal chin straps, however, occur in some tombs of the Northern Wei period[16] and may continue into the Tang.[17] It is possible that in Chinese burials cloth was used to bind the jaw and has not survived; the well-preserved mummies of Xinjiang, belonging to the first millennium BCE, show the lower jaws tightly bound with cloth strips.[18] Gold chin straps are found in western Central Asia in the graves at Tillya Tepe (northern Afghanistan), dated from the second half of the first century BCE to the first half of the first century CE.[19]

Although these parallels for Shi Daode's mask exist in Sogdian territory, the Shi family was from Kesh, in the Sogdian heartland, south of Samarkand, where Zoroastrian burial practices were preva-lent. There is no evidence for face masks in such a context. Questions have been raised about Shi Daode's ethnic group, with some Chinese scholars rejecting his Sogdian affiliation.[20] Yet a Sogdian or a more generalized Iranian tradition for the mask is supported by its headdress, which consists of a crescent topped by a globe (most likely the sun) as the central decoration, mounted on a headband of which only two side elements survive.

A similar crescent and globe is a characteristic feature of the Sasanian kings' crowns from the fifth century on (see the coins of Peroz, Chapter 9: fig. 3a, nos. 93–96), and more importantly, it also appears in funerary contexts in Choresmia, to the northwest of Sogdiana. Ossuaries of the seventh and eighth centuries, discovered in the necropolis at Tok-kala (northwest Uzbekistan), are decorated with astral emblems; one ossuary, an alabaster chest painted with a scene of mourning, shows the entry to a sepulcher capped with a crescent holding a globe.[21] A crescent with a globe or the sun, its base tied with ribbons in the manner of the Sasanian crown, surmounts a chest of the same form as the Tok-kala ossuary in the center of a silver dish found near Bartym in the Perm region of Russia (fig. A). Although Bartym is well north of Choresmian territory, the dish is of Choresmian manu-facture and can be dated by its inscription to the seventh century.[22] The image in the medallion refers to a Choresmian and Sogdian rite, in which homage was made to the remains of important ancestors, which were kept in an urn and displayed for the ceremony.[23] This confirms the funerary connection of the crescent and globe on Shi Daode's mask and ties the image (if not the actual use of funerary masks) to a Sogdian origin.

JAL

Fig. A. Silver dish found near Bartym, Perm region, Russia, Choresmian, seventh century. A chest or ossuary is represented in the central medallion. It is pro-tected by a canopy and supported by a pedestal formed by a pair of lions (photo courtesy of the State Historical Museum, Moscow)

91. *Belt buckle and belt plaques*

Tang dynasty (618–906), seventh century
From the tomb of the Shi Daode (d. 678) in the southern suburbs of Guyuan, Ningxia
Gold
Buckle: length: 4.6 cm; greatest width: 3.2 cm; thickness: 0.5 cm
Plaques: length: 2.2 cm; width: 1.9 cm; thickness: 0.5 cm
Guyuan Municipal Museum, Ningxia Hui Autonomous Region

These objects are examples of several belt buckles and decorative plaques found in the tombs of Shi family members.[1,2] They and the others were attached by means of small holes to a leather or fabric backing to form a belt set, one of the expressions of status and rank held by the Chinese aristocracy and officials. A set consisted of a buckle with movable tongue; a pointed or rounded tail piece, which covered the other end of the belt and was pulled through the buckle to tighten the belt; and various plaques, either sewn or riveted onto the leather backing, along with various pendant forms.[3] The belt plaques were slit in their lower section for suspended straps with smaller buckles, from which decorative pendants or implements could be hung.

These complex belts were worn by mounted horsemen for both utility and display. Additional straps with buckles could be used to suspend weapons and other necessities, such as purses and similar noncombat items (see no. 41). Such pendants are a feature specifically associated with Turkic-Mongolian belts (fig. A).[4] Their use spread from the Turkic tribes on China's northern borders to China as well as to the West, where, by the end of the sixth century, belts with this kind of ornamentation were worn in Central Asian, Sasanian, and Byzantine territories.[5]

Belt sets come in a variety of materials—jade, gold, silver, brass, copper, and iron. Under the Tang, imperial decrees regulated the type of metal and even the number of belt plaques. A seventh-century edict "conferred girdles of gold and jade on civil and military officials above the third grades, gold girdles on those of the fourth and fifth grades, silver girdles on those of the sixth and seventh grades, brass girdles on those of the eighth and ninth grades, and assigned copper and iron girdles to the people at large."[6]

Shi Daode's belt buckle and plaques were manufactured from thin gold sheets, somewhat crudely cut and shaped over a rectangular form. The loop of the buckle was cut from the same sheet of gold as the rectangular portion that attaches to the belt; the movable tongue is a strip of gold wrapped around a hole punched in the buckle. Holes were then punched into the cut sheets for attachment to the backing. The use of such thin sheet gold for the buckle would have made it too fragile for the belt to be worn in life; and this suggests the belt was only for funerary use.[7]

As the commander of a horse farm in Yuanzhou, Shi Daode had obtained the rank of the fifth grade, albeit at a low level, and so was entitled to wear a gold girdle. It is curious, then, that he was not buried with it. It is possible, of course, that the girdle he actually wore was taken by tomb robbers, but, if so, then the mystery remains that a second, funerary, girdle accompanied him to his grave.

JAL

1. For Shi Daode's belt buckle and plaques, Luo 1996, p. 91, fig. 66:3, 4; p. 92; pl. 71; *Yuanzhou* 1999, no. 136.

2. Luo 1996, Tomb of Shi Shewu, p. 15:4 (buckle, with remains of leather on the back), 5 (square plaques), 6 (semicircular plaques), 7 (rings); colorpl. 12 (buckle), all of gold; Tomb of Shi Hedan, p. 60, fig. 43: 9 (gilded buckle), 10 (gold tail piece); Tomb of Shi Tiebang, p. 81, fig. 59:9 (gilded bronze semicircular plaque), 12 (gold tail piece).

3. For the possible arrangement of belt plaques based on evidence from excavated tombs, see Sun 1994, p. 62.

4. For a range of belt decorations and stone grave monuments showing Turkic warriors wearing them, see Pletneva 1981, pp. 128–129, fig. 23.

5. Sun 1993, pp. 54, fig. 10. One of the most notable examples of belts with pendants are those worn by the Sasanian king and his attendants at the boar hunt relief at Taq-i Bustan, in northwestern Iran (Fukai and Horiuchi 1969, vol. 1, pls. XXXV–XXXIX, XLVI–L, LVII, LX, LXII, LXIV, LXVI–LXVII).

6. Laufer 1912, pp. 286–87.

7. The buckles of Shi Shewu's and Shi Hedan's belts were cast and so are more substantial and thus functional.

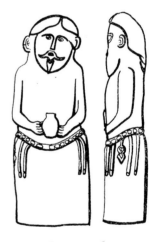

Fig. A. Drawing of a stone grave monument of a Turkic warrior (*above*), wearing a belt with pendants, and detail showing how the pendants hung from the belt plaques. Tuva, Russia, probably eighth century (after Pletneva 1981, p. 128, figs. 23:19, 20)

92a,b. *Ornamental bracteates*

Tang dynasty (618–906), seventh century
From the tomb of the Shi Daode (d. 678), southern suburbs of Guyuan, Ningxia
a. Lion bracteate: gold foil
Diameter: 2.82 cm
b. *Taotie* bracteate: gold foil
Height: 2.57 cm; width: 3.07 cm
Guyuan Municipal Museum, Ningxia Hui Autonomous Region

The small holes punched in these ornaments indicate that they were meant to be sewn onto clothing.[1] The designs of these appliqués were created by hammering the thin sheets of gold over a mold. The details on the lion appliqué were then punched and chased.

The lion bracteate is in the form of a lotus medallion formed by an outer circle of petals and an inner one of beading. Within, the beast sits alertly with forepaw raised, his tail curling between its haunch and up behind him. Cloudlike forms serve as filler motifs. The lion's body is incised with dots, while short lines indicate his mane. The background is covered with ring-punching, a technique that enters the Tang goldsmith's repertory from Sogdian metalwork (see nos. 111 and 118). The

no. 92a

beaded or pearled lotus medallion with a single figural motif becomes prominent on Tang textiles, though not until the eighth or ninth century.[2]

The lion is not an indigenous Chinese animal, but with the introduction of Buddhism, it begins to be a popular motif in the fifth century, continuing through the Sui and into the Tang. The kingly lion was associated with the strength of the Buddha's teachings and thus lions abound on Buddhist sculpture (nos. 47, 52, 68). They also are incorporated into Sui and Tang mirror designs, particularly the so-called "lion and grape" (nos. 116 and 117). Although lionlike creatures guard Han burial grounds ("spirit road"), more recognizably leonine guardians protect Tang imperial tombs. The distinctive placement of the lion's tail occurs earlier on the Northern Zhou stele of Wang Lingwei (no. 67), commissioned in 573 and then is found on one of the stone guardians lining a mid-seventh-century Tang general's spirit road (fig. A); it recurs at eighth- and ninth-century burial sites in Dulan (Qinghai) and Tibet.[3]

The bracteate in the shape of a *taotie* (animal mask) harks back to the ancient ritual vessels of the Shang dynasty (c. 1200 BCE) on which the masks were the dominant form of a very complex decorative scheme. Long after the Shang, the mask remains a widespread motif often used as a protective device (no. 17). In this rendition, the *taotie* has taken on a more leonine character than is typical. Stylistically, the distinct arrises that demarcate the different compartments that form the lion head recall nomadic work from northwest China, though of a much earlier period. A cast-bronze harness ornament dated to the sixth century BCE in the shape of a bovine mask is distinguished by deeply grooved curved bands that follow the contours of the face and horns.[4] If survival of such stylization is to account for this rendition of the *taotie*, the northwest

no. 92b

1. Luo 1996: p. 91, fig. 66:1; pl. 69; col-orpl. 22 (lion bracteate), p. 91, fig. 66:2, pl. 70; colorpl. 21 (*taotie* bracteate); *Yuanzhou* 1999, pls. 134 (lion), 135 (*taotie*).

2. In the Dunhuang Cave 158, dated to the ninth century, the reposing Buddha rests on a stone pillow painted with this textile pattern (Whitfield 1995, p. 123, fig. 7).

3. Heller 1998, pp. 101, fig. 46; p. 99, fig. 45.

4. So and Bunker 1995, p. 118, no. 33.

Fig. A. Stone lion from the spirit road of General Li Ji at Zhao Ling, eighty miles west of Xi'an, Tang, mid to late seventh century (after Juliano 1981, p. 151, bottom left)

border of China, with its mix of nomadic cultures, is a likely source. The Tang's interest in the exotic might also explain the revival or continuation of such a motif.

It is interesting to note that this bracteate has an alternative orientation. When turned upside down the mask becomes a typical Tang floral configuration, a lobed floral head that rises between a pair of volutes. The overall floral shape is reminiscent of the upright lotus-like buds that decorate the Buddha's canopy on the Wang Lingwei stele.

Of all the Shi tombs so far discovered, the three objects from Shi Daode's burial—the two bracteates and the mask (no. 90)—are the most mysterious. This may be due to Shi Daode's deliberate choice of grave goods, or to the fortuitousness of archaeology and the depredations of tomb robbers.

ALJ and JAL

9

Coins and the Silk Road

MICHAEL ALRAM

The Importance of Coins

Our knowledge of international trade and cultural relations during the fourth to seventh century CE is based in great part on the coins that have been excavated and found in settlements and oases along the Silk Road. Coins reached Central Asia and China through both mercantile activity and the Buddhist missionaries and pilgrims who traveled back and forth between China and India. As the primary medium of trade, such coins are often found thousands of miles from their place of manufacture, well beyond the issuing country's borders. This allows us to reconstruct trade routes and gain insight into the active commercial and cultural exchanges that occurred as both coins and goods changed hands.

As primary sources of a particular time, coins are often the only evidence of long-forgotten rulers, as they bear portraits and names; through the internal correlation of these coins we can develop a chronological framework to serve as a crucial support for history, art history, and archaeology. Not only do coins allow us to develop a chronology for the rulers who issued them, they also reveal their cultural and ethnic identities. The legends and designs of coins provide important information about language and religion; their images and symbols bear witness to artistic influences and developments of the period. Coins also attest to the economic conditions of the times in which they were minted, as revealed by their particular standards of weight, the actual metals employed, and the denominations in which they are issued.

Since the invention of coinage in the Greek world in the late seventh century BCE, coins have not only been used as payment; they have also been saved and hoarded. Typically, such coins are made of precious metals and consist of denominations of high value. These hoards (which may have been gathered during the whole lifetime of a single individual or only during a very short period of time) are a valuable source of information about the economic and political developments of a particular time period. Some of these hoards were buried in times of emergency; others were stashes, forgotten because the owners died before they could tell (or because they did not want to tell) their heirs where their money was hidden. Other coin finds are simply the present-day outcome of long-ago accidental losses in which coins were dropped by their owners but can now be analyzed to provide a glimpse into the daily life and commercial activities in market places and settlements.

Finally, coins, particularly those of gold and silver, have non-monetary uses. As religious offerings, they served as foundation deposits for temples, palaces, and, other buildings—a practice still in use at the end of the nineteenth century.[1] In Gandhara the coins

OPPOSITE: Painting of a military officer without armor but in court dress—a long robe and a small cap (*pinshance*). From the tomb of Shi Shewu (d. 609), Sui dynasty (photo: Guyuan Muncipal Museum, Ningxia)

that were used as relic deposits in Buddhist stupas were considered sacred objects, no matter how worn they were. The stupa of Ahinposh, in Afghanistan, contained fifteen Kushan and three Roman gold coins dating to the first half of the second century CE, along with an amulet case that held a relic and two more Kushan gold coins.[2] This practice traveled with the Buddhist monks and pilgrims who went to China, and coins have been discovered in the foundation deposits under the pagodas at Dingxian, Tianziyu, Yaoxian,[3] and Changanxian near Xi'an.[4]

Coins have also been used as jewelry, serving as parts of necklaces, bracelets, and rings. They have been given a single perforation or several to enable them to be sewn onto garments and headdresses, and to be hung as pendants (nos. 97–99, 101–102, 104). Some may have been used as talismans, for good luck or for religious purposes. Certainly, they were considered to be objects of prestige by their owners and accompanied the deceased in their graves. Common to many ancient cultures is "Charon's obol," so called after the ancient Greek practice of placing a coin in the mouth or on the eyes of the deceased as passage-money for Charon, the ferryman who transported the newly dead across the river Styx. This practice was not confined to Greece; it was followed in Central Asia and in China, as attested by the burials of the Northern Zhou general Tian Hong (nos. 97–100) and one of the Sogdian Shi family members, Shi Daode (no. 104).[5]

The Roman-Byzantine and Sasanian Monetary Systems

The merchants, monks, and pilgrims who traveled to China during the fourth to seventh century CE were confronted with many different currency systems in the numerous kingdoms, principalities, city states, and oases along the routes of the Silk Road. Most of these locally produced coins were of "barbaric style," made of debased silver or copper and circulated mainly within the boundaries of the authority that issued them. The value of this token money was not based on the intrinsic value of the metal content, but was fixed by each political unit by law.[6] These local coins were not very attractive for international trade, and the merchants were forced to use other means of payment for bigger transactions. According to written sources, the use of silver bullion, which was exchanged by weight, played a significant role. Uncoined silver was accepted everywhere, being measurable and easy to handle. Other forms of payment were valuable goods like spices, fragrances, and measured lengths of silk.

However, foreign gold and silver coins played an important role in the trade along the Silk Road. During the fourth to seventh century, two major currency systems based on precious metals existed in the world. In the western hemisphere, the coinage system of the Late Roman-Byzantine Empire predominated, while in Western Asia and Iran that of the Sasanian Empire served as the medium of exchange far beyond the borders of the Sasanian state. Both were distinguished by their extraordinary stability and continuity over centuries.

The monetary system of the Late Roman-Early Byzantine Empire underwent a fundamental change at the beginning of the fourth century with, among other reforms, the introduction of the gold *solidus* by Constantine the Great (r. 306–337) in 309. This new denomination, set at 4.5 grams, was an economic success and remained nearly unchanged in weight and fineness for centuries (nos. 97–101). It was used for official payments by the emperor to his soldiers and the civil service, as well as for tax payments to the state. It

Byzantine coin: Obverse and reverse of unclipped gold *solidus* of Justin I (518–527), mint of Constantinople, struck between 518 and 522 (cf. no. 98). Weight: 4.42 g; diameter: 2.0 cm. Kunsthistorisches Museum, Vienna (photo: M. Alram)

became the ideal medium for savings and trade and circulated all over the ancient world. For smaller payments and daily use on local markets, various denominations of copper coins were struck that stand in a fixed relation or rate to the *solidus*. Silver coins were also issued but actually played no role in the normal monetary circulation. The Roman-Byzantine *solidus* continued the Roman imperial coinage practice of showing the emperor on the obverse. But Christian motifs and symbols on the reverse grew increasingly frequent with the triumph of Christianity under Constantine and became standard with the adoption of Christianity as the state religion of the Roman Empire under Theodosius I (r. 379–395).[7]

Sasanian coin: Obverse and reverse of original silver *drachm* of Peroz (r. 459–484) with mint abbreviation AW (cf. no. 95). Weight: 3.99, diameter: 2.8 cm. Kunsthistorisches Museum, Vienna (photo: M. Alram)

As the other leading power of the ancient world, Sasanian Iran was often in opposition to Rome, and then with Constantinople. Despite their numerous conflicts, Sasanian Iran continued to engage with the West in trade and cultural exchange. The main denomination of the Sasanian monetary system was the silver *drachm*, which was based on the Greek Attic weight standard of about 4 grams and was used for all kinds of payments. Like the Roman *solidus*, the Sasanian *drachm* was never struck of debased metal and never suffered a weight reduction. It was a stable coin through centuries and, therefore, like the Roman *solidus*, an ideal medium for transnational trade. This was especially the case in the different principalities of Central Asia to the north and east of Sasanian Iran, where no good silver coins were minted.

For small exchange and daily use on the markets, the Sasanian mints issued copper coins in various denominations, but not in the same quantities as the Roman state. Unlike Rome, the Sasanian state struck gold coins only for ceremonial purposes; these *dinars* played no role in the monetary circulation and trade. It is interesting to note that the weight of the Sasanian gold *dinar* was based on the Roman model: a heavier one with about 7 grams followed the Roman *aureus*, and a lighter one of about 4.25 grams was influenced by the *solidus*. Like the Roman coins, the obverse of the Sasanian issues always shows the imperial portrait (in this case, the King of Kings, whereas the reverse shows a religious image, specifically, the Zoroastrian fire altar flanked by two attendants).[8]

The Chinese Monetary System

In contrast to the Late Roman–Early Byzantine and Sasanian Empires, the monetary system in China was based exclusively on bronze (and later brass) coins, which first appear in the fourth century BCE. Also in contrast with Western practice, Chinese coins were cast and not struck, and they were nearly always of a single denomination.[9] Several different forms of coinage were in use until the Qin emperor Shu Huangdi (r. 221–210 BCE) decreed a unified currency in the form of the *banliang* ("half-ounce," or 12 *chu*), a round coin with a square central hole and weighing from about 10 grams to about 6 grams. In 118 BCE, a new coin type, the *wuzhu* (5 *chu*, weighing about 3.5 grams on average), was introduced by the Han emperor Wudi (r. 141–87 BCE). For the Chinese state and the demands of its economy the *wuzhu* coins (followed by the *kai yuan tong bao* coins of the Tang dynasty and its many successors) became a perfect medium, and they were maintained in size, shape, and weight for nearly seven hundred years until the late nineteenth century. For use in large transactions, however, the very low value of these bronze or brass coins (known in English as *cash*) was not very suitable; normally they were strung together in strings of a thousand, each string weighing more than three kilograms.[10] Not surprisingly, the use of coin spread slowly and irregularly. Salaries and taxes were sometimes paid in cash, grain, or a mixture of both. With the political confusion that gripped northern China during the four centuries between the end of the Han dynasty and the beginning of the Tang, monetary transactions typically consisted of grain and cloth currencies, although the use of coin was never abandoned.

In light of these developments, it is understandable that the consistent Sasanian silver *drachm* was used for large transactions in the bazaars and trading stations along the Silk Road.[11] It is also understandable that the Chinese used gold and silver ingots in large transactions from the earliest historical period. In Qin and Han tombs, copies of such ingots in bronze, lead, and even clay have been found as grave goods (no. 1).[12] To sum up, the Chinese monetary system and economic structures were very conservative, showing no fundamental changes over centuries. Although the Chinese were familiar with the concept of coining precious metals, they never adopted it for their own purposes.[13]

Western Coins in China

The first official contacts between China and the western countries are dated to the second century BCE, when the emperor Wudi sent his ambassador Zhang Qian to Bactria as early as 139 BCE. In 121 the first Chinese embassy visited the Parthian court (Anxi), and much new information about the unknown western countries reached China. In the Chinese historical accounts, the *Shiji* and the *Hanshu*, great attention is drawn to the fact that the Parthians used inscribed silver coins, which show on the obverse the image of the ruling king.[14] Although no Parthian silver coins have so far been recorded from China, we can surmise from these sources that foreign coins of precious metals had a special attraction for the Chinese. This is further attested by the Han lead ingots with imitation Greek legends (no. 1).

The first foreign coins of precious metals that reached Xinjiang in considerable quantities are the Sasanian silver *drachm*s of Shapur II (r. 309–379 CE) and his immediate successors, Ardashir II (r. 379–383) and Shapur III (r. 383–388). Shapur II strengthened the Sasanian power in the east with his successful wars against the Kushans, as well as against the first wave of Hephthalite Huns. Coin production under Shapur II was concentrated in the eastern part of the empire; the main mint for his military expeditions in the east was probably Kabul where great quantities of silver *drachm*s were produced.[15] In the city of Gaochang (Qocho in the Turfan area), three hoards were discovered that contained only *drachm*s of Shapur II, Ardashir II, and Shapur III from the Kabul mint.[16] Other Sasanian coins were found in several tomb sites in the Turfan area: the majority were found in the mouths of the deceased,[17] as were the Byzantine coins in the burials of Tian Hong (nos. 96–99) and Shi Daode (no. 104). The Sasanian coins from the Gaochang tombs, however, are of considerably later dates. They start with the reign of Peroz (r. 459–484), reach their peak under Khosro II (r. 590–628), and end with two Arab-Sasanian *dirhems* struck after 651.[18] It is has been suggested that these Sasanian coins in Gaochang are the result of the local authorities' taxation of merchants passing through the oasis.[19] It is likely, then, that such taxes were levied on merchants as they passed into Gansu and that such taxes may be the explanation, in part, for the appearance of Sasanian coins in China proper.

In contrast to Xinjiang, the peak of Sasanian silver coins in China dates to the middle of the fifth century, that is, from the time of Peroz.[20] In addition to the pagoda deposit from Dingxian (see above, p. 272), dated to 481 with coins of Yazdgard I (r. 438–457) and

Peroz,[21] there is the hoard found on the way to the temple of Chenghuang at Xining (Qing-hai), which contained 76 *drachms* of Peroz.[22] Found together with Chinese coins cast in 621 and after, the hoard dates to the early years of the Tang. These two examples may show that Peroz coins reached China even during the lifetime of the king and were kept in circulation for a considerable time. As tomb finds, Peroz *drachms* are attested in northwest China, dating from the time of the Northern Wei and Sui (nos. 93, 95). This is confirmed by another Peroz coin that was recently excavated in one of the caves at the north end at Dunhuang, dated to Sui–early Tang (no. 94).

By 439, the complete reunification of northern China, including Gansu, under the Northern Wei created greater political stability and allowed the reorganization of economic structures. This paved the way for the Central Asian merchants to fulfill the increasing demand for foreign goods by the Chinese.[23] Mercantile activities were supported by the Peroz *drachms* that were struck in huge quantities to finance the Sasanians' war against the Hephthalites, a Hunnish people who had settled in eastern Khorasan and Tokharistan in the fifth and sixth centuries and made numerous incursions into the Sasanian state. The climax to these conflicts was the Hephthalites' capture of Peroz in 476 and the payment of a ransom said to be thirty mule loads of silver *drachms*. This may account for the predominance of Peroz coins in northern China and along the southern route of the Silk Road in Xinjiang.[24] Indeed, it seems that most of the Peroz *drachms* acquired by the Hephthalites as booty, ransom, and subsidies served to propel trade between Xinjiang and China.[25]

Once they had left their own currency area, Sasanian silver *drachms* lost their monetary character (i.e., as a piece of money) and were taken as little ingots to be measured by weight.[26] Exceptions were made if a local government officially legalized the circulation of foreign silver coins, as was the case in the Turfan area during the sixth and seventh centuries.[27]

Unlike Sasanian silver *drachms*, Byzantine gold *solidi* have never been found as hoards in China.[28] They occur in Xinjiang and northwest China only sparsely,[29] although they must have been considered precious and "exotic," as they are found primarily in graves. Most of them remained in circulation for a rather long time and were clipped and pierced and used as jewelry and talismans, but their former character as a piece of money was not forgotten by their owners. Finally, imitations were produced, and some of them were struck as bracteates on a very thin flan (unstamped metal disk) or with only one die. Imitations of Byzantine *solidi* and bracteates have been found in Central Asia, and it seems likely that those found in the Shi family tombs (nos. 96, 102–103) came from these western countries.[30] During the sixth and seventh centuries in Central Asia and Xinjiang, Byzantine *solidi* may have initially also functioned as money, as did Sasanian silver *drachms*.[31] But the *solidi* soon became highly appreciated objects of prestige and were taken out of circulation to serve mainly as jewelry and luxury gifts. It is difficult to know precisely how Byzantine gold coins reached Central Asia and China, but certainly the Silk Road trade helped to satisfy the demands of the Byzantine upper class for luxury goods from the East.[32] Also, *solidi* moved eastward with the Byzantine embassies sent to Central Asia, as well as in the subsidies paid to the Sasanian state.[33]

The greatest number of Byzantine gold coins found in China occurs in the second half of the sixth century, with the *solidi* of the Byzantine emperors from the Chinese tombs of this same time span.[34] The oldest coin in this context dates from the reign of Theodosius II (r. 408–450) and was in circulation for more than a hundred years before it was buried.[35]

The most recent coin is that of Justinian I (r. 527–565), buried during the lifetime of the emperor.[36] This may indicate that most of the Byzantine *solidi* reached China during or shortly after the reign of Justinian I. This date corresponds approximately with the beginning of the second great influx of Sasanian *drachms* to China after the death of Peroz (484) and culminates during the reign of Khosro II (r. 590–628), as well as with the earliest Turfan documents that mention silver coins.[37]

The above evidence for the influx of Western coinage into northwest China corresponds with the coins in the exhibition from Guyuan. The earliest Western coins are the silver *drachms* of the Sasanian king, Peroz. Thus, the tomb with the Northern Wei lacquer sarcophagus, which dates to the fifth century, contains one *drachm* of Peroz (no. 93); Byzantine coins are absent. The Sasanian *drachms* are immediately followed by Byzantine *solidi*, which culminate in the third quarter of the sixth century. Of the five Byzantine *solidi* buried in the tomb of Tian Hong (d. 575), the oldest was that of Leo I (r. 457–474) (no. 97), followed by one of Justin I (r. 518–527) (no. 98), two of Justin and Justinian I (r. 527) (nos. 99a, b) and one of Justinian I (r. 527–565) (no. 100), struck in Constantinople between 537 and 542.

After the middle of the seventh century, only imitations of coins (nos. 95, 104) and bracteates (nos. 96, 102, 103) occur in the tombs; only number 101, that of Justin II from the tomb of Shi Daoluo (d. 658), is a genuine coin. All the coins are pierced, indicating that they had lost their monetary function and were used as jewelry, as were all but one bracteate (no. 103). Clearly, these coins and bracteates were considered by their owners, members of the Shi family, as prestigious objects, much as the gold ring (no. 85), Sasanian intaglio (no. 86), and pendant (no. 87) that accompanied them in their graves.

NOTES

1. For example, gold coins of Emperor Franz Joseph I (r. 1848–1916) of Austria were deposited in the foundation of the Opera House, Vienna, in 1862.

2. Errington and Fabrègues 1992, pp. 176–77.

3. Thierry 1993, p. 103–4.

4. Fontein 1995, p. 24.

5. For the derivation of this custom, see Thierry 1993, pp. 100–2; Skaff 1998, p. 69 n. 10. One of the five Byzantine *solidi* found in Tian Hong's tomb is reported to have been in his mouth (see entries for nos. 99, 100 in this catalogue).

6. For the local coinage in Central Asia, see Zeimal 1994, and Baratova 1999.

7. For an introduction to the Late Roman–Byzantine monetary system, see Hendy 1985.

8. For an introduction to Sasanian coinage, see Göbl 1971.

9. For a concise history of Chinese coinage, see Thierry 1998.

10. According to a Khotanese document found near Khotan dated in the year 781 the price of a camel was fixed with sixteen thousand copper coins; that means that at least 50 kilograms (100 pounds) of copper would have had to change hands (Kumamoto 1999).

11. Thus the use of foreign silver coins for large transactions is attested by an undated Sogdian sales contract, found in a tomb at Turfan, Xinjiang, that cites "120 *drachms* of very pure struck [coins]" as the price for a female slave (Frye 1993, p. 73). One of the last documents from Turfan, which mentions silver coins and dates to 692, gives a rate of thirty-two Chinese bronze coins for one *dirhem* (Skaff 1998, pp. 101, 109, D45).

12. Cribb 1978, pp. 76–78; Cribb 1979, p. 191.

13. As imperial or private gifts, contemporary bronze cash coins were also imitated in gold and silver, but these coins had no monetary function and were only used as talismans or ornaments and accompanied the dead in their graves (Cribb 1979, p. 191).

14. For the Chinese written sources about the Parthians, compare Posch 1998.

15. Göbl 1984, pp. 49–55.

16. It is reported that one of these hoards had about a hundred coins. cf. Skaff 1998, p. (72), As Skaff pointed out, (p. 81), the Turfan hoards contain nearly the same coins as the famous hoard from Tepe Maranjan, buried near Kabul at the end of the fourth century CE, cf. Göbl 1984, pp. 55–56, pls. 145–55; Göbl 1993, pp. 27–29; Alram 1996, pp. 521–22.

17. Skaff 1998, p. 69f.

18. Skaff 1998, p. 74. However, Skaff points out that, according to the dated documents found in the tombs that mention "silver coins," the second phase of silver coin circulation in Turfan started not under Peroz, but in the 580s (pp. 77–79). Variations in coin distribution between Turfan (Xinjiang) and China during the fourth and fifth centuries may be explained by political events and shifts in trade routes (pp. 80–81; Thierry 1993, pp. 107–11).

19. Skaff 1998, p. 98. With the Tang occupation of Gaochang in 640, Chinese bronze coins (such as no. 105) and monetary silk began to replace Sasanian silver *drachms* as the medium of taxation.

20. Thierry 1993, pp. 99–100.

21. Ibid., p. 93, no. 32: the hoard contained four coins of Yazdgard II and thirty-seven of Peroz.

22. Ibid., p. 91, no. 12, p. 99. Xining is approximately 190

kilometers west of Lanzhou (Gansu). Thierry notes his surprise that so vital a passage as the Gansu corridor should not yield any hoards.

23. Ibid., pp. 109–11; Skaff 1998, p. 81.

24. That is, at Tashkurgan, Yarkand, and Khotan (Skaff 1998, pp. 82–84). The Hephthalites took control of Khotan in 498 (Thierry 1993, pp. 113–14).

25. It should also be noted that during this time the maritime trade from Persia via the Indian Ocean and Ceylon (Sri Lanka) to south China was also active. This is corroborated by a coin hoard that came to light in Suikai (Guangdong) in south China. The majority of the coins, which were stored together with gold and silver objects in a clay pot, are again from the reign of Peroz. Moreover, three Peroz *drachms* were found in a tomb in Yingdak (Guangdong) and were buried in 497—only thirteen years after Peroz's death (for Sasanian coins found in south China, see Thierry 1993, p. 93, no. 27; p. 95, nos. 47, 52, pp. 123–25).

26. Skaff (1998, pp. 103–4) advances the hypothesis that from the fourth through the seventh century CE, Sasanian *drachms* replaced silver ingots in the Chinese monetary economy. Ingots reappeared in China during the eighth century (cf. Cribb 1979, pp. 203–4, app. 5), and a new ingot standard was developed that forced the merchants to carry silver in the form of bullion instead of coins to China. Cribb (p. 192) argues that "most of the Iranian coins entering China were presumably melted down and cast into ingots"; however, no such ingots that can be dated to our time period (fourth to seventh century) have been recorded so far. This conversion to ingots may have begun at the beginning of the eighth century, and so may explain the nearly complete lack of Islamic *dirhems* in Xinjiang and China; see also Skaff 1998, pp. 99–100.

27. Ibid., pp. 104–5.

28. For Byzantine coins found in China, see Morrisson and Thierry 1994.

29. Ibid. Morrisson and Thierry record only twenty-seven pieces. They do not, however, include the coins from the tombs of Tian Hong and Shi Daoluo; moreover, according to Morrisson and Thierry, no. 15 (tomb of Shi Tiebang) is not a *solidus* but a bracteate following the type of the Sasanian king Ardashir III. (no. 96).

30. For Byzantine *solidi*, imitations and bracteates found in Panjikent, see Raspopova 1999. Raspopova (p. 454) argues

that some of the imitations were produced especially for burials. She also reports that most of the bracteates at Panjikent were not found in the necropolis, but in private houses and temples (p. 457).

31. Ibid. Raspopova refers to a Sogdian inscription on a sixth-century silver, bowl from Munchak-tepe (near Bukhara) in which *dinars* (i.e., gold coins) together with *drachms* are mentioned (p. 456). When the Buddhist monk Xuanzang visited Karashahr and Kucha in 630, he also reported the use of gold, silver and copper coins (Morrisson and Thierry 1994, p. 121).

32. The official price for one pound of silk (c. 327 grams) was fixed by Justinian I at fifteen *solidi*.

33. For example, in 533 Justinian I paid 11,000 pounds of gold (about 800,000 *solidi*) to Khosro I for a peace treaty. In 552 Justinian sent an expedition to Central Asia in order to import silkworms to Constantinople. In 569, following the successful trade negotiations between Constantinople and the Sogdian-Turkic mission, Justin II sent his ambassador, Zemarkhos, back with the mission to the Turks' territory (Miyakawa and Kollautz 1984).

34. Thus, the *solidi* of Justin I (r. 518–527) and Justinian I (r. 527), Justinian I (r. 527–565), and Justin II (r. 565–578) that were found in tombs in Zanhuangxian (Hebei), Cixian (Hebei), and Xianyang (Shaanxi); see Morrisson and Thierry 1994, nos. 19, 24, 25, 27; no. 99b in this catalogue.

35. Morrisson and Thierry 1994, no. 23. The *solidus* of Theodosius II (r. 408–450) was found together with two *solidi* of Justin I and Justinian I (r. 527) in the Zanhuangxian tomb, which dates to 576.

36. Morrisson and Thierry 1994, p. 113, no. 27 (Cixian, Hebei), buried in 550. The latest *solidus* is reported from Khotan and was struck by Constantine V (r. 741–775), see ibid., no. 1. In China proper the latest genuine *solidus* dates from the time of Phocas (r. 602–610), found in Tianshui (Gansu); see ibid., no. 18. A *solidus* imitation from Heraclius and Heraclius Constantine (d. 641) was part of the famous hoard from Hejiacun (Xi'an), buried c. 756 (ibid., no. 21); a bracteate of this type was found in Panjikent (Raspopova 1999, fig. 7).

37. Nine Byzantine gold coins and imitations have been found in the Turfan area (Skaff 1998, p. 67 n. 9; and Morrisson and Thierry 1994, p. 111).

1. *Yuanzhou* 1999, pl. 27; Thierry 1993, no. 51.

2. See Göbl 1971, pp. 6–13, for a discussion of the crowns and how to "read" them.

3. At first, Peroz was only able to raise twenty mule loads and was forced to give his son Kavad as hostage to the Huns until the rest of the debt was discharged.

93. *Silver* drachm *of Peroz*

Sasanian, fifth century, Peroz (r. 459–484)
From the lacquer sarcophagus tomb (no. 16), Northern Wei dynasty (c. 470–480),
of Guyuan, Ningxia
Weight: 3.50 g; diameter: 2.74 cm; broken into six pieces,
with one small fragment missing
Guyuan Municipal Museum, Ningxia Hui Autonomous Region

Obverse. Bust of Peroz right, wears a mural crown with a crescent in front, above two spreading wings,
surmounted by a crescent containing a globe; a diadem tie floats over either shoulder; blundered
middle Persian inscription (not fully readable): "the Mazda worshiping 'divinity,' king Peroz."

Reverse. Zoroastrian fire altar flanked by two attendants with raised hands, in the left field a star,
in the right field a crescent; the name of the king in the left field is not readable,
in the right field mint abbreviation ShY (probably Shiraz, in southwestern Iran).
Cf. The coin type corresponds to Göbl 1971, type III/1 or III/3.

The crown of the Sasanian king is the main means of identifying the individual rulers of the dynasty.[1] Each Sasanian king had his own particular crown, designed especially for him. Because the crown symbolized the *khwarrah*, or divine aura, of a ruler, if a reign was interrupted by captivity or usurpation, the king was considered to have lost his *khwarrah*. If and when he returned to the throne he had to assume a new crown.

Peroz was the first to have three different crowns in succession.[2] His first, distinguished by one merlon and a crescent between the crown cap and the globe, dates to the first two years of his rule (459–461), during which he fought his brother Ohrmazd for the throne. Once he had secured his rule, he added a second merlon. His third crown shows the addition of the wings of Verethragna, the Iranian god of victory, and refers to his release from the Hephthalites, a Hunnish people who had settled in eastern Khorasan and Tokharistan during the fifth and sixth centuries and, as the leading power in Central Asia, made numerous incursions into the Sasanian state.

This coin type shows Peroz with this third crown. It was probably struck after 476–477, when Peroz freed himself from Hephthalite captivity after suffering a devastating defeat. His ransom was said to be thirty mule loads of silver *drachms*. Since the maximum load that can be carried by a mule is approximately 150 kg, it means that Peroz paid a maximum of 4,500 kg of silver or 1,250,000 silver *drachms*.[3] Even after the ransom was paid, large sums of *drachms* continued to flow to the Hephthalites as tribute. Once freed, Peroz made peace with the Hephthalites but soon began a new campaign. In 484, he was defeated a second time and lost his life in battle.

Twenty-four different mint locations in Iran are recorded for Peroz's reign. To control production, each mint had to put its signature (the abbreviation of its name) in the right field of the reverse. In the left field is either the name of Peroz, the date of issue according to his regnal year, or a monogram, probably consisting of the Middle Persian letters *M P*, meaning, "king Peroz."

From hoard evidence and statistical analyses, we learn that this third coin type of Peroz was struck in huge quantities and in different mints of the Sasanian Empire. It probably served to finance the second war against the Hephthalites and was also used to pay subsidies and tribute (see also nos. 94–95).

Peroz *drachms* represent the first big influx of Sasanian silver coins into China (see p. 274–76). They reached Xinjiang and China proper as early as Peroz's lifetime (like this coin) and remained in circulation until the early Tang period.

MA

1. *Wenwu* 1998.10, p. 13, fig. 15; p. 23, fig. 1.

94. *Silver* drachm *of Peroz*

Sasanian, fifth century, Peroz (r. 459–484)

Found in 1998 in North End Caves, Dunhuang

Weight: 3.88 g; diameter: 3.1 cm

Dunhuang Research Institute, Gansu

Obverse. Bust of Peroz facing right, wears a mural crown with a crescent in front, above two spreading wings, surmounted by a crescent containing a globe; a diadem tie floats over either shoulder; blundered middle Persian inscription: "the Mazda worshipping 'divinity,' king Peroz."

Reverse. Zoroastrian fire altar flanked by two attendants with raised hands, in the left field a star, in the right field a crescent; Middle Persian inscription "Peroz" to the left, and to the right the mint abbreviation NY (Nihavand in Media, western Iran).

Cf. Göbl 1971, type III/1.

This coin was found in Cave 222 of the North End Caves, Dunhuang, in an early Tang context (early seventh century), and is of a type similar to the Peroz *drachm* found in the Northern Wei tomb with the lacquer sarcophagus (no. 93).[1]

As noted for number 93, Peroz *drachms* represent the first big influx of Sasanian silver coins to China. This coin, showing Peroz's third crown, dates to as early as 476–477 and so remained in circulation for at least 140 years.

MA

1. *Yuanzhou* 1999, pl. 96; Luo 1996, pls. 9, 10, colorpls. 13, 14; Thierry 1993, no. 53.

2. Zeimal 1994, pp. 251–57.

95. *Imitation of a silver* drachm *of Peroz*

Sasanian, fifth century, Peroz (r. 459–484)
From the tomb of Shi Shewu (d. 609), Sui dynasty
vicinity of Guyuan, Ningxia
Weight: 3.30 g; diameter: 2.6 cm; pierced twice
Guyuan Municipal Museum, Ningxia Hui Autonomous Region

Obverse. Bust of Peroz facing right, wears a mural crown with a crescent in front, above two spreading wings, surmounted by a crescent containing a globe; a diadem tie floats over either shoulder;
blundered Middle Persian inscription.

Reverse. Zoroastrian fire altar flanked by two attendants with raised hands, in the left field a crescent,
in the right field a star; blundered Middle Persian inscription and mint abbreviation (probably AW).

Cf. Göbl 1971, type III/1.

This Peroz *drachm* seems to be an imitation.[1] This is indicated by the completely blundered Middle Persian inscriptions and mint abbreviation, as well as by the reversed positions of the star and the crescent on the reverse. As the two holes in this coin show, it had lost its function as money and was used as jewelry or an appliqué, perhaps even before it arrived in China.

As previously noted (no. 93), Peroz spent his entire life fighting the Hephthalites. By the sixth century, the Hephthalites controlled great parts of Central Asia, including Sogdiana. At first, the Hephthalite rulers did not strike their own coins but used the Sasanian *drachms*, which they acquired through booty and tribute. In a second phase of their rule, the Hephthalites countermarked the Sasanian *drachms* to express their own authority and to legalize the circulation of these coins in their territories. In a third development, they imitated Peroz's coin type, and this served as a local cur-rency, especially in northern Tokharistan (southern Tajikistan and Uzbekistan).[2] At the beginning of this imitation phase it is sometimes difficult to determine whether a coin is an original, struck by a Sasanian mint, or an imitation minted beyond the borders of the Sasanian state. During Peroz's final battle, which resulted in his death (484), the Hephthalites seized not only the royal treasure and account books but possibly also the royal mint, which traveled with the king. Thus, captive Sasanian mint workers working for the Hephthalite conquerors may explain the close stylistic cor-respondence of some Peroz imitations with Sasanian originals.

MA

96. *Gold bracteate after a coin of Ardashir III*

Seventh century

From the tomb of Shi Tiebang (d. 666, buried 668), Tang dynasty, southern suburbs of Guyuan,
Ningxia

Diameter: 2.45 cm; thickness: 1 mm; weight: 7.00 g; pierced

Guyuan Municipal Museum, Ningxia Hui Autonomous Region

Obverse: Bust of Ardashir III facing right, wears a mural crown surmounted by a crescent containing a
globe; a diadem tie floats over either shoulder; star in left field; star and crescent in right field; crescent on
his left shoulder; Middle Persian inscription "Ardashir", ("strength.")

Reverse: Blank, except for the impression of image on the obverse

Cf. Göbl 1971, type 1 (obverse).

1. Published in *Yuanzhou* 1999, pl. 29.

2. Thierry 1993, nos. 21–26, 29, 36, 38–42.

3. Ibid., no. 18.

4. Ibid., no. 33.

5. Ibid., no. 30.

6. Ibid., no. 19.

The die for this bracteate was modeled directly from a silver *drachm* of Ardashir III.[1] The image of the king, as well as the Middle Persian legend, is rendered without any mistakes. No gold coins (*dinars*) of Ardashir III are recorded. The Sasanians struck gold coins only sporadically and used them mainly as festival issues. The last *dinars* so far known were minted by Khosro II (r. 590–628), dated to his thirty-seventh regnal year (626), and by his daughter, Boran (r. 630–631).

The diameter of the bracteate is slightly larger than the inner field of an actual *drachm*. It is cut sharply around the circle, so that the symbols (star and crescent) at the three cross points, which in actual coins are always placed outside the circle (at 3, 6, and 9 o'clock), as well as the upper part of the crown (crescent with globe, at 12 o'clock) are missing. Only the short ribbons that bind the globe and crescent at the crown cap are visible. The flan out of which the bracteate was struck is quite thick, so that a negative image of the obverse is only slightly visible on the reverse side. The bracteate is pierced directly above the middle of the crown cap at the ribbons and so was probably used as pendant.

Although Ardashir III reigned for only two years, his *drachms* were struck in considerable quantities. Whereas his first crown type, as it is represented on the bracteate, was used in his first and second regnal year, his second crown type, showing the wings of Verethragna (the Iranian god of victory) as an additional emblem, is recorded only from his second year. This was a time of great political instability and internal struggle in Iran. In 628 Khosro II, who led the Sasanian state to a final blossoming, had lost his throne. In the following four years not fewer than six rulers fought against each other, until the last Sasanian king, Yazdgard III, was enthroned in 632. But the time of the Sasanians was over. The Arabs, pushed forward by the new religion of Islam, rushed into Iran and defeated the Sasanian troops in two battles. In 651 Yazdgard III was murdered, and the surviving members of the Sasanian dynasty fled to the Chinese court to live in exile.

Shi Tiebang died in 666 (his epitaph was written in 670), so that the bracteate must have been manufactured in the forty years between 630 and his death. No coins of Ardashir III have yet been recorded in China. The *drachms* from his immediate predecessor, Khosro II, however, form the last big influx of Sasanian coins into Xinjiang and China proper. In the tombs of Astana, many of Khosro II's *drachms* were found. The majority date from 619 to 628, the last decade of his reign, and were buried between 626 and 706.[2] The largest hoard of Sasanian coins was found in Ulugh Art (Wuqia, Xinjiang), west of Kashgar, and must have been buried in the second half of the seventh century. It contained 567 *drachms* of Khosro II, 281 Arab-Sasanian *dirhems*, and thirteen gold bars.[3] A small hoard is recorded from Xi'an (near the monastery of Guoqing), where six coins of Khosro II were found in a silver box.[4] One coin of Boran, Khosro's daughter and the immediate successor of Ardashir III, was found in a tomb at Astana, dating to 685[5]; another is recorded from the aforementioned hoard from Xi'an. The latest Sasanian coins found in China are those of Yazdgard III, which were buried at Astana in 653,[6] only three years after the last King of Kings was murdered in Merv and Iran became part of the Arab Caliphate.

MA

97. *Gold* solidus *of Leo I*

Late Roman–Byzantine, fifth century, Leo I (r. 457–474),
mint of Constantinople, struck probably 462 or 466

From the tomb of Tian Hong (d. 575); Northern Zhou dynasty
western suburbs of Guyuan, Ningxia

Weight: 2.55 g; diameter: 1.62 cm; clipped, pierced four times,
scratch on the helmet (obverse)

Guyuan Municipal Museum, Ningxia Hui Autonomous Region

Obverse: D(ominus) N(oster) LEO PERPET(uus) AVG(ustus);
helmeted bust of emperor three-quarter facing right, diademed, cuirassed,
spear in right hand held over right shoulder behind head, on left arm decorated shield
with horseman riding down enemy.

Reverse: VICTORIA AVGGG(ustorum) I (*officina* 10); Victory standing left,
supporting long jeweled cross; star in right field; in exergue CONOB.

Cf. Kent 1994, no. 605.

98. *Gold* solidus *of Justin I*

Byzantine, sixth century, Justin I (r. 518–527), mint of Constantinople,
struck between 518 and 522

From the tomb of Tian Hong (d. 575), Northern Zhou dynasty
Western suburbs of Guyuan, Ningxia

Weight: 2.80 g; diameter: 1.72 cm; clipped, pierced three times

Guyuan Municipal Museum, Ningxia Hui Autonomous Region

Obverse: D(ominus) N(oster) IVSTINVS P(er)P(etuus) AVG(ustus);
helmeted bust of emperor, three-quarter facing right, cuirassed,
spear in right hand held over right shoulder behind head, on left arm shield.

Reverse: VICTORIA AVGGG(ustorum) I (*officina* 10); Victory standing left,
supporting long cross topped with the Greek *rho* (*chrismon*) turned to the left
(not visible on this coin); star in left field; in exergue CONOB.

Cf. Hahn 2000, no. 2.

99a. *Gold solidus of Justin I and Justinian I*

Byzantine, sixth century, Justin I and Justinian I (ruled as co-emperors 527),
mint of Constantinople

From the tomb of Tian Hong (d. 575), Northern Zhou dynasty,
western suburbs of Guyuan, Ningxia

Weight: 3.10 g; diameter: 1.79 cm; clipped, pierced three times

Guyuan Municipal Museum, Ningxia Hui Autonomous Region

Obverse: D(omini) N(ostri) IVSTIN(us) ET IVSTINIAN(us) P(erpetui) AVG(usti);
the two emperors sitting on throne with straight back, each holding globe;
cross above back, in exergue CONOB.

Reverse: VICTORI-A AVGGG(ustorum) Σ (*officina* 6); angel standing frontal,
long cross in right hand, globe surmounted by a cross (*globus cruciger*)
in left hand; star in right field, in exergue CONOB.

Cf. Hahn 2000, no. 2c.

99b. *Gold solidus of Justin I and Justinian I*

Byzantine, sixth century, Justin I and Justinian I (ruled as co-emperors 527),
mint of Constantinople

From the tomb of Tian Hong (d. 575), Northern Zhou dynasty,
western suburbs of Guyuan, Ningxia

Weight: 2.50 g; diameter: 1.62 cm; clipped, pierced four times

Guyuan Municipal Museum, Ningxia Hui Autonomous Region

Obverse: D(omini) N(ostri) IVSTIN(us) ET IVSTINIAN(us) P(erpetui) AVG(usti);
the two emperors sitting on throne with lyre back, each holding globe;
cross above back, in exergue CONOB.

Reverse: VICTORI-A AVGGG(ustorum) I (*officina* 10); angel standing frontal,
long cross in right hand, *globus cruciger* in left hand; star in right field, in exergue CONOB.

Cf. Hahn 2000, no. 3b.

100. *Gold* solidus *of Justinian I*

Byzantine, sixth century, Justinian I (r. 527–565), mint of Constantinople,
struck between 537 and 542
From the tomb of Tian Hong (d. 575), Northern Zhou dynasty
western suburbs of Guyuan, Ningxia
Weight: 2.50 g; diameter: 1.65 cm; clipped
Guyuan Municipal Museum, Ningxia Hui Autonomous Region
Obverse. D(ominus) N(oster) IVSTINIANVS P(er)P(etuus) AVG(ustus); helmeted bust of
emperor facing, cuirassed, globe cruciger in right hand, shield in left hand.
Reverse. VICTORIA AVGGG(ustorum) A (*officina* 1); Angel standing frontal, long cross in right
hand, *globus cruciger* in left hand; star in right field, in exergue CONOB.
Cf. Hahn 2000, no. 6.

The five Late Roman–Byzantine *solidi* that were found in the tomb of Tian Hong (d. 575) cover a time span of more than one hundred years.[1] The oldest was struck by Leo I (r. 457–474), whereas the most recent dates to the reign of Justinian I (527–565 r.) and was minted in Constantinople between 537 and 542. One of these *solidi* had been placed in the mouth of the deceased.

All the coins are in good condition and show no heavy traces of wear. However, all have been clipped. Clipping coins to extract some small portion of their precious metal was a common practice all over the ancient world, as people used the clipped bits of gold or silver for their own purposes. Further, four have been pierced, signifying that at some point they had lost their function as money and were used as jewelry. Only the most recent coin, that of Justinian I, is not pierced. It was only in circulation for about 38 years, while the *solidus* of Leo I circulated for a maximum of 113 years. All five coins either had come from a single hoard or had been collected by Tian Hong himself.

A close parallel to the appearance of these coins in Tian Hong's tomb are those found in the Northern Qi tomb of Li Xizong and his wife, at Zanhuangxian (Hebei). His wife was buried in 576, only one year after Tian Hong, and was accompanied by one *solidus* of Theodosius II and two from Justin I and Justinian I.[2] Only the *solidus* of Theodosius II is pierced[3]; the other two coins are clipped but not pierced.

The *solidus* had been introduced into the late Roman monetary system by Constantine the Great (r. 306–337) (p. 272). Because of its purity and stability it became one of the most successful gold coins in monetary history. It provided satisfactorily for the economic needs of the Late Roman and Byzantine state and became a perfect medium for international trade. In shape, weight, and fineness the *solidus* remained nearly unchanged until the tenth century.

In the Byzantine state the minting of precious metals was under the direct control of the *comes sacrarum largitionum*, the Secretary of the Treasury, who resided in the capital of Constantinople. The *solidi* of the early Byzantine coinage bear the formula CONOB, normally placed on the reverse, in the exergue (the lower segment of the coin, marked off by a horizontal line). CON stands for Constantinopolis; OB is an abbreviation for *obryzum*, the technical term in Latin for pure gold, as well as the Greek numeral 72. This indicates that the *solidus* was struck of "pure gold of Constantinople quality," on a weight standard of 72 to the Roman pound, and thus weighing 4.55 grams (the weight of the Roman pound was about 327 grams). The *moneta auri*, the special mint that produced gold coins, was situated in the palace of Constantinople; it was subdivided into ten workshops called *officinae*, each of which put its mark—a Greek numeral—at the end of the legend on the reverse (A–I = 1–10).

Under Justinian I one of the most striking and permanent changes in the design of the *solidus* occurred: instead of the traditional spear, the emperor is depicted with the *globus cruciger* in his right hand. This signifies that the whole world is subject to the emperor; the cross above the globe is the emblem by which he has obtained both his empire and victory in war. Moreover, the bust of the emperor is no longer in three-quarter view but is in full-face. The reverse design, showing a completely frontal angel holding a long cross, had already—under Justin I's rule—replaced the traditional Victory.

The extraordinary popularity of the Late Roman–Byzantine *solidus* throughout the ancient world and into China forced the Byzantine state to proclaim strict laws for the export of precious metals. The *Codex Justinianus* (CJ IV.63.2) clearly states, "If, henceforth, gold is supplied by merchants to the barbarians, either for sale or in exchange for whatever kind of commodities, they shall suffer not just a fine but even heavier punishment."[4] Merchants, however, were always trying to circumvent government controls on the outflow of gold, since its export to countries where gold was not minted proved to be a lucrative business. Furthermore, the Byzantine emperor himself had to pay large amounts of gold and silver as subsidies or tribute to the "barbarians" as a means of keeping the peace. In addition, the huge sums that the Roman or Byzantine upper class spent on luxury goods from the East, such as Chinese silk, were mainly paid in gold coins.

As already noted, most of the Byzantine *solidi* that reached China are clipped. It seems unlikely that this happened in China. It was probably done even before the coins left the Byzantine Empire or perhaps later on their way through Central Asia. In most cases it was an illegal practice to gather gold and silver bullion from the coins in circulation.[5] If a coin was clipped, its weight was diminished; it thus lost its function as money and had to be withdrawn from circulation.

MA

1. *Tian Hong* 2000, color pl. 28 (all five coins); *Yuanzhou* 1999, pl. 82 (Leo I).

2. Morrisson and Thierry 1994 nos. 23–25, pl. xvi; *Kaogu* 1977. 6, pl. 6: 1–3.

3. The two holes are placed above the head of the emperor. This practice is well attested on Roman and Byzantine gold coins found in India, so that it might be possible that this particular coin traveled via India to China (Berghaus 1993, pp. 305–10, figs. 11, 12; Turner 1989.

4. For the legislation about the control of outward flows in the Late Roman–Byzantine Empire, see Hendy 1985, pp. 257–79.

5. Ibid., pp. 316–20.

1. *Shi Daoluo* 2000, pl. 25 top, pp. 202–6.

2. Morrisson and Thierry 1994, p. 112, no. 19.

101. *Gold* solidus *of Justin II*

Byzantine, sixth century, Justin II (r. 565–578), mint of Constantinople
From the tomb of Shi Daoluo (d. 658), Tang dynasty, southern suburbs of Guyuan, Ningxia
Weight: 4.6g.; diameter: 2.1 cm; pierced twice
Guyuan Municipal Museum, Ningxia Hui Autonomous Region
Obverse: D(ominus) N(oster) I·VSTI·NVS P(er)P(etuus) AVG(ustus); helmeted bust of emperor
facing, cuirassed, globe with Victory in right hand, shield in left hand.
Reverse: VICTORI·A AVGGG(ustorum) H (*officina* 8); Constantinopolis enthroned frontal,
head turned right, scepter in right hand, *globus cruciger* in left hand; in exergue CONOB.
Cf. Hahn 1975, no. 1 or 5.

This *solidus* of Justin II remained in circulation for eighty to ninety years and shows considerable traces of wear.[1] By the time it was buried with Shi Daoluo, it had been used as an ornament, as indicated by the two holes, one above the head of the emperor and one beneath the bust.

The only other gold coin of Justin II so far recorded from China was buried in the tomb of Dugu Luo (534–599) at Dizhangwan, Xianyang (Shanxi); it had circulated for only twenty-five years.[2]

Under Justin II, a considerable change took place in the design of the *solidus*. On the obverse, he replaced the cross on the globe with a small Victory crowning him with a wreath. On the reverse, the angel with the long cross was replaced by the enthroned Constantinopolis, the old personification of the imperial capital. This reversion to a pagan type, following the ancient tradition, was remarkable. Justin II's own people had difficulty recognizing the image of Constantinopolis and identified it with the Roman goddess Venus.

MA

102. *Gold bracteate, imitating a Byzantine* solidus

Place of manufacture unknown, but probably Central Asia,
sixth–seventh century
From the tomb of Shi Suoyan (d. 656; buried 664), Tang dynasty (618–906),
southern suburbs of Guyuan, Ningxia
Diameter: 1.9 cm; thickness: 0.35 mm; weight: 0.85 g; pierced twice
Guyuan Municipal Museum, Ningxia Hui Autonomous Region
Obverse: helmeted bust of emperor three-quarter facing right, cuirassed,
spear in right hand held over right shoulder behind head,
on left arm shield; totally blundered legend.

1. *Yuanzhou* 1999, p. 113; Luo 1999, p. 48, colorpl. 17; Morrisson and Thierry 1994, no. 16.

2. Other bracteates are known in Xinjiang and in China proper: for example, those recorded from Astana (Morrisson and Thierry 1994, no. 7) and Xi'an (Ibid., no. 7; Thierry 1993, no. 22).

3. Raspopova 1999, p. 455, fig. 5.

4. Göbl 1967, vol. I, pp. 255–56; vol. III, pl. 87, B1–B3.

The prototype of this gold bracteate is the obverse of a Byzantine *solidus* of the fixth through sixth century.[1] The image of the emperor is recognizable in its main details, but the Latin legend is completely blundered and remains only as decoration to fill the empty space around the bust. This bracteate was not modeled after a genuine *solidus* but from an imitation. Moreover, it is unlikely that it was manufactured in China but was instead imported from Central Asia.

Although the bracteate is based on an imitation, the barbarized but still legible letters identify its prototype as a *solidus* of the emperor Anastasius (r. 491–518).[2] A similar bracteate was found in Panjikent in a house dating to the seventh through eighth century.[3] Other gold bracteates were manufactured in Afghanistan and northwest India by local Hunnish rulers in the sixth and seventh centuries in imitation of the official Hunnish coin types that circulated in the area.[4]

These bracteates were struck or pressed with only one die using a very thin sheet of metal for the flan, or metal blank. They had no monetary function but were used for ornaments, such as jewelry, and for grave goods.

MA

1. *Yuanzhou* 1999, pl. 121; Luo 1996, pl. 28, colorpl. 16; Morrisson and Thierry 1994, no. 17; *Put Svile* 1996, p. 167, no. 91.

103. *Gold bracteate, imitating a Byzantine* solidus

Place of manufacture unknown, but probably Central Asia,
sixth–seventh century
From the tomb of Shi Hedan (d. 669), Tang dynasty (618–906),
southern suburbs of Guyuan, Ningxia
Diameter: 2.4 cm; thickness: 0.4 mm; weight: 2.00 g
Guyuan Municipal Museum, Ningxia Hui Autonomous Region
Obverse: Helmeted bust of emperor three-quarter facing right,
cuirassed, spear in right hand held over right shoulder behind head,
on left arm shield; totally blundered legend.

This bracteate is similar to that from the tomb of Shi Suoyan (no. 102); it was buried only five years later.[1] The fabrication, however, is completely different, and it must have been manufactured in a different workshop. The flan, or metal sheet, is thicker than that of number 102, and the emperor's bust is drawn in a more careful manner. The helmet, the spear, and even the shield are clearly depicted, as are the letters, which are engraved more accurately, although the inscription itself, like that on Shi Suoyan's bracteate, is totally blundered. Overall, this bracteate is closer to its Byzantine prototype than is Shi Suoyan's. The most interesting feature, however, is the broad, undecorated border, which is not common on Byzantine coins but is a characteristic of Sasanian ones.

The prototypes of this bracteate are Byzantine *solidi* from the fifth to sixth century. The type of the three-quarter facing bust of the emperor with helmet, spear, and shield goes back to the time of Constantine the Great (r. 306–337), who introduced it for an exceptionally rare issue. From the time of Constantius II (r. 337–361) onward, it was used more frequently for festival issues and finally became the main *solidus* type in the East shortly after the death of Theodosius I (r. 379–395). This type of three-quarter facing bust remained unchanged until the time of Justinian I (r. 527–565), who put the facing bust with the *globus cruciger* on the obverse of his *solidi* (no. 100).

MA

104. *Imitation of a Byzantine gold* solidus

Made after the middle of the fifth and before the middle of the seventh century

From the tomb of Shi Daode (d. 678), Tang dynasty (618–906),
southern suburbs of Guyuan, Ningxia

Diameter: 1.89 cm; weight: 4.00 g; pierced

Guyuan Municipal Museum, Ningxia Hui Autonomous Region

Obverse: [–]VS P(erpetuus) F(elix) AVG(ustus); helmeted bust of emperor
three-quarter facing right, diademed, cuirassed, spear in right hand held over right shoulder
behind head, on left arm decorated shield.

Reverse: Blundered Latin legend; Victory standing right, supporting long jeweled cross.

1. *Yuanzhou* 1999, pl. 137; Luo 1996, pl. 73.

2. Morrisson and Thierry 1994, no. 14. The authors consider a *solidus* from Theodosius II (r. 408–450) as a prototype.

3. Ibid., nos. 4, 5, 9, 20, 21.

4. Burnett 1998, pp. 179–89.

The prototype of this crude and rather worn imitation dates to the time from Marcian (r. 450–457) to Anastasius I (r. 491–518),[2] although it was buried in the second half of the seventh century. The obverse shows the common type of the three-quarter facing bust of the emperor, but only part of the legend is readable. On the reverse the image of Victory is reversed (on the genuine coins Victory always stands to the left; see, for example, no. 98) and the legend is completely blundered. The hole directly above the head of the emperor indicates that whoever pierced the bracteate considered the obverse as the main side and most likely wore it as a pendant.

Other imitations so far found in China copy Byzantine *solidi* from the time of Justinian I (r. 527–565) up to Heraclius (r. 610–641).[3] This time span corresponds with the evidence of Late Roman and Byzantine coin finds from Central Asia, as well as from India where many imitations were also manufactured. The import of Byzantine gold coins to India resumes with Theodosius II in the early fifth century and finds its end with Heraclius in the early seventh century, as is the case in China.[4] We also cannot exclude that this imitation came to China via India.

The coin was found in Shi Daode's mouth.

MA

1. *Shi Daoluo* 2000, colorpls. 26, 27 (all fifteen coins), pp. 208, 214.

2. Thierry 1991, pp. 209–49; see Thierry 1998 for a general introduction.

3. Zeimal 1994, fig. 2, no. 14; Thierry 1991, no. 102.

4. Cribb 1979, p. 188.

5. Thierry 1998a, pp. 209–12.

105. *Ten* kai yuan tong bao *coins*

Tang dynasty, 621 and later
From the tomb of Shi Daoluo (d. 658), Tang dynasty (618–906),
southern suburbs of Guyuan, Ningxia
Base silver (?)
Weight: 3.5–4.4 g; diameter: 2.52–2.45 cm
Guyuan Municipal Museum, Ningxia Hui Autonomous Region
Obverse: Chinese inscription *kai yuan tong bao* ("Current money of the Kai yuan [new] era")
Reverse: Plain

A total of fifteen *kai yuan tong bao* coins were found in Shi Daoluo's grave.[1] *Kai yuan tong bao* coins were introduced by the Tang dynasty in 621 and continued to be issued under the Five Dynasties and the Ten Kingdoms period (907–976).[2] They were cast for more than 350 years and circulated far beyond the borders of the Chinese empire. In the second half of the seventh to the beginning of the eighth century, they were also imitated in Sogdiana (Bukhara region), with the device of the issuing locality appearing on the reverse.[3]

The coins that accompanied Shi Daoluo in his grave are from the earliest phase and must be dated between 621 and the time of his burial in 658. Regularly, *kai yuan tong bao* coins are cast of copper, but the pieces in Shi Daoluo's tomb seem to be made of base silver alloy, showing on some parts of the surface heavy traces of corrosion. Silver imitations of official bronze cash coins were not used as current money but as talismans for good luck and ornaments. They were produced as gifts and symbolized largesse and wealth.[4]

The Chinese monetary system is characterized by an extraordinary continuity and persistence. The immediate predecessor of the *kai yuan tong bao* coins, the *wuzhu* coins (see p. 273), were issued for more than seven hundred years and still remained in circulation after the *kai yuan* coins were introduced. The *kai yuan* coins also circulated over centuries and it is quite possible to find them in hoards of the fifteenth century. Any copper coin could circulate freely, no matter when it was produced. The value of the coins was not based on their intrinsic value, i.e., the weight or metal content, as was the case in the western Byzantine or Sasanian Empires; instead the coins were a fiduciary currency like paper money, based on a general agreement between the issuing authorities and the users.[5]

The characteristic shape of the Chinese coins—round with a square hole in the middle—has a cosmological background and symbolizes heaven (round) and earth (square). In contrast to Western countries, where coins were normally struck between two dies, all Chinese coins were cast in molds. First an ancestor coin was produced, which was used to make mother coins. Then the mother coins were sent to the different workshops in the provinces to make the molds from which the ordinary coins for circulation were cast. Molten metal was poured into the stacked molds and once the metal had cooled, the coins were broken out.

MA

PART IV

CONCLUSION

10

Cosmopolitanism
and the Tang

Annette L. Juliano
and Judith A. Lerner

. . . Good fortune falls on the gold-pillared gateway . . . .
The prophecies of Taizong are supreme,
The empire is firmly established and reaches the sky!

Du Fu (712–770)[1]

"Chineseness"

The great Tang dynasty in 618 strengthened the unity achieved by the short-lived Sui, and created a culture that was rivaled perhaps only by the earlier Han. Tang culture is characterized by its cosmopolitanism, its taste for the exotic, and its artistic use of foreign imagery and techniques. It is marked by communities of foreigners residing in Chinese cities and towns, by a flood of foreign influences and goods acquired through commerce and diplomacy, and by the flowering of distinctively Chinese Buddhism thought and art.

However, these phenomena had already emerged in the centuries before the Tang. The influx of foreign merchants and Buddhist monks, exotic goods, and even more exotic ideas into China from the end of the Han into the seventh century wrought great changes to Chinese society—changes that had a powerful impact on the succeeding Tang. This growing openness to and adoption of foreign ideas was, to some degree, opposed to accepted notions of who and what is "Chinese."

The definition of "Chinese" has long been an issue for those dwelling within the "Middle Kingdom," the term by which the Chinese came to call their country, one that reflects their distinctly sinocentric view of the world.[2] From ancient times, the Chinese view of itself was based on cultural and political rather than ethnic criteria. It involved a complex set of usages, sometimes known as *li*, defined as "what the former Kings received from Heaven and Earth, in order to govern their people."[3] By the Han dynasty (206 BCE–220 CE), the notion of what it means to be Chinese was firmly established, so that those who considered themselves Chinese called themselves "Han" and termed all others "not Han." To be considered Han, one had to live according to specific political and cultural norms; "Han"

OVERLEAF: Tiantishan (Celestial Ladder Mountain) in a remote valley of the Qilian Mountains near the city of Wuwei (Gansu). Thirteen caves in a magnificent setting of stone cliffs overlook a broad valley.

OPPOSITE: A detail of a face from the Northern Wei carved sandstone pagoda (no. 52) showing a crouching figure holding a plate with fire overhead. This central figure is flanked by Buddhas, while beaked human-headed bird-bodied creatures confront each other below

came to be an ethno-cultural designation, regardless of a person's actual origins. Indeed, to this day, the Chinese call themselves Han, to distinguish themselves from all non-Chinese. Yet those who are Han may, as recently as two generations earlier, have come to China from elsewhere, having descended from ancestors who were considered not Han. This is a familiar process in which newcomers become so much a part of the national culture that they perceive other, later arrivals as outsiders and themselves as natives.

The centralized and autocratic government of the Han dynasty, with the emperor as its cosmic pivot, depended on Confucian ideology as a moral regulator of society. This ideology was shared by an elite, educated class, which formed the bureaucracy that administered the state.[4] After the disintegration of the Han, this bureaucratic structure survived to provide cultural continuity and stability against the challenge of nomadic invasions and the inroads of Buddhist teachings. Also providing important cultural continuity as well as ethnic and cultural identity was the Chinese language. Although its spoken form has changed over the centuries, its written form, distinguished by an ideographic, non-alphabetic system, has persisted unchanged for the two thousand years since Han times.[5]

Adaptation, Acculturation, and Assimilation

In the post-Han to Tang period, Gansu and Ningxia in the northwest provided a major stage for viewing the process of cultural and ethnic interaction and assimilation between the Han and other cultures. The combination of this region's geographic location and the survival of its material culture from this period create the opportunity to explore this process. The interaction and assimilation that took place in Gansu and Ningxia are revealed in two ways: by the acculturation of outsiders to Han customs and practices and by the maintenance, often by these same outsiders, of their distinctive cultures. An example of acculturation of non-Chinese to Han society is the adoption of names in the Chinese style. Whether such names were conferred upon these outsiders by state decree or were voluntarily used is difficult to say. In the case of the nomadic Xianbei, the emperor himself ordered that the distinctive names of this people be altered to become traditional Chinese.[6] The Shi family of Yuanzhou (modern Guyuan, Ningxia), along with the descendants of other Sogdian immigrants (those whom the Chinese called *zhaowu jiuxing*, "the nine clans of *Zhaowu*"), accepted surnames in the Chinese style (see Chapter 8).

These complex crosscurrents of acculturation and assimilation are also evident in the interaction between Buddhist and Chinese popular and traditional imagery beginning as early as the second half of the Han dynasty, third and fourth centuries. Depictions of the Buddha and related Buddhist symbols placed in traditional Chinese contexts appear on the walls and ceilings of tombs, on bronze mirrors, and on ceramic vessels. Separated from his own religious milieu during the Han and after, the Buddha appeared to the Chinese to have affinities with popular Daoism and became a "Buddha-like Chinese deity."[7] He was subsumed into the Daoist pantheon of the immortals associated with Han immortality cults. Incorporated into programs of tomb decoration, Buddha-like images and lotus flowers mingle with historical and legendary Confucian heroes and auspicious figures. In the post-Han period, this process is visible in Gansu and Ningxia and is evident on the late-fifth-century lacquered coffin (no. 16) and the associated bronze plaques (nos. 17, 18) from the same tomb. The painted decor of the coffin, as well, reflects the multi-ethnicity of the culture, with Buddhist elements placed with Chinese Daoist deities and Confucian parables of filial piety. On the bronze plaques, the image of the infant Buddha is converted into the auspicious Chinese legend of the Dragon Tamer. The process continues through the Tang; for example, the *lokapalas,* temple guardians of the Indian Buddhist universe (nos. 74, 78), remain virtually unchanged in form but become clay *mingqi,* renamed and moved underground as Chinese tomb guardians.[8]

The stupa pillar, dated 428, and Caves 285 and 249 at Dunhuang, dated Western Wei (535–557), offer three striking examples of efforts to accommodate or integrate Buddhist and traditional Chinese cosmology. The Buddhist stupa pillar (no. 48) with its seven Buddhas, Maitreya, and sutra text, also shows unquestionable Chinese elements in the eight incised trigrams from the *Book of Changes.* The incorporation of these ancient Chinese cosmological elements into the Buddhist system reflects the complex and continuing process of cultural adaptation, perhaps in a conscious attempt to create a unified and orderly universe. Finally, the ceiling of Cave 285 brings together both universes in an extraordinary set of images.[9] Directly overhead, the trapezoidal form of the ceiling teems with Buddhist images including *apsaras* and lotus flowers, as well as with many traditional Chinese creatures such as nine-headed dragons and the mythic Chinese cultural heroes, Fuxi and Nukwa, and dragon-pulled sleds carrying Xiwangmu (Queen Mother of the West) and Dongwangkong (King Father of the West). At the ceiling's lower edge, painted Buddhist monks sit calmly meditating in their caves.

Adaptation also was critical to the advancement of Buddhism in China.[10] When Buddhism arrived during the Han dynasty, this Indian religion was introduced into a traditional culture whose fundamental Confucian values emphasized the worldly commitment to build a good society based on the family and on the practice of filial piety. This emphasis conflicted directly with Buddhist teachings, with the monastic ideal of the otherworldly, and with the Buddhist concept of enlightenment outside the family.

Buddhists met with opposition from Confucian scholars and officials, angered by such practices as withdrawal from society and family to a life of celibacy. Recognizing the challenge of conflicting value systems, Buddhists began reinterpreting scriptures incompatible with filial piety and created new or apocryphal sutras, making them more consistent with Chinese cultural values.[11] New genres such as the narrative murals, called *bianxiang* ("transformation illustrations") on the walls of the Dunhuang caves, particularly during the Sui and Tang, reinforced Buddhist versions of filial piety.[12]

China may also have reshaped at least some of the religious practices of the Sogdian settlers. Although we have no real evidence of their religious beliefs, members of the Shi family may have worshiped in a local Zoroastrian temple. Even though they interred their dead, they may have held to some interpretation of Zoroastrian practices, considering the stone and brick platforms on which the bodies were laid as protection against polluting the soil into which the tombs were dug.[13] The use of a stone funerary couch (such as the Tianshui [no. 106] Xi'an, Miho, and Zhangdefu couches) or sarcophagus (like that from Taiyuan) would also prevent the body from coming into contact with the earth. Although funerary couches and sarcophagi serve as tomb furniture in "Chinese" tombs,[14] their occurrence in the tombs of foreigners and their descendants reveals the blending of Chinese and Sogdian practice.

Such adaptation or assimilation of one culture's form to suit another culture's needs is balanced by an apparent desire of those who are "not Chinese" to differentiate themselves from those who are. Even as the sinicized heirs of Sogdian immigrants, integrated into the

Fig. 1. Banquet scene with Central Asian dancer and musicians from a marble funerary couch, Miho Museum, Shigaraki. Among the characteristically non-Chinese elements in the banquets are the images of a dancing Central Asian and the drinking of wine by the deceased from a rhyton, a distinctive Iranian vessel (see no. 106, fig. E) (Courtesy, Miho Museum)

Chinese military and court establishments, the men who bore the Shi surname still married within the *zhaowu jiuxing* (see Chapter 8 and note 20). Although not all the Shi so far found in the Guyuan cemetery were directly related, a feeling of connection to a shared descent from people from Kesh seems to account for the clustering of their tombs in the cemetery.

The desire to maintain one's ethnic identity through marriage and religious customs also manifests itself through the objects that are chosen for one's tomb.[15] Among the traditional grave goods in the tombs of certain Northern Qi and Sui nobles and officials are distinctive ceramic objects, elaborately decorated with vegetal and other motifs applied in relief. The owners of these tombs were closely connected to the Gao family—Northern Qi rulers of nomadic origin—and were themselves of non-Chinese descent.[16] In the Shi family tombs, the use of an epitaph stone (no. 83) and the ceramics, guardian figures, and *mingqi* conform to standard Chinese burial practices of the period.[17] Yet other objects, such as Shi Hedan's

Sasanian seal (no. 86), Shi Suoyan's crystal pendant (no. 87), and, most spectacularly, Shi Daode's gold mask (no. 90), are so closely linked to the region these men's ancestors came from that one can assume that these objects were consciously chosen for their connection to this foreign heritage. Similarly, the necklace of the young Sui princess Li Jingxun (no. 87, fig. A) and other objects from her tomb speak of some connection with places distant both in time and space. The necklace may represent simply an interest in the exotic, which increased with the advent of the Tang, but it may also speak of some memory or association with a past that had specific meaning to the little girl and her family. Some of Li Jingxun's possessions may have been family heirlooms, passed to her from her great-grandfather Li Xian, who had in his lifetime acquired objects from western lands (nos. 30–32).[18]

Further evidence that at least some of the Central Asians or their descendants living in China consciously indicated their non-Chinese heritage is their choice of certain motifs—even an entire decorative program—on the stone couches or sarcophagi in their tombs. Based on currently known examples, there seem to be two distinct iconographies that are utilized on funerary furniture in tombs from the mid-sixth century into the early Tang. One is more traditional, depicting Chinese mythology, such as the *sishen* or *siling* (the animals of the four directions) and Fuxi and Nukwa, and Confucian stories of filial piety.[19] The other shows specifically Central Asian subjects, such as hunting and banquet scenes with non-Chinese participants (fig. 1).[20] Interestingly, the differences between Chinese and non-Chinese iconographies are paralleled by differences in style: the Chinese carving tends to be incised or in very low relief, while the non-Chinese reliefs tend to be higher and more sculptural.

The Cosmopolitan Tang

Elements of Tang cosmopolitanism already existed in China before the Tang period, driven by the constant movements of monks and merchants and their influence on ideas and the arts. What prevented this earlier period from having the great artistic and cultural coherency of the Tang was the political and cultural fragmentation of the country.[21] The absence of a strong central government resulted in multiple patronage centers and mitigated the development of a unified national style. In Gansu and Ningxia, the city of Guzang (present-day Wuwei) was the capital of the Northern Liang kingdom (398–439), under the enlightened nomadic ruler Juqu Mengxun. Under his aegis, Guzang became the cultural center of the mid-Gansu corridor, supporting both a Confucian academy and an active Buddhist translation center, the Buddhist caves at Jintasi, Tiantishan, and Wenshushan were opened and the vast program of cave temple decoration begun (no. 49). In southeast Gansu, the important commercial center of Tianshui supported the establishment of the unique Buddhist cave site of Maijishan (nos. 61–71). Compared to other caves in Gansu, Maijishan's painting and sculpture are distinguished by stylistic and iconographic influences from southern Chinese Buddhist art. In southern Ningxia, the lacquered coffin (no. 16) unites a variety of Chinese and foreign elements, the latter apparently influenced by imported textiles.

Buddhist sculpture in the Tang period achieves an exquisite synthesis of foreign influences balanced with Chinese aesthetic values. During the second half of the sixth century, Buddhist sculpture reflected an emerging interest in naturalism inspired by renewed vigorous contacts with the Western Regions, including India, and the elegant, restrained, and yet taut forms of Indian Gupta and post-Gupta sculpture. Chinese Tang Buddhist sculptures

Fig. 2. *Bian hu* decorated on the sides with relief of figures among vines. Stoneware with dullish brown glaze. Tang, seventh or early eighth century. (photo: Victoria and Albert Museum, London)

reveal an intensified naturalism and humanism conveyed with more organic articulation of the full, rounded body. Drapery clings, caresses, and falls, conveying a tactile sense of the cloth. These sensual forms are restrained by the abstract linear patterning of the cloth as it defines the body. This distinctive style is visible in the abundant Tang sculpture remaining in Dunhuang and from Tiantishan cave temple sculpture preserved in the Gansu Provincial Museum (nos. 72, 77–79).

One of the hallmarks of the Tang is the rich floral and vegetal vocabulary that is found in virtually every medium (nos. 109, 111, 117–120), even on stone funerary furniture (nos. 80, 83). After the fall of the Han dynasty, such motifs as undulating and foliate vines, inhabited vines, palmettes, and floral medallions enter China through trade and imported Buddhist imagery. For example, vines inhabited by birds, insects, animals, and humans are popular on Tang metalwork and ceramics. However, this motif occurs as early as the mid-fifth century, as on the lacquered coffin from Guyuan (no. 16a,c,d) and the stone pillar support from the tomb of Sima Jinlong (d. 484), near Datong (Shanxi) (no. 16, fig. D). Inhabited vines also figure as border decoration in Buddhist cave temples in northern China.[22] In these early versions, the vines tend to be decorative rather than naturalistic, incorporating palmettes and other vegetal forms that do not occur botanically. The early interest in decorative vines may have been inspired by such imported Central Asian metalwork as the gilt bronze bowls found at Datong.[23] One of the most distinctive types of inhabited vine is identifiable as a grapevine, from which grow heavy grape clusters and leaves. This relatively naturalistic rendering appears in the Sui and early Tang, primarily on mirrors (nos. 116, 117).[24] The naturalism of the mirror decoration may have derived from metalwork more directly linked to Western, i.e., Roman or Hellenistic, sources. The provincial Roman silver platter, found in Gansu (no. 115), is an example of the kind of work that could have influenced the design of these mirrors.[25]

A widespread element in Chinese art is the beaded border, which embellishes works in a range of media. It is found emphasizing the mandorlas of Buddha images in painting and sculpture (nos. 55, 59) and decorating objects, such as the bronze dragon plaque (no. 18) and a bodhisattva's offering tray (no. 56). One of its earliest appearances is as the edging of the Buddhas' mandorlas in the paintings in Cave 169, Binglingsi, dated 420. The beaded border seems to be linked with works produced along the Silk Road: it is pervasive at Dunhuang, bordering individual scenes as well as decorating images of Buddhas and bodhisattvas[26]; it frequently occurs at Yungang (Shanxi) and Longmen (Henan).[27] It appears on funerary couches, as on the Miho couch (fig. 1), on the base of that from Tianshui (no. 106), and on the panels from Zhengdefu (no. 106, fig. E).

By the Tang, the beaded border had become a favorite device for ceramics, metalwork, and textiles, both as an independent decorative feature and as a means of enclosing roundels (nos. 84, 112).[28] Emblematic of this usage are the ceramic animal-headed rhyta, inspired by

Fig. 3. Bull's-head rhyton, light green glazed earthen-ware. Tang, seventh–eighth century. (photo: courtesy of the Royal Ontario Museum©ROM, 927.19.7, Bishop White Collection)

Fig. 4. Lead-glazed pillow decorated with a half-pal-mette scroll against a stippled ground imitating silver. Tang, eighth–ninth century, (photo: ©The British Museum)

Central Asian vessels and ranging from the sixth to the eighth century, on which beaded borders define the faceted walls of the cup part (fig. 3). Although the origin of the beaded border is Western, no single source can be cited for its appearance in China; instead, multiple influences in many media and from many cultures are responsible for the motif. Parthian and Kushan clothing with beaded decoration (nos. 17, 18, figs. A, B); textiles from Persia, Sogdiana, and Xinjiang[29]; Sasanian and Byzantine coins (nos. 93, 96, 97, 104)[30]; and metalwork from the Roman and Iranian worlds (no. 31)[31] are only some of the sources. The jewelry technique of granulation, which entered northwest China at least as early as the Han (no. 5), may also have served as an impetus for beading. The use of granulation as a border for gemstones (nos. 20, 21) may have suggested the kind of border that encloses the cabochons and plaques applied to the highly ornate ceramics associated with high-ranking personages of non-Chinese origin.[32]

Ring-punching, a technique used by Tang metalsmiths to decorate the backgrounds of gold and silver work, was first introduced to China via the northwest in the early Tang with imports of Sogdian silver (no. 118). The ring-punch pattern was so popular that it became part of the ceramic vocabulary as a background effect (no. 111 and fig. 4). It became an almost ubiquitous metalworking device throughout the Tang period and continued into the Song dynasty (960–1279).

Despite continued exposure to foreign influences, the Tang developed an art that was quintessentially Chinese, while using forms, motifs, and techniques from outside. With the re-establishment of a strong centralized government and the expansion beyond previous imperial boundaries, China reaffirmed its ethno-cultural identity and its sinocentric outlook. In the visual arts, this affirmation emerged as a unified style that is national in scope and international in outlook. This style uses imagery and techniques—many of them foreign borrowings—that were already part of the art of the preceding periods and adds newly arrived motifs and techniques, synthesizing and transforming all into an aesthetic that reflects foreign inspiration yet remains decidedly Chinese. Tang art and culture could not have attained their richness and complexity without the preceding "interregnum" of the fourth to early seventh century and the interactions in Gansu and Ningxia of merchants, monks, and nomads with Chinese civilization.

NOTES

1. Quoted by Munro 1971, p. 91.

2. As Reischauer and Fairbank observe (1960, vol. I, p. 37), the Chinese "considered China the unique land of civilization, surrounded on all sides by the 'four barbarians.'" Thus they called China *zhongguo*, meaning "Central Country," which is most often translated as "Middle Kingdom," and is still the Chinese name for China.

3. Creel 1970, vol. I, p. 197. As early as the late second millennium BCE, the issue of who is and who is not "Chinese" arose with the invasion of the Zhou peoples. The settled Shang viewed them as "uncultivated intruders," although as soon as the Zhou established themselves as rulers, their non-Chinese origins became moot as they adopted existing Chinese cultural values.

4. Pirazzoli-t'Serstevens 1982, p. 8.

5. The form of the Chinese characters as used even today were standardized by the publication in 100 CE of the *Shuo Wen* dictionary, compiled by Hu Shan (Karlgren 1971, p. 52).

6. Dien 1977, p.139. In his desire to sinicize the court, in 496 the Northern Wei emperor Xiao Wendi, himself of Xianbei origin, ordered that Xianbei names be altered to more Chinese forms. Although Chinese, the names adopted by Xianbei were different enough to convey their non-Chinese origin. Chinese had multi-syllabic surnames, but the double multi-syllabic names were unusual; Xianbei and Xiongnu names, such as Kudi Huilo and Juqu Mengxun, were often distinctively multi-syllabic.

7. See Wu 1986, p. 263; Wu Hung believes as do Professors Seiichi Mizuno and Toshio Nagahiro of Japan and Zeng Zhaoyue of Beijing that these earliest representations of Buddha images should be classified as Buddha-like Chinese deities. Yu Weichao also discusses early Han images of the Buddha in Yu 1980, pp. 68–77.

Erik Zürcher proposes that penetration of Buddhism into Han China was not a gradual process of diffusion but rather "long-distance transmission," part of a huge Buddhist expansion that started with the Mauryans and Kushans (Zürcher 1990, pp. 158–82).

8. *Yuanzhou* 1999, tomb guardians in Tang tomb of Shi Daoluo, dated 658 CE, nos. 98–99.

9. *Dunhuang* 1981, pls. 97–107 (Cave 249); 130, 140–143 (Cave 285).

10. Ch'en 1973. This book focuses on the process of adaptation of Buddhism to Chinese cultural conditions. As Ch'en

points out that, as the same time Indian ideas were gaining ground, the Chinese were changing Indian ideas and practices, "so that Buddhism became more and more Chinese and more acceptable to the Chinese" (p. 5).

11. Sun 2000, pp. 281–83.

12. Ibid., p. 282.

13. A brick platform bore the remains of the skeletons of Shi Suoyan and his wife, while one of the stone slabs bore those of Shi Hedan (Luo 1996, pp. 33, 57); Shi Daoluo's tomb was lined with brick. The other Shi burials used earthen platforms, which were perhaps thought to pose no danger of pollution from the decomposing flesh because they were not made of fertile soil.

14. Thus the bases of the funerary couches in the Freer Gallery of Art (Sickman and Soper 1971, p. 121, fig. 79) and that published by Loo 1940, pl. XXVII, no. 35); the sarcophagus in the Nelson Gallery of Art of the Northern Wei (Soper 1948, pp. 180–86, figs. 6–9), and the sarcophagus of the Sui princess Li Jingxun (*Tang Changan* 1980, pls. I, II). The backs and sides of the funerary couches have been dispersed into other collections, such as the stone panels said to have been excavated at Zhangdefu (Henan): two of the panels are in the Museum of Fine Arts, Boston (Juliano 1992, figs. XI, XII); and one panel is in the Musée Guimet (*Sérinde, Terre de Bouddha* 1995, pp. 57–58, no. 25). Another set of stone with scenes in an unquestionably Chinese style of the first half of the sixth century, and incised in dark limestone, is in the Asia Art Museum, San Francisco (d'Argencé 1974, p. 108, no. 44).

15. For a discussion of how material culture may be used to emphasize group identity in an archaeological context, see Whitehouse and Wilkins 1989, p. 122. Further discussion of the "archaeological detection of ethnic groups" and the ability to distinguish ethnic identity from acculturation, see Bartel 1989, pp. 174–77.

16. Valenstein 1997–98, pp. 4–12. The ceramics in these tombs seem to reflect a northern, nomadic sensibility; a similarly elaborate vessel, found near Nanjing in the south, is close enough in its fabric and decoration to be considered a northern ware (Feng 1982, pp. 164–65, colorpl. 11).

17. *Yuanzhou* 1999, nos. 93, 98–101, 109–111, 120, 124–25.

18. The phenomenon of the geographic transfer of images between cultures via the actual object as well as the memory of an initial image is discussed in Hay 1999, p. 6.

19. Such as on the Nelson Gallery of Art sarcophagus and the Asian Art Museum panels (above, note 14).

20. The Miho couch also depicts a specific Zoroastrian funerary rite, the *sagdid* (Lerner 1995).

21. It is important to remember that this fragmentation was between northern and southern China. The north, which has been the focus of this exhibition, was ruled by successive and contemporaneous nomadic dynasties, while the south was under the control of a series of Chinese dynasties that saw themselves as inheritors of and preservers of the Chinese or Han imperial tradition. In contrast to the north, the southern dynasties ruled from the same capital, Qiankang (present day Nanjing).

22. *Yungang* 1977, Cave 10, pl. 56 and *Longmen* 1977, Cave XVI, after Bush 1976, fig. 31.

23. For pieces from the Datong hoard, see *Wenhua* 1972, pp. 150–52. Jessica Rawson notes that these cups "were evidently based on provincial Central Asian copies of Hellenistic or Roman plate" (Rawson 1986, p. 36).

24. See also Rawson 1982, pp. 15–16.

25. For example, the so-called "Chalice of Antioch," also from the fifth-century Datong hoard (*Wenhua* 1972, p. 151)

26. *Dunhuang* 1981, vol. 2: in Sui Caves, beaded borders abound (see figs. 62, 63, 70, 71 [Cave 420]; fig. 89 [Cave 425]; fig. 96 [Cave 406]; fig. 102 [Cave 403]; figs. 108, 109 [Cave 282]).

27. *Longmen* 1991, vol. 1: Guyang Cave, north wall, top tier, niche 3, 4 (Buddha: beaded border edging the garment across his chest), pls. 160, 161; *Yungang* 1977, pl. 93. Mandorlas in Cave 169 in the Binglingsi cave temples, near Lanzhou, Gansu, have painted beaded borders (Dong 1994, pl. 33).

28. Rawson 1977, pp. 42–43.

29. See, for example, the textiles represented on wall-paintings at Afrasiab (ancient Samarkand) on which ducks stand on beaded platforms; animal motifs are enclosed in pearled, rather than beaded, roundels (Frumkin 1970, pl. L). Beading decorates the lozenge pattern framework design on the trousers of the mummy from Yingpan (Xinjiang) (Mallory and Mair 2000, p. 201, fig. 115).

30. Beading is a device used for the rims of the coins and the crowns and dress of the rulers.

31. Beaded rims figure prominently on fourth-century Roman metalwork (*Wealth of the Roman World* 1977, pp. 34–35, nos. 56–61; p. 50, no. 99; p. 53, no. 103).

32. See note 16 above. For another example, see the footed cup from the tomb of Duan Boyang (d. 667), embellished with square floral appliqués and cabochons, outlined by beading (Watson 1986, p. 163, fig. 1).

106. *Funerary couch*

Sui dynasty (589–618), early seventh century
Found in the environs of Tianshui[1]
Gray-pink granite with remains of polychrome painting and gilding
Overall dimensions of the couch and base:
height: 123 cm; width: 218 cm; depth: 115 cm
Couch: average height of panels: 87 cm
From right to left (following the order in the original Chinese publication):
a. Drinking scene: width: 38 cm
b. Tropical landscape with sun: width: 30 cm
c. Figures on the balcony of a pavilion: width: 33 cm
d. Ox cart and gateway: width: 40 cm
e. Architectural scene: width: 43 cm
f. Feast scene in a pavilion: width: 46 cm
g. Procession on horseback: width: 41 cm
h. Architectural scene: width: 39.5 cm
i. Brewing scene: width: 33 cm
j. Boating scene with moon: width: 31.5 cm
k. Hunting scene: width: 37.5
Base (includes lion figures): height: 36 cm
l. width: 137.5 cm
m. width: 80.5 cm
Tianshui Municipal Museum, Gansu

no. 106f (detail)

This couch consists of eleven rectangular stone panels, carved in relief and painted and gilded, that form a screen at the back and sides; four plain rectangular stones that serve as the platform; and two front panels, carved in relief and painted and gilded, with four side and rear undecorated panels that form the base.[1] The upright stone panels are secured to each other by two sets of dovetailed clamps, while the horizontal slabs of the platform are mortised to each other. The carved vertical panels thus formed a backdrop for the deceased and his wife. Wood and skeletal remains found on the couch indicate that the bodies were placed in a wooden coffin or coffins (fig. A). Also on the couch were a stone pillow and a gold hairpin, presumably near the heads of the deceased, and a silvered bronze mirror at the center of the couch (no. 108a–c). Stone carvings of kneeling musicians flanked the couch, two on one side and three on the other (no. 107).

The couch belongs to a class of funerary furniture that only in the last few years can be recognized as a distinctive group with foreign associations.[2] Two complete couches with their bases (one from Tianshui and one from Xi'an)[3] and a sarcophagus from Taiyuan have been excavated[4]; acquired on the art market were two other couches, one reputedly from Zhangdefu (Anyang, Henan), incomplete and divided among four museums,[5] and the other in the Miho Museum, also incomplete.[6] The manufacture of the couches and sarcophagus was concentrated within an approximately fifty-year period, from the Northern Qi (550–577) and Northern Zhou (557–581) through the Sui (581–618). The excavations of the Xi'an couch and Taiyuan sarcophagus revealed epitaphs that identify the respective owners as foreigners and *sabaos:* An Qie (d. 579), the owner of the Xi'an couch, was originally from Wuwei (Guzang), but his ancestors were Sogdian; Yu Hong (d. 593), the occupant of the Taiyuan sarcophagus, had some affiliation with nomadic rulers and had served the Northern Zhou and Sui courts.

Whereas each of these monuments has its own distinct iconographic program and style of execution, they share many themes, which ultimately seem to be connected with religious beliefs and conceptions of an afterlife. All but the Zhangdefu couch (which is incomplete) have hunting scenes; and all have scenes of drinking and feasting: on the Tianshui couch, the central panel (f) shows a couple in a pavilion drinking from shallow bowls (identified in Chinese as *poluo*), while panel a shows

another pavilion with a man drinking from a horn rhyton—a non-Chinese vessel—and his companion from a cup; the Zhangdefu panels, the An Qie and Miho couches, and the Yu Hong sarcophagus also show feasting and drinking couples in pavilions, with the rhyton used as a drinking vessel in one of the Zhangdefu scenes (fig. E).[7] Central Asian musicians and dancers performing the "Sogdian whirl" (see p. 298, fig. 1 and fig. E; see also nos. 81, 82) appear on all but the Tianshui couch. Perhaps there was no need to depict such entertainers on the couch because Central Asian musicians were included as stone *mingqi* in the tomb itself (no. 107).

The panels on which the hunts, banquets, and other activities appear are organized either into two levels of landscape or by architectural structures. Each of the panels of the Tianshui couch is composed as a single, coherent garden landscape that contains architectural elements—pavilions, covered walkways, bridges, and walls—along with small lakes and waterways, rocks, and shrubbery. These compositions bring to mind the format of later Chinese vertical landscape scrolls and actual Chinese gardens.[8] Specific architectural details, such as hipped and tiled roofs and brackets, mark

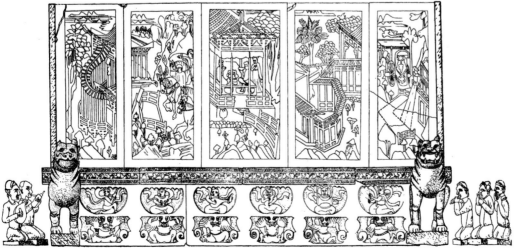

Fig. A. Elevation drawing of the front view of the couch, showing the five rear panels, the base, and the five musicians (after *Kaogu* 1992.1, p. 47, fig. 2)

This page, top to bottom:

Fig. B. Elevation drawing of the left and right side panels of the couch (after *Kaogu* 1992.1, p. 48, fig. 3)

Fig. C. Elevation drawing of the side views of the couch, showing the dovetailed clamps and the lions of the base (after *Kaogu* 1992.1, p. 49, fig. 5)

Fig. D. Plan of the tomb showing placement of the couch (1), the musicians in front of the couch (7–11), and the pillow (2), hairpin (3) and mirror (6). Also indicted in front of the couch are a ceramic candlestick (4) and a chicken-head spouted pitcher (5) (after *Kaogu* 1992.1, p. 46, fig. 1)

Opposite page, left to right:

Fig. E. Detail of a limestone panel from a funerary couch showing a Central Asian drinking from a horn rhyton, thought to have come from Zhengdefu (Henan), Northern Qi (550–577). Museum of Fine Arts, Boston, Denman Waldo Ross Collection and Gift of G. M. Lane (photo © Museum of Fine Arts)

Fig. F. Banqueter drinking from a horn rhyton that ends in a caprid head, wall painting from room XXIV/1, Panjikent, Sogdian, first half of the eighth century (after Belenizki 1980, fig. 55).

Fig. G. Detail of a gilded silver lobed dish, showing a nude male figure holding a wineskin and drinking from a horn rhyton that ends in a bull's head. Sasanian, sixth or seventh century. Cleveland Museum of Art, purchase from the John L. Severance Fund.

Fig. H. Paradise scene set in a water garden, with pavilions, jeweled canopies, and entertainers, Dunhuang Cave 172 (after *Dunhuang* 1981, vol. 4, pl. 13)

the pavilions as Chinese. These features distinguish the Tianshui couch from the other monuments and make it the most "Chinese" in appearance.[9]

A further indication of its Chinese character is the fact that the Tianshui couch is the only one of these funerary monuments that does not contain an overt reference to Zoroastrianism. A specific Zoroastrian ceremony is represented on the Miho couch, (chapter 8, fig. 6)[10] and more generalized allusions to Zoroastrian fire ceremonies appear on Yu Hong's sarcophagus and the Zhangdefu couch gateposts; the lintel of An Qie's tomb shows what may be another kind of Zoroastrian ceremony.[11]

The Tianshui couch, however, may imply some Zoroastrian—and certainly a non-Chinese—connection for its owner. The rhyton, from which the man in the pavilion drinks (panel a), is a quintessential Iranian vessel; it also seems to have a religious, Zoroastrian, connotation. The rhyton, essentially a horn-shaped vessel with a pouring spout, has a long history in the Iranian world, although by the fifth century CE it had disappeared from the repertory of luxury vessels produced in the western part of that region, Sasanian Iran.[12] A shortened form, ending in a caprid or bovine head, remained in use in Central Asia, particularly in Sogdiana (fig. F.), and by the seventh century it had spread into China (p. 301, fig. 3).[13] Even though the rhyton was no longer made in Iran, this truncated form appears on late Sasanian vessels of the sixth and seventh centuries in a ritual or even eucharistic context; in one, a male figure holding a wineskin crouches within a grapevine that grows treelike from between two mountains and drinks from a short rhyton that terminates in a bull's head (fig. G). Writing about this bowl, Dorothy Shepherd observes that the figure "is performing a ritual act"; citing a Zoroastrian text, she notes that "our little tippler is not drinking wine but Haoma, the liquor of immortality," from the sacred Hom tree, the tree of life.[14] On one of the Zhangdefu panels, too, the rhyton—also ending in a bull's head—is held by the deceased as he sits within a grape arbor (fig. E).[15] These drinking scenes on the couches and the sarcophagus—represented within a grape arbor or a garden—evoke the image of paradise.

A further evocation of paradise and the afterlife is suggested by the extensive architectural, aquatic, and landscape elements on eight of the eleven Tianshui panels. These same elements become important metaphors in Chinese Buddhist visions of the Western Paradise and in the private gardens, which increase in importance in China during this period. On the Tianshui couch, the drinking figures sit in pavilions that rise from the water (panels c and f). These and the other, often interconnected, pavilions standing in lotus-filled lakes resemble on a smaller, simpler scale the architectonic visions of the Buddhist Western Paradise painted on the walls of Buddhist cave temples in Gansu. In particular, the western walls of several Tang caves at Dunhuang show elaborate panoramas containing water gardens with budding lotuses, ornate pavilions, jeweled canopies, and small orchestras accompanying dancers (fig. H).[16] At about the same time, private walled gardens for the privileged were also evolving, their pavilions, bridges, and lakes serving as both walled islands of repose and as microcosmic universes, and perhaps even as replicas of paradise on earth.

1. *Kaogu* 1992.1, pp. 46–54; p. 46, fig. 1; p. 47, fig. 2; p. 48, figs. 3, 4; p. 49, figs. 5, 6; p. 50, figs. 7, 8:1; pls. 6,,7. The tomb was first discovered when farmers were preparing a terrace and was then excavated by local archaeologists.

2. Only the carved panels and base allegedly from a tomb at Zhangdefu (Anyang, Henan) had been known until 1991, when Annette L. Juliano published the first extensive discussion of the date and iconography of the couch panels that are now in the Miho Museum (Juliano 1991). At the time of publication, these panels provoked considerable controversy about their authenticity; the simultaneous publication of the Tianshui couch and subsequent discoveries of the Taiyuan sarcophagus and Xi'an couch have now dramatically changed this assessment.

3. Yin, Li, and Xing 2000.

4. Zhang and Jiang 2000; Xu and Zhang 2000.

5. Scaglia 1958: two panels are in the Museum of Fine Arts, Boston; one panel is in the Musée Guimet, Paris; the two gateposts are in the Museum für Ostasiatische Kunst, Cologne; and the base is in the Freer Gallery, Washington, D.C.

6. Juliano 1992; Shumei 1996, pp. 142–45, no. 73; Juliano and Lerner 1997a; Juliano and Lerner 1997b. Two bases, also on the art market, are believed to have belonged to the Miho couch; one is now in a private collection in New York. In Yin, Li, and Xing 2000, p. 23, Xing offers the provenance for the Miho couch as a Northern Qi tomb in Shanxi and notes a Sogdian origin for the owner.

7. That the figure drinking from a rhyton on the Zhangdefu panel is non-Chinese is attested by his garments and headgear; by analogy, the figure drinking from the rhyton on the Tianshui couch is also non-Chinese, as he wears the same hat with two points as the rhyton-drinker and others on the Zhangdefu panels.

8. For the evolution and symbolism of the Chinese garden, see Keswick 1978,

pp. 116–554 ("Architecture in Gardens") and pp. 193–200 ("Meanings of the Chinese Garden").

9. On the Tianshui couch, all but one building is in the Chinese style, and that is the one containing the foreigner drinking from the rhyton. On the Zhangdefu panels not all the architecture is identifiably Chinese.

10. Lerner 1995. The ceremony depicted is the *sagdid* funerary rite.

11. Performing the ceremonies on the Zhangdefu posts and An Qie's lintel are half-human, half-bird creatures; similar beings help tend the fire on the base that may have supported the Miho couch.

12. Harper 1988, p. 158; Harper 1991a, p. 95.

13. The agate rhyton with antelope-head terminal, found in a hoard deposited at Xi'an sometime before 726, is a possible import from Sogdiana or from Khotan, a supplier of agate to Tang China (Parlasca 1975, fig. 1. Parlasca dates the rhyton to the second-century BCE Egypt, which would have made it at the time of burial some nine hundred years old).

14. Shepherd 1966, p. 301.

15. A rhyton was reportedly discovered in the tomb that contained the Miho couch (Yin, Li, and Xing 2000, p. 23).

16. *Dunhuang* 1981, vol. 3, 1981, pls. 5, 6 (Cave 341); pls. 44, 45 (Cave 329); pl. 54 (Cave 321); pl. 62 (Cave 338); pl. 103 (Cave 217). Even earlier images of the Buddhist paradise appear carved onto the backs of Buddhist stele dating from the first half of the sixth century (*China 5,000* 1998, no. 151).

17. Bambling 1996, p. 82.

18. See Keswick 1978, chapter 10, n. 14, and the large tripartite panel in the Nelson Gallery (Keswick 1978, p. 41, no. 39).

Additional Buddhist paradisiacal features can be found on the base of the Tianshui couch. Along with heavenly musicians, the frontal lion on each end recalls the lions that support the Lion Throne of the Later Jin (383–417) and the gilt bronze Buddha (no. 47).

The iconography of the Tianshui couch also may refer to Daoist ideas of eternity and the associations of the "sun and moon" motif with Daoist seasonal iconography. Michelle Bambling has pointed out the positioning of the couch at the rear or south wall of the north-facing burial chamber and the placement of the side-wing bearing the sun (panel b) at the east and of the side-wing with the moon (panel j) at the west. She notes that the panels "depict a sequence of events that appear to unfold from spring to autumn, which, together with the sun and moon, align with the directions" and result in the deceased being "surrounded by a world in which the seasons and sun and moon revolve eternally in the screen's panels."[17] Daoist associations are implied further by the images on the late-fifth-century Northern Wei lacquered coffin (no. 16a), on which the rulers of Eastern and Western Daoist paradises sit in pavilions on either side of the stylized River of Life.

In contrast with the Tianshui couch and the other couches and sarcophagus, another group of stone couches, coffins, sarcophagi, and panels from similar kinds of funerary furniture exist in China and in Western collections.[18] Almost all have scenes, incised like a drawing or brush painting or carved in low relief, depicting traditional Chinese subjects, such as stories of filial piety or of winged Daoist immortals (*xian*) leading a male or female on winged tiger or dragon mounts. All are carved from the dark gray-black limestone that is characteristic of northern China, but none depicts non-Chinese being entertained by Central Asian musicians and dancers or non-Chinese drinking from a rhyton.

ALJ and JAL

Fig. I: The most "Chinese" of the images on the marble Miho funerary couch (*top left*), the two-wheeled ox cart is a common feature in Chinese tombs and Buddhist stelae and cave paintings from the fourth century on (photo: Miho Museum, Shigaraki)

Fig. J: Double panel from the Miho couch (*top right*): on the left, male and female riders move through rocky terrain; on the right, a four-armed goddess (the Sogdian Nana) peers down on two bodhisattva-like beings playing instruments, while below them musicians accompany a female dancer. (photo: Miho Museum, Shigaraki)

Fig. K: An encampment scene from the Miho couch (*bottom left*), showing long-haired Turks attending to their leader, who rests in a yurt. Below them, in the foreground, a group of riders hunt fleeing game, (photo: Miho Museum, Shigaraki)

Fig. L: A camel laden with goods, accompanied by long-haired Turks on horseback, from the Miho couch (*bottom right*) (photo: Miho Museum, Shigaraki).

1. *Kaogu* 1992.1, p. 46, fig. 1.

2. Ibid., p. 51, fig. 9; pp. 52–53.

3. Zhou and Gao 1988, pp. 76, 244–45.

4. Luo 1996, pp. 24–26, Sui tomb of Shi Shewu, died 609 CE; Yun 1993; Fourteen Northern Zhou tombs, eight with epitaph stones, were excavated near Xianyang Airport outside Xi'an in Shaanxi. None of these figures wear this wrapped and tied cloth covering on their heads.

5. Zhang 1997, p. 92.

6. Juliano 1988, nos. 72–74. Similar questions have been raised around some of the stone sculptures that have been for sale or have been purchased on the art market and added to private collections in the West.

107. *Five musicians*

Sui dynasty (581–618), early seventh century
Excavated from Tianshui
Granite with pigment and traces of gilding
Heights range from 32–33 cm
a. lute player (*pipa*)
b. reed pipe player (*sheng*)
c. transverse bamboo flute (*hengdi*)
d. cowrie-shaped calabash or ocarina? (*beili*)
e. panpipes (*paixiao*)
Tianshui Municipal Museum, Gansu

Accompanying the Tianshui stone couch are five exceptionally fine stone sculptures of seated musicians; these were placed in front of the couch, near the lions. Two were placed to the left (a,b) and three to the right (c–e); (see tomb plan in entry number 106, fig. A).[1] By their distinctive dress, cloth hats, and facial features, including deep-set eyes and pronounced straight noses, the musicians have been identified as *hujen*, non-Chinese or non-Han peoples living in the north and west.[2] Intently playing their musical instruments, the figures sit on square bases with their legs tucked to the right or left under their robes. All wear identical long, belted robes with thin, rolled collars, round necks, and tight sleeves that fasten to the left. The pointed shape of the foot visible on one musician (d) suggests that the figures wear boots and most likely have trousers under their robes. Several have extensive remains of pigment. In particular, one musician (c) playing the transverse flute displays what was clearly a painted band of lighter color, simulating fabric, perhaps embroidery; his upper arm has an armlet with extensive traces of gilding.

Apparently, this type of dress was a Sui style that continued into the early seventh century.[3] With the exception of the *sheng* player (b), the heads are covered with a type of hat consisting of a cloth wrapped around the head to the forehead and rolled and knotted in the front and back with two ends left hanging free. The slight variations in headgear visible on the four musicians (a, c–e)

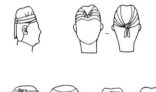

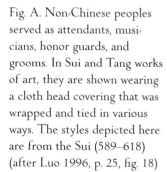

are also found on figures in Sui tombs (fig. A).[4] A group of donors from Cave 8, dated to Northern Zhou or mid-sixth century, shows similar dress, head coverings, and facial features.[5] By Tang, this kind of hat assumed a higher profile with an indentation that forms two characteristic bumps and with two ties hanging from the back. Foreign musicians, music, instruments, and dancers were a common feature of life during the late sixth and early seventh centuries and are also visible on stone couches discussed in no. 106 and Chapter 10.

Keenly observed and sensitively modeled, these five musicians offer many pleasures as figural sculpture. Although at first glance, all seem to sit in the same position with legs tucked to the side and arms raised to play their instruments, each figure's position and facial expression is actually slightly different. The individual musicians lean or twist lightly one way or another and may even kneel rather than sit, but all appear completely absorbed in their music making.

Of exceptional quality, this group of musicians is an extraordinary discovery. Stone sculptures buried in tombs are rarely found and excavated, and this group of five was uncovered in relatively good condition and in their original positions within the tomb. Most Sui and Tang stone sculpture occurs on a much larger scale, as massive honor guards lining the Spirit Road that approaches the tomb mound. The few scattered finds of stone sculpture within tombs raise a fundamental question about these objects: Were these stone sculptures in essence *mingqi*, spirit objects, replicas usually fashioned from clay and made specifically for burial? Or did these figures serve another purpose during the deceased's life and then were buried?[6] Interestingly, no clay *mingqi* were found in this tomb, as might have been expected.

ALJ

Fig. A. Non-Chinese peoples served as attendants, musicians, honor guards, and grooms. In Sui and Tang works of art, they are shown wearing a cloth head covering that was wrapped and tied in various ways. The styles depicted here are from the Sui (589–618) (after Luo 1996, p. 25, fig. 18)

no. 107a

no. 107b

no. 107e, c, d

108a–c. *Pillow, hairpin, and mirror*

Sui dynasty (589–618), early seventh century
From the tomb containing the couch and musician sculptures,
found in the environs of Tianshui
Tianshui Municipal Museum, Gansu

These objects were found on the couch described in the entry for number 106, so they mostly likely had been enclosed in the wooden coffin that contained the body or bodies.[1] We do not know whether the tomb had a sole occupant or a couple, but the hairpin and mirror probably belonged to a woman.

a. Pillow

Granite
Length: 14.5 cm; depth: 8.6 cm; height: 5.4–6.2 cm

Fig. A. Carved stone pillow, top and side views, dated to Northern Zhou dynasty (557–581) (after Osaka 1976, p. 39 fig. 4:6)

Crafted from the same granite as the mortuary couch, this rare stone pillow, rectangular in shape, with a flat bottom and a concave top, was found on the couch next to the gold hairpin (no. 106, fig. D). Nearly all the other known pillows are glazed ceramic; such pillows in ceramic became very popular later, during the tenth through fourteenth century. Although literary evidence suggests that ancient pillows were made from highly perishable materials, such as wood, woven bamboo, and lacquer, the origins of the pillow and its ceramic version remain obscure. At present, no tangible evidence of their use in the Han dynasty exists, and only a very few clay examples have been uncovered that date from the Tang. One late-Tang ceramic, lead-glazed pillow, dated to the eighth or ninth century, is in the collection of the British Museum, London (p. 305, fig. 4).

The question remains: When were stone pillows first made or introduced into China? There is one comparable stone pillow of similar shape and size, which has been embellished with relief carving and dated to the Northern Zhou dynasty (557–581) (fig. A). At one end is a deeply undercut dragon with one front paw raised; carved into the top is a clearly non-Chinese figure with large eyes, prominent hooked nose, and sharp chin, wearing a long, belted tunic and boots. The figure is enclosed in a lush border, a sinuous vine with half palmettes.

b. Hairpin

Gold

Length: 14 cm; weight: 9.7 g

The gold hairpin is the double-prong kind that has been known as early as the Han period (see the jade examples, nos. 44 and 88). It is a simple form that changed very little since its first appearance.[2] Although this plain U-shape form continues into the Tang period,[3] hairpins with molded and engraved decoration, often incorporating floral and vegetal shapes, became fashionable during that time. Since the late Han (first century CE), gold was the preferred material for such ornaments, its bright gleam showing up dramatically against the dark, heavy hair of Chinese women.

c. Mirror

Silvered bronze

Diameter: 14.5 cm; thickness: 1 cm

This bronze mirror was found lying in the center of the funerary couch near the outer edge. Broken in several pieces and reassembled, the surface also appears corroded or worn, which makes it very difficult to read the decoration accurately. The decoration has been organized into five concentric bands of varying widths. After the outer plain rim is a narrow band filled with a standard saw-tooth pattern followed by a slightly wider band of double line zigzag. Here a high plain ridge divides the central field of decoration, which is enclosed by a narrow band of parallel raised lines, and another band of sixteen evenly spaced raised bosses. A round knob handle sits in the center, surrounded by a field of unidentifiable creatures. The excavation report describes these as confronted auspicious beasts.[4] Aside from these ambiguous animals, the concentric rings have the standard mirror design decor that reaches back to at least the Han dynasty and continues through early Tang. Very few Sui mirrors are extant for comparison.

ALJ and JAL

1. *Kaogu* 1 (1992), p. 46, fig. 1:2 (pillow), 1:3 (hairpin), 1:6 (mirror); p. 52, fig. 10:2 (pillow); p. 52, figs. 11:3 (hairpin), 11:4 (mirror).

2. For the variations of this type, see Zhou and Gao 1991, p. 71, as well as the group of gold single- and double-pronged hairpins from a fifth-century tomb near Nanjing (*Wenwu* 1972.11, p. 41, fig. 44).

3. Michaelson 1999, pp. 64–65, no. 31.

4. *Kaogu* 1 (1992), p. 53: described by the director of the Tianshui Municipal Museum as possibly sea creatures because of the crablike bodies and what appear to be pincers.

1. The rosette appears as early as the fifth millennium BCE on the painted pottery of ancient Mesopotamia (present-day Iraq) (Amiet 1979, figs. 180–81).

2. Schmidt 1953, vol. 1, pl. 198; Amiet 1967, pl. 141 (guards at Susa). Rosettes, either woven or embroidered, also decorate the garments of the ninth–seventh-century BCE Assyrian kings (Amiet 1980, p. 292, fig. 122, p. 302, fig. 129).

3. Fukai and Horiuchi 1969, vol. 1, pls. LI, LVIIb, LXII; vol. II, pls. XLIV–XLVII, LIII.

4. Lukonin 1983, p. 741.

5. Shepherd 1983, p. 1107–8.

6. Watson 1983, p. 550.

7. Xu and Zhao 1996, pp. 13–27.

109. *Brocade with floral roundel motif*

Chinese; Tang dynasty (618–906), eighth century
Unknown provenance
Silk, six fragments, warp-faced compound twill
Width: 8 cm; length: 18.8 cm
Gansu Provincial Museum, Lanzhou

The main motif of this textile is a six-lobed or six-petaled rosette from which radiate six lotus buds. An undulating half-palmette scroll encircles the rosette to complete this floral roundel. Although the rose medallion was a persistently popular motif in silks of the Tang dynasty, the rosette as a textile pattern can be traced back to ancient Western Asian sources.[1] In the relief sculpture at the late-sixth–fifth-century BCE Persian Achaemenid palaces at Persepolis and Susa in Iran, rosette-filled medallions embellish the king's robes and those of some of the royal guards, while bands of rosettes decorate the canopy over the king's throne.[2] On the textiles represented in the seventh-century CE Sasanian reliefs at Taq-i Bustan in Iran, rosettes appear as isolated design units or as part of a rectangular network that encloses another motif.[3]

Persian silks with rosette designs would have been traded over the Silk Road and served as diplomatic gifts; indeed, as a prime commodity of the Persian Empire, silk was presented in tribute to kings and ambassadors and was also used to purchase allies and pay soldiers.[4] Instead of relying on China for its silk, during the fourth century Persians began to create their own sophisticated silk fabric after the Sasanian king Shapur II (r. 309–379 CE) relocated a group of weavers from Mesopotamia to Susa and other cities in the heartland of the Persian Empire.[5] There new types of silks and brocades were introduced, and it is likely that such Persian silk fabrics with rosette designs appear on the seventh-century royal reliefs of Taq-i-Bustan.

By the Sui dynasty, Persian silk had already become highly regarded in China, and several sources refer to Persian brocades and their "gold thread weave."[6] After the fall of the Sasanian Empire in 651,

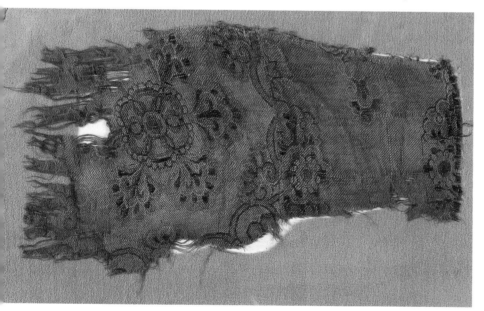

Persian textiles accompanied the Sasanian court in its exile at the Tang capital of Xi'an. It was the introduction of Persian silk with the rosette motif that proved to have a major artistic influence on Chinese weavers.

It is easy to see why exotic Persian fabric would appeal to the Chinese court. That clothing with rosette designs was fashioned for the elite is reflected in the motifs painted onto the clothing of wood tomb figures, decorating the garments of glazed pottery tomb figures, and patterning the gowns of court women featured on wall paintings. Throughout the Tang dynasty, Chinese weavers continued to transform and refine this Persian pattern, creating many complex variations similar to this example. With its elegant, naturalistic central motif, woven in blue and brown against a yellow ground, this example contains distinctive characteristics found in many Chinese brocades of the period.[7] Such Persian-inspired brocades were, in turn, popular in Sogdiana, appearing on cushions and clothing on the wall paintings at Varakhsha and Panjikent (Chapter 7, fig. 8).

JS

110. *Brocade with pheasants*

Sogdian or Chinese; Tang dynasty (618–906); eighth century
Unknown provenance
Silk, four fragments, weft-faced compound twill
Width: 10 cm; length: 20 cm
Gansu Provincial Museum, Lanzhou

By the sixth century, the *hanshou niao* motif—standing, confronted birds within a roundel, like the example featured here—had become a popular textile design in western China. It originated, however, in Persia, where it was considered a symbol of royal power and the desire for good fortune.[1] It was also a favored motif of the Sogdians, who, by the fourth century had established a series of trading posts along the famed Silk Roads into western China.[2]

Indeed, wall paintings in areas dominated by the Persians and Sogdians document the popularity of the standing-bird design. It can be seen on the clothing of attendants of the Sasanian king Khusro II (r. 591–628) on his reliefs at Taq-i Bustan, decorating the walls of the sixth–seventh-century cave at Kizil, and patterning the clothing of Sogdian nobles painted on the mid-seventh-century walls of the palace at Afrasiab (Old Samarkand).[3]

Textiles featuring *hanshou* motifs appear in wall paintings in the Sitra Cave (K-17) at Kahar-Khojo (Xinjiang) and in Cave 130 at Dunhuang (Gansu), and actual fabrics have been excavated in the cemeteries at Dulan (Qinghai).

By the fifth century, Persia was creating its own unique fabric, and expensive Persian silks imported into the Eastern Roman Empire were damaging the balance of foreign commerce to such an extent that the Byzantine emperor was advised not to purchase them.[4] Documents unearthed in Xinjiang indicate that by the late fifth century, Persian silk had already entered the Western Regions.[5] By then, the Sogdians had also mastered the production of silk fabric and began to trade directly with Constantinople, bypassing Persia.[6] Moreover, local histories document that during the Sui and early Tang periods, a Sogdian descendant was in charge of Sichuan province's imperial weaving workshops and that reproductions of Persian polychrome fabric with roundels were created there.[7]

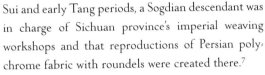

Brocades with this motif attributed to the West or its weavers (either Persian or Sogdian) have distinctive features: a weft-faced pattern with warp threads that are Z-twisted; birds that appear more geometric in shape with sharp outlines; and changes of color within the linked pearls or petal roundels, to name several.

To differentiate between Persian and Sogdian examples is a more difficult task. Sogdian silks are generally muted in color and often feature pairs of confronted birds standing on a split palm leaf tree, as opposed to their Persian counterparts, which are featured on brightly colored cloth, often with a single bird standing on a string-of-pearls platform.[8]

Although a mid-seventh-century Chinese painting of a visiting Tibetan minister depicts him wearing a robe decorated entirely of repeated *hanshou* patterns, it is believed that such fabric was usually reserved for collar, bodice, and sleeve trimming.[9]

JS

1. Xu 1996, pp. 17–21.

2. *Xinjiang daxue Xuebao* 1997.4, pp. 62–66. Xue Zongzheng states that the Sogdians migrated from their homeland to the Western Regions of China beginning in the third century BCE; however, they actually began to migrate during the fourth century BCE military campaign of Alexander the Great.

3. See *Ancient Silk Routes* 1982, p. 82, no. 19 (Kizil); Al'baum 1975, pl. VI (Afrasiab).

4. The sixth-century Byzantine historian Procopius states that monks from India advised Justinian I to begin his country's own silk industry, thus preventing the Romans from purchasing expensive Persian silks (*Wenwu tiandi* 1996.4, pp. 12–15).

5. The Chinese term for Persian silk, *bosi jin*, first appears in a manuscript unearthed at Khara Khojo (tomb M90) of the Kan dynasty in Qoco (Xinjiang), dated to 482, and in tomb inventory of objects in the later tomb M170, unearthed at Astana (Xinjiang), dated to 543 (Xu 1996, pp. 17–18).

6. Segraves 1996, pp. 54–62.

7. Watt and Wardwell 1997, pp. 23–24.

8. Xu 1996, pp. 17–21.

9. Ibid. pp. 3–10; Reynolds 1995, p. 89, fig. 3.

Fig. A. A similar textile in the Abegg-Stiftung, Riggisberg, shows roundels with pairs of confronted pheasants alternating with roundels enclosing pairs of confronted doves, Sogdian or Chinese, eighth century (after Otavsky 1998, p. 37, fig. 10)

1. Marshak 1986, figs. 55, 56, 68. A Sogdian silver ewer with a tall neck and a long handle topped by a small head in the round was found in a tenth-century tomb in Inner Mongolia and predates the burial (Rawson 1991, p. 144, with reference).

2. Rawson 1977, p. 41: "Indeed, the whole concept of working the metal cold rather than by casting, was alien to the Chinese tradition."

3. Watson 1986, p. 162.

4. See the tomb of Sima Jinlong, *Wenwu* 1972.3, pp. 20–33.

5. Watson 1986, p. 169.

6. Watson 1991, pp. 193–94. Cockerel-spouted ewers, now with dragon handles, of the Northern Qi tombs are white-glazed and embellished with applied "flamboyant ornamentation" and are themselves based on Western models. For a discussion of ceramics with molded-relief decoration, see Valenstein 1997/98, pp. 4–7.

7. Lovell 1975, p. 340. Lovell points out that there is no evidence in the Western or Sasanian work to suggest, as some have claimed, that "the 'phoenix-headed ewer is the result of contact with the Near East.' It is not until the 12th and 13th centuries that one finds such a feature on Persian ceramics of the Seljuk dynasty, in the form of rooster heads at the mouth of pottery ewers."

8. Rawson 1986, p. 43, n. 9.

111. *Phoenix-headed ewer*

Tang dynasty (618–906), second half of seventh–first half of eighth century
From a Tang dynasty tomb, discovered in the 1950s in Wushan county,
between Tianshui and Xi'an
Yellow, green, and brown lead glazes over buff earthenware
with molded relief decoration
Height: 31 m
Gansu Provincial Museum, Lanzhou

One of several lead-glazed ceramic ewers that terminate in a phoenix head, this ewer epitomizes the adaptation of foreign artistic ideas to the Chinese ceramic tradition that distinguishes Tang art. In its shape and surface treatment, the ewer reveals its debt to metalwork of Western origin, particularly that of Sogdiana. The high foot, the flattened bulbous body, the slender neck, and the elongated handle are based on Sasanian and Central Asian models, but the attachment of the upper part of the handle to the back of the bird's head, just below the rim of the vessel, is evidence of Central Asian—specifically, Sogdian—influence (fig. A), and not Sasanian, which characteristically has the upper part of the handle attached to a ewer's body instead of its rim (no. 31, fig. A).[1] The actual form of the handle is additional proof of a Sogdian heritage, for the bird's (possibly duck's) head and the sprouting tendril of the Gansu ewer handle correspond to the dragon's head and foliate attachment of the Sogdian ewer illustrated here.

The use of Sogdian rather than Sasanian metalwork models is further revealed by the background surface of the ewer's body. The raised pattern of dots is actually a molded imitation of the ring-punching used on the grounds of Sogdian silver vessels. The technique is alien to Chinese metalwork but was adopted and refined by Tang craftsmen to decorate the grounds of their silver and gold vessels.[2] Further recalling Western metalwork is the raised molded decoration of the body and foot, which imitates the repoussé technique.

The lead polychrome glaze that characterizes this ewer and others like it may be an additional mark of Western influence. Although lead glazing was known in China since at least as early as Han times, it was equally at home in Western and Central Asia.[3] Lead glazes in more than one color can be documented in China from at least as early as the late fifth century,[4] and the use of three-color technique, or *sancai*, is a hallmark of Tang ceramics. On this vessel, the way in which the splashed glaze highlights the raised and smooth areas is testimony to the technological expertise of the potter. Such polychrome application has been likened to the gilding that covers contemporary silver dishes.[5]

Despite these strong parallels with Western, and especially Central Asian, metalwork, the ewer and others like it grew out of a Chinese ceramic tradition that goes back to at least the third century

Fig. A. Gilded-silver ewer with a winged camel on each side, found at Malzewa, Perm region, Russia. Sogdian, end of the seventh century–beginning of the eighth century (photo courtesy of the State Hermitage Museum, St. Petersburg)

CE. A standard form of stoneware ewer, embellished with a cockerel-headed spout, had developed in eastern China and expanded north and west, where it occurs in sixth-century Northern Qi tombs and continues into the Sui dynasty.[6] The modeled bird's head of the spout also seems to be a Chinese invention.[7]

The ewer belongs to a group of vessels manufactured in north China specifically for burial in tombs. Made in shapes that are appropriate to metalwork, they served as substitutes for the more precious materials, silver and gold.[8]

JAL

1. Fontein and Wu 1973, p. 149. For examples, see Watson 1962, pl. 67b; So 1995, vol. III, pp. 279, 282, fig. 50.3.

2. Another is the greenish glazed *bian hu* with an upright spiky, five-lobed palmette (see Tseng and Dart 1964).

3. On the white glazed *bian hu* from the tomb of the Sui princess, Li Jingxun (d. 608) and an identical one in Toronto (Fontein and Wu 1973, p. 162, figs. 80 and 77, respectively).

4. Watson 1984, p. 23, fig. 11 (in the Museum für Ostasiatische Kunst, Berlin).

5. Mowry 1996, no. 2, pp. 82–85 (in the Metropolitan Museum of Art); Vainker 1991, p. 63, fig. 45 (in the British Museum).

6. Watson 1984, p. 144, fig. 123 (in the British Museum).

7. Rawson 1982, p. 8.

8. Valenstein 1997–98, pp. 2–13.

9. See note 3 above. A band of "pearls," not raised as from a mold, but incised, decorates the almost heart-shaped body of a celadon-glazed stoneware *bian hu* that is dated to the third or fourth century CE; it seems to be an intermediary form, between the Late Eastern Zhou bronzes and the Northern Qi and later ceramic models (Tseng and Dart 1964, vol. I, no. 14).

10. Medley 1981, p. 20, figs. 4, 5 (this unusual rhyton is of white porcelaneous ware with an octagonal top terminating in a lion's head, British Museum).

11. Rawson 1991, p. 145, fig. 7. Such ewers decorated with beading, figural roundels, and floral motifs in high relief are related to the ewer discussed under entry number 110.

112. *Pilgrim flask* (bian hu *or "flattened jar"*)

Northern Zhou or Sui dynasty, c. 550–600
Unknown provenance
Reddish earthenware with molded relief decoration
Height: 21 cm; greatest width: 18.6 cm; thickness: 9.5 cm
Gansu Provincial Museum, Lanzhou

This vessel is characterized by its prominent lip, short cylindrical neck, flattened ovoid body, high splayed foot, and horizontal loop handle on each shoulder. Although similar examples in bronze are known as early as the Late Eastern Zhou period (fourth–third century BCE),[1] ceramic examples, both glazed and unglazed, with molded decoration seem to begin in the Northern Zhou and Northern Qi, and flourish in the Sui and Tang periods.

These so-called pilgrim flasks are typically ornamented with a single bold image in relief that fills each of the two identical sides, a stylized foliate shape (like the hanging palmette here),[2] a winged monster mask,[3] an eagle trampling on a monstrous snake,[4] a phoenix amid scrolling grapevines,[5] or a complex figural scene, such as that from the Northern Qi tomb at Anyang, depicting a Central Asian dancer and musicians (no. 81, fig. B).[6] The palmette is not an indigenous Chinese motif but an import from the West, having reached China by the fifth century.[7] From the beaded border at the neck of the Anyang *bian hu*, a palmette hangs above the dancing Central Asian. Large jars with heavy applied decoration that feature hanging (as well as upright) palmettes, along with monstrous faces and lotus petals, have been found in China, in tombs of the Northern Qi and Sui; interestingly, many of these tombs belong to nobles of nomadic origin. The decoration of these jars can be related to that found on earthenware from the oasis area of Khotan (Xinjiang) on the southern Silk Road, which, in turn, can be traced to several Western sources, Greece and Gandhara included.[8]

The use of beads or pearls to form rosettes in the spaces around the palmette, to punctuate its leaves and to frame the entire composition, is a decorative device known from Central Asian textiles and employed extensively in the Sui and Tang. A pearled or beaded band also surrounds the monster mask on the *bian hu* found in the Sui princess Li Jingxun's tomb,[9] while bands and rosettes formed of beads or pearls figure prominently in the decoration of a ceramic rhyton of the Tang period,[10] as well as on some of the phoenix-headed ceramic ewers so characteristic of the Tang.[11]

JAL

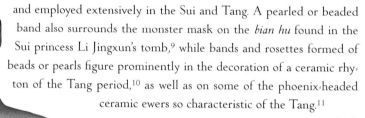

113. *Figure of a dwarf (Kubera?)*

Tang dynasty (618–906), seventh–eighth century
From Longxi county, between Lanzhou and Tianshui, Gansu
Earthenware
Height: 9.5 cm; greatest width: 5 cm
Gansu Provincial Museum, Lanzhou

The Tang fascination with the exotic may account for this figure's appearance in China. Wearing a cloak that seems too long for him, his short legs swathed in leggings and placed wide apart, the figure turns slightly to his right to grasp a jar close to his body. The blunt features of his oversize head and his shortened limbs mark him as a dwarf. His garb and his hair, which is combed forward to end in a row of forehead curls and bound with a fillet, identify him as non-Chinese.

Although dwarfs occasionally appear among Chinese tomb sculpture (*mingqi*), none looks quite like this fellow,[1] nor do the so-called *kunluns*, foreigners with short, curly hair and dark skin who were a favorite subject for *mingqi* in the Tang period.[2] While *kunluns* wear draped garments and some are rendered with exaggerated features, none share the ill proportions or fierce expression of this figure.

In this regard, the figure's glaring eyes, his corpulence, and his association with a vessel that could hold wine or coins suggest a link with the Indian Kubera, king of the *yakshas*, lord of the northern quadrant, and god of wealth and prosperity, who is typically depicted as a pot-bellied dwarf clutching a wine cup or with a vessel containing money.[3] In the Buddhist art of Gandhara and Bactria, Kubera appears in an Indian dhoti in bacchanalian scenes, an equivalent of the Hellenistic Dionysus[4]; as late as the seventh to eighth century, he occurs at the Buddhist site of Kuva (present-day Uzbekistan) as a wine-drinking deity.[5] In Gandhara, Kubera is also correlated with Panchika, general of the army of *yakshas*, who, with his consort Hariti, is associated with riches and fertility. Images of Panchika often show him wearing a cloak, along with a short, belted tunic and leggings.[6] Although both Kubera and Panchika wear fillets on their heads, the very specific hairstyle of straight locks ending in waves on the forehead is closest to classicizing heads found in Sogdiana on metalwork of the seventh century.[7]

The figure is made in a single mold and so is flat on the back. It has been suggested that such frontality is a reflection of Buddhist sculpture, which emphasized the frontal view for use in temples.[8] Indeed, small terracotta sculptures of seated Buddhas and bodhisattvas have been found at Buddhist sites in Uzbekistan, each made from a single mold and curved on the back as if to fit into a devotee's hand.[9] A further reflection of Buddhist sculpture is in the lotus petals that decorate the base of the figure.

In the highly syncretic world of Buddhist art as it developed in Gandhara and continued in Bactria and elsewhere in Central Asia, this figure seems to represent some beneficent demon or guardian, meant to be carried and kept as a personal talisman. Perhaps some monk or other traveler lost it as he passed through what is today Longxi, or some resident of the area returning home brought it with him and chose to have it accompany him in his tomb.

JAL

1. See the dwarfs from the tomb of Zheng Ren Tai (buried 664) (*Wenwu* 1972.7, p. 42, figs. 5–6) and those gathered for a China House Gallery Exhibition (Schloss 1969, nos. 21–28).

2. Although *kunlun* refers specifically to those countries bordering on the South China Sea—a source of gold and other luxuries—and to the people who lived there, the term was also applied to any person with curly hair and dark skin; hence, East Africans, who entered Tang China as slaves, are also called *kunlun*. See Mahler 1959, pp. 84–88, pls. XXIII–XXIV.

3. One Indian text states that Kubera, as well as the other *yakshas*, should have big bellies, hold treasures in their hands, and be shown fierce because of drunkenness (Sahai 1975, p. 60). I wish to thank Vishakha Desai for suggesting the figurine's resemblance to Kubera.

4. See the Kushan seated Kubera of the third–fourth century CE (Czuma 1985, no. 54, pp. 126–27) and the stone capital of similar date from Kara-tepe in Bactria (Stavisky 1997, p. 50, fig. 21).

5. Thus, on a bronze disk a seated Kubera is shown in the dhoti, a nimbus surrounding his head and a rhyton raised to his lips (Abdullaev, Rtveladze, and Shishkina 1991, vol. 2, p. 84, no. 501). Kuva is on the road that links the Ferghana Valley of Uzbekistan-Kyrghyzstan with the northern route through the Taklamakan Desert by way of Kashgar.

6. For example, the third–century relief group from Takht-i-Bahi and the fourth-century gold plaque from Taxila (Errington and Cribb 1992, no. 136, pp. 134–35, no. 144, p. 144.)

7. Marshak 1986, fig. 70 (silver cup from the Firunze region, Kyrghyzstan); Abdullaev, Rtveladze, and Shishkina 1991, vol. 2, p. 81, no. 498 (bronze disk from the Koktash cemetery, Ferghana, Kyrgyzstan).

Such Hellenistic features and themes survive in Central Asia and are also evident in some ceramics of the Chinese Tang. See Watson 1984, p. 147, fig. 126, pilgrim flask decorated with Greek-like figures among vines (Chapter 10, fig. 2).

8. Kosei Ando, "Burial Objects—Models of Worldly Comfort," in Akiyama 1968, p. 145.

9. See Staviskij 1998, pp. 138–41, 145, figs. 102–105, 107 (on a lotus base); these images range from the second into the sixth century CE. Throughout Central Asia representations of other deities (specifically a goddess with a mirror) appear as single-mold sculptures.

1. Zhou and Gao 1988, p. 76. See also a chart (pp. 244–45) on the dynastic evolution of male costume.

2. Mahler 1959, p. 115. See also p. 187, fig. 9.

3. Zhou and Gao 1988, p. 77.

4. Zhang 1995, p. 107. This fresco on the west wall of the passageway in Li Xian's tomb shows a foreign envoy with similar dress and without a hat.

5. Barnhart 1997, pp. 60–61. This painting is attributed to Yan Liben of the Tang dynasty but may be a Song copy. See also Zhou and Gao 1988, pp. 82–83.

6. Ibid.

7. Mahler 1959, p. 115.

Fig. A. Foreign envoy painted on west wall in the passage of the tomb of Li Xi'an, prince Zhang Huai (buried 706) (after Zhang 1995, p. 107, no. 118)

114. *Figure of a foreigner*

Tang dynasty (618–906), seventh–eighth century
Found in Shandan, Gansu
Clay with remains of black pigment
Height: 29.5 cm
Shandan Municipal Museum on loan to Gansu Provincial Museum, Lanzhou

This earthenware figure of a man still retains traces of unfired black pigment. He has curly hair, a prominent nose, and wide-set eyes with pupils far apart; his mouth is slightly open. The figure wears a robe that falls to mid-calf, with round collar and narrow sleeves, and leather boots. His hands are clasped on his chest above his bulging belly. Although the figure was made in a mold, there is some modeling by hand on the elements of the face.

The dress of this figure is typical of male costumes in the seventh century, which follows the patterns of the Sui dynasty.[1] However, in the Tang dynasty, the typical outfit had changed from a long robe to this

style of medium-length tunic with a high, round neck, worn over trousers and cinched with a narrow belt.[2] Before this time, men had to wear shoes when entering the imperial court, but beginning in the Tang, they were permitted to wear boots.[3] The costume on this figure resembles that of a foreign envoy painted on the west wall of the tomb of Li Xian, who was reburied in 706 with the title Prince Zhang Huai, near Xi'an in Shaanxi province (fig. A).[4] It is also similar to that of a foreign envoy depicted in the painting *The Imperial Sedan Chair* attributed to Yan Liben of the Tang dynasty. The colophon on this painting records the event as taking place in 641 CE.[5] In addition, the costume also resembles that of figures in wall paintings in the Tang-dynasty tomb of Li Zhongren in Qian county in Shaanxi province.[6] By the eighth century, men's fashion changed again. Although the tunics were similar in appearance, they were longer, usually reaching the ankles, and men wore distinctive black caps.[7] During the Tang, figurines of foreigners were often placed in tombs, reflecting both the cosmopolitan nature of society and the many foreigners who entered China across the Silk Road.

SB

115. *Platter*

Provincial Roman, second–third century CE?
Accidental find, Beitan township, Jingyuan county, Gansu
Silver with traces of gilding
Height: 4.4 cm; diameter: 31 cm; weight: 3,180 g
Gansu Provincial Museum, Lanzhou

This elaborately decorated platter is divided into three concentric bands that surround a central medallion.[1] The outermost band, executed in repoussé, is filled with a complex interlace of grapevines and ivy, inhabited by birds, insects, and reptiles. A narrow beaded border separates it from a circular band that contains the busts of the twelve Olympian gods accompanied by their symbols. In the center, in high relief, an epicene Dionysous lounges on the back of a feline, his cloak draped behind him and his thyrsus, or staff, resting against his shoulder.

The Roman silver expert François Baratte notes the uniqueness of the platter's style and imagery and hence the difficulty in dating and attributing it to a particular part of the Roman world.[2] However, a workshop in an eastern province of the Roman Empire, such as Egypt or Syria, is likely. Enhancing this attribution is, as Martha Carter observes, its "coherent iconographic program with overtones of Neoplatonism."[3] A Late Roman philosophy, which originated in Egypt, Neoplatonism holds Dionysous as the highest divinity, embodying all the other Olympian gods. The band of deities framing a central divine image has parallels in Western art in the celestial or zodiacal ring enclosing the frontal bust of a deity or ruler that is a device of exaltation[4]; in fact, the bust of Dionysus is placed at the uppermost part of the band. By placing Dionysus in the center of the platter in high relief and again in the intermediary band in a position of honor among the Olympian gods, and then

1. *Wenwu* 1990.5, pp. 1–9; Pirazzoli-
t'Serstevens 1982, pp. 21–22; Laing
1995, p. 10; Carter 1995, pp. 260–61;
Baratte 1996, pp. 142–47.

2. Baratte 1996, p. 146.

3. Carter 1995, pp. 260, 265 n. 12.

4. Richard Brilliant in Weitzmann 1979,
no. 160, pp. 181–82: a first–second-century CE relief from Jordan with the bust
of Atargatis/Tyche surrounded by a
ring with the signs of the Zodiac, a
telling example of "the assimilation of
classical forms and images into an
indigenous artistic mode in the service
of ritual," and a "common phenomenon
in the eastern provinces of the late
Roman empire."

5. Baratte 1996, p. 145.

6. Martha L. Carter, entry no. 24 in
Harper 1978, pp. 72–73, no. 24.

7. Sims-Williams 1995, p. 225. In the
original Chinese publication and that of
Pirazzoli-t'Serstevens, the inscription
appears upside down.

8. Carter (Harper 1978, p. 265 n. 12)
makes the tantalizing observation that
the platter might have been owned by a
follower of Neoplatonism, perhaps even
by the last imperial advocate of that
philosophy, Julian, who lost his life in
363 at Ctesiphon (in present-day Iraq)
while at war with the Sasanian king
Shapur II (r. 309–379). She notes that
Shapur II went on from this victory to
defeat by Hunnish armies in the territory of the old Kushan Empire in the
East. Might that explain how the platter traveled from the Sasanian capital
of Ctesiphon all the way to Bactria?

Bactrian inscription (*above*)
in *pointillé* on the underside
of the platter (after Sims-
Williams 1995, p. 225)

Drawing of the platter (*right*)
(after *Wenwu* 1990.5, p. 2, fig. 1)

surrounding him with luxuriant and densely populated vegetation, the artist shows the dominance and rule of the god of wine over a truly universal "golden age."[5]

The interwoven vines that fill the outer zone of the platter belong to the classical repertoire of Dionysiac motifs that had spread by the third century CE from the Roman East into Kushan Bactria and India and eventually into China (nos. 116, 117).[6] Their dense regularity betrays a *horror vacui* that may be characteristic of its place of manufacture. Whatever its origins, the platter is a provin-cial Roman work. The figure of Dionysous is awkwardly rendered; his animal mount has the spots of a panther, as in classical Dionysian images, but its mane is that of a lion, a variant found in provin-cial workshops.

On the back of the platter, on the inside of the foot, is an incised inscription. Written in *pointillé*, the script is a variety of the Greek cursive used in Bactria in the Sasanian period.[7] Basing evidence on some of the letter forms, Nicholas Sims-Williams has dated the inscription to "not later than the early sixth century." He interprets the letters as indicating the weight of the silver, i.e., 1,000 + 20. Since the weight of the platter is given as 3,180 grams, the unit of measurement, according to Sims-Williams, would be approximately 3.12 grams, smaller than the Sasanian *drachm* of approximately 4 grams (see glossary and p. 273), and perhaps representing a local Bactrian standard.

The platter was found during the construction of a peasant's house, on the northern route to Xi'an, which ran from Wuwei or Lanzhou, north of the Yellow River to the administrative center of Guyuan. Perhaps buried for safekeeping or part of the contents of a plundered tomb, the platter exemplifies the "life" of a luxury object on the Silk Road: fashioned somewhere in the Roman West in the second or third century CE, exported to Bactria where it acquired its inscription sometime before the early sixth century, and eventually brought or traded into the Gansu corridor, where it remained, first in use and then buried, until its discovery in 1988.[8]

JAL

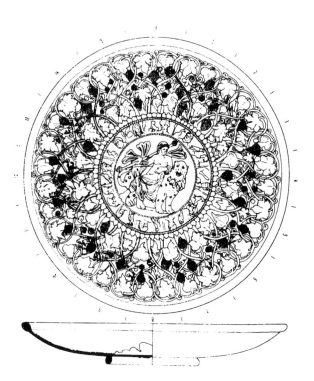

116. *Mirror*

Sui (589–618) to Tang dynasty (618–906), late sixth–early seventh century
Silvered bronze
Diameter: 13.7 cm
Gansu Provincial Museum, Lanzhou

117. *Mirror*

Tang dynasty (618–906), early eighth century
Silvered bronze
Diameter: 20.7 cm
Gansu Provincial Museum, Lanzhou

The "lion and grape" pattern is perhaps the best-known decorative program appearing on the famous bronze mirrors of the Tang. Both these bronze silvered mirrors (nos. 116, 117) have been embellished with this rich and complex decor. Lush vines laden with bunches of grapes and sometimes inhabited by birds, insects, and small animals are combined with four to as many as nine lionlike creatures as well as other animals. Although these mirrors were immensely popular in the Tang, this decor was abandoned by the mid-ninth century shortly before the fall of the dynasty and did not reappear.[1]

Twelfth-century Song dynasty antiquarians catalogued several lion-and-grapevine mirrors in the Imperial Palace Collection, assigning them a Han-dynasty date, which they established by the introduction of the grape from Bactria upon the return of Zhang Qian, the court emissary, in 126 BCE. These Song scholars assumed that this fruit-laden vine had made a deep impression on Han culture.[2]

Early artistic representations of the grapevine reached China from the West, carried by trade and Buddhism during the centuries following the collapse of the Han dynasty. From the fifth through the late sixth century, a small number of examples are found on western metalwork in China and in a Buddhist context. An extraordinary interlacing of grapevines and ivy inhabited by birds, insects, and reptiles fills the surface of the silver platter, most likely of provincial Roman manufacture that eventually found its way to Gansu (no. 115). Another inhabited and tendriled grapevine embellishes the chalicelike gilt-bronze cup dated to the fifth century, also believed to be eastern Roman, found

1. The late Schuyler Cammann proposed that "marriage mirrors" with their imagery of paired phoenixes and other auspicious animals obviously referring to marriage symbolism eventually supplanted the lion-and-grape motif (Cammann 1953, pp. 278–91).

2. The historiography of the lion and grapevine mirror has been recounted by Thompson 1967, p. 26, and Cammann 1953, pp. 265–70. The Song scholars who attributed the lion and grapevine mirrors to the Han dynasty, Wang Fu and his assistants, compiled the well-known illustrated catalogue of the Song imperial bronze collection, the *Bogu tulu* about 1125. Although grapes were brought from Central Asia during the Western Han, there is not much evidence for Chinese either making or drinking grape wine before the Tang dynasty. A sixth-century agricultural treatise, *Qimin yaoshu* (Essential Arts of the Common People), compiled between 533 and 544 by Jia Sixie, a local official in the north, contains a long citation on methods for growing and storing grapes but does not mention wine (Knetchges 1997, pp. 231–32, 238).

3. *Wenhua* 1972, p. 151.

4. *Longmen* 1991, pls. 81, 82; Yungang, Cave 12, around the window; Rawson 1982, p. 52, no. 44. These are not true grapevines but half palmettes with bunches of grapes attached.

5. Juliano 1992, fig. XI (slab in Boston).

6. Soper 1967a. addendum, p. 55.

no. 116

no. 117

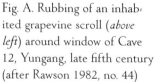

Fig. A. Rubbing of an inhab‑
ited grapevine scroll (*above
left*) around window of Cave
12, Yungang, late fifth century
(after Rawson 1982, no. 44)

Fig. B. Gilt‑bronze footed cup
(*above center*) from Datong
(Shanxi) (after *Wenhua* 1972,
p. 151)

Fig. C. Carved grapevines
(*above right*) from mandorla
from Milei niche outside
Cave XVI at Longmen
Cave Temple, Luoyang,
Henan, end of fifth century
(after *Longmen* 1991, pl. 82)

with a group of other vessels in a southern suburb of Datong, Shanxi province, dated to the fifth cen‑
tury (fig. B).[3] At the cave temples of Yungang in Shanxi and Longmen in Luoyang, carved borders
are filled with inhabited grapevines, part of a mandorla framing a Buddha image (figs. A, C); they
also border a window entrance, both dating to the late fifth century.[4] In another example, stone slabs
from a funerary couch said to have been found in Zhangdefu near Anyang in Henan, dated to the
Northern Qi (550–577) and now in Boston, depict Central Asians sitting on a Chinese‑style plat‑
form under an arbor dense with grapevines and drinking from a rhyton and shallow cups (see no.
106, fig. E).[5] During the late sixth and early seventh centuries, or Sui and Tang dynasties, grapevines
were combined with animals and adapted to the mirror format in a motif that gained in popularity
to the mid‑eighth century.

Two types of lion‑and‑grape pattern mirrors have been found in Gansu, the emerging Sui and
the fully developed Tang. The decor on the mirror in number 116, which falls into the "Sui" type,
divides into two concentric bands with the outer band containing a Chinese poem in twenty‑four
characters and the inner with five foxlike animals energetically chasing each other around the cen‑
tral knob against a background of grapevines. The poem consists of six lines, each line with four
characters. A group of these mirrors inscribed with elegant, somewhat artificial but evocative poems
has been ascribed to the Sui, particularly since a few of the poems included the two characters *jen
shou* (benevolence and longevity), which are closely associated with the reign of the first Sui
emperor (r. 601–604).[6] None of the inscribed poems offer specific dates, and the poems are usu‑
ally not connected to the imagery of the mirror. The decor on these earlier mirrors begins with a
focus on the animals symbolic of the four directions[7] and then moves to auspicious creatures that
later become identified as lions.[8] This example of a Sui‑type mirror does have a poem, although
without the *jen shou* characters. The poet rhapsodizes about the shining moon and its reflection in
the water, relating the sheen of the moon to the mirror and citing the four directional animals that
are not represented on this mirror.[9] The combination of the five animals, which are not yet lions,
with the grapevine on this mirror suggests that it represents a transitional type bridging from the
end of the Sui into the early Tang.[10]

As noted above, there was a small number of representations of grapevines in the sixth century.
By the mid‑seventh century, interest in the grape and grapevine was revitalized in a new context as trib‑
ute gifts of grapes and cuttings were sent to the capital, and wine was made not only from imported
grapes but also from local varieties of small wild grapes.[11] This second type of mirror (no. 117) reflects

the full development of the luxuriant Tang lion and grape mirror decor.[12] As on the provincial Roman plate, the surface of the mirror teems with dense grapevines, birds, and auspicious animals. However, the birds, insects, and reptiles on the plate truly inhabit the grape and ivy vines, deftly tucked into and perched on vines or grapes, while the Chinese version superimposes the animals on top of the vines.

This Tang mirror reflects the early eighth-century style with three concentric rings: an outer border of evenly spaced small flowers composed of clusters of seven small, raised dots, like granulation, enclosing a band with grapevines and creatures, including flying birds; a raised ridge delineates the central field with six animals presumed to be lions accompanied by a pair of phoenixes. The seventh lion forms the central knob. A very similar mirror without the narrow border at the edge was excavated from the Tang-dynasty tomb of Li Shouyi, dated 694 from Henan. The mirror contains four lions in the center field with a fifth as the central knob, and on the outer rim, grapevines with ten long-tailed birds, possibly parrots.[13]

These mirrors have long been admired for their beauty but have also stirred considerable controversy among western scholars in the first half of the twentieth century.[14] What does the combination of the lion and grapevine symbolize? Explanations have ranged from the Tang fascination with the exotic to the symbolism of the grape as embodying luxurious eating, drinking, and plenty[15] to the popularity of the five-lion dance introduced into the Tang court from Kucha.[16] Almost all potential interpretations acknowledge the connection to the auspicious symbols fundamental to the Chinese decorative vocabulary. Amorphous lionlike creatures, some more authentically leonine than others, appear on Sui mirrors before the grapevine was incorporated. These creatures became accepted alternatives to the animals of the four directions. The lion also carries strong Buddhist connotations and never completely loses its exoticism. Although not indigenous to China, lions began arriving at the Chinese capital as tribute starting in the Han; Parthia sent a lion in 87 CE, and the practice continued into the Sui and Tang. Two years after Taizong ascended the throne in 628 CE, a lion was sent from Samarkand (city state of Sogdiana) as tribute. It was uncrated in the market place of the capital, Changan, and described as follows: "It glares its eyes, and lightning flashes; it vents its voice, and thunder echoes."[17] Still, few artists would have had the opportunity to observe real lions but rather relied on the familiar, copying Buddhist versions or basing their depictions on traditional Chinese representations of imaginary beasts.[18]

ALJ

7. The animals of the four directions, *siling* or *sishen*, included the White Tiger of the West, Green Dragon of the East, Red Bird of the South, and Black Warrior (turtle wrapped with snake) of the North.

8. Soper argues that this Sui mirror type most likely originated under the Liang dynasty in the south and was probably imported by the Northern Qi court in the mid-sixth century to decorate the palace; the mirror design was continued by the Sui and Tang (Soper 1967a, addendum, pp. 59–66).

9. The poetry is highly formulaic, a familiar type of composition called the "Palace Style," that developed in the Liang Dynasty (502–557) in the south and flourished in sophisticated circles during the second half of the sixth century (Soper 1967a, addendum, pp. 55–56).

10. Thompson 1967, pp. 34–35.

11. Schafer 1963, 1981, pp. 141–44; according to Laufer 1919, p. 232, about 640, the Chinese learned from people of Turkestan to ferment grapes and make wine. However, it appears that the Chinese may have known how to make wine from grapes as early as the third century CE as Cao Pi, the Emperor Wen of the Wei dynasty (220–264), one of the Three Kingdoms, paid an early tribute to the grape and grape wine. "They also can be used to brew wine, which is sweeter than brewed from ale. From it, one can get goodly drunk but easily recover" (quoted in Knechtges 1997, p. 238).

12. Tang mirror, *Sichou* 1994, no. 118; *Maijishan* 1991, no. 86.

13. *Kaogu* 1986.5, p. 431, fig. 4, pp. 429–57.

14. A review of the footnotes in the three articles about lion and grape mirrors will provide a cross section of the literature and the various interpretations (Cammann 1953; Thompson 1967; Soper 1967, addendum).

15. Cammann 1953, p. 275.

16. Ibid., pp. 274–75. Camman discusses what he believes is a connection between the lion and grape mirror symbolism and the Manichean religion, or "Religion of Light." The "five lion" imagery could symbolize the Manichean Five Bodies of Light, Five Elements, and grapes as "fruits of light" suitable fare for ascetic adepts (pp. 284–91).

17. Munro 1971, p. 81.

18. Thompson 1967, p. 37.

1. Ring punching is a non-Chinese metalworking technique that is found on Sogdian metalwork as a background motif. It was also adapted as a decorative pattern in ceramics (see Phoenix-headed ewer, no. 111 in this catalogue).

2. The detailed evolution of comb shapes and materials is described in Zhou and Gao 1988, pp. 80–81.

3. Gyllensvard 1957, p. 49.

4. *Wenwu* 1986.5, pp. 68–69, 77, pl. 5.

5. *Wenwu* 1980.5, pl. 5.

6. Gyllensvard 1957, fig. 12e.

7. *Ladies Preparing Newly Woven Silk* by Emperor Huizong; copy of an eighth-century painting by Zhang Xuan. In Barnhart 1997, pp. 78–79.

8. Tait 1986, p. 115, fig. 255, Stein painting 47.

9. Gyllensvard 1965a, p. 166. See also a similar Tang silvered-bronze comb with birds and flowers, fig. 1-A.

10. Bush 1976, pp. 40–83.

Fig. A. Tang-dynasty gilt-bronze comb (*bottom right*). The British Museum, London (photo: © The British Museum)

118. *Comb with birds*

Tang dynasty (618–907), eighth century
Found near Qingyang, Gansu
Gilded bronze
Height: 10.7 cm; weight: 12.8 cm
Gansu Provincial Museum, Lanzhou

This comb is made of a thin sheet of hammered bronze, which was then gilded. The handle is decorated in repoussé with two large birds on a ground of scrolling leaves. The birds have delicate detailing of the hairs on their heads and under their necks, and their feathers are carefully defined. The raised birds are placed among foliage on a ring-punched background.[1] The central part of the design is separated from the outer rim by two rows of repoussé dots, which mimic granulation; these dots also form the outer border of the handle. The outer rim is further decorated with leaves that radiate along the border. The teeth of the comb are cut from the same piece of bronze as the top, with the end prong thicker than the others, and the right-end prong missing.

This general comb shape, crafted from wood, emerges in the Warring States period.[2] Although the shape was not popular during the Qin and Western Han dynasties, it became the standard type commonly found from the Eastern Han through the Tang dynasty. During that period the comb handle became wider and the materials used changed from wood and bone to gold and gilded metals. An excavated wood comb from the Han tomb at Lolang is similar in shape.[3] Similar combs have also been excavated from a Tang tomb at Yangzhou in Jiangsu province[4] and a Northern Song tomb in Jiangxi province.[5] Another comparable gilt-bronze Tang comb with birds is in the British Museum, London (fig. A).[6]

During the Tang dynasty, combs as well as hairpins and large headdresses were the most important piece of jewelry that women wore. Combs were worn as decoration high atop women's hair, as can be seen from paintings from the Tang dynasty such as *Ladies Preparing Newly Woven Silk* by Zhang Xuan,[7] as well as in a painting of a donor patron from Dunhuang.[8] The bird and flower motif on this comb (no. 118) became especially popular during the Tang, when flowers were a common decorative design in part because of the rising influence of Buddhism.[9] Floral motifs enter the decorative vocabulary during the Period of Disunity; the vocabulary is rich and varied and by the Tang becomes quite lush.[10]

SB

119. *Horse trapping*

Tang dynasty (618–907), seventh–eighth century
Found near Huachi, Gansu
Gilded bronze
Height: 7.7 cm; width: 6.5 cm
Gansu Provincial Museum, Lanzhou

This ornament is called an apricot leaf, or *xingye*, and was placed on the crupper, breast strap, and other parts of a horse's harness, hung by the small round hole that is molded into its top. Such ornaments were hung from the harness around a horse's neck and also on its haunches.[1] This object's borders are filled with foliage in deep relief. The top-right register shows a horseman in full gallop twisting backward in his saddle to shoot at a bird. His left arm is bent, and his fingers are poised for the shot as his body remains taut. This "Parthian shot" motif is common in Sasanian silver vessels and is an import from Persia. Above the hunter is a bird that floats in midair on delicately striated wings. Below is a deer with branching antlers. In the lower left register, another horseman lances a large animal, perhaps a lion, which is leaping toward him. The exquisite detailing of this object complements its balanced composition.

Xingye ornaments entered China across the Silk Road from Persia. These and other harness adornments were influenced by Sasanian equestrian decorative elements.[2] In Han times, however, a brow ornament called *mayang* or *danglu* was also an antecedent of the *xingye* and is shown in pottery figures found at Yangjiawan, Xianyang, Shaanxi province. These Han ornaments may in turn have been influenced by equestrian elements found in the Altai at Pazyryk in Central Asia, which are dated fourth to third century BCE.[3]

The horse was an instrument of diplomacy and military policy in Tang China. Hunting themes were common in Tang art, as can be seen from the famous murals painted in the tomb of Prince Zhanghui, whose remains were reburied in a large tomb completed no later than 706 near Xi'an. The deer motif with branching antlers was popular with the Xiongnu in the Spring and Autumn and Warring States periods, after this motif had entered China from Bactria. By the Tang, however, deer were rarely depicted with such antlers; when presented in this way, the antlers were usually flat and were meant to resemble *lingzhi* fungus, which was a sign of immortality.[4]

A similar *xingye* gilded-bronze horse ornament was excavated from the tomb of Princess Yongtai near Xi'an. Although slightly smaller than this treasure from the Gansu Provincial Museum, it has similar foliage on its borders and a bird in the center of the ornament.[5] The ornament also has a round hole in its top. Other *xingye* ornaments have been found with purely floral motifs, a pair of lions or a pair of birds surrounded by foliage, and a supernatural horse flying over mountains and also surrounded with foliage,[6] an allusion to the divine horses of Ferghana from Central Asia. Ceramic horses with similar ornaments hanging from their harnesses have been excavated from Tang tombs in Henan province and in Shaanxi province (fig. A).[7] The ceramic ornaments are the same shape as the *xingye* ornament displayed here and also have foliage decorating their borders.

SB

1. *Kaogu* 1992.11, p. 1008, detailed drawing fig. 8.

2. Sun 1981, pp. 82–88, 96: English abstract by Chauncey Goodrich in Dien 1985, pp. 1982–87. Also see Yang 1984, pp. 45–54, 76.

3. Ibid., p. 85.

4. Qi 1996, pp. 15–18.

5. This was seen by the author in June 2000 at the museum adjacent to Princess Yongtai's tomb near Xi'an, Shaanxi province. The museum label noted that eight such ornaments had been found in the tomb, although only one was on display.

6. Sun 1981, p. 85, fig. 7, nos. 4–8.

7. Pottery horse with harness in *sancai* glaze, no. 68 in *Treasures of Chang'an* 1993, pp. 186–87, excavated in 1959.

Fig. A. *Sancai* pottery horse with similar *xingye* ornaments hanging from the harness and also hanging from the bridle below the horse' ears (from Hong Kong 1992, p. 99, no. 66)

120. *Set of nested reliquaries*

Tang dynasty (618–907), dated 649

Excavated in 1964 from the Temple of the Great Clouds (*Dayunsi*) in Jingchuan County, Gansu

a. Stone sarcophagus box: height: 42.5 cm; width: 49.5 cm; length: 50.5 cm

b. Gilded-bronze reliquary: height: 13.2 cm; width: 12.3 cm;
length: 12.3 cm; weight: 590 g

c. Silver reliquary: height: 9.3 cm; width: 8.4 cm; length: 8.4 cm; weight: 350 g

d. Gold reliquary: height: 6 cm; width: 5.4 cm; length: 7.5 cm; weight: 110 g

e. Glass *sarira* bottle with relic of fourteen grains: diameter of body: 2.1 cm; diameter of mouth: 0.5
cm; height: 2.6 cm

Gansu Provincial Museum, Lanzhou

This set of nested reliquaries was excavated from the underground burial chamber of the pagoda at the Temple of the Great Clouds (*Dayunsi*). The five-part set was found intact inside a stone chamber that had guardian figures, *apsaras*, and heavenly kings carved on its walls and door lintels.[1]

Fig. A. Reliquaries and glass bottle from Qingshan Temple, Lintong, Shaanxi (after *Zhongguo* 1996, vol. 10, p. 37, pl. 75)

The outermost container is a nearly square stone box (sarcophagus); a separate top bears a nine-character inscription on its flat center and has four beveled edges decorated with a scrolling floral pattern, a form resembling *muzhiming*, or epitaph stone tablets (no. 83). The inscription in clerical script reads: "Reliquary Box of the Temple of the Great Clouds of Jingchuan during the Great Zhou Dynasty containing fourteen grains of *sarira* relics." On the lower half of the box, all four sides are inscribed with donor names and a detailed epigraph described below. The more than a thousand characters include the names of some sixty donors who helped pay for this pagoda deposit.[2]

Inside the stone box was a gilded-bronze box of similar shape, decorated on all sides with scrolling lotuses. The top bears a twelve-petal silver lotus and the front, a silver lock with a five-petal flower latch and hinge. A lock and key are gilded bronze with a silver chain. Between the stone box and this bronze reliquary were found gold hairpins and bronze coins.

Within this bronze box was a silver reliquary shaped like a Chinese coffin, with a fence on its platform base and two ring handles on each side. It is decorated with scrolling flowers on a ring-punched ground (nos. 111, 119).

Within this silver box is a gold reliquary, also shaped like a Chinese coffin with a similar fence at its base. This is the most intricately designed of the four reliquaries and has inlaid pearls[3] and striated turquoise stones set in floral motifs, each setting surrounded by granulation (see no. 5a–c). The

no. 120b–e

no. 120a

no. 120d

1. Original excavation report, *Wenwu* 1966.3, p. 8; This reliquary was exhibited in Memphis, Tennessee. See Lei, Yang, and Zhao 1995, pp. 120–21; in *The Silk Road*, pp. 118–19; *Zhongguo* 1986, vol. 10, pp. 38, figs. 78–80, p. 22; *Zhongguo* 1993, p. 127, fig. 117.

2. Ibid., p. 12.

3. Pearls were imported to China across the Silk Road from India and Persia and along with gold and silver made up part of the Seven Treasures (*sapta-ratna*) of the Buddhist ideal world.

4. *Wenwu* 1965.8, pp. 47–51. This article details Tang-Dynasty reliquaries in the shape of Chinese houses used as coffins. The shape of the wooden coffin is identical to both the silver and gold reliquaries from Jingquan. See also p. 50, fig. 10. Whitfield 1989, p. 135.

5. Schafer 1963, pp. 136–37.

6. *Wenwu* 1966.3, p. 13.

7. Reischauer and Fairbank 1960, p. 157. When Empress Wu usurped the throne, she changed the name of the dynasty from Tang to Zhou.

8. Ch'en 1973, p. 223.

9. In Ningan county in Heilongjiang province, at the site of Longquan, capital of the Tang kingdom of Bohai, a glass *sarira* bottle was found in an oval silver box inside a square silver box, which was in turn contained in a bronze casket, an iron chest, and two stone chests. These were found in the pagoda deposit of a large Buddhist temple, according to An 1984, p. 19; *Zhongguo Meishu*, vol. 10, no. 75.

10. According to Roderick Whitfield, nested reliquaries like those at Famensi provide a three-dimensional version of the usual two-dimensional mandala diagram. Whitfield 1990, p. 85. There is also some indication at Famensi, where more than one set of nested reliquaries was found, that these sets of reliquaries also formed a mandala. *Wenwu* 1988.10, pp. 1–43.

11. An 1984, p. 19.

tops of both the silver and gold reliquaries are shaped like Chinese roof tiles. The use of Tang coffin shapes for the boxes themselves not only shows the sinicization of Buddhism in the Tang dynasty but also establishes parallels between the sacred and the secular worlds.[4]

Within this final gold reliquary, on a sandalwood board, rested the *sarira* glass bottle with the relics inside. Sandalwood, considered a luxury, had religious significance; it most likely originated in India and was traded across the Silk Road.[5] The sandalwood board and the glass bottle were wrapped in silk brocade. The glass bottle, handblown in China (no. 89a–b), contained the fourteen relic grains referred to in the inscription of the outermost stone box. These grains are presumed to be made from pearls and resemble small rice kernels through which tiny holes have been drilled. The smallest grain is 0.01 mm long and the largest is barely 0.5 mm.[6] According to Buddhist texts, the ancient Indian king Asoka placed the ashes of Sakyamuni Buddha, called *sarira*, in 84,000 exquisite caskets to be distributed for worship both within and outside of India. If true *sarira* were not available, then precious substances like pearls could be used.

The inscription on the outermost stone box, dated 694, describes how the *sarira* bottle and fourteen relic grains were found in a stone coffin, originally dating from the Sui dynasty. Emperor Wendi, after founding the Sui dynasty, relied on Buddhism as a state ideology to unify and to consolidate his power and empire. In 601 he sent monks throughout his empire to enshrine *sarira* relics in Temples of Great National Prosperity (*Daxing Guosi*), thus emulating King Asoka. This glass *sarira* bottle and these relic grains were originally from the Daxing Guo Temple in Jingchuan, eastern Gansu, which was later destroyed.

In 690 Empress Wu Zetian usurped the throne, assuming the title of emperor for herself, the only time a woman did this in China.[7] According to the inscription on the reliquary, after the empress Wu Zetian ascended the throne, she had the monastery rebuilt in 694. The empress Wu had the Great Cloud Sutra (*Dayunjing*), which was part of the Mahamegha Sutra, distributed throughout her empire and decreed that Dayun temples be erected in all prefectures of the empire. At that time, the original glass bottle and *sarira* relics were provided with the new reliquaries of stone, gilded bronze, silver, and gold that are shown here and were reburied in the underground pagoda deposit where they remained until excavated in 1964. The Great Cloud Sutras and temples were designed by Empress Wu to legitimize her ascension to the throne, since the sutra states that a woman would be reborn as a universal monarch. Chinese monks at that time designated Empress Wu as an incarnation of Maitreya on earth, capitalizing on the prevailing idea in the Tang that Maitreya would soon be reborn on earth as its future Buddha. This bolstered her claim to imperial power and legitimized her rule as successor to the Tang emperors. Some Dayun temples were established by Chinese monks even in Central Asia, emphasizing the extent of the Chinese Empire by the end of the seventh century.[8]

Similar sets of nested reliquaries have been excavated at Longquan in Heilongjiang province, in Dingxian county in Hebei province, at Famensi Temple located near Xi'an in Shaanxi province, and from Qingshan Temple, Lintong, in Shaanxi province (fig. A).[9] At Famensi, more than one set of nested reliquaries was excavated in the base of the pagoda, and there is some indication that they were buried positioned in the shape of a mandala.[10] Similar glass *sarira* bottles have been found in all three of the above sites, as well as in a gilt-bronze box in a reliquary pagoda dated 719 in the eastern suburbs of Xi'an.[11]

SB

MONKS AND MERCHANTS

Glossary

abhaya mudra: a Buddhist ritual hand position, a gesture of protection or blessing or of fearlessness; generally, the hand is shown with palm facing outward and fingers extended upward.

anjali mudra: a Buddhist ritual hand position, a gesture of prayer or devotion; generally, the hands are held to the chest with palms touching and fingers extended upward.

apsara or *apsaras*: *tianjen* (heavenly beings) or *feitian* (flying beings) in Chinese; type of deva or heavenly or radiating being who lives in heavenly realms and is invisible. Usually depicted flying, playing musical instruments, or bearing offerings, and trailing drapery and ribbons.

Avalokitesvara: (Guanyin, Chinese): a bodhisattva, known as the compassionate one and rescuer from perils; the most popular figure of the Buddhist pantheon.

bezel: the decorative part of a finger ring, visible when the ring is worn on the hand and shaped as a seal or stone setting; a bezel setting is the projecting strip or flange of metal that surrounds and secures the stone.

bo or bodhi tree: bodhi means awakened or enlightened and refers to the tree the Buddha sat under when he achieved enlightenment.

bodhisattva: enlightened being in Mahayana Buddhism, embodying the concept of compassion in the Mahayana Buddhist ideal. As emanations of the Buddha, the bodhisattvas continually work for the salvation of the world.

bracteate: very thin coin or imitation coin struck on one face only. The term is derived from the Latin *bractea*, a thin metal sheet. It is also applied to stamped gold plaques perforated with holes or fitted with rings on the reverse.

brocade: a textile to which extra decorative threads have been added during the weaving process. Brocaded threads "float" over parts of the ground weave, resulting in a raised design

Buddha: the "awakened one." Most commonly used to name the historic Buddha born in 563 BCE, the son of the prince of the Shakyas, a kingdom in the foothills of the Himalayas, present-day Nepal. Generically, any person who has achieved enlightenment.

dharma: the teachings or law discovered and proclaimed by the Buddha as summed up in the four noble truths; also philosophically, the elements of existence, things, phenomena.

dhoti: a loincloth

drachm: the main denomination of the Sasanian monetary system, struck of silver and based on the Greek Attic weight standard, but reduced to about 4 grams.

granulation: an intricate and highly skilled jewelry technique whereby small gold granules or beads are soldered to a solid gold background to form a decorative pattern. Hinayana: the "small vehicle," or school of Buddhism, that considers itself closest to the original form of Buddhism; emphasis on meditation practice and liberation of the individual; also known as Theravada or "teaching of the elders."

ingot: a cast piece of metal based on a defined weight standard that can come in different shapes

intaglio: an engraved design or a seal or gemstone with an incised design on its face

jataka tales: a collection of 550 stories of the former lives of the Buddha

lakshana: a divine mark or characteristic; the Buddha has thirty-two.

Mahayana: the "greater vehicle," one of three bodies of Buddhist doctrine, emphasizes compassion and the acknowledgment of the universal Buddha-nature; the bodhisattva is the ideal figure of Mahayana.

Maitreya: the "kindly-loving." The name of the future Buddha, waiting in Tusita Heaven, who eventually will appear on earth; often represented as a bodhisattva.

mingqi: funerary objects or replicas made specifically for burial usually fashioned from clay; mass-produced with molds but then hand-finished, painted and sometimes gilded. Mingqi can also be made from wood and sometimes metal like the famous Flying Horse and accompanying mounts.

mudra: a Buddhist ritual hand pose or position

nirvana: the extinction of the passions, calm, absolute; may be attained in this life but may not be continuously realized until after death.

ossuary: a receptacle for holding the bones of the deceased. In Zoroastrian belief, the earth may not be defiled by decomposing flesh. Instead of burial in the ground, the corpse is exposed to beasts and birds of prey and the bones then gathered for storage in a stone or ceramic container, an ossuary.

pagoda (*ta*, in Chinese): a multi-storied tower that became the Chinese equivalent of the stupa, the primary Buddhist monument for ritual and worship

parinirvana: synonym for nirvana. In sculpture and painting, the Buddha is represented reclining on his right side at the time of his death; this scene is often misnamed as sleeping or reclining Buddha.

repoussé: the technique of hammering thin metal from the underside to form a pattern or design in relief

rhyton (pl. rhyta): a drinking vessel in the shape of a horn or an animal's head or body, with the spout at the tip of the horn, in the animal's mouth, or in an opening in the animal's chest

sancai: tri-colored lead glazes predominant during the Tang dynasty (618–906)

saptaratna: the seven marks or signs of the universal ruler that also become associated with the seven precious treasures for the worship and patronage of the Buddha including silver, gold, lapis lazuli, red coral, pearls, agate, crystal or quartz. There are occasional variations in Buddhist texts; rubies or red carnelian can substitute for red coral.

sarira: originally the sarira (ashes) of Sakyamuni Buddha placed inside 84,000 caskets (reliquaries) by Indian King Asoka to be distributed for worship inside and outside India. If true sarira are not available, other precious substances can be used, such as pearls.

solidus: late Roman-Byzantine gold denomination (weighing about 4.5 grams) introduced by Constantine the great (306–337)

stupa: a tumulus or funerary mound symbolizing the Buddhist universe. It generally consists of a platform surmounted by a dome shape containing the relics of the Buddha buried inside.

sutra: "thread," a discourse attributed to the Buddha, collected in the second part of the Buddhist canon (*Tripitaka*) and preserved in Pali and Sanskrit as well as in Chinese and Tibetan translations

tribhanga: "three bends" pose with the body bending at the neck, waist, and one knee

Tusita Heaven: the "Heaven of Bliss." A bodhisattva, before reaching his last birth as a Buddha on earth, is living in the Tusita Heaven. Tusita Heaven becomes increasingly associated with the Maitreya, the Buddha of the Future image, often depicted cross-ankled with the garments of a bodhisattva, princely jewelry, and a crown.

urna: "hairy mole," a Buddhist iconographic mark, one of the *lakshanas*, which appears on the foreheads of the Buddha and bodhisattvas; sometimes represented by a jewel, a small proturberance, or as a third eye inserted between the eyes of the Buddha and bodhisattva images.

usnisa or ushnisha: the proturberance on the skull of the Buddha—the first and most important of the 32 marks (lakshanas)

xiangrui: "good omen," a concept that figured prominently in Chinese art and culture beginning in the Han period. The term refers to auspicious, generally zoomorphic phenomena that were considered good omens because their appearance was thought to indicate the approval of Heaven.

warp: the thread running lengthwise or vertically on a loom. These vertical threads are interlaced by the weft threads, which are introduced from the side and run across or horizontally on the loom.

vara or *varada* mudra: a Buddhist ritual hand position, the gift bestowing or charity mudra; the hand is shown with extended palm facing outward and fingers extended.

Bibliography

Abdullaev, Rtveladze, and Shishkina 1991
K. A. Abdullaev, E. V. Rtvedladze, and G. V. Shishkina. *Kul'tura i iskusstvo drevnego uzbekistana. Katalog vystavki* [Culture and art of ancient Uzbekistan. Exhibition catalogue]. Vol. 2. Moscow, 1991.

Abe 1990
Stanley K. Abe. "Art and Practice in a Fifth Century Chinese Buddhist Cave Temple." *Ars Orientalis* 20 (1990): 1–20.

Akiyama 1968
Terukazu Akiyama, et al. *Arts of China: Neolithic Cultures to the T'ang Dynasty: Recent Discoveries.* Tokyo and Palo Alto, 1968.

Akiyama 1969
Terukazu Akiyama and Saburo Matsubara. *Arts of China, Buddhist Cave Temples, New Research.* Tokyo and Palo Alto, 1969.

Al'baum 1960
L. I. Al'baum. *Balalyk-Tepe: K Istorii material'noj kul'tury i iskusstva Tokharistana* [Balalyk Tepe: Toward a history of material culture and art of Tokharistan]. Tashkent, 1960.

Al'baum 1975
L. I. Al'baum. *Zhivopis' Afrasiab* [Painting from Afrasiab]. Tashkent, 1975.

Alekseyeva 1987
E. M. Alekseyeva. "Antique City of Gorgippia." In *Shedevry drevnego iskusstva kubani* [Art treasures of ancient Kuban], edited by A. M. Leskov and V. L. Lapushnian, 159–77. Moscow, 1987.

Alram 1996
Michael Alram. "Alchon und Nezak: Zur Geschichte der iranischen Hunnen in Mittelasien." In *Convegno internazionale sul tema: La Persia e l'Asia centrale da Alessandro al X secolo (Roma, 9–12 novembre 1994).* Atti dei Convegni Lincei, no. 127 (Rome, 1996): 517–54.

Ambroz 1986
A. K. Ambroz. "Kinzhaly VI–VIII v.v.s. dvumia vystupami na nozhnakh." *Sovietskaia Arkheologiia* 4 (1986): 53–73.

Amiet 1967
Pierre Amiet. "Nouvelles acquisitions: Antiquités parthes et sassanides." *La Revue du Louvre* 17 (1967): 280.

Amiet 1980
Pierre Amiet. *Art of the Ancient Near East.* Translated by John Shepley and Claude Choquet. New York, 1980.

Amorai-Stark 2000
Shua Amorai-Stark. "The Crouching Lion Motif in Sassanian Glyptic: A Seal Found in China." In *International Symposium on Chinese Archaic Seals*, edited by Wang Yan Chung and Yau Hok Wa, 201–26. Hong Kong, 2000.

An 1984
An Jiayao. "Early Chinese Glassware." Translated by Matthew Henderson. *Oriental Ceramic Society Transactions* 12 (London: n.d.). English translation of *Kaogu xuebao* 1984.4, 413–57.

An 1986
An Jiayao. "A Glass Bowl from Li Xian's Tomb of the Northern Zhou Dynasty: The Discovery of and Research on Sasanian Glassware " (in Chinese). *Kaogu* 1986.2, 173–81.

Azarpay 1969
Guitty Azarpay. "Nine Inscribed Choresmian Bowls." *Artibus Asiae* 31 (1969): 185–203.

Azarpay 1981
Guitty Azarpay. *Sogdian Painting: The Pictorial Epic in Oriental Art.* Contributions by A. M. Belenitskii, Boris I. Marshak, and Mark J. Dresden. Berkeley and Los Angeles, 1981.

Bagchi 1955
Prabodh Chandra Bagchi. *India and Central Asia.* Calcutta, 1955.

Bagchi 1981
Prabodh Chandra Bagchi. *India and China: A Thousand Years of Cultural Relations.* Calcutta, 1981.

Bailey 1982
Harold W. Bailey. "The Culture of the Sakas in Ancient Iranian Khotan." *Columbia Lectures on Iranian Studies* 1 (Delmar, N.Y., 1982).

Baker 1999
Janet Baker. "Sui and Early Tang Period Images of the Heavenly King in Tombs and Temples." *Orientations* no. 4 (April 1999): 53–57.

Bambling 1996
Michele Bambling. "The Kongô-ji Screens: Illuminating the Tradition of Yamato-e 'Sun and Moon' Screens." *Orientations* 27, no. 9 (1996): 70–82.

Baratova 1999
Larisa Baratova. "Alttürkische Münzen Mittelasiens aus dem 6.–10. Jh. n. Chr." *Archäologische Mitteilungen aus Iran und Turan* 31 (1999): 219–92.

Baratte 1996
François Baratte. "Dionysos en Chine: remarques à propos de la coupe en argent de Beitan." *Arts Asiatiques* 51 (1996): 142–47.

Barfield 1989
Thomas J. Barfield. *The Perilous Frontier: Nomadic Empires and China.* Cambridge, 1989.

Barnhart 1997
Richard Barnhart, et al. *3000 Years of Chinese Painting.* New Haven, 1997.

Bartel 1989
Brad Bartel. "Acculturation and Ethnicity in Roman Moesia Superior." In *Centre and Periphery: Comparative Studies in Archaeology*, edited by Timothy C. Champion, 173–85. London, 1989.

Barthold 1966
V. V. Barthold. *Sochineniia.* Vol. 6. Moscow, 1966.

Basham 1959
A. L. Basham. *The Wonder That Was India.* New York, 1959.

Beishi 1974
Beishi. Beijing, 1974.

Belenitskii 1954
A.M. Belenitskii. *Zhivopis' drevnogo Piandzhikenta* [Painting of ancient Panjikent]. Moscow, 1954.

Belenitskii 1959
A.M. Belnitskii. *Skul'ptura i zhivopis' drevnego Pijandzhikenta* [Sculpture and painting of ancient Panjikent]. Moscow, 1959.

Belenitskii 1973
A. M. Belenitskii. *Monumental'noe iskusstvo Pendzhikenta* [Monumental art of Panjikent]. Moscow, 1973.

Belenizki (Belenitskii) 1980
A. M. Belenitskii. *Mittelasien: Kunst der Sogden.* Leipzig, 1980.

Belenitskii, Marshak, and Raspopova 1979
A. M. Belenitskii, Boris I. Marshak, and Valentina I. Raspopova. "Sotsial'naia struktura naselaniia drevnego Pendzhikenta"[Social structure of ancient Panjikent]. In *Tovarno-denezhnye otnosheniia na Blizhnem i Srednem Vostoke v epokhu srednevekov'ia* [Commodity-money relationships in the medieval Near and Middle East]. (Moscow, 1979): 19–26.

Belenitskii, Marshak, Raspopova, and Isakov 1977
A. M. Belenitskii, Boris I. Marshak, Valentina I. Raspopova, and A. I. Isakov. "Raskopki na gorodishche drevnego Pendzhikenta v 1973 godu" [Excavations in the ancient city of Panjikent in 1973]. *Arkheologicheskie raboty v Tadzhikistane* [Archaeological excavations in Tajikistan]. Vol. 13. Dushanbe, 1977.

Benkó 1992/1993
Mihály Benkó. "Burial Masks of Eurasian Mounted Nomad Peoples in the Migration Period (1st Millennium A.D.)." *Act Orientalia Academiae Scientiarum Hungarium* 46 (1992/1993): 113–31.

Bercholz and Kohn 1993
Samuel Bercholz and Sherab Chodzin Kohn. *Entering the Stream, An Introduction to the Buddha and His Teachings.* Boston, 1993.

Berghaus 1993
Peter Berghaus. "Indian Imitations of Roman Coins." In *Proceedings of the XIth International Numismatic Congress, Brussels, September 8th–13th 1991.* Vol. 2. (Brussels, 1993): 305–10.

Bielenstein 1997
Hans Bielenstein. "The Six Dynasties, Vol. II." *Bulletin of Far Eastern Antiquities* 69 (1997): 5–246.

Binglingsi 1989
Yongjing Binglingsi [Bingling cave temples at Yongjing]. The Grotto Art of China Series. Beijing, 1989.

Bivar 1969
A. D. H. Bivar. *Catalogue of the Western Asiatic Seals in the British Museum. Stamp Seals II: The Sassanian Dynasty.* London, 1969.

Black and Green 1992
Jeremy Black and Anthony Green. *Gods, Demons and Symbols of Ancient Mesopotamia: An Illustrated Dictionary.* Austin, Tex., 1992.

Blockley 1985
R. C. Blockley. "The History of Menander the Guardsman. Introductory Essay, Text, Translation, and Historiographical Notes." *ARCA: Classical and Medieval Texts, Papers and Monographs* 17 (Liverpool, 1985).

Boodberg 1979
Selected Works of Peter A. Boodberg. Compiled by Alvin P. Cohen. Berkeley and Los Angeles, 1979.

Boulnois 1966
Luce Boulnois. *The Silk Road.* New York, 1966.

Boyce and Grenet 1991
Mary Boyce and Frantz Grenet. "A History of Zoroastrianism." In Vol. 3, *Zoroastrianism Under Macedonian and Roman Rule.* Handbuch der Orientalistik. Erste Abteilung: Der Nahe und der Mittlere Osten. Leiden, 1991.

Brinker and Goepper 1980
Helmut Brinker and Roger Goepper. *Kunstschätz aus China. 5000 v. Chr. bis 900 n. Chr. Neuere archäologische Funde aus der Volksrepublik China.* Zurich, Berlin, Hildesheim, and Cologne, 1980.

Brough 1962
John Brough. *The Gandharan Dharmapada.* London Oriental Series, vol. 7. London, 1962.

Brunner 1978
Christopher J. Brunner. *Sasanian Stamp Seals in the Metropolitan Museum of Art.* New York, 1978.

Bukhoro 1991
Bukhoro. Ochlik osmon ostodagi muzei [Bukhara. A Museum in the Open]. Tashkent, 1991.

Bulling 1966
Anneliese Bulling. "Notes on Two Unicorns." *Oriental Art,* n.s., 3 (Spring 1966): 109–13.

Bunce 1997
Frederick W. Bunce. *Buddhist and Hindu Iconography.* New Delhi, 1997.

Bunker 1993
Emma Bunker. "Gold: A Cultural Puzzle." *Artibus Asiae* 53, no. 1/2 (1993): 27–50.

Burnett 1998
Andrew Burnett. "Roman Coins from India and Sri Lanka." In *Origin, Evolution and Circulation of Foreign Coins in the Indian Ocean,* edited by Osmund Bopearachchi and D. P. M. Weerakkody, 179–89. Proceedings of the numismatic workshop, "Origin and Evolution of Coins," and the international seminar, "Circulation of Foreign Coins in Sri Lanka and Ancient Sea Routes in the Indian Ocean," Colombo, September 8–10, 1994. New Delhi, 1998.

Bush 1976
Susan Bush. "Floral Motifs and Vine Scrolls in Chinese Art of the Late Fifth to Early Sixth Centuries, A.D." *Artibus Asiae* 38, no. 1 (1976): 40–83.

Cammann 1953
Schuyler Cammann. "The Lion and Grape Patterns on Chinese Bronze Mirrors." *Artibus Asiae* 16, no. 3 (1953): 265–91.

Cao 1960
Cao Shibang. "Lun Liang Han qi Nanbeichao Hexi zhi kaifa yu Ruxue shijiao zhi jinzhan" [A discussion of the development of the Gansu corridor from the Han to the Northern and Southern Dynasties and the advances of Confucianism and Buddhism]. *Xinya xuebao* 1960.1, 49–57.

Carpino and James 1989
A. Carpino and J. M. James. "Commentary on the Li Xian Silver Ewer." *Bulletin of the Asia Institute* 2 (1989): 71–76.

Carter 1995
Martha L. Carter. "Metalwork from the Hellenistic East." *Bulletin of the Asia Institute,* n.s., 9 (1995): 257–66.

Caswell 1988
James O. Caswell. *Written and Unwritten: Buddhist Caves at Yungang.* Vancouver, 1988.

Chavannes 1903
Edouard Chavannes. *Documents sur Les Toukiue (Turcs) Occidentaux.* St. Petersburg, 1903.

Chen 1988
Chen Bingying, "Bei Wei Cao Tianhu fangshi ta" [Northern Wei Square Stone Pagoda of Cao Tianhu] (in Chinese). *Wenwu* 1988.3, 83–85, 93.

Chen 1998
Chen Chien-wen. "Further Studies on the Racial, Cultural, and Ethnic Affinities of the Yuezhi." In *The Bronze Age and Early Iron Age Peoples of Eastern Central Asia,* edited by V. Mair. Washington, 1998.

Ch'en 1972
Kenneth K. S. Ch'en. *Buddhism in China: An Historical Survey.* Princeton, 1972.

Ch'en 1973
Kenneth K. S. Ch'en. *The Chinese Transformation of Buddhism.* Princeton, 1973.

Cheng 1996
Cheng Yue. "A Summary of Sogdian Studies in China." *China Archaeology and Art Digest* 1 (January–March 1996): 21–30.

China 5,000 1998
China 5,000: Innovation and Transformation in the Arts. Selected by Sherman Lee. New York, 1998.

Chou 2000
Ju-hsi Chou. *Circles of Reflection: The Carter Collection of Early Chinese Bronze Mirrors.* Cleveland, 2000.

Chu 1924
Chu sanzangjiji [Collection of notes concerning the translation of the *Tripitaka,* a bibliography compiled by Sengyou in 510–518]. In *Taisho shinshoji Daizokyo* [The *Tripitaka* newly compiled in the Taisho era], edited by Takakusu Junjiro and Watanabe Kaiyoku. 85 vols. Tokyo, 1924–32 (hereinafter referred to in the text as T.)

Clairmont 1959
Christophe Clairmont. *Das Parisurteil in der Antiken Kunst.* Zurich, 1959.

Conze 1954
Edward Conze. *Buddhist Texts through the Ages.* New York, 1954.

Coomaraswamy 1964
Ananda K. Coomaraswamy. *Buddha and the Gospel of Buddhism.* New York, 1964.

Creel 1965
Herrlee G. Creel. "The Role of the Horse in Chinese History." *The American Historical Review* 70, no. 3 (1965): 647–72.

Creel 1970
Herrlee G. Creel. *The Origins of Statecraft in China.* Chicago and London, 1970.

Cribb 1978
Joe Cribb. "Chinese Lead Ingots with Barbarous Greek Inscriptions." *Coin Hoards* 4 (1978): 76–78.

Cribb 1979
Joe Cribb. "An Historical Survey of the Precious Metal Currencies of China." *The Numismatic Chronicle* (1979): 185–209.

Cribb 1999
Joe Cribb. "The Early Kushan Kings: New Evidence for Chronology. Evidence from the Rabatak Inscription of Kanishka I." In *Coins, Art and Chronology: Essays on the Pre-Islamic History of the Indo-Iranian Borderlands,* edited by Michael Alram and Deborah Klimburg-Salter, 177–205. Vienna, 1999.

Curtis 1995
John Curtis. "Gold Face-Masks in the Ancient Near East." In *The Archaeology of Death in the Ancient Near East,* edited by Stuart Campbell and Anthony Green, 226–31. Oxford, 1995.

Czuma 1985
Stanislaw J. Czuma. *Kushan Sculpture: Images from Early India.* Cleveland, 1985.

d'Argencé 1974
René-Yvon Lefebvre d'Argencé, ed. *Chinese, Korean and Japanese Sculpture: The Avery Brundage Collection, Asian Art Museum of San Francisco.* Tokyo, New York, and San Francisco, 1974.

Davidson 1954
J. Leroy Davidson. *The Lotus Sutra in Chinese Art.* New Haven, 1954

Debaine-Francfort, Idriss, and Wang 1994
Corinne Debaine-Francfort, Abdurassul Idriss, and Wang Binghua. "Agriculture irriguee et art bouddhique ancien au coeur du Taklamakan Karadong, Xinjiang, II–IV siècles." *Arts Asiatiques* 49 (1994): 34–52.

De Marco 1957
Giuseppe De Marco. "The Stupa as a Funerary Monument: New Iconograpical Evidence." *Monumenta Serica* 16, fasc. 1 and 2 (1957): 1–56.

de Menasce 1973
Jean de Menasce, trans. *Le troisième livre du Dēnkart.* Paris, 1973.

Demiéville 1968
Paul Demiéville et al. *Repertoire du Canon Bouddhique sino-japonais.* Paris and Tokyo, 1968.

Dengxian 1959
Dengxian caise huaxiang zhuanmu [Dengxian tomb tiles with color painted images]. Beijing, 1959.

de Rosny 1891
Leon de Rosny L.L.P. *Chan hai king, antique geographie chinoise* [The Classic of the Mountains and Seas: An ancient Chinese geography]. Vol. 1. Paris, 1891.

Di Cosmo 1994
Nicola Di Cosmo. "Ancient Inner Asian Nomads: Their Economic Basis and Its Significance in Chinese History." *The Journal of Asian Studies* 53, no. 4 (November 1994): 1092–1126.

Dien 1962
Albert E. Dien. "The 'sa-pao' Problem Re-examined." *Journal of the American Oriental Society* 82 (1962): 335–46.

Dien 1977
Albert E. Dien. "The Bestowal of Surnames Under the Western Wei-Northern Chou. A Case of Counter-Acculturation." *T'oung Pao* 63, no. 2–3 (1977): 137–77.

Dien 1981–1982
Albert E. Dien. "A Study of Early Chinese Armor." *Artibus Asiae* 43, no. 1/2 (1981–1982): 5–56.

Dien 1986
Albert E. Dien. "The Stirrup and Its Effect on Chinese Military History." *Ars Orientalis* 16 (1986): 33–56.

Dien 1987
Albert E. Dien. "Chinese Beliefs in the Afterworld." In *The Quest for Eternity: Chinese Ceramics Sculpture from the People's Republic of China,* edited by Susan. L. Caroselli, 1–15. Los Angeles, 1987.

Dien 1990a
Albert E. Dien. "The Role of the Military in the Western Wei/Northern Zhou State." In *State and Society in Early Medieval China,* edited by Albert E. Dien, 331–67. Stanford, 1990.

Dien 1990b
Albert E. Dien, ed. *State and Society in Early Medieval China.* Stanford, 1990.

Dien 1991
Albert E. Dien. "A New Look at the Xianbei and Their Impact on Chinese Culture." *Ancient Mortuary Traditions of China: Papers on Chinese Ceramic Funerary Sculptures,* edited by George Kuwayama, 40–59. Los Angeles and Honolulu, 1991.

Dien 1997
Albert E. Dien. "Six Dynasties Tomb Figurines: A Typological Survey and Analysis." In *Integrated Studies of Chinese Archaeology and Historiography.* Symposium series of the Institute of History and Philology, Academic Sinica, no. 4 (1997): 961–81.

Dong 1983
Dong Yuxiang. "Maijishan shiku fenqi" [Classification of Maijishan grottoes]. *Wenwu* 1983.6, 18–33.

Dong 1994
Dong Yuxiang. *Binglingsi yiliujiu ku* [Binglingsi's Cave 169]. Haitian, 1994.

Dong n.d.
Dong Yuxiang. "Jingmei de Bei Wei shi zao xiangta" [The beautiful Northern Wei stone image pagoda]. *Zhongguo Yishu,* no. 5 (Gansu zhuanji), n.d. : 35–39.

Duan 1978
Duan Wenjie. "Dunhuang zaoqi bihua de minzu zhuantong he wailai yingxiang" [Indigenous traditions and foreign influences on the early wall paintings at Dunhuang]. *Wenwu* 1978.12, 8–20.

Dunhuang 1981
Dunhuang Mogaoku [Dunhuang Mogao grottoes]. China's Cave Temple Series, 4 vols. Beijing, 1981.

Durt, Riboud, and Lai 1985
Hubert Durt, Krishna Riboud, and Lai Tungtung. "A propose de 'stupa Riboud, and Lai miniatures' votifs du V siècle découverts à Tourfan et au Gansu." *Arts Asiatiques* no. 40 (1985): 92–106.

Egami 1988
Namio Egami. "The Silk Road and Japan." In *The Grand Exhibition of Silk Road Civilizations: The Silk Road: The Oasis and Steppe Routes.* (Nara, 1988): 12–24.

Emmerick 1983
Ronald E. Emmerick. "The Iranian Settlements to the East of the Pamirs." In Vol. 3, *The Cambridge History of Iran,* edited by Ehsan Yarshater, 263–75. Cambridge, 1983.

Enoki 1994
K. Enoki, G. A. Kosholenko, and Z. Haidary. "The Yuieh and Their Migrations." In *History of Civilizations of Central Asia,* edited by János Harmatta. Vol. 5, *The Development of Sedentary and Nomadic Civilizations: 700 B.C. to A.D. 250.* Paris, 1994.

Errington and Cribb 1992
Elisabeth Errington and Joe Cribb, eds. *The Crossroads of Asia: Transformation in Image and Symbol in the Art of Ancient Afghanistan and Pakistan.* Cambridge, 1992.

Errington and Fabrègues 1992
Elizabeth Errington and Chantal Fabrègues. "Stupa Deposit from Ahinposh, Jalalabad District, Afghanistan." In *The Crossroads of Asia: Transformation in Image and Symbol,* edited by Joe Cribb and Elizabeth Errington, 176–77. Cambridge, 1992.

Feng 1982
Feng Xianming, et al., eds. *Zhongguo taoci shi* [The history of Chinese ceramics]. Beijing, 1982.

Filanovič 1991
M. I. Filanovič. "Les relations historiques, culturelles et idéologiques et les échanges entre le Čač, la Sogdiane et la Chorasmie au début du Moyen-Âge, d'après les données de l'étude des residences fortifiées au VIe –VIIIe s. de notre ère." In *Histoire et cultes de l'Asie centrale préislamique: Sources écrites et documents archéologiques*, edited by Paul Bernard and Frantz Grenet, 205–12. Paris, 1991.

Foltz 1999
Richard C. Foltz. *Religions of the Silk Road: Overland Trade and Cultural Exchange from Antiquity to the Fifteenth Century.* New York, 1999.

Fong 1991
Mary H. Fong. "Tomb-Guardian Figurines: Their Evolution and Iconography." In *Ancient Mortuary Traditions of China: Papers on Chinese Ceramic Funerary Sculptures,* edited by George Kuwayama, 84–105. Los Angeles and Honolulu, 1991.

Fontein 1995
Jan Fontein. "Relics and Reliquaries, Texts and Artifacts." In *Function and Meaning in Buddhist Art*, edited by K. R. van Kooij and H. van der Veere, 21–31. Proceedings of a seminar held at Leiden University, October 21–24, 1991. Groningen, 1995.

Fontein and Hickman 1970
Jan Fontein and Money Hickman. *Zen Painting & Calligraphy.* Boston, 1970.

Fontein and Wu 1976
Jan Fontein and Wu Tung. *Han and Tang Murals.* Boston, 1976.

Fontein and Wu 1973
Jan Fontein and Wu Tung. *Unearthing China's Past.* Boston, 1973.

Forte 1996
Antonino Forte. "On the Identity of Aluohan (616–710), a Persian Aristocrat at the Chinese Court." In *Convegno internazionale sul tema: La Persia e l'Asia Centrale da Alessandro al X Secolo (Roma, 9–12 novembre 1994).* Paper presented at a conference at the Accademia dei Lincei, no.127 (Rome, 1996): 187–97.

Frank 1992
Andre Gunder Frank. *The Centrality of Central Asia.* Amsterdam, 1992.

Fraser
Sarah Fraser. "Regimes of Production: The Use of Pounces in Temple Construction." *Orientations* 27, no. 10 (1996): 60–69.

Frodsham 1967
J. D. Frodsham. *An Anthology of Chinese Verse.* Oxford, 1967.

Frumkin 1970
Grégoire Frumkin. *Archaeology in Soviet Central Asia.* Handbuch der Orientalistik. Vol. 3, *Innerasien.* Leiden: 1970.

Frye 1993
Richard N. Frye. "Sasanian-Central Asian Trade Relations." *Bulletin of the Asia Institute,* n.s., 7 (1993): 73–77.

Fukai 1977
Shinji Fukai. *Persian Glass.* Translated by Edna B. Crawford. New York and Tokyo, 1977.

Fukai and Horiuchi 1969
Shinji Fukai and Kiyoharu Horiuchi. *Taq-i-Bustan.* Vol. 1. The Tokyo University Iraq-Iran Archaeological Expedition, Report 10. Tokyo, 1969.

Fukai and Horiuchi 1972
Shinji Fukai and Kiyoharu Horiuchi. *Taq-i-Bustan.* Vol. 2. The Tokyo University Iraq-Iran Archaeological Expedition, Report 13. Tokyo, 1972.

Fu 1995
Fu Xinnian. *Gu yu zhuo ying.* Hong Kong, 1995.

Gahli-Kahil 1955
L. B. Gahli-Kahil. *Enlèvements et retour d'Hélène dans les texts et les documents figures.* Paris, 1955.

Gale 1931
Esson Gale. *Discourses on Salt and Iron.* Leiden, 1931.

Gaosengzhuan
Gaosengzhuan [Accounts of Eminent Monks] by Huijiao (497–544) in Takakasu Junjiro, ed. *Taisho shinsho Daizoko kankokai.* Vol. 50, 1960–78: 2059.

Getty 1962
Alice Getty. *The Gods of Northern Buddhism.* 3rd ed. Tokyo and Palo Alto, 1962.

Ghirshman 1962
Roman Ghirshman. *Persian Art, 249 B.C – A.D. 651: The Parthian and Sassanian Dynasties.* Translated by Stuart Gilbert and James Emmons. New York, 1962.

Ghirshman 1963
Roman Ghirshman. "Notes iraniennes XIII: Trois epées sassanides." *Artibus Asiae* 36, no. 3–4 (1963): 293–311.

Ghirshman 1979
Roman Ghirshman. "La Ceinture en Iran." *Iranica Antiqua* 14 (1979): 167–96.

Ghose 1998
Rajeshwari Ghose, et al. *In the Footsteps of the Buddha, An Iconic Journey from India to China.* Hong Kong, 1998.

Giles 1923
H. A. Giles. *The Travels of Fa-hsien (399–414 A.D.) or Records of the Buddhist Kingdoms.* London, 1923.

Giles 1956
Herbert A. Giles. *The Travels of Fa-Hsien (399–414 A.D.).* 2nd ed. London, 1956.

Göbl 1967
Robert Göbl. *Dokumente zur Geschichte der iranischen Hunnen in Baktrien und Indien.* 4 vols. Wiesbaden, 1967.

Göbl 1971
Robert Göbl. *Sasanian Numismatics.* Brunswick, 1971.

Göbl 1984
Robert Göbl. *System und Chronologie der Münzprägung des Kusanreiches.* Vienna, 1984.

Göbl 1993
Robert Göbl. *Donum Burns: Die Kusanmünzen im Münzkabinett Bern und die Chronologie.* Vienna, 1993.

Gongxian 1989
Gongxian Shikusi [Gongxian stone cave temples]. Chinese Temple Series. Beijing, 1989.

Goodrich 1984
Chauncey S. Goodrich. "Riding Astride and the Saddle in Ancient China." *Harvard Journal of Asiatic Studies* 44, no. 2 (1984): 279–300.

Goodrich 1956
L. Carrington Goodrich. "Trade Routes to China from Ancient Times to the Age of European Expansion." In *Highway in Our National Life, A Symposium,* edited by Jean Lanatut and Wheaton J. Lane. Princeton, 1956.

Gorjačeva 1987
V. D. Gorjačeva. "La practique des sepultures en *naus* dans le Sémiretchié (d'après les fouilles de la nécropole de Krasnorečenskoe)." In *Cultes et monuments réligieux dans l'Asie centrale préislamique,* edited by Frantz Grenet, 73–79. Paris, 1987.

Grancsay 1930–1931
Stephen V. Grancsay. "Two Chinese Swords Dating about A.D. 600." *Bulletin of the Metropolitan Museum of Art* 25 (1930–1931): 194–96.

Grand Exhibition 1996
Grand Exhibition of Silk Road Buddhist Art (in Japanese with English catalogue list). Tokyo, 1996.

Grenet 1984
Frantz Grenet. *Les Pratiques funéraires dans l'Asie centrale sedentaire de la conquête grecque à l'islamisation.* Paris, 1984.

Grenet 1986a
Frantz Grenet. "L'Art Zoroastrian en Sogdian." *Mesopotamie* 21 (1986): 97–131.

Grenet 1986b
Frantz Grenet. "Les Pratiques funéraires dans l'Asie centrale préislamique." In *Le Grand Atlas de l'Archéologie.* Encyclopaedia Universalis. (Paris, 1986): 236–37.

Grenet 1994
Frantz Grenet. "The Second of Three Encounters between Zoroastrianism and Hinduism: Plastic Influences in Bactria and Sogdiana (2nd – 8th c. A.D.)." *Journal of the Asiatic Society of Bombay, James Darmesteter (1849–1894) Commemoration Volume,* n.s., 69 (1994): 41–57.

Grenet 1996
Frantz Grenet. "Les Marchands sogdiens dans les mers du Sud." In "Inde-Asie centrale: Routes du commerce et des idées." *Cahiers d'Asie centrale* 1–2 (Tashkent and Aix-en-Provence, 1996): 65–84.

Grenet and Marshak 1998
Frantz Grenet and Boris Marshak. "Le Mythe de Nana dans l'art de la Sogdiane." *Arts Asiatiques* 53 (1998): 5–18.

Grenet and Sims-Williams 1987
Frantz Grenet and Nicholas Sims-Williams. "The Historical Context of the Sogdian Ancient Letters." In *Transition Periods in Iranian History: Actes du Symposium de Fribourg-en-Brisgau (22–24 Mai 1985).* (Leuven, 1987): 101–22.

Grierson 1975
Philip Grierson. *Numismatics.* London, 1975.

Griswold 1958
A. B. Griswold. "Prolegomena to the Study of the Buddha's Dress in Chinese Sculpture." *Artibus Asiae* 26 (1958): 85–131.

Gropp 1974
Gerd Gropp. *Archaologishche Funde aus Khotan Chinesische-Ostturkestan.* Bremen, 1974.

Gu 1956
Gu Zuyu. *Dushi fangyu yiiao* [Summary of historical geography]. Taipei, 1956.

Gu 1962
Gu Jiguang. *Fubing zhidu kaoshi* [Textual analysis of the *fubing* system]. Shanghai, 1962.

Guyuan 1988
Guyuan Bei Wei mu qiguanhua. [Lacquer coffin painting from a Northern Wei tomb, Guyuan]. Ningxia, 1988.

Gyllensvard 1965a
Bo Gyllensvard. "Botanical Excursion in the Kempe Collection." *Bulletin of the Museum of Far Eastern Antiquities* 37 (1965).

Gyllensvard 1965b
Bo Gyllensvard. " Tang Gold and Silver." *Bulletin of the Museum of Far Eastern Antiquities* 37 (1965): 1–230.

Hahn 1975
Wolfgang Hahn. *Moneta Imperii Byzantini.* Vol. 2, *Von Justinus* II *bis Phocas (565–610).* Vienna, 1975.

Hahn 2000
Wolfgang Hahn. *Money of the Incipient Byzantine Empire (Anastasius I – Justinian I, 491–565).* Vienna, 2000.

Han 1985
Han Shunfa. "Bei Qi huangyou ci bianhu yuewu tuxiang de chubu fenxi." [Preliminary Analysis of the Dancing Scene on Yellow-Glazed Pilgrim Bottles of the Northern Qi]. *Wenwu* 1980.7, 39–41. English translation by Albert E. Dien in *Monumenta Archaeologica* 11 (1985): 1564.

Hannestad 1955–1957
K. Hannestad. "Les Relations de Byzance avec la Transcaucasie et l'Asie Centrale aux 5ième et 6ième siècles." *Byzantion* 25–27 (1955–1957): 421–56.

Hanshu 1962
Hanshu. Beijing, 1962.

Harada 1967
Harada Yoshito. *Kan rikucho no fukusho* [Chinese dress and personal ornaments in the Han and Six Dynasties] (English summary). Tokyo, 1967.

Harmatta 1971
János Harmatta. "The Middle Persian-Chinese Bilingual Inscription from Hsian [Xi'an] and the Chinese-Sâsânian Relations." In *Atti del convegno internazionale sul tema La Persia nel Medioevo (Roma, 31 marzo–5 aprile 1970).* Problemi attuali di scienza e di cultura, Accademia Nazionale dei Lincei, no. 160. (Rome, 1971): 363–76.

Harper 1978
Prudence O. Harper. *The Royal Hunter: Art of the Sasanian Empire.* New York, 1978.

Harper 1988
Prudence Oliver Harper. "Sasanian Silver: Internal Developments and Foreign Influences." In *Argenterie romaine et Byzantine,* edited by François Baratte, 153–62. Paris, 1988.

Harper 1990
Prudence O. Harper. "An Iranian Silver Vessel from the Tomb of Feng Hetu." *Bulletin of the Asia Institute,* n.s., 4 (1990): 51–59.

Harper 1991a
Prudence Oliver Harper. "Luxury Vessels as Symbolic Images: Parthian and Sasanian Iran and Central Asia." In *Histoire et cultes de l'Asie centrale préislamique,* edited by Paul Bernard and Frantz Grenet, 95–100. Paris, 1991.

Harper 1991b
Prudence O. Harper. "The Sasanian Ewer: Questions of Origin and Influence." In *Near Eastern Studies Dedicated to H. I. H. Prince Takahito Mikasa on the Occasion of His Seventy-Fifth Birthday,* edited by M. Mori, 67–84. Wiesbaden, 1991.

Harper 1998
Prudence Oliver Harper. "Sasanian and Early Islamic Silver and Bronze Vessels." In "Entlang der Seidenstrasse: Frühmittelalterliche Kunst zwischen Persien und China in der Abegg-Stiftung." *Riggisberger Berichte,* vol. 6 (Riggisberg, 1998): 215–38.

Harrist 1997
Robert E. Harrist, Jr. *Power and Virtue: The Horse in Chinese Art.* New York, 1997.

Hartman 1975
Joan M. Hartman. *Ancient Chinese Jades from the Buffalo Museum of Science.* New York, 1975.

Hay 1999
Jonathan Hay. "Toward a Theory of the Intercultural." *Res* 35 (Spring 1999): 5–9.

Hayashi 1991
Hayashi Minao. *Chugoku Kogyoku no kenkyu.* Tokyo, 1991.

Heller 1998
Amy Heller. "Two Inscribed Fabrics and Their Historical Context: Some Observations on Esthetics and the Silk Trade in Tibet, 7th to 9th Century." In "Entlang der Seidenstrasse: Frühmittelalterliche Kunst zwischen Persien und China in der Abegg-Stifftung." *Riggisberger Berichte,* vol. 6. (Riggisberg, 1998): 95–118.

Hendy 1985
Michael Hendy. *Studies in the Byzantine Monetary Economy, c. 300–1450.* New York and Cambridge, 1985.

Herold 1975
Robert J. Herold. "A Family of Post-Han Ritual Bronze Vessels." *Artibus Asiae* 37, no. 4 (1975): 259–77.

Hexi 1987
Hexi shiku [Cave temples of the Hexi corridor]. Beijing, 1987.

Hou Han Shu 1965
Hou Han Shu. Beijing, 1965.

Howard 1988
Angela F. Howard. "Tang Buddhist Sculpture of Sichuan: Unknown and Forgotten." *Bulletin of the Museum of Far Eastern Antiquities* 60 (Stockholm, 1988): 1–164.

Howard 1991
Angela F. Howard. "In Support of a New Chronology for the Kizil Mural Paintings." *Archives of Asian Art* 44 (1991): 68–83.

Howard 1996
Angela F. Howard. "Buddhist Cave Sculpture of

the Northern Qi Dynasty: Shaping a New Style, Formulating New Iconographies." *Archives of Asian Art* 49 (1996): 7–25.

Howard 1999
Angela F. Howard. "The Eight Brilliant Kings of Wisdom of Southwest China." *Res* (Spring 1999): 93–107.

Howard 2000
Angela F. Howard. "Liang Patronage of Buddhist Art in the Gansu Corridor during the Fourth Century and the Transformation of a Central Asian Style." In *Between Han and Tang: Religious Art and Archeology in a Transformative Period*, edited by Wu Hung, 235–75. Beijing, 2000.

Hsieh 1973
Hsieh Chiao-min. *Atlas of China.* Edited by Christopher L. Salter. New York, 1973.

Hu 2000
Hu Tongqing. "A Tentative Analysis of the Artistic Characteristics of Early Sui Wall Paintings at Dunhuang." Summary in *China Archaeology and Art Digest* 3 (June 2000): 241.

Huang 1993
Huang Ti. "The Variegated and Magnificent Wall Paintings of Kizil." *Orientations* 24, no. 3 (1993): 62–67.

Hung 1975
Hung Shih-ti. "The Age in which Ch'in Shih-huang was born." *The First Emperor of China*, Edited by Li Yu-ning, 9–15. New York, 1975.

Huntington 1987
John C. Huntington. "Pilgrimage as Image: The Cult of the *Astamahapratiharya*, Part I." *Orientations* 18, no. 4 (1987): 55–63.

Hurvitz 1976
Leon Hurvitz. *Scripture of the Lotus Blossom of the Fine Dharma.* New York, 1976.

Idries 1994
Idries Abdurassul. "Agriculture iriguess et art bouddiques ancien au coeur du Taklamakan Karakdong, Xinjiang, II-IV siècles." *Arts Asiatiques* 49, (1994): 34–42I.

Idries and Zhang 1997
Idries Abdurassul and Zhang Yuhong. "A Brief Survey of Archeology Along the Keiya River Since 1993." *Xiyu yanjiu* 1997.3, 39–42.

Ierusalimskaia 1972
Anna A. Ierusalimskaia. "K Slozhenniyu Shkoly Khudozhestvennogo Shelkotcachestva v Sogde" [On the formation of the Sogdian school of artistic silk weaving].

Sredniaia Aziia i Iran [Central Asia and Iran]. (Leningrad, 1972): 5–58. English summary, 178–79.

Jenner 1981
W. F. J. Jenner. *Memories of Loyang, Yang Hsuan-chih and the Lost Capital (493–534).* Oxford, 1981.

Jerusalimskaia (Ierusalimskaia) and Borkopp 1996
Anna A. Jerusalimskaia and Birgitt Borkopp. *Von China nach Byzanz: Frühmittelalterliche Seiden aus der Staatlichen Ermitage Sankt Petersburg.* Munich, 1996.

Jettmar 1991
Karl Jettmar. "Sogdians in the Indus Valley." In *Histoire et cultes de l'Asie centrale préislamique: Sources écrites et documents archéologiques*, edited by Paul Bernard and Frantz Grenet, 251–54. Paris, 1991.

Jiang 2000
Jiang Boqin. "The Zoroastrian Art of the Sogdians in China." *China Archaeology and Art Digest* 4, no. 1 (December 2000): 35–71.

Jin 1964
Jin Fagen. *Yongjia luanhou beifang di haozu* [Northern landed magnates after the Yongjia disturbances]. Taipei, 1964.

Jinshu 1974
Jinshu. Beijing, 1959.

Juhl 1995
Susanne Juhl. "Cultural Exchange in Northern Liang." In *Cultural Encounters: China, Japan and the West*, edited by Soren Clausen, Roy Starrs, and Anne Wedell-Wedellsborg, 55–82. Aarhus, Denmark, 1995.

Juliano 1975
Annette L. Juliano. *Art of the Six Dynasties: Centuries of Change and Innovation.* New York, 1975.

Juliano 1980
Annette L. Juliano. "Teng-Hsien: An Important Six Dynasties Tomb." *Artibus Asiae Supplementum.* (Ascona, 1980).

Juliano 1981
Annette L. Juliano. *Treasures of China.* New York, 1981.

Juliano 1988
Annette L. Juliano. *Bronze, Clay and Stone, Chinese Art in the C. C. Wang Family Collection.* Seattle, 1988

Juliano 1991
Annette L. Juliano. "The Warring States Period–The State of Qin, Yan, Chu, and Pazyryk: A Historical Footnote." *Source* (special issue) 10, no. 4 (1991): 25–29.

Juliano 1992
Annette L. Juliano. "Northern Dynasties: A Perspective." In J. J. Lally & Co., *Chinese Archaic Bronzes, Sculptures and Works of Art.* 1–15. New York, 1992.

Juliano and Lerner 1997a
Annette L. Juliano and Judith A. Lerner. "Cultural Crossroads: Central Asian and Chinese Entertainers on the Miho Funerary Couch." *Orientations* 28, no. 9 (1997): 72–78.

Juliano and Lerner 1997b
Annette L. Juliano and Judith A. Lerner. "Eleven Panels and Two Gate Towers with Relief Carvings from a Funerary Couch." *Miho Museum: South Wing.* (Shigaraki, 1997): no. 125, 247–57.

Karetzky and Soper 1991
Patricia Eichenbaum Karetzky and Alexander Soper. "A Northern Wei Painted Coffin." *Artibus Asiae* 51 (1991): 5–20.

Karlgren 1971
Bernhard Karlgren. *Sound and Symbol in Chinese.* Rev. ed. Hong Kong, 1971.

Keall 1983
Edward J. Keall. "A Persian Castle on the Silk Roads." In *Silk Roads: China Ships*, edited by John E. Vollmer, E. J. Keall, and E. Nagai-Berthrong, 34–44. Toronto, 1983.

Kecier 1989
Kecier Shiku [Cave temples at Kizil]. 2 vols. Chinese Stone Grottoes Series. Beijing, 1989.

Keightley 1983
David N. Keightley, ed. *The Origins of Chinese Civilization.* Berkeley and Los Angeles, 1983.

Kent 1994
John P. C. Kent. *Roman Imperial Coinage.* Vol. 10, *The Divided Empire and the Fall of the Western Parts 395-491.* London, 1994.

Kervran 1994
Monica Kervran. "Fortress, entrepôts et commerce: une histoire à suivre depuis les rois sasanides jusqu'aux princes d'Ormuz." In *Itinéraires d'Orient: Hommages à Claude Cahen*, edited by Raoul Curiel and Rika Gyselen, 325–51. *Res Orientales* 6 (Bures-sur-Yvettes, 1994).

Keswick 1978
Maggie Keswick. *The Chinese Garden.* New York, 1978.

Knauer 1998
Elfriede R. Knauer. *The Camel's Load in Life and Death: Iconography and Ideology of Chinese Pottery Figurines from Han to Tang and Their Relevance to Trade Along Silk Routes.* Zurich, 1998.

Knechtges 1997
David R. Knechtges. "Gradually Entering the Realm of Delight: Food and Drink in Early Medieval China." *Journal of the American Oriental Society* 117, no. 2 (April–June 1997): 229–39.

Koch 1999
Alexander Koch. "Überlegungen zum Transfer von Schwerttrag⸝ und Kampfweise in frühen Mittelalter am Beispiel Chinesischer Schwerter mit P⸝förmigen Tragriemenhaltern aus dem 6.–8. Jahrhundert n. Chr." *Jahrbuch des Römisch⸝ Germanischen Zentralmuseums Mainz* 45 Jahrgang 1998, part 2. (Mainz, 1999): 571–98.

Kossolapov and Marshak 1999
Alexander J. Kossolapov and Boris I. Marshak. *Stennaja zhivopis' srednej i tsentral'noj Azii(Istoriko⸝khudozhestvennoe i laboratornoe issle⸝ dovanie)* [Murals along the Silk Road (Com⸝ bined art historical and laboratory study)]. St. Petersburg, 1999.

Krahl 1999
Regina Krahl. *The Dawn of the Yellow Earth.* New York, 1999.

Kumamoto in press
Hiroshi Kumamoto. "A Khotanese Document from St. Petersburg—A Sales Contract of a Camel." Paper read at the fourth European con⸝ ference of the Societas Iranologica Europaea, Paris, September 6–10, 1999. Paris, in press.

Kuznetsov 1996
V. A. Kuznetsov. "Fire Sanctuary in the Humara Castle." *Acta Orientalia Academiae Scientiarum Hungaricum* 49 (1996): 197–204.

Laing 1991
Ellen Johnston Laing. "A Report on Western Asian Glassware in the Far East." *Bulletin of the Asia Institute*, n.s., 5 (1991): 109–20.

Laing 1995
Ellen Johnston Laing. "Recent Finds of Western⸝ Related Glassware, Textiles, and Metalwork in Central Asia and China." *Bulletin of the Asia Institute*, n.s., 9 (1995): 1–18.

Larsen 1987
Mogens Trolle Larsen. "Commercial Networks in the Ancient Near East." In *Centre and Periph⸝ ery in the Ancient World*, edited by Michael Row⸝ lands, Mogens Larsen, and Kristian Kristiansen, 47–56. Cambridge: 1987.

Laufer 1912
Berthold Laufer. *Jade: A Study in Chinese Archaeology and Religion.* Chicago, 1912.

Laufer 1914
Berthold Laufer. *Sino⸝Iranica, Chinese Contribu⸝ tions to the History and Civilization in Ancient Iran.* Field Museum of Natural History, Publi⸝ cation 177. Anthropological Series 13, no. 2. Chicago, 1914.

Laufer 1919
Bertold Laufer. *Sino Iranica.* Chicago, 1919.

Lee 1953
Sherman E. Lee. "Two Early Chinese Ivories." *Artibus Asiae* 16, no. 4 (1953): 257–64.

Lee 1955
Sherman E. Lee. "The Golden Image of the New⸝Born Buddha." *Artibus Asiae* 18, no. 3/4 (1955): 225–37.

Legge 1893
James Legge. *The Confucian Analects.* Oxford, 1893.

Lei, Yang, and Zhao 1995
Lei Congyun, Yang Yang, and Zhao Gushan. *Imperial Tombs of China.* The Memphis Interna⸝ tional Cultural Series. Memphis, 1995.

Leidy 1989
Denise Patry Leidy. "The Ssu⸝wei Figures in the Sixth⸝Century A.D. Chinese Buddhist Sculp⸝ ture." *Archives of Asian Art* 43 (1989): 21–37.

Leidy 1998
Denise Patry Leidy. "Avalokitesvara in Sixth⸝ Century China." In *The Flowering of a Foreign Faith: New Studies in Chinese Buddhist Art*, edited by Janet Baker, 88–103. Mumbai, 1998.

Lerner 1995
Judith Lerner. "Central Asians in Sixth⸝Century China: A Zoroastrian Funerary Rite." *Iranica Antiqua* 30 (1995): 179–87.

Leslie 1981–1983
Donald Daniel Leslie. "Persian Temples in T'ang China." *Monumenta Serica* 35 (1981–1983): 275–303.

Levi 1912
Sylvain Levi. "L⸝Apramada⸝varga, Etude sur les resensions des Dharmapadas." *Journal Asiatique* 20 (1912): 203–94.

Li 1998
Li Chongjian. *Jin Tong Fo* [Bronze Buddhist sculpture]. Shanghai, 1998.

Li 1998
Li Jingjie. "Buddhist Sculptural Stelae." *Dun⸝ huang jikan* 1998.1, 81–86. English summary in *China Archaeology and Art Digest* 3, no. 4 (2000): 397–98.

Li 1985
Li Xueqin. *Eastern Zhou and Qin Civilizations.* Translated by K. C. Chang. New Haven, 1985.

Li 1973
Li Yaobo. "Liaoning Xian Xiguanxingzi Bei Yan Feng Sufu mu" [Northern Yan tomb of Feng Sufu from Xiguanxingzi Beipiao County, Liaon⸝ ing]. *Wenwu* 1973.3, 2–28, pls. 1–5.

Liang 1987
Liang Xinmin, "Qian Liang Zhangshi zengzhu hou Guzang cheng di bianqian" [The changes in Guzang city after the expansion by the Zhang line of the former Liang]. *Xibei shidi* 1998,4: 34.

Lin 1997
Lin Meicun. "On the Seal Bearing Persian Characters from a Sogdian Tomb in Guyuan and Related Issues." Summary in *China Archae⸝ ology and Art Digest* 2, no. 1 (1997): 170–71.

Litvinskii 1994
Boris A. Litvinskii. "The Archaeology and Art of Central Asia: Studies from the Former Soviet Union." *Bulletin of the Asia Institute*, n.s., 8 (1994).

Liu 2000
Liu Panxiu. "A Discussion of the Fashion for Riding in Ox⸝Drawn Carriages Among the Upper Classes in the Wei⸝Jin and Southern and Northern Dynasties Period." *Zhongguodianji yu wenhua (Chinese Classics and Culture)* 4 (1998): 96–101. English summary in *China Archaeology and Art Digest* 3, no. 4 (2000): 274–88.

Liu 1976
Liu Ts'un⸝yan. "Traces of Zoroastrian and Manichaean Activities in Pre⸝Tang China." In *Selected Papers from the Hall of Harmonious Wind.* (Leiden, 1976): 3–24.

Liu 1988
Liu Xinru. *Ancient India and Ancient China: Trade and Religious Experience, AD 1–600.* New Delhi, 1988.

Livshits 1962
Vladimir A. Livshits. "Iuridischeskie doku⸝ menty i pis'ma" [Legal documents and letters]. In Vol. 2, *Sogdiiski dokumenty s gory Mug* [Sog⸝ dian documents from Mount Mug]. (Moscow, 1962): 69–70.

Loehr 1975
Max Loehr. *Ancient Chinese Jades from the Grenville L. Winthrop Collection in the Fogg Art Museum, Harvard University.* Cambridge, Mass., 1975.

Loewe 1979
Michael J. Loewe. *Ways to Paradise: The Chinese Quest for Immortality.* London, 1979.

Loewe 1982
Michael J. Loewe. *Chinese Ideas of Life and Death: Faith, Myth and Reason in the Han Period (202 BCE–CE 220).* London, 1982.

Long n.d.
Long Xuli. "Qiantan Wuwei Handai mudiao de yishu fengge" [Discussion of the style of Han Dynasty wood carving from Wuwei] *Zhongguo Yishu*, no. 5 (Gansu), n.d.: 24–31.

Longdong 1987
Longdong shiku [Longdong stone grottoes]. Bei⸝ jing, 1987.

Longmen 1991
Longmen shiku [Longmen Caves Temples]. Vol. 1. Beijing, 1991.

Loo 1940
C. T. Loo and Company. *An Exhibition of Chinese Stone Sculptures.* New York, 1940.

Los Angeles County Museum of Art 1987
The Quest for Eternity, Chinese Ceramic Sculptures from The People's Republic of China. Los Angeles, 1987.

Louis 1999
François Louis. *Die Goldschmeide der Tang- und Song-Zeit. Archäologische, sozial- und wirtschafts-geschichtliche Materialien zur Goldschmiedekunst Chinas vor 1279.* Schweizerische Asiengesellschaft Monographie 32. Bern, Berlin, Frankfurt am Main, New York, Paris and Vienna, 1999.

Lovell 1975
Hin-cheung Lovell. "Some Northern Chinese Ceramic Wares of the Sixth and Seventh Centuries." *Oriental Art* n.s., 21 (1975): 328–41.

Lu 1993
Lu Liancheng. "Chariot and Horse Burials in Ancient China." *Antiquity* 67 (1993): 824–38.

Lukonin 1983
Vladimir G. Lukonin. "Political, Social, and Administrative Institutions, Taxes and Trade." In Vol. 3, *The Cambridge History of Iran,* edited by Ehsan Yarshater, 681–746. Cambridge, 1983.

Luo 1988
Luo Feng. "Further Discussion of Shi Daode's Ethnicity and Related Issues" (in Chinese). *Wenwu* 1988.8, 92–94.

Luo 1990
Luo Feng. "Lacquer Painting on a Northern Wei Coffin." *Orientations* 21, no. 7 (July 1990): 18–29.

Luo 1994
Luo Feng. "The Spread of the *Huxuan* Dance Between Central Asia and China, Focused on the Tang Tomb Doors from Yanchi in Ningxia" (in Chinese). *Chuantong wenhua he xiandaihua* [Traditional culture and modernization] 1994.2, 50–59.

Luo 1996
Luo Feng. *Guyuan nanjiao Sui-Tang mudi* [A Sui and Tang graveyard in the southern suburbs of Guyuan]. Beijing, 1996.

Luo 1998
Luo Feng. "A Central-Asian-Style Gilt-Silver Ewer." *Orientations* 29, no. 7 (1998): 28–33.

Luo 2000a
Luo Feng. "Bei Zhou Li Xian mu chutu de Zhongya fengge liujin yinping" [A gilded silver vase in the Central Asian style from Li Xian's Tomb of the Northern Zhou period]. *Kaogu xuebao* 2000.3, 311–30.

Luo 2000b
Luo Feng. "Central Asian Shi People Who Migrated to China" (in Chinese). *Guoxue Yenjiu* 2000.7, 235–78.

Luo 2000c
Luo Feng. "A Gilded Vase in the Central Asian Style from Li Xian's Tomb of the Northern Zhou Period" (in Chinese). *Kaogu xueba* 2000.3, 311–30.

Luo 2000d
Luo Feng. "*Sabao*: Further Consideration of the Only Post for Foreigners in the Tang Dynasty Bureaucracy." *China Archaeology and Art Digest* 4, no. 1 (December 2000): 165–91.

Ma, Qi, and Zhang 1994
Ma Shunying, Qi Xiaoshan, and Zhang Ping. *The Ancient Art in Xinjiang, China.* Urumqi, 1994.

Mänchen-Helfen 1924
Otto Mänchen-Helfen. "The Later Books of the Shan-Hai King." *Asia Major* 1 (1924): 550–86.

Maenchen-Helfen 1973
J. Otto Maenchen-Helfen. *The World of the Huns: Studies in Their History and Culture.* Berkeley and Los Angeles, 1973.

Mahler 1959
Jane Gaston Mahler. *The Westerners Among the Figurines of the T'ang Dynasty of China.* Istituto Italiano per il medeo ed Estremo Oriente, *Serie Orientalia Roma* no. 20 (Rome, 1959).

Maijishan 1954
Maijishan shiku [Cave temples of Maijishan]. Beijing, 1954.

Maijishan 1972
"Maijishan shiku de xintong ku." [The Recently Accessible Caves in Maijishan]. *Wenwu* 1972.12, 47–54. English summary in *Monumenta Archaeologica* 11 (1985): 1634–38.

Maijishan 1987
Maijishan shiku [Cave temples of Maijishan]. Tokyo, 1987.

Maijishan 1992
Zhongguo Maijishan shiku zhan [Exhibition from China's Maijishan stone grottoes]. Tokyo, 1992.

Maijishan 1998
Tianshui Maijishan shiku [Maijishan's stone grottoes at Tianshui]. Chinese Stone Grottoes Series. Beijing, 1998.

Maillard 1973
Monique M. Maillard. "Essai sur la vie matérielle dans l'Oasis de Tourfan pendant le haut moyen-âge." *Arts Asiatiques* (special issue) 29 (1973).

Mair 1994
Victor H. Mair, ed. *The Columbia Anthology of Traditional Chinese Literature.* New York, 1994.

Mair 1998
Victor Mair, ed. *The Bronze Age and Early Iron Age Peoples of Eastern Central Asia.* Washington, D.C., 1998.

Mair and Skjaervø 1991
Victor Mair and Prods Oktor Skjaervø. "Chinese Turkestan II: In Pre-Islamic Times." In Vol. 5, *Encyclopaedia Iranica,* edited by Ehsan Yarshater, 463–69. London, 1991.

Mallory and Mair 2000
J. P. Mallory and Victor H. Mair. *The Tarim Mummies: Ancient China and the Mystery of the Earliest Peoples from the West.* New York and London: 2000.

Marschak 1986
Boris I. Marschak. *Die Silberschätz des orients: Metallkunst des 3.–13. Jahrhunderts und ihre Kontinuität.* Leipzig, 1986.

Marshak 1994
Boris I. Marshak. "Le programme iconographique des peintures de la 'Salle des ambassadeurs' à Afrasiab (Samarkand)." *Arts Asiatiques* 49 (1994): 1–20.

Marshak 1998
Boris I. Marshak. "The Decoration of Some Late Sasanian Silver Vessels and Its Subject-Matter." In *The Art and Archaeology of Ancient Persia: New Light on the Parthian and Sasanian Dynasties,* edited by Vesta Sarkosh Curtis, Robert Hillenbrand, and J. M. Rogers, 84–92. London and New York, 1998.

Marshak 1999a
Boris I. Marshak. "L'Art sogdien (IV au IX siècle)." In *Les Arts de l'Asie Centrale,* edited by P. Chuvin. Paris, 1999.

Marshak 1999b
Boris I. Marshak. "A Sogdian Silver Bowl in the Freer Gallery of Art." *Ars Orientalis* 29 (1999): 101–10.

Marshak (forthcoming)
Boris I. Marshak. "So-called Zandanījī Silks in Comparison with the Art of Sogdia." *Riggisberger Berichte,* vol. 7 (forthcoming).

Marshak and Anazawa 1989
Boris I. Marshak and Wakou Anazawa. "Some Notes on the Tomb of Li Xian and His Wife under the Northern Zhou Dynasty at Guyuan, Ningxia and Its Gold-Gilt Silver Ewer with Greek Mythological Scenes Unearthed There." *Cultura Antiqua* 41, no. 4 (1989): 49–58.

Marshak and Raspopova 1990
Boris I. Marshak and Valentina I. Raspopova. "Wall Paintings from a House with a Granary, Panjikent, 1st Quarter of the Eighth Century A.D." *Silk Road Art and Archaeology* 1 (1990): 123–76.

Marshak and Raspopova 1991
Boris I. Marshak and Valentina I. Raspopova. "Cultes communautaires et cultes privés en Sogdiane." In *Histoire et cultes de l'Asie central préislamique*, edited by Paul Bernard and Frantz Grenet, 187–95. Paris, 1991.

Marshak and Raspopova 1997/1998
Boris I. Marshak and Valentina I. Raspopova. "A Buddha Icon from Panjikent." *Silk Road Art and Archaeology* 5 (1997/1998): 297–305.

Marshall 1960
Sir John Marshall. *The Buddhist Art of Gandhara: The Story of the Early School, Its Birth, Growth, and Decline*. Cambridge, 1960.

Masterpieces 1968
British Museum. *Masterpieces of Glass: A Selection Compiled by D. B. Harden, K. S. Painter, R. H. Pinder-Wilson, Hugh Tait*. London, 1968.

Matsubara 1966
Saburo Matsubara. *Chinese Buddhist Sculpture: A Study Based on Bronze, Stone Statues Other than Works from Cave Temples*. Tokyo, 1966.

Mayers 1964
William Frederick Mayers. *The Chinese Reader's Manual*. (Taipei, 1964): 127 no. 389.

Medley 1981
Margaret Medley. *T'ang Pottery and Porcelain*. London, 1981

Melikian-Chirvani 1976
Assadullah Souren Melikian-Chirvani. "Iranian Silver and Its Influence in T'ang China." In *Pottery & Metalwork in T'ang China, Their Chronology & External Relations*, edited by William Watson, 12–26. Colloquies on Art and Archaeology in Asia, no. 1. Percival David Foundation of Chinese Art. 2nd ed. London, 1976.

Memphis 1995
Imperial Tombs of China. Memphis 1995.

Metropolitan Museum of Art 1982
Along the Ancient Silk Routes. New York, 1982.

Michaelson 1999
Carol Michaelson. *Gilded Dragons: Buried Treasures from China's Golden Ages*. London, 1999.

Miyakawa and Kollautz 1984
H. Miyakawa and A. Kollautz. "Ein Dokument zum Fernhandel zwischen Byzanz und China zur Zeit Theophylakts." *Byzantinische Zeitschrift* 77 (1984): 6–19.

Mizuno 1960
Seiichi Mizuno. *Bronze and Stone Sculpture of China from the Yin to the T'ang Dynasty*. Translated by Yuichi Kajiyama and Burton Watson. Tokyo, 1960.

Mizuno and Nagahiro 1952–1956
Seiichi Mizuno and Toshio Nagahiro. *Yunkang, The Buddhist Cave Temples of the Fifth Century A.D. in North China* (in Japanese). 16 vols. Kyoto, 1952–1956.

Mode 1993
Markus Mode. "Sogdien und die Herrscher der Welt. Türken, Sasaniden und Chinesen in Historiengemälden des 7. Jahrhunderts n. Chr. Aus Alt-Samarqand." *Europäische Hochschulschriften/European University Studies*, Series 28. Art History, vol. 162. Frankfurt am Main, Berlin, Bern, New York, Paris, and Vienna, 1993.

Morrisson and Thierry 1994
Cecile Morrisson and François Thierry. "Monnaies byzantines en Chine." *Revue Numismatique* 36 (1994): 109–45.

Morton 1994
W. Scott Morton. *China: Its History and Culture*. 3rd ed. New York, 1995.

Mowry 1996
Robert D. Mowry. *Hare's Fur, Tortoiseshell, and Partridge Feathers: Chinese Brown-and-Black-glazed Ceramics, 400–1400*. Cambridge, Mass., 1996.

Müller 2000
Shing Müller. "Pingcheng—the Emerging of the Tuoba Culture in Northern China." Abstract of paper presented at a national conference, "Cultural and Artistic Interaction Between the Han and Tang," at Beida University. (Beijing, 2000): 33–42.

Munro 1971
Eleanor C. Munro. *Through the Vermilion Gates: A Journey into China's Past*. Toronto, 1971.

Myer 1986
Prudence R. Myer. "Bodhisattvas and Buddhas: Early Buddhist Images from Mathura." *Artibus Asiae* 46, no. 1/2 (1986): 107–42.

Nagel's 1978
Nagel's Encyclopedia-Guide, China. Geneva, Paris, Munich, 1978.

Narain 1990
A. K. Narain. "Indo-Europeans in Inner Asia." In *The Cambridge History of Early Inner Asia*, edited by Denis Sinor, 151–76. Cambridge, 1990.

Nickel 1973
Helmut Nickel. "About the Sword of the Huns and the 'Urepos' of the Steppes." *Metropolitan Museum Journal* 7 (1973): 131–42.

Ning 1992
Ning Qiang. "The Emergence of the 'Dunhuang Style' in the Northern Wei Dynasty." *Orientations* 23, no. 5 (1992): 45–48.

Ning 1996
Ning Qiang. "Buddhist-Daoist Conflict and Gender Transformation: Deciphering the Illustrations of the Vimalakirti-nirdesha in Medieval Chinese Art." *Orientations* 27, no. 10 (1996): 50–59.

Ning 2000
Ning Qiang. "Patrons of the Earliest Caves: A Historical Investigation." In *Between Han and Tang: Religious Art and Architecture in a Transformative Period*, edited by Wu Hung, 489–529. Beijing, 2000.

Northern Wei tomb 1984
"Ningxia Guyuan Bei Wei mu qingli jianbao" [Brief report on the excavation of a Northern Wei tomb at Guyuan, Ningxia]. *Wenwu* 1984.6: 46–56.

Ogasawara 1957
Senshu Ogasawara. "Kosho Bukkyo no kenkyu" [A study of Buddhism in Gaochang]. *Ryukoku shidan* 1957.42, 1–13.

Osaka Municipal Museum 1976
Rikucho no bijitsu [Art of the Six Dynasties]. Osaka, 1976.

Otavsky 1998
Karel Otavsky. "Stoffe von der Seidenstrasse: Eine neue Sammlungsgruppe in der Abegg-Stiftung." In "Entlang der Seidenstrasse: Frühmittelalterliche Kunst zwischen Persien und China in der Abegg-Stiftung." *Riggisberger Berichte*, vol. 6 (Riggisberg, 1998): 13–41.

Paine and Soper 1975
Robert Treat Paine and Alexander Soper. *The Art and Architecture of Japan*. Harmondsworth, 1975.

Paludan 1991
Ann Paludan. *The Chinese Spirit Road: The Classical Tradition of Stone Tomb Statuary*. New Haven, 1991.

Paludan 1992
Ann Paludan. "A New Look at the Han Tomb of Huo Qubing." *Orientations* 23, no. 10 (1992): 64–82.

Pan 1997
Pan Yihong. "Chinese Foreign Policy Before Sui: Theory and Practice." In *Son of Heaven and Heavenly Qaghan: Sui-Tang China and Its Neighbors*. Studies on East Asia, no. 20 (Bellingham, Wash., 1997): 50–54.

Parlasca 1975
Klaus Parlasca. "Ein hellenistisches Achat-Rhyton in China." *Artibus Asiae* 37, no. 4 (1975): 280–90.

Pavchinskaia 1994
L. V. Pavchinskaia. "Sogdian Ossuaries." *Bulletin of the Asia Institute*, n.s., 8 (1994): 209–25.

Pirazzoli-t'Serstevens 1982
Michèle Pirazzoli-t'Serstevens. *The Han Dynasty*. New York, 1982.

Pirrazoli-t'Serstevens 1994
Michèlle Pirazzoli-t'Serstevens. "Pour une archéologie des échanges: Apports étrangers en Chine (transmission, reception, assimilation)." *Arts Asiatiques* 49 (1994): 21–33.

Pletneva 1981
S. A. Pletneva, ed. *Stepi Evrazii v epokhu sredn-evekov'ya* [The Eurasian steppes in the Middle Ages]. Moscow, 1981.

Posch 1998
Walter Posch. "Chinesische Quellen zu den Parthern." In "Das Partherreich und seine Zeug-nisse," edited by Josef Wiesehöfer. *Historia Einzelschriften* 122 (Stuttgart, 1998): 355–64.

Pugachenkova 1994
Galina A. Pugachenkova. "The Form and Style of Sogdian Ossuaries." *Bulletin of the Asia Insti-tute*, n.s., 8 (1994): 227–43.

Pulleyblank 1952
Edwin G. Pulleyblank. "A Sogdian Colony in Inner Mongolia." *T'oung Pao* 1952.41, 317–56.

Pulleyblank 1983
Edwin G. Pulleybank. "The Chinese and Their Neighbors in Prehistoric and Early Historic Times." In *The Origins of Chinese Civilization*, edited by David N. Keightley, 411–466. Berke-ley and Los Angeles, 1983.

Pulleyblank 1991
Edwin G. Pulleyblank. "Chinese-Iranian Rela-tions I: In Pre-Islamic Times." In Vol. 5, *Ency-clopaedia Iranica*, edited by Ehsan Yarshater, 424–31. London, 1991.

Put Svile 1996
Put Svile (The Silk Road). Zagreb, 1996.

Qi 1996
Qi Dongfang. "A Silver Bowl with Deer Design Unearthed at Shapo Village in Xi'an." *China Archaeology and Art Digest* 1, no. 1 (January–March 1996): 15–18.

Raspopova 1980
Valentina I. Raspopova. *Metallischeskie izdeliia rannesrednevekovogo Sogda* [Early medieval metal-work of Sogdia]. Leningrad, 1980.

Raspopova 1990
Valentina I. Raspopova. *Zhilishcha Pendzhikenta: opyt istoriko-sotsial'noi interpretatsii* [The dwellings of Panjikent: Historical-social interpretations]. Leningrad, 1990.

Raspopova 1999
Valentina I. Raspopova. "Gold Coins and Barcteates from Pendjikent." In *Coins, Art and Chronology: Essays on the Pre-Islamic History of the Indo-Iranian Borderlands*, edited by Michael Alram and Deborah Klimburg-Salter, 453–60. Vienna, 1999.

Raspopova (forthcoming)
Valentina I. Raspopova. "Textiles Represented in the Sogdian Murals." *Riggisberger Berichte*, vol. 7 (forthcoming).

Rawson 1977
Jessica Rawson. "Chinese Silver and its Western Origins." *The Connoisseur* 196 (1977): 36–43.

Rawson 1982
Jessica Rawson. *The Ornament on Chinese Silver of the Tang Dynasty (AD 618–906)*. British Museum Occasional Paper, no. 40. London, 1982.

Rawson 1984
Jessica Rawson. *Chinese Ornament: The Lotus and The Dragon*. New York, 1984.

Rawson 1986
Jessica Rawson. "Tombs or Hoards: The Sur-vival of Chinese Silver of the Tang and Song Periods, Seventh to Thirteenth Centuries A.D." In *Pots and Pans: A Colloquium on Precious Met-als and Ceramics in the Muslim, Chinese and Graeco-Roman Worlds*. Oxford Studies in Islamic Art, vol. 3. (Oxford, 1986): 31–56.

Rawson 1987
Jessica M. Rawson. "China." In *Jewelry, 7000 Years: An International History and Illustrated Survey from the Collections of the British Museum*, edited by Hugh Tait, 114–19. New York, 1987.

Rawson 1991
Jessica Rawson. "Central Asian Silver and Its Influence on Chinese Ceramics." *Bulletin of the Asia Institute*, n.s., 5 (1991): 139–51.

Rawson 1995
Jessica Rawson. *Chinese Jade from the Neolithic to the Qing*. London, 1995.

Rawson 1996
Jessica Rawson. *Mysteries of Ancient China: New Discoveries from the Early Dynasties*. London, 1996.

Reichelt 1931
Hans Reichelt. *Die soghdischen Handschriften-reste des Britischen Museums*. Vol. 2. Heidelberg, 1931.

Reischauer and Fairbank 1960
Edwin O. Reischauer and John K. Fairbank. *East Asia: The Great Tradition*. Boston, 1960.

Ren 1997
Ren Shumin. "Guanzhong Di, Qiang yu Bei Wei Xianbei zhengquan" [Di and Qiang within the passes and the Northern Wei regime]. *Beichao yanjiu* 1997.2, 20–24.

Reynolds 1995
Valrae Reynolds. "Silk in Tibet." In *Asian Art: The Second Hali Annual*, edited by Jill Tilden, 86–97, 190–91. London, 1995.

Reynolds 1999
Valrae Reynolds. *From the Sacred Realm: Trea-sures of Tibetan Art from the Newark Museum*. Munich, London, and New York, 1999.

Rhi 1994
Ju-Hyung Rhi. "From Bodhisattva to Buddha: The Beginning of Iconic Representations in Buddhist Art. *Artibus Asiae* 54 nos. 3/4 (1994): 207–25.

Rhie 1976
Marilyn M. Rhie. "Some Aspects of the Rela-tion of 5th-Century Chinese Buddha Images with Sculpture from N. India, Pakistan, Afghanistan and Central Asia." *East and West*, n.s., 26, no. 3/4 (1976): 439–61.

Rhie 1982
Marilyn M. Rhie. "Late Sui Buddhist Sculpture: A Chronology and Regional Analysis." *Archives of Asian Art* 35 (1982): 27–54.

Rhie 1988
Marilyn M. Rhie. "Interrelationships Between the Buddhist Art of China and the Art of India and Central Asia from 618–755 A.D." *Annali* (supplement) 48, no. 54, fasc. 1 (1988): 1–44, pls. 1–31.

Rhie 1995
Marilyn M. Rhie. "The Earliest Chinese Bronze Bodhisattva Sculptures." *Arts of Asia* 25, no. 2 (1995): 86–98.

Rhie 1998
Marilyn M. Rhie. "Buddhist Sites of Gansu." *The Flowering of a Foreign Faith: New Studies in Chinese Buddhist Art*, edited by Janet Baker, 104–17. Mumbai, 1998.

Rhie 1999
Marilyn M. Rhie. *Early Buddhist Art of China & Central Asia*. Vol. 1. Leiden, Boston, and Cologne, 1999.

Riboud 1977
Krishna Riboud. "Some Remarks on Face Cov-ers (Fu-mien) Discovered in the Tombs of Astana." *Oriental Art* 23 (1977): 438–54.

Rice 1965
Tamara Talbot Rice. *Ancient Arts of Central Asia*. New York and Washington, 1965.

Roberts 1979
Laurence Roberts. *Treasures from the Metropoli-tan Museum of Art*. New York, 1979.

Rogers 1968
Michael Rogers. *The Chronicle of Fu Chien: A Case of Exemplar History*. Berkeley and Los Angeles, 1968.

Rong 2000a
Rong Xinjiang. "The Juqu Anzhou Stele and the Daliang in Qoco." *China Archaeology and Art Digest* 3, no. 4 (June 2000): 318–21.

Rong 2000b
Rong Xinjiang. "The Migrations and Settlements of the Sogdians in the Northern Dynasties, Sui and Tang." *China Archaeology and Art
Digest* 4, no. 1 (December 2000): 117–63.

Rong 2000c
Rong Xinjiang. "Research on Zoroastrianism in
China 1923–2000." *China Archaeology and Art
Digest* 4, no. 1 (December 2000): 7–13.

Rosenfield 1967
John M. Rosenfield. *The Dynastic Arts of the
Kushans.* Berkeley and Los Angeles, 1967.

Rowland 1934
Benjamin Rowland, Jr. "Chinese Sculpture of
the Pilgrimage Road." *Bulletin of the Fogg Art
Museum* 4, no. 1 (November 1934): 22–28.

Rowland 1960
Benjamin Rowland, Jr. *Gandhara Sculpture from
Pakistan Museums.* New York, 1960.

Sahai 1975
Bhagwant Sahai. *Iconography of Minor Hindu
and Buddhist Deities.* New Delhi, 1975.

Sammlung Uldry 1994
*Die Sammlung Pierre Uldry: Chinesisches Gold
und
Silber.* Zurich, 1994.

Sanguo Zhi 1938
Sanguo Zhiji peizhu zanghe yinde. Harvard
Yenching Institute, 1938.

Sarianidi 1985
Victor Sarianidi. *The Golden Hoard of Bactria:
From the Tillya-tepe Excavations in Northern
Afghanistan.* New York and Leningrad, 1985.

Scaglia 1958
Giustina Scaglia. "Central Asians on a Northern Ch'i Gate Shrine." *Artibus Asiae* 21, no. 1
(1958): 9–28.

Schafer 1951
Edward H. Schafer. "Iranian Merchants in
T'ang Dynasty Tales." In *Semitic and Oriental
Studies: A Volume Presented to William Popper on
the Occasion of His Seventy-Fifth Birthday,* edited
by W. J. Fischel, 403–22. University of Califor-
nia Publications in Semitic Philology, no. 11.
Berkeley and Los Angeles, 1951.

Schafer 1963
Edward H. Schafer. *The Golden Peaches of
Samarkand: A Study of Tang Exotics.* Berkeley,
Los Angeles, and London: 1963.

Schloss 1969
Ezekiel Schloss. *Foreigners in Ancient Chinese Art
from Private and Museum Collections.* New York,
1969.

Schmidt 1953
Erich F. Schmidt. *Persepolis I, Structures, Reliefs,
Inscriptions.* Oriental Institute Publications, 68.
Chicago, 1953.

Schopen 1988/1989
Gregory Schopen. "On Monks, Nuns and 'Vul-
gar' Practices: The Instruction of the Image
Cult into Indian Buddhism." *Artibus Asiae* 49,
no. 1/2 (1988/1989): 153–68.

Segraves 1996
Julie M. Segraves. "Preliminary Findings on the
Evolution of the Rosette Motif Found on Chinese Silks." In *First International Symposium on
the Reproduction of Silk Relics.* Paper presented at
a symposium at the China Reproduction Center of Silk Weaving and Embroidery Relics and
the Suzhou Silk Museum. (Suzhou, 1996):
54–62.

Sekel 1964
Dietrich Sekel. *The Art of Buddhism.* New York,
1964.

Sérinde 1995
Galeries nationales du Grand Palais. "Sérinde,
Terre de Bouddha. Dix siècles d'art sur la
Route de la Soie." *Connaissance des Arts* no. 79
(Paris, 1995).

Serruys 1969
Henry Serruys. "A Note on China's Northern
Frontier." *Monumenta Serica* 28 (1969): 442–61.

Shandong 1999
*Shandong Qingzhou Longxisi chutu fojiao shike
zaoxiang jingpin* [Masterpieces of Buddhist statuary from Qingzhou City, Shandong]. Beijing,
1999.

Shandong 1991
Shandong Provincial Museum. *Shandong Sheng
Bowuguan Zang Pin Xuan* [Selections from the
Shandong Provincial Museum]. Shandong,
1991.

Sheng 1999
Angela Sheng. "Woven Motifs in Turfan Silks:
Chinese or Iranian?" *Orientations* 30, no. 4
(April 1999): 45–52.

Shepherd 1966
Dorothy G. Shepherd. "Two Silver Rhyta." *Bul-
letin of the Cleveland Museum of Art* 53, no. 8
(October 1966): 289–317.

Shepherd 1983
Dorothy Shepherd. "Sasanian Art." In Vol. 3,
The Cambridge History of Iran, edited by Ehsan
Yarshater, 1055–1112. Cambridge, 1983.

Shi 2000
Shi Anchang. "A Study on a Stone Carving
from the Tomb of a Sogdian Aristocrat of the
Northern Qi: A Preliminary Study of an
Ossuary in the Collection of the Palace
Museum." *China Archaeology and Art Digest* 4,
no. 1 (December 2000): 72–84.

Shi 1992
Shi Pingting. "A Brief Discussion of the *Jingbian*
Buddhist Illustrations at Dunhuang." *Orienta-
tions* 23, no. 5 (1992): 61–64.

Shi 1980
Shi Shuqing. "Bei Wei Cao Tiandu zao wanfo
shita" [The Northern Wei thousand Buddha
stone stupas made by Cao Tiandu]. *Wenwu*
1980.1, 68–71.

Shi 1985
Shi Weixiang. "Dunhuang Mogaoku de Fu Tian
Jing Bian Bihua" [Two illustrations of the Fu
Tian Jing from Dunhuang's Mogao caves].
Wenwu 1980.9, 44–48. English summary in
Monumenta Archaeologica 11 (1985): 1623–26.

Shi Daoluo 2000
Yuanzhou Archaeological Joint Excavation in
1995. *The Tomb of Shi Daoluo of the Tang
Dynasty: The Yuanzhou Archaeological Joint
Excavation in 1996* (in Chinese and Japanese).
Tokyo, 2000.

Shih 1980
Shih Hsio-yen. "New Problems in Tun-huang
Studies." *Proceedings of the International Confer-
ence on Sinology,* Section of History of Art,
Taipei, 1980: 211–46.

Shih 1983
Shih Hsio-yen. "Gold and Silver Vessels Exca-
vated in North China: Problems of Origin."
New Asia Academic Bulletin 4 (1983): 63–82.

Shih 1968
Robert Shih, trans. and ed. *Biographies des
Moines
eminents (Kao Seng Tchouan) de Houei-Kiao.* Vol.
54. Louvain, 1968.

Shiji 1959
Shiji. Beijing, 1959.

Shumei 1996
Ancient Art from the Shumei Family Collection.
New York, 1996.

Sichou 1994
*Sichou zhilu, Gansu Wenwu Jinghua [The Silk
Road: The Best of Gansu's cultural relics].*
Lanzhou, 1994.

Sickman and Soper 1971
Laurence Sickman and Alexander C. Soper.
The Art and Architecture of China. First inte-
grated ed. London and New York, 1971.

The Silk Road 1988
*The Grand Exhibition of Silk Road Civilizations:
The Silk Road: The Oasis and Steppe Routes.*
Nara, 1988.

Silk Road 1997
The Silk Road: Treasures of Tang China. Singa-
pore, 1997.

Sims-Williams 1989–1992
Nicholas Sims-Williams. *Sogdian and Other Inscriptions of the Upper Indus*. 2 vols. Corpus Inscriptionum Iranicarum. London, 1989–1992.

Sims-Williams 1995
Nicholas Sims-Williams. "A Bactrian Inscription on a Silver Vessel from China." *Bulletin of the Asia Institute*, n.s., 9 (1995): 225.

Sims-Williams 1996
Nicholas Sims-Williams. "The Sogdian Merchants in China and India." In *Cina e Iran da Alessandro Magno alla dinastia Tang*, edited by Alfredo Cadonna and Lionello Lanciotti, 45–67. Florence, 1996.

Singer 1966–1967
Paul Singer. "Black Lacquer." *Archives of Asian Art* 20 (1966–1967): 82–83.

Singh 1965
Madanjeet Singh. *Ajanta Painting for the Sacred and the Secular*. New York, 1965.

Sinor 1990
Denis Sinor. "The Establishment and Dissolution of the Türk Empire." In *The Cambridge History of Early Inner Asia*, edited by Denis Sinor, 285–316. Cambridge, 1990.

Skaff 1998
Jonathan. K. Skaff. "Sasanian and Arab-Sasanian Silver Coins from Turfan: Their Relationship to International Trade and Local Economy." *Asia Major* 11, no. 2 (1998): 67–115.

Snelling 1998
John Snelling. *The Buddhist Handbook*. Vermont, 1991. Reprint, New York, 1998.

So 1995
Jenny So. *Eastern Zhou Ritual Bronzes from the Arthur M. Sackler Collections*. Vol. 3. Washington D.C., 1995.

So and Bunker 1995
Jenny F. So and Emma C. Bunker. *Traders and Raiders on China's Northern Frontier*. Washington, D.C., 1995.

Soper 1947
Alexander C. Soper. "The 'Dome of Heaven' in Asia." *Art Bulletin* 29, no. 4 (1947): 241ff.

Soper 1948
Alexander C. Soper. "Life, Motion, and the Sense of Space in Early Chinese Representational Art." *Art Bulletin* 30 (1948): 164–86.

Soper 1949a
Alexander C. Soper. "Aspects of Light Symbolism in Gandharan Sculpture." *Artibus Asiae* 12, no. 3 (1949): 252–83.

Soper 1949b
Alexander C. Soper. "Aspects of Light Symbolism in Gandharan Sculpture: Hero and Serpent God." *Artibus Asiae* 12, no. 3 (1949): 314–30.

Soper 1949c
Alexander C. Soper. "Literary Evidence for Early Buddhist Art in China, I: Foreign Images and Artists." *Oriental Art* 2, no. 19 (1949): 28–35.

Soper 1950
Alexander C. Soper. "Aspects of Light Symbolism in Gandharan Sculpture: The Light Shining in the Darkness." *Artibus Asiae* 13, no. 1/2 (1950): 63–85.

Soper 1953
Alexander C. Soper. "Literary Evidence for Early Buddhist Art in China, II: Pseudo-Foreign Images." *Artibus Asiae* 16, no. 1/2 (1953): 83–110.

Soper 1958
Alexander C. Soper. "Northern Liang and Northern Wei in Kansu." *Artibus Asiae* 21, no. 2 (1958): 131–64.

Soper 1960
Alexander C. Soper. "South Chinese Influence on the Buddhist Art of the Six Dynasties Period." *Bulletin of Museum of Far Eastern Antiquities* no. 32 (Stockholm, 1960): 47–112.

Soper 1961
Alexander C. Soper. "A New Tomb Discovery: The Earliest Representations of a Famous Literary Theme." *Artibus Asiae* 24, no. 2 (1961): 79–86.

Soper 1966a
Alexander C. Soper. *Chinese, Korean and Japanese Bronzes: A Catalogue of the Auriti Collections Donated to ISMEO and Preserved in the Museo Nazionale D'Arte Orientale in Rome*. Rome, 1966.

Soper 1966b
Alexander C. Soper. "Imperial Cave-Chapels of the Northern Dynasties: Donors, Beneficiaries, Dates." *Artibus Asiae* 28, no. 4 (1966): 241–70.

Soper 1967a
Alexander C. Soper. "Addendum: The 'Jen Shou' Mirrors." *Artibus Asiae* 29, no. 1 (1967): 55–66.

Soper 1967b
Alexander C. Soper. "Textual Evidence for the Secular Arts of China in the Period from Liu Sung through Sui (A.D. 420–618), Excluding Treatises on Painting." *Artibus Asiae Supplementum* 29 (1967): 54.

Soper 1990
Alexander C. Soper. "Whose Body? (With apologies to Dorothy L. Sayers)." *Asiatische Studien* 44, no. 2 (1990): 205–16.

Splendeur des Sassanides 1993
Louis Vanden Berghe and Bruno Overlaet, eds. *Splendeur des Sassanides: L'empire perse entre Rome et la Chine (224–642)*. Brussels, 1993.

Sponberg and Hardacre 1988
Alan Sponberg and Helen Longacre. *Maitreya, the Future Buddha*. Cambridge, 1988.

Staviskij 1995
Boris I. Staviskij. "Central Asian Mesopotamia and the Roman World. Evidence of Contacts." In *In the Land of the Gryhpons: Papers on Central Asian Archaeology in Antiquity*, edited by Antonio Invernizzi, 191–202. Florence, 1995.

Stavisky 1997
Boris Stavisky. "Bactria and Gandhara: The Old Problem Reconsidered in the Light of Archaeological Data from Old Termez." In *Gandharan Art in Context: East-West Exchanges at the Crossroads of Asia*, edited by Raymond Alchin, et. al., 29–53. New Delhi, 1997.

Staviskij 1998
Boris Ja. Staviskij. *Sud'by buddizma v srednij azii* [The fate of Buddhism in Central Asia]. Moscow, 1998.

Steensgaard 1973
Niels Steensgaard. *Carracks, Caravans and Companies: The Structural Crisis in the European-Asian Trade in the Early 17th Century*. Copenhagen, 1973.

Stein 1904
Marc Aurel Stein. *Sand-Buried Ruins of Khotan*. London, 1904.

Stein 1912
Sir Marc Aurel Stein. *Ruins of Desert Cathay*. 2 vols. London, 1912.

Stein 1921
Sir Marc Aurel Stein. *Serindia*. 5 vols. Oxford, 1921.

Stein 1928
Sir Marc Aurel Stein. *Innermost Asia*. Oxford, 1928.

Steinhardt 1998
Nancy Shatzman Steinhardt. "Early Chinese Buddhist Architecture and Its Indian Origins." In *The Flowering of a Foreign Faith: New Studies in Chinese Buddhist Art*, edited by Janet Baker, 104–17. Mumbai, 1998.

Sterckx 1996
Roel Sterckx. "An Ancient Horse Ritual." *Early China* 21 (1996): 47–79.

Su 1986
Su Bai. "Liangzhou shiku yiji he 'Liangzhou mushi'" [Liangzhou cave temples and the "Liangzhou" type]. *Kaogu xuebao* 1986.4, 435–45.

Su 1996
Su Bai. *Zhongguo shikusi yanjiu* [Studies concerning cave temples in China]. Beijing, 1996.

Sullivan 1969
Michael Sullivan. *The Cave Temples of Maijishan.* Berkeley and Los Angeles, 1969.

Sun Ji 1981
Sun Ji. "Tangdai de maju yu mashi" [The equestrian gear and ornament of the Tang Dynasty]. *Wenwu* 1981.10, 82–88, 96. English abstract by Chauncey Goodrich in Albert Dien, et al. *Chinese Archeological Abstracts* 4 (Los Angeles, 1985): 1782–87.

Sun 1989
Sun Ji. "Guyuan Bei Wei qiguan hua yanjiu" [Research on the Northern Wei lacquer coffin painting from Guyuan]. *Wenwu* 1989.9: 38–44.

Sun 1993
Sun Ji. "The Gold and Silver Wares of the Turk and Turk Styles Unearthed in Inner Mongolia in Recent Years" (in Chinese). *Wenwu* 1993.8, 48–58.

Sun 1994
Sun Ji. "Gold and Silver Belt Buckles of the Pre-Qin Period and the Han and Jin Dynasties" (in Chinese). *Wenwu* 1994.1, 50–64.

Sun Xiushen 2000
Sun Xiushen. "A Comparative Study of Filial Piety in Confucianism" (in Chinese). *Dunhuang yanjiu* Xiushen 1998.4 (1998): 1–11. English summary in *China Archeology and Art Digest* 3, no. 4 (June 2000): 281–83.

Taaffe 1990
Robert N. Taaffe. "The Geographic Setting." In *The Cambridge History of Inner Asia,* edited by Denis Sinor, 19–40. Cambridge, 1990.

Taddei 1998
Maurizio Taddei. "Ten Years of Research in the Art of Gandhara, 1987–1997." In *In the Footsteps of the Buddha, An Iconic Journey from India to China,* Rajeshwari Ghose, et al., 51–56. Hong Kong, 1998.

Tait 1986
Hugh Tait, ed. *Jewelry 7000 Years: An International History and Illustrated Survey from the Collections of the British Museum.* New York, 1986.

Takakusu 1924–32
Takakusu Junjiro and Watanabe Kagyoku, eds. *Taishōshinshû daizokyō* [The Tripitaka newly compiled in Taisho era]. 85 vols. Tokyo, 1924–32.

Takashi
Takashi Kozuka. "Mogaoku di 275 ku jiaojiao pusa xiang Yu Jiantuolou de xianlie" [Precedents in Gandharan art for the image of the crossed-legged Bodhisattva of Mogaoku Cave 275]. *Dunhuang yanjiu* 1990.1.

Tang Changan 1980
Tang Changan Chengjiao Sui Tang Mu [Excavations of the Sui and Tang tombs at Xi'an]. Beijing, 1980.

Tangdai 1993
Tangdai guizu de wuzhi shenghuo [Daily life of aristocrats in Tang China]. Hong Kong, 1993.

Tang 1963
Tang Yongtung. *Han Wei Liang Nanbeichao Fojiaoshi* [History of Buddhism in the Han Wei Jin and Northern and Southern Dynasties]. Beijing, 1963.

Tao 1988
Tao Jing-shen. *Two Sons of Heaven: Studies in Sung and Liao Relations.* Tucson, 1988.

Tarn 1951
W. W. Tarn. *The Greeks in Bactria and India.* 2nd ed. Cambridge, 1951.

ten Grotenhuis 1999
Elizabeth ten Grotenhuis. *Japanese Mandalas, Representations of Sacred Geography.* Honolulu, 1999.

Thierry 1991
François Thierry. "Typologie et chronologie des *kai yuan tong bao* des Tang." *Revue Numismatique* (1991): 209–49.

Thierry 1993
François Thierry. "Sur les Monnaies sassanides trouvées en Chine." In *Circulation des Monnaies, des marchamdises et des biens,* edited by Rika Gyselen, 89–139. *Res Orientales* 5 (Bures-sur-Yvettes, 1993).

Thierry 1995
François Thierry. "Bulletin Bibliographique." *Revue Numismatique* 150 (1995): 304–309.

Thierry 1998a
François Thierry. "Maritime Silk Routes and Chinese Coin Hoards." In *Origin, Evolution and Circulation of Foreign Coins in the Indian Ocean,* edited by Osmund Bopearachchi and D. P. M. Weerakkody, 209–12. Proceedings of the numismatic workshop, "Origin and Evolution of Coins," and the international seminar, "Circulation of Foreign Coins in Sri Lanka and Ancient Sea Routes in the Indian Ocean," Colombo, September 8–10, 1994. New Delhi, 1998.

Thierry 1998b
François Thierry. "The Origins and Development of Chinese Coins." In *Origin, Evolution and Circulation of Foreign Coins in the Indian Ocean,* edited by Osmund Bopearachchi and D. P. M. Weerakkody, 15–62. Proceedings of the numismatic workshop, "Origin and Evolution of Coins," and the international seminar, "Circulation of Foreign Coins in Sri Lanka and Ancient Sea Routes in the Indian Ocean," Colombo, September 8–10, 1994. New Delhi, 1998.

Thompson 1967
Nancy Thompson. "The Evolution of the T'ang Lion and Grapevine Mirror." *Artibus Asiae* 29, no. 1 (1967): 25–40.

Tian Hong 2000
Yuanzhou Archaeological Joint Excavation in 1996. *Tomb of Tian Hong of the Northern Zhou Dynasty: The Yuanzhou Archaeological Joint Excavation in 1996* (in Chinese and Japanese). Tokyo, 2000.

Tokyo 1988
Illustrated Catalogues of Tokyo National Museum: Chinese Ceramics I. Tokyo, 1988.

Toronto 1974
The Exhibition of the Archeological Finds of the People's Republic of China. Toronto, 1974.

Treasures of Chang'an 1993
Chang'an Guibao: Silu zhidou [Treasures of Chang'an: Capital of the Silk Road]. Hong Kong, 1993.

Trever and Lukonin 1987
Kamilla V. Trever and Vladimir G. Lukonin. *Sasanidskoe serebro, Sobranie Gosudarstvennogo Ermitazha: Khudozhestvennaya kul'tura Irana III–VIII vekov* [Sasanian silver, Collection of the State Hermitage: Artistic culture of Iran, 3rd–8th centuries]. Moscow, 1987.

Trousdale 1975
William Trousdale. *The Long Sword and Scabbard Slide in Asia.* Smithsonian Contributions to Anthropology, 17 (Washington, D.C., 1975).

Tseng and Dart 1964
Tseng Hsien-Ch'i and Robert Paul Dart. *The Charles B. Hoyt Collection in the Museum of Fine Arts: Boston.* Vol. 1, *Chinese Art: Neolithic Period through the T'ang Dynasty and Sino-Siberian Bronzes.* Boston, 1964.

Tsien 1962
Tsuen-hsuin Tsien. *Written on Bamboo and Silk: The Beginnings of Chinese Books and Inscriptions.* Chicago, 1962.

Tsukumoto 1942
Zenryu Tsukumoto. *Shin Bukkyoshi kenkyu: Hoku giahn* [A study of the history of Buddhism in China: Northern Wei Section]. Tokyo, 1942.

Tsukumoto 1956
Zenryu Tsukumoto. "Wei Shou. Treatise on Buddhism and Taoism: An English Translation of the Original Chinese Text of Wei-shu CXIV and the Japanese Annotation of Tsukumoto Zenryu." Translated by Leon Hurvitz. In Seiichi Mizuno and Toshio Nagahiro, *Yun-kang, the Buddhist Cave Temples of the Fifth century A.D. in North China.* Vol. 16, Supplement and Index. Kyoto, 1956.

Tsukumoto 1957
Zenryu Tsukumoto. "The Sramana Superinten-

dent T'an-Yao and His Time." Translated by Galen Eugene Sargent. *Monumenta Serica* 16 (1957): 363–97.

Tsukumoto 1979
Zenryu Tsukumoto. *A History of Early Chinese Buddhism*. Tokyo, New York, and San Francisco, 1979.

Turner 1989
Paula Turner. *Roman Coins from India*. London, 1989.

Twitchett 1979
Denis Twitchett. Introduction in *The Cambridge History of China*. Vol. 3, *Sui and T'ang China, 589–906*, edited by D. Twitchett and M. Loewe, 1–47. Cambridge, 1979.

Umehara 1955
Sueji Umehara. "Gold Granulation Works of the Han and Six Dynasties Period" (in Japanese with English summary). *Yamato Bunka: Quarterly Journal of Eastern Arts* 16 (June 1955): 2–8 (English); 68–76 (Japanese).

Vainker 1991
Shelagh J. Vainker. *Chinese Pottery and Porcelain from Prehistory to the Present*. London, 1991.

Valenstein 1989
Suzanne Valenstein. *A Handbook of Chinese Ceramics*. New York, 1989.

Valenstein 1997/1998
Suzanne G. Valenstein. "Preliminary Findings on a 6th-Century Earthenware Jar." *Oriental Art* 43, no. 4 (1997/1998): 2–13.

Waldron 1990
Arthur Waldron. *The Great Wall of China from History to Myth*. Cambridge, 1990.

Wang 1999
Eugene Y. Wang. "What Do Trigrams Have to Do with Buddhas? The Northern Liang Stupas as a Hybrid Spatial Model." *Res* 35 (Spring 1999): 70–91.

Wang 1998
Wang Huimin. "An Account of Dong Baode's Pious Deeds and the Sui Sairira Stupa in the Changjiaosi (Temple) at Dunhuang" (in Chinese). *Dunhuang yanjiu* 3 (1997): 69–83. English summary in *China Archaeology and Art Digest* 2, no. 3–4 (December 1998): 272–73.

Wang 1984
Wang Yi-t'ung. *A Record of Buddhist Monasteries in Lo-yang*. Princeton, 1984.

Wang and Li 1983
Wang Zongyuan and Li Bingcheng. "Wuwei luzhou chengzhen di xingcheng yu bianqian" [The formation of and changes in the cities and towns of the Wuwei oasis]. *Xibei shiyuan xuebao* 1983.4, 103–11.

Watson 1962
Burton Watson. *Records of the Grand Historian of China, Translated from the Shi chi of Ssu-ma Ch'ien*. 2 vols. New York and London, 1962.

Watson 1962
William Watson. *Ancient Chinese Bronzes*. London, 1962.

Watson 1983
William Watson. "Iran and China." In Vol. 3, *The Cambridge History of Iran*, edited by Ehsan Yarshater, 537–58. Cambridge, 1983.

Watson 1984
William Watson. *Tang and Liao Ceramics*. London, 1984.

Watson 1986
William Watson. "Precious Metal—Its Influence on Tang Earthenware." In *Pots and Pans: A Colloquium on Precious Metals and Ceramics in the Muslim, Chinese and Graeco-Roman Worlds*. Oxford Studies in Islamic Art, vol. 3. (Oxford, 1986): 161–74.

Watson 1991
William Watson. *Pre-Tang Ceramics of China. Chinese Pottery from 4000 BC to 600 AD*. London and Boston, 1991.

Watt and Wardwell 1997
James C. Y. Watt and Anne E. Wardwell. *When Silk Was Gold: Central Asian and Chinese Textiles*. New York, 1997.

Wealth of the Roman World 1997
J. P. C. Kent and K. S. Painter, eds. *Wealth of the Roman World: Gold and Silver, AD 300–700*. London, 1977.

Weber 1967–1968
Charles Weber. "More on the Little Black Figurines of Ancient China." *Archives of Asian Art* 21 (1967–1968): 73–74.

Weihrauch und Seide 1996
Wilfried Seipel, ed. *Weihrauch und Seide: Alte Kulturen an der Seidenstrasse*. Vienna, 1996.

Weishu 1974
Weishu. Beijing, 1974 ed.

Weitzmann 1943
Kurt Weitzmann. "Three Bactrian Silver Vessels with Illustrations from Euripides." *Art Bulletin* 24 (1943): 289–324.

Weitzmann 1979
Kurt Weitzmann, ed. *Late Antique and Early Christian Art, Third to Seventh Century*. New York, 1979.

Wenhua 1972
Wenhua dageming qijian chutu wenwu [Historical relics unearthed in New China]. Beijing, 1972.

Whitcomb 1985
Donald S. Whitcomb. *Before the Roses and Nightingales: Excavations at Qasr-i Abu Nasr, Old Shiraz*. New York, 1985.

White and Bunker 1994
Julia M. White and Emma C. Bunker. *Adornment for Eternity: Status and Rank in Chinese Ornament*. Denver and Hong Kong, 1994.

Whitehouse and Wilkins 1989
Ruth D. Whitehouse and John B. Wilkins. "Greeks and Natives in South-East Italy: Approaches to the Archaeological Evidence." In *Centre and Periphery: Comparative Studies in Archaeology*, edited by Timothy C. Champion, 102–26. London, 1989.

Whitfield 1989
Roderick Whitfield. "Buddhist Monuments in China: Some Recent Finds of Sarira Deposits." In *The Buddhist Heritage*, edited by Tadeusz Skorupski, 129–41. Paper presented at a symposium by the Institute of Buddhist Studies, Tring, 1989.

Whitfield 1990
Roderick Whitfield. "The Significance of the Famensi Deposit." *Orientations* 21, no. 5 (May 1990).

Whitfield 1995
Roderick Whitfield. "Vision of Buddha Lands: The Dunhuang Caves." In *Asian Art: The Second Hali Annual*, edited by Jill Tilden, 118–35. London, 1995.

Whitfield and Farrer 1990
Roderick Whitfield and Anne Farrer. *Caves of the Thousand Buddhas: Chinese Art from the Silk Route*. London, 1990.

Wolpert 1981
R. F. Wolpert. "The Five-Stringed Lute in East Asia" *Musica Asiatica* no. 3 (Oxford, 1981): 97–106.

Wong 2000
Dorothy C. Wong. "Women as Buddhist Art Patrons During the Northern and Southern Dynasties." In *Between Han and Tang: Religious Art and Archaeology in a Transformative Period*, edited by Wu Hung, 535–66. Beijing, 2000.

Wright 1948
Arthur F. Wright. "Fo-t'u-teng: A Biography." *Harvard Journal of Asiatic Studies* 11 (1948): 321–71.

Wright 1959
Arthur F. Wright. *Buddhism in Chinese History*. Stanford, 1959.

Wright 1978
Arthur F. Wright. *The Sui Dynasty*. New York, 1978.

Wu 1986
Wu Hung. "Buddhist Elements in Early Chi-

nese Art (2nd and 3rd Centuries A.D.)." *Artibus Asiae* 47, no. 3/4 (1986): 263–303.

Wu 1987
Wu Hung. "Xiwangmu, the Queen Mother of the West." *Orientations* 18, no. 4 (1987): 25–33.

Wu 1987
Wu Shouzhi. "Wu Liang Fojiaoshi jianyi" [A brief discussion of Buddhist history during the Five Liang States period]. *Xibei shiyuan xuebao* 1987.1, 76–83.

Wu 1989
Wu Zhou. "Notes on the Silver Ewer from the Tomb of Li Xian." *Bulletin of the Asia Institute* 2 (1989): 61–70.

Xia 1961
Xia Nai. "East Roman Gold Coin Excavated in the Sui Tomb in Dizhangwan in Xianyang" (in Chinese). *Collected Writings on Archaeology*. Beijing, 1961.

Xi'an 2000
Xi'an Beilin Bowuguan [Xi'an Forest of Stone Tablets Museum]. Xi'an, 2000.

Xiangshan
"A Short Report of the Discovery of Tombs Nos. 5, 6, 7 at Xiangshan, near Nanjing" (in Chinese). *Wenwu* 1972.11, 23–41.

Xie 1967
Xie Zhicheng. "The Sichuan Han Dynasty Buddhist Stupa Relief" (in Chinese) *Szechwan Wenwu* 1967.4, 62 and 1992.11, 40 and 1993.3, 16.

Xinjiang 1975
Xinjiang chutu wenwu [Cultural relics unearthed in Xinjiang]. Beijing, 1975.

Xiong and Laing 1991
Victor Cunrui Xiong and Ellen Johnston Laing. "Foreign Jewelry in Ancient China." *Bulletin of the Asia Institute* 5 (1991): 163–73.

Xu and Zhang 2000
Xu Gaozhe and Zhang Xinming. "The Excellent Sculptures in the Yu Hong Tomb" (in Chinese). *Wenwu Shijie* [World of Antiquity] 2000.36, 4–8.

Xu 1995
Xu Pingfang. "The Silk Routes within China in View of Archaeology" (English summary). *Yanjing xuebao* 1995.1, 342–44.

Xu 1996
Xu Xinguo. "A Study of the *Hanshou-niao* ('bird with ribbon in its bill') Motif Woven on Silk Polychrome Fabric Unearthed from Ancient Tibetan Tombs in Dulan County" (in Chinese). *Zongguo Zangxue* 1996.1, 3–21. Xu and Zhao 1996 Xu Xinguo and Zhao Feng. "Preliminary Study of the Silk Textiles Excavated at Dulan." *China Archaeology and Art*

Digest 1, no. 4 (October–December 1996): 13–27.

Xumishan 1997
Xumishan shiku nei rong zonglu [Record of the contents of the Xumishan stone caves]. Beijing, 1997.

Xumishan 1988
Xumishan shiku [Xumishan stone grottoes]. Beijing, 1988.

Yang 1963
Yang Hong. "Some Major Changes in the Costume of the Buddhist Sculptures of the Early Southern and Northern Dynasties" (in Chinese). *Kaogu* 1963.6, 331–37. English summary in *Monumenta Archaeologica* 6 (1978): 295–96.

Yang 1984
Yang Hong. "Zhongguo gudai maju de fazhan he duiwai yingxiang" [The development and external influence of ancient Chinese horse's harness]. *Wenwu* 1984.9, 45–54, 76.

Yang 1996
Yang Jinyu. "A Study of Lazulite Used as Pigment at the Dunhuang, Maijishan, and Binglingsi Grottoes" (in Chinese). *Kaogu* 1996.10, 77–92.

Yang 1998
Yang Xiaoneng, ed. *Golden Age of Chinese Archeology*. Washington, 1998.

Yetts 1929
Walter Percival Yetts. *Chinese and Korean Bronzes in the Eumorfopoulos Collection*. Vol. 3. London, 1929.

Yi 1981
Yi Shui. "Han Wei liuchao di junyue—'guchui' he 'hengchui'" [Military music of Han, Wei, and Six Dynasties—drum and wind instruments and drum and long horn]. *Wenwu* 1981.7, 85–89.

Yin 1977
Yin Guangming. "Stone Stupas of the Northern Wei" (in Chinese). *Wenwu* 1977.1, 179–88.

Yin 1991
Yin Guangming. "Three Northern Liang Stone Stupas in the Dunhuang City Museum" (in Chinese). *Wenwu* 1991.11, 64, 76–83.

Yin 1996a
Yin Guangming. "On the Relationship between the Incised Figures on the Base of the Northern Stone Stupas and the Spirit Kings" (in Chinese). *Dunhuang yanjiu* 1996.4, 8–19.

Yin 1996b
Yin Guangming. "The Twelve Hetupratayaya Sutra and Related Questions on the Northern Stupas" (in Chinese). *Dunhuangxue jikan* 1996.2, 61–71.

Yin 1997a
Yin Guangming. "A Tentative Periodization of

Stone Stupas of the Northern Liang" (in Chinese). *Dunhuang yanjiu* 1997.3, 84–94.

Yin 1997b
Yin Guangming. "Eight Trigrams and Seven Buddhas and Maitreya Carved on the Northern Liang Stone Stupas" (in Chinese). *Dunhuang yanjiu* 1997.1, 81–94

Yin 1998
Yin Guangming. "A Discussion of Northern Liang Stone Stupas" (in Chinese). *Dunhuangxue jikan* 1998.1, 87–107.

Yin, Li, and Xing 2000
Yin Shenping, Li Ming, and Xing Fulai. "Notes on the Excavation of the Tomb of An Qie." *China Archaeology and Art Digest* 4, no. 1 (December 2000): 15–29.

Yong 1999
Yong Xinjiang. "Migration and Colonies of the Sogdians in the Northern Dynasties and Sui and Tang" (in Chinese) *Guoxue Yenjiu* 6 (1999): 27–86.

Yu 1994
Yu Taishan. "Xi Liang, Bei Liang yu Xiyu guanxi shukao" [A critical discussion of the connection between the Western Liang/Northern Liang and the Western Regions]. *Xibei shidi* 1994.3, 1–5.

Yu 1985
Yu Weichao. "Notes on the Eastern Han Dynasty Images of Buddha" (in Chinese). *Wenwu* 1980.5, 68–77. English summary in *Monumenta Archaeologica* 10 (1985): 1375–81.

Yu 1964–1965
Yu Ying-shih. "Life and Immortality in the Mind of Han China." *Harvard Journal of Asiatic Studies* 25 (1964–1965): 80–122.

Yu 1967
Yu Ying-shih. *Trade and Expansion in Han China: A Study in the Structure of Sino-Barbarian Relations*. Berkeley and Los Angeles, 1967.

Yuanzhou 1999
Zhong Ri Yuanzhou Lianhe kaogudui [Collection of the ancient tombs in Yuanzhou]. Beijing, 1999.

Yun 1993
Yun Anzhi. *Zhongguo Beizhou zhengui wenwu* [Northern Zhou's precious historical relics]. Xi'an, 1993.

Yungang 1977
Yungang shiku [Yungang stone grottoes] (in Chinese with English summary). Beijing, 1977.

Yungang 1988
Zhongguo Meiji quanji. Vol. 10, *Yungang shiku diaoke* [Carvings of Yungang cave temples]. Complete Works of Chinese Arts Series. Beijing, 1988.

Yutaka 1996
Yoshida Yutaka. "Additional Notes on Sims-Williams' Article on the Sogdian Merchants in China and India." In *Cina e Iran da Alessandro Magno alla dinastia Tang*, edited by Alfredo Cadonna and Lionello Lanciotti, 69–78. Florence, 1996.

Zadneprovskiy 1994
Yuri A. Zadneprovskiy. "The Nomads of Northern Central Asia After the Invasion of Alexander." In *History of Civilizations of Central Asia*. Vol. 2, *The Development of Sedentary and Nomadic Civilizations: 700 B.C. to A.D. 250*, edited by János Harmatta, 457–72. Paris, 1994.

Zalesskaya et al. 1997
V. N. Zalesskaya, Z. A. L'vova, Boris I. Marshak, I. A. Sokolova, N. A. Foniakova. *Sokrovishcha Khana Kubrata: Pereshchepinskii klad* [Treasures of Khan Kubrat: The hoard from Pereshchepino]. St. Petersburg, 1997.

Zeimal 1994
Evgeniy Zeimal. "The Circulation of Coins in Central Asia during the Early Medieval Period (Fifth–Eighth Centuries A.D.)." *Bulletin of the Asia Institute* 8 (1994): 245–67.

Zeng 1956
Zeng Zhaoyu, et al. *Yinan gu huaxiangshi mu fajie baogao* [Excavation report of the Yinan tomb with ancient stone relief carvings]. Beijing, 1956.

Zhang 1986
Zhang Anzhi. *Zhongguo meishu quanji* [Complete Works of Chinese Art]. Vol. 1: *Huihuabian*. Beijing, 1986.

Zhang 1994
Zhang Baoxi. *Gansu shiku yishu diaosu bian* [Gansu Grotto Art-Sculpture]. Lanzhou, 1994.

Zhang 1997
Zhang Baoxi. *Gansu shiku yishu pihua bian* [Gansu Grotto Art—Frescoes]. Lanzhou, 1997.

Zhang 1995
Zhang Hongxiu. *Zhongguo Tang mu bihua ji* [A collection of China's Tang dynasty frescoes]. Shenzhen, 1995.

Zhang 1998
Zhang Hongxiu. *Sui-Tang shike yishu* [Stone carving arts of the Sui and Tang dynasties]. Xi'an, 1998.

Zhang and He 1994
Zhang Xuerong and He Jinzhen. "Lun Liangzhou fojiao ji Juqu Mengxun de chongfo zunru" [On the Buddhist religion in the Liangzhou area and Juqu Mengxun's belief in Buddhism and Confucianism]. *Dunhuang yanjiu* 1994.2, 98–110.

Zhang and Jiang 2000
Zhang Qingjie and Jiang Boqin. "Brief Reports on the Stone Sarcophagus of Yu Hong." *China Archaeology and Art Digest 4*, no. 1 (December 2000): 30–34.

Zhao 1997
Zhao Feng. "Silk Roundels from the Sui to the Tang." *Hali* 92 (May 1997): 80–85, 120.

Zhao 1996
Zhao Xiangqun. *Wu Liang shitan* [Explorations of the history of the five Liang states]. Lanzhou, 1996.

Zhao 1960
Zhao Yiwu. *Wu Liang wenhua shulun* [A discussion of the culture of the five Liang states]. Lanzhou 1989.

Zheng 1987
Zheng Binglin. "Shiliu shiqi Guzang jiandu ziran he renkou tianjian" [The ecological and population conditions of the capital Guzang in the Sixteen States period]. *Xibei shidi* 1987.3, 22: 21–29.

Zhongguo 1991
Zhongguo meishu quanji [Complete works of Chinese art]. Vol. 9, *Jade*. Beijing, 1991.

Zhongguo 1993
Zhongguo wenwu jinghua [Gems of China's Cultural Relics].Beijing, 1993.

Zhongguo 1996
Zhongguo meisue quanji [Complete works of Chinese art]. Vol. 4, *Qin, Han, and Northern and Southern Dynasties*. Hebei, 1993.

Zhongguo yinyue 1964
Zhongguo yinyue shican kaotu pian [Chinese musical history reference pictures]. No. 9, *Beizhao de yue tian he yue jen* [Northern Dynasties heavenly musicians and male musicians]. Beijing, 1964.

Zhongguo n.d.
Zhongguo yishu [Chinese Arts], no. 5. Gansu. Beijing, n.d.

Zhou and Gao 1988
Zhou Xun and Gao Chunming. *5000 Years of Chinese Costume*. Hong Kong, 1988.

Zhou and Gao 1991
Zhou Xun and Gao Chunming. *Zhongguo Lidai Funu Zhuangshi* [The history of women's clothing and ornament in China]. Hong Kong, 1991.

Zhoushu 1971
Zhoushu. Beijing, 1971.

Zhu 1960
Zhu Longhua, ed. *Gudai shijie shi cankao tu* [Compendium of ancient world history]. Beijing, 1960.

Zürcher 1962
Erik Zürcher. *Buddhism, Its Origins and Spread in Words, Maps, and Pictures*. London, 1962.

Zürcher 1972
Erik Zürcher. *The Buddhist Conquest of China: The Spread and Adaptation of Buddhism in Early Medieval China*. Vol. 2. 2nd ed. Leiden, 1972.

Zürcher 1990
Erik Zürcher. "Han Buddhism and the Western Region." In *Thought and Law in Qin and Han China*, edited by W. L. Edema and E. Zürcher, 158–82. Leiden, New York, Copenhagen, and Cologne, 1990.

Zürcher 1995
Erik Zürcher. "Buddhist Art in Medieval China: The Ecclesiastical View." In *Function and Meaning in Buddhist Art*, edited by K. R. van Kooij and H. van der Veere, 1– 20. Proceedings of a seminar held at Leiden University, October 21–24, 1991. Groningen, 1995.

Zwalf 1985
Vladimir Zwalf. *Buddhist Art and Faith*. London, 1985.

CHINESE JOURNALS

Dunhuang yanjiu
1990.1, 16–24 (Cave 275, Dunhuang).
1994.2, 98–110 (Juqu Mengxun's Buddhism and Confucianism).1996.1, 59–75 (Early caves near Jiuquan).1996.4, 8–19; 22–36 (Early Caves at Zhangye).1997.1, 42–156 (Early Tiantishan Grottoes).1997.3, 81–89 (Northern Liang Stone Stupas).1997.4, 56–72 (Sculpture at Dunhuang).

Gugong Bowuguan yuankan
1986.4, 30–31. (Fragment Northern Wei Square Stone Stupa).
1998.2, 30–42, 32 (Regionalism, Buddhist Stone Sculpture).

Huaxia kaogu
1989,3, 109 (Tang Tombs, San Menxia, Henan).

Kaogu
1965.8, 383–385, 388 (Pagoda Vessel, Tang tomb, Xi'an, Shaanxi).
1966.5, 252–59 (Stone Coffin, Dingxian, Hebei).
1972.5, 33–35 (Northern Wei Tomb, Quyang, Hebei).
1973.4, 218–24, 243 (Tomb of Yuan Shao, Henan).
1974.3, 191–99 (Jin Tombs at Dunhuang, Gansu).
1977.6, 391–402; 403–6 (Eastern Wei tomb of Li Xi Zong).
1977.7, 372, 382–390 (Tomb of Li Xizong).
1983.10, 906–14 (Southern Buddhist Grottoes, Jingchuan, Gansu).
1984.7, 622–26 (Grottoes at Wangmugong, Jingchuan, Gansu).
1986.5, 429–57 (Six dated Tang tombs, Henan).

1986.9, 841–48 (Epitaph of He Wenshe, Xi'an, Shaanxi).

1992.1, 46–54 (Mortuary Couch, Tianshui, Gansu).

1992.11, 1000–1010 (Tang Tomb, Yanxi, Henan).

1995.5, 451–65 (Origins, Early Gilt Bronze Buddhas).

Kaogu xuebao

1957.1, 103–118 (Warring States—Han Tombs, Fenshuiling, Shanxi).

1974.2, 87–109, pls. 1–15 (Unicorn, Wuwei, Gansu).

1979.3, 377–402 (Northern Qi Tomb of Kudi Huiluo, Shanxi).1984.6

Kaogu yu wenwu

1989.1, 32–44 (Cliff Tomb at Honghua Village, Sichuan).

2000.3, 5–6 (Tang Zhaoling Spirit Road, Shaanxi).

Wenwu

1956.4, 37–44 (Buddhist sites of Matisi, Jintasi).

1964.6, 58–59 (Wei-Jin Gilt Bronze Seals, Gansu).

1965.8, 47–51 (Reliquaries, Wooden House Model, Jiangsu).

1966.1 (Tomb of Li He).

1966.3, 8 (Tang reliquary, Jingchuan, Gansu).

1971.2, 66 (Southern Dynasties Tomb, Danyang, Jiangsu).

1972.2, 16–24 (Han Bronze Horses, Wuwei, Gansu).

1972.2, 54–60 (Northern Wei Embroidery, Dunhuang).

1972.3, 20–33 (Tomb of Sima Jinlong, Datong, Shanxi).

1972.8, 39–48 (Hebei, Dingxian).

1972.12, 47–54 (Maijishan Caves, Tianshui, Gansu).

1973.1, 8–20 (Han Tomb, Dingxian, Hebei).

1973.11, 8– 20 (Han Tomb no. 43, Dingxian, Hebei).

1974.2, 44–56 (Southern Dynasties Tomb, Danyang, Jiangsu).

1975.6, 85–88 (Tomb of Wang Zhenbao, Gansu).

1975.9, 1–8 (Han Tomb 168, Jiangling, Hubei).

1977.1, 44–51; 64–73 (Southern Dynasties Tomb, Danyang, Jiangsu).

1977.6, 17–22 (W. Han Tomb, Hensu).

1978.12, 5–6 (Dunhuang).

1978.12, 65–68 (Mogao Caves, Dunhuang).

1979.3, 17–31 (Gao family Tomb, Jing County, Hebei).

1979.6, 1–14 (Jin Tomb, Jiayuguan, Gansu).

1980.5, pl. 5 (Combs).

1981.7, 85–89 (Military Band).

1981.11, 1–11 (Eastern Jin Tomb, Nanjing).

1981.12, 14–23 (Southern Liang Tombs, Yaohuamen, Nanjing).

1983.8, 1–4; 5–8; 9–12 (Tomb of Feng Hetu, Datong, Shanxi).

1983.10, 1–23 (Tomb of Lou Rui, Taiyuan, Shanxi).

1984.4, 1–9; 10–15; 16–22 (Tomb of Ruru Princess, Cixia, Hebei).

1984.6, 35 (Eastern Jin Tomb, Liaoning).

1984.6, 46–56 (Lacquered Coffin, Guyuan).

1984.8, 46–48 (Shu Han Tomb, Wudaoqu, Sichuan).

1984.9, 45–54, 76 (Ancient horse harnesses).

1985.11, 1–12 (Tomb of Li Xian, Guyuan, Ningxia).

1986.5, 68–69, 77, pl. 5 (Tang Dynasty Combs).

1987.9, 87–93 (Wei-Jin Tomb at Nantan, Gansu).

1987.10, 77–79 (Gold necklace and bracelet from the
tomb of Li Jingxun, Xi'an, Shaanxi).

1988.2, 19–43 (Western Han Tomb, no. 101, Jiangsu).

1988.2, 69–71 (Northern Zhou "Wang Ling-wei" Stele, Gansu).

1988.3, 83–85, 93 (Miniature Stone Stupa of Cao Tianhu, Jiuquan, Gansu).

1988.6, 49–56 (Tuoshan Cave Temples, Shandong).

1988.9, 26–42 (Tombs at Pengyang, Ningxia).

1988.9, 43–56 (Tang Tombs at Yanchi, Ningxia).

1989.9, 59–86 (Spring Autumn Period Tomb, Taiyuan, Shanxi).

1989.10, 1–43 (Famen temple pagoda).

1990.1, 1–9 (Han Cemetery at Yangyuan, Hebei).

1990.5, 1–9 (Silver Plate, Jingyuan, Gansu).

1993.9, 55–59 (Western Zhou Jades).

1994.1, 50–64 (Qin, Han, and Jin Buckles).

1996.7, 4–38 (Wei-Jin Tomb at Xigou, Jiuquan, Gansu).

1997.1, 13 (Clay Pagoda Vessel).

1997.4, 42–45 (Stone Pagoda, Cleveland).

1997.12, 44–51 (Gaotai, Painted Brick Tomb, Gansu).

1998.6, 47–56 (Tuoshan Cave Temples, Shandong).

1998.7, 60–66 (Cave Shrine Zhangjiakou, Hebei).

1998.9, 64–66 (Buddhist Cultural Relics, Gansu).

1998.10, 4–21 (North End Caves, Dunhuang); 22–27 (Peroz Drachm from Dunhuang).

1998.11, 4–20 (Buddhist Sculpture, Xi'an Road, Chengdu).

1999.1, 4–16. English summary (Yingpan Mummy, Xinjiang).

1999.2, 46 (Pagoda Vessel in Tang Tomb, Luoyang, Hebei).

1999.4, 18–28 (Tomb 2, Jingzhou, Hebei).

2000.5, 50–61 (Buddhist Sculpture, Qingzhou, Shandong).

Wenwu cankao ziliao

1955.12, 59–65 (Tomb of Shao Zhen).

Wenwu tiandi

1996.4, 12–15.

Wenwu ziliao congcan

1983.3, 74–76 (Gilt Bronze Buddha, Shijiazhuang, Hebei).

Xinjiang daxue Xuebao

1997.4, 62–66 (Migrations of the Sogdians, Tang Dynasty).

Zhongyuan wenwu

1982.3, 21–26 (Tomb of An Pu).

Index